DISCARDED

Finding Her Voice

Finding Her Voice

The Saga of Women in Country Music

By

MARY A. BUFWACK

and

ROBERT K. OERMANN

CROWN PUBLISHERS, INC. NEW YORK

For our mothers,
Mary Jane Oermann and Agnes Mary Bufwack,
the first singing voices we ever heard.

Photos and illustrative material were obtained from such institutions as the Country Music Foundation, *Music City News, The Tennessean,* Mars Hill College, the Historical Center for Southeast New Mexico, the Academy of Motion Picture Arts and Sciences, the Country Music Association, and Broadcast Music Inc. The Rounder, Bear Family, and Flying Fish record labels were gracious enough to open their files.

Jo-Ann Campbell, Patsy Montana, Gene Wiggins, Charles Wolfe, Jean Miles Catino, and Kay Baker Gaston loaned images; while Wanda Jackson, The Carter Family, Skeeter Davis, Gail Davies, and Jean Ritchie all gave us a look at their personal archives.

Also, such photographers as George Pikow, Alan L. Mayor, Beth Gwinn, Gerald Holly, Mary Bufwack, Robert K. Oermann, and P. Casey Daley provided prints. To the best of our knowledge the illustrations used here are used with permission of copyright holder or are not covered by current copyrights. In cases where we have not learned names of photographers, artists, or publishers we shall appreciate credit-line data.

Published by Crown Publishers, Inc., 201 East 50th Street, New York, New York 10022.
Member of the Crown Publishing Group.
Random House, Inc. New York, Toronto, London, Sydney, Auckland
CROWN is a trademark of Crown Publishers, Inc.

Manufactured in the United States of America

Book design by Kay Schuckhart

Library of Congress Cataloging-in-Publication Data
Bufwack, Mary A.
    Finding her voice : the saga of women in country music / by Mary
A. Bufwack and Robert K. Oermann. — 1st ed.
    Includes bibliographical references and index.
    1. Country music—History and criticism   2. Women musicians—
Biography.   I. Oermann, Robert K.   II. Title.
ML3524.B83   1993
781.642'082—dc20
                                                                    92-44269
                                                                    CIP
                                                                    MN

ISBN 0-517-58114-0
10 9 8 7 6 5 4 3 2 1
First Edition

CONTENTS

ACKNOWLEDGMENTS

In 1978, in a '68 Cutlass, the two of us took to the road with a preliminary draft of this manuscript and a box full of note cards in hand. During the next six months we went through 30 states and more than 13,000 miles gathering information. It changed our lives: The trip brought us to Nashville, where we have remained.

We had been initially encouraged in this endeavor after we presented our early research at academic conferences in 1976–1977. Jim O'Brien of The New England Free Press produced an early essay as a pamphlet. Our send-off in that cold January was given at Syracuse University by Professor Antje Lemke and at Colgate University by Margaret Mauer and Carl Peterson, who had read and commented on early drafts of the manuscript. New York City artists Bob Huot and Carol Kinne were consistently enthusiastic supporters.

In Maryland, Joe Bussard's collection was a great boon, while Richard Spottswood's hospitality and information gave the project a further boost. Lynne Burkhart, President Carter's Deputy Secretary of Transportation and a friend, made helpful comments as she hosted us. At the Library of Congress Joe Hickerson, Gerry Parsons, and Mark Mattucci were most helpful as we made our way through the Archive of Folk Song holdings.

In Charlotteville, Virginia, we met Chuck and Nan Perdue, scholars and performers. They guided us to further materials. In Amissville, we encountered Dick and Ginny Pierson, whose charm and hospitality were immense and whose record collection was invaluable.

In North Carolina, the Appalachian Collection in Boone attracted us. Social worker Carol Teal and computer wiz Bill Wilson fed us, housed us, and showed us the Tarheel State while we explored the folklore collection at Chapel Hill that Daniel Patterson had introduced us to. Tiny hillbilly record stores throughout rural South Carolina and Georgia provided more primary documents for study as we made our way southward to Florida.

In Bartow, Florida, Tom Rowland and his family were generous and kind as we worked our way through his extensive collection of 78 r.p.m. records. It was southern cooking and love of music at its best. In Roanoke, Alabama, old-time musicians Robert and Claudene Nobley guided us patiently through more antique sounds. Later, in Clarksville, Tennessee, Robert kindly introduced us to Ivan Tribe and other old-time music enthusiasts.

Nashville, of course, is where we struck gold. When we arrived in Music City we were warmly greeted by folklorists Patty Hall and Charles Wolfe. Their *Banjo Pickin' Girl* compilation LP was an inspiration. At the Country Music Foundation is the rock upon which country music scholarship so often rests, the ever-generous, ever-kind Bob Pinson. Throughout this project he has tirelessly provided information and guidance. He remains the touchstone of all country music research. Tony Russell provided further discographic help during the following years of research. Ronnie Pugh was always there to help during the final writing, and CMF director Bill Ivey has remained a supporter throughout.

Memphians Paul Ross, Nina Etkin, and Charlie McNutt talked blues and gospel with us as we explored Mississippi's resources. Thanks to the kindness of Robin and Shirley Mathis and radio station WCPC in Houston, Mississippi was one of our favorite stops. The gospel groups who perform live broadcasts at the station were our accompaniment as we sorted through the enormous amount of material Robin had stored. Together we drove to Meridian to meet Miss Elsie McWilliams, who could still belt out a fine "Mississippi River Blues" in those days.

In St. Louis, George and Dru Lipsitz, who had initially egged us on, introduced us to the radio gospel singers Slim and Zella Mae Cox, further reminding us of the vigor of this tradition. After a stop at the Ozark collection in Fayetteville, Arkansas, the music of countless small radio stations across Oklahoma and Texas sang us to New Mexico. In Albuquerque, Lenny and Lois Weslowski housed us while James B. Wright provided expert guidance to the University of New Mexico's folk music tapes.

D. K. Wilgus at UCLA was not only a pioneer among country music scholars but a charming and generous man who with his wife, Ebby, showed us great hospitality. Paul Wells at the John Edwards Memorial Foundation is owed another thank-you. In Los Angeles, folklorists Frankie Farrell and Dianne Dugaw shared their experiences as struggling female musicians in their band Darlin' Cory. Further up the coast the Archive of Recorded Sound at Stanford provided information on vaudeville and the early years of recording. Bonnie Malone offered relaxation in Oroville, California, as we returned eastward. Austin and Alta Fife's collection at Utah State in Logan and libraries in Nebraska and Iowa provided information on pioneer women. In Chicago, Jean Hardisty cared for two weary travelers and kept us updated on the development of feminist music. We bought records by the carload in St. Louis, Nashville, West Virginia, and Pennsylvania.

Others helped through correspondence, including Gerald Vaughn, Bill Grant, the late Milford H. Fargo, Elvis E. Fleming, and many more. One very special acknowledgment must go to the late Will Roy Hearne, one of the grand ole men of country music discography. He provided us with our initial list of contacts of record collectors.

Country scholar Archie Green became a booster, as did record collector Pete Loesch, friends Bob Millard and Lucinda Smith, writers John Lomax III and Thomas Goldsmith, rockabilly expert Mike Smyth, music mavens Holly George-Warren and Martha Hume, film collector Boyd Magers, researcher Meagan Gurley, and Bud Schaetzle's High Five production team, particularly Michael McNamara. This book could not have been written without the dedication of our singing secretaries in Music City, LouAnn Bardash and Molly Felder.

The women who made it a reality are our caring agent and friend, Sarah Lazin, and our visionary editor, Betty Prashker.

INTRODUCTION

T his book is a journey of discovery.

It's a new look at country music history that searches for its roots beyond Nashville, beyond the contemporary hit records, and beyond the male superstars. It's an attempt to place music in its social context and to explain why songs happen when they do. And it's an attempt to preserve and appreciate the music of the disenfranchised, the overlooked, and the ignored.

Finding Her Voice is a view of American society through the songs and styles of the working class. Country music is art created by the population that author Tillie Olsen calls "our silenced people." "For century after century their beings [are] consumed in the hard, everyday essential work of maintaining human life. Their art [is] . . . anonymous; refused respect, recognition; lost."

This book finds those "silenced" voices.

Most important, it is a document of women's lives. The biographies of the women in this book put us in touch with the personal dimension of political, economic, and social trends. Our written histories exclude these ordinary women, the backbone and lifeblood of America, but these women have documented their own saga in song. The women in this book carry the music and culture of the ordinary mothers, grandmothers, and matriarchs who worked in the field, the women who bore children and watched them die without medical assistance, the women who made homes from practically nothing, the women who worked in the textile mills, the women who sold their bodies to survive.

Looking to country music for information about working-class women uncovers a rich and expressive tradition. Along with the blues, country music stands nearly alone as a record of the thoughts and feelings, the fantasies and experiences of this invisible and often silent group of women. It stands as one of the only documents of working-class women's thoughts created by working-class women for working-class women.

The story of women in country music is a window into the world of the majority of American women. It describes poverty, hardship, economic exploitation, sexual subjugation, and limited opportunities. Sometimes it is self-defeating and reactionary, painful and despairing. But it also contains outspoken protest and joyful rebellion, shouts of exaltation and bugle calls of freedom. There is humor as well as sadness here, victory as well as heartache. The history of women's country music reveals a rich vein of positive images, self-assertive lyrics, and strong female performers.

We find women's voices ringing loudly in our folk culture. There was a female musical tradition in America long before the advent of entertainment industries. Women's activities as collectors of songs and as singers reflected their central family role as provider and mother. As music, work, and leisure intermingled, women also had an important community role as bearers of tradition. And because women were so central as teachers and keepers, a distinct female point of view was passed through the generations.

With urbanization, capitalism, and the commercialization of culture came a growing separation of work/public life and leisure/family life. It was difficult for women to enter public life in general and show business in particular, because accompanying the division of work and family was the belief that women belonged in the home, protected from the wicked ways of the world. Public entertainment was associated with prostitution. Small wonder that so many women's voices we find in early entertainment were in family groups projecting images and singing songs of hearth and home.

With the Depression the down-to-earth music of the rural South and the popularity of its folksy performers spread nationwide on radio. The country found symbols of unity in the strength, integrity, and ingenuity of its poor. We find women's voices broadcasting the images of self-reliance, compassion, and familial love in these troubled times.

World War II meant women had to enter the work force in great numbers. Professional opportunities flourished for morale-boosting female performers. Their voices helped develop women's sense of independence and build female self-confidence.

The difficulties and stress of postwar life were experienced very differently by men and women. In country culture honky-tonk music was the voice of the loneliness, alienation, and loss of community in industrial mass society.

Women were blamed as men expressed their feelings of victimization; but the culture responded with the women's point of view, and the argument about who victimized whom became institutionalized in the country sound. Southern gospel music emerged as the fevered response to the new morality of the nuclear age.

The rockabilly style was another response, one of restless rebellion and aggressive self-expression. Despite the suburban conformity of the fifties, women as well as men expressed themselves in this new, youth-oriented style. Women became leaders in the next musical protest movement, the highly political folk revival of the sixties.

The modern women's liberation movement's tensions were played out in female country music in a way that produced some of the most creative women's songs in pop-culture history. And as songwriters, singers, performers, and businesswomen, women made themselves heard in ever-greater numbers. We find their voices loudly proclaiming working-class pride as well as expressing their distinct identities as women.

In the seventies and eighties, female country performers spread their message beyond the working class. Their images became powerful symbols of female achievement as women took on careers, became single parents, and entered all areas of American life.

Women's lives have changed greatly from the time of country music's folk origins, but they are still not like those of men. Going to work has become the rule rather than the exception, and with the escalation of divorce, women have also taken on the primary duties of parenting and wage earning. They still do most of America's domestic work, and although there is a blending of working-class and middle-class culture and experience, the United States has never experienced a wider gap between the rich and the regular people. We do not doubt that country music's women will continue to give voice to this reality—for women and for men.

This book has a thousand heroines, a thousand voices, a thousand stories, and a thousand points of view. It's a search for our heritage through a myriad of styles, attitudes, and images. As we listen to these voices, we hear ourselves—our inner conflicts, our foolishness, and our wisdom.

In the end, this book is about music, but these words and pictures are no substitute for the power of a song that speaks to your own heart. No book can convey the strength, individuality, and creativity of these voices. Read about the extraordinary person who becomes a country music woman. But go and listen, too. For the whole thrill is in finding her voice.

Finding Her Voice

1

THE SPIRIT
OF THE
MOUNTAINS

Women in American

Folk Music

To thirteen-year-old Emma Bell, the mist-shrouded Appalachian Mountain vales around her hometown were places of thrilling romance, of wild beauty, of escape from her stiff-necked Presbyterian home life. The dark-eyed dreamer didn't know the people who lived in the hollows and hills near Walden's Ridge, Tennessee, but she could see blue-gray plumes of smoke that curled above the treetops. And she'd catch a glimpse of a life-style quite unlike her own starched, evangelical upbringing when some rugged mountaineer would appear in her village to sell furs or wood. No buggy could take her up to their remote cabins. In 1891 the only way to find them was by walking up streambeds or centuries-old Indian trails. She had no books to read about them, no radio documentaries to tell her of their lives.

But Emma could hear them. The ring of the banjo and the scrape of the fiddle bow beckoned her. By the time she was fifteen, she was practically living in the woods. She rode her horse astride like a man, scandalizing the neighbors. During her explorations she began to meet mountain children, mountain women, and—fatefully—a mountain man.

His name was Frank Miles, a handsome and engag-

ingly shy fellow with sensitive eyes, a poet's heart, and a knowledge of wildflowers and plants passed down from his mother, a folk herbalist. Emma was nineteen when they met. When they eloped in 1901, her family disowned her.

Emma spent the rest of her life in hardship, a bride of Appalachian poverty. To make ends meet, she'd come down from the hills to give speeches and recite nature poetry to the wellborn ladies of Chattanooga. She sold them her paintings of Appalachian flora and fauna and told them of the culture she both loved and endured. By 1903 she had delivered two of her five babies under the care of mountain midwives and had begun to publish her poems. In 1905 Emma Bell Miles published a collection of her writings called *Spirit of the Mountains,* a landmark and forerunner of hundreds of books about traditional country culture. In its pages is the first appreciation of mountain music written by a literary figure.

"Here, among the mountains of Kentucky, Tennessee and the Carolinas, is a people of whose inner nature and its musical expression almost nothing has been said," Emma wrote. "The music of the Southern mountaineer is not only peculiar, but like himself, peculiarly American.

"Nearly all mountaineers are singers. Their untrained voices are of good timbre, the women's being sweet and high and tremulous, and their sense of pitch and tone and rhythm remarkably true."

In those crude mountain cabins—built much the same way they had been when Daniel Boone opened the Appalachians to white settlers in 1775—Emma listened to women's voices singing ballads that had been handed down for centuries, songs whose ancestry is as old as the English language itself.

"The mother is crooning over her work, some old ballad of an eerie sadness . . . something she learned as a child from a grandmother whose grandmother again brought it from Ireland or Scotland. As she bends above the loom, sending the shuttle back and forth, her voice goes on softly, interrupted by the thump of the batten. . . ."

At loom, butter churn, cooking pot, or spinning wheel a housewife's mind might escape to tales of lords and ladies in faraway castles who loved tragically and violently, the stuff of which romance novels are written to this day. The daydream-in-song might be of love in the arms of "Black Jack Davey," "The Gypsy Rover," "The House Carpenter," or "The Daemon Lover."

Mrs. Maud Long, who sang for British folklorist Cecil Sharp in 1917, picked up a baby before she sang, saying that she always felt more like it when she was holding a young one.

"When I was left a widow with a kit and bilin' of younguns, I'd keep myself company at nights singing them," said Mrs. Ida Rice to folk song collector Dorothy Scarborough. "Pore folks ain't got so many ways to pleasure themselves."

Emma Bell Miles's music chapter in *Spirit of the Mountains* was first published as an article called "Some Real American Music" in *Harper's Monthly* in 1904. It was probably the first appreciation of Appalachian music to appear in a popular magazine; it was certainly one of the first to appear *anywhere*, following by only four years the academic writing on the subject by William Wells Newell in *The Journal of American Folklore*. Three years after Emma's article appeared, the same academic journal published Appalachian folk songs that had been collected by Kentucky schoolteacher Katharine Pettit. Then North Carolina schoolteacher Olive Dame Campbell enthusiastically showed her song collection to Cecil Sharp, spurring the creation of his cornerstone work on traditional music, *English Folk Songs from the Southern Appalachians*.

Sharp did his song collecting from 1916 to 1918, using Campbell's mountain home as his base and with the assistance of Maud Karpeles. The women guided the venerable scholar along dirt roads and muddy trails, from crude cabin to rustic schoolhouse. The preliminary 1917 version of Sharp's magnum opus was coauthored by Campbell, and it was Karpeles who edited the two-volume landmark after Sharp's death in 1924.

Among the mountain families who sang their traditional songs for Sharp was the Ritchie clan of Viper, Kentucky. There were eleven daughters and three sons born to Balis and Abbie Ritchie, and all were folk song lovers. Daughters Una and May were among Sharp's song sources, and their younger sister Jean became a major popularizer of American folk music in the 1940s and 1950s.

Jean Ritchie recalled that the social worker women who established mountain schools in the early 1900s were the people most responsible for saving the ancient folk songs: "If it hadn't been for the settlement schools, many of the old mountain songs would have died out when the ways of the world came in on us. But the women loved our music and plays. . . . Every new girl or boy that'd come in, the women'd soon find out what ballads she or he knew, and that song'd be written down and taught to all the other children."

Folklorists poured into rural and mountain areas from roughly 1910 to 1940, documenting and preserving America's unwritten music heritage. Dozens of the most important musical explorers were women.

The song most commonly found by all the collectors was "Barbara Allen." Told from a woman's point of view, it is about the irrational power of love. In the song Sweet William pines to death after being spurned by a disbelieving Barbara Allen. In remorse she wastes away, too. Scholars have dated "Barbara Allen" to Scotland in the early 1600s. A London entertainer named Mary Knep delighted diarist Samuel Pepys with it in 1666. Folklorist Alan Lomax believes the ballad has had such remarkable longevity because "the song is the vehicle for the aggressive fantasies of women." In fact, Lomax asserts that *most* Appalachian ballads are concerned with "sexual conflict as seen through feminine eyes."

The central character of "The Butcher's Boy" commits suicide over love when she finds that her intended loves a wealthier woman. "The English Lady Gay" scorns and spurns her young suitor, then dies of remorse. Both the highborn damsel and her peasant lover are murdered by her outraged brothers in "The Lady and the Shepherd." In "Lord Lovell" a deserted young woman dies of grief, while in "Fair Margarat" a young man dies because his lover is accidentally killed. In "Lady Isabel and the Elf Knight" her devil lover turns against her and tries to kill her, but she outwits him. In "The Unquiet Grave" the dead sweetheart speaks to the lover who mourns at her tomb, urging him to join her. In some versions of the "Lady Alice"/"Earl Colvin" ballads he dies of venereal disease, and she pines away at his coffin. "Queen Jane" dies in childbirth while her beloved King Henry mourns. "Silver Dagger" is a double suicide, à la *Romeo and Juliet*. There are "eternal triangle" lyrics, such as those of "Lord Bateman" and "The Brown Girl"/"Fair Ellender" ballads. The woman who loves "Mattie Groves" defies her husband, and both are stabbed to death by the betrayed man.

In addition to tales of violent events, folk women's songs occasionally speak of love affairs with happy endings, as in the thematically related songs "The Constant Damsel," "Pretty Fair Maid Out in a Garden," and "John Riley." But far more numerous are the broken hearts of "The Soldier and the Lady," "All for the Love of a Man," "The Poor Girl's Warning," "The Deceived Girl," and "I'll Give You My Story," wherein women are seduced and abandoned.

These ballads were preserved not because of their connection to English ancestry, but because the singers believed in their messages. An old Virginia lady named Grandma Ball told Dorothy Scarborough that she did not like the violent, tragic love songs, but that she was able to tolerate some because "they spoke the truth." After singing a version of "Billy Grimes" for North Carolina folk song collector Maude Minnish Sutton, an old woman said she admired the song character's sensible approach to money and marriage. "That woman was right. . . . Ef you've got a chance at a feller that's well fixed, you take him, hon. . . . This [song] was talkin' sense."

Jean Ritchie wrote that the lords and ladies of the ballads were real to her when she was an imaginative mountain child, that singing was part of her fantasy life. "These old story songs, now. We sang and listened to them, for themselves, for the excitement of the tale . . . for the romantic tingle we got from a glimpse of life in the long-ago past, for the uncanny way the old, old situations still fit the present."

The preservation of folk ballads is also part of women's "rag bag" tradition.

Country women saved scraps of cloth for quilts, balls of string, boxes of buttons, human hair for funeral wreaths, postcards, mementos, and all manner of potentially decorative or useful materials. It was just a pleasure to collect.

Kentucky-bred traditional folksinger Sarah Ogun Gunning told her interviewers that she preserved old songs because they reminded her of her mother, and that she wanted to keep her memory alive. Other traditional folksingers have said that they wrote down lyrics they'd heard or clipped poems from newspapers and saved them, much as later generations would keep scrapbooks of movie or music stars. Teenage girls frequently traded and shared these paper scraps and eagerly tried to add to their song collections. As an old woman, Emma Dusenberry of Arkansas recalled that when she was a girl, her "aim was to learn all the songs in the world."

"Mothers handed the songs down much more than the fathers," observed Appalachian singer Jim Garland, "for they would stay at home with the children during the long winter months. . . . There were few other recreational things to do, except for an occasional medicine or Punch-and-Judy show. . . . Girls then didn't have much to look forward to except marriage, because the rule of their parents was so strict. So they went in for the folk songs and stories more than the men and boys."

In some states the number of women folksingers found by folklorists was double the number of men. And their repertoires were huge; it was not uncommon to find ladies who knew fifty to a hundred songs by heart.

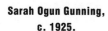

**Sarah Ogun Gunning,
c. 1925.**

Scarborough wrote of one singer who could sing all night without repeating herself. Such performers were considered community treasures.

The violent and sexual content of these women's repertoires frequently astonished the post-Victorian academics who ventured into the mountains seeking the remnants of Elizabethan balladry and Anglo-Saxon culture. These middle-class moralists—expecting the old song culture to reflect their own repressed sexuality—were also shocked at the promiscuity, incest, unwanted pregnancy, and premarital sex they found among the mountaineers.

Emma Bell Miles wrote with great insight about the consequences of mountaineers' open sexuality, about women made old before their time—as she was—by repeated pregnancies. Both *Spirit of the Mountains* and Kay Baker Gaston's biography based on Emma's diary and letters reflect the mountain writer's ambivalence about sex.

In 1914 Emma wrote in her diary, "It drives me wild to remember how, from the time Joe was born, I have begged Frank not to lay this burden on my sick body . . . and how at each of the two births and miscarriages since then I have tried to make him understand it is bound to kill me sooner or later."

By this time what Emma once called the "sex magic" between her and Frank was gone. Life with him through mountain winters in a crude, unheated log cabin aggravated the tuberculosis that became evident when she was thirty-three. Poverty had killed three-year-old son Mark when they were too poor to afford a doctor to treat his scarlet fever in 1913. But Emma submitted to Frank's sexual urges; and he kept forcing himself on her despite the danger of another debilitating pregnancy and the frailty of her health.

Once married, the average nineteenth-century housewife had seven or more children, initially one every two years. A mother's advice on birth control might consist of "If you don't want butter, pull the dasher out in time." Babies were delivered at home by "grannies," with little sanitation beyond boiling water. There were no painkillers. Any birthing complications, such as torn flesh, a dislocated uterus, or hemorrhoids, went untreated. At the turn of the century, one in every thirty mothers died during her childbearing years, and the number was perhaps double that in the mid-1800s. (Today it is approximately two per ten thousand.) Because of extended bleeding, miscarriages could be as dangerous as births one hundred years ago. If a woman had nearby female relatives, they might pitch in to do her housework for as much as a week. After that, the new mother was expected to take up her chores where she left off.

Emma wanted to be left alone during her pregnancies, but Frank was persistent about his marital rights. When she broached the subject with her mother-in-law, Grandma Miles told her how she handled Grandpa: "I told him that he'd have to go elsewhere. I told him I didn't care nothing about hit if only I didn't have to see hit. And he let me plumb alone."

Maude Minnish Sutton was especially fond of a group of about fifty songs she collected in 1915 that all warned young ladies against the sexual wiles of men. "The shocking unmorality . . . might be explained in that underlying idea that man's infidelity is a natural sort of thing," Sutton wrote. "No wonder these attractive rascals are bad. They are expected to be. . . . They are so vital that they have a certain easily explained charm, but there's no sense in the he's-got-to-sow-his-wild-oats attitude of these fool women. I believe these songs have a good deal to do with it."

Sutton was referring to such enduring odes as "Come All You Fair and Tender Maidens," which has an attitude of regret that is echoed by women throughout country music history: "Come all you fair and tender maidens / Take warning how you court young men / They're like the stars in the summer morning / First they appear and then they're gone."

There is a very large group of similar Anglo-American ballads that folklorists have grouped together as "come-all-ye" women's warning songs. The first song quoted in Emma's touching *The Spirit of the Mountains* is one such number. She called it "The Cuckoo," but portions of it became more widely known as "On Top of Old Smoky": "Courting's a pleasure and parting's a grief / But a false-hearted lover is worse than a thief / A thief will but rob you, and take all you've saved / But a false-hearted lover will lead you to your grave / The grave will consume you and turn you to dust / And where is the young man a woman can trust?" This timeless female lament spans centuries of English-language culture. The lines above appeared almost verbatim in a Scottish song quoted in 1788 by James Johnson in *The Scots Musical Museum*. And "On Top of Old Smoky" endured 163 years later as a chart-topping hit for the folk group The Weavers in 1951.

Missionary Campbell heard much the same sentiment in a song she collected from mountain women who had migrated to North Carolina's cotton mill communities in 1909: "He'll hug you and kiss you / He'll roll you all about / Then he'll leave you as I were left / To roll the baby out."

Saddest of all the betrayed-by-love ballads is the immortal "I Never Will Marry," in which the heartbroken woman chooses suicide. "I'll be no man's wife," the deserted woman sings as she throws herself into the sea, "I expect to live single all the days of my life."

Considering the prevalence of these heartache/inconstant-lover songs and their relatives like "Careless Love," "Hard Ain't It Hard," and "When a Woman Blue," is it any wonder that one of the largest groups of Appalachian women's folk songs is about single life? After hard-hearted "Barbara Allen," the female most commonly sung about in the mountains of Virginia was the "Single Girl," or her older counterpart the "Old Maid." Indeed, the preoccupation with marital status far outweighs all other concerns in women's folk songs. "Don't you never get married," said one old woman to Sutton in 1915. "There's as much again satisfaction in being an old maid."

Appalachian folk songs are rich in this theme. The verse to one goes: "Seven long years I've been married / And I wish I'd lived an old maid / My husband has taken to drinking / And now he won't work at his trade."

One of the most colorful folksingers encountered by Maud Karpeles during her ground-breaking 1916 trip through the Appalachians with Cecil Sharp was a mountain gal who was fed up with marriage. "We spent many long hours with her and a friend who lived with her," Maud recalled, "delighting in her racy talk and enjoying the songs the two women gave us. They both smoked pipes, although when we visited them they had only one between them. She told us she had been married three times: the first husband had killed a man and was serving a long sentence in a penitentiary; the next one drank, so she kicked him out; and the third wouldn't work and so had to depart in the same summary fashion. She had a three-roomed house and each room contained an enlarged photograph of one of the husbands, which she showed us with great pride."

The widespread folk song "Single Girl" contrasts the careworn married drudge with the carefree unmarried woman:

Single girl, single girl, going dressed so fine;
Married girl, married girl, goes ragged all the time.
Single girl, single girl, she goes to the store and buys;
Married girl, married girl, she rocks the cradle and cries.
Single girl, single girl, she's going where she please;
Married girl, married girl, baby on her knees.

Emma Bell Miles was a weary mother aged twenty-six when she wrote, "At twenty the mountain woman is old in all that makes a woman old—toil, sorrow, child-bearing, loneliness and pitiful want....

"A rift is set between the sexes at babyhood that widens with the passing of the years, a rift that is never closed even by the daily interdependence of a poor man's partnership with his wife.

"The pathos of the situation is nonetheless terrible because unconscious. They are so silent. They know so pathetically little of each other's lives.

"Of course, the woman's experience is the deeper. . . . Her position means sacrifice, sacrifice and ever sacrifice. . . ."

The "Wagoner's Lad" is fatalistically philosophical about the burden of work housewives bore: "Hard is the fortune of all womankind / They're always controlled, they're always confined / Controlled by their parents until they are wives / Then slaves to their husbands the rest of their lives."

From nineteenth-century Illinois comes "The Housewife's Lament," which details the daily grind of being a homemaker. "I spend my whole life in the struggle with dirt," it goes. And in its finale the hapless woman loses her lifelong battle and is buried in—what else?—dirt.

In the "Father Grumble"/"Old Man in the Woods" group of related folk songs a farmer challenges his wife to trade places after she complains about how hard housework is. She succeeds in plowing and doing heavy farm labor while he botches all the household chores of milking, chicken feeding, egg gathering, cream churning, calf feeding, fat boiling, pig feeding, lard fixing, and various other tasks. The farmer surrenders: "He swore by all the leaves on the tree / And all the stars in heaven / His wife could do more work in a day / Than he could do in seven."

At the turn of the century most everyday southern families lived, at best, in a three- to four-room house with whitewashed walls, unpainted floors, bare essentials for furniture, kerosene lanterns, and only minimal decorations, perhaps a calendar and some curtains. Housework began before daylight and was not over until after dark. There was no running water. There was no electricity. There were no modern appliances, time-savers, or conveniences.

Most time-consuming was cooking. Poor women made everything from scratch—they milked cows, churned butter, baked, drew water, grew and picked vegetables, and tended chickens or pigs during a typical week. In addition, they canned food for future use. Men bought their overalls, but almost all the garments worn by women and children were sewn in the home. Household cleaning was a round of emptying chamber pots, scrubbing floors, and sweeping.

Washing was the heaviest and hardest chore. The scarcity of clothing and linens made this a weekly necessity. It took a full day. Wood was chopped for burning to heat the water. One washing, boiling, and rinse might use fifty gallons of water—four hundred pounds—all of which had to be drawn and hauled from the well or stream. Homemade lye soap was fiercely caustic to the skin. Diapers and men's filthy farming overalls were particularly vexing.

No wonder the careworn mothers sang "Single Girl" and advised their daughters to stay single and free as long as they could. When Emma went to live among the mountaineers, she gravitated toward such wise matriarchs. She wrote, "I have learned to enjoy the company of these old prophetesses almost more than any other. The range of their experience is wonderful; they are, moreover, repositories of tribal lore—tradition and song, medical and religious learning. They are the nurses, the teachers of practical arts, the priestesses, and their wisdom commands the respect of all." She thought that an aged mountain woman's "strength and endurance are beyond imagination to women of the sheltered life."

Sutton's song searches led her to many such women. "When I find the real ballad singer," she wrote, "I bow my spirit before her. She is the successor of the Greek myth makers, the northern Skalds, the desert storyteller. The absorbed interest the hearers give her makes it perfectly plain that these stories . . . have nearly all been tested by the attrition of centuries and have never worn out."

Jean Ritchie wistfully recalled her girlhood learning folk songs: "We'd set there before the fire and pretty soon Granny'd begin to hum and sing. . . . I guess she sung with me and learnt me more songs than anybody. . . . And she never quit one till I'd learned to sing it by heart all alone. . . . just think now, that little tiny girl 'bout eight years old and that old white-headed woman with her cob pipe and her little coals of fire a-setting way out in . . . a log house miles from any neighbors, a-singing them old lonesome songs and the frogs a-hollering and no light but an old coal-oil lamp."

Country music can be directly traced to such women in hollows and remote communities throughout Appalachia. In Tennessee Dolly Parton's grandmother was learning songs from an "old prophetess" relative, and those songs would in turn be passed through the family's generations. In Virginia young Sara Dougherty was beginning to swap songs with her cousins that would resonate through country music as the repertoire of The Carter Family. In Kentucky Clara Butcher's mother was singing to her babies the songs that Clara would sing to *her* daughter, Loretta Lynn.

The really feisty lyrics were in songs of the "troublesome" or "shrewish" wife. "Devilish Mary," "The Scolding Wife," "The Dumb Wife," and "The Unwilling Bride" are just a few such musical characters. In "The Wife Wrapt in Wether's Skin" the difficult woman is beaten into submission. But in "The Farmer's Curst Wife"/"The Old Lady and the Devil" she gets the upper hand. The devil comes to steal a scolding wife. But the old gal is so mean, the devil returns her, more quarrelsome than ever. Cries the husband, "I am to be cursed: She's been to Hell and come back worse!"

The ballads and songs of complaint were sung around the fire or as accompaniment to housework. But other folk songs were for social occasions. After a hard week's work eking out a subsistence living in the remote reaches of the southern highlands, mountaineers would gather to play musical games. Their "play-party" folk songs were accompanied by simple dances or parlor games involving shifting chairs, opposing lines of boys and girls, or circles of courting young people. In many of the courtship "play-party" games, the girls have the upper hand in choosing their make-believe lovers. And in almost all of them the sexes are at least equal.

In "Slap Out," for instance, the girl claps her hands if the wrong boy joins her, and the game continues until each girl is satisfied with her suitor. In "Chimney Sweeper" boys and girls alternate as the dominant partners, stepping over a broom to kiss their intended while singing. "Jumping the broomstick" became a country euphemism for marriage or lovemaking.

When not accompanied by dancing, many of the "play-party" songs are of the "answer-back," or riddle, variety, such as "Billy Boy"/"Charming Billy," "I Gave My Love a Cherry," "Cambric Shirt," and "Soldier Won't You Marry Me." The boy questions the girl, and she resists his musical advances with sassy comebacks. In "Paper of Pins" he tries bribing her with all kinds of material goods. She continues to turn him down until he gets to his "chest of gold."

The accompaniment to these amusements during the early 1800s would probably have been the dulcimer or the fiddle. Later in the century came the banjo, brought from Africa by slaves and introduced to white audiences via minstrel shows, which abounded by the 1840s. Then came the guitar. In better-off communities the piano and wheezing pump organ would have arrived.

The dulcimer is strongly identified with mountain women instrumentalists. The long, lap-held dulcimer is one of the simplest instruments to make by hand. This ancient music maker is mentioned in the book of Daniel in the Bible and was brought to England as the psaltery during the Crusades. Since women were the repositories of old English ballads, it fol-

The sprightly "Banjo Pickin' Gal" is a character who occurs in American folklore repeatedly. This anonymous 1890s picker was probably one of the earliest photographed.

lows that they would also play dulcimer, for the instrument is in modal tunings, survivals of medieval scales born in non-Western music.

By all accounts, the fiddle was the dominant instrument in rural American music until the 1930s. Known as "the devil's box" because of its association with drinking and dancing, it was played mainly by men.

Emma Bell Miles believed the sexes had two distinct musical traditions: "Men do not live in the house," she observed. "They commonly come in to eat and sleep, but their life is outdoors. . . . Let the woman's part be to preserve tradition. His are the adventures of which future ballads will be sung. . . . His first songs are yodels. Then he learns dance tunes, and songs of hunting and fighting and drinking. . . . It is over the loom and the knitting that the old ballads are dreamily, endlessly crooned. . . . The woman belongs to the race, to the old people."

But writing in 1909, Louise Rand Bascom noted: "The women are . . . endowed with musical talent; but they regard it as the man's prerogative and rarely touch an instrument when their husbands or sons are present. The author has known a certain woman for a dozen years and never dreamed that she could handle a fiddle bow till, on one occasion when much was said in admiration of her son's skill, she mentioned casually that she hadn't 'knowed the time' when she couldn't fiddle."

Contemporary country fiddler and quilter Vivian Williams has pointed out an odd convergence in American folk culture: Many quilt patterns have the same names as fiddle tunes or square dances— "Twin Sisters," "Arkansas Traveler," "Nelson's Victory," "Rippling Water," "Soldier's Joy," "Virginia Reel," and "Hands All Around" among them.

The numerous references to the "Banjo Pickin' Girl" in southern folk-lore indicate an active female instrumental tradition. The old-time banjo tune "Rachel" salutes Andrew Jackson's controversial wife Rachel Donelson, reputed to have been a backwoods banjo player, singer, and guitarist of the 1790s. In 1916 Maude Minnish Sutton collected songs from a "Banjo Pickin' Girl" of the mountains: "She was the usual, drab, flat-chested, snaggle-toothed, colorless crone, with her mouth full of snuff. The house was clean, though, and she had a big loom in the corner. I was looking at her woven counterpanes when I noticed a banjo hanging up. 'Do you play it?' I asked. 'I kin make that banjer talk,' she said. And she could."

Women also appear as the brash, rough-and-tumble subjects of many banjo songs, including "Cindy," "Liza Jane," and "Black-Eyed Susie": "Black-eyed Susie about half grown / Jumps on the boys like a dog on a bone / I asked her to be my wife / She come at me with a barlow knife."

Perhaps the most closely female-identified instruments were the piano and pump organ. Keyboard instruments sold in enormous quantities between 1860 and 1920 in rural America. The picture of the mother leading the family singing at the old parlor keyboard is one of the most common in American rural culture.

When they weren't coaching juvenile sopranos, mothers might have been dangling babies on their knees, rocking or bouncing them to the strains of pattycake tunes, nursery rhymes, and lullabies. Then as now, the first music nearly all babies heard was a mother's soft cradle song.

In 1719 Boston's Thomas Fleet published *Songs from the Nursery or Mother Goose's Melodies for Children*. According to one theory, this bible of kiddie rhymes was based on the songs he heard his British mother-in-law, Mrs. Isaac Goose (or Vertigoos), sing to her six grandchildren.

The female "song-saving" tradition also gave us our first folk song book. Lucy McKim Garrison was nineteen when she heard slave spirituals sung in war-torn Port Royal, South Carolina, in 1862. Moved, she published "Roll, Jordan, Roll" and "Poor Rosy, Poor Gal." During the next five years Lucy corresponded with other song enthusiasts and became the driving force behind the 1867 publication of *Slave Songs of the United States*.

Women have been enthusiastic chroniclers of folk music ever since. Indeed, the preservation of America's musical heritage was that rare area of work where women participated on a nearly equal footing with men. Ten-

The character of Mother Goose might be based on a Colonial grandma named Mrs. Isaac Vertigoos. Even if she wasn't the original, there's no denying women's deep and abiding association with children's folk tunes.

nessean Emma Bell Miles's fascination with mountain culture soon gripped many other women of her day. Josephine McGill, Susannah Wetmore, Ethel Park Richardson, Loraine Wyman, Annabell Morris Buchanon, Mary Wheeler, and Louise Rand Bascom were among the many female scholars captivated by Appalachian folk music.

Several left us vivid accounts of the culture. Dorothy Scarborough's tale of song collecting in the highlands of Virginia and North Carolina, *A Song Catcher in Southern Mountains*, rivals Emma's *Spirit of the Mountains* in rich detail and telling anecdote. Jean Thomas and Jean Ritchie both wrote books from the perspective of having grown up in the mountains. Thomas was a court stenographer who began her song collecting as a seventeen-year-old in 1898. Dubbed "The Traipsin' Woman" because of her song wanderings, she founded Kentucky's durable American Folk Song Festival.

Newspaper writer Maude Minnish Sutton, who collected in the North Carolina mountains from 1915 to 1925, left behind a lively diary of her experiences and opinions. After listening to one mountain mother sing a lullaby to her baby while sitting on a homemade chair on a log cabin's porch, Sutton wrote, "She might have been an Italian madonna with her blue-black hair combed smoothly back from her olive brow. She had the sweetest voice—low and clear with a plaintive note like a ring dove."

Jean Thomas, "The Traipsin' Woman," in 1939.

These women firmly believed that they were cherishing and preserving something of incalculable value. Jean Thomas incessantly reminded her readers and audiences that this was culture preserved from Elizabethan England. Sutton wrote of women old in the 1920s who had gotten songs from their female ancestors, who were old in the 1880s. And the generation of women before those grandmothers was alive during the birth of the United States.

"No songs are so popular as the ones that tell stories," she wrote. "How I hate to see the stupidly obvious moving picture take the place of this real literature, and jingling syncopated ragtime replace the living wail of these 'lonesome tunes.' Their crudities are as much a part of the folk to whom they belong as the rhododendrons are a part of the mountains. . . . When the present generation sneers these old songs away and the cheap gramophones have brought the . . . atrocities in, I wonder where they'll get their stories?"

Her sentiments were shared by an entire generation of folk-saving women. Sea chanteys, lumberjack songs, and African-American work songs were diligently preserved and published by female collectors as these melodies began to fade from American life. The first person to write of American cowboy folk songs was also a woman, Mary J. Jacques. She documented them in her 1894 book *Texas Ranch Life*.

Early cowboy lore is dominantly male, but the Wild West had its share of folk heroines, too. Tough mountain girls such as "Black-Eyed Susie," "Cindy," and "Liza Jane" had counterparts out west such as outlaws Cattle Kate and Rose of Cimarron, gamblers Poker Alice and Madame Moustache, prostitutes Kitty Le Roy and Little Gold Dollar, and colorful drunks Calamity Jane and Peg Leg Annie. All inspired folklore among the old-time cowboys.

So did many women who worked as cowhands alongside men in the Old West. "Arizona Boys and Girls," "Little Joe the Wrangler's Sister Nell," "The Fair Lady of the Plains," and "The Little Cowgirl" commemorate the able-bodied skills of these pioneer women.

"Pecos River Queen" salutes Texas cowgirl Patty Moorhead: "She's known by all the cowboys on the Pecos River wide / They know full well that she can shoot, that she can rope and ride / She can rope and tie and brand it as quick as any man / She's voted by all the cowboys as A-1 top cow hand." Similar skill is demonstrated by "The Cowboy's Girl," who "lived on the plains / She helped me herd cattle / Through mist, storm and rain." Rough and ready Miss Pompey Stiles appears in the cowboy song "The Dying Desperado": "She ain't much on the figger and don't give a damn for styles," but Pompey "Could spin the longest windy, could rope the biggest steer / And ride the wildest bronco that stands upon its ear."

Women began migrating westward with their families following the economic depression of the late 1830s. Approximately a quarter of a million Americans made the two-thousand-mile trip to California and Oregon between 1840 and 1865. The journey usually took nearly a year, during which they experienced immeasurable hardship. Hundreds of women's diaries have survived from this period, painting grim pictures of pioneer

Artist Paul Laune created this block print to illustrate the woman-to-woman folk-music preservation that resulted in books such as Dorothy Scarborough's *A Song Catcher in Southern Mountains* of 1937.

life. One out of every five migrating women either was pregnant or had a baby during the trip. In addition to "women's work" of cooking and washing, the pioneer mothers generally had to do heavy labor, too. Illness and death were ever present, but many women wrote that the most difficult part of their experience was their separation from other women.

Many did not survive, as many a sad cowboy has sung in "Colorado Trail." The hardship killed men by the thousands, too. Often women were widowed or left alone when husbands went hunting or prospecting. In such conditions, they were forced to become independent heads of households. Or independent otherwise. When it was a matter of sheer survival, women took on many untraditional roles.

Some became outlaws. Cowboy folksinger Jack Thorp collected two tunes about distaff bandits, "The Overland Stage" and "Women Outlaws." One of the most famous of all western songs, "Bucking Bronco"/"My Love Is a Rider," has long been ascribed to the outlaw queen Belle Starr. The hypothesis isn't unreasonable, since Myra Belle Shirley is known to have sung ballads and Confederate songs as a teenager in her father's Missouri tavern. She later became notable as a saloon pianist and entertainer in the boomtown of Dallas, Texas. Furthermore, the famed song dates from around 1878, which fits comfortably within Belle's life span, 1846 to 1889. And some of the song's bawdy stanzas certainly reflect her sexual reputation:

'Twas near the arroya he first laid me down
He was dressed for the round-up and I wore a gown
And he wiped off his chaps so the stain wouldn't show
And he turned and rode off on his bucking bronco.

My love had a gun that was dirty and long
But he wore it to visit the lady gone wrong
Though once it was strong and it shot straight and true
Now it wobbles and buckles and it's red, white and blue.

Young maidens take warning, where'er you reside
Beware of a cowboy who swings the rawhide
He'll love you, he'll lay you, then one day he'll go
In the spring up the trail on his bucking bronco.

Lie still ye young bastard, don't bother me so
Your father's off riding another bronco.

Lest that seem too outspoken for a woman of that era, consider the anecdote that Belle once forced a doctor who ridiculed her to kiss the anus of his horse at gunpoint.

The theatrical Belle wasn't the only woman who contributed to cowboy folk music. Cowgirl Jean Beaumondy may have had a hand in composing the once widely sung "Fightin' Mad." Montana Kate (Kate Childs) is given credit for originating the 1860s overlander ballad "California Trail." Agnes Morley Cleveland wrote the 1880s cowboy chestnut "When Bob Got Throwed."

Best known of all the western folk song heroines are "Clementine" and "Sweet Betsy from Pike." Betsy survives the journey west, separating from her husband, Ike, shouting, "Goodbye you big lummox, I'm glad you backed out."

The famous western song "Streets of Laredo" began life in America as a prostitute song variously known as "The Young Girl Cut Down in Her Prime," "When I Was a Young Girl," "The Bad Girl's Lament," or "One Morning in May." All of them are about women dying of syphilis or dissipation bemoaning their fate.

Prostitution has long been reflected in folk music. "Greensleeves," which first appears in print in 1580 in England, documents a man's infatuation with a lady of the streets. At the time, prostitutes were recognized by the green sleeves on their garments, green being the color of wantonness. In the American folk song "Home Daughter Home," a whore raises her daughter to be one, too, and sees no harm in it. The anonymous women who worked in nineteenth-century houses of prostitution reportedly gave us "A Hot Time in the Old Town Tonight," "Bang Bang Lulu," "Ta-Ra-Ra-Boom-De-Ay," "The Bully Song," "Who Stole the Lock on the Henhouse Door?," and numerous other familiar American tunes. Belle Starr's daughter Pearl Starr operated the Fort Smith, Arkansas, brothel that popularized the cowboy folk song "Boring for Oil."

The best-known woman's song from this subculture is undoubtedly "Rising Sun Blues,"

Belle Starr, c. 1880.

sung from the point of view of the rueful prostitute and notable for its woman-to-woman warning stanza: "Go tell my baby sister / Never do like I have done / Tell her shun that house in New Orleans / They call the Rising Sun." The heroine of "Cocaine Lil" fares no better than her prostitute sisters, dying of an overdose.

Women outside the realm of law and respectability are a breed one encounters time and again in our folklore. "The Female Smuggler" tells the tale of a lady pirate and may be based on the careers of Mary Read, Anne Bonney, or other lady adventurers who operated in the Atlantic in the 1700s. Another distinctly American outlaw character is the female moonshiner, immortalized as "Darlin' Corey" and her bluegrass relative "Little Maggie."

The ultimate crime of murder is the basis of the renowned "Frankie and Johnny." For generations, folksingers have told the tale of wronged Frankie gunning down her cheating Johnny in the barroom. Sung by both blacks and whites, this nineteenth-century song concludes, "This story has no moral / This story has no end / It only goes to show you / There ain't no good in men."

Besides "Frankie and Johnny," the most noteworthy American murderess ballad is "Frankie Silvers." Frances Silvers killed her husband, Charlie, in Burke County, North Carolina, in 1831 and allegedly recited the song that bears her name at her hanging in 1833. Less well known is Sarah Ann Legg. When she disposed of her husband in West Virginia in 1904, it inspired a ballad called "The Murder of Jay Legg." The Arkansas Ozark ballad "Love Henery" tells the story of a woman who stabs and drowns her lover because he is married to another. There is a woman's version of "Greenback Dollar" with the threatening lines "I don't want your greenback dollar / I don't want your diamond ring / All I want is a .38 special / To blow out your dirty brains." Family-murdering women such as Lizzie Borden (1892) and Lydia Sherman (1864) have also entered American folklore in rhyme.

In song as in life, women are far more often the victims of violence than its perpetrators. The archetypal folk ballad in this country is the murder of a hapless, pregnant girl by a boyfriend who is unwilling to marry her. There are some examples of this in British-originated folk songs such as the murder of "Pretty Polly" by Willie, and the "Rose Connally"/"Down in Willow Garden" songs. But in general this is an American-born genre, typified by songs such as "Banks of the Ohio."

Pregnant "Naomi Wise" was murdered in 1808 by Jonathan Lewis near Ashboro, North Carolina. Pregnant "Poor Ellen Smith" was murdered by Peter DeGraff in 1892 in Forsyth County, North Carolina.

Pregnant "Pearl Bryan" was mutilated and disposed of by Scott Jackson and Alonzo Welling after she died during their abortion attempt in Cincinnati in 1896. Factory worker "Little Mary Phagan" was assaulted and murdered in Atlanta in 1913. Laura Foster met her death at the hands of "Tom Dooley"/"Tom Dula" in 1866 near Ferguson, North Carolina. Ella Mae Cropsey, known in song as "Ella Crappy" or "Nellie Cropsey," was murdered by James Wilcox, also in North Carolina.

Little Nellie Meeks survived the "Meeks Murders" committed by the Taylor family at Browning, Missouri, in 1894 and subsequently appeared in tent shows around the state. She'd brush back her hair to reveal the dent in her head caused by the ax blow and sing "Nellie's Lament."

These kinds of songs have held their fascination for singers of both sexes for generations. Early country star Moonshine Kate sang the saga of "Little Mary Phagan" in the 1920s; and you can still hear Wilma Lee Cooper wailing the sad tale of "Poor Ellen Smith" on the stage of the Grand Ole Opry today.

The tragic deaths of fair young women were popular ballad topics even if the women weren't murdered. Often these tragedies had strong morals attached. "Young Charlotte" tells the story of an excitable, headstrong girl who refuses her mother's offer of a blanket on a New Year's Eve sleigh ride with her boyfriend and freezes to death. Little girls' china dolls in the nineteenth century were dubbed "frozen Charlottes" after this 1840s ballad. "The Orphan Girl" also freezes to death, but the moral is drawn against the rich man on whose doorstep she perishes begging.

Tales of the hardship and exploitation of downtrodden poor women also provided a framework for the earliest American labor protest songs. The first factory system in the United States was established by the textile industry in New England around 1815 with a work force composed principally of women and children. The women were the daughters of nearby farmers, housed in company boardinghouses and worked fourteen hours a day for pitifully low wages. Since then, the female-dominated textile industry has produced more topical and social protest song material than any other labor group, with the exception of miners. "The Lowell Factory Girl" dates from the 1830s and has been found in various forms in Massachusetts, Maine, Florida, and Texas. One North Carolina variant is called "No More Shall I Work in the Factory." Among the dozens of songs spawned by women's deplorable working conditions in nineteenth-century factories are "All the Doo Da Day," "Factory Girl's Come-All-Ye," and "Thirty Cents a Day."

The only other significant group of work songs from women came from store clerks. "The Victory" and "Oh Let the Girls Sit Down" both

THE MURDERED WOMEN OF AMERICAN FOLK SONG

Among the dozens of victims commemorated in American folk and country songs are the following fair maidens:

LOTTIE SHORN, FANNY MOORE, FRIEDA BOLT, LULA VRIES, GRACE BROWN, POLLY WILLIAMS, FLORELLA, CATHERINE BERRINGER, MARY ANN WYATT, SARAH FURBER, SERVILLA, NELLIE PAGET, JOSIE LANGMAID, LOTTIE YATES, SALLY COCHRAN, GLADYS KINCAID, KITTY GING, LURA PARSONS, THE LAWSON FAMILY, AND LITTLE MARION PARKER

Emma Bell Miles, 1900.

resulted from a strike waged by girls working in the department stores of St. Louis in the 1870s.

Industrialization came late to the South. The Civil War transformed Dixie's agrarian economy, and in its aftermath mines and textile mills both proliferated. In the West, timber cutting, mining, and railway construction boomed. By the turn of the century even the most remote areas were not immune to the spread of wage labor.

"My people . . . are being swept away by the oncoming tide of civilization," mourned Emma in the last chapter of *Spirit of the Mountains*. "Good roads are built in place of the old creek beds and trails, and rubber-tired carriages whirl past the plodding oxen and mule teams." She realized that the advent of businesses meant her neighbors would lose their way of life. "A host of evils follow. Here is an easy way of making money, and the old pursuits are abandoned. Men neglect their farms and the fashioning of sturdy home-made implements and utensils. It is easier, by far, to buy tools with the city money. . . . The homespuns, with their delightful dull colors of root and bark, are ousted by aniline-dyed calicoes which do not wear more than a season. . . . the loom and wheel are consigned to a barn loft, where they fall to pieces with dry-rot, and the woman forgets her coverlet patterns. . . . The old music is supplanted by cheap Sunday-school songbooks."

Emma wrote that country people realized too late the folly of the new-fangled life-style. Around mines and mills, owners built rows of cheap clapboard houses and company stores where workers were required to shop. Women and children labored in the factories for sixteen hours a day and barely made enough to cover the owners' rent and food charges. Sanitary conditions were abominable, and education nearly completely lacking. Industrial accidents crippled thousands of laborers. Those not felled by inhuman working conditions might fall victim to tuberculosis, hookworm, malnutrition, flu, or pellagra.

Women fought alongside men in the struggle to better working people's lives. Before he was executed in 1915, labor organizer Joe Hill sent out his song "The Rebel Girl" as a salute to all the women who supported the union movement. The 1930 passing of the widely beloved labor organizer Mary Harris Jones was saluted even by Gene Autry in "The Death of Mother Jones." During a 1929 unionizing struggle, Ella May Wiggins composed "Mill Mother's Lament," the song that was sung at her funeral after she was gunned down by mill-boss goons. The North Carolina factory laborer had become a workers' activist after losing four of her nine children to whooping cough because she couldn't afford medical care on her wages.

Emma Bell Miles also died in tragic poverty, unable to buy proper treatment for the tuberculosis that ravaged her body. Frank became increasingly dissolute—malingering about imagined illnesses, becoming subject to angry outbursts, unable or unwilling to work, wasting the little money they had. In the throes of TB she was forced to provide for herself and her four surviving children. She tried selling her drawings and paintings, writing a nature column for the Chattanooga newspaper, giving lectures on mountain culture, and selling herself as a ghostwriter for others.

But by 1916 her strength had faded so much that often she could scarcely leave her bed. She prepared for suicide by gathering wild poisonous thorn apples. Her society friends formed a charity organization to provide for her so that she could finish another book.

Emma wrote that she could not bear this "sense of loss, of defeat and degradation, the hopelessness of Frank's character, and the trap in which he holds me helpless." Her love for him was dead, and weighing less than ninety pounds, she was dying; yet he still insisted on his conjugal rights.

In 1917 she vowed to stop giving Frank money and to die in peace. By 1918 she was beginning to think of death as a joyous release from the poverty and hardship she had endured.

". . . after my escape I shall no longer have to work for money which does no one any good, being wasted by self-willed mismanagement. . . . I shall not be compelled to yield my body to sexual torture. . . . I shall not be pinched by continual want."

She got her release on March 19, 1919, two weeks after the publication of *Our Southern Birds,* the collection of drawings and prose that was her last idyll to mountain life.

She was thirty-nine years old.

SOUTHERN SENTIMENTS

Country Females in Nineteenth-Century Show Business

Abby Hutchinson, 1847.

They called them "crackers," "dirt eaters," "wool hats," "low-downers," "po' buckra," "white trash," "sand-hillers," "piney woods tackies," "tar-heels," "peck-erwoods," "mean whites," "no-'counts," and "hillbillies."

As early as the 1840s, popular literature and entertainment had created negative stereotypes of poor white Southerners. Folk humorists characterized male mountaineers as degenerate, inbred, illiterate, dirty, immoral, drunken, foolish, shiftless, and lawless, and their female counterparts as pipe smoking, snuff dipping, work-laden, slutty, and ugly.

Hicks first appear as American stock characters in stage shows of the 1820s, though they weren't necessarily from the South, just rural. They were comedic rustic figures—generally innocents whose guileless nature masked an earthy wisdom. At times, as in the 1830s' rise of Davy Crockett and Johnny Appleseed as pop culture figures, backwoods ways were even portrayed as heroic. They often poked fun at the rich and powerful.

The poor-but-proud sentiment has been in American song from the time of "Yankee Doodle," our first hit tune. It turned a British ditty mocking colonials as bumpkins into a rallying song in the 1760s. The tune was spread in

colonial America by several theatrical troupes, including Nancy Hallam's. She and Maria Storer emerged as the colonies' first female stage stars.

The association of stage entertainment with drinking and prostitution precluded all but a few women from the profession prior to the Civil War. Virtually every religious sect officially declared the theater a den of sin. Any woman choosing it as her livelihood was an immoral slut by association.

Literature and sermons of the nineteenth century unendingly emphasized the home as a woman's proper sphere of activity. A lady was to be chaste and pure. She was expected to be the bearer of the family's religious and moral conscience. Piety, submissiveness, and domesticity were preached. Public activity of any kind was frowned upon. The 20 percent of women who worked were generally domestics and laundresses, textile factory girls, or cigar makers. In marriage women lost all civil rights, including the right to hold property or control their own wages. Women did not have the right to vote. They could not attend college.

But some women turned the ideal of piety and purity on its head. They entered public life in the mid-1800s carrying the banner of morality. Women formed religious and reform associations aiming to improve the world, not just the living room. Orphanages, single women's homes, temperance societies, prostitution reform groups, slavery abolition groups, and widows' benevolent societies sprang up. Evangelists and social reformers were America's first big female public personalities as a series of religious revivals swept across the land.

The most female-dominated of the revivals was the Shaker sect, inspired by the prophetess Mother Ann Lee. She wrote or inspired all its songs. Likewise, the Holy Roller churches were often led by female singing visionaries. The shape-note, "fa-so-la" singing tradition was another gospel music style where women's contributions became important.

American Sunday schools got one of their first musical guidebooks with 1804's *Hymns for Infant Minds* by Ann and James Taylor. One of the earliest collections of camp-meeting hymns was compiled and published in 1816 by Peggy Dow. The era's female poets provided the lyrics to some of our most enduring gospel songs. "Jesus Loves Me," "Just as I Am," "Will the Circle Be Unbroken," and dozens of other religious lyrics are by nineteenth-century women. In the 1850s, Mary Ann Kidder created dozens of Baptist hymns.

The women who might be called America's first "country sweetheart" performers also grew from religious roots. The singing, moralistic Hutchinson Family made its debut in 1838. By the end of the century the clan was an American institution.

New Hampshire farmer Jesse Hutchinson and his wife Mary had

thirteen children who survived to adulthood. Sons John, Asa, and Judson defied Jesse's will and began singing in local inns. But it was youngest daughter Abby Hutchinson (1829–1892) who became the family's star.

Although there was no such term at the time, the Hutchinsons were "country music." The siblings were self-taught as fiddlers, and a number of reviewers commented on their rustic, offbeat vocal harmony. In their early years they were criticized for their "farm talk" vocabulary. In an era that idolized the art singing of "Swedish Nightingale" Jenny Lind, Abby Hutchinson's simple, untrained voice was refreshingly different. A British reviewer described Abby in 1846 as "sweetly unassuming." He added, "There are no meretricious smiles—no rouged cheeks—nothing at all about her that in the least savors of affectation. As the little Yankee girl stands, dressed in a plain . . . gown, without a single ornament . . . many a nod of delighted approbation is exchanged amongst the . . . audience. It is indeed something new to them to behold one so utterly artless in so public a position."

At their earliest shows the Hutchinsons sang the ageless folk song "Barbara Allen." Later Abby arranged and popularized such black spirituals as "Nobody Knows the Trouble I've Seen." During an 1842 visit to Lowell, Massachusetts, a factory girl gave her "Hannah's Binding Shoes," which became one of Abby's favorite concert songs. "Kind Words Can Never Die," Abby's own simple composition, was for some years a backwoods favorite.

Her big showstopper was "The Snow Storm," which told the tale of a young woman struggling through drifts, carrying her baby. The mother tears the clothes off her body to cover the infant and dies of exposure. The Hutchinsons also popularized such sentimental fare as "Sweet By and By," "Lorena," "The Drunkard's Wife," and "Home Sweet Home." Their concert songs "From Greenland's Icy Mountains" and "Praise God from Whom All Blessings Flow" are still familiar to churchgoers today. The Hutchinsons are particularly associated with the Civil War standards "Tenting Tonight on the Old Camp Ground," "We Are Coming Father Abraham," and "The Battle Cry of Freedom."

The family was supportive of slavery's abolition, women's rights, temperance, communal living, clothing reform, international peace, and other progressive ideals of the day. "Get Off the Track!," sung to the tune of the minstrel song "Old Dan Tucker," was one of their big antislavery numbers. The activist Hutchinsons helped sing "log cabin" candidate William Henry Harrison into the presidency with "Tippecanoe and Tyler Too" in 1840.

The concert tours and her volatile brothers' bickering were hard on

In the wake of the fabulously successful Hutchinson Family in the 1800s came a myriad of touring family troupes. Among the most popular were the following:

THE ALLEGHENIANS

THE BAKER FAMILY

THE BARKER FAMILY

THE DEMOSS FAMILY BARDS

THE FLOWERS FAMILY

THE FOX SISTERS

THE GIBSON FAMILY

THE HARMONIUM FAMILY

THE HAUSER FAMILY

THE HIGGINS FAMILY

THE LUCA FAMILY

THE McGIBENEY FAMILY

THE STENYAN FAMILY

Abby, who dropped out of the act for a time in the 1850s. This prompted brother Judson to tour with his daughter Kate as Abby's substitute. For the sake of the Civil War effort, Abby reunited with John and Asa, but when she retired again after the war, the brothers split into two singing groups.

Brother John's included as Abby's replacements his wife, Fanny; his daughter, Viola; and his daughter-in-law, Lillie. They popularized the future country standard "Root Hog or Die." Brother Asa toured with his wife, Lizzie, and daughter, Little Abby, as stand-ins for the original "sweetheart" of the family. Then Lizzie and Asa began "adopting" a series of pseudodaughters in the 1870s, creating a dynasty of country misses. To nineteenth-century music lovers, the myriad of family members wasn't important; the very name Hutchinson meant entertainment.

By the end of the century the plain-speaking, plain-singing New Englanders were nationally revered. During the U.S. centennial celebration of 1876 in Washington, D.C., Fanny, Viola, and Abby raised their voices for women's rights with Lucretia Mott and Elizabeth Cady Stanton with "Nearer My God to Thee" and "A Hundred Years Hence." Abby's last major singing appearance was in 1892 in a trio with brother John and the great black libertarian Frederick Douglass.

The Hutchinson Family spawned a whole series of professional singing families. More than a dozen popular Hutchinson imitators toured the United States between 1840 and 1890. Such acts established the song themes adopted by the early professional country music women in decades to come—home and hearth, religion, sentiment for the downtrodden, praise for rural virtues.

It was as members of family acts or evangelical groups that most women initially appeared before rural audiences. But not all. In frontier areas churches weren't as powerful; audiences were hungry for entertainment, and women weren't bound to middle-class conventions.

The West was where America's first homegrown, homespun solo woman headliner rose to fame. Lotta Crabtree (1847–1924) was the first major female stage personality to capture the spirit of common folks in a down-to-earth image. Born Charlotte Mignon Crabtree in New York in 1847, she was taken west to California in 1853 after her father caught gold fever. Mama Mary Ann Livesay Crabtree ran a boardinghouse in Grass Valley, California, where the tot met dancer Lola Montes.

Irish-born Montes, known as "The Divine Eccentric," was then all the rage with her celebrated spider dance. Kiddie performers were enjoying a vogue at the time, and Lola was impressed by the elfin Lotta. She wanted to take the talented child on the road. Mama turned the star down, but when a local theater needed a replacement for a juvenile act in 1855, she made her eight-year-old daughter an Irish costume and put her on the stage. Lotta danced jigs and reels and sang popular ballads of the day, launching her career.

Lotta and her mother hit the road, traveling by horseback from mining town to mining town, performing in saloon after saloon. The child refined her act to please the commonfolk, the rowdy-but-sentimental adventurers who populated California. She learned to play the banjo and developed skills as a mimic and mime. She became a boisterous, vivacious hoyden, full of rambunctious tomboy charm.

Hers was a very physical act. Lotta threw her legs about, showed her petticoats, and rolled around wildly. She was reportedly quite an ad-libber, with most of her humor centered in character parts, including old ladies, newsboys, blackface children, gypsies, poor little girls, and Irish immigrants. Lotta had the ability to be flirtatious and risqué, yet remain naive and innocent. Mugging and winking, she'd sing the coy "The Captain and His Whiskers Gave a Sly Wink at Me," recorded sixty-five years later as a country tune. Garbed in a soldier's uniform, she'd belt out the Civil War anthem "Rally 'Round the Flag, Boys." The lollapalooza was her closing number. Clad in angelic white, Lotta would sing a tear-jerking ballad, such as "Dear Mother I'll Come Home Again." The misty-eyed miners would toss gold at her feet. By the time she died in 1924, Lotta Crabtree had amassed four million dollars.

Lotta Crabtree, c. 1870.

In 1864 she began appearing in custom-written musical plays, the most famous of which was a comedy based on the Charles Dickens poor-waif character Little Nell. By the 1870s Lotta was a national celebrity. "The Lotta Polka" and "The Lotta Gallop" were widely popular dance songs published to salute her fame.

Her chaperone mother remained with her throughout, living until Lotta was sixty and long retired. Reportedly the stage mother to end all stage mothers, Mama Mary Ann discouraged all Lotta's suitors and shrewdly invested the little star's money in property in numerous cities where the show stopped. Lotta never married.

She quit show business at age forty-three in 1890, while still quite popular. "I think I am a lucky lady," she said. "I had the money to leave the hard grind while I was still young enough to enjoy life." She took up painting, tended expertly to her real estate investments, and became a philanthropist.

Despite her millions, she was denied membership in a society women's club in New York in 1893 because of her unladylike stage career. When she died at age seventy-seven, Lotta Crabtree left her money to war veterans, art and music students, hospitals, prisoners, and animal shelters.

When she began, she was virtually alone as a female star. By the time she retired, Lotta Crabtree had contemporaries from coast to coast who would influence the direction country music would take in the twentieth century. In the Northeast, for instance, vocalist Rose Merrifield was the popularizer of 1855's "Listen to the Mockingbird," later a fiddle standard. In the South, "Dixie" was introduced by singers Mrs. John Woods and Susan Denin in New Orleans in 1860. "The Bonnie Blue Flag" was written in 1861 by the brother-sister team Harry and Marion Macarthy as the finale to their stage act.

After the Civil War, there was a huge outpouring of sentimental tunes nostalgically portraying the defeated Confederacy. Pity for the degraded South was reflected in minstrel numbers such as "Carry Me Back to Ole Virginny" (1878) and "The Little Little Old Log Cabin in the Lane" (1871), all inspired by Stephen Foster's immortal output of 1843–1864, including "The Old Folks at Home" and "My Old Kentucky Home." This sentimental Southern material later became strongly associated with female performers in the early days of sound recording, as well as with country entertainers.

Many Southern stage stereotypes, including those of women, had been established in blackface minstrelsy. Often associated with showboats, this show-biz genre rose to enormous popularity with common people between 1830 and 1870. From minstrel shows came the sentimental figures of the wise old aunt or granny and the assertive, comedic farm gal, usually portrayed by men in drag.

Vaudeville replaced minstrelsy in the 1870s. In minstrel show times the only women generally in a theater were prostitutes or hostesses selling drinks. Vaudeville, on the other hand, was marketed as no-alcohol "family entertainment." Female entertainers were welcomed after the integration of women into its audiences around the mid-1880s. Around this same time, mocking ethnic groups with stereotypes like the Jewish tightwad, the Irish drunk, and the German immigrant became increasingly unfashionable, but hicks in the South were still a safe target for vaudevillians. Southerners and country folk became the main objects of ridicule, derision, and disdain. Audiences and show people alike called them "rubes."

Vaudeville featured clog dancers, banjo and fiddle players, ocarina soloists, yodeling acts, jug bands, and other entertainments associated with rural people. In the 1890s it expanded female country stereotypes with such stock figures as the man-hungry old maid, the innocently sexy farm girl, the brash tomboy, the virginal sister/sweetheart, and other personalities. These remained on view a century later on the television program "Hee Haw."

So with vaudeville came female stars. Indeed, during its full flower in the late 1890s and early 1900s, its *biggest* stars were women—Eva Tanguay, Nora Bayes, Lillian Russell, Elsie Janis, May Irwin.

Sophie Tucker (1884–1966) influenced such diverse country performers as cowgirl singer Texas Ruby, radio barn dance star Louisiana Lou, and torchy teen sensation Brenda Lee. In vaudeville she was "The Last of the Red Hot Mamas." "Oh, show business was flourishing. In those days," recalled Sophie in her vivid autobiography, *Some of These Days*, "if you wanted to tap your foot to a swell new tune . . . or laugh away your worries, you went to a show. You didn't just sit home and twiddle a button" on a radio or TV.

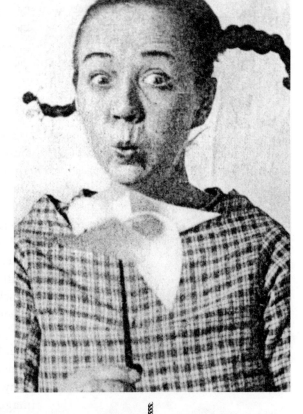

Rose Melville as "Sis Hopkins," c. 1910.

"Vaudeville, playing daily matinees, depended on women. You had to please the women patrons to be and stay a headliner." Vaudeville's women were first and foremost for the working class. Vaudeville was earthy, inexpensive, and proletarian. It aired the complaints and concerns of the poor as nothing before it had, establishing a tradition that country music took as its own in the twentieth century.

Although developed in the cities, its touring circuits eventually reached virtually every state, knitting America together with mass musical culture and low comedy. *Sis Hopkins, the Country Girl* was the blueprint for vaudeville's female rubes. Performer Rose Melville was linked inseparably to this role in her shapeless dress, pigtailed hair, and hanging petticoat. For decades after, female vaudevillians imitated this portrayal.

Ida and Pearl Melville were established midwestern vaudevillians when little sister Rose joined them on the road in 1889. Two years later

Ida and Rose worked up a show called *Zeb,* in which the latter introduced an ungainly country girl character. In 1894 the sisters became a New York vaudeville sensation as "Two Little Jays from Indiana," with Rose doing the singing and dancing. After Ida retired, Rose renamed the act "Sis Hopkins" and portrayed "Sis" successfully for more than twenty years thereafter, eventually translating her popularity into a newspaper column called "Sis Hopkins' Sayings" and a 1914 series of "Sis Hopkins" silent-movie comedies.

Rubes hit their stride at the turn of the century. Between 1885 and 1915 there were more than a dozen Broadway shows with country, southern, and western themes. By the early 1900s, rural humorists such as the husband-wife Sidmans team were common on vaudeville bills. Mrs. Neil Litchfield performed hick routines with her husband, too. Mr. and Mrs. Jimmie Barry's big skit at the turn of the century was "The Rube," wherein he was the yokel and she the city girl. Martin and Fabbrini did a novelty dance act as a hick schoolboy and his gal. *Variety* said of Rae Samuels, "There's no girl who sings a rube number as well as she does." Jane Green was "The Kentucky Speedball" of Los Angeles from 1908 to 1916, delighting audiences with trick riding in cowgirl fringe and singing "My Old Kentucky Home." Jane was part Cherokee and was sometimes billed under her Indian name, Mikigado.

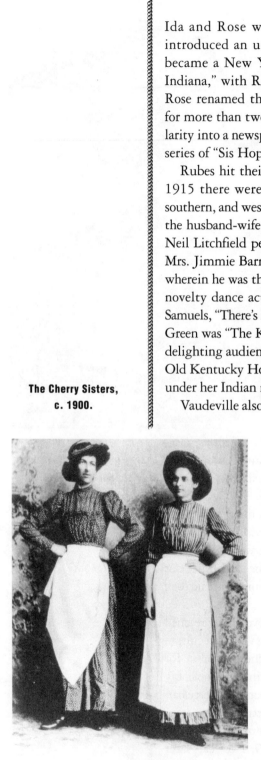

The Cherry Sisters, c. 1900.

Vaudeville also enthusiastically welcomed a host of singing sister acts, many of which traded on innocent, girl-next-door images. Early favorites included Lulu and Mabel Nichols performing "plantation songs and dances," and the banjo-playing Tobin and Carmen sisters. In addition to their "Topsy and Eva" *Uncle Tom's Cabin* burlesque, the Duncan Sisters performed rube dialogue skits. By 1917 the Fuller Sisters were renowned for singing the folk song "Raggle-Taggle Gypsies," now better known as "Black Jack Davey."

But it is doubtful that any such sibling sweethearts could have sufficiently prepared audiences for the amazing Cherry Sisters, who began performing in 1893. Despite universal panning from critics, these Iowa farm girls resolutely continued moaning their homey songs with piano accompaniment billed as "The World's Worst Sister Act."

The Cherrys were the originators of the "so-bad-it's-good" show, the queens of high camp of their time. There were originally five of them—Ella, Jessie, Lizzie,

32 *Finding Her Voice*

Addie, and Effie—farm girls from near Cedar Rapids. Wrote *Coronet* magazine, "Their voices were twangy and irritating; they were personally ungainly and their choice of apparel—usually home-made calico creations—was a modiste's nightmare."

Addie and Effie were the mainstays. The two eventually had to play behind netting to protect them from flung produce. After a particularly vicious review appeared in 1900, the bucolic team sued for libel. In a landmark decision, the Iowa Supreme Court held that newspapers have the right to criticize freely and even to hold public figures up to ridicule.

"As terribleness, their skit is perfection," opined *Variety*. The Cherrys were recalled generations later every time country music's Minnie Pearl or "Hee Haw"'s Roni Stoneman intentionally sang loudly and off-key for a laugh.

If the bizarre Cherry Sisters had done rope tricks, they might have gotten some respect. Rubes were comics; but westerners got the heroic treatment. The cowgirl image in show business dates from at least the 1850s, when Mary Ann Whittaker gave public exhibitions of her western horseback riding abilities. Dime novels of the 1870s and 1880s told of Hurricane Nell, the queen of the saddle and lasso, of Bess the Trapper, of Wild Edna, and of Rowdy Kate, all of whom rode and shot in buckskin and leather as the equals of frontier men. A highly embellished autobiography by hell-raiser Calamity Jane (Martha Jane Canary, c. 1852–1903) was quite popular in 1896, and her many personal appearances furthered her alleged cowgirl exploits.

Sheet music tunesmiths did their part to popularize the Golden West, turning out a rash of songs with Indian characters between 1903 and 1910, followed by a flood of western titles from 1905 to 1919. These included the widely sung "Sierra Sue," "Cheyenne (Shy Ann)," "Rio Grande," "Pride of the Prairie," and "The Girl I Loved Out in the Golden West."

Cowgirl images were sensationally popular in the touring Wild West troupes. One of the star attractions of Buffalo Bill Cody's Wild West Show from 1883 to 1902 was sharpshooter Annie Oakley (Phoebe Ann Moses, 1860–1926). Her "dead shot" ability to fire holes through the spots on playing cards became so legendary that tickets with punched holes were called "Annie Oakleys" in show business parlance. By 1887 more than a dozen other cowgirls were in Buffalo Bill's Wild West Show.

Kitty Lee (1868–c. 1949) was a trick rider who trouped with Buffalo Bill and Annie beginning in 1893. The two women became buddies, and in later years Kitty liked to recall target shooting with her celebrated contemporary. In 1895 Kitty married fellow Buffalo Bill headliner Powder River Jack Lee, and together they formed one of the pioneering western music acts. Jack popularized traditional

"COUNTRY" PLAYS AND MUSICALS

Western, country, frontier, and Dixie themes enjoyed a vogue in the theater world around the turn of the century. Among the productions that incorporated them, in either musical or melodrama, were the following:

The Maid and the Moonshiner (1886)

In Old Kentucky (1893)

The Ogallallas (1894)

Westward Ho (1894)

The Glad Hand (1897)

Tennessee Tess, the Queen of the Moonshiners (c. 1898)

When Johnny Comes Marching Home (1902)

The Girl from Dixie (1903)

The Southerners (1904)

Pioneer Days (1906)

Louisiana Lou (1911)

cowboy tunes like "Red River Valley," and Kitty was his guitarist.

Billy McGinty was another of Buffalo Bill's stars. He, too, used the show business smarts he learned in Cody's troupe to start a traveling cowboy band. His female singer was his wife, Mollie.

The McGinty musicians eventually merged with the cowboy band led by Oklahoman Otto Gray and his singing wife, "Mommie." Otto provided the business savvy and showmanship, but by many reports it was Mommie's plain, no-frills singing of sentimental ballads that was their act's drawing card. She also performed rope tricks on stage.

Mommie (c. 1889–c. 1946), who was born Grace Means, came by her western and old-time repertoire naturally, having been one of twelve children in a Kansas ranching family. As a youngster, Mommie was reportedly a song collector, in the folk tradition of ballad-saving women.

Around 1905, when she and Otto were still teenagers, they married, and she began living the rough life of a farm wife. A drought and a cholera epidemic wiped them out in 1907, and they migrated from Oklahoma to Wyoming. There, Mommie lived in a tent on the prairie with Otto, cooked for thirty working cowboys, churned butter, carried a child, helped to milk sixty-three cattle, chopped cotton, did housework, and still had the energy to sing with the cowpunchers at night. "Her hands are those of a woman who has worked hard," was the understatement in a 1934 story about Otto Gray and His Oklahoma Cowboy Band.

Otto and Mommie Gray, c. 1928.

The song saving of Mommie's girlhood proved to be invaluable. Otto and Mommie began singing at fairs and circuses, forming their first western music band in 1918. Initially dubbed Otto and His Rodeo Rubes, the band "drew upon her storehouse of . . . songs she had learned from the cowboys who rode with her father," according to Otto's publicity. The act could reportedly perform for eighteen straight hours without repeating a song or looking at a sheet of music. "We acted like we were in the bunkhouse back at the ranch," Otto said. "People had never heard anything like us."

After merging with McGinty's group, the Grays hit the road in 1924, and by 1926 they were on the Orpheum vaudeville circuit. They blazed a trail eastward, giving many people their first exposure to cowboy music. By the time the group disbanded in 1936, the couple had made a fortune.

Mommie's most popular numbers were the nineteenth-century motherhood songs "Your Mother Still Prays for You, Jack" and "Where Is My Wandering Boy Tonight." She also handled cowboy fare such as "Bury Me on the Lone Prairie" and such vintage tragic pieces as "In the Baggage Coach Ahead," "Drunkard's Lone Child," and "Blind Child."

Despite her stage popularity, she remained consistently in the background in the act's publicity, always allowing Otto to have the lion's share of the limelight. Mommie Gray once said, "If I had four dozen [children] I'd want them all to be boys. There are too many temptations for girls these days, and once a girl falls by the way she cannot come back. But a man—well, it's a man's world, in spite of all the talk of women's freedom."

The cowboy/cowgirl was a completely American cultural metaphor for people's unfulfilled dreams and aspirations. It represented a simple life. It emphasized freedom and adventure. And for women it was totally unlike the confining ideals of turn-of-the-century America.

In 1905 authentic Oklahoma ranch hand Lucille Mulhall (1886–1940) appeared in Madison Square Garden, demonstrating her skills at lariat twirling, riding, and steer lassoing. Lucille was a western superstar of 1900–1915, and a media sensation for her equestrian feats of derring-do in her father's Wild West show. President Teddy Roosevelt dubbed her a "cowgirl," making the term nationally popular for the first time; within a decade her image was copied by more than sixty other entertainers.

In 1911 Sophie Tucker encountered cowgirl Texas Guinan on a vaudeville bill in Seattle. "She was doing a western act," Tucker recalled. "She had something that made everyone feel instantly at ease and ready for a good time. And she had a heart as big as her native state." Both Texas Guinan and Lucille Mulhall became silent-screen stars. Later Texas was the queen of New York's speakeasies during Prohibition, becoming legendary in show business for her catchphrase, "Give the little girl a great big hand!" and her brassy barroom greeting, "Hello, suckers!"

Touring at the turn of the century was no picnic, whether you came from Texas or Tennessee. "Sometimes I used to stare at the four walls of my boarding-house bedroom and wonder if I had really ever had any other home," Sophie Tucker recalled. "I look back at some of the theaters we played—drafty old firetraps, no toilets, filthy dirty cracked walls that let in the wind and the rain, old broken floors. . . . Never enough heat. I would come into one of these places, take a look around, and then roll up my sleeves. I would borrow a hammer and nails, get a heavy cardboard to

The cowgirl image was developed in Wild West shows, in dime novels, and on the covers of popular pieces of sheet music such as 1919's "Rio Grande."

cover up the ratholes in the wall and ceiling of my dressing room."

And those were accommodations for a *headliner.* Most acts played under worse circumstances. Out in the boondocks, hundreds of itinerant thespians, evangelists, medicine-show troupes, comics, and musicians labored from town to town in makeshift tents, on flatbed wagons, or in barns.

One of the earliest professional hillbilly groups was The Carver Family. The leader was Lorenzo Dow Carver, a blind man who was joined by his five brothers and four sisters playing fairs throughout Kentucky and Tennessee around 1904–1905. Brother Henry's daughter Emmy began doing road shows with the act in 1911, when she was eight. She continued to combine country music with vaudeville showmanship in adulthood as Cousin Emmy (1903–1980). The brassy, blond Kentuckian survived decades of shifting musical tastes to be rediscovered by collegiate folk fans of the 1960s.

"We started traveling with our music in 1918," recalled Ada Powers, the youngest of the three daughters who accompanied champ fiddler Cowan Powers in a family string band that toured the southern mountains. "We made our best money on those West Virginia and Kentucky mining towns. It was not unusual in there to take in over two hundred dollars a night—at twenty-five cents an adult and fifteen cents a child." Cowan Powers and his wife, Tilda, were Virginia mountain musicians who married in 1900. Charles, born to them in 1902, was taught banjo. Orpha, born in 1904, became the family mandolinist. Carrie, born in 1908, learned guitar. Ada, the baby, was taught to dance and play ukulele by her fiddling parents. After Tilda died of TB at age thirty-five in 1916, Cowan took the children on the road as a band. "At first we traveled by train," Ada recalls, "but then Daddy bought one of the first . . . Model T Fords . . . and we went in that. I can still hear those old curtains in the back flapping in the cold wind." Fiddlin' Powers and Family eventually made it onto radio and records in the 1920s.

Missouri's Leon "Abner" Weaver liked to bill himself as vaudeville's first rube. He began in show business in 1902. After some medicine-show work he brought brother Frank into

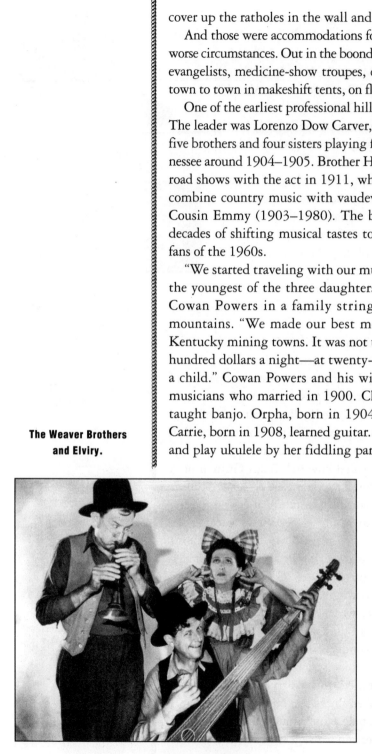

The Weaver Brothers and Elviry.

the act as "Cicero" Weaver. And after they met Chicago-bred June Petrie in 1913, the star hillbilly attraction The Weaver Brothers and Elviry was born.

Elviry Weaver (1891–1977) was the niece of the husband-wife vaudeville attraction Petrie and Fish, so Elviry naturally gravitated toward show business. She got a job in a tent show—taking tickets, cranking the silent-picture machine, playing the piano, and singing. While "learning the ropes," she also walked a tightrope, juggled, and modeled in a draping act. From tent and medicine shows, she worked her way up to small-time vaudeville, where her path often crossed the brothers' on the circuit. At one stop "mother got up a costume, one similar to her famous Elviry dress, and she and Leon did some . . . old routines—and they stopped the show," recalled Elviry's daughter Loretta Weaver Torbett. "Three years later Leon and June married."

The act graduated from rinky-dink shows to headlining status after World War I, earning five thousand dollars a week at its peak and making its way to Hollywood movie stardom. During their heyday, the Weavers worked on bills with Al Jolson, George Burns and Gracie Allen, Jack Benny, the Foys, Beatrice Lillie, and many other top vaudevillians.

"Leon and mother divorced in 1924, I think," daughter Loretta recalled. "Then in 1928 mother married Frank/Cicero. Mother married brothers and they all got along and worked in harmony. Mother still bossed [ex-hubby] Leon around, and he loved it. He would say, 'Now, Ellie.' They were longtime friends and remained so."

The trio's entertainment mixture was homespun humor, tossed together with country tunes and rural caricatures. Leon/Abner played mandolin, guitar, fiddle, and handsaw. Loretta believed he originated the musical saw, which his guitarist brother, Frank/Cicero, also took up. The latter patented a number of novelty instruments, including a spinning banjo and a one-man band. Elviry's instruments were piano, mandolin, and ukulele.

"Elviry can change 'Le Jazz Hot' to 'La Musique Corn' and make you like it," said a critic in Dallas. But it was her drawling, deadpan comedic style that was the real attraction. Reviewing one Broadway appearance, a *New York American* critic wrote, "Sis Elviry is the best straight-faced comedienne in captivity." She had the original stern, poker-faced look later adopted by movie stars Marjorie Main ("Ma Kettle") and Margaret Hamilton ("The Wicked Witch of the West"). Her hilariously bossy ire, blunt delivery, and snake-eyed frowns were the counterpoint to the Weaver Brothers' shenanigans.

"The character of Elviry is a unique one," said one Hollywood publicist. "Belligerent, self-assertive, she carries a permanent chip on her shoulders and insults her audience raucously—to their huge delight."

Elviry's catchphrase was "If I had my druthers, I druther...," and among her musical mainstays was the 1895 "fallen woman" song "Just Tell Them That You Saw Me." She reportedly had an uncanny ear for music and was able to memorize songs on first hearing.

She also led the singing of her "Home Folks," a troupe of nineteen country musicians who were incorporated into the act in 1927–1928. Eleven of Elviry's troupe were relatives, including her daughters Loretta and Willa, niece Jessie, and sisters-in-law Bessie, Lillian, and Wreatha. There was also a trick dog named Nancy. For decades Elviry Weaver trouped through dingy, run-down, podunk "opera houses," doing three shows a day, six days a week, for boisterous, tobacco-spitting audiences who wanted their money's worth for that seventy-five-cent ticket.

One of the roughest circuits was the Southwest. The Oklahoma Territory's oil boom of 1903 resulted in a crop of dance halls, opera houses, and honky-tonks eager to serve the wild-and-woolly workers. A half–Cherokee Indian named Margaret Lillie (c. 1880–1942) and her husband, George Hall, were there. The country-singing couple hired a line of ten chorus girls and began packing in the rowdy wildcatters at a dollar a head on makeshift pine benches. A niece of Wild West show star Pawnee Bill, Margaret was still going strong after the Sooner State's admission to the Union in 1907. But the coming of silent movies and the death of her husband in the 1920s put an end to her top-grossing days.

She retreated to Lake Taneycomo in the Missouri Ozarks to operate a tavern, and that is where Elviry Weaver found the vaudeville veteran when she was recruiting her Home Folks. The two women were physically similar, so in addition to having her own spots in the Weavers' shows, Margaret filled in for Elviry when the star was unable to perform. She also met and married second husband Chappy Chapman while in Elviry's troupe. As the humorist A'nt Idy, Margaret Lillie achieved fame a third time as a country music star of the 1930s.

The rigors of raising children on the road encouraged most show-business women of the nineteenth century to work behind the scenes. Many became successful composers, turning out a profusion of sentimental "parlor songs." There was already an established tradition of women composing magazine poetry for money; also, songwriting could be done at home. The parlor song tradition began in Europe in the late 1700s, when guitar and piano performances by highborn young ladies became a big craze. The fad trickled down to the U.S. middle class around the time of the Civil War. Sheet music for these home recitals sold in vast quantities during the late 1800s and early 1900s, particularly after the advent of national retailers such as Montgomery Ward and Woolworth's in the 1870s. By 1890 sheet music sales tallied $1.7 million, and by 1909 business had boomed to the $5.5 million level, with 30 million copies of songs sold. Before the advent of records and radio, this was how most music was popularized. "The largest audience for inexpensive sheet music, with its mushy titles, sentimental art covers and lyrical inanities, were shop girls, most of whom . . . were steady customers of the dime and novelty stores," observed scholar William McKinley Randle, Jr.

The first piece of copyrighted sheet music in America was both southern-themed and by a woman. It was "The Kentucky Volunteer" of 1794, registered by "a Lady of Philadelphia" and melodist Raynor Taylor. Female lyricists were set on a path that was paved with golden oldies of nineteenth-century America. Sarah Josepha Hale's "Mary Had a Little Lamb" (1832), Emma Willard's "Rocked in the Cradle of the Deep" (1839), Mrs. Marion Dix Sullivan's "Blue Juniata" (1844), and Caroline A. Mason's "Do They Miss Me at Home?" (1852) were the first big secular favorites written by American women. Maud Irving's "I'll Twine Mid the Ringlets" (1860) is now known as the country standard "Wildwood Flower."

The Confederacy's "Maryland My Maryland" was born in 1862 when Jennie Cary put a James Ryder Randall poem to the German melody "O Tannenbaum" and added the words "my Maryland" every second line. She and her sister Hetty sang it to Maryland's troops, and thereafter the South adopted it as its "Marseillaise," second only to "Dixie" in impact. In the North the same year, Julia Ward Howe heard Union troops singing "John Brown's Body" near Washington, D.C. Stirred and haunted, she awoke from a fitful sleep in the gray predawn of the next morning and scribbled the words to "The Battle Hymn of the Republic" for the melody. The apocalyptic fervor and messianic intensity of "The Battle Hymn of the Republic" are so strong that it was still sung by such women as Barbara Mandrell, Jan Howard, Anita Bryant, and Dottie West more than a century after its creation. Yet another Civil War standard from a woman's pen was "All Quiet Along the Potomac Tonight." Popular with both sides during the conflict, it was born when John Hewitt put a melody to a poem by New York State housewife Ethel Beers.

Despite writing massive hits, these women did not get rich. Songwriters worked for a flat fee, were routinely robbed, and had their works bootlegged by quick-buck printers. Charlotte Bernard, who wrote under the name "Claribel," was the trailblazer in protecting songwriters' works.

Songwriter Anita Owen found a good thing and stuck with it with "Sweet Bunch of Daisies" (1894), "Daisies Won't Tell" (1904), and "Daisies Will Tell You So" (1913).

Among her big hits was 1868's "Come Back to Erin," said to be the first song paid royalties instead of an outright sum.

Euphemia Allen's descendants would be zillionaires if they had a penny for every time her instrumental has been played. In 1877 she composed "Chopsticks." In 1884 fifteen-year-old Effie J. Crockett was baby-sitting a crying infant. Trying to still the fitful child, she improvised a melody for the Mother Goose rhyme "Rock-a-Bye Baby," creating the most famous lullaby in history. Mildred J. and Patty Hill were Louisville teachers when they adapted their 1893 composition "Good Morning to All" to be "Happy Birthday to You." Their schoolhouse ditty is now the most frequently sung composition in America.

New Englander Katherine Lee Bates also created a classic in 1893. Invited to teach in Colorado, she took her first trip west and was stunned by the beauty of the American landscape. After standing atop Pike's Peak and gazing at nature's splendor, she wrote "America the Beautiful." Lyricist Ada Blenkhorn had an invalid nephew who always wanted her to push his wheelchair down the sunny side of the street. In 1899 she turned the request into "Keep on the Sunny Side of Life," which became The Carter Family's radio theme of the 1930s and later a bluegrass standard.

The early country favorite "In the Shadow of the Pines" (Hattie Lummis, 1895), the square dance melody "Li'l Liza Jane" (Countess Ada deLachau, 1916), "Shine On Harvest Moon" (Nora Bayes, 1908), and the first million-copy sheet music song by a woman, "Sweet Rosie O'Grady" (Maude Nugent, 1896), are among the many turn-of-the-century standards with female lyricists. In 1915 Utah's Mary Hale created a poem called "When It's Springtime in the Rockies," which later became known as "the national song of the West." Nashville's Beth Slater Whitson cowrote two sentimental songs that define the era, 1909's "Meet Me Tonight in Dreamland" and 1910's "Let Me Call You Sweetheart." Women were almost always the writers of lyrics rather than tunes. But Anita Owen composed her own melodies for "Daisies Won't Tell" (1904) and "Sweet Bunch of Daisies" (1894), both of which became country string band songs.

Also capable of both lyrics and tunes was Fanny J. Crosby (1820–1915), the most famous female songwriter of the nineteenth century. She began her composing career in 1854–1855 by collaborating with

Turn-of-the-century composers turned out a profusion of sentimental "parlor songs" of wistful antebellum landscapes, orphaned children, forsaken ladies, crippled and blind tots, tragic deaths, fallen women, sad slaves, lovelorn Indian maids, and downtrodden poor folks. Mothers—widowed mothers, silver-haired mothers, praying mothers, dead mothers, and sweetly remembered mothers who taught their children to sing—were big sellers. This sheet music example dates from 1914.

George F. Root on the big hits "Rosalie the Prairie Flower," "The Honeysuckle Glen," and "There's Music in the Air," and went on to write the gospel standard "Pass Me Not O Gentle Savior," the homeless mission staple "Rescue the Perishing," the Salvation Army's "The Blood-Washed Throng," and the future Billy Graham Crusades theme "Blessed Assurance." Fanny Crosby's eight-thousand-plus song output is all the more impressive because she was blind.

Fanny, who was born in upstate New York, had her sight destroyed by an incompetent doctor who applied hot poultices to her inflamed eyes when she was six months old. Blindness condemned a person to a lifetime of charity, dependency, and poverty, but when Fanny was fifteen, her widowed mother sent her to the then-new New York Institution for the Blind in Manhattan. There, Fanny learned to read by touching books with raised letters. She developed as a poet, singer, guitarist, pianist, organist, and songwriter. "We had fine music in our school," she recalled in her 1903 auto-biography; "for as is well known, some of the best musicians in the world come from among the blind. . . . We often had 'musical soirees' and invited our neighbors in the city." Music made both Fanny and the school famous in New York.

Fanny Crosby, 1906.

Fanny answered the altar call at an 1850 revival meeting, and from then on she was evangelical in the extreme. She used to say she was glad she was blind, so that the first face she would ever see would be her Savior's in heaven. Fanny's hymns have been sung worldwide for a hundred years. Gospel entertainers still record them today. "There's Music in the Air" later served as the basis for both the Hawaiian standard "Aloha Oe" and Princeton University's "Whoop 'er Up." With its advice of "hold fast to the right," her "Mother's Goodbye" became a favorite with country acts.

Despite her songs' universal acceptance, Fanny Crosby was content to write for three dollars a song for forty-seven years as an employee of the gospel publisher Bigelow & Main. She wrote under more than two hundred pseudonyms and sometimes with no credit at all. Fanny was such a song factory that she often composed both melody and words on the spot, singing them to her bosses in a clear, sweet soprano.

She was completely unmaterialistic, and throughout her life Fanny maintained a concern for the poor. She often spoke at mission meetings in the Bowery among the homeless, was active in the Salvation Army, attended meetings of railroad workers, addressed revival services, and was a tireless saver of "lost men." "The merciful God has put His hand over my eyes, and shut out from me the sight of many instances of cruelty and bitter unkindness and misfortune, that I would not have been able to relieve, and must simply have suffered in seeing," she wrote. "Why should the blind be objects of pity? Darkness may . . . throw a shadow over the outer vision; but there is no cloud . . . that can keep the sunlight of hope from the trustful soul."

During Fanny's extraordinarily long life, women's lives were revolutionized. By 1890 a third of Americans were living in urban centers. The U.S. population doubled from thirty-eight million in 1870 to seventy-six million in 1900. Gigantic slums developed. Poverty was epidemic. It is estimated that there was one prostitute for every fifty men in the 1890s. When the International Ladies Garment Workers Union was founded in 1900, sweatshop girls worked seventy-hour weeks for thirty cents a day. This was the industrial revolution.

Women continued to be at the forefront of social reform during this grim era. In 1887 newspaper reporter Nellie Bly published her exposé of mental institutions after having herself committed to one. Helen Hunt Jackson crusaded for the rights of Native Americans in the 1890s. In 1889 Jane Addams opened Hull House in Chicago to aid the poor, and in 1890 the National American Women's Suffrage Association was formed. In 1900 six-foot Carry Nation swung her hatchet in Kansas saloons as a temperance activist, then went on the road as a vaudeville attraction with her message. In 1903 Mary Harris "Mother" Jones led a march of one hundred mill children from Philadelphia to Washington, D.C., to publicize the plight of child labor. In 1915, the year Fanny Crosby died, New York slum nurse Margaret Sanger was jailed for obscenity for publishing birth control information; three years later she opened the first birth control clinic. Also in 1915 Nevada passed the first easy-divorce law.

The technological progress of the time was unprecedented. The telephone, elevator, X rays, automobiles, airplanes, jazz, movies, electric lights, the radio, and mass transit were all brought into American life between 1880 and 1920. America was also developing a consumer culture. Montgomery Ward (1872), Woolworth's (1879), and Sears (1890) were thriving as national retailers by the turn of the century. The first self-service supermarket appeared in 1916, offering the canned food and packaged cereal that made housewives' food preparation easier for those who could afford them. Advertising evolved to create a demand, rather than merely sell goods—soap was a "beautifier," not just a cleaner.

By 1910 women's hoops and corsets were replaced by the ankle-revealing sheath, and the one-piece bathing suit was introduced. Working girls had begun to throw away their bustles around the turn of the century. By then industry was using women to operate new machines like the electric sewing machine, carpet sweeper, electric iron, telephone switchboard, and modern typewriter. In 1880 just four percent of office clerks were women; ten years later twenty-one percent were. Between 1870 and 1900 the number of women wage earners grew from 1.5 million to 5 million, of whom 2 million were in factories.

In West Orange, New Jersey, Thomas Edison employed young girls in his Phonograph Works factory of the 1880s. He had them recording nursery rhymes like "Jack and Jill" and "Little Bo Peep" on tiny cylinders for use in talking dolls. Edison thought that dolls, dictaphones, and telephone answering machines were going to be the main uses of sound recording.

By 1897, when a home market for records began developing, the public was proving him wrong. The end of the 1893–1895 recession and the introduction of less-expensive models took phonographs out of the penny arcades and into living rooms. At first consumers were edified by military bands and classical *artistes*, but it wasn't long before mass-appeal music took over: By 1905 three-quarters of the Victor company's offerings were discs by popular singers and musicians, but female voices were in the distinct minority. During recording's infancy, higher-pitched women's voices were difficult to record: Before the invention of microphones a woman singer had to "put her head as far as it will go into the [recording] horn when she's on her very low notes, and when she soars to the heights she must draw her head quickly back and sing straight to the ceiling," instructed a Columbia Records executive in 1898.

Women rose to the acrobatic challenge—records were soon offered by sassy vaudevillians, singers of sentimental southern songs, and rube character performers. Among the pioneers was Marguerite Newton. One of her turn-of-the-century Edison cylinders was the period's most famous "fallen-woman" song, "She Is More to Be Pitied Than Censured." Newton also recorded "I Don't Like No Cheap Man" and "Take Your Clothes and Go" for inventor Edison. But by the early 1900s other companies were beating Edison at his own game, all of them offering southern tunes singers and self-assertive dialect comediennes.

The sentiment singers were usually billed as women singing "native American melodies," "home songs and familiar melodies," or "southern songs and plantation airs." They included Marie Tiffany ("Listen to the

Mockingbird," "Darling Nellie Gray"), May Peterson ("My Old Kentucky Home," "Dixie"), and Florence Easton ("Old Folks at Home," "Hard Times Come Again No More"). The Victor, Columbia, Gennett, Okeh, and Vocalion companies advertised more than forty such stylists in catalogs between 1910 and 1925. Several were billed as Southerners to add to their authenticity in presenting this material, including Georgia's Ann Wheaton, Kentucky's Clarice Vance, Tennessee's Brox Sisters, and South Carolina's Marguerite Dunlap. Columbia Records soprano Alice Nielson was from Nashville.

By far the most successful was Alma Gluck, whose Victor disc of "Carry Me Back to Ole Virginny" (1915) was the first female record to sell a million. She also recorded "The Little Old Log Cabin in the Lane," the song that would later launch the country music industry. (Gluck was the mother of Hollywood star Efrem Zimbalist, Jr., who starred in "The F.B.I.," "77 Sunset Strip," and other popular programs.)

The vaudeville character comediennes were recorded just as much as the "heart" singers; and the themes of their high-spirited songs would later be echoed in country music. The queen of the "coon singers" was May Irwin (1862–1938). Her big 1907 hit, "The Bully Song," later became a hillbilly music standard. Blossom Seeley's (1891–1974) "Bringing Home the Bacon" found new life in the 1930s on "The National Barn Dance." Nashville's Kitty Cheatham (1864–1945) did "Scandalize My Name–Satidy Night–Georgia Buck" in country/"coon" dialect and also gave serious presentations of such African-American folk songs as "Swing Low, Sweet Chariot." Kitty, who left Tennessee for the bright lights of Broadway at age seventeen, was also a pioneer in children's music.

Anna Chandler's 1917 record "She's Good Enough to Be Your Baby's Mother and She's Good Enough to Vote with You" urged the passage of the women's suffrage amendment, which occurred three years later. Bessie Lestina, Louise Marshall, and Robert B. Tessemann treated the same issue in rube terms with their comic "Uncle Henry Sees the Suffragette Parade" in 1913.

"Uncle Henry" had several country peers who commented on the rapidly modernizing society. Around 1915 Mr. and Mrs. Cal Stewart donned doltish facial expressions, old-fashioned clothes, and wire-rim glasses to perform and record rube comedy such as "The Wedding of Uncle Josh and Aunt Nancy Smith" and "Uncle Josh and Aunt Nancy Go to Housekeeping."

Columbia, the first record company to specialize in lowbrow music, was advertising "barn dances" as a category of records by 1913. Its female superstar was Ada Jones (1873–1922), the first woman to achieve worldwide fame on records.

Ada's 1904–1921 recorded work for Columbia, Victor, Edison, and more than fifty other labels is an encyclopedia of female show business stereotypes of the day. On more than two thousand cylinders and discs this versatile dialect queen portrayed Irish, German, British, Jewish, Italian, and Scottish women. She was a "coon shouter," a society dame, a Bowery "tough," a schoolgirl, a vamp, an old lady, and a modern suffragette. Her "working-girl" characters included washerwoman, salesgirl, manicurist, actress, and housekeeper. Ada Jones was also famed on records as a cowgirl and a country bumpkin.

She knew she was no grand opera diva: "I have come to take a delight in interpreting the songs that are born of the people and sung by the people," Ada once said. "They express the real sentiments of the times. . . . And I believe that the world is enriched by the melodies . . . that come from the masses.

"It may seem to you that a singer like myself, who sings the everyday songs for everyday people, may not have a highly appreciative audience, but I believe that it would be hard to find people more grateful than those comprising the invisible listening audience to which I sing. Unable to indicate their approval by applause, they express their appreciation by letters. I have hundreds of these . . . from all kinds of people."

Ada was born in England in 1873, the daughter of an innkeeper. The family immigrated to the United States when she was five. Her stepmother managed her early career, promoting her as "Little Ada Jones, the Child Wonder." The tot made her debut in a Philadelphia variety show at age seven. At seventeen Ada starred in a Broadway farce called *A Knotty Affair*. In 1894 her stepmother arranged for Ada to make cylinders for Edison, leading to the star's claim that hers "was the first woman's voice ever successfully recorded by a phonograph." It wasn't, but she was still a pioneer.

By 1904 Ada was evidently a bit down on her luck, singing in a little freak show in Greenwich Village called Huber's Museum. She was heard there by singer Billy Murray, who suggested her as the comedic partner for Len Spencer, then a major star. Spencer was a master in compacting sketches into two-minute records, and he brought out Ada's natural gifts of mimicry. Her popularity rapidly eclipsed her mentor's, and she went on to record with a half dozen other partners, as well as on her own. Her Irish, German, Jewish, Bowery, and black accents were recorded during the first few years, followed by her country comedy efforts.

Ada's biggest solo hit was probably "Just Plain Folks," which tells the story of an old couple from the country who visit their rich son in the big city. He treats them coldly at his mansion, leading the oldsters to

sadly head for home, feeling "out of place here, 'cause we're just plain folks." Her many southern favorites included "Are You from Dixie?," "All Aboard for Dixie," "In Alabama Dear with You," and "Let Me Live and Stay in Dixie Land." The question-answer Jones/Spencer 1905 number "Reuben and Cynthia" became the mountaineer play-party ditty "Reuben and Rachel."

She portrayed rube characters on "Down on the Farm" (1909), "Si Perkins' Barn Dance" (1909), "Return of the Arkansas Traveler" (1910), "Hay Ride" (1912), and at least eighteen other records, including several portraying "Aunt Nancy" opposite Cal Stewart after his wife dropped out of the "Uncle Josh and Aunt Nancy" series. During these sketches, her male partners would almost inevitably ask her to sing an old-timey tune.

Among Ada's western titles were 1907's "Bronco Bob and His Little Cheyenne" and 1910's "Cowboy Romance." In "Queen of the Ranch" (1910) she is cattle queen "Little Nellie," courted by Spencer as a visiting Kentuckian. "Protect me?" she saucily responds. "Why, I'm not afraid of anything." Ada's 1909 version of the jaunty "My Pony Boy" helped make it the most enduring of the many turn-of-the-century western romance songs.

Despite her position as the best-selling nonoperatic woman on disc, the buxom blonde was never a big live attraction. Perhaps this is because she was epileptic. "Any number of times," her finest vocal partner, Billy Murray, recalled, "we'd be recording duets. I'd hear a 'plop' and look around, and there would be poor little Ada, writhing on the floor. We'd have to wait until she got over the spell, then try again to make a satisfactory record." Epilepsy was not treatable by medication until the 1950s.

She'd married a little-known, Irish-born actor named Hughie Flaherty, six years her junior, in 1904. They had a daughter and a home on Long Island, but when Ada's disc career began to falter, she was apparently forced to leave them for the road. Unlike those of most of her contemporaries, Ada's records sold better in rural areas than urban, so in spite of her health, in 1918 she played whistle-stops in the South. As "Aunt Nancy" she also appeared on stage with Stewart in his "Pumpkin Center" vaudeville sketches. The following year she was on the road again, appearing in little Marion, Virginia, and Rocky Mount, North Carolina, among other places.

Members of her troupe found her semiconscious in her hotel room the day after the Rocky Mount show. She went into a coma and died at the local hospital of acute uremia, kidney failure, and hypertension at age forty-eight.

While on tour, she was introduced as "Ada Jones, the mother of the phonograph." "It made me feel quite ancient, I assure you," she remarked.

Ada Jones, Len Spencer, and Billy Murray had many contemporaries as record pioneers. None became more popular than Vernon Dalhart; his "The Prisoner's Song" of 1924 was country music's first million-seller. One of the biggest hits of all time, the thing was such a colossal success that it sold for thirty years, eventually topping perhaps twenty million in overall sales.

Dalhart was a Texas-bred operetta tenor who'd performed on New York stages from 1910 to 1915 before entering the recording business. One of his jobs was demonstrating the wonders of Edison's invention on the vaudeville circuit. Fiddler, pianist, and insouciant southern singer Adelyne Hood (1897–1958) was an "Edison Tone Tester," too. She had pert good looks, a vivacious wit, flirtatious charm, and a Deep South drawl of honeysuckle in summer. Vernon Dalhart and Adelyne Hood met on the road; she became his musical partner and mistress.

Born in South Carolina, Adelyne was initially tutored by her pianist mother. She later attended colleges in North Carolina, South Carolina, and Alabama, receiving a musical education far beyond the level of most women of her day. But after hooking up with Dalhart around 1917, she tossed her classical studies aside in favor of show biz.

Dalhart fired his fiddler to hire her, much to the displeasure of his then partner Carson Robison. Nevertheless, Dalhart, Robison, and Hood went on to make a superb series of records in 1927 and 1928, capturing the vocal vitality of fading vaudeville, prefiguring country sounds with Robison's rural guitar work, and spotlighting Adelyne's deft, lively fiddling. The trio's most popular record was "Sing On Brother, Sing" backed with "Oh! Susanna." They followed this with several toe-tapping "darky" dialect numbers—"Heah Dem Bells," "Climbing Up de Golden Stairs," and "Golden Slippers." A secular romp called "Razors in de Air" was even more zippy. On the sentimental southern side were "On Mobile Bay" and "Old Plantation Melodies." These charming performances continued to sell into the 1930s.

Adelyne's natural Dixie accent, playful vocal style, and flair for comedy are highlighted on the minstrely Dalhart-Hood duets "Sing Hallelujah" and "Hallelujah There's a Rainbow in the Sky." Their finest together was unquestionably "The Frog Song," which featured absurdly funny amphibian imitations: She trills merrily in high soprano while Dalhart croaks "Kneedeep, Kneedeep, Ratherdeep-Ratherdeep-Ratherdeep" on the choruses.

The fun and games in the studio masked some serious personality clashes. Dalhart was arrogant, difficult, and prone to temper outbursts. Adelyne was an ambitious, if talented, gold digger. Robison was the country boy who was supplying the songs and being exploited. Fed up with the whole arrangement, he quit in 1928. Stripped of his gifted collaborator, Dalhart saw his career go into a steady decline.

Adelyne Hood, on the other hand, was poised to make her finest records. "Calamity Jane" (1929) was the most popular. Her two recordings of this number are billed as duets—the first with Dalhart and the second with "Lonesome Cowboy" John White—but both are really her own, with Adelyne acting the part of the famous 1870s carouser and hell-raiser: "I'm the famous Calamity Jane," she bragged. "I've blazed the trail and rode the plain / I'm fast on the draw, don't care for the law." When her male partners challenged her, she added, "When it comes to drinkin' likker, I can take a dozen men / And drink 'em under the tables, and up on their chairs again / And if I haven't got a corkscrew, I never give a snatch / I bite off the neck of the bottle, and throw 'er right down the hatch." Adelyne's boast of toughness, athletic prowess, and ability to whip men on their own ground appeared on at least ten record labels.

Brassy women dominate Adelyne's recordings. "The Daughter of Calamity Jane," a 1930 sequel to her big hit, was backed by the humorous divorce-and-alimony revenge song "Westward Ho for Reno." She also treated that topic in "Song of the Old Ding Dong" ("Ding means matrimony / Dong means alimony"). In "The Lady That's Known as Lou" Adelyne declares herself to be better than other western folk heroines Cattle Kate, Calamity Jane, and Poker Alice, as well as male desperadoes like Jesse James. "Clementine the Bargain Queen" is a gum-chewing teenage dime store clerk, fending off the advances of guys who get fresh. "Alaska Ann and Yukon Steve," a duet with Dalhart, finds her gunning him down in a dispute and shouting triumphantly, "So drink up, boys, for another notch on the six-gun of Alaska Ann, Whooee!"

Dalhart had an expensive Tudor home in suburban Mamaroneck, New York, for his wife, children, Cadillacs, and maid, but he was seldom there. He lived mainly in a suite at the Knickerbocker Hotel in Manhattan. But the stock market crash of 1929 ruined him, and Adelyne left the obnoxious fading star. "After the Crash, she walked out on him," said one observer. "She took him for just about all he had while he was in New York."

After concert and recording work in London she returned to America around 1936 for national broadcasts on NBC Radio as folksinger "Betsy White." Her comic flair was still evident in "Since Nellie Got the Gong" and "Don't Swat Your Mother, It's Mean." Adelyne's vivid country, cowgirl, and "coon" character sketches had always been her forte. She'd carried her dialect style into the 1930s on such Dalhart duets as "Madam Queen" and "He's on the Chain Gang Now." In 1939 Quaker Oats hired Adelyne as its first radio "Aunt Jemima." After two seasons of this she moved to Pittsburgh, where she introduced mammy "Aunt Caroline" as a morning radio favorite from 1941 through 1945.

Her Carolina inflections led Pittsburgh blacks to believe the radio star was one of their own, sending her invitations to "jive parties and other assorted social activities."

In the mid-1940s this survivor of rube and "coon" vaudeville married a Pittsburgh food broker. She retired and became a respectable socialite before her death at age sixty. Her *Pittsburgh Press* obituary mentioned parenthetically that the plump dowager "had made several phonograph records of Negro, Southern and hillbilly songs."

Adelyne Hood, 1929.

When Adelyne began her career in the teens, record companies were recording women in increasingly diverse styles. Lady whistlers and female Hawaiian bandleaders were big. In 1920 Mamie Smith made the first black blues record (when Sophie Tucker was unavailable for a recording session), launching an industry. Mr. and Mrs. McNiff-Locke were an accordion-banjo combination who recorded jigs and reels. Maude Powell was a violinist who was advertised as having learned in a rural style.

In retrospect, it seems almost inevitable that the booming record industry would develop a taste for real rural music. And having absorbed Anglo-American folk music, gospel anthems, parlor songs, and nineteenth-century show business, country music's women had a recipe ready.

SINGLE GIRL, MARRIED GIRL

The Carter Family and

the Birth of Country

Music Recording

The Carter Family's image, as illustrated on this 1941 songbook cover, was simple and placid. But beneath the surface, emotions seethed. Sara, right, took the then-revolutionary step of divorcing her husband, A.P., which meant country music's model "family" wasn't really one after all.

It was so hot that patches melted off the tires as the old Ford chugged along the rutted Virginia dirt road leading to Bristol in August 1927.

One woman on board held a crying infant. Her eighteen-year-old sister-in-law shifted in her seat after every bumpy jolt, trying to ease the discomfort of being eight months pregnant with her first child. At the wheel was a lean, somber, thirty-six-year-old dreamer who'd sold fruit trees, been a carpenter, worked on railroads, farmed, and collected songs in Scott County, Virginia. He believed he could turn the two Appalachian women into recording stars.

The three had been performing in churches, living rooms, and schoolhouses in Maces Spring and the other tiny communities in the shadows of the thickly forested mountains above Poor Valley. Twenty-six miles away was Bristol, then the biggest town in the southern Appalachians. A Victor Records talent scout was there in that blistering summer of 1927, trying to find rural musicians to market in the company's "New Southern Series." In the wake of Vernon Dalhart's 1924 million-seller "The Prisoner's Song" the Victor firm was keen to find more hit country sounds.

Would-be Dalhart mountaineers were pouring into

town to audition, lured by an article in the Bristol paper about the visiting New Yorker. Alvin Pleasant "A.P." Carter heard the news and announced his plans.

"He came back home and said, 'We're going to Bristol tomorrow to make a record,'" recalled Maybelle Addington Carter five decades later. "And I just fluffed him off. I didn't think about makin' a record. The next morning he said, 'Y'all get ready, we're goin' to Bristol.' And I said, 'Well, should I take my guitar?' He said, 'Well, how you gonna make a record if you don't take your guitar?' I said, 'Well, okay.' And we all got ready and took off."

"'Course we didn't think anything about it," recalled A.P.'s wife, Sara Dougherty Carter. "Just thought it was more or less just a trip."

"I was right there with 'em," said Sara's oldest daughter, Gladys. Then an eight-year-old, she was taken along as a baby-sitter for her still-nursing baby brother, Joe. "It was *hot.* We had three flats going to Bristol that day. . . . It took you about all day to get to Bristol back then; the roads were bad."

"They just had an old buildin' that we recorded in," said Maybelle. "It wasn't a regular studio. It was just an old warehouse up there. Everything we recorded on one mike. Only me and Sara were the musicians."

There were more than twenty other acts milling around Bristol during that historic twelve-day Victor recording marathon—gospel singers, vaudevillians, old-time string bands, mountain blues moaners, traditional folk performers, family groups, and rustic instrumentalists. The reserved, distinctly unflashy Carter Family was shy about setting up for the recording equipment. But once the women began to sing, the Victor scout was mesmerized.

"As soon as I heard Sara's voice," recalled Ralph Peer years later, "that was it. I knew that it was going to be wonderful."

That voice can still work its magic, for the stark, raw-boned Carter Family records have an eerie power. Sara Carter's resonant alto is as deep and dark as a cool underground mountain spring. It has brokenhearted shards of repressed emotion, trouble, regret, and pain. There's a chilly pang of loneliness in it. There is fervor and yearning. In its lower, throatier moments, it takes on an almost masculine tone. At other times it has a mournful, bluesy quality. That remarkable voice, A.P.'s vivid song constructions, and Maybelle's treble harmonies and instrumental ability were the act's tickets to immortality.

There have been Carters, Doughertys, and Addingtons in southwestern Virginia as long as there has been an American nation. Maybelle was a direct descendant of Revolutionary War soldier William

Addington, who settled in the Clinch Mountains with twelve other families around 1782. In 1784 A.P.'s ancestor Thomas Carter built a fort on the old wilderness road near Rye Cove. A.P. was born in 1891 in a log cabin that's still standing in his valley, the oldest of farmer Robert and Mollie Carter's nine children.

Mother Mollie Bayes Carter, a mountain midwife, was a ballad-singing woman. She taught her children to love "The Wife of Usher's Well," "Brown Girl," "Sinking in the Lonesome Sea," and other Anglo-American folk songs. As teenagers, A.P. and his sister Vergie began singing in a gospel quartet with their uncles. He is also reported to have briefly performed in a bucolic medicine show before trying his hand at selling fruit trees door to door.

Sara Dougherty Carter (1898–1979) also grew up musical. Her mother died when she was a baby, and Sara was raised by her childless Aunt Melinda and Uncle Milburn Nichols in Copper Creek, just across Clinch Mountain from A.P.'s family home in Maces Spring. A quarter of a mile from the Nichols place lived Sara's cousins Madge and Maybelle Addington. Madge and Sara amused themselves for hours playing guitars, autoharps, and banjos, and singing the lonesome mountain tunes.

Fruit tree salesman A.P. arrived in Copper Creek in 1914, heard That Voice singing the train wreck ballad "Engine 143," and instantly fell in love with the bewitching Sara. She was tall and buxom, with lustrous brown hair and penetrating black eyes. They wed in 1915, a month before her seventeenth birthday.

Dancing among the grown-ups at the wedding celebration was Sara's six-year-old cousin Maybelle, by then almost as musical as the bride and groom. Maybelle Addington Carter (1909–1978) was one of ten children born into a somewhat merrier mountain clan of music makers. "I have loved music all my life; I guess I was just born that way," she said. "My sister used to play the banjo some; my mother would play banjo and I would pull the autoharp down off the table to the floor and try to play it. . . . I played the banjo too when I was a kid and me and my brothers used to play for squaredances. . . . and then when I was about twelve or thirteen one of my older brothers gave me a guitar and I started trying different ways to pick it, and came up with my own style, because there weren't many guitar pickers around.

"The songs we learned were taught to us by my mother who had learned them from her mother before her, who had, in turn, learned them from her parents." Momma Margaret Addington was the leader of the Women's Chorus of the Fair Oak Methodist Church, so little Maybelle learned gospel songs as well as the family's traditional ballads and the community square dance melodies. On weekends nearby neighbors would set aside their labors to swap songs. "They'd all get together and play," Gladys recalled. "Both sides of the house was musical people. It was just nature for them to get together on weekends or whenever. It was the only way they had of entertaining themselves back then . . . singin' or goin' to church or something like that."

A.P., Vergie, baby sister Sylvia, Sara, and her cousin Maybelle were the most gifted, and in various combinations with other kin, they were soon playing at ice-cream socials, schoolhouses, dances, family gatherings, and church events. At one schoolhouse show, A.P.'s brother Ezra fell in love with Maybelle's pale blue eyes and gentle disposition.

Maybelle recalled, "I was six years old when I met him the first time, at Sara and A.P.'s wedding. I was just a kid, and he was eleven years older than I was, but I had never forgotten him. . . . Then the next time I saw my husband was when I was sixteen and I'd gone to Sara and A.P.'s to do a show at a schoolhouse. . . . I had never thought too much about getting married . . . but then, all of a sudden, the first thing I knew we were married." The whirlwind courtship lasted just four months before Maybelle and Ezra eloped in 1926.

"A.P. was a brother to my husband; and his wife Sara was my first cousin. And we married brothers. That's how we got 'The Carter Family.'" A year later the family trio sang its way to stardom.

A.P. apparently saw music as a way out of rural poverty. The average Scott County family in those days made less than two hundred dollars a year. Farming the mountain land wasn't easy; there were no jobs, and now he and Sara had Gladys, born in 1919; Janette, born in 1923; and Joe, born in early 1927. He'd heard that record companies paid fifty dollars per song. With his store of tunes and Sara's penetrating voice, he was certain he had something they'd pay for. The duo had auditioned unsuccessfully a few months before for a Brunswick Records scout in nearby Kingsport, Tennessee. The Brunswick man was encouraging, saying, "there was no need to worry about getting to make records, for someone would be sure to want them," recalled Gladys; "and there was no need for them to be poor folks with voices like theirs." With the addition of Maybelle's extraordinarily full, driving guitar and harmony vocals, A.P. hit pay dirt in Bristol on that hot 1927 summer day.

After the historic Victor session "they didn't say nothin' much about it," Gladys recalled. "Maybe that they were glad it was over with or they thought they had done all right or something like that. No, they never talked a bit about their music. It was just everyday life. To them, it was just a little somethin' to make money with. It never did go to their heads or nothin'."

On the way home the rickety car died while fording a stream and had to be pushed out by the trio to dry. After that, life in Maces Spring returned to normal. With grandma Mollie Carter as her midwife, Maybelle gave birth to Helen a month later.

The Carters' first records appeared in November. "I had the surprise of my life when we went into Bristol one day and saw a crowd of people gathered around listening to Jimmie Rodgers and Carter Family records that were being played over the loudspeakers," Maybelle said. "This was something new and caught on like wildfire."

What it was was the birth of the country music industry. Rodgers and the Carters, both discovered during Victor's 1927 trip to Bristol, had made the first nationally popular rural records.

Records were expensive—at seventy-five cents apiece they could be double a southern worker's hourly wage in the twenties—but they captivated consumers nonetheless. Prices had plunged to ten dollars for record players around the turn of the century, and the wind-up Victrolas particularly appealed to country people, since they didn't require electricity. Records didn't have much competition, either. The movie palaces that were all the rage after 1915 were only in towns, and radio did not blanket the nation until the mid-1920s. In 1921 the disc business boomed with record-setting sales of $105.6 million. The development of portable recording equipment made rural experimentation possible, and rural dwellers' hunger to hear their own stars made that experimentation pay off.

It would be hard to overstate The Carter Family's importance to popular music history. Country music's first star group is unmatched as a preserver and popularizer of folk and parlor songs. Maybelle's then-revolutionary guitar style helped transform the instrument from background rhythm to the dominant lead sound in pop culture. Her playing and Gene Autry's marketing of the instrument in Sears catalogs are perhaps the most significant factors in bringing the guitar to the forefront. In addition, Sara and Maybelle were essentially a duet with occasional bass vocals from A.P. and were thus the foundation female act of country music history.

From the Carters have come Emmylou Harris's "Hello Stranger," Roy Acuff's "Wabash Cannonball," Elvis Presley's "Are You Lonesome Tonight," Linda Ronstadt's "I Never Will Marry," and The Kingston Trio's "Worried Man." The Carters' "I'm Thinking Tonight of My Blue Eyes" provided the melody for three country music classics—Acuff's "Great Speckled Bird," Hank Thompson's "Wild Side of Life," and Kitty Wells's "It Wasn't God Who Made Honky-Tonk Angels." Its "Little Darling Pal of Mine" became the basis for "You Are My Sunshine." Woody Guthrie borrowed the melody of the Carters' "When the World's

The following are British folk ballads brought from Appalachian Mountain hollows into commercial music by the Carters:

"I HAVE NO ONE TO LOVE ME" (1928)

"I NEVER WILL MARRY" (1933)

"SINKING IN THE LONESOME SEA" (1935)

"NEVER LET THE DEVIL GET THE UPPER HAND" (1937)

"WHO'S THAT KNOCKING AT MY WINDOW" (1938)

"BLACK JACK DAVID" (1940)

"WAVE ON THE SEA" (1941)

"RAMBLING BOY" (1941)

on Fire" for "This Land Is Your Land," used "Wildwood Flower" for "Reuben James," and co-opted "John Hardy Was a Desperate Little Man" for "Tom Joad." Joan Baez launched her career with Carter Family favorites such as "Engine 143," "Wildwood Flower," and "Little Moses." Maybelle's picking on "Wildwood Flower" is still the standard for young guitarists. "Will the Circle Be Unbroken" remains a definitive country anthem, serving as the theme song for two hugely successful all-star Nitty Gritty Dirt Band collections. Minnie Pearl sings "Jealous Hearted Me." And bluegrass bands everywhere know "Keep on the Sunny Side," "Gold Watch and Chain," "Foggy Mountain Top," and dozens of other Carter Family melodies.

The song that emerged as the hit from the 1927 Bristol sessions was "Single Girl, Married Girl." "I didn't want to sing that song; I didn't like it," Sara said later. "When we got our first royalty check, why the 'Single Girl, Married Girl' had sold the most, the very one that I didn't want to sing." The song bemoans the lot of the married girl with a baby on her knees and shabby clothes. And Sara Carter had traveled to fame that August with a screaming baby in tow and auditioned in plain country clothes rather than city finery.

When the royalty checks started to come in, A.P. began pushing the shy women to record and perform more. They traveled to Victor headquarters in Camden, New Jersey; to Louisville; to Memphis; to New York; to Chicago; to Atlanta; to Charlotte, North Carolina—they went wherever and whenever they were summoned to record. The trio is one of the few country acts that was in the studio at least once a year throughout the Depression, when the rest of the record business nearly died. On each of these occasions, the Carters were so tightly rehearsed that they rarely required more than one or two takes of a number to get a finished product. During a memorable two-day session in 1940, The Carter Family recorded twenty songs in a row in one take each. The group left us more than 250 songs in its fifteen years as a recording act.

The Carter Family was widely applauded during the folk revival of the late 1950s and early 1960s for having preserved much American folk material, but the bulk of its repertoire was nineteenth-century parlor songs and gospel tunes. A.P. assembled the trio's immortal output by putting together fragments of lyrics and images he heard other mountain people singing. Often these were half-remembered leftovers from sentimental pieces about tragic lovers, orphan children, blind beggars, and sadly departed mothers. Many have a funereal tone or a sad, pent-up emotional intensity that spoke of hardship, poverty, and death that was never far away in Appalachia.

In addition to "Single Girl, Married Girl," the Carters' 1927 records included such melancholy fare as "Bury Me Under the Weeping Willow." From the following year's session came "Will You Miss Me When I'm Gone." The unhappy "Grave on the Green Hillside" and "Motherless Children" were recorded in 1929. During the grim Depression came "Poor Little Orphaned Boy," "The Dying Mother," "Will the Roses Bloom in Heaven," and the like.

The Carters invariably sang these like backwoods church harmonizers, solemn and sober. But beneath their gravestone demeanors, emotions seethed. Despite their name and image, they were not a "family" for most of their professional career. Sara separated from A.P. Carter in 1933 and lived apart from him throughout the next ten years of the trio's existence.

The rustic schoolhouse bookings increased in the 1930s, the three often performing for twenty-five or fifty dollars a night on crude planks atop sawhorses, lit by kerosene lamps. Sara began to balk. When she wouldn't or couldn't go, A.P's sister Sylvia sang her part. He'd advertise the dates with little handbills in store windows or tacked to trees that promised, "The Program Is Morally Good." Domineering over his female partners, he had the trio touring weekly into West Virginia, North Carolina, Tennessee, Virginia, and occasionally Maryland, Pennsylvania, and New England. In general it was low-paying, small-time stuff, for he never really exploited possibilities in the wider show-business world of country radio barn dances or vaudeville bills.

A.P. was a nervous, eccentric man with a stubborn, taciturn nature. He had such a lack of concentration that he would wander offstage or out of the studio in midsong. He could be chatty and gentle one minute, difficult and sulking the next. The women soon learned to rely on their own abilities, rather than on their moody, undependable boss.

"If he felt like singing, he would sing," Maybelle said. "If he didn't, he'd look out the window. So we never depended on him. We just let him sing when he got ready." His oddball behavior "drove my mother and Maybelle up a wall," Janette once remarked. In retrospect, the two women could have probably done as well without him were it not for constraints against unchaperoned country women at that time.

That is, if they'd wanted to. In a way it is ironic that The Carter Family's music became so commercially popular, for it belongs to the tradition of homemade, private, living room music that had long been the province of mountain women. Sara, whose voice took the songs out of the parlor and into country music tradition, was never comfortable as a concert performer. Quiet and strong-willed, she wanted something that had nothing to do with fame or fortune. She wanted happiness. She

These Carter Family songs have been collected by scholars as American folk tunes:

"JOHN HARDY WAS A DESPERATE LITTLE MAN" (1928)

"ENGINE 143" (1929)

"WESTERN HOBO" (1929)

"DON'T FORGET THIS SONG" (1929)

"IF ONE WON'T ANOTHER ONE WILL" (1933)

"COWBOY JACK" (1934)

"MY HEART'S TONIGHT IN TEXAS" (1934)

"HE TOOK A WHITE ROSE FROM HER HAIR" (1935)

"JIM BLAKE'S MESSAGE" (1937)

"THE RECKLESS MOTORMAN" (1938)

wanted a normal home life. "Of all the three, I think music interested my mother the least," said Janette. "She could take it or leave it. She wasn't a-tryin' to reach no goals. If she had a performance or a job to do, she done it. And she done it excellent; she done it well. . . . She wasn't seekin' no fame or nothin'. She was just a gifted singer that enjoyed singing."

Sara bore the brunt of A.P.'s neurotic, distracted behavior. "He would go out and hunt for songs, leavin' all the chores to Mother," son Joe told a *Life* magazine interviewer. "She'd be cuttin' wood, pullin' mining timbers outta the mountains—and him out somewhere tryin' to learn a song! He never stopped to think what effect it might have on his family." Six years after leaving him, Sara got a divorce in 1939. These steps were so extreme, so bold, and so rarely taken by women of her time and place that it is virtually impossible for us to grasp their enormity. After seventeen years of marriage, why?

None of the original Carter Family would discuss it, although A.P. is said to have carried a torch for Sara until the day he died in 1960. Helen, June, and Anita—Maybelle and Ezra's daughters—don't seem to know the exact cause of the marriage breakup. Gladys, Janette, and Joe—Sara and A.P.'s children—remain mute on the subject.

"As far as I can remember, it was the first separation that ever occurred in the valley, so we never talked about it," June said. Janette turns testy when asked: "Daddy was a man who didn't like to talk about his personal life. If you ever interviewed him, he talked about his *music*. And I'm the same way. When you start to talk to me about my personal life, that's it. I just clam up. I think everybody should be that way."

Gladys said, "Why they chose separate lives, no one ever knew but them. . . . They were people that never did like to tell too much about their business and their private life. That was their concern. It wasn't nobody else's. Daddy, especially. He kept everything to hisself. He just thought it wasn't nobody's business. And Mommy and Maybelle was a lot the same way."

Victor executive Ralph Peer asked Sara to set aside her feelings so that the act could continue, and instructed the group not to reveal personal matters. He feared sales would suffer if people knew Carter Family members were not really a family, so despite internal tensions and emotional distance, the image was maintained.

Whatever the enigma, whatever the turmoil, that image, presented to an America in crisis, was home, hearth, family, and religion. "Mid the Green Fields of Virginia," "Picture on the Wall," and "You Are My Flower" rang with nostalgia for a time that was fast slipping away as the world rocked through the Jazz Age, plunged into economic chaos, and

slid inexorably toward
World War II. The Carter
Family sometimes com-
mented on contemporary
times, as in 1938's "Coal
Miner's Blues" and 1936's
"No Depression in Heaven,"
but more often it took its lis-
teners to that "Church in the
Wildwood" to hear "Hold
Fast to the Right," "Meeting
in the Air," and "There'll Be
No Distinction There."

Theirs was a universe of
old-fashioned female ideals,
of traditional male domi-
nation. Sara and Maybelle's
musical sisters were few. Only about five percent of country's earliest
recordings feature female performers. Those that do are mostly by families.

Fiddler/singer Hattie
Stoneman takes her
place in the Blue Ridge
Corn Shuckers band in
this 1929 portrait. She
had twenty-three
children during her per-
forming career.

At the Bristol Victor sessions, the reigning star was Ernest V. "Pop"
Stoneman. By 1927 he had already recorded more than any other country
artist; and among his hundred-plus sides were collaborations with his
fiddling wife, Hattie, and her little sister, Irma Frost. Hattie Frost
Stoneman (1900–1976) performed regularly with her husband during
the early years of his career, 1926 to 1934, but recorded only a smat-
tering of titles. That she was able to participate at all is a wonder, since
the Stonemans had twenty-three children, fifteen of whom survived.
Three daughters—Patsy, Donna, and Roni—all later became country
music professionals.

Hattie and Irma, who played the pump organ, were used particularly
on gospel songs such as "Are You Washed in the Blood," "Going Down
the Valley," and "When the Redeemed Are Gathered In." Hattie's
piercing, reedy soprano leads the singing on these and several other discs
by Stoneman's groups. Victor Records publicity described them as "gospel
songs as they sing them only in the South. This organization of five artists
who play while they are actually singing to you, will bring back to you the
memories of many a stirring revival night. A woman's voice leads."

Tennessee's enormously popular Pickard Family was similar to the
Stonemans. Again there was leader Obed "Dad" Pickard; again there was
dutiful helpmeet, Leila May Wilson Pickard (1885–c. 1955). And again
there were daughters who took the family name into the modern era,

Women occur most frequently in old-time country music as members of gospel acts. These were among those recorded or performing between 1925 and 1935, plus some representative songs:

THE ALABAMA SACRED HARP SINGERS ("Religion Is a Fortune," 1928)

J. T. ALLISON'S SACRED HARP SINGERS ("The Old Ship of Zion," 1928)

OLIVE BOONE WITH HER PARENTS, THE REV. AND MRS. EDWARD BOONE ("He Answers Prayers Today," 1929)

VIRGIL AND BLANCHE BROCK ("Today Is Mine, Tomorrow May Not Come," "Beyond the Sunset," 1920s–1930s)

THE CHARLES BUTTS SACRED HARP SINGERS ("I Would See Jesus," 1928)

THE CHUMBLER FAMILY ("Jacob's Ladder," 1929)

THE CORLEY FAMILY ("Give the World a Smile," 1930)

THE DEAL FAMILY ("Everybody Will Be Happy Over There," 1927)

DENSON'S SACRED HARP SINGERS ("The Christian's Hope," 1928)

MR. AND MRS. C. A. DOUGHERTY ("No Disappointment in Heaven," 1926)

DYE'S SACRED HARP SINGERS ("New Hosanna," 1929)

THE FLAT CREEK SACRED SINGERS ("Mother, Tell Me of the Angels," 1928)

THE FOREMAN FAMILY ("The Dying Nun," "The Poor Old Slave," 1929)

THE GRISHAM FAMILY ("Angels Tell Mother I'll Be There," 1928)

BILLIE HOLSTEIN WITH HER BROTHER, THE REV. CALBERT HOLSTEIN ("Zion's Hill," 1928)

ED AND GRACE MCCONNELL ("I Want to Be Like Jesus," 1928)

THE MIXED CHOIR OF THE ORIGINAL SACRED HARP ("Canaan's Land," "The Christian Warfare," 1923)

THE MORRIS FAMILY ("Mary Don't You Weep," 1930)

THE MOUNT VERNON QUARTET ("Tenting Tonight on the Old Camp Ground," 1928)

THE NANCE FAMILY ("Old Rugged Cross," 1930)

ERNEST PHIPPS AND HIS HOLINESS SINGERS ("If the Light Has Gone Out in Your Soul," 1928)

MR. AND MRS. WILLIAM SHIVELY, "THE BUCKEYE SONGBIRDS" ("Nearer My God to Thee," 1931)

THE SPARKMAN TRIO ("Living for Christ Each Day," 1929)

MR. AND MRS. J. DOUGLAS SWAGERTY ("Life's Railway to Heaven," "Shall We Gather at the River," 1924)

THE TENNESSEE MOUNTAINEERS ("Standing on the Promises," 1927)

THE THRASHER FAMILY ("I Have a Friend," 1931)

THE TILLMANS ("My Mother's Bible," 1925)

WILLIAMS AND WILLIAMS ("In the Garden," 1926)

Ruthie and Ann. The Pickards were from Ashland City, Tennessee, about twenty-five miles down the Cumberland River from Nashville. In 1926 Dad and his "Little Mother" began broadcasting on WSM's six-month-old Saturday night radio barn dance show, later to become world-renowned as "The Grand Ole Opry." Thus began a thirty-year odyssey that took the Pickards and their four children to more than forty radio stations, three national networks, and eventually movies and television. Like western stars Otto and Mommie Gray, Obed and Leila May Pickard were trailblazers in popularizing country music in such Northeast markets as Philadelphia and New York.

The Pickards recorded some forty numbers between 1927 and 1930, but it was as homespun radio personalities that they really popularized "She'll Be Comin' 'Round the Mountain," "Buffalo Gals," "Little Red Caboose Behind the Train," "The Old Gray Goose Is Dead," and other campfire favorites.

This Pickard Family songbook of 1930 has the look of an old-time family photo album. The image was bolstered by the presence of Leila May "Mom" Pickard and was carried into the 1960s by daughters Ruthie and baby Ann.

The community-and-family values of acts like the Pickards and Carters spoke to a nation cast spiritually adrift in the rampaging social waters of the twenties. On one hand were religious upholders of the pre–World War I Victorian morality. On the other were cigarette smoking, scandalous confession magazines, science, flimsy dresses and bare arms, drinking, ethnic groups, movies, and jazz.

The brutal realities of World War I had destroyed the nation's optimistic view of unlimited progress. In the wake of this loss of faith, there was a cultural tug back to an idealized past of simple, sentimentalized values. This culminated in the Agrarians' 1930 literary manifesto that held up the South as a perfect society, a place of serenity in a morally disintegrating world. Early country music was marketed similarly.

Female revivalists became a huge phenomenon—Bishop Alma White; Elder Lucy Smith; and the famous Aimee Semple McPherson, known as "The Mary Pickford of Revivalism." The beauteous McPherson (1890–1944) used her husky contralto to become a Columbia Records star, developed a fabulous California show-biz gospel empire, and became a media sensation before overdosing on sleeping pills.

The religious boom led to the development of down-home family gospel

The Speer Quartet
of DOUBLE SPRINGS, ALA.
Will Appear in Concert *at*

The Program will consist of both Sacred and Secular Songs.
A clean program that you will enjoy.

EVERYBODY COME!

Admission: 25 and 35 Cents

Lena Brock Speer, left, initially teamed up with her husband, his sister, and his sister's husband to form the original Speer Quartet in 1921. From the start, the presence of the women's voices in the rural southern gospel act created a stir.

troupes, as well. Other than the Carters and Stonemans, only one country music family active today has its roots in the 1920s, gospel's Speer dynasty. The Speer Family, which featured the penetrating lead voice of Lena Brock ("Mom") Speer (1900–1967), began performing in 1921, started recording in 1947, and is still going strong.

It was as unbilled members of such family gospel acts that women often marched through the pages of early country music history. More than a dozen were recorded between the Carters' 1927 breakthrough and the onset of the Depression. Most were promoted by Columbia Records in an attempt to duplicate the success of Victor's star Carters.

Paramount, Gennett, and the American Record Company all tried with the Welling & McGhee Trio, formed when West Virginia's John McGhee and Frank Welling added the former's daughter, Alma McGhee, or the latter's wife, Thelma Welling, to their duo. Billed under such family-oriented pseudonyms as The Mitchell Family Trio, The Harper Family Trio, and The Baxter Family Trio, this extensively recorded act's output of 1929 through 1931 included such parlor song fare as "In the Garden," "A Flower from My Angel Mother's Grave," Anita Owen's 1894 chestnut "Sweet Bunch of Daisies," and Fanny Crosby's standard "Pass Me Not O Gentle Savior."

Columbia unknowingly stumbled on its best Carter Family rival on April 21, 1930, in Atlanta, when it recorded ten tunes by The Blue Ridge Mountain Singers. The combo had the whole package—lovely female duet singing, autoharp-guitar accompaniment, an occasional male voice, and exquisite, old-timey performances—but the company apparently failed to see it.

The Blue Ridge Mountain Singers is a group still shrouded in mystery. Despite researchers' efforts, they remain audio shadows with no names. The act's sound is like no other in country music. The female voices have an unearthly timbre and beautiful, flawless harmony. As they weave their duets, the women trade parts back and forth, the melody sometimes falling to the intense alto and sometimes to the ethereal high soprano. All the performances are ultraprofessional. Why weren't they Carter-size hits?

Some old-time music fans think it was because of their content. The Blue Ridge Mountain Singers recorded family-harmony/parlor-song fare such as "I'll Remember Your Love in My Prayers" and "Lorena"; but fully six of the ten Blue Ridge Mountain Singers songs deal with betrayal, two-timing, adultery, or another of the darker aspects of love. While these themes later became common—indeed, dominant—in country music, they were not prevalent in the twenties and thirties. The act's "I Wish I Had Never Met You" and "Christine LeRoy" are the first women's "cheating" songs in country music history. Columbia chose not to release these profoundly un-Carter-like lyrics; they remained unheard until a 1979 LP of old-time-music women.

Georgia's capital city was the mecca for early country music talent scouts, the undisputed headquarters for early hillbilly recording. The metropolis was the hub of eight railroads by the early 1900s and one of the first southern cities to boast paved roads.

When Okeh Records scouts arrived in Atlanta in 1924 looking for hillbilly talent, they found a huge pool of ready-made country celebrities. The Jenkins Family, for instance, was well on its way to regional fame. The trio was headed by "Atlanta's Blind Newsboy Evangelist," a local character called Blind Andrew Jenkins who operated a newsstand in front of the city's Transportation Building. He was a widower when he married his second wife, Frances, in 1919. With her and her grown daughters, Irene Spain and Mary Lee Eskew, he formed The Jenkins Evangelist Family.

The Jenkins Family, including keyboardist Irene Spain, 1924.

Andy, Irene, and Mary Lee went into music professionally when they hit the airwaves of Atlanta's new WSB radio station on August 14, 1922, likely making the sisters the first country music women to broadcast. They continued to be heard on the station, doing fiddle music, folk songs, and religious numbers throughout the next two years. The powerful WSB boasted that it "covered Dixie like the dew," so Atlantans were well acquainted with the trio by the time The Jenkins Family first stepped into Okeh's studio in 1924 to become country music's first recorded family harmony group.

When the women led the singing,

the trio's records were generally billed as The Irene Spain Family. Among the Jenkins' fifty-some tunes of the twenties on Okeh are sturdy versions of the gospel anthems "Leaning on the Everlasting Arms," "On Christ the Solid Rock I Stand," and "We Are Going Down the Valley." The trio also revived Annie Walker's 1864 chestnut "Work for the Night Is Coming."

Among the Jenkins secular discs are "Picture from Life's Other Side" and "That Little Old Hut." On the play-party folk song "Charming Billy" (1926), Mary Lee asks the questions. Blind Andy answers, then laughs crazily along as she sings the chorus. "I Got Mine" (1924) is a religious parody of Ella Shields's vaudeville tune about a no-account crapshooter. It was one of the ten tunes included in *Christian Love Songs*, probably the first songbook published by a country act. Issued by Blind Andy, Irene, and Mary Lee in 1924, the collection was "Dedicated to the Unseen Circle of WSB" listeners.

The road to Atlanta as a hillbilly center was paved by phonograph dealer Polk Brockman. He was in Manhattan on a business trip when he saw a silent newsreel of a Virginia fiddlers' contest. He immediately thought of his hometown's popular Fiddlin' John Carson and wondered if there might be a market for records by the old geezer.

Atlanta had hosted a fiddle convention as early as 1885 and had been staging one annually since 1913. These events attracted thousands of whooping, screaming, crowing, dancing fans and considerable local newspaper coverage in the teens and twenties. Grizzled old mountaineers with their ancient tunes dominated these well-publicized hillbilly get-togethers, but a stubborn minority strain of female instrumentalists showed up, too. A fourteen-year-old named Louise Hall took second place at the 1916 Georgia Old-Time Fiddlers' Convention. Anita Sorrells, then fifteen, played "Casey Jones" to win the second prize in 1920. As Mrs. Anita Wheeler, the same contestant was crowned champion in 1931 and 1934. North Carolina's Samantha Bumgarner attended the 1927 convention. Savannah Singley (1913), Nancy Hall (1916), and a Miss Brown (1916) were also noted in Atlanta papers as participants.

When fiddler Emilia Wells tried to enter in 1929, the men had had enough. "Looks like the women are running the men out of every kind of job, from driving cars to flying," fumed convention organizer Aleck Smart. "But up in the mountain regions where most of our fiddlers come from they have always figured that the place for a woman is in the cabin, doing the cooking and looking after the children, with some plowing and hoeing in season. And they certainly are not used to women fiddlers. I reckon we'll have to take a vote on it." Emilia, rest assured, competed.

Brockman had these colorful contests on his mind when he approached

Okeh Records about making some authentic country discs. His overture coincided with the development of new portable recording equipment, so the company sent a reluctant Ralph Peer to Atlanta in 1923 to record Fiddlin' John Carson's "The Little Old Log Cabin in the Lane"/"The Old Hen Cackled and the Rooster's Going to Crow." Peer pronounced Carson "pluperfect awful," but when sales in Atlanta topped fifteen thousand within a week, he changed his mind. Four years later a more enthusiastic Peer was in the mountains of Virginia making country music history with Jimmie Rodgers and The Carter Family.

Cotton mill worker Carson, the seven-time fiddle champ, was Atlanta's flamboyant hillbilly ambassador. A master of the droll one-liner, he was a veteran of carnivals, square dances, and traveling medicine shows by 1900. He was also the first hillbilly act to make the transition to radio on WSB (*Welcome South, Brother*). Fiddlin' John's wife, Jennie Nora Carson, provided rhythm accompaniment during his radio performances by beating his fiddle strings with straws. An even more important part of the show was daughter Rosa Lee Carson Johnson, known as "Moonshine Kate."

"Moonshine Kate" and Fiddlin' John Carson, 1925.

Born in 1909, she began doing a buck-and-wing dance on stage to his fiddle accompaniment at age seven. By age fourteen she was playing guitar and banjo, and a year later she was a permanent part of her father's act. Her Moonshine Kate comic character was a brassy, slow-drawling mountain gal who offered wisecracks to her father's stage (and apparently real-life) role as a sly, boozy reprobate. She sassed the revenuers looking for his still and hid moonshine flasks in her bosom. On comedy skits preserved on records, she outguffs her dad considerably. "Pa's Birthday Party," "The Old Gray Horse Ain't What It Used to Be," and "Kate's Snuff Box" are among these. Although just a teenager, Moonshine Kate could be remarkably sassy and acidic. She was our first outstanding female hillbilly comic personality.

The two were closely connected with the Populist movement and used their music to draw crowds to rallies and political events. Fiddlin' John's campaign song "Georgia's Three-Dollar Tag" was an important factor in the election of Governor Eugene Talmadge, and the Carsons also campaigned for Georgia's Populist senator Tom Watson. During the Talmadge campaign, "We'd go from town to town . . . and he would have a big truck for us to get up there and make some music," Kate recalled. "We'd sing and I'd buck-and-wing dance, and Pa would tell a few jokes in the courthouse square." Moonshine Kate and Fiddlin' John recorded the Populist anthems "The Honest Farmer" and "The Farmer Is the Man Who Feeds Them All" to protest taxes, middlemen, and the credit system.

In addition to recording frequently with her father, Moonshine Kate did several solo records, from 1925 to 1934. Among her finest moments as a singer and guitarist were "My Man's a Jolly Railroad Man" (1931), "Poor Girl's Story" (1930), "The Lone Child" (1925), and "Last Gold Dollar" (1930), the last-named better known as the country-blues standard "Don't Let Your Deal Go Down." Kate sang with a sliding, lazy, bent-note ease that does, indeed, reflect some blues influence. "Texas Blues" (1930) is her variation of Jimmie Rodgers's "T for Texas," complete with yodeling and Rodgers-style guitar runs. On its flip side was "Raggedy Riley." In this feisty "shrewish wife" number, Kate makes it clear who's going to wear the pants in the family. Considering her dad's life-style, her reworking of the nineteenth-century temperance song "The Drinker's Child" (1925) might be her most autobiographical performance. But it is as the vocalist of "Little Mary Phagan" that Moonshine Kate is best remembered. The 1913 murder of fourteen-year-old Atlanta pencil factory girl Mary Phagan became one of the most sensational cases of the day when an anti-Semitic mob lynched innocent Jewish factory supervisor Leo Frank for the crime. John and Kate's lyrics support the prevailing view of the day that Frank was guilty; he wasn't cleared until 1986. The melody, credited to Irene Spain, was also used for Ella May Wiggins's notable labor protest song "Mill Mother's Lament."

John and Kate continued to perform until the Depression torpedoed the record industry. A grateful Talmadge gave John a patronage job running the elevator in the state capitol building. Fiddlin' John died at age eighty-one in 1949. Kate went to work for Atlanta's recreation department.

"Every now and then, I still like to get out my old guitar and play some of those old hillbilly songs," she said wistfully, fifty years after she drawled and sassed her way into country music history. A nephew who visited Nashville once asked her why country music's first star and his wisecracking daughter aren't in the Country Music Hall of Fame. "Honey," she replied, "we weren't country musicians. We were hillbillies."

Georgia fiddler Rob Stanley was the man who'd beaten Anita Sorrells in that 1920 Atlanta fiddle contest. Like Fiddlin' John Carson, Stanley had a musical daughter. Roba Stanley (1910–1986) was fourteen years old when she made country music's first solo female record. Later called "America's first country sweetheart," Roba never achieved the fame of Atlanta's Jenkins Family or Moonshine Kate. Her entire recording career consisted of just nine performances, but her charming, youthful, fresh-as-Georgia-peaches voice was a female milestone on the country music road.

Roba and daddy Rob came down to Atlanta from Gwinnett County, a farming area in the hills of north Georgia. As a tot Roba would pick up her older brother's guitar when he was out in the fields working. Soon she was backing her father at square dances. "I know I was the only girl playing," she recalled in 1977. "At least, I don't remember seeing any more girls."

Rob, who was sixty-five at the time, evidently thought it a cute novelty to have little Roba along. They began to tour a little, eventually coming to the

Roba Stanley, 1924.

attention of WSB, where the Stanleys debuted in early 1924. Back home everyone around gathered at the village jailhouse to hear the performance on the town's one radio set. Radio exposure led to the offer to record for Okeh that summer.

Roba's best-selling effort from the session was "Devilish Mary," again a tale of that combative gal who wants to wear the pants in a marriage. "I was crazy back then, wasn't I?" Roba said with a lilting laugh when reminded years later of her spunky attitude. "Still am." As a spry, plump, little old lady she used the name "Devilish Mary" as her CB "handle."

Four months later Okeh had the teen back in the studio, this time singing the slightly salty "All Night Long" and a version of "Frankie and Johnny" she called "Little Frankie." Henry Whitter, one of the biggest of the early hillbilly stars, came to Atlanta to record with her and invited the youngster to tour with him. She didn't go, and the 1925 records with Whitter were her swan songs. "Old Maid Blues" was an "I-ain't-got-nobody" blues number. Then came her masterpiece, "Single

Life." With a wry drawl, Roba announced, "I am single and no man's wife / And no man shall control me." It was strikingly feminist stuff, even by today's standards.

Despite her free-as-a-bird youthful boast, Roba married impulsively a few months after recording "Single Life" at age fifteen. "I just quit everything and got married. My parents were a little concerned about how young I was, but they liked Mr. Baldwin a lot." Newlyweds Bob and Roba Baldwin moved to Florida, where Roba raised three children and lived to be seventy-six.

"My husband didn't like for me to play out in public much," Roba told *Old Time Music* magazine. "There was no way to keep recording— they were up there in Georgia and I was in Miami, and lucky to get home once a year. They kept playing, but when I left it almost broke things up. I carried my guitar with me but I played very, very little, and in just two or three months I wasn't playing at all." Eventually she gave the old guitar away to some nephews and forgot about her singing career. Roba was unaware that she was country's trailblazing solo female singer until she was rediscovered by folklorists in the 1970s. One grandson moved to middle Tennessee, and in her old age Roba's accomplishment was finally saluted from the stage of "The Grand Ole Opry" during a visit with his family.

You can count the other solo female country acts of the 1920s on the fingers of both hands. Veterans of the vaudeville era Adelyne Hood (1929) and Mommie Gray (1928) were on disc by the end of the decade. Excluding Mommie, who recorded mainly parlor songs, the era's first singing cowgirl was Billie Maxwell (1906–1954). Sometimes accompanied by her father, fiddler E. Curtis Maxwell, Billie recorded six sides for Victor in El Paso in July 1929. And "The Cowboy's Wife," with its odd minor-key melody, lonely sound, and fatalistic attitude, is perhaps our best view of what it meant for a western woman to live in such desolation.

Raised near the western frontier town of Springerville, Arizona, Billie and her father rode horseback to play at back-country cowboy dances in the early 1920s. She was a fine guitarist, but music making was never her full-time career. Billie married Alvin Chester Warner in 1929 and was pregnant with their first child when she recorded. She dropped out of music to raise her family and died before her songs were rediscovered by cowboy-song folklorists in the 1960s. Equally obscure is Billie's only singing cowgirl contemporary, Buerl Sisney, who issued a handful of tunes as "The Lonesome Cowgirl" in 1931 on Indiana's small, short-lived Superior label.

Female country duets were as rare as soloists prior to the 1930s. The banjo-guitar team Ruth and Wanda Neal were another Okeh Records

Atlanta discovery. Their "Round Town Girls" (1927) is a version of the familiar "Buffalo Gals" folk song. Shortly after the Neals' session came one by The Moore Sisters. These Atlantans revived Anita Owen's 1908 song "Daisies Won't Tell." The Brock Sisters, Allie and Pearl, checked in with their "Broadway Blues" in 1929. Like Moonshine Kate and Roba Stanley, Jennie and Pauline Bowman were the teenage daughters of a famed fiddler, Tennessee's Charlie Bowman. The Bowman Sisters recorded in the bluesy, jazz-baby mode of "Railroad Take Me Back" and "Old Lonesome Blues" in 1929.

These young "country flappers" were a distinct minority, but it is logical that they went to work. Unmarried daughters were expected to help support country families. Families with many female children often moved to mill towns, where the girls could all be employed. Work gave these young women spending money and independence; so in imitation of their city sisters, they turned into sassy, pint-size flappers. Thus, Moonshine Kate, Roba Stanley, and the Bowmans combined saucy modern attitudes with traditional styles.

Women performing in families were a reassurance that the traditional social order endured, and record companies wanted to stick with their successful "family" formula. After all, The Carter Family's "Anchored in Love" (1928) sold almost a hundred thousand copies. "Little Moses"/"God Gave Noah the Rainbow Sign" (1929) sold sixty thousand, and even during the Depression "Diamonds in the Rough" managed to sell forty thousand. During one two-year period, sales of fourteen Carter discs totaled seven hundred thousand. This was at a time when a giant country hit would be a sale of fifty thousand, and million-sellers were practically unheard of. Carter records exceeded the sales of many country 78s by ten times.

If it was families record buyers wanted, it was families they got. Woman after woman was chaperoned to the recording studio by her mate during country music's infancy. There were at least eleven husband-wife duos recorded, in addition to the profusion of family groups in the twenties.

Willie Sievers was billed as "the girl guitar-playing wonder of the world" in a 1929 Brunswick Records promotional blurb. "Plays with the guitar held behind her—plays the instrument with her feet. Right this way to hear Willie Sievers—Champion Woman Guitarist of the World." The subject of this tub-thumping was the nineteen-year-old guitarist of The Tennessee Ramblers. Born in 1909, Willie was from a dynasty of musical women that also included her mother and grandmother. The group was—surprise—a family act headed by her fiddling father, Bill. The Tennessee Ramblers 78s of 1928–1930 mainly showcase his work. Willie was seen and heard to better

THE EARLY COUNTRY FEMALE SOLOISTS

Women who recorded solo were rare in country music of the 1920s. These were the pioneers:

ROBA STANLEY (1924)

CONNIE SIDES ("In the Shadow of the Pines," 1924)

MOONSHINE KATE (1925)

FLORA NOLES ("Little Mohee," 1925)

DAPHNE BURNS ("Weeping Willow Tree," 1927)

SUE MORGAN ("Just Plain Folks," 1928)

LULU JACKSON ("Little Rosewood Casket," "So You're Going to Leave the Old Home Jim," "Careless Love," 1928)

NETTIE ROBERTSON ("The Island Unknown," 1929)

JOSSIE ELLERS ("Old Maid Song," "Dying for Someone to Love Me," 1929)

BILLIE MAXWELL ("The Cowboy's Wife," 1929)

BESS PENNINGTON ("Jack and May," 1930)

advantage at the band's live appearances, which continued long after the recording industry left The Tennessee Ramblers behind.

As you might expect, there were a plethora of pianists among old-time music women. They were the piano, organ, and melodeon accompanists for the period's many male gospel quartets, as well as for several string bands. Clarice Blackard Shelor's work in Virginia's Shelor Family was notable. Theron Hale & His Daughters were among the pioneer "Grand Ole Opry" acts of the twenties. This family band featured Elizabeth Hale on piano, and Theron's other daughter, Mamie Ruth, played twin fiddle with him on such charming outings as "Listen to the Mockingbird."

Several female instrumentalists popularized more exotic instruments during country music's infancy. The Opry's first solo woman performer was Westmoreland, Tennessee's, Kitty Cora Cline, who performed on a twenty-string hammered dulcimer. She was given her own segment on WSM's new show in 1928. After seeing a gruesome automobile accident on the highway en route to the Opry one evening in 1932, she commuted no more. The hammered-dulcimer wonder retired to raise her family and died in the late 1960s at nearly ninety years of age.

The cello and the banjo-uke were played by The Blankenship Family's teen daughters Darius and Daphna. To Willie Spainhour Greer goes the distinction of being the only commercially recorded Appalachian dulcimer player of the 1920s. Dyke's Magic City Trio included Myrtle Vermillion on autoharp. Female harmonica players were quite rare, but Cordelia Mayberry of Blue Gap, Virginia, was a hot shot on the instrument. In 1929 she strutted her stuff—imitating a chugging train and performing "Oh Susanna" with The Blue Ridgers band—for the Warner/Vitaphone cameras to become the first country entertainer captured on sound film.

For individuality, vision, and melodic splendor, none could hold a candle to the remarkable Nonnie Smith Presson (c. 1897–1977). Although never as widely recorded as the Stonemans, as popular as the Carters, or as historic as the Speers, Nonnie's Perry County Music Makers were indisputably among the greatest family acts in old-time music. Her instrument was a giant, fifty-four-string zither. Her great gift was her songwriting. Her flowery Victorian metaphors were as poetic as her fluid, entrancing picking style.

Nonnie Smith Presson and her brother Bulow Smith recorded four captivating tunes in Knoxville in 1930. The ringing, bell-like tones of Nonnie's unusual instrument ripple and roll through the numbers in an achingly beautiful way. Bulow echoes her on guitar, and the two sing harmony in natural, unaffected voices. When the records appeared on Vocalion Records in August 1930, Nonnie and Bulow put together a band and headed out on tour to promote them. When the Depression caught up with the show in Arkansas—leaving the group broke and stranded in the Ozarks—they headed for home and eventual obscurity.

After thirty years of inactivity, The Perry County Music Makers were rediscovered by old-time music scholar Charles Wolfe. The old pickers were featured at the Smithsonian Folk Festival, and Wolfe persuaded them to record again, issuing two albums on Davis Unlimited Records, in 1974 and 1976. Nonnie's niece Virginia Clayborne pitched in on harmony vocals, but otherwise the sound was untouched by time. The albums were Nonnie's last testament. After a brief illness she died in 1977.

"You might say music is, and always has been, a big part of my life," Nonnie wrote the year before she passed away. "I have known music as long as I've known anything. Words cannot express just how I feel about it. To me it is a link between Heaven and Earth. In fact, it has been said that music ties the Two Worlds together, and I find this is very true."

Of all the female pickers of the twenties, the one who was the strongest link between Appalachian folk music and the emerging commercial country

OLLIE HESS ("Sleep Baby Sleep," "Mammie's Lullaby," 1931)

BUERL SISNEY, "THE LONESOME COWGIRL" ("My Mother Was a Lady," 1931)

Nonnie Smith Presson with her brother Bulow, 1976.

Country music pioneer Samantha Bumgarner lived long enough to find her music appreciated anew during the folk-music revival. This photo was taken at a festival appearance in 1955.

scene was Samantha Bumgarner (c. 1880–1960). Samantha was once praised by folk festival king Bascom Lamar Lunsford as being the best all-around musician he'd ever met. She was also a bona fide North Carolina mountain legend: probably the first five-string banjo player to record; an enduring folk festival favorite; a perennial instrumental competition champion; and the leader of one of the first recorded country string bands.

Moonshine Kate, Roba Stanley, Billie Maxwell, the Bowman Sisters, and Willie Sievers were all country pioneers who were fiddlers' daughters. So was Samantha. But in her case we have the first star representative of the assertive, independent "banjo-pickin' girl" tradition. When Samantha was a little girl, her father, Has Biddix, wouldn't let her touch his fiddle. So she snitched it to practice whenever he wasn't home. She also taught herself banjo on an instrument that was "a gourd with a cat's hide stretched over it and strings made out of cotton thread waxed with beeswax," she recalled. She started playing in public at age fifteen in 1895.

Samantha's husband, Carse Bumgarner, was very supportive of his wife's abilities. He bought her the first fiddle she ever owned and witnessed her triumphs in old-time instrumental competitions.

"We was in Canton [North Carolina], and they was havin' a fiddlers' convention," she recalled of her first such experience. "Somebody entered me in the banjo contest. First banjo contest I was ever in, and I was nervous. I knew I couldn't hit a string. Besides, I had that old ten-cent banjo. And here I looked up and saw all these fine banjos coming in from Asheville. I wanted to leave, but they wouldn't let me. I tell you I was so nervous I didn't know I was hitting the strings. . . . But I won the contest. And I've been winning them ever since."

By the time she and her friend Eva Davis traveled to New York in April 1924, the native of tiny Silva, North Carolina, had confidence. She was a tall, bony woman of forty-two when they walked into the Columbia Records studio on the top floor of the Gotham National Bank Building and introduced themselves. Nashville's Fisk Jubilee Singers finished singing a spiritual called "Hope You'll Join the Band." Then it was Samantha's turn. She and her partner ripped into "Cindy in the Meadows," the first of twelve spirited banjo and fiddle tunes they performed for what must have been a somewhat puzzled group of New Yorkers. At the time, the label had recorded only one other string band.

But after Okeh's experience with Fiddlin' John Carson, Columbia must have figured something was up. On June 15, the company put an ad in *Talking Machine World* that said optimistically, "The fiddle and guitar craze is sweeping northward! Columbia leads with records of old-fashioned southern songs and dances." Bumgarner and Davis were pictured and described as "quaint musicians" who will "go over big with your trade."

The records apparently sold respectably, but Samantha didn't return to the studio for thirty years. Instead, she hit the road. Eva Davis eventually dropped out of the picture, but Samantha became the headliner of the Mountain Dance and Folk Festival in Asheville, North Carolina, every year between 1928 and 1959.

"Aunt Samantha" died on Christmas Eve 1960. The Asheville *Citizen-Times* noted that her death "marked the passing of one of this mountain region's most colorful and picturesque individuals." Said the Associated Press, "She was the last of the old-time balladeers, and the cry of her fiddle and the twang of her banjo were known wherever music-making folks gathered. She wandered up and down the country and across the land."

They were wrong about one thing. Independent country music woman Samantha Bumgarner wasn't the end of the line. She was a beginning.

GEORGE AND ODA ROARK ("I Truly Understand You Love Another Man," "My Mother's Hands," 1928)

SELMA AND DEWEY HAYES ("Broken Heart," 1931)

Mr. and Mrs. Westbrook ("Will the Circle Be Unbroken," 1929)

"THE NATIONAL BARN DANCE"

Country Women, Radio, and the Great Depression

I t is an era we think of in grainy black-and-white images—images of gaunt, careworn mothers sitting on Dust Bowl porches surrounded by raggedy children; images of urban women in threadbare dresses, waiting in breadlines and living in shantytowns; images of mountain girls made old before their time by years of poverty and hunger. The Great Depression of the 1930s produced bleakness and misery of awesome proportions.

The statistics are staggering: 28 percent of the nation's households did not have an employed wage earner. Three-quarters of the nation's workers were on part-time schedules. Unemployment increased and wages fell steadily between 1929 and 1933. In cities, adults and children dug through garbage dumps for food. People in the countryside were no better off. From Harlan County, Kentucky, came reports that entire families were subsisting on dandelions and blackberries. There was no national relief program until after Franklin Roosevelt's inauguration in 1933. Public welfare funds were depleted from Philadelphia, Mississippi, to Philadelphia, Pennsylvania.

Desperation drove the poor and unemployed into America's railroad boxcars and onto its newly paved roads in search of a job, any job. Thousands of families from

poverty-stricken rural areas headed for California or to the industrial cities of the North.

By 1931 several hundred homeless and unemployed women were sleeping nightly in Chicago's parks. The city had just one shelter—with only a hundred beds—available to women at the time. Nearly 20 percent of the city's schoolchildren suffered from malnutrition, and in 1932 five hundred ragged and gaunt students marched to the Board of Education asking for food in their classrooms.

Arkansas farm girl Rubye Blevins was in Chicago in 1930 looking for a job. She found it as Patsy Montana, the singing cowgirl. Indiana's Jean Meunich was twenty years old and trying to make it in the Windy City as a singer. She found her niche as Linda Parker, the ideal country sunbonnet sweetheart. North Carolina's Myrtle Eleanor Cooper was a convicted moonshiner's daughter who arrived in Chicago as a teenager. The family was looking for a better way of life and found it when ne'er-do-well John Cooper took the nineteen-year-old to audition for radio executives. Four years later as Lulu Belle, she was the most popular woman on America's airwaves.

These young women and their contemporaries became country music's first national radio stars. They were headliners at the biggest and best hillbilly show of the day, "The National Barn Dance" at station WLS in Chicago. They landed choice jobs in one of the few areas of American life that boomed during the Depression's darkest days. As it has done in every recession since, country music thrived, providing escape and inspiration for its listeners, as well as employment for its performers.

Chicago was not the Cooper family's first stop in their quest for financial stability. Myrtle/Lulu Belle was born on Christmas Eve 1913 in Boone, North Carolina, while Papa John was working on the Ohio River locks in West Virginia. Chronically unemployed, he moved his brood to Indiana, Tennessee, Florida, South Carolina, and Kentucky during the next few years.

"Daddy was a great guy, but he wouldn't stay in one place very long," Lulu Belle recalled years later. "He was a rambler, big ideas. He invented things and never could find anybody to back them. . . . Then he'd pack us all up, take what we could carry and away we'd go.

"My mother knew every song—you'd call them country songs now. Mom knew them and she sang *all* the time when she was working around the house. . . . 'Barbara Allen,' things like that. She sang all the time. I remember so well her rolling out a pie crust one time with [little brother] Pete and me right under her feet . . . I think that's the way I learned 'The Little Rosewood Casket,' 'Little Mohee.'"

Myrtle was fourteen when the family moved back to Tennessee. In Elizabethton she went to work in the local hosiery mill. Lying about her age, the energetic tomboy got a meager $8.20 a week on the 7 A.M. to 5 P.M. shift. The girl's wages were welcome. In those days many country girls left school at age fourteen or fifteen to become domestics in cities, sending money home when they could. Others, like Myrtle, became factory laborers earning subsistence wages.

So instead of marrying young, as was the norm in earlier decades, the outgoing Myrtle Cooper stayed home and provided extra family income. Because of the economic uncertainty of the times, marriages were often postponed—there were twenty-five thousand fewer marriages in 1932 than in 1929, despite population growth. Myrtle and others like her made the thirties the first big era of "the single girl."

Papa John was jailed for selling moonshine in Tennessee; he escaped in the summer of 1929 and headed north for the anonymity of Chicago. The family arrived just in time for the Crash. "It was just a lot of poor folks, but not as poor as we were. I don't know where Daddy got the money that we lived on. He managed to bring food home every night—where he got it, I don't know." Myrtle took jobs as a maid and a department store clerk to help her ex-con papa make ends meet. As was later widely publicized by WLS, the bighearted country gal was fired from her job at the candy counter in a department store after the manager found out she was giving away peanuts and hunks of chocolate to a hungry old lady every day. At a Chicago hotel Myrtle advanced from maid to a five-dollar-a-week job as the baby-sitter for guests' children. Next she got nine dollars a week in the china department of a five-and-dime.

One-fourth of American women were working outside the home like young Myrtle. Not everyone found decent employment: Prostitution increased, and for the first time since the days of the outlaw queens of the Old West, female criminals such as Ma Barker and Bonnie Parker made headlines. Unemployment was compounded by homelessness in urban areas. In 1933 the YWCA estimated that it had served 145,000 homeless women.

Author Meridel Le Sueur spent the Depression interviewing her sisters in the streets. In *Women on the Breadlines* she wrote, "There is a great exodus of girls from the farms into the cities now. . . . Some are made brazen too soon by the city. . . . The prettier ones can get jobs in the stores when there are any, or waiting on table, but these jobs are only for the attractive and the adroit. The others, the real peasants, have a more difficult time."

The "attractive and adroit" had another option: show business. Myrtle Eleanor Cooper was no raving beauty and possessed a merely adequate

WLS's "National Barn Dance"— Chicago (launched 1924)

WSM's "Grand Ole Opry"—Nashville (1925)

WWVA's "Jamboree"— Wheeling, West Virginia (1926)

KMOX's "Old-Fashioned Barn Dance"—St. Louis (1930) Starred Cousin Emmy and others, including Uncle Henry's Original Kentucky Mountaineers, a popular troupe featuring as its singers leader Henry Warren's wife, Wava Ilene Shockley, and Warren with his brother Grady (as "Sally and Coonhunter") and his sister Essie Mae (as "Judy Lane")

WOWO's "Hoosier Hop"—Fort Wayne, Indiana (1932)

WHO's "Iowa Barn Dance Frolic"—Des Moines (1932) The Calico Maids, the Lem and Martha comedy team (Tom and Ann Lewis), Texas Ruby, Peggy Anne

singing voice, but she had enough verve and personality to get in the door of America's most powerful country music radio station, WLS. Its fifty-thousand-watt signal boomed across the plains and prairies, reaching millions.

The call letters originally stood for "World's Largest Store," for WLS was founded by Chicago's mighty Sears empire in 1924. From the beginning, it promoted an idealized rural wholesomeness. When *Prairie Farmer* magazine acquired the station in 1928, this country image was strengthened. And by then the station's Saturday-night barn dance variety show was already the most powerful and influential in America.

Fort Worth's WBAP, Atlanta's WSB, and Pittsburgh's KDKA had already offered country shows by 1924, but WLS launched the blockbuster when it beamed "The National Barn Dance" into the American heartland that year. It set the radio barn dance prototype—square dance bands, heart singers, barbershop quartets, rube comics, and next-doorneighbor announcers blended in a weekly repertory company. The show's pattern was traced by dozens of other stations in the 1930s; its barn dance format coalesced and united the country music audience, giving the young industry a focus.

Despite the might of WLS, "in those days you could get in without having to fill out an application and all that," Lulu Belle/Myrtle recalled. Her father pestered the station's brass into listening to his daughter, who by this time was supplementing her wages with five-dollar performances at local chamber of commerce events. Her vim and let-'er-rip vocal style didn't initially impress the radio men, and her sheer volume drove the audio engineers crazy. She flunked the audition, but two weeks later John was back with a toned-down daughter, and this time he got her on the air. She was given a spot on WLS's 5:30 A.M. "Smile-a-While" show for $7.50 a week. Before graduation to the big time on "The National Barn Dance" she needed a few pointers. Barn Dance boss John Lair instructed Papa John to take her to see vaudeville rube star Elviry Weaver.

"She was real feisty," Lulu Belle recalled years later. "I think that's what he wanted me to do. Well, I know he did. And so I did it insofar as I could, but she was older and knew more about what she was doing; I was young and ignorant. But so far as the *costume* went, that was from her."

She knew she couldn't pull off Elviry's vinegar, but she could certainly manage the older star's self-assertion. Myrtle was presented to "National Barn Dance" audiences as the aggressive mountain girlfriend of Red Foley, a member of Linda Parker's popular Cumberland Ridge Runners band. Mother Sidney Olive Marie Cooper did her part by sewing Myrtle an Elviry-style "Mother Hubbard" hillbilly dress for her WLS debut. Wearing her mother's calico creation, a pair of laced-up nineteenth-century high-topped shoes, and a pinned-on hair braid, Myrtle made her entrance with spirits high.

Lair dubbed her Lulu Belle after that first show, and in the months to come she solidified her image. Lulu Belle's trademarks became her pantaloons, gingham dresses, high-topped shoes, and ever-present chewing gum, which she snapped and chawed with a vengeance. Her stage personality evolved into the quintessential man-hungry mountain gal. She was unladylike. She was forward. She was lovably foolish.

The year she stepped onto the Barn Dance stage, 1932, is also the year the show began playing to capacity *paying* audiences weekly. Hundreds of country enthusiasts were turned away at ninety cents a seat at a time when going to the movies cost only a dime and money was at its scarcest. She made the most of that fan devotion. The big, lefthanded tomboy became the show's resident cutup, frequently galloping across the stage and out into the aisles, shrieking in hot pursuit of Foley or running from a musician. "I'd clown around . . . and get into mischief all the time.

"If I *moved* the audience would laugh, whether it was funny or not . . . the announcer got very nasty with me, even on the air. . . . But Mom said . . . 'You just come right back at him.' So I got to be a smart aleck. Anything he'd say to me, I'd talk right back to him. The audience just loved that, because here's this dumb kid and he's being mean to her, so they took me right under their wing," she recalled in a 1987 *Journal of Country Music* article.

"I was headlining my own show after being there less than a year. I don't know what people liked about me—I was crazier than a bed bug! But they took me right into their hearts." She was brash, forthright, uninhibited, and altogether irrepressible. She was at once shy and boisterous, bashful and boastful—she communicated lovable honesty and a certain blundering ingenuousness that audiences adored. Lulu Belle's considerable charisma was something never captured on records, yet it was this zest, enthusiasm, and assertiveness that formed the basis for her vast radio popularity.

In 1933 Lulu Belle's partner Red Foley married Eva Overstake of WLS's Three Little Maids singing trio. Eva insisted that the duo break up the boyfriend-and-girlfriend act, so Lair instructed Lulu Belle to work up routines with Barn Dance newcomer Scott Wiseman. Scotty played the shy, soft-spoken bachelor to her sassy, extroverted, hayseed character, and the team's popularity soared. Theirs was the hillbilly version of the formula used by their contemporaries Gracie Allen and George Burns and by such later teams as Lucille Ball and Desi Arnaz.

Coon, "Maids of the Prairie" Faye and Cleo, headliner Louisiana Lou, old maid Tillie Boggs (Shari Morning), and other female stars

WBT's "Crazy Barn Dance"— Charlotte, North Carolina (1934)

KMBC's "Brush Creek Follies"— Kansas City (c. 1935) The Kasper Sisters, The Kentucky Girls (Mrs. H. S. Berry and her daughter Helena Berry Edmonson), Joy and Jane

WLW's "Midwestern Hayride"— Cincinnati (1936) Ma and Pa McCormick, The Owens Sisters, "Canadian Cowgirl" Helen Diller, "Ozark Sweetheart" Eileen Graham and The Yodelettes, and others

WRVA's "Old Dominion Barn Dance"— Richmond, Virginia (1938)

WHAS's "Renfro Valley Barn Dance"— Louisville (1939)

WSB's "Barn Dance"—Atlanta (1940)

By 1935 WLS was touting its musical comedy sensation as "the recipient of the largest personal mail in radio. . . . with the greatest number of admiring letters of any star." In 1936 Lulu Belle drew more votes than actresses, jazz singers, Broadway entertainers, and all other popular female performers in *Radio Guide* magazine's poll for the title of "Radio Queen of America." This rollicking, rambunctious singer was the most popular woman on American radio, the only country star to have attained this level of fame. She remained a radio superstar for the next twenty years.

The couple's marriage in December 1934 and the birth of daughter Linda Lou in January 1936 were eagerly followed by radio fans. Lulu Belle's love for Scotty was one of country music's great romances. They were dubbed "The Hayloft Sweethearts," then simply "The Sweethearts of Country Music."

Their radio success led to recording for more than a dozen labels. Hollywood offered still wider renown. The pair appeared in eight motion pictures between 1938 and 1950, among them *Shine On, Harvest Moon, Village Barn Dance, Swing Your Partner,* and *National Barn Dance.* Their own "Breakfast in the Blue Ridge" radio show was nationally syndicated, and their Armed Forces Radio transcriptions were heard worldwide. The Wisemans were among the earliest stars to make the transition to television, broadcasting regularly over WNBQ-TV in Chicago from 1949 to 1957.

Lulu Belle and Scotty are perhaps best remembered today as composers. Scotty was particularly important in this regard, with "Remember Me (When the Candle Lights Are Gleaming)," "Homecoming Time in Happy Valley," and "Tell Her You Love Her" to his credit. But Lulu Belle's name appears as the cowriter on their best-known song, "Have I Told You Lately That I Love You?" In 1945 Scotty was hospitalized for minor surgery, and one day while visiting him, his wife said softly, "Have I told you lately that I love you?" and inspired a classic recorded by everyone from Bing Crosby to Elvis Presley. Lulu Belle and Scotty were also important as the popularizers of several standards in the American songbag, including "Did You Ever Go Sailing" (1940), "Does the Spearmint Lose Its Flavor on the Bedpost Overnight" (1948), "This Train" (1939), and "Turn Your Radio On" (1939). "Mountain Dew" (1939) even has a popular soft drink named after it.

Several numbers were from a strong women's perspective. Lulu Belle's "What Are Little Girls Made Of?" was a particular radio favorite. "The Farmer's Daughter Named Loueller" humorously warned of an innocent girl led astray on "sassperilly" by a city slicker. "Be Careful Girls" warned women not to get too involved with men because of potential heartbreak.

In 1939 the ever-spunky Lulu Belle recorded one of the most famous versions of the folk favorite "I Wish I Was a Single Girl Again." This humorous ditty laments, "When I was single I used to be afraid / No one would ever wed me and I'd die a sour old maid." Then, "Now I am married, and oh what do you think? / He bought a gingham apron and he showed me to the sink." And finally, "Lord, I wish I was a single girl again."

Lulu Belle's reign as "Radio Queen" in the 1930s means she is the first Queen of Country Music, for no other show of its kind was as widely heard as Chicago's "National Barn Dance." The creation of this fountainhead of all hillbilly radio frolics was the most important step in bringing broadcast country music to national popularity, for it was radio, not sheet music, records, or concerts, that spread the music throughout the Depression.

The radio craze had begun in the late teens. KDKA in Pittsburgh launched commercial broadcasting in 1920. A year later there were eight stations. By 1922 there were 30, and by 1923 there were 556. National networks were created in 1926 (NBC) and 1928 (CBS). Their ad revenues rocketed from three million dollars in 1927 to seventy-five million dollars in 1929.

By the time of the Depression, radio had become the central fact of American culture. Social workers of the day found that Americans would rather sell their refrigerators, telephones, or beds to pay the rent than part with the boxes that provided entertainment and escape from the nation's wretched economic condition.

Of all the forms of pop culture at the time, none was cheaper or more accessible than radio. In 1933 more than 3 million sets were produced. By 1938 radio was in 82 percent of U.S. homes. Broadcast programming exploded simultaneously. Between 1931 and 1939 the number of commercial stations more than tripled in America. And at one time or another, nearly all of them programmed some kind of country music.

"The National Barn Dance" went on the air on April 19, 1924, a week after its host station crackled to life. A year after Lulu Belle's arrival "The National Barn Dance" became the first coast-to-coast country music

Lulu Belle was so popular that WLS ran a contest promoting her after she was voted Radio Queen of 1936.

Lulu Belle and Scotty's
-- Mountain Melodies --

Published by Lulu Belle and Scotty
1230 W. Washington Blvd., Chicago, Ill.

Radio's biggest country stars of the Depression maintained their popularity well into the 1950s. This Lulu Belle and Scotty songbook was published in 1947.

show. During its two decades of top network ratings on Saturday nights, the country shindig had all America tuned in. NBC carried it nationally for nearly a decade before WSM's "Grand Ole Opry" had such exposure from Nashville.

From the start WLS had the ears of the populous Midwest rather than WSM's rural South. More than three-fourths of the nation's radios were in the Northeast and Central states in 1930 (only 12 percent of the receivers were in Dixie). "The National Barn Dance" not only popularized southern culture over the air, it was the first to send out touring road companies of country stars.

The show's gentle, reassuring ambience, celebration of rural culture, and homey presentation were popular during the nation's darkest days of economic catastrophe. A key to the comforting sound was the presence of female voices. Unlike more tradition-bound southern barn dances, WLS hired women abundantly. It was not only the trailblazer for national country popularity, it was the pioneer in presenting women's country music.

The Wisemans retired to their native North Carolina in 1958, but continued to record sporadically in the 1960s and 1970s. Lulu Belle also remained in the public eye by parlaying her fame into a seat in the state house of representatives. In 1974 she became the first woman ever elected from her mountain district. The most crucial vote in the state house during the 1976 session was on the passage of the Equal Rights Amendment. The woman who had won fame as a self-assertive tomboy voted no in a close roll call that defeated it by a margin of only five votes. The ERA died in 1982, three states shy of the thirty-eight needed for ratification.

Representative Wiseman was reelected for the legislative term of 1977 to 1978. In 1977 she gave an emotional testimony on the house floor during discussions of bills on capital crimes, relating a harrowing tale of being raped at gunpoint in the 1960s and calling for the death penalty for rapists. After Scotty's death in 1981 she remarried and moved to Goodland, Florida.

Lulu Belle was the biggest star of "The National Barn Dance," but she wasn't its first. That distinction belongs to another woman, the matronly Grace Wilson. The lively comic was also preceded by sunbonneted country sweetheart Linda Parker.

Grace Wilson (1890–1962) was a faded vaudevillian who found new life at the station by singing the golden oldies of the turn of the century. She parlayed the nostalgia for these numbers into the longest career of any Barn Dance performer, broadcasting from the show's birth in 1924 to its demise in 1960.

A native of Owosso, Michigan, Grace was the daughter of veteran concert singer Amalia Kelp. She made her stage debut as a four-year-old vaudeville tot and was among the first to popularize the 1902 classic "Bill Bailey, Won't You Please Come Home." Grace then entered musical comedy, touring with Nora Bayes and other vaudeville greats before making her radio debut in 1922 in Elgin, Illinois. So she was already a show-biz vet by the time she became known as "The Girl with a Million Friends" on "The National Barn Dance."

One reason she made the transition into country music so successfully was that she astutely pinpointed her just-folks appeal. "I'm not a glamour girl and haven't tried to be," she said. "I'm a homey person and like people—just 'Grace Wilson, your old friend and neighbor,' singing the songs everyone likes to hear." Grace Wilson's contralto radio style was later echoed by the monumentally popular "Songbird of the South," Kate Smith (1909–1986), in "When the Moon Comes Over the Mountain" and "God Bless America."

WLS's other pioneer female star was Linda Parker (1912–1935), radio's first major "country sweetheart." As "The Little Sunbonnet Girl" she projected much the same image as the silent-screen star Mary Pickford. Linda's songs were variously described in WLS publicity as "plaintive notes," "quaint old ballads of the hills," and songs "just as her mother and grandmother sang." Her demeanor was demure, her smile shy, her bearing girlish, and her voice sweet and low. Both her appearance and her singing were quite lovely in an artless, natural way, and these were heavily promoted. Show publicity also emphasized her Kentucky roots.

Linda Parker was born Genevieve Elizabeth Meunich in Covington, Kentucky, a bustling little city across the river from Cincinnati, Ohio. She was raised in Hammond, Indiana, which is part of metropolitan Gary. When WLS music director John Lair discovered her, she'd been a radio pop singer since her teens and at twenty was a struggling nightclub chanteuse.

He added her to his Cumberland Ridge Runners group, renamed her, and introduced her to WLS listeners in early 1932. She learned a new repertoire to go with her new stage persona. "The Little Sunbonnet Girl" popularized several folk tunes over WLS, among them the venerable women's numbers "Single Girl" and "Who's Gonna Shoe Your Pretty Little Foot." Her signature songs were the 1879 weeper "I'll Be All Smiles Tonight" and Lair's senti-

Grace Wilson, 1945.

We dedicate this book to the memory of Linda Parker, Our little Sunbonnet Girl.

Her sweet voice first brought you many of the songs which you will find in this book. Below is her favorite.

Linda Parker, 1933.

mental "Take Me Back to Renfro Valley." Linda Parker occasionally stepped out of character for rowdier numbers like "Gonna Raise a Ruckus" and the 1850s minstrel tune "Wait for the Wagon."

Publicity photos tended to go overboard in projecting her country "roots." She was pictured with banjo, guitar, fiddle, piano, clarinet, and dulcimer, and was said to be proficient on all of them, although there is no recorded evidence that she was. Linda's records do reveal a lovely, liquid alto delivery that was simple and unassuming. The overall effect is quite soothing, and this dulcet quality became characteristic of many "National Barn Dance" vocalists who succeeded Linda.

Radio was called "the housewife's companion," and programming reflected this. The network sponsor of "The National Barn Dance" was the newly introduced Alka-Seltzer, and women were the main targets of its ads. WLS carried a great many domestic shows about cooking, canning, and gardening, and its many female stars were groomed to appeal to the woman at home.

But family appeal didn't mean the WLS women got much of a family life. When they weren't on the air, they were on the road. In 1932, the year Linda became a radio star, she married Arthur Janes, the baritone singer in WLS's Maple City Four. This fact wasn't widely publicized, perhaps because of her virginal sweetheart image. And perhaps because of Depression-era economics she continued to work after the marriage. This included touring: Linda was featured in the first traveling "National Barn Dance" troupe, and she toured with the Cumberland Ridge Runners throughout the next two years.

Her last appearance was on August 3, 1935, in Elkhart, Indiana. According to later WLS publicity, Linda was racked with pain during the show, but continued to perform. Nine days later she died of what was reported to be a "perforative appendix" in nearby Mishawaka, Indiana. She was twenty-three.

Following Linda's burial, it was revealed to WLS listeners that "Bury Me Beneath the Willow" had been the last song she'd sung. The station was soon deluged with mail requests for the lyrics and sheet music. In fact, the two most requested WLS songs for 1935 were "Bury Me Beneath the Willow" and "Take Me Back to Renfro Valley," both popularized by Linda. The outpouring of sentiment after her death was considerable; the station received hundreds of cards and letters of sympathy. "The Little Sunbonnet Girl" had passed away in the bloom of her youth like some poetic character or a maiden in a folk ballad. The Cumberland Ridge Runner duo Karl & Harty offered the tribute record "We Buried Her Beneath the Willow."

Linda Parker's sweetheart image remained with female country performers for decades to come. Indeed, the gingham dress was practically a uniform for female country soloists until the 1960s.

By the mid-thirties country music was firmly associated with the disadvantaged working class and with fading rural life. These early radio women traded on this, turning the hayseed's lack of sophistication into a virtue. But to the stylish and modern, the overall image was still a negative one: A comic bumpkin was still a bumpkin.

The cowboy was the one American working stiff who had a positive image of dignity and romance. The dime novel and Wild West show fascination with this image blossomed into a full-blown American craze during the 1930s, and country musicians were quick to call it their own. A country string band could don cowboy regalia and give its music much more respectability than it could in an overalls-and-straw-hat getup.

Female musicians became accepted in the rough-and-tumble western role, as well as men. In contrast to the silk, satin, and furs of the movies' Jean Harlow and Mae West, country music's cowgirls were clad in clean, outdoorsy, functional garb. The cowgirl image wasn't an unachievable peroxide fantasy for women; it matched the sewing skills and pocketbook of the country audience. And as with the other major female stereotypes—mother, sweetheart, tomboy/comic—it was a WLS star who was the outstanding example, Patsy Montana.

Montana's cowgirl guise rolled the sweetheart and tomboy into one, giving traditional values an updated image. And with this new image Montana achieved a landmark—her 1935 "I Want to Be a Cowboy's Sweetheart" became the first record by a woman in country music to pass the million mark in sales. That these sales took place during the Depression years, when record retailing was down, makes them all the more impressive. The advent of radio had eroded the booming disc sales of the early twenties, and the Depression did the rest of the dirty work. From approximately seventy-five million dollars in sales in 1929, the record industry tumbled to forty-six million dollars a year later; by 1933 the record business was worth just five and one-half million dollars. The infant country music disc business did proportionally better than the industry as a whole, accounting for a quarter of all records sold in 1930. It also survived because of the introduction of budget-priced, thirty-five-cent hillbilly 78s. These included Victor's Bluebird line (1933), Decca Records (1934), and the numerous labels sold by Woolworth's, Montgomery Ward, Sears, and other retailers. The new barn dance radio stars also stimulated country record sales, as only the biggest acts were given recording studio time.

Patsy Montana's sunny voice, sparkling yodeling, and energetic style made the grade. Her indomitable, will-to-win personality played a part, as well. She thinks her spunk came from being the only girl raised with ten brothers on an Arkansas farm when times were tough.

For Southerners like Lulu Belle and Patsy, the Depression started long before Black Friday in 1929. Agricultural prices began falling in the early 1920s—cotton, the mainstay of the South's economy, dropped from forty-three cents a pound to eleven cents a pound in 1920; sugar descended to five cents a pound; the cost of raising rice and tobacco exceeded their selling prices. Farm income was down 50 percent in 1921; hundreds of rural banks failed. A mass exodus of farm laborers to the cities was under way by 1921. One of every two American farmers did not own his own land by 1930. By 1932 there were twenty thousand farm foreclosures a month. Compounding the problem was a farm family birthrate that was three times the national average.

Down in Hope, Arkansas, not far from the Texas border town of Texarkana, Augustus and Victoria Blevins were struggling to maintain a farm and raise eleven children. Their one daughter was born in 1912. They named her Ruby.

She grew up as "one of the guys," scrapping, playing, and making music with her brothers. Independent and plucky, Ruby had stars in her eyes by the time she was a teenager. An adept guitarist and fiddler, she decided at age seventeen that her name was too homespun, so she added an "e" to the end of it. A year later older brother Ron Blevins and his wife left the farm to head for the Land of Opportunity—California—and young Rubye went, too. Her upbringing as a forward tomboy served her well. She took violin lessons at the University of the West (now UCLA), but was more often found in the company of Los Angeles hillbilly musicians. In 1931 she won a talent contest singing Jimmie Rodgers's "Blue Yodeler" songs and got a job on KTMR radio as Rubye Blevins, "The Yodeling Cowgirl from San Antone."

Handsome, rugged singer/songwriter Stuart Hamblen had his own new radio show on nearby KMIC in Inglewood, and he invited Rubye to join his troupe. At the time, the only other women in Los Angeles who were performing western material were Lorraine McIntire and Ruthy DeMondrum. They did shows with Hamblen and cowboy star Montie

Montana as "The Montana Cowgirls." Rubye joined them to form a female trio and adopted the new moniker Patsy Montana. The Montana Cowgirls quickly became L.A. country favorites, riding in rodeos, singing on radio, and making movie shorts.

When the Montana Cowgirls went their separate ways, Patsy headed back home to Arkansas. She got a week's booking on nearby Shreveport, Louisiana's, KWKH so her family could hear her as the singing cowgirl she had become. This proved to be a fateful decision, for she was heard by Victor Records star Jimmie Davis. He invited her to accompany him to the Victor headquarters in Camden, New Jersey, to fiddle and sing backup on his records. The Depression was at its peak, and Patsy was in no position to refuse job offers of any kind, much less one to travel east to the Victor studios. After serving as Davis's accompanist, Patsy made her disc debut at the Victor sessions with 1932's "When the Flowers of Montana Were Blooming."

Patsy Montana's songbook, 1941

Upon returning once more to the Blevins farm, Patsy and brothers Kenneth and Claude decided to take "the world's biggest watermelon" to the Chicago World's Fair. At WLS a female vocalist was being sought to add to The Kentucky Ramblers. Patsy auditioned and got the job. At age twenty-one she had become a member of one of the hottest, jazziest, most accomplished string bands in the history of country music.

The group had been together since late 1931 and was composed of fellow Kentuckians Floyd "Salty" Holmes (guitar and vocals), Shelby "Tex" Atchison (fiddle), Jack Taylor (bass), and Charles "Chick" Hurt (mandolin). When Patsy joined in mid-1933 she was accomplished on fiddle, vocals, and guitar; but her main contributions to the act were her sense of showmanship and distinctive image. To accommodate their new member's western style, the four men renamed themselves The Prairie Ramblers.

The new act built its reputation on the road. Patsy Montana & The Prairie Ramblers toured the Midwest, performing two matinees and three evening shows daily at movie theaters in town after town. The yodeling cowgirl learned to sleep on backstage chairs and travel in one car holding five people plus instruments for her $7.50 a day in earnings.

Patsy fell in love with Paul Rose, one of the organizers of the WLS road shows. They wed in 1934, but she kept working after the nuptials. On sabbatical from "The National Barn Dance" Patsy, Paul, and The Prairie Ramblers saddled up for New York City to appear for a year on WOR.

By 1935 the market for records was quite low. Few new artists were being recorded, and female country acts, in particular, were not considered good prospects. Nevertheless, American Record Company (ARC, the predecessor to CBS Records) producer Art Satherley believed in Patsy and The Prairie Ramblers enough to take a chance. In August 1935 he took them into the studio in New York. They came out with the biggest records that both she and the band ever had.

The Ramblers recorded "Nobody's Darling But Mine," one of the country's biggest Depression-era hits. Patsy recorded "I Want to Be a Cowboy's Sweetheart," country's first female million-seller. Despite its title, "I Want to Be a Cowboy's Sweetheart" is not about a traditional sweetheart. It expresses a woman's desire for independence, alongside her cowboy lover as an equal. This notion of being a cowboy's cohort and lover was repeated over and over again in Patsy Montana's subsequent recordings.

"I never knew I was doing anything important for women until people started writing about me," said an amazed Patsy when fifty years later articles began appearing that praised her point of view. "I didn't understand it until it was explained to me. At the time, I was just tryin' to make a living."

Her own explanation for the success of "I Want to Be a Cowboy's Sweetheart" is that it was a lively polka, which appealed to both rural country music fans and ethnic groups in northern cities. At the very least the sprightly record appealed to the dance spirit that was sweeping the nation following the 1934 repeal of Prohibition.

"The amazing thing was, it's a *girl's* number, and that ain't 'sposed to happen. . . . There were girls on the radio then. . . . but they had no personality. So maybe in that way, maybe I did break the ice . . . for the Dolly Partons and the Loretta Lynns. . . . But I wasn't aware of breaking the ice for anybody. . . . Maybe it was time for a change and I happened to be there."

Patsy elaborated her cowgirl image during the next five years. "Sweetheart of the Saddle" (1936) is about being a cowpuncher alongside her "cowboy pal." "I Wanna Be a Western Cowgirl" (1939) expresses dissatisfaction with dull city life to the accompaniment of the band's hot fiddle and accordion breaks. In "Ridin' Old Paint" (1935) Patsy sings that she "won't settle down and be a wife." Most independent-spirited of all are the "man-hatin' lassie" of "The She-Buckaroo" (1936) and the "tough as I can be" heroine of "A Rip-Snortin' Two-Gun Gal" (1939). The fusion of her exuberant yodels and sunny singing with the sizzling instrumental work of the Ramblers reached its peak with the likes of "Cowboy Rhythm" (1938) and "Swing Time Cowgirl" (1940). The team continued to record together sporadically in the 1940s, but Patsy was a solo touring star from 1940 on.

The 1946–1947 radio season featured her own network show, "Wake Up and Smile," on ABC. Her broadcast greeting, "Hi pardner! It's Patsy Montana!" accompanied by the stamping of horses' hoofs, was familiar to millions. She found time to appear in Gene Autry's film *Colorado Sunset* in 1940, but was often on the road during these years. In 1948 she starred on the "Louisiana Hayride" radio barn dance. The program was carried nationally by CBS, bringing her renewed fame as Patsy Montana, "The Girl with the Million-Dollar Smile." (A 1939 single had been titled "My Million Dollar Smile.")

With the coming of TV westerns in the 1950s, Patsy's cowgirl image was revived. Patti Page and Dale Evans repopularized "I Want to Be a Cowboy's Sweetheart." In the 1960s yodelers such as Bonnie Owens and Judy Lynn brought the number back again. Patsy rerecorded her signature tune herself in 1966, hiring the then-obscure Waylon Jennings as her guitarist on the session. "Cowboy's Sweetheart" is now a female country staple, becoming a 1988 single for Suzy Bogguss, and a 1992 CD title tune for Lynn Anderson.

Like her song, Patsy became a country institution. One of the most durable troupers in the business, she continued to book appearances and record albums into the 1990s. By 1992 her concert appearances numbered well over seven thousand. No other performer of her era has demonstrated such continuing popularity. "I'm a pretty good example of 'sticking around,'" says the pioneer singing cowgirl. "What I've achieved wasn't all due to luck. I've had to work hard for it."

By popularizing the cowgirl image—the strong, good-humored saddle pal—Patsy Montana gave female country performers their first new solo style. The cowgirl was an alternative to the shy country sweetheart, yet it sidestepped the lone-woman sexuality of the cabaret torch singers, jazz chanteuses, and Broadway stars of the day. Patsy found a respectable way to swing. This independent yet compassionate image was soon adopted by dozens of other Depression-era female entertainers.

The one WLS star who could claim to be an *authentic* cowgirl was Louise Massey (1908–1983). Her parents had settled in Texas in the nineteenth century. Henry Massey moved into even wilder country when he relocated his wife and eight children to a ranch in southeastern New Mexico in 1914, just two years after the desert territory had been granted statehood.

Louise grew up to be an accomplished horsewoman, with ribbons and trophies to prove it. She could sing, too. Three of the eight Massey offspring became musicians—Victoria Louise and her brothers Allen and Curt. Dad Massey was an old-time fiddler, who formed a family band with these youngsters for home entertainment. When piano-playing Louise married bass player and composer Milt Mabie in 1919, he joined the group, as well.

She and Milt had a daughter named Joy in 1922, and it was around this same time that Dad Massey began seriously grooming his little family act for professional show biz. When Louise met the owner of the Chautauqua and Lyceum touring circuits in downtown Roswell, New Mexico, in the spring of 1928 and invited him home to hear The Massey Family, the band was ready.

"I went down to the tent where the show was playing," Louise recalled years later. "I walked up to him, and of course he didn't know me. And I said, 'Would you like to come up to my house for a while?'" She laughed merrily relating the anecdote. "He looked at me like, 'Does she mean it?'" She explained, and he followed the beguiling brunet home. In the living room "he took a pill and said, 'I have ulcers.' I said, 'When you finish listening to us, you ain't never had no ulcer like you're going to have.' And he laughed. But when he started to leave, he said, 'Consider yourselves under contract.'"

The group spent that summer touring the United States, then a second season in rugged Canada, traveling between dates in everything from roadsters to dogsleds. Dad retired, but the rest of the troupe landed a five-year radio stint at KMBC in Kansas City that was picked up by the CBS network. A WLS talent scout found the Masseys there and brought them to "The National Barn Dance" in 1933, just in time for the show's jump to national network radio on NBC.

The group quickly made the transition from family bunkhouse band to slick urban entertainment unit. Louise was breathtakingly beautiful, and she soon adopted an image considerably more glamorous than that of pert Patsy Montana. Both women wore cowgirl garb, but Louise's costumes were generally fancier and more flowing; her deportment was rather more ladylike, as well. Once described as "The Perfect Face" by the *New York Times*, Louise Massey added glamour to the cowgirl image.

"We were never hillbilly," she explained to historian Elvis E. Fleming in 1976. "We were western from the beginning and loved to be called western. . . . We didn't just play a number; we had arrangements. . . . We had beautiful costumes. We had a Spanish costume for 'Ramona' as our big number and two or three other Mexican tunes with Spanish words. That was my job in the act, to see that we were dressed right. I had a French designer design the boys' outfits out of white gaberdine; the lapels were white satin trim. And mine were beaded with wide belts and pretty things with lots of sequins. And I wore my satin boots; I never wore any other kind."

Dubbed Louise Massey & The Westerners, the group left Chicago for New York in 1936. There they introduced their own NBC Tuesday-night program, "The Log Cabin Dude Ranch." The show's fictional setting was "Miss Louise's dream Bar-Z ranch."

"While we were in New York, I still say that was the beginning of acceptance in the East of any kind of music except their very modern. I feel like my brothers and I did an awful lot toward furthering the acceptance of that. We played 'Home on the Range,' and we played it beautifully. We had just enough finesse that they had to look back a second time. If it had been just 'country' music, I doubt seriously if they would have listened at all."

Louise Massey, 1936.

The group made several follow-the-bouncing-ball movie musical short subjects, and appeared in the Tex Ritter film *Where the Buffalo Roam.*

Returning to Chicago, Louise and her Westerners starred on NBC's "Plantation Party" show. A young Mike Wallace was one of their announcers during this second sojourn in the Windy City. "We never had to walk the streets, and it was during the Depression; and that was a wonderful thing. . . . I'm very proud of it."

All of the Westerners could double on several instruments, giving the band's music more complexity and variety than most of its country contemporaries. A look at the more than one hundred titles the act recorded between 1933 and 1943 gives some idea of its wide-ranging ability—in the repertoire are polkas, waltzes, traditional fiddle tunes, ragtime piano numbers, folk songs, pop ditties, German schottisches, gospel numbers, vaudeville novelties, minstrel tunes, cowboy songs, and Mexican music.

Louise either sang or wrote most of the group's biggest hits. One of the band's earliest recording successes featuring her dreamy, languid voice was 1934's lilting "When the White Azaleas Start Blooming." In 1939 her liquid vocals on "South of the Border (Down Mexico Way)" and "I

Only Want a Buddy (Not a Sweetheart)" provided two more sizable hits. And in 1941 she wrote and recorded the song that earned the group country immortality, "My Adobe Hacienda." In 1946 and 1947 "My Adobe Hacienda" became the first country song to be listed simultaneously on the hillbilly and pop music hit parades, the first authenticated "crossover" hit. It was subsequently recorded by more than twenty other acts, including Bob Wills, Eddy Howard, The Dinning Sisters, and virtually all singing cowboys and cowgirls worth their spurs.

Ironically, Louise and Milt were thinking of retiring to ranch life at the time it hit. Louise Massey & The Westerners were on national radio on NBC in 1947, and now they had a million-selling hit record, too. But the following year Louise abruptly moved back to New Mexico at the height of her success. Twenty years of bright lights and fame had never turned her pretty head.

"We had done all the things we had set out to do," she recalled shortly before her death. "I wanted to come home. I wanted to *have* a home. I had just traveled and traveled and traveled. . . . I was getting awfully tired. We went back to New York and recorded one more year's worth of shows and then we said good-bye. . . . We quit for good. It was time for us to enjoy our own life. . . . we decided to retire to our 'Adobe Hacienda.' We went to our ranch, and I never looked back once. All the past was completely out of my mind."

For the next thirty-five years her mellifluous crooning could be heard only when she gave her two annual local concerts in Roswell, New Mexico. In 1982, the year before her death, Louise became the first western singer inducted into the National Cowgirl Hall of Fame in Hereford, Texas. At the time, she was hailed as "the original rhinestone cowgirl."

Younger brother Curt went to Hollywood and enjoyed considerable later success doing music for movies and TV. In the 1960s he was the musical director for the highly popular "Beverly Hillbillies" series. He wrote its theme song ("Come and listen to my story 'bout a man named Jed . . ."), then sang as well as wrote the theme to its spin-off show, "Petticoat Junction."

Perhaps the most striking feature of Louise Massey's repertoire of the 1930s and 1940s is her large number of Spanish-language recordings. She was bilingual. "The National Barn Dance" seems to have realized quite early that its audience was ethnically diverse, for Louise was one of several women on the show who represented non-Anglo culture.

One of the longest-lasting personalities on "The National Barn Dance" was Christine, "The Little Swiss Miss Yodeler." Another WLS woman cast in an ethnic role was Princess Tsianina. In the early 1930s this Cherokee Indian was featured performing songs and legends of native

Americans. Gospel singer Sophia Germanich, known as "Our Singing Stenographer," was a native of the Ukraine, and this fact was heavily promoted by WLS. Sophia's on-air image of a strong, docile East European earned her more than twenty-five marriage proposals in a week's mail in 1937, many from immigrants looking for a "good girl from the old country."

Whatever their ethnic heritage, members of the U.S. working class shared the reality of family disintegration as the Great Depression dragged on. Although divorce rates declined in the 1930s, desertion rates soared. By 1940 there were more than a million and a half women living apart from their husbands. The number of children placed in custodial institutions rose 50 percent during the first two years of the Depression. More than 200,000 vagrant children wandered the country as a result of broken homes. Couples began to think of pregnancy as a misfortune; the birthrate declined; the Sears catalog sold contraceptive devices. The inability to support families devastated many blue-collar workers. Reports from the era repeatedly stress that men were overwhelmed by guilt and low self-esteem.

In the face of a disintegrating social fabric, popular magazines, radio shows, and films placed a new emphasis on familial affection and mutual support. Of all the radio fare, none was more family-oriented than country music. The nation's most powerful country show paraded a series of mothers, aunts, and wives in front of its microphones, and singing sisters proliferated at "The National Barn Dance."At least a dozen sister acts were broadcast by WLS during the thirties.

From Glasgow, Kentucky, came the charming old-time sound of Jo and Alma Taylor. They not only recorded in sisterly harmony, but teamed up with their brother Jack Taylor and his Prairie Rambler bandmate Chick Hurt to form WLS's answer to The Carter Family. As The Happy Valley Family, they issued several fine family harmony records in the mid-1930s, including "When the Bees Are in the Hive," "Lorena," and "Going Down the Valley."

By far the most historically significant of the WLS sister acts was The Three Little Maids. Evelyn, Eva, and Lucille Overstake had their musical roots singing in the Salvation Army in the bustling central Illinois city of Decatur. They became WLS regulars as teens in 1931, and their early repertoire drew on their Bible-thumping background. "I Ain't Gonna Study War No More" was probably learned in the Salvation Army.

Alto Evelyn, born in 1913, was the oldest Overstake sister. Her low tones are perhaps the outstanding feature of the trio's records. After going solo in 1935, she sustained the longest WLS career of the three, per-

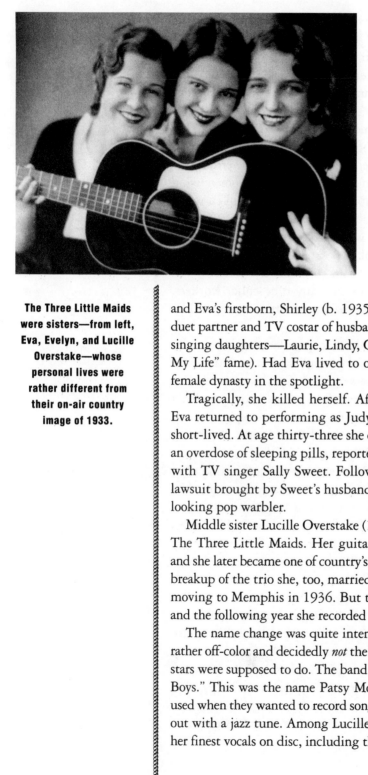

The Three Little Maids were sisters—from left, Eva, Evelyn, and Lucille Overstake—whose personal lives were rather different from their on-air country image of 1933.

forming steadily there for the next two decades.

Soprano Eva Overstake (1918–1951) was the youngest sister. Eva was just thirteen when she began singing professionally with her sisters and only sixteen when she married Red Foley, thereby breaking up both The Three Little Maids and the Foley/Lulu Belle partnership. Foley's first wife had died in childbirth, so to Eva fell the responsibility of raising baby Betty, as well as the three daughters she bore during the next six years.

Both Betty Foley (1933–1990) and Eva's firstborn, Shirley (b. 1935), became entertainers, Shirley as the duet partner and TV costar of husband Pat Boone. Shirley also raised four singing daughters—Laurie, Lindy, Cherry, and Debby (of "You Light Up My Life" fame). Had Eva lived to old age, she'd have seen her religious female dynasty in the spotlight.

Tragically, she killed herself. After her girls all reached school age, Eva returned to performing as Judy Martin, but her revived career was short-lived. At age thirty-three she committed suicide in Nashville with an overdose of sleeping pills, reportedly after learning of Foley's adultery with TV singer Sally Sweet. Following a nasty alienation-of-affections lawsuit brought by Sweet's husband, Foley did indeed marry the flashy-looking pop warbler.

Middle sister Lucille Overstake (1915–1978) was the real musician of The Three Little Maids. Her guitar was the act's sole accompaniment, and she later became one of country's pioneer female songwriters. After the breakup of the trio she, too, married, becoming Mrs. Jack Dumbald and moving to Memphis in 1936. But two years later she was back at WLS, and the following year she recorded under the pseudonym Lucille Lee.

The name change was quite intentional, for the resulting records were rather off-color and decidedly *not* the sort of things "National Barn Dance" stars were supposed to do. The band on these discs was "The Sweet Violet Boys." This was the name Patsy Montana's fun-loving Prairie Ramblers used when they wanted to record songs about drinking and sex or to swing out with a jazz tune. Among Lucille's 1939 collaborations with them are her finest vocals on disc, including the jazzy female "cheating" complaint

"Chiselin' Daddy" and the swinging "Widow's Lament," about being roped in by a cowboy gigolo. Her "I Married a Mouse of a Man" seems to be about male impotence. Still more suggestive is "I Love My Fruit." The verses contain double entendres about cherries being eaten in bed, nuts being chewed on, and bananas being gobbled. Patsy Montana says she wasn't allowed in the studio when the band was working on these numbers.

The 1940s found Lucille Overstake reborn as singing cowgirl Jenny Lou Carson on radio and Decca Records. This was her name as the songwriter of "Let Me Go Lover," "Jealous Heart," and several other country classics of the 1940s and 1950s. Her composing talents developed during an affair with Country Music Hall of Fame songwriter Fred Rose. Her marriage in 1946 to obese bandleader Tiny Hill also proved to be good for her career, as he became the folk music director for Mercury Records, her final label.

That the Overstake sisters' real lives were considerably more colorful than the homey family image they projected on WLS was typical of the station. "National Barn Dance" publicity relentlessly stressed the "family" nature of the station and its stars. In reality things were a mite spicier—show veterans recall that almost everyone in the cast was embroiled in some romance or affair with another member of the "family." This was, after all, a group of largely single, young people working in an exciting urban setting, many with the bohemian attitudes one associates with musicians.

Country veteran Zeke Clements performed at virtually all the important radio barn dances, and he recalls humorously of Chicago's, "Oh, they were all screwin' each other left and right up there. You didn't dare bend over." Lulu Belle said, "One thing I didn't like about it [the Barn Dance] . . . all the fellows, and these men on the show were always trying to get around you—you know, young girl, free—trying to get you somewhere in a bed."

Intercast marriages and babies abounded at "The National Barn Dance," most of them duly reported in its widely circulated *Stand By!* magazine and annual *WLS Family Album* (1931–1957). WLS defined and popularized all the basic tenets of country stardom—clean humor, family entertainment, moral uprightness, just-folks humility, fan appreciation, next-door-neighbor friendliness, direct appeal to the working class. Women on the air were expected to conform to the station's wholesome sweetheart/sister/mother/saddle-pal images. Lulu Belle and Scotty were forbidden to sing "Mountain Dew" because it was about booze. Chicago's nationally famed "Love Me or Leave Me"/"Ten Cents a Dance" torch singer Ruth Etting (1896–1978) was barred from WLS for her sultry singing, as well as her stormy, gangster-dominated personal life. "Her voice is too sexy for our type station," declared the WLS music directors.

Sister acts came to
Chicago's WLS in bewil-
dering profusion during
the Depression. The
biggest of them were the
following:

THE ASHLEY
    SISTERS—billed as
    The Three Prairie
    Daisies

THE OZARK
    SISTERS—folk song
    specialists

THE JENSON
    SISTERS—changed
    their names to
    Winnie, Lou, and
    Sally to match the
    WLS call letters

"THE THREE WIS-
    CONSIN HONEY-
    BEES"—farm-girl
    sisters Vern and Lee
    Hassel, plus their
    childhood friend Mary
    Brygger, also billed
    as Vern, Lee, and
    Mary

THE DUNCAN
    SISTERS—
    vaudeville veterans
    who turned up at WLS
    in their "Topsy" and
    "Eva" guises

THE FLANNERY
    SISTERS—a duo
    from upper Michigan
    with a homespun
    style

WLS brought professional public relations to the young country business, and its image development clung to country music culture until the 1980s. The WLS publications contained idealized, embellished biographies of the show's stars to go along with their homespun images.

Given the station's acute image consciousness and superb publicity machinery, it comes as no surprise that the most popular of all the sister teams had a totally fictitious cowgirl identity that was accepted as fact among country fans for more than fifty years. Dolly and Millie Good arrived at WLS in 1933. Their real last name was Goad. Their billing was The Girls of the Golden West, and they were said to hail from the colorful-sounding birthplace of Muleshoe, Texas. In reality they were from East St. Louis and had never set foot in cowboy country.

But singing cowgirls seemed stylish, so cowgirls they became. A radio station manager had dubbed them The Girls of the Golden West when they got their first on-air job, but there wasn't much in their background that was even rural. In 1978 older sister Millie (b. 1913) recalled that they moved off the Goads' Mount Carmel, Illinois, farm when she was ten and Dolly was eight. Papa Goad then tried being a shopkeeper, but failed. "He just didn't have the knowledge on how to run a business," Millie said, "so my mother was always the go-getter, and she took over and made a little restaurant out of it, because she was always a good cook, and that brought them out of it." Father next tried his hand at selling insurance, again unsuccessfully. Then he moved the eight-child family to East St. Louis, where he took a factory job. By this time Mama Goad had taught younger daughter Dolly (1915–1967) how to play guitar and sing old-time songs.

"Dolly took it [singing professionally] up on her own," Millie recalled. "I had already started working as a salesgirl when I was fourteen, and then I went with her on my lunch hour for an audition at KMOX in St. Louis. She was more aggressive with it than I was." The younger Goad sister was twelve at the time.

With their last name restyled Good and their Girls of the Golden West moniker in place, they became full-time entertainers when they were fifteen and seventeen. They went to Abilene, Kansas, where their program got national exposure over the powerful Mexican-border radio station XER. Back in St. Louis in 1933 on KMOX they were discovered by WLS talent scouts.

The Girls of the Golden West performed western songs in a relaxed, silken, close-harmony style. It was a warm, glowing sound, perfectly in keeping with the honeyed gleam of the millions of radio dials lit for Saturday night's "National Barn Dance" broadcasts. WLS set up a prop campfire on the Barn Dance stage for the duo's segment.

The sisters not only sang flawless harmony, they augmented Dolly's guitar accompaniment by vocally imitating the sound of Hawaiian guitars and even yodeled with perfect-pair precision. "Mom said Dolly could sing before she could talk." Millie recalled, "And whatever Dolly could learn, I could sing harmony to."

The Girls of the Golden West recorded prolifically for Vocalion/Okeh, Columbia, and Bluebird. They repopularized the Belle Starr song "Bucking Bronco"/"My Love Is a Rider" in 1934, albeit with cleaned-up lyrics. Many other western folk songs were also given the Good harmony treatment, as were customized cowgirl numbers such as Millie's compositions "Lonely Cowgirl," "Will There Be Any Yodelers in Heaven," and her tale of the "Two Cowgirls on the Lone Prairie," who sang "married life won't do for me."

"Texas Moon" and the assertive "Give Me a Straight Shootin' Cowboy" were tailored for them by fellow Barn Dance headliner Lucille Overstake, who also composed their most popular number, "I Want to Be a Real Cowboy Girl." In it the Girls sang that they want to strut around in all the buckles, straps, six-shooter, spurs, chaps, and gear of a macho cowboy.

In 1935 The Girls of the Golden West became regulars on Rudy Vallee's national radio show in New York City, and for several months they had their own NBC program from Radio City. The move to Manhattan was in the interest of family unity. Dolly was married, predictably, to a WLS musician, the boyishly handsome Tex Atchison of Patsy Montana's Prairie Ramblers. When the Montana entourage went east, so did the Goods.

Millie's husband, Bill McCluskey, was the duo's road show and radio emcee at WLS. When he got a job as a promotion man at WLW's "Midwestern Hayride" in 1937 and Dolly's marriage foundered, both sisters relocated to the show's hometown of Cincinnati, where the Girls of the Golden West remained popular well into the 1950s. Millie had five children and became less active than her always more driven younger sister. Dolly remarried, but remained in show business full-time, becoming hostess of a kiddie program and doing pop hit parade material as a solo on other WLW shows.

JO AND ALMA TAYLOR—from Glasgow, Kentucky, billed as The Kentucky Girls, also part of the Happy Valley Family quartet

THE THREE LITTLE MAIDS—Eva, Evelyn, and Lucille Overstake from Decatur, Illinois

THE PLAY PARTY GIRLS—folksingers

The Girls of the Golden West, 1934.

The Girls of the Golden West were the most popular sister duo in country music history. Their influence was enormous, leading to the creation of a host of similar sister acts. Virtually every barn dance of the thirties and forties had such a duo.

If The Girls of the Golden West represent the peak of commercial success, the DeZurick Sisters surely represent the zenith of musical creativity. No one who has ever heard the incredible DeZuricks would ever forget their sound. WLS billed them as "trick yodelers," a phrase that only dimly suggests their astounding vocal gymnastics. Their unique, birdlike style featured complex chirps, whistles, trills, and vocal effects executed with precision timing. The sisters' ability to hear musical possibilities in the sounds of barnyard animals, cuckoo clocks, whippoorwills' songs, and nature's noises, plus their devotion to practice and presentation, made them one of the most original acts in the annals of pop music.

At the Barn Dance the DeZuricks were promoted as farm girls, milkmaids, and hayloft lovelies, images they came by naturally enough. Of Dutch descent, they were born on a dairy farm in Royalton, Minnesota, and raised in a family of six girls and a boy. Mary Jane (b. 1917) and Carolyn (b. 1919) formed the original duo, but sisters Lorraine and Eva were both capable of filling in when either of them was unable to perform.

In the mid-1940s the team came to the attention of the Ralston-Purina Company. Recognizing the promotional potential of having an act that could cackle like chickens in harmony, the farm-feed firm hired the DeZuricks to represent it during its portion of "The Grand Ole Opry." Beginning in 1945, the sisters commuted back and forth between Chicago and Nashville, performing as The Cackle Sisters on the Opry and retaining their original billing on WLS. They are the only women to have achieved stardom on both of the two most important radio programs in country music history.

As was true of virtually every other "National Barn Dance" woman, the DeZuricks married WLS musicians—Mary Jane married Augie Klein, little sister Eva married Augie's brother Ray, and Carolyn married Rusty Gill. Mary Jane's child-rearing and homemaker duties caused her to withdraw from the act in 1947. Her slot was taken over by fourth sister Lorraine DeZurick, and in Nashville The Cackle Sisters' yodels became more complicated than ever. They developed "triple-tongue," "machine-gun" yodels, gaining a measure of fame that carried them into the early 1950s.

The DeZuricks' smile-and-a-wink personalities were not a small factor in their Depression-era popularity. Chicago's kaleidoscope of culture was nothing if not a nest of comedic possibilities. In addition to Lulu Belle, the city's radio stages were platforms for several funny, down-home ladies. Marian Jordan (1898–1961) was the ultradry, female half of the ultimate proletarian pair Fibber McGee and Molly. Marian and hubby Jim Jordan were teen sweethearts from Peoria, Illinois, who began their career as a singing duo with rural fare like "The Little Old Log Cabin in the Lane." They arrived at WENR in the Windy City in 1927 and shortly afterward began experimenting with their hokum comedy characters Luke and Mirandy. The "Fibber McGee and Molly" format came in 1935, and by the end of the Depression it was one of the most popular radio programs in America.

"Molly" needled her mate's pomposity, tall tales, bragging, and endless get-rich-quick schemes. Her exclamation "Heavenly days!" deflated "Fibber's" ego, and every time she deadpanned "T'ain't funny, McGee!" forty-eight million listeners burst into laughter. Fibber McGee's junk-filled closet and the couple's fictional address of 79 Wistful Vista were famous, as was Marian's catchphrase "You're a hard man, McGee." Board games, comic books, spinning tops, and a variety of products from their sponsor, Johnson's Wax, promoted the couple. So did the movies *This Way Please, Look Who's Laughing, Here We Go Again,* and *Heavenly Days* (1937–1944).

Folksy fare, hokum humor, country nostalgia, small-town pleasantry, and sentimentality for the Old South characterized much Depression-era culture. The radio ratings successes of "The National Barn Dance" and "Fibber McGee and Molly" coincided with the launch of such popular "people's" programs as "Lum and Abner" (1931), "Farm and Home Hour" (1929), "Ma Perkins" (1933), "Amos 'n' Andy" (1925), and "Main Street" (1929), not to mention President Roosevelt's neighborly "Fireside Chats" (1933). The "country" climate of the time was also fueled by stage productions like *Tobacco Road* (1933) and *Porgy and Bess* (1935), newspaper comics such as *L'il Abner* (1934) and *Snuffy Smith* (1934), and the novels *Gone with the Wind* (1936), *Cimarron* (1929), and *The Yearling* (1938), not to mention the multiformat craze for all things connected with the American cowboy.

In Washington there was a purposeful push to develop a national identity with roots in a native culture. The Roosevelt administration promoted folklore, national theater, public mural painting, historical pageants, public building projects, and all sorts of Americana. As respect for folk traditions and rural values grew, country musicians like Gene Autry and Lulu Belle became idols. A nation looking for strength found it in its common people.

By the middle of the Depression there were hay bales–and-gingham barn dance shows beaming from cities throughout America. These

THE LEATHERMAN SISTERS—Lucille and Lillian, who dressed in western garb, but stressed old-time tunes such as "Just a Little While" and "Lonesome for You, Darling" on their 1936 Bluebird discs

THE RODIK TWINS— Verna and Verda, elaborately coiffed Minnesota blondes with cowgirl outfits but an old-time sound on their 1941 Decca disc "Did You Ever Go Sailing (Down the River of Memories)"

JUDY AND JEN—stars of "The Hoosier Hop," "Midwestern Hayride," "Brush Creek Follies," and "Old Dominion Barn Dance," who carried the soft harmony style into the 1940s and early 1950s

THE SWEENEY SISTERS—toured with "Grand Ole Opry" troupes of the early and mid-1930s

The DeZurick Sisters, as they appeared on the cover of WLS's fan magazine *Stand By* in 1937.

programs were enormously popular; after all, 48 percent of Americans were still rural dwellers in the mid-1930s. But on radio, as on records, country women were in the distinct minority, accounting for only 10 to 15 percent of barn dance acts during the Depression. Midwestern radio jamborees generally welcomed women more than their counterparts in the Deep South.

Mountain gals got a pretty fair shake on the WWVA "Jamboree" radio barn dance in West Virginia, although the Wheeling radio station had an irritating tendency to refer to them exclusively by catchy monikers such as "Sunflower," "Cricket," or "Little Shoe" rather than their names.

The greatest of the women who rose to fame on Mountain State radio was the flamboyant Cousin Emmy (1903–1980), perhaps the greatest distaff showman of her era. This hillbilly gal was a star not only at WWVA, but at Louisville's WHAS, St. Louis's KMOX, Atlanta's WSB, Knoxville's WNOX, and anyplace else she performed. "Oh, she was awfully popular," recalls Grandpa Jones of his old WWVA costar. "She was pretty wild, I guess. . . . She had them big, wide teeth and, you know, she'd grin and they'd just shine. And she was mighty good on the old five-string banjo. She played a little fiddle and everything else on her show. She was a good showman, I'll tell you that."

Emmy's wide-mouthed grin, crimson lipstick, platinum hair done up in gaudy ribbons, boundless get-up-and-go, hellzapoppin' delivery, and full-throttle musical antics brought souped-up style to her old-timey tunes. She was part carnival barker and part mountain folk song preserver, part medicine show huckster and part sincere sentimentalist. She was innocent and brash, yet shrewd and savvy. Emmy's formal schooling reportedly consisted of just two weeks, and she learned to read by poring over mail-order catalogs, but she was as sharp and canny as any business college grad. "I ain't educated," she once remarked, "but I'm sincere."

One of eight children in a tobacco sharecropper's family near Lamb, Kentucky, outside Glasgow, Emmy was born Cynthia May Carver. Home was a two-room log cabin with "cracks between the walls so big that you could a-throwed a cat betwixt them without tetching a hair." Her cousins were entertainers, her father was a fiddler, and "In the dancing contests for women, nobody ever beat my mother." But Emmy said she learned her musical skills on her own: "I reckon I allus was a show-off, because I can remember when Mama would leave me in the tobacco patch and tell me to do one row, I'd sing and dance and slap my legs and entertain the seven other kids to git them to do my work for me."

In a 1943 article *Time* magazine annotated her skills as "a voice like a locomotive whistle and a heart of gold . . . immense enthusiasm and a masterly capacity for mugging. She also plays at least 15 musical and questionable instruments," including fiddle, banjo guitar, French harp, ukulele, accordion, dulcimer, harmonica, handsaw, rubber glove, "and a tune I makes by just slopping against my cheeks with my hands." She could execute "Turkey in the Straw" this way, and her rubber glove technique consisted of blowing it full of air and coaxing out "You Are My Sunshine" by controlling the escaping air.

In 1935 Emmy became the first woman to win the National Old-Time Fiddlers Contest in Louisville. Cousins Warner and Noble "Uncle Bozo" Carver gave Emmy her professional show business start, and then she joined Frankie Moore's Log Cabin Boys at WWVA in Wheeling. That's where she taught future Country Music Hall of Famer Grandpa Jones to play banjo. From 1937 to 1940 Emmy hit the road from West Virginia with her own Kin Folks band.

"In two weeks I was the biggest thing that ever hit any man's radio station," she recalled of her WHAS stint in Louisville. Emmy was never one to sell herself short. "Darlin'," she told one interviewer, "I'm the sweetest singer of mountain ballads that ever came out of the foothills. I know and can prove that I can outdraw . . . anybody else. So you just go ahead and put me on top of that there pile where I belong."

She relied on her native wit and intelligence to survive as country music's first independent, unmarried, self-supporting female touring attraction. "I ain't got time to do no courtin'," she said. Feisty and fearless, Emmy learned to handle her money carefully, to be pushy when needed, and to protect her tunes with copyrights.

"I learned that right quick when they began stealing them songs from everybody and making money on us poor hillbillies, and we didn't get a dime out of it. I thought it's time to do something about it. I learned this right fast, after I got out of them sticks. . . . I thank God thousands of times that He gave me the talent and the good common sense to get out of there . . . don't send me back there no, never no more."

Emmy reached the height of her radio fame in St. Louis over KMOX between 1941 and 1944. This is where the apparently wonderstruck *Time* reporter found her. A Washington University professor was also charmed by Emmy and invited her to perform with him at the St. Louis Art Museum to illustrate his lecture on "The Ballad." In 1947 she recorded her *Kentucky Mountain Ballads* album for producer/folklorist Alan Lomax, preserving versions of "Come All You Virginia Gals," "Free Little Bird,"

"I Wish I Was a Single Girl Again," "Pretty Little Miss Out in the Garden," and other folk traditionals. Her biggest hit was "Ruby (Are You Mad at Your Man)," which she wrote. "Ruby" became a huge bluegrass hit when it was recorded by The Osborne Brothers in 1970.

In 1944 Emmy went west to appear in the movie *Swing in the Saddle.* In the late 1940s she continued to divide her time among the St. Louis, Louisville, and Atlanta stations, by now piling into her Cadillacs a series of adopted children and sundry strays who'd become Kin Folks members. By the 1950s she was living in Los Angeles, and she appeared again on screen in 1955's *The Second Greatest Sex.* She also entertained at Disneyland before beginning a second career as a star of the 1960s folk revival movement.

During this last phase of her performing life Emmy offered a country gal's words to live by to collegiate audiences: "Don't give up. If you set out to do something, do it or bust, honey. Just keep on and you'll get it."

Only one other Kentucky performer of the Depression could match Cousin Emmy for female pluck and independence. Lily May Ledford (1917–1985) learned there was safety in numbers in 1937 when she fronted The Coon Creek Girls, country's first all-female string band. The group teamed the woman known as the original "Banjo Pickin' Girl" with fiddler/bass player Evelyn "Daisy" Lange, mandolinist Esther "Violet" Koehler, and Lily May's sister, guitarist Rosa Charlotte "Rosie" Ledford (1915–1976).

"We were so happy back then," Lily May recalled years later. "Daisy and Sis, being good fighters, would make short work of anybody . . . who would tease us or torment us. We all made short work of the 'wolves,' as they were called, who tried to follow us home or get us in their cars.

"I remember having a fight one time in Georgia at a little theater. . . . Us girls was loading the car out in the alley. We'd had to work that night . . . and I had to stop two or three times and tell these hoodlums to be quiet, that we were trying to put on a simple country show. It wasn't burlesque or anything. Well, about three of these characters followed us back in the alley.

"We were as mad as could be, but our hands were full of guitars, and we had our high-top shoes tied together and slung around our necks. Just as soon as we got our stuff down in the station wagon—we hadn't said a word to one another—we attacked those boys and run them off with their tails between their legs, embarrassed to death!" The heels of old-time footwear made dandy weapons, and even in street shoes Lily was nearly six feet tall.

"All my life [Mama Ledford] . . . had scolded and lectured me saying,

Cousin Emmy hams it up
in the 1944 movie
Swing in the Saddle.

'Toughen up! If the rest can make it, you can!'" The Ledford family, with ten children, scraped to make ends meet in Pinch-'em-Tight Holler near Stanton, Kentucky. Lily May's first instrument was a homemade groundhog-hide banjo. At age eleven she fell in love with the fiddle.

"I never learned enough in school. I wasn't worth a dime. My mind was on music and that's all. I was a daydreamer, very absent-minded, and just made the worst grades in the world." When she was seventeen and an eighth-grade dropout, she began hiking eight miles out of the hills to a train station to fiddle for tips. An entrepreneur took her north to perform in movie theaters between screenings. In the summer of 1936 Lily May won first place in a talent contest, with the prize being a slot on "The National Barn Dance."

"My daddy . . . was tickled to death, he was so proud. But Lord, what a time we had with Mama! She'd heard stories where the young girls who went to the cities were captured and sold into white slavery, and she was scared to death of cities and the things which could happen to young girls there. . . . But she needn't have worried . . . I was pretty sharp.

"I had never heard of Cousin Emmy until I had that [WLS] contract," Lily May told an interviewer in 1977. "I heard her on someone's radio and

Country's pioneering all-female string band The Coon Creek Girls were, from left, Rosa Charlotte "Rosie" Ledford, Esther "Violet" Koehler, Lily May Ledford, and Evelyn "Daisy" Lange. This edition of the act headlined shows from 1937 to 1939.

everyone began talking about Cousin Emmy, a banjo player and fiddler. And I thought, 'Oh Lord, if they hear her before I can get up there, they will take her instead because she's so much smoother and better.'" But Emmy's whoop-it-up delivery would have been louder than anything else on the show, and her brassy image was certainly not demure enough. Lily May was nineteen and could be more easily molded to the WLS philosophy. The station's John Lair got her to tone down her exuberant singing to blend in with WLS's fireside sound; he also encouraged her to switch to banjo as her primary instrument and to learn more mountain tunes than the ones her mother had taught her. The homesick but determined Lily made her debut in late 1936, complete with the usual WLS publicity ballyhoo and even a comic strip called "Lily May—The Mountain Gal."

"Mr. Lair discouraged my buying clothes, curling my hair, going in for make-up or improving my English. 'Stay a mountain girl, just like you were when you came here. Be genuine and plain at all times,' he said."

Lily May wrote in her 1980 autobiography, *Coon Creek Girl.* "I was always a little timid and modest. Mr. Lair . . . encouraged me to get out there and kick up my heels a little and show Lulu Belle. Lulu Belle had been voted Radio Queen that year [1936], and they thought she needed big competition, but I didn't relish the idea of trying to compete with her."

After a year in the Windy City at sixty dollars a week for radio and eleven dollars a week for the road tours, Lily May went to Cincinnati with Red Foley, Eva Overstake, The Girls of the Golden West, Sophia Germanich, and some other WLS defectors to form the core of the "Renfro Valley Barn Dance" cast. Here Lair formed The Coon Creek Girls, named all the members after flowers, and had them sing "Flowers Blooming in the Wild Wood" as a theme song. "We took like a house afire the first week. And it was mostly the middle-aged and old people, farm people, and the very, very poor that went for the Coon Creek Girls. . . . they would be lined up way down the block and way round to the next just trying to crowd into that studio. And us girls got baskets of fan mail and cakes and homemade candy . . . flowers . . . crocheted little things and embroidered handkerchiefs . . . marriage proposals and I couldn't tell you what all."

The Renfro stars made forty dollars a person for a week's work, minus a 20 percent management fee to Lair. A family of five needed a minimum of twenty-five dollars a week to make it in the thirties. The average woman made ten dollars a week, less than half of what most men earned. Although their wages were higher than most, barn dance women maintained grueling, seven-day-a-week schedules to earn their pay.

"Violet and Daisy were becoming unhappy and begged Sis and me to leave Renfro and find a better-paying job. . . . We called WSM in Nashville, which was beginning to come up big. . . . However, we were surprised when they offered us only twelve dollars per week! They explained to us what their policy was: You 'made it' through records, pictures, songbooks and bookings. The station furnished the broadcasting for publicity only. You did the rest . . . sink or swim."

Daisy and Violet dropped out of The Coon Creek Girls in late 1939. Teenage Ledford sister Minnie Lena "Black-Eyed Susan" (1922–1987) joined The Coon Creek Girls in 1940, making it a sister trio. Their unique status as a female band kept the act busy constantly. "We stayed tired all the time," Lily May said.

That, plus increasing family duties, led to their retirement in 1957. Rosie raised 1980s country singer Clyde Foley Cummins. Black-Eyed Susan became the editor of the *Renfro Valley Bugle*. Lily May was married to Glenn Pennington from 1945 until their divorce in 1967. Their son J. P. Pennington topped the rock charts as the leader of Exile with 1978's "Kiss You All Over," then took the group into country music in the eighties with "She's a Miracle," "Woke Up in Love," and fifteen other hits.

Lily May Ledford's Coon Creek Girls served as the training ground for many female musicians of the 1940s. During various absences by her sisters, Lily May hired such notables as "Mattie, Marthy, and Minnie" Amburgey, Inez Coffee, Betty Callahan, Little Jo Depew, and Molly O'Day. More importantly, her rollicking "Banjo Pickin' Girl" became the anthem for all free-spirited country music women with a yen to ramble.

Lily May's headlining status at the "Renfro Valley Barn Dance" was matched by only a handful of female contemporaries. At "The Grand Ole Opry," the comedy team of Sarie and Sally was a major draw of the 1930s. Sunshine Sue became the superstar of "The Old Dominion Barn Dance." The queen of WHO's "Barn Dance Frolic" in Des Moines was Louisiana Lou.

WHO was a fifty-thousand-watt giant like WLS, WWVA, and WSM, and Lou was its biggest star between 1933 and 1939. But only a few documents from her Depression-era career remain. Barn dance performers were itinerant workers, gypsies who moved from station to station. A few were fixtures like Lulu Belle at "The National Barn Dance."

For unknown reasons, virtually all the women performing country music during the thirties and forties in West Virginia did so behind odd, diminutive nicknames. Listed below are the radio monikers and the real names behind them.

SUNFLOWER (Mary Calvas)

LITTLE SHOE (Alma Crosby)

BROWN EYES (Mrs. James "Slim Carter" Conwell)

CRICKET (Celia Mauri)

LAUGHIN' LINDY (Elizabeth Margaret Lindsay)

LITTLE SHIRLEY (Barker)

PENNY (Thelma Woodford)

LITTLE MONTANA (Evalina Stallard)

CHEROKEE SUE (Hattie Dickenhoff)

But most country music women's lives were like that of the always-rambling Cousin Emmy. And unless you had a publicity machine like WLS's or WSM's, you could expect mainstream newspapers and magazines of the day to ignore both your low-class music and your blue-collar fans, whether you were at WHO in Des Moines, KMBC in Kansas City, KSTP in Minneapolis/St. Paul, or WNAX in Yankton, South Dakota, all of which starred Louisiana Lou.

The general pattern was to move to a barn dance and collect between fifteen and fifty dollars a week for seven days of radio work, using the airtime to plug your upcoming personal appearances in the listening area. The station would have you for a daily show, usually in the early morning, plus its Saturday night frolic. In between, on week nights, you'd drive all the narrow highways within a hundred-mile radius of your station, playing schoolhouses, movie theaters, and small-town auditoriums. There, you'd sell your songbooks, souvenir picture albums, or records to pick up extra money. You'd split the take with your band, pile everyone back into your well-worn 1930s sedan, drive half the night to get back for the morning radio show, then go back out on the road. After a few seasons of this, you'd "played out" the region, so you headed for another station in another town for another grind.

And when all was said and done, all that remained of Louisiana Lou and dozens of country women like her were some faded old publicity photos and a few scratchy 78s. Lou was born Eva Mae Greenwood around 1907 in central Mississippi, graduated from Clarke College in 1923, taught school, and made her radio debut on Jackson, Mississippi's, WJDX. Her first marriage evidently occurred during this time, for shortly thereafter Lou's name is given as Eva Mae Sargent. By the early 1930s she was Mrs. Dutch Conn and living in Des Moines, Iowa. She joined the "Barn Dance Frolic" in 1933, taking her stage name from the hit Sophie Tucker musical of 1911.

"Lou was very popular," recalls WHO veteran Zeke Clements, "a 'loverly' person. Very, very country with a no-good husband and a houseful of children. Didn't hardly have enough to eat. But she was just a lovely person."

In the spring of 1933 Louisiana Lou, "The Southern Songbird," recorded six numbers for Bluebird Records in Chicago. In keeping with her image and life-style, the discs reveal a jaunty, "ramblin' gal" stylist, with Lou giving a bluesy lilt to "Go 'Long Mule" and "With My Banjo on My Knee Blues." "When the Moon Shines Down" is a wandering girl's lament for the boy she left behind. All her songs are delivered forcefully, with the unself-conscious directness that is the hallmark of country's other great songsters of her era.

Lou became known as "The Veteran's Sweetheart" because of her work with VFW posts. She toured to Boston on behalf of war vets in 1939, the same year she headlined at Iowa Day at the New York World's Fair and appeared in the Roy Rogers movie *Wall Street Cowboy*. In 1938 she made the cover of *Rural Radio* magazine. By 1940 she was on radio in Kansas City, and the following year she was a regular in Yankton. Next her KSTP "Sunset Valley Barn Dance" stint in Minneapolis was carried on the Minnesota Radio Network. Then she went back to Yankton to lead an all-girl band called The Pine Cabin Girls on WNAX during World War II. In 1946 Lou's "Night-Time on the Trail" broadcasts from Kansas City were carried on the CBS network on Monday nights, but this is her last documented activity.

Louisiana Lou, 1936.

One of the few who remembers Lou is Nashville musicians' union executive and "Grand Ole Opry" entertainer Vic Willis, who worked with her in Kansas City. He says he knew her under a third married name, Nichols, and recalls fondly that Lou "always acted like one of the boys, playing poker and telling jokes" with the members of his Willis Brothers band on the road.

You just about had to be "one of the boys" to survive from barn dance to barn dance. The hours were long, the traveling was rugged, and the pay wasn't great, but at least the work was plentiful. By the late 1930s there were approximately five thousand radio shows in the United States using live country music. About five hundred were large-cast barn dances, from KVOO's "Saddle Mountain Round-Up" in Tulsa to WFIL's "Sleepy Hollow Ranch" in Philadelphia. In addition to the Opry and "The National Barn Dance," "Hill Billy Champions," "Shady Valley Jamboree," "Hayloft Hoedown," "The Corn Cob Pipe Club," "Dude Ranch," "Carson Robison's Buckaroos," "Plantation Party," and "Renfro Valley" all aired as national network shows. The biggest hillbilly radio stars drew ten thousand pieces of mail a week. On the road at the height of the Depression, barn dance troupes sometimes played to crowds numbering between ten thousand and fifty thousand.

"Turn the dial this way or that, before long you are perfectly sure to hear some songs that are as wholly and originally American as cornbread," noted Avis D. Carlson in *Better Homes and Gardens* in 1931. "It is safe to say that no program of oldtime tunes is without a sprinkle of some genuine folk music. . . . In the days when static and interference were nothing to fret about, only a few scholars and collectors were interested in the songs which have sprung up from the very soil of our country. But now interest is rapidly spreading to people in general." In 1938 *Collier's* magazine put it more succinctly: "Thar's Gold in Them Hillbillies."

HUNGRY DISGUSTED BLUES

Women in Protest

Aunt Molly Jackson, 1939.

A low, mournful alto reverberates through the barbed wire of a remote Texas cattle ranch in 1938. The puzzled cowboys pause in their labors to wonder at the ghostly music resonating through the fence, miles from the nearest radio. "For fear, the hearts of men are failing," she sings. "The Great Depression now is spreading."

In Atlanta a businessman tries in vain to tune to WSB. But the woman's voice blasts through the speakers, obliterating all other nearby signals with her song of woe. On the chorus a moaning soprano and a soft bass join her. "I'm going where there's no Depression," they harmonize solemnly. "To the lovely land that's free from care."

Children on the Kansas prairie fashion homemade receivers out of tin cans and wire, knowing they'll hear that woman and her sad, sad song. "My home's in Heaven," she sings. "In that bright land, there'll be no hunger, no orphan children crying for bread."

In Saskatchewan and Nebraska and West Virginia you can hear her graveyard intonation, her ineffable weariness, her stark sense of loss, her arid and forlorn desolation. "I'm going where there's no Depression." From Philadelphia to Phoenix her voice rings through the air with the power to vibrate tooth fillings and rattle radio

tubes. "I'm going where there's no Depression. . . . My home's in Heaven. I'm going there."

The voice belongs to Sara Carter, and it is riding the gargantuan wattage of the most powerful radio station in the world. By an odd quirk of fate, the reserved Appalachian alto is taking part in one of the most rebellious chapters in the history of broadcasting—border radio.

Broadcasting was a freewheeling and almost unmanageable thing during its early years. Prior to the late 1920s there were no standards of conduct or codes of behavior. When the government began to impose rules and regulations, radio wildcatters defied them flagrantly. Beginning in 1930 a platoon of quack medicine men and an army of mystics, astrologers, psychics, political kooks, and shady evangelists constructed a series of megastations just south of the Mexican border to sidestep Washington's control. They defiantly boosted their power to one hundred thousand watts, five hundred thousand watts, and a million watts when the ceiling for major U.S. stations such as Chicago's WLS and Nashville's WSM was fifty thousand watts. You could hear border radio in telephone lines and electric fans.

Mexican-border stations such as XERA, XENT, XEPN, and XEAW were titans that reached into everyday Americans' homes to peddle patent medicines, cosmetics, and unsavory cures. Drug companies were the nation's biggest radio advertisers by 1932, when there were no regulations on either drugs or advertising. The airwaves were wide open, and none more so than over border radio. There, hucksters offered Lash Lure, a beauty aid that had the unfortunate side effect of rendering some users blind; Marmola, a fat reducer that also caused headaches and fever; Koremlu, a depilatory made from rat poison; and Kolorbak, a hair dye capable of causing lead poisoning. Lysol was advertised as a safe douche. Lucky Strike cigarettes were offered as "slenderizers" and "throat balms." On border radio, Dr. John R. Brinkley advertised that he could restore sexual potency in his Mexican clinic, where he transplanted tiny slivers of billy-goat gonads into men's scrotums. Purple-suited Norman G. Baker promised a cancer cure. Crazy Water Crystals, the first of the border radio nostrums, supposedly cured arthritis.

The border broadcasters' pitches were aimed at gullible rural and working-class Americans, so from the start, the stations featured plenty of country music. Some scholars, in fact, credit the border stations with bringing country music to mass popularity. Women such as Rose Maddox, The Herrington Sisters, Molly O'Day, Texas Rose, and Patsy Montana all became widely heard via the programs they beamed over the megawatt giants. South-of-the-Border superstars Rosa Dominguez ("Mexico's Nightingale") and Lydia Mendoza ("The Lark of the Border") were other notable women who spread their music via border radio. Many acts prerecorded their shows on sixteen-inch transcription discs—often complete with commercials—for airing on border radio. The blind harmonizers Ma and Pa Smithers had ads on their show for Willard's Tablets. The homey shows of The Pickard Family and The Carter Family were sponsored by Kolorbak.

"Don't let gray hair cheat you out of your job and cause you a lot of worry," went the Pickards' border radio pitch in 1937. "No sirree, that isn't necessary anymore. Not when it's so easy to get rid of gray-hair worries and handicaps. And here is all you have to do. Get a bottle of Kolorbak . . . scientifically imparts color and charm to gray hair." Dad Pickard did the sales pitches while daughters Ruthie and Ann charmed listeners with song.

At their peak, the Pickards were pulling in twenty thousand Kolorbak orders a week. In 1940 the Tennessee family pressed westward, heading to Hollywood from San Antonio. Border radio fame led to movie appearances, then to starring on the first live television show in Los Angeles, from 1949 to 1954.

The Pickards met The Carter Family in Texas in 1938. The Pickard children remember Sara and A.P. as sad people. The estranged couple came into the studio and sang songs without looking or speaking to each other. Patsy Montana, who was also recording transcriptions for border radio use, recalls, "At that time, A.P. and Sara were separated. Whenever A.P. wanted to say something to Sara, he'd call me over, and I'd have to relay his message. It sure was awkward."

Sara Carter got her divorce in 1939 and married A.P.'s handsome cousin Coy Bayes. A.P. sat silently in the back of their whitewashed Virginia mountain church while Maybelle stood up front as her singing partner's matron of honor. When the trio resumed its border radio broadcasts, A.P. became ever more taciturn and withdrawn.

"Mother and Aunt Sara did most of the songs," Maybelle's daughter June remembers. "He and Aunt Sara didn't talk too much. . . . I don't remember having any compassion for my Uncle A.P. at this time. Maybe once when I realized that Janette was doing all the cooking, and she was just about sixteen by now. I guess they were all a little sad."

Janette came to Texas to sing with her parents during The Carter Family's first border radio season; Maybelle brought along her little soprano, Anita. In 1939 ten-year-old June and twelve-year-old Helen joined the act; in fact, Maybelle put her trio of daughters to work recording their own border radio shows. When they went back to Virginia after that second season, five thousand fan letters were waiting at home. Carter Family record sales soared as a result of their "outlaw" broadcasts. So did sales of Kolorbak.

"Hello there, Mother, you little sweetheart," crooned silver-tongued country bandleader W. Lee O'Daniel on his radio show. "How in the world are you, anyway, you little bunch of sweetness?" A political ultraconservative, supersalesman O'Daniel parlayed border radio fame into a Fort Worth real estate empire, the 1939 governorship of the Lone Star State, and a 1941 Senate seat in Washington. "Sing it, Texas Rose!" was his shout on the campaign trail. O'Daniel's female singer/fiddler was a recording veteran from a family act called The Three Williamsons who'd warbled the saucy "Rooster Rag" and "A Good Man Is Hard to Find" on Bluebird Records in 1937. She was put on O'Daniel's government payroll, but Texas Rose (Kitty Williamson) couldn't help him once he was in office. By the late 1940s O'Daniel's widely broadcast anti-Roosevelt, prosegregation diatribes became an embarrassment to Texas.

Even more controversial on border radio were the women "spooks," so called because of their stargazing and quasireligious ravings. The Reverend Ethel Duncan was one of several astrologers banned by U.S. broadcasting laws who operated along the Rio Grande. One of the most popular radio stars in history was Rose Dawn. She not only divined listeners' fates by horoscopes, but would pray for specific matters or give love advice for the fee of one dollar. The self-billed "Patroness of the Sacred Order of Maya" was married to an enigmatic guy in a turban called Koran. "The couple were an ethereal sight on the streets of Del Rio as they glided past gawking onlookers in their pink Chrysler with orchid wheels," report border radio historians Gene Fowler and Bill Crawford. Sister White was a border radio faith healer. Even more dramatic was border radio evangelist A. A. Allen, who claimed to be able to raise the dead. One of Brother Allen's last tent-revival singers in the fifties was a little ol' country gal who grew up to be Tammy Faye Bakker, the most famous female TV evangelist of the 1980s.

The popular media steadily and surely filed down America's roughest and most radical cultural edges during the Depression. Extremes on both left and right were discouraged or excluded. Minority messages and minority voices were gradually eliminated from the airwaves, the mainstream press, the recording studio, and the Hollywood soundstage.

These characters were drawn to border radio stations because U.S. authorities gagged their wild expressions, extravagant claims, unorthodox business practices, and radical theologies. The flamboyant Aimee Semple McPherson's case was typical. The glamorous, vaudeville-style religious showboat and Columbia Records gospel artist of 1926 through 1932 raised the ire of federal officials by repeatedly shifting her Los Angeles radio station's frequency. Beset by bullies who tried to make her obey the broadcasting laws, the Queen of the Heavens wired President Hoover to "order your minions of Satan to leave my station alone."

The radio renegades were drawing upon a deep-seated dissatisfaction. People were hungry. People were angry and agitated. More than ten million were unemployed by 1934. The old values of hard work being rewarded, of keeping your nose to the grindstone, and of facing problems with square-shouldered toughness seemed bankrupt. The era spawned unprecedented numbers of spontaneous rebellions, as well as organized anticapitalist movements. Picket lines, hunger marches, and meetings of the unemployed sprang up everywhere. The sitdown strike was a new tactic in the 1930s and was quickly adopted by workers in various industries. The Union Party of the Midwest ran a candidate for president on a platform based on radical agrarian reform. In Louisiana master radio orator Huey Long was swept into the governorship and then a Senate seat by championing the common man. He advocated shifting the taxation burden to large corporations to make them "share the wealth." By 1935 the international communist movement was campaigning among the unemployed and among blacks to help form the Congress of Industrial Organizations (CIO) as a union of unskilled workers.

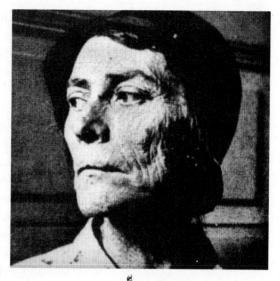

Aunt Molly Jackson, 1939.

The county with the biggest Kentucky coal-mining strikes of the thirties became nationally known as "Bloody Harlan" and became the archetype of worker-versus-owner, good-versus-evil in these struggles. Those coal fields became the meeting ground for political leftists and folk musicians. Urban radicals organized efforts to feed and support the miners. In turn, the proletarian rebels taught the intellectuals about a country culture that addressed social problems on a grass-roots level.

The scene is New York City's Coliseum in 1931. More than twenty-one thousand people have gathered to express support for Kentucky miners struggling for social justice, better living conditions, and decent wages. On stage, a plainspoken, plain-dressed Appalachian woman of fifty stills the crowd with her stark, searing singing. "I am soliciting for the poor Kentucky miners," her song begins. "While the coal operators and their wives all went dressed in jewels and silk / The poor coal miners' babies starved to death for bread or milk."

Her name was Aunt Molly Jackson (1880–1960). Her father was a Kentucky preacher, miner, and union organizer who taught his daughter to stand for the rights of common people. She was writing songs by age four, walking picket lines with her father at age five, and landing in jail at age ten because of her family's union beliefs. Molly married at fourteen and was working as a nurse-midwife among the poor mountaineers shortly afterward. Her father and a brother were blinded in mining accidents. Her first husband, son, and another brother were killed working in an industry that paid them barely enough to subsist. Her neighbors were felled by black lung, TB, and malnutrition. During her lifetime seventy thousand men were killed in the mines, and thousands of women and children lived in agonizing deprivation. She saw her fellow union organizers shot and killed in cold blood by mining company thugs. "I have often wondered why they have not killed me," she once said.

Her second husband divorced her because he feared reprisals from her fiery crusading. The Depression only intensified the struggle between wealthy coal company bosses and workers making thirty-three cents per ton of coal extracted. In 1931 Aunt Molly Jackson was forced to leave the coal fields by Kentucky authorities. But evicted into the wide world beyond the mountains, she brought national attention to the shameful working conditions, pitiful wages, and cruel inhumanity.

Molly chronicled thirty-five years of miners' miseries and struggles in her songs, delivered in the powerful, unaccompanied, declamatory style of old-time Appalachian ballad singing. In 1930 she recorded "Kentucky Miner's Wife (Ragged Hungry Blues)" for Columbia Records' country market. A year later she was giving her ringing musical testimony before the thousands at that New York rally; she subsequently toured with her message to thirty-eight states. Her "Poor Miner's Farewell," "Hard Times in Coleman's Mines," and "Hungry Disgusted Blues" lay bare the wretched reality of the miner's life.

In 1935 and 1939 Molly recorded 150 of her songs for the Library of Congress Archive of Folk Song; some of these performances became a Rounder Records LP in 1971. Along with Leadbelly, Josh White, Burl Ives, W. C. Handy, and others, Molly appeared in the 1940 stage show *Cavalcade of American Song*. This production, some subsequent tours, and Molly's participation in New York's earliest "hootenannies" in Greenwich Village formed the foundation of the folk music revival and established a long-lasting link between left-wing politics and folk songs.

Toward the end of her life Molly claimed to be the inspiration and first popularizer of the 1944 megahit "Pistol-Packin' Mama." According to her, she threatened her moonshine-making husband with a gun in Kentucky, leading her cousin to compose the strikingly similar "Pistol-Packin' Woman." Molly said she performed this in New York and that country and pop singers copied her, creating the immensely popular war-era catchphrase.

Molly moved to California. Her health began to fail in the 1950s, and she died at age eighty in extreme poverty and relative obscurity. Shortly before her death she wrote to the *Sing Out!* folk song magazine: "I compose a lot of songs that teaches people right from wrong. . . . I believe I have seen more poverty and suffering than any other poor woman that has ever lived under the sun. . . . I have never received one cent from anyone out of all the protest songs I have composed."

"Aunt Molly Jackson and Texas Gladden were the finest traditional singers I met in the United States," eulogized folklorist Alan Lomax in 1961. "Her songs of protest can only be matched by those of Woody Guthrie, but they were more passionate than his, and they cut deeper."

Molly was not the only country woman rabble-rouser of the Depression. Her half-sister Sarah Ogun Gunning (1910–1983) followed Molly to New York in 1935; starred at the 1939 New York World's Fair; took part in the early folk song hootenannies of 1940; sang at the Newport Folk Festival in 1964; rose to prominence on the folk circuit from 1965 to 1975; and released albums in 1964, 1973, and 1976. Sarah's repertoire included such well-burnished Appalachian gems as "Silver Dagger," "Oh Death," "The House Carpenter," "The Drunkard's Dream," and "The Lonesome Dove." But her original songs were shaped by the same Depression forces that molded Aunt Molly's.

"I was a coal miner's daughter and a coal miner's wife," Sarah said. "In some of the mines you had to work for so long, and load so many tons of coal before you was allowed to even rent one of them old company houses. And they was just what you'd call a shack now. . . . What little money you made, they paid you in scrip and you had to spend it at the company store. Everything cost at least three times as much as it would if you could go downtown to shop. But you wasn't allowed to do that. . . . In the early thirties I had one of my babies starve to death. It literally happened, people starved to death. . . . And all you could do was go over and help . . . lay them out and sit with the mothers until they could put them away. . . . These and other things in my life, is what I composed the songs about."

Sarah's fame rests on her six cornerstone songs of the miners' union struggle—"Come All You Coal Miners," "Dreadful Memories," "I'm Going to Organize, Baby Mine," "I Hate the Capitalist System," "Down on the Picket Line," and "I Am a Girl of Constant Sorrow." Folklorists Mary Elizabeth Barnicle and Alan Lomax recorded Sarah for the Library of Congress in 1937 and 1938. The following year she and her fellow mountain women Mamie Quackenbush, Hazel Garland, and Dorothy Barton sang as Jim Garland and His Kentucky Mountain Singers on a

Sis Cunningham, 1940.

thirty-minute weekly show on WNYC in Manhattan and in a one-week stand at the New York World's Fair at the Kentucky Exhibit. In later years Sarah was hailed as "the best of the living bards" because of her rich repertoire of traditional folk music.

"Which Side Are You On?" became one of the left's most enduring songs from the Depression era. It was written by miner's wife Florence Reece (1900–1986) in the aftermath of the violent and failed National Miners Union strike of 1931. In the 1960s the native Tennessean's song became even more famous when adapted for the civil rights movement.

Agnes "Sis" Cunningham came to the social justice struggles from the Dust Bowl. Born in Oklahoma in 1909, Sis worked her way through school as a waitress after her family lost its farm in a bank foreclosure. She became a music teacher who put her melodies to work in labor organizing for the Southern Tenant Farmers Union. In 1939 she performed topical skits and tunes for Okie sharecroppers as a member of The Red Dust Players. Two years later the singer, accordion player, and composer joined New York's leftist Almanac Singers, a loose-knit communal group that also included Woody Guthrie, Pete Seeger, Lee Hays, and Bess Lomax. The best-known songs Sis wrote were "Mr. Congressman" and "Strange Things Happenin' in This Land." She was also responsible for "Fayette County," one of the earliest songs about the struggle for black equality. But she was at her most eloquent with such Okie-themed numbers as "Song of the Evicted Tenant," "My Oklahoma Home (It Blowed Away)," and her extraordinarily piquant "Sundown" of 1937. Her song "How Can You Keep On Movin'" was repopularized by pop star Ry Cooder in the 1970s.

Sis continued to write and perform into her late seventies. She founded and edited the long-running folk magazine *Broadside.* Published between 1962 and 1988, it was devoted to topical songs. Among the female troubadours who were introduced in its pages were Janis Ian, Malvina Reynolds, and Buffy Sainte-Marie. *Broadside* was also the first to publish and record Bob Dylan.

Lita Auville and her husband, Ray, were perhaps the most radical country songsters of the Depression. Introduced in the pages of the *Daily*

Worker in 1935, these West Virginians were Communist Party members who sang political songs to working-class audiences. The John Reed Club, named for the man commemorated in the Oscar-winning movie *Reds,* published the Auvilles' songbook. It included "Painting the Old Town Red," "The Ghost of the Depression," "Mighty Fine Country," and other strong statements.

While Sis Cunningham was chronicling the Depression-era woes of Okie farmers and Sarah Ogun Gunning and Aunt Molly Jackson were singing on behalf of Kentucky miners, Nancy Dixon was singing of Carolina textile workers. Nancy was the older sister of The Dixon Brothers, Dorsey and Howard, best known as the originators of the Roy Acuff hit "Wreck on the Highway (I Didn't Hear Nobody Pray)." In 1936 and 1937 the Dixons also recorded "Weave Room Blues" and "Weaver's Life."

Just about everyone in East Rockingham, North Carolina, worked as "lintheads" at the looms and shuttles of its textile mill. Nancy went to work as a child spinner in 1899, when she was eight. She and the other girls made eight cents a day. If a worker fell asleep on the job, she was beaten and tied to her work station. At home Nancy repeated the tunes she'd learned from the older mill hands, "Hard Times in Here" and "Factory Girl," the latter of which is one of America's oldest labor songs. Nancy taught her singing brothers some of their numbers, but spent her

Sarah Ogun Gunning, Hazel Garland, Mamie Quackenbush, and Dorothy Barton were Jim Garland's "Kentucky Mountain Singers" at the New York World's Fair of 1939.

entire working life as a textile girl; she didn't record until folklorists visited the Dixons in 1962 for the album *Babies in the Mill*. Dorsey's wife, Beatrice, also a mill worker, recorded six gospel songs with him for Bluebird Records in 1937 and 1938.

Cotton mill worker Georgia Dell (Adelle Bassett) also attempted to escape from factory life by recording for Bluebird. With her husband, Rupert McClendon, and his McClendon Brothers group she sang several numbers for the label between 1936 and 1938. In turn, Georgia alerted the company to her singing mill hand brother and his wife, Dewey and Gassie Bassett. They recorded twenty-two charming old-timey duets for Bluebird in 1939 and 1940, including the rakish novelty ditty "Good Evening Mama."

Most of the record companies experimented with such working-class female singers during the Depression. And because of the times, country music women's statements became a little stronger. Hazel Scherf issued "Married Girl's Troubles" and "You Can't Blame Me for That" on Champion Records in 1934. Charlotte Miller, the wife of country song-writing great Bob Miller, recorded the outlaw-girl tunes "Dangerous Nan McGrew" and "Poker Alice" for Columbia in 1930. Evelyn Harding and Sylvia Porter issued several numbers for Champion between 1933 and 1935 as The Blue Ridge Mountain Girls, but the company chose not to release the pair's political "Depression Medley."

Easily the most unconventional female country recordings of the era were those of North Carolinian Betty Lou (DeMorrow). With the Hartman's Heartbreakers band, Betty Lou sang such lascivious lyrics as "Let Me Play With It," "Give It to Me Daddy," and "My Southern Movements." Her ten bawdy Bluebird sides of 1936 and 1937 are the first "party" records in country music history. Betty Lou's daughter is Hope Powell, the doyen of Nashville's country music photographers.

Zora Layman, a product of the Kansas prairie, was the first woman to curse on a country record. Her "hell" and "damn" on Decca discs are mild by today's standards, but were considered unbecoming for civilized women in the thirties and are still not in the recording vocabularies of country music women today.

Zora Layman (c. 1900–1981) was the country queen of New York City's airwaves during the Depression. She and her husband, Frank Luther, first came to prominence after Carson Robison's breakup with Vernon Dalhart and Adelyne Hood in 1928: Robison was looking for a substitute fiddler/singer for Hood and a baritone like Dalhart to reconstitute a Carson Robison Trio. Zora was certainly qualified. The cattle-ranch child was a violin prodigy who became a concertmaster for the orchestra on the summer Chautauqua touring circuit in her home state at age seventeen. After toying with a film career in Hollywood, Zora married fellow Kansan Francis Luther Crow in 1926 and moved to Manhattan. After the Luthers' four-year introduction to hillbilly recording with Robison, they split amicably from him and formed their Frank Luther Trio with Leonard Stokes in 1933.

Zora didn't have the comic flash, vocal expertise, or fiddle dexterity of her predecessor, Adelyne Hood, but she performed adequately on such Luther-Layman-Robison discs as "Home on the Range" and "Rocking Alone in an Old Rocking Chair." Zora sang lead on "Poor Unwanted Children" (1933), a plea for the adoption of orphanage children. "The Old Ladies' Home" (1933) dealt with the sad loneliness of aged mothers wishing for letters from their children.

The Frank Luther Trio graduated to Big Apple radio in the mid-1930s. Zora was featured on "The Fleischmann Hour"; the Maxwell House, Standard Oil, and Crazy Water Crystals programs; "Hillbilly Heart-Throbs"; and "Heart-Throbs of the Hills." The last two were written and produced by folklorist Ethel Park Richardson and were dramatizations of the stories of mountain songs. Frank and Zora were deeply influenced by Richardson, and as folk music enthusiasm spread in the late 1930s and early 1940s, the couple embarked on a trailblazing series of folk albums for Decca, plus singles of "Sweet Betsy from Pike," "Clementine," and "Barbara Allen."

A large part of Frank and Zora's output was family-harmony fare such as "Picture from Life's Other Side" and "I'll Be with You When the Roses Bloom Again," or such women's religious standards as Sarah Adams's "Nearer My God to Thee" of 1841 and Katharine Purvis's "When the Saints Go Marching In" of 1896. But they also did novelty tunes such as "Barnacle Bill the Sailor," "I'm Popeye the Sailor Man," and "Who Stole the Lock Off the Henhouse Door?"

Zora was unquestionably at her best with lighter material, which she often recorded as the lead singer of Zora and the Hometowners between 1934 and 1937. She answered the huge country hit "Seven Years with the Wrong Woman" with the exaggerated hillbilly flair of, naturally, "Seven Years with the Wrong Man." In it Zora asked the musical question, "Girls, why are we saving for some no-good man? / They've had the same habits ever since time began," and opined, "You can find more real friendship in ownin' a dog," before concluding, "Seven years with the wrong man is like livin' in hell."

Zora's other "answer" records included the responses to the big Depression-era hit "21 Years"—"New 21 Years" and "Last of the 21-Year Prisoner." On "I'll Be Hanged if They're Gonna Hang Me" (1937) she

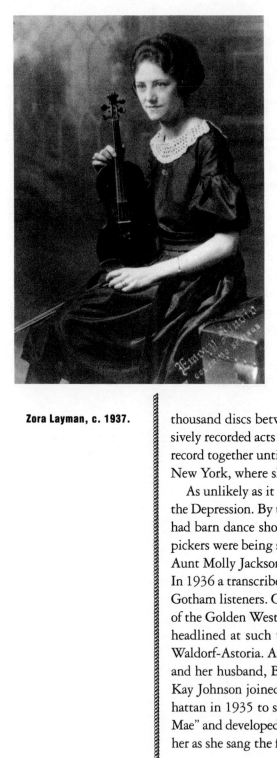

takes the part of the jailbird vowing to bust out while Luther and Stokes echo her sentiments with sung interjections. All three deliver "The Beer Song" in a rollicking tempo in celebration of the 1933 repeal of Prohibition, singing "It'll be a glorious day, sir, when we get back our beer!" As a duo, Frank and Zora shine on "A Hillbilly Wedding in June" (1934).

Zora continued her woman-oriented recordings with 1934's "I've Got Man Trouble," "The Wrong Man and the Wrong Woman," a version of the Roba Stanley song "All Night Long," and a celebration of divorce called "Hurray, I'm Single Again." The last-named offered the pointed observation, "No man's worth a damn / They're so low they'd crawl under a snake."

In addition to singing (and swearing) assertive women's lyrics, Zora made musical history in other ways. Beginning with an album of Mother Goose nursery rhymes in 1936, Frank and Zora recorded a long series of children's discs, virtually defining the art of kiddie records. During the next decade 85 percent of children's records sold in the United States were recorded by them. With more than two thousand discs between them, the Luthers were among the most extensively recorded acts of their day. They divorced in 1940, but continued to record together until 1948. Zora Layman remarried and retired to upstate New York, where she died blind and nearly forgotten in 1981.

As unlikely as it seems, New York was a country music hotbed during the Depression. By the mid-1930s New York's WOR and WHN stations had barn dance shows, country was thriving in nightclubs, and country pickers were being showcased on Broadway. Zora Layman, Pearl Pickens, Aunt Molly Jackson, and Sarah Ogun Gunning were heard on the radio. In 1936 a transcribed radio show by The Carter Family was popular with Gotham listeners. Cowgirls Louise Massey, Patsy Montana, and The Girls of the Golden West all migrated to New York during this period. Louise headlined at such uptown showrooms as the Rainbow Room and the Waldorf-Astoria. At the swank Stork Club, Kansas-bred Tex Ann Nation and her husband, Buck, were the western headliners. Philadelphia-born Kay Johnson joined her singing-cowboy husband Ray Whitley in Manhattan in 1935 to sing on the WHN "Barn Dance." She became "Cassie Mae" and developed a routine that included twenty-nine chorines backing her as she sang the female folk favorite "Get Away, Old Man, Get Away."

The city originally caught "hillbilly fever" in 1930 from a new downtown nightclub and its trio of singing siblings who called themselves The Three Georgia Crackers. Their name was Canova, and their talent was unstoppable. Diane, Juliette, and Leon Canova were middle-class children of a cotton broker from Starke, Florida. Juliette was trained as an opera vocalist, and Diane as a pianist. Mother Henrietta Perry Canova had been a concert singer and encouraged her children's theatrical ambitions, particularly after their father died and money got tight. As youngsters, the trio began playing around with the hillbilly accents they heard on vacations in North Carolina. By the time they hit the airwaves on Jacksonville's WJAX in 1928, their country comedy characters were Anne, Judy, and Zeke, The Three Georgia Crackers. The team adopted Unadilla, Georgia, as its hometown because Juliette/Judy was fascinated with the sound of the name.

With hillbilly gags, dance routines, and songs in place, the trio hit New York in mid-1930. They had just enough money to share a four-flight walk-up room on West Sixty-fifth Street "that was so small if you ate a square meal you couldn't get in," Judy recalled years later. The landlady "allowed no rehearsals, so we used to go to Central Park to practice. . . . Our yodels, grunts, and hog-calls opened windows to see what jungle animals were now invading Broadway." They haunted theatrical agents' offices in search of vaudeville bookings and recorded briefly for Gennett Records before landing their first nightclub engagement: "We grabbed a fifty-dollar job and dinner at Jimmy Kelly's," Judy said. "I just wanted the dinner." A guitar player familiar with their rube routines suggested auditioning at the new Village Barn, which Judy described as "a fine, neighborly institution: If you sat down, you soon found one of the customers on your lap."

The Canovas' cornpone antics were quite a novelty in Manhattan. They went over so big at the Barn that they were held over for seven months as Zeke and the Happiness Girls.

Packed houses at the Village Barn led to vaudeville bookings. The Georgia Crackers were on their way. "Only thing that can possibly stand in the way of this trio clicking . . . on the Orpheum route is that they are following comparatively close on the heels of The Weaver Brothers and Elviry," opined *Billboard*'s reviewer in 1931 after catching Anne, Judy, and Zeke at the Chester Theatre in the Bronx. "Similarity of their act with the Weavers may rub the fur of some audiences . . . the wrong way. . . . Both girls affect hillbilly dress and mannerisms, with one, Judy, furnishing comedy. . . ."

Within ten years Judy Canova (1916–1983) was the biggest woman

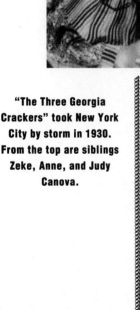

"The Three Georgia Crackers" took New York City by storm in 1930. From the top are siblings Zeke, Anne, and Judy Canova.

hillbilly comedian in history. "Evidently, I got it [comedy flair] at school. My teachers used to say, 'Judy, you are not on a vaudeville stage.'" In classic plain-Jane fashion, the goofy-looking kid learned to develop "personality." "I thought it was terrible that I didn't look like [silent-screen star] Clara Bow or Evelyn Brent. But no matter how I tried, I didn't. So one day, I got smart and not only accepted my lack of glamor, but made the most of it."

A New York sophisticate once suggested that Judy was great as a hillbilly character because she really was one. "Brother, you are making history with them true and beautiful remarks," wisecracked the well-trained professional. "We walked up here from Florida in our bare feet, subsisting on betel nuts and the bark of trees along the way. It took two traffic cops, a bouncer and a plain-clothes dick to hold me down while they got shoes on me."

By 1932 the Canovas were guesting on Rudy Vallee's NBC radio variety show. The American Record Company started issuing both authentic folk songs and vaudeville hillbilly hokum discs by the act in 1931 and 1932. In the former category were Judy and Anne's duet on "Frog Went A-Courtin'" and Judy's solo on "I Wish I Was a Single Girl Again." On "I've Been Hoo-Dooed" and "The Poor Little Thing Cried Mammy" Anne, Judy, and Zeke recall the merry style of Dalhart, Robison, and Hood. On the cornball side were such trio numbers as "Me and My Still," "The Fatal Shot," and "Snake-Eyed Killing Dude"; while "Reckless Love," "When the Sun Goes Down Behind the Hill," and "Don't Let My Mother Know" amply demonstrated the Canovas' family-harmony abilities. Most of the discs appeared on Romeo Records, the twenty-five-cent ARC label sold during the Depression by the S. H. Kress dime store chain.

In addition, a 1934 songbook from the "famous radio hill-billies Anne, Judy and Zeke" was marketed under the title *Collection of Original Songs of the Hills and Popular Old-Time Mountain Tunes.* Twenty-one of its thirty-three melodies were composed by Anne.

The Canovas hit Broadway in *Calling All Stars* with Martha Raye, which opened in late 1934. Warner Bros. Pictures financed the show, and when it closed, the family was contracted by the company for three 1935 films in Hollywood. In January of the next year Judy was signed without her siblings to appear on the Great White Way in the *Ziegfeld Follies of 1936,* where Judy did her usual hillbilly burlesque. The Canovas were, by this time, full-blown New York celebrities, and they became regulars on radio's "Rippling Rhythm Revue" (1936–1937) and "The Chase and Sanborn Hour" (1938).

Paramount offered a second film contract. Anne, Judy, and Zeke trudged west again. Two 1937 films fizzled, and the studio did not renew the Canovas' six-thousand-dollar-a-week contract. The increasingly outspoken Judy snapped, "I would have done better getting eighteen bucks a week and a good part." The team returned to vaudeville, including a two-week stand in London, and Judy kept her name in the news by staging a fake feud with ventriloquist Edgar Bergen and his dummy Charlie McCarthy. In May 1939 the Canovas took part in an NBC experiment in New York and became probably the first hillbilly act videocast on commercial television. Cousin Emmy was in a similar Philco TV experiment in Louisville around the same time.

Next the cracker comic and her siblings were signed to star in 1939's *Yokel Boy* on Broadway. Mugging, braying, yodeling, and prancing opposite Buddy Ebsen and Phil Silvers, Judy was a smash. She got solid notices and was the toast of the town. Hollywood came calling a third time, with contract offers coming from virtually all the major studios. The shrewd Judy reflected on her experiences with Warner Bros. and Paramount and opted to sign with the smaller Republic Studio, noted for its westerns with John Wayne, Gene Autry, and Roy Rogers. Republic specialized in features for the sticks and small towns of America, the places that would take Judy's bumpkin character to heart. So rather than be a lovable freak opposite big-name glamour queens and be forever consigned to specialty numbers, Judy opted to become ruler of her own rustic, B-movie kingdom.

She packed her bags and never looked back. Like millions of other displaced hillbillies of the Depression, Judy Canova migrated to the Land of Golden Opportunity—California.

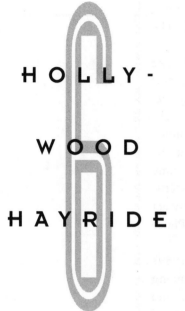

HOLLY-WOOD HAYRIDE

Country Music Women in World War II

Dale Evans, c. 1947.

L ula and Charlie Maddox sold what was left of their possessions for thirty-five dollars in 1933. Trailing five of their children, the sharecropper couple hitchhiked from the god-forsaken dirt-farm poverty of Boaz, Alabama, to the railroad yards of Meridian, Mississippi. The family of seven picked up a few pointers from the hoboes and the dispossessed to learn the tricky and sometimes dangerous art of hopping boxcars. Then they climbed aboard the first train heading west.

Mama Maddox had her heart set on a better life in California, the land of opportunity. "It was supposed to be a land of milk and honey where you could reach up and practically pick gold off the trees," recalled her daughter Rose years later. The saga of Rose Maddox, who was just six years old when she learned to ride the rails, is one of the most cinematic in country music history.

Sympathetic railroad workers hid the family from the violent "bulls" and rail-yard cops along its westward odyssey. During boxcar checks the children were sheltered by a friendly brakeman. On stopovers the Maddoxes slept in charity shelters and were aided by the Salvation Army. The jolting, rumbling, freight-train journey brought the dazed brood into the blinding sunshine of Los Angeles.

From there, the hungry, rawboned, ragtag clan climbed aboard a northbound freight to Oakland. They took shelter there at Pipe City, a community of hundreds of indigents living inside lengths of drainage culverts. "Family Roams U.S. for Work" headlined the *Oakland Tribune* on April 11, 1933, after a human interest reporter found the weary but resolute Maddox clan living in their pipe. Clinging to her California dream, Lula boarded the train with her brood one more time, to the end of the railroad line at Tuolumne, up in gold rush country in the foothills of the Sierra Nevada. But panning for gold didn't pan out.

Like thousands of other displaced tenant farmers, the Maddox family wound up in the fertile San Joaquin Valley near Modesto, working as "fruit tramps," living in tents and following the harvest seasons of local crops as migrant workers. Charlie made twelve and a half cents an hour. The kids made three cents a box for their crop harvesting. "We were classified as 'Okies,'" Rose recalls, "which was fine. That didn't bother us, because there was a lot of us all goin' through the same thing at the same time."

Lula Maddox was the "Ma Joad" of her Dust Bowl migrant family. Rose didn't have to read John Steinbeck's *The Grapes of Wrath*; she lived it. As if ten million people unemployed and 2,300 bank failures by the end of 1931 weren't enough, the spring, summer, and autumn of 1933 had been so desperately dry and hot that the earth began to blow away in dust. A black cloud whirled over Middle America, choking livestock and creating darkness at noon. Tons of topsoil blew out to sea; despairing farm families deserted the land. In northern cities they were greeted by unemployment—half couldn't get jobs. In the West they were greeted with hostility, violence, and exploitation by resentful rural residents.

Between 1935 and 1939 an estimated 350,000 Dust Bowl farmers entered the Golden State looking for a better way of life; by the fall of 1936 there were 175,000 people living in tents and shanties in the government-sponsored labor camps. They moved into only a few agricultural counties of the San Joaquin Valley, causing the population of some of the counties to grow more than 50 percent. The Okies and Arkies found work in vineyards, orchards, and truck gardens. Most were employed by one of the three thousand large-scale California operators, the foundation of today's agribusiness conglomerates. The owners formed an organization that conspired to pay the Okies starvation wages and keep them hungry for work.

Life for the Dust Bowl migrants was an endless cycle of backbreaking labor and spirit-breaking prejudice. The immigrants were spat upon by the state's natives. One movie theater in Bakersfield had a sign that read, "Negroes and Okies Upstairs." Roadblocks were set up to turn the immigrants away, and a law was passed prohibiting any person or corporation from bringing any indigent migrant into the state.

Upon their arrival, families lived in camps built along irrigation ditches where typhoid, TB, malaria, and pneumonia were endemic. As soon as picking season arrived, they were forced off the relief rolls and into the fields and orchards for twenty cents an hour, at best. An Okie made approximately $289 a year, half of what was necessary to survive. Violence against the Okies escalated in 1937 when the CIO attempted to unionize them.

Country music was one of the few pleasures of the Farm Services Administration camps, especially where cooperative self-government was emphasized. The government administrators encouraged the "quaint" music, and in 1941 the Woodville camp hosted the first folk festival of migrants.

The Maddox Brothers and Rose, c. 1948.

Both of Rose's parents were musical, but singer/mandolinist Lula Maddox was the one with the drive. Sons Cal, Fred, Henry, and Don all picked up instruments. Older brother Cliff and sister Alta, left behind in Alabama but eventually reunited with the clan in California, also had musical gifts. But little Rose became the star.

"Mama was forever sayin', 'Will you get outta here and leave me alone? I'm tired of listenin' to ya. Go sing to your daddy for a while.'" Rose was just eight when she began harmonizing with her family in the migrant labor camps at night. Fred Maddox, always the most talkative and gregarious of the Maddox children, was desperate to escape pennies-a-day peach picking. He maintained humorously, "I can't stand to work," and decided to try his salesmanship on the Rice Furniture Company in Modesto. In 1937 he and Lula talked the firm into sponsoring the family on a country music radio show. The owners' only stipulation was that the act have a female singer.

"Fred told 'em, 'We've got the greatest girl singer that's ever been.' He didn't tell 'em I was just a little kid or that all he'd ever heard me do was holler around the campfires." Ten-year-old Rose didn't even know enough songs to fill a radio program. "I just started learnin' songs as hard as I could. We all did. I was too young to be pushed into doing anything;

didn't even know anything about it. To me, it was just a job that I was supposed to do and I did it. It was pretty unusual for a woman back in those days to be doin' things like that. Very unusual; especially for a kid like me. But I always had my four big brothers to look after me. And Mama."

Using KTRB, the Modesto station, as a base, the Maddox Brothers and Rose began following rodeos from town to town, asking nearby club owners if they could set up and play for tips. Rambling folk hero Woody Guthrie and his brother Jack were on the same circuit. Rose saw them play when she was twelve and incorporated Woody's "Philadelphia Lawyer" into her act. The saga of the rich city slicker being gunned down by a cowboy became Rose's first hit and Woody's biggest country classic.

Lula and Charlie Maddox eventually divorced. She became the proverbial stage mother, as tough, outspoken, and ambitious as they come. She chaperoned her brood through central California's rough honky-tonks and dives where the desperate and down-and-out gathered to blow off steam.

"Show business was something she always wanted to do and she found out that she could do it through us kids. There was no smokin' and no drinkin'. Mama wouldn't put up with that. She would'a slapped me across the room if I'd talked back. And as far as she was concerned, there was no such thing as a man for Rose."

As part of the 1939 California State Centennial Festival, Sacramento's KFBK sponsored a talent contest. The first prize, won by the Maddoxes, was a syndicated show sponsored by Anacin that broadcast throughout California, Arizona, Oregon, and Washington. The act's popularity soared.

"But the war came along and changed a lot of things," recalls Rose. The brothers were drafted. At sixteen she married a man named E. B. Hale. "It lasted 'til I got pregnant, which was about six months. And then he was gone, into the army. He came back from the war, but not to me. That was the end of that story. . . . After the war I had a kid to raise. I *had* to work. Prior to the war we worked for tips, mostly. Then after the war we started getting paid for doing dances and stuff. So we had to change our style some, to really *entertain*. We'd play these big barns and dance halls, sittin' out in the middle of nowhere, and you'd think, 'How is anybody gonna be here?' That night, the place would be just packed to the rafters."

Lula took The Maddox Brothers and Rose to N. Turk, the North Hollywood tailor who outfitted movie cowboys. He designed more than a dozen sets of eye-popping band costumes for the Maddoxes, all resplendent with satin sleeves, long fringes, colorful embroidered patterns, spangled trim, elaborately tooled boots, and flowing kerchiefs. In them, the group lifted country costuming to a new level. Its fabulously gaudy, flower-encrusted cowboy/Mexican outfits of the 1940s defined the country music look for a generation to come. The onstage behavior was equally showy as the siblings incorporated shrieking comedy routines, loud honky-tonk wailing, hepped-up hillbilly versions of rhythm and blues tunes, close-harmony gospel show stoppers, uproariously zany ad-libbing, sound effects, and cackling laughter into their performances. They traveled in a fleet of five matching, gleaming black Cadillacs. They were flashier than anything seen in country music, before or since.

Before long, the five spangled crazies were billed as "The Most Colorful Hillbilly Band in the Land." In years to come Rose Maddox would be hailed as a key figure in the development of both honky-tonk and rockabilly, would bring superstar Buck Owens to fame as her duet partner, and would be revered by such female successors as Dolly Parton and Emmylou Harris. But at the dawn of World War II she was a sassy teenager with flashing eyes and a brassy voice blaring the suggestive "Sally Let Your Bangs Hang Down" at the center of the gang of howling wiseguys in rowdy West Coast bars. Rose's whoop-it-up delivery was the perfect soundtrack for the restless country folks on the loose in the Golden State. They wanted pizzazz, and she had it.

Just as Atlanta had served as country's cradle in the 1920s and Chicago had taken it through childhood in the 1930s, Los Angeles became country's adult mecca of the 1940s. During World War II the city became host to tens of thousands of blue-collar defense plant workers; 1943 was like the second gold rush to California, with the population growing 10 percent in that year alone. Shipbuilding employed 300,000, and the number of aircraft factory workers grew from 1,000 to 280,300 between 1940 and 1943. The state's employed grew by 1,150,000, and its population swelled from 7 million in 1940 to over 9 million by 1945.

California had first attracted a huge number of rural Americans when its petroleum, agricultural, and auto industries were booming in the 1920s. They brought their dreams of owning a small farm with them. And they brought country music.

California country's female pioneers were in such acts as Uncle Pete and Louise (Collins), Mirandy, Bea Rhodes, and The Crockett Family, all active in the late 1920s and early 1930s.

California's emerging country culture was soon featured in the state's most famous export, movies. By 1935 every American town with ten thousand people or more had at least two movie houses. Double bills were popular and were changed three times each week. Film production soared to meet the demand. The major studios developed B-movie departments, and new independent companies like Republic, Mascot,

Grand National, and Columbia cranked out low-budget films to fill the bills. Singing-cowboy westerns rose to wide popularity in the thirties and became even bigger in the forties. Hillbilly musicals rode in on the coattails of this B-movie cowboy craze. Big-city critics sneered at the features geared for small-town specialty markets, but many of these films were big-grossing studio money makers.

Prior to the 1940s only a handful of country music women were captured on film. Harmonica-playing Virginian Cordelia Mayberry led her Blue Ridgers band in a Warner/Vitaphone short of 1929. Two years later Otto and Mommie Gray were signed to make six shorts for Film Exchange in New York. After Gene Autry led the singing cowboy charge in 1935, the way was paved for dozens of other country acts to cavort for the cameras. Mirandy (Marjorie Bauersfeld, 1890–1974) parlayed L.A. radio stardom into roles in the movies *Mountain Music* (Universal, 1937) and *Comin' Round the Mountain* (Paramount, 1940).

No other career better illustrates the transition between small-time hillbilly entertainment and the modern country music industry than Judy Canova's. In 1928 she was part of a regional southern musical family act. By 1936 she was a star of the New York stage. By 1940 she'd mugged her way into Hollywood, and by 1955 she was a millionaire. Already a New York radio star, a hillbilly recording artist, the toast of Broadway as a rube thespian, and the marketer of a successful country songbook, the tenacious and ambitious comic became the queen of Republic Studios during the war. Judy Canova's humor was broad; she overacted; her plots were simple; her rubber-faced shenanigans were outrageous. And she was absolutely lovable.

Judy, then twenty-four, became a Hollywood heroine with *Scatterbrain* (1940), the first in a fifteen-year string of features dedicated to the proposition that guileless country honesty and simplicity will triumph over sophisticated urban duplicity and corruption every time. The formula worked. As one show-biz scribe put it, Judy Canova became "the Beatrice Lillie of Marked Tree, Arkansas . . . the Fanny Brice of Pawhuska, Oklahoma . . . the Lily Pons of Tucumcari, New Mexico," and "the Duse of the sticks, the Bernhardt of the canebrakes." Her Republic films of the 1940s made her the studio's top money-making female. Only the westerns of Gene Autry, John Wayne, and Roy Rogers were more popular than her hokum comedies.

Movie stardom led to her own national radio show. Her weekly listening audience swelled to more than eighteen million. "The Judy Canova Show" ranked among America's ten most popular radio programs of the mid-1940s. By 1946 she was getting 250,000 fan letters a week and mailing out more than 150,000 publicity photos. At a time when most country acts were working for peanuts, Judy formed her own production company and negotiated percentages of her movies' and radio shows' profits.

"Sure, they were fairy tales that had a little upbeat lesson," she said of her films. "I started out as a plain Jane, an ugly duckling, and ended up as a beautiful girl decked out in fancy dresses. I was the . . . country bumpkin, honest and straightforward, who won out in the end."

Several of Judy's movie plots were about country gals dealing with World War II. In *Joan of Ozark* (1942) her rustic character shoots down a carrier pigeon carrying a Nazi-spy message and becomes a nationwide heroine. Her comedic bungling and lovable pluck eventually result in the capture of the spies and the destruction of a Japanese sub in U.S. waters. In between slapstick action sequences Judy sings "The Lady at Lockheed," "Backwoods Barbecue," and "Wabash Blues." In *True to the Army* (1942) she impersonates a GI at Fort Bragg. She battled gangsters in *Sleepytime Gal* (1942); in the course of the filming she was required to fall off a fire escape, be frozen in a refrigerator, eat five cream puffs filled with soap, take a dozen spills during a dance sequence, be walked on as a rug, and get knocked over by a line of waiters. Said Judy during these darkest days of World War II,

Judy Canova, 1955.

"The world today needs a laugh. If a couple of broken bones and flock of bruises will give it to them—well, here we go." In *Sleepy Lagoon* (1943) Judy is elected town mayor by the women's reform party. Her platform is to close down the saloons and build an amusement park to offer good, clean fun to the defense workers who've come to Sleepy Lagoon to help the war effort.

Throughout 1943 she toured army camps and embarked on war bond selling trips. During her World War II radio broadcasts she dropped her traditional closing number, "Go to Sleep Little Baby," in favor of the moving "Good Night, Soldier." Like millions of other women, Judy found her life turned upside down during the war years. She made headlines in 1941 when she married army corporal James H. Ripley while on vacation in Hawaii. That same night he was arrested by military police and jailed for being AWOL. At first she denied the marriage; then she decided to deal with it using hillbilly humor. "I don't know what hit me on the head the hardest, that uniform of Ripley or that soft

Hawaiian moon," she said. "Anyhow, we upped and got married, and now my poor groom is in the jailhouse." Back home in Los Angeles she got an annulment, stating that he had "deceived me and told me lies; his being a soldier didn't have anything to do with it."

Judy never found lasting love. She was married to Chester B. England from 1943 to 1950. Their daughter, Julietta, appeared in several Judy Canova movies. Her third marriage was her stormiest, a 1950–1964 union with Cuban musician Philip Rivero. Their daughter, Diana Canova, became a TV comedian of the 1980s in such shows as "Soap," "I'm a Big Girl Now," "Foot in the Door," and the music-business comedy series "Throb."

Republic studio boss Herbert Yates reportedly took a more than personal interest in his biggest box office female. When Judy rebuffed the boss's advances, he cut her film production budgets. She retaliated by becoming a fierce negotiator, demanding—and getting—script, cast, and director approval. She also became co-owner of her features.

"I hate to say it, but it's a dog-eat-dog business, the toughest in the world," Judy said in a 1980 *TV Guide* interview. "They used to call me the toughest woman in Hollywood to drive a deal with," she added with pride.

But constant conflict and studio battles took their toll on her films; they are wildly uneven. Her earliest efforts got the best reviews and made the most money. In *Scatterbrain* she was a hillbilly singer who is transformed into a glamorous movie starlet. Next, Republic dusted off the old Rose Melville play *Sis Hopkins* as a 1941 Judy feature. Originally filmed as a Mabel Normand silent, the movie was updated with Judy as the bumpkin cousin of snobbish Susan Hayward, then a movie newcomer. Judy's talent upstages Hayward's in the college musical so the snob tricks the innocent into appearing in an embarrassing burlesque show. The underdog eventually wins out, of course, giving the hepcats a lesson in plain farmer values. *Sis Hopkins* is one of Judy's most impressive vocal showcases, including everything from opera excerpts to "Cracker Barrel County." The movie also introduced her trademark expression "You're telling I." Budgeted at $750,000, it cost more than ten Gene Autry Republic pictures put together.

At the end of 1941 the barnyard bumpkin beat Rita Hayworth, Joan Crawford, and James Stewart in the movie fan popularity polls. Her CBS radio show was launched in 1943, and she became an even bigger success over NBC beginning in 1945. Soon Judy's gags were standard "filler" items in newspapers.

Chatterbox (1943) and *Singin' in the Corn* (1946) had comedic western plots. In *Oklahoma Annie* (1952) gun-toting sheriff's deputy Judy, billed as "Queen of the Cowgirls," rids her town of crooked gamblers. Along the way she warbles tunes including "Billy Boy," "Have You Ever Been Lonely," and "Oh Dear What Can the Matter Be." By this time she was in constant dismay over her chintzy plots and low budgets. Judy's great ambition was to play the lead in the movie version of the 1946 Annie Oakley musical *Annie Get Your Gun.* Despite her hard Hollywood campaigning, MGM bought the show for Judy Garland, and when Garland was too ill to film, Betty Hutton got the part.

Consigned to B-movie purgatory, Judy Canova was apprised by a snippy columnist that she had been voted by magazine readers as "the corniest actress in the movies." Retorted the pride of the farm folks, "I'm deeply flattered to be called an actress."

During her lifetime few ever pointed out that Judy Canova was also a gifted singer. Although most of her recording was done back east in the 1930s, when she was at her most "country," Judy's California years are dotted with fine studio performances. During the war she waxed patriotic fare such as "Stars and Stripes on Iwo Jima Isle," "Good Night, Soldier," and "A Tiny Little Voice and a Tiny Little Prayer." In the immediate postwar era Judy Canova issued her masterpiece, a 1947 disc that coupled "No Letter Today" and "Never Trust a Man." On the former she engages in vocal pyrotechnics including yodeling, jazz phrasing, and leaping octaves. The hillbilly-jazzy "Never Trust a Man" is delivered in hilarious, listen-sisters-take-my-advice asides: "Never, never trust a man / He'll try to fool you if he can / If you're thinkin' of a wedding, gal, you better change your plan."

Judy's unique blend of jazz phrasing and country yodeling was also displayed on her lone record album, released in 1958. Backed by the sizzling steel guitar riffs of Speedy West and the scampering fiddle notes of Harold Hensley, she was particularly gymnastic as a vocalist on "Just Because," "Wabash Blues," and the infectious "Blow the Whistle."

Radio, not records, was Judy's primary medium. At her peak in the late 1940s she made $8,500 per weekly show. Its skits and gags were the prototypes of such later TV series as "The Beverly Hillbillies," "Petticoat Junction," "Green Acres," and "Hee Haw." Despite ruling the radio airwaves until 1953, Judy failed to make the transition to television. Her slapstick abilities should have made her a rustic rival to Lucille Ball, but Judy's series pilots for "Li'l Abner" (1967) and "The Murdocks and the McClays" (1970) found no network buyers. Her last starring feature was in 1955, and thereafter she made cameo appearances in such films as *Huckleberry Finn* (1960) and *Cannonball* (1976). She did several commercials, took dramatic roles in TV series, and guest-starred on variety shows.

On "The Colgate Comedy Hour" in 1952 she costarred with Zsa Zsa

Gabor in a train skit that involved the two fighting over a Pullman berth. Gabor, in a frilly negligee, brags that her perfume is "Spring Night in Venice." Judy, in a flannel nightgown, informs her bunkmate that she is wearing "Hot Night on a Chicken Farm."

When job offers for her canyon-mouthed hayseed characters got fewer, she retired to her San Fernando Valley mansion, emerging for occasional parts. Judy died of cancer in 1983 at age sixty-six.

Judy wasn't Republic's only lady with country appeal. Those popular vaudeville veterans The Weaver Brothers and Elviry landed in thirteen Hollywood features. In Elviry's movies, like Judy Canova's, the message was that simple, decent rural folk could always triumph over slick, sophisticated urban deceit.

Elviry Weaver was certainly the woman for the job. In *The Old Homestead* (1940) small-town mayor Elviry battles big-town gangsters. In *Mountain Rhythm* (1943) Elviry and her cohorts did their bit for the war effort by buying a California farm away from the Japanese and tilling the soil for victory. Faced with prejudice from snobs at a nearby boys' school, they convert the students to manual war work and expose the headmaster as an enemy agent. Her irascible character was given top billing in *Grand Ole Opry*, the 1940 feature that introduced such Nashville radio barn dance stars as Roy Acuff and Uncle Dave Macon to movie audiences. Up-and-coming singing cowboy Roy Rogers had supporting parts in the Weaver films *Jeepers Creepers* (1939) and *Arkansas Judge* (1940); the trouper introduced future headliner Alan Ladd in 1940's *In Old Missouri*.

The notoriously cheesy Republic scripts and budgets irritated Elviry. The act abruptly quit Hollywood in 1944 with her curt explanation, "We play 'A' houses and these are 'B' movies." The Weavers reappeared briefly on the dying vaudeville circuit in 1950 and declined offers to appear on TV before retiring gracefully.

The country-star vehicles of Elviry Weaver, Judy Canova, and their cinema sisters were part of a big boom in "pix for the sticks" of the 1940s. The domestic, folksy humor of Fibber McGee and his droll Molly was translated from radio to the silver screen in four pictures made between 1937 and 1944. Marjorie Main (Mary Tomlinson, 1890–1975) created her most memorable role when she introduced Ma Kettle in the 1947 Claudette Colbert movie *The Egg and I*. Ma/Marjorie's crow-voiced yokel delivery, sassy lines, and crusty demeanor won her an Oscar nomination. After graduating to hayseed stardom in 1948's *Feudin', Fussin' and A-Fightin',* the rambunctious, headstrong, raucous rural matriarch, her hesitant Pa, and their brood of a dozen country kids were given their own seven-film series from 1949 to 1953. Then Ma continued for two more features alone. When the series ended in 1957, Marjorie Main retired.

"National Barn Dance" radio stars Lulu Belle and Scotty made the pilgrimage to Hollywood for a series of eight films between 1938 and 1943. They got their best notices for *Swing Your Partner* (1942), wherein we find top-billed Lulu Belle working in a cheese factory. The millionairess owner decides to go incognito as a worker to find out what the lives of Lulu Belle, The Dinning Sisters, and the other proletarians are like. As a result she softens and becomes kinder to the workers. Dale Evans, third-billed as the owner's secretary, "looks like a film comer," said *Daily Variety*.

"You ain't missed a thing if you ain't seen those films," wisecracked Lulu Belle of her cinematic efforts. But of Paramount's *National Barn Dance* (1944), *The Hollywood Reporter* said, "It is quite the best picture of its kind yet made. . . . All the entertainers are tops, but special commendation is due The Dinning Sisters, an engaging trio of vocalists who not only can give out with the hot stuff, but are exceptional in 'sweet' numbers."

The trio that stood out in *Swing Your Partner* and *National Barn Dance* was composed of identical twins Jean (Eugenia) and Ginger (Virginia) Dinning (born 1924) and their older sister Lou (Lucille, born 1920). There were nine children in the Dinning farmhouse, and the struggling family moved to Kentucky, Kansas, and Oklahoma during the 1920s and 1930s. As teenagers in Enid, Oklahoma, the three girls with perfect pitch got their own radio show. In 1939 they moved to Chicago, following in the footsteps of older sister Marvis, by then a singer with the Freddy Owen Orchestra.

The Dinning Sisters starred on "The National Barn Dance" from 1941 through 1945 as "The Sweethearts of Sunbonnet Swing." Their style was that of a homier Andrews Sisters. Unlike the brassier and more popular trio, the Dinnings seduced the ears with soft, glowing, muted-trumpet harmonies and a gentle, shoulder-shaking rhythmic sense. The Dinnings became NBC radio regulars and graduated to their own "Dinning Sisters Show" as "The Loreleis of the Airwaves" before heading for Hollywood for cameo work in six war-era features. Their largest acting roles were in 1946's *That Texas Jamboree*. The Dinnings did soundtrack work in Disney animated shorts. They also made Soundies, two in 1942 and eight more between 1945 and 1946. These were musical film clips, the ancestors of today's music videos, that were shown on visual jukeboxes in clubs and bars of the mid-1940s.

More than two thousand Soundies were produced between 1940 and 1947, preserving the performances of urban blues acts, swing orchestras, supper club stylists, singing cowboys, and a wide variety of other entertainers. By 1941 some 4,500 Panoram machines were in use in U.S. cafés and bars. Each had a small screen with a sixteen-millimeter projector inside that was activated by a dime.

The Dinnings did film shorts for the Soundie and Snader Telescription companies. Besides being superb singers, twins Jean and Ginger were drop-dead gorgeous on screen. That alone should have encouraged a Hollywood buildup, but despite many people's fondness for their country-leaning style, the girls were never as big as the swinging Andrews trio. "Let's face it—The Andrews Sisters were way ahead of us," Lou recalled in an *Esquire* article. "We tried our darnedest to be as commercial as they were, but we weren't flashy enough. We were all kind of shy. We came from a farm in Oklahoma. We never took dancing lessons or anything."

After signing with Hollywood's infant Capitol Records label in 1945, The Dinning Sisters made musical history as the first act to debut on disc in the then-new long-playing record album format. The trio hit the Top 10 with a delightfully jazzed-up version of Louise Massey's "My Adobe Hacienda" in 1947, and in 1948 scored a million-selling smash with the bucolic "Buttons and Bows." There were a string of sweetly scampering vocal workouts on Capitol, including the zany, tongue-twisting "Iggedy Song" (1946), the merry "Bride and Groom Polka" (1948), and the toe-tapping "Oh Monah" (1949).

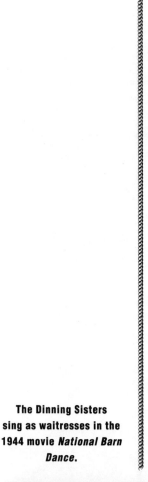

The Dinning Sisters sing as waitresses in the 1944 movie *National Barn Dance*.

Always the least aggressive of the sisters, alto Lou quit the act in 1946 after marrying star songwriter Don Robertson ("Please Help Me I'm Falling," "I Really Don't Want to Know," "I Don't Hurt Anymore," etc.). "She helped him with a lot of the numbers," says Jean. "She didn't get any credit, but she wrote. . . . When they got a divorce, the judge could see that the rise in his career had happened after their marriage. So he gave her almost 50 percent of everything that was written, in spite of the fact that her name wasn't on it." Her spot in the trio was first taken by Jayne Bundesen from 1946 to 1949, then by youngest sister Delores Dinning.

Little sister Delores became a successful Nashville studio singer, appearing weekly in the Nashville Edition vocal backup group on TV's "Hee Haw". In the mid-1950s soprano Jean became a successful songwriter, penning the giant 1960 pop hit "Teen Angel" for baby brother Mark Dinning and the 1977 Christmas duet "Fall

Softly Snow" for country stars Jim Ed Brown and Helen Cornelius.

The B-movie boom of the 1940s attracted several other country music women as supporting players, among them Cousin Emmy, Louisiana Lou, The Sunshine Girls, Louise Massey, Kitty Wilson, Sarie and Sallie, Laura Lee McBride, Patsy Montana, and Radio Dot (Dorothy Marie Henderson Swan, 1916–1972). None was more prolific than yodeling Carolina Cotton. Although never a top-billed star, the curvaceous Carolina popped up in the casts of more than a dozen features of the era.

A petite, blue-eyed blonde with a vivacious personality, Carolina was the definition of sunshine. Born Helen Hagstrom Braunsdorf in Arkansas in 1926, Carolina grew up in San Francisco. She began singing there in a western swing band at age fourteen. In 1942 she arrived in Hollywood and caught the eye of western swing bandleader Spade Cooley, who instantly hired the sixteen-year-old as a vocalist. Her scintillating stage presence and brilliantly showy yodeling style also made her a favorite

Carolina Cotton, c. 1950.

with western swinger Deuce Spriggins, to whom she was married for three months in 1945. She divorced him in 1946, stating that he had affairs with others during their brief union. The blond bombshell hit the screen in 1944 through 1954 in a string of films that featured such top stars as Eddy Arnold, Gene Autry, Roy Acuff, and Bob Wills. She was also country music's most prolific female maker of Soundies for the visual jukeboxes of the mid-1940s.

She wrote her biggest hit record, "Three Miles South of Cash in Arkansas," and recorded it in 1951 for MGM with Bob Wills and his Texas Playboys. But her finest vocals were captured on the silvery yodel showcases "I Love to Yodel" and "Mockingbird Yodel," issued on King Records in 1949.

Carolina was one of several singing cowgirls Republic Studios chose to costar alongside Gene Autry and Roy Rogers. Arkansas native Gail Davis (b. 1925)—TV's "Annie Oakley" of 1953 through 1956 and a Columbia Records act with "Tomboy"/"I'm a Female Through and Through"—costarred with Roy Rogers, Monte Hale, and Ray Whitley in the 1940s. The pert, green-eyed, strawberry blond sparkler caught Gene Autry's eye in 1950; he starred her in a dozen of his films, featured her on many episodes of his TV show, toured with her in his musical act, and produced her TV series. Gail was a fine rider with a dead-eye aim and an appealing, spunky, pistols-and-pigtails image that could have made her a major singing cowgirl if only she'd been blessed with a better voice.

Republic's B-movie neighbor, Grand National Pictures, built up the independent and spirited Dorothy Page with three 1939 features, *Singing Cowgirl, Water Rustlers,* and *Ride 'Em, Cowgirl.* But the studio went bankrupt before Dorothy could develop into the female equivalent of Autry or Rogers. Instead Republic's Dale Evans was crowned "Queen of the West."

Chipper, plainspoken Dale was the right personality in the right place at the right time. Many western movie heroines of the 1940s mirrored the "Rosie the Riveter" era by being self-reliant personalities. The singing cowgirl, as exemplified by Dale Evans, was a blend of tough and tender. She had a no-nonsense manner. She could shoot and ride. Dale's characters had minds of their own. They had chin-up vitality and spunk. Dale's hard-headed quality endeared her to the masses. She had her own line of comic books, kiddie novels, and paraphernalia. She was a role model for millions of little girls of the 1940s and 1950s who grew up wearing fringed Dale Evans outfits and toting cap guns like their brothers'.

As she was the first to confess in a series of candid Christian books, Dale was far from a role model when she was climbing the show-business ladder. Born on Halloween in 1912 to a farmer/hardware store owner in Uvalde, Texas, Frances Octavia Smith moved with her family to Osceola, Arkansas, at age seven. Her mother was fiercely religious, but Dale was a willful and headstrong daughter.

"As a small child, my mother says, I was quite vain and pirouetted in front of a mirror when someone gave me new clothes," Dale recalled in her 1971 book, *My Personal Picture Album.* "I also was ready to pose for the camera. . . . Having already been taught the basics of reading, writing and math by my mother, I entered school at age 7. After half a year in the first grade, I was advanced all the way to the third. I would later also skip the seventh, thus arriving at the eighth grade at the ripe age of 11. And I promptly had a nervous breakdown. . . . I had pushed myself too hard. I was, Mother would remind me years later, a child who never went about any activity at a normal speed. For me it was full throttle or not at all.

"Boys fascinated me. . . . I felt that I was fully capable of coping with the opposite sex. When my parents tried to divert my interest, to prolong my enjoyment of childhood until I was a little more mature, I was resentful and began to strain at the leash. . . . I grew up fast."

Lying about her age, she married a man named Tom Fox when she was fourteen. During the first six months of their marriage he left her twice. After she bore son Tommy at age fifteen, Fox deserted her for good, leaving a letter saying he was too young to be tied down to a wife and kid. "Totally disillusioned, I struck out in all directions, literally daring anyone to knock the sizable chip off my shoulder. . . . I declared independence against the world."

Determined to raise her baby, rather than taking her mother's offer to raise him, Dale enrolled in a Memphis business school and took a job as an insurance secretary. Her boss heard her singing in the office and offered to put her on a local radio program the company sponsored. Frances Fox made her debut on the airwaves with songwriter Ethelbert Nevin's 1901 melody "Mighty Lak a Rose." In time the singer would follow in Nevin's footsteps as a major female composer. Armed with some early songwriting efforts, Dale headed north to Chicago in 1934.

Dale Evans, c. 1945.

"And proceeded to very nearly starve to death. . . . [I] still remember watching large groups of down and defeated men, victims of the Depression, standing in soup lines in Chicago and sleeping beneath old newspapers on the cold cement sidewalks along Wacker Drive. . . . For almost two years I beat my head against that wall—still stubborn, still ambitious to a fault, still holding my grudge against the world like a shield."

Suffering from acute malnutrition, she swallowed her pride and wired home for money. After recuperating with her folks in Texas, she took little Tommy and struck out for Louisville and WHAS. There she was christened Dale Evans as she repopularized Nora Bayes's vaudeville standard "Shine On Harvest Moon." Dale first rose to fame at WFAA in Dallas, becoming a *Rural Radio* magazine cover girl in 1938. She married pianist Robert Dale Butts in 1939, and they both landed good jobs in Chicago, she as the lead vocalist with the Anson Weeks Orchestra. Dale composed the leap year ditty "Will You Marry Me, Mr. Laramie?" and it made her the toast of the swank Chez Paree. She starred on daily radio as "That Gal from Texas."

"My greatest goal was to make a name for myself in show business," Dale recalled many years later. "I felt I *had* to make a lot of money. . . . I was torn between my desire to be a good housekeeper, wife, and mother, and my consuming ambition as an entertainer. It was like trying to ride two horses at once, and I couldn't seem to control either one of them."

A Hollywood agent heard her on the radio and offered her a screen test. Paramount was looking for a new face to star opposite Bing Crosby and Fred Astaire in *Holiday Inn.* Tinsel Town moguls tinted Dale's hair, capped her teeth, changed her makeup, lied about her age, had her lose twelve pounds, and told her to refer to thirteen-year-old Tommy as her brother. But despite the best efforts of an elocution teacher, they couldn't eradicate her Texas twang. She also couldn't dance. Marjorie Reynolds, with a singing voice dubbed by Martha Mears, got the part in the movie blockbuster that introduced "White Christmas." Dale went to bit-part purgatory at 20th Century Fox.

Her cinema pickings were slim, but the plucky singer stayed busy. Following the outbreak of World War II she threw herself into wartime morale-building and sang at more than six hundred USO shows in full cowgirl regalia. Republic Pictures picked up her movie contract in 1942. Her big break was in *Swing Your Partner,* starring the popular "National Barn Dance" radio team Lulu Belle and Scotty. During the next year she appeared in nine more low-budget musicals, including *Hoosier Holiday* and *Here Comes Elmer.* Opposite John Wayne she sang "Put Your Arms Around Me Honey" in 1943's *In Old Oklahoma.* In 1944 Republic boss Herb Yates attended a performance of the smash hit musical *Oklahoma!* and decided that his Roy Rogers features needed to be snazzed up with a female singer at once.

"His was not the most exciting proposal I'd ever heard," Dale groused. "B-westerns were directly opposite from the way I wanted my career to go. . . . 'Mr. Yates,' I said, 'are you sure you want me?' . . . He was sure. 'Rehearsals for *The Cowboy and the Senorita* will begin next week,' he said. 'You're the senorita.' Period." The team clicked. Roy and Dale were teamed in three more features before the year was out. By 1947 Republic had them in nineteen films.

"I usually played a reporter [as in 1946's *Home in Oklahoma*], or some other kind of smart-alecky girl. I think the fans enjoyed watching me because they liked to hate me. . . . Before I realized what was happening . . . I was being typecast as a western player." Dale Evans began receiving more fan mail than she'd ever gotten in her career and in 1947 became the first and only woman ever ranked in the Top 10 in the movie cowboy popularity polls.

"It began to occur to me that there were far worse fates than working with Roy Rogers on a daily basis." Like everyone else who ever worked with him, Dale fell under Roy's spell. His genuine humility, sensitivity to children, decency, honesty, and gentle, easygoing personality were a marked contrast to her brassy, pushy manner. Roy was a devoted family man with two daughters when his son, Dusty, was born in 1946; two days later his wife Arlene died suddenly of a blood clot. He was shattered.

Roy and Dale drew closer during the following year as they filmed and did promotional tours together. After years of living separate lives, she and Butts were divorced in 1945. The King of the Cowboys and the Queen of the West were married on New Year's Eve 1947. Fans were ecstatic. Dale quit smoking to improve her image with her stepchildren and threw herself into motherhood with the same zeal she'd devoted to her career. Her own mother's fundamentalist teachings, the prompting of son Tommy, and a particularly vivid Sunday sermon sent Dale back to religion. She bought Roy a Bible and urged him to join her as a born-again Christian. He did.

Their daughter Robin was born with Down's syndrome in 1949. She died two years later, and Dale dealt with her sorrow by writing the best-seller *Angel Unaware*. Proceeds went to the National Association for Retarded Persons, and the book became the first of twenty-five inspirational Dale Evans volumes. Roy and Dale adopted a Choctaw Indian daughter, a battered baby boy, a girl with Down's syndrome, and a Korean orphan, and became foster parents to a Scottish waif. A series of tragedies such as daughter Debbie's death in a bus accident and son Sandy's accidental alcohol poisoning in the army deepened their religious convictions. They became associated with the popular preachers Billy Graham and Norman Vincent Peale.

Roy and Dale became national radio costars in 1948. After twenty-eight films together they left Republic in 1951. Their TV series of 1951 through 1964 featured Dale as the owner of the Eureka Cafe in mythical Mineral City. But each episode she would saddle up Buttermilk to help Roy and Trigger, wonder dog Bullet, and Pat Brady with his jeep Nellybelle solve crimes and right wrongs. The husband and wife became wildly successful on the rodeo circuit and branched out into gospel music.

On her gospel records Dale revived such female religious standards as Fanny Crosby's "Near the Cross" and "Pass Me Not," Anna and Susan Warner's "Jesus Loves Me," and Catherine Hankey's "I Love to Tell the Story." But Dale Evans will be best remembered as a composer in her own right. Her country and gospel classics include "Aha San Antone," "My Heart Went That-a-Way," "I Wish I Had Never Met Sunshine," "The Bible Tells Me So," and her immortal "Happy Trails" TV show theme song.

Dale belongs to country music's first wave of female professional songwriters, a group that also includes Cindy Walker and Jenny Lou Carson. All of them came to prominence during the 1940s.

During World War II doors were opened to women in dozens of occupations that had been dominated by males. Women were encouraged by government posters, magazine ads, and radio shows to leave the home, do their patriotic duty, and contribute to the war effort by working. "If you've sewed on buttons, or made button holes, on a machine, you can learn to do spot welding on airplane parts," read one billboard. "If you've used an electric mixer in your kitchen, you can learn to run a drill press. If you've followed recipes exactly in making cakes, you can learn to load shell."

In the absence of men, women became fire fighters, train conductors, miners, pilots, lumberjacks, professors, and scientists. Many states allowed them to sit on juries for the first time during this decade. In 1945 the Boston Symphony hired its first female musician. The number of women elected as state legislators increased from 144 in 1941 to 228 in 1945. Women grew from 25 percent of the overall labor force to 36 percent during World War II. In addition, the proportion of married women working grew from 15 percent to 25 percent. This was the first time in U.S. history that the "single girl" in the factory was no longer the norm. Half of all women workers were now thirty-five years old or older.

A third of working women were in factories during the war. Those who entered the defense plants became known collectively as "Rosie the Riveter." Overall, more than 500,000 "Rosies" were enlisted in building bombers and planes, wielding riveting machines, and driving cranes while garbed in overalls.

The still-young country music business, previously noted for its religious-leaning family groups and chaperoned women, developed its first female radio DJs, songwriters, movie headliners, bandleaders, managers, and independent solo stars during the 1940s. The era's female country DJs included West Virginians Millie Wayne, Bonnie Baldwin, and Cherokee Sue, as well as New York City's Rosalie Allen and Esmereldy. During the war a woman named Gerry Rice became the emcee of the popular Herrington Sisters radio show from Texas. Marge Engler produced the radio barn dance in Toledo, Ohio. "Miss Maudie" Shreffler produced, directed, and played piano for "Kansas Round-Up Time" in Topeka. In Pittsburg, Kansas, Lois Shook took charge of the "Town Talk Bread Program." Bess Farmer became the musical director of the "Renfro Valley Barn Dance."

The shortage of men opened up some starring slots on radio for country music women. Among the headliners who emerged during the war were "Lucky Penny" West (Delois Jane Maxedon), Minnie Pearl (Sarah Ophelia Colley), Linda Lou Martin (Wanda Frances Arnold), Little Texas Daisy (Rhodes), Mary Ann Estes, Nancy Lee, and Judy Dell. Numerous country bands of the era were led by women, and it was women who took country to the city during the war years. The Kendall Sisters, Dolly and Polly, were the most popular radio act in Cleveland. Philadelphia's country queen was Kitty O'Brien. Viola, Bella, and Yvonne, The Moore Sisters, delighted audiences with "Boogie Woogie Cowboy" over WOR in New York City. The "Jersey Jamboree" in Trenton starred Prairie Maid Norma.

Show promotion, booking, song publishing, and radio engineering also admitted women. During World War II Margaret Lowe was the station engineer at the mighty, fifty-thousand-watt WWVA in Wheeling, West Virginia. Barbara Bennett became the manager of the popular late-1940s West Coast stars Carolina Cotton, Hank Penny, and Spade Cooley. By the end of the decade there were two female-owned country labels, Lois Nettles's Red Bird Records and Macey Henry's Macey Records. Women launched country music journalism as the first wave of hillbilly fan magazines developed. They became the main writers in such pioneering country periodicals as *Rural Radio* (1938–1939), *The Mountain Broadcast and Prairie Recorder* (1939–1947), *The Jamboree* (1940–1942), *Cowboy Music World* (1944), *National Hill-Billy News* (1945–1950), *Tophand* (1946), *Record Roundup* (1946–1949), *Song and Picture Barn Dance* (1947–1948), and *National Jamboree* (1949).

Songwriting was the biggest growth profession for country music women of the 1940s. Pearl Clark entered professional songwriting in 1943 and 1944 with "We're One Day Nearer to Victory," "We'll Have a Rodeo in Tokyo," and "Shoot a Dime for Victory." Likewise, Texan Kahl RaFaun contributed "Uncle Sammy Needs Your Dough" and "Blackout in My Heart." The "Down Hoosier Way" theme song of Fort Wayne, Indiana's, "Hoosier Hop" radio barn dance of the forties was written by the distaff team of Eleanor Smythe and Ruth Franks. Edith Berbert used the name "Ed Burt" on the 1945 Bob Wills hit "Silver Dew on the Bluegrass Tonight": "When I took the song to my publisher, he advised me to use a pseudonym because ordinarily women don't get very far," she recalled.

In its earliest days the hillbilly music field had just one female songwriter of consequence. That was Elsie McWilliams (1897–1985). She was Jimmie Rodgers's sister-in-law and was the source of many of his

After 1930s "National Barn Dance" stardom, Lucille Overstake reinvented herself as cowgirl Jenny Lou Carson, the star of her own 1944 songbook publication.

most famous songs. Elsie had a hand in more than a third of the Singing Brakeman's 110-song recorded repertoire, including such favorites as "Daddy and Home," "You and My Old Guitar," "My Rough and Rowdy Ways," "Never No Mo' Blues," and "Waiting for a Train." She also helped Rodgers compose many of his famous "blue yodels," but refused to have her name put on that type of song. "I've always been mighty straight laced," said Elsie, though she plunked the piano in Rodgers's dance bands and for silent movies.

"I said, 'Jimmie, I can't write any songs.' He says, 'Well, I know you can: You write plays and poems and things for children . . . to sing in church . . . and you play and you make up songs all the time on the piano. So I know you can do it, so just do it.' And so I wrote a few. . . . Sometimes . . . my name's not on there at all ["Waiting for a Train," for instance], but . . . that's the way it went. . . . I told Jimmie when I was writing them, 'No, don't put my name on them. You're the inspiration of them, and you change them anywhere you want to. . . . I'm just trying to help you make a living for my sister and the baby.' I didn't care anything about the fame or the money, either, at that time. . . . I was more busy with my children; they were growing up; they needed me. And that's all I've ever been, is just a homebody." In later years "Miss Elsie" became the warmhearted hostess in Meridian, Mississippi, at the annual Jimmie Rodgers Days celebrations. Her piano now rests in the Jimmie Rodgers Museum there, and in 1979 she was inducted into the Nashville Songwriters Hall of Fame.

In the 1930s Lucille Overstake provided The Girls of the Golden West with their most popular numbers. But her blossoming as a songwriter came in the 1940s as Jenny Lou Carson. Her affair with songwriting great Fred Rose and her marriage from 1946 to 1949 to bandleader Tiny Hill probably helped her achieve the new heights of her huge hits "Jealous Heart," "Don't Rob Another Man's Castle," and "Let Me Go, Lover." Jenny Lou often wrote specifically from the woman's point of view, notably in the late-forties songs "Your Key Don't Fit My Lock Anymore," "I'll Never Trust You Again," and "I Wasn't Born Yesterday."

Jenny Lou was one of the most prolific composers of World War II material, contributing "Dear God, Watch Over Joe," "May God Be with

You Sailor Boy," and "When the Boys Come Marching Home" to the war-morale musical trend of 1943. For "adopting" wounded war heroes and tirelessly corresponding with servicemen, she was dubbed "The Radio Chin-Up Girl."

Jenny Lou soon had company. Songwriter Cindy Walker drove west to Los Angeles with her parents in 1941. They stopped the car when Cindy spotted Bing Crosby's office. The gutsy Texan marched in, talked her way past the receptionist, declared herself a songwriter, went out to the car to get her piano-playing mother, Oree, sang for Crosby's brother, and wound up with Bing's hit "Lone Star Trail" plus a Decca Records contract of her own. With Oree as her accompanist, companion, and supporter, Cindy went on to write more than five hundred other classics and become the first female inductee into the Nashville Songwriters Hall of Fame.

"Papa was going to Los Angeles on a business trip and asked Mama and me if we wanted to go," Cindy recalled of her fateful journey to song-writing fame. "Does a sinner want to go to heaven? L.A. meant music to me. Mama worried about clothes while I worried about getting all my songs in one briefcase. . . . Papa said I was squirrelly."

"Foxy" is more like it. Cindy Walker soon had songs recorded by more than ten top stars of the late 1940s, including such women as Dale Evans, Margaret Whiting, Rose Maddox, Jo Stafford, and Patti Page. During her thirteen years in Hollywood, Cindy custom-tailored tunes for cowboy movies and wrote on demand for everyone from pop crooners to honky-tonk moaners. Her ability to wed her songs to specific voices made her legendary in songwriting circles and is illustrated by such diverse creations as "Dream Baby" (Roy Orbison), "Distant Drums" (Jim Reeves), "I Don't Care" (Webb Pierce, revived by Ricky Skaggs), "You Don't Know Me" (Eddy Arnold, revived by Ray Charles and Mickey Gilley), "In the Misty Moonlight" (Jerry Wallace, revived by Dean Martin), "China Doll" (The Ames Brothers), "Blue Canadian Rockies" (Gene Autry), "The Gold Rush Is Over" (Hank Snow), "Take Me in Your Arms and Hold Me" (Eddy Arnold, Les Paul & Mary Ford), and "Lorelei" (Elton Britt). The time-lessness of her tunes is such that contemporary country women such as Lacy J. Dalton and k.d. lang still sing the songs of Cindy Walker.

In Hollywood Cindy's good looks made her a natural for Soundies, the pre-MTV video-jukebox clips. When she sang "Seven Beers with the Wrong Man" for Soundie cameras in early 1941, Cindy became country's first "music video" star. In features Cindy appeared with Gene Autry in *Ride Tenderfoot Ride* (1940) and *Trail to San Antone* (1947). She also made waves as a recording artist, scoring a Top 10 hit on the hillbilly hit parade with "When My Blue Moon Turns to Gold Again" in 1944. Her Decca singles of the time included the feisty feminist statements "Why I Don't Trust the Men" and "Don't Talk to Me About Men."

In 1947 Cindy turned her back on her budding movie and recording career to concentrate on songwriting full-time. One of her best Hollywood connections turned out to be western swing king Bob Wills. "I saw this huge white bus with his name painted on the side," she recalled. "I knew he had to be in Hollywood, so I started calling all the hotels." Her perseverance paid off. Within a week after she'd met Wills, he recorded five of her tunes, including "Dusty Skies" and "Cherokee Maiden." Cindy eventually wrote more than fifty Bob Wills classics, including "Bubbles in My Beer," "Miss Molly," "Blue Bonnet Lane," "Sugar Moon," and "You're from Texas."

In 1954 the Walkers left L.A. to return to Mexia, Texas, and thereafter Cindy did her highly profitable songwriting at home, far from the show-biz whirl. She never married and lived with her mother until Oree died in 1991.

"I couldn't do without my mama. She plays piano for all my tapes. I'm not a musician, I'm strictly a songwriter. My words and melodies come to me together. I won't sing my songs to anybody until they're finished. When I'm ready, all I have to do is call for Mother. I sing it for her and she can play it after she's heard it twice."

"She taught me everything," Cindy recalled the day after her mother's death. "She was a wonderful piano player. I was singing and dancing at age seven because I was her 'play-party.' I was her little doll. Besides being my mother, she was my very best friend. She was 'The Wind Beneath My Wings.'" Hundreds of hillbilly hits are the proof: Oree Walker raised the greatest female songwriter in the history of country music.

Cindy, Carolina Cotton, and The Dinning Sisters weren't the only women making those pre-MTV Soundies in Hollywood. Around 10 percent of the two thousand Soundies made featured country acts, and in contrast to records of the day, nearly *half* of the country clips included females. Most of the country gals showcased were blondes—Cindy and Carolina, for example, as well as two other headliners of the day who were filmed, Esmereldy and Rosalie Allen.

Soundie maker Esmereldy was known as "The Streamlined Hillbilly." Verna Sherrill, her real name, was a Middleton, Tennessee, native who first attracted attention on Memphis radio. She adopted her nickname while doing radio and nightclub work in New York. Her musical movie shorts were filmed there in 1941 and 1944. Both Esmereldy and Rosalie Allen became trailblazing country disc jockeys, as well as Soundie filmers. In a field still overwhelmingly dominated by men, each had her own radio program in the nation's largest city during World War II.

Rosalie Allen did her Soundies from 1943 to 1945, and also appeared in a 1949 feature called *Village Barn.* During this era when women were breaking into male occupations, Rosalie owned New York City's first country record shop; was a pioneer woman DJ with her "Prairie Stars" show (1944–1956); hosted a country TV show in Manhattan (1949–1953); and wrote columns for the *Hoedown* (1954), *National Jamboree* (1949), and *Country Song Roundup* (1950) magazines. But Rosalie Allen's name is written even larger in country history as "The Queen of the Yodelers."

Born Julie Marlene Bedra in 1924 in Old Forge, Pennsylvania, Rosalie was one of eleven children of Polish parents. Even in a culture as full of poverty and hard luck as the country music world, Rosalie's story stands out.

"I still wonder if any moment, now, I won't waken to find it's all a dream," she told writer Ellsworth Newcomb at the peak of her fame during World War II. "But it's all true and it came true the hard way. . . . When I think back over the way I've come, I can say again what I've been saying all these years, 'Nothing can stop me.' I don't remember when I first said those words or when I first knew . . . I wanted to be a singer. But it was when I was just a little tow-headed girl . . . living near the Pennsylvania coal mines where my father worked until his health failed.

"I longed for a doll. . . . But there was never quite enough money for food, much less for toys, and I didn't dare even to hope. Finally, though, with pennies I earned by helping neighbors with housework . . . I actually got my doll. . . . She was so beautiful she brought a lump to my throat. But almost since I could walk I had been helping Mother iron and scrub; I had fed the chickens and milked our cow. There had never been time for anything but work and now that I had my lovely doll I didn't know how to play with her. Tenderly I put her back in her box and closed the lid softly as a tear fell on my small, work-roughened hand. I never saw my doll again. . . . our house burned to the ground one cold September night. . . . Next day, while neighbors sheltered the rest of our big family, I got work [washing dishes] at a nearby restaurant and went to board there. My salary was $2 a week and I walked the three miles to and from school so I could save bus fare and turn the whole amount over to Mother."

Music became the nine-year-old's escape from drudgery. Rosalie listened

Cindy Walker, the greatest female country composer in history, c. 1941.

intently to the radio, memorized the songs, and began singing at local banquets. When she moved back home with her dreams, her mother dismissed them as so much foolishness. "She believed that girls should stay at home until it was time for them to marry. Then they should raise a family and stay home some more. . . . Mother put her foot down hard. She enforced her arguments with a strap."

Rosalie began sneaking out of the house to enter amateur contests. When her mother found out, she forbade her daughter to even listen to the radio. Rosalie would wait until the family was asleep to sneak downstairs and listen to her beloved music with the radio tuned to a whisper. At age thirteen she won a contest, sang on local radio, and got an offer to spend the summer in Vermont with a hillbilly band. For the next five years she toured, entertaining at New England's then-popular country music parks, perfecting the yodel trills and sunny stage demeanor that became her trademarks.

Rosalie's yodeling was more elaborate than her predecessor Patsy Montana's, and she quickly became a celebrity after arriving in New York with Denver Darling's Swing Billies cowboy troupe in 1943. Darling's band was drafted, leaving Rosalie to build a solo career, blaze a trail as a female DJ, and open Rosalie Allen's Hillbilly Music Center on Broadway near Carnegie Hall. Her singing style was showcased on a number of RCA Victor records of the late 1940s, including "Guitar Polka," "Yodel Boogie," "Yodeling Bird," and her biggest hit, "He Taught Me to Yodel." Her decorative yodeling was also in peak form in a series of duets with Elton Brit.

Rosalie and her country contemporaries were nothing like their mothers. These DJs, songwriters, and bandleaders of the 1940s came on the scene during the first big era of the "career girl." Strong-minded Joan Crawford, Bette Davis, Rosalind Russell, Barbara Stanwyck, and Jean Arthur ruled the silver screen in working-woman roles. First Lady Eleanor Roosevelt's energetic, public-spirited activity made her a role model for millions. Anthropologist Margaret Mead, publishing magnate Clare Boothe Luce, choreographer Agnes de Mille, playwright Lillian Hellman, radio broadcaster Mary Margaret McBride, and Congresswoman Margaret Chase Smith all gained national fame during the decade. The All-American Girls Baseball League was founded in 1943 with ten teams. Nurses in the military blazed a trail by becoming the first women to get equal pay and equal rank with men. Reflecting the new independence, Wonder Woman made her comic book debut in 1941, soon to be followed by Sheena, Queen of the Jungle. A wave of "all-girl" jazz groups that began in the 1930s with the bands of Rita Rio and Ina Ray Hutton crested in the 1940s. Professional female instrumental troupes such as The International Sweethearts of Rhythm, Tiny Davis and Her Hell Divers, The Harlem Playgirls, Phil Spitalny's All-Girl Orchestra, The Hormel Girls' Caravan, The Victory Belles, and The All-American Girls were particularly popular during the decade.

The "Rosie the Riveter" social climate broke down barriers for country's female instrumentalists, too; and it wasn't long before "all-girl" string bands were serenading barn dance audiences. Billie Gale saddled up with her Hollywood Cowgirls in Texas in 1945. In Pennsylvania Erma Mae Reed and Her Melodiers were formed as an all-girl lineup. A female kiddie country band called The Texas Dollies was active in Rhode Island. Betty Lee and Her Cowgirls hit the trail in Boston. In West Virginia Frankie More's Log Cabin Boys became the Log Cabin Girls from 1938 through 1941, and member Little Shoe (Cousin Emmy's niece Alma Crosby) then formed her own all-female war-era band, The Polka Dot Girls. The Girls of the Sunny South were active in Kentucky. Veteran Louisiana Lou fronted The Pine Cabin Girls in South Dakota during the war. Patricia Reed and The Rancherettes were popular in Kansas.

There were two all-girl country bands active at WLW in Cincinnati. Former Coon Creek Girl Daisy Lange headed The Rangerettes beginning in 1940. Ramona Riggins, Jane Allen, Sue Workman, and Irene Martin teamed up as The Happy Valley Girls from 1942 to 1943. In years to come Ramona would gain national fame as an old-time fiddler and as the wife/duet partner of Grandpa Jones, while bandmate Sue would rise to country renown as Sunshine Sue, the top star at "The Old Dominion Barn Dance."

With her daughters Helen, June, and Anita on accordion, autoharp, and bass, respectively, Mother Maybelle Carter hit the airwaves of Richmond, Virginia, in 1943. The transition from the old-timey Carter Family trio to their all-female band had been gradual. The once-shy Maybelle had gained strength and confidence during the trio's Mexican-border radio broadcasting years. In Texas and during a 1940 radio stint in Charlotte, North Carolina, she'd introduced her daughters to show business. By this time the Carter name had national renown: In September

The Carter Sisters and Mother Maybelle pose with their instruments as they launch their career on WRVA in 1946. From left are Helen, Anita, Maybelle, and June.

1941 *Life* magazine reporters traveled to Maybelle's Virginia home to do a photo spread on the famous mountain music family, but the outbreak of war bumped the Carters from the weekly's December 7 issue. Then lead singer Sara quit for good, and the family's saga seemed to be at an end. Maybelle tried settling down to gardening and child rearing, but after six months, Ezra Carter said to his wife, "I can't stand seeing your long face anymore. Go out and find someplace to sing. . . . If the money is good, take it. The mountains will always be here."

So the three teenage girls became full-time musicians. Helen developed into the most capable instrumentalist, Anita into the finest singer, and June into the best showman of the three. June recalls their juvenile act as "pathetic," but the female foursome rapidly gained wide country popularity.

"I hoofed away—one of the silliest-looking vaudeville jigs that a girl could ever do," June recalled of her pantaloon-clad "Aunt Polly" comedy character in the act. "Between singing Carter Family songs we sang pop tunes. I played the autoharp, Mother Maybelle played 'The Wildwood Flower,' Helen played the accordion, and Anita stood on her head and played the bass fiddle. We did old vaudeville skits and we sold pictures for twenty-five cents apiece. While everyone was dating, I was busy riding everywhere in our old Cadillac, setting up the PA system, and taking up money at the door."

June remembers that men in uniform were everywhere during the war years in Richmond and that the thrill of her fifteen-year-old life was becoming a "sponsor" for a military cadet there. But by the time she graduated from high school in 1946, her future was mapped.

"I cried because I wasn't going to college . . . I couldn't understand why it was more important for me to work. But it was. Our family show was a unit. . . . So we had our homemade college. . . . I learned to do what was necessary to make a good show. . . . The old circuits sometimes called for five shows a day. I learned to sleep in the car, get ready in five minutes, and tune a guitar in two. Sometimes I felt like I had little wool sweaters on my teeth. My body ached. Then I stopped a show with a routine, and I finally had to face it—I was hooked. There would be no turning back now. I would be an entertainer. My life would be different. I would not go to college, would not marry Freddie Fugate back home and raise children, cook three meals a day, and be an average American housewife."

Mother Maybelle and The Carter Sisters became top stars at "The Old Dominion Barn Dance" in Richmond in 1946. Two years later the act moved to the "Tennessee Barn Dance" on WNOX in Knoxville. There Maybelle picked up a promising young guitarist named Chet Atkins and added him to the band. They joined the Ozark Jubilee in Springfield, Missouri, in 1949, and in 1950 the group took up permanent residence at "The Grand Ole Opry" in Nashville.

The other major female family band of the 1940s was composed of Kentucky's Amburgey sisters. Fiddler Bertha (born c. 1920), guitarist Irene (born 1921), and banjoist/mandolinist Opal (born c. 1925) were the daughters of a coal miner/farmer from Neon, Kentucky.

"My dad played old-time banjo, my mother played organ, and they formed a quartet to sing sacred songs," Irene reminisces. "They traveled throughout the Southeastern states to singing conventions. . . . As just kids, we started entertaining around our community. We'd go play for the coal mining meetings, for church gatherings, for somebody that was running for sheriff, and various places. . . . We would ride around in the back of an old truck, playing and singing all day long for ten dollars . . . to split between us.

"We first left home [in 1938] to go to WLAP in Lexington, Kentucky, and worked there for a man that had an all-girl band. And, boy, I could write a book on that job. . . . That was the first time we was away from home without one of our parents, and o-o-o-h yes it was frightening. . . . This was a married man, but everybody knew he was married but *him*. He was shackin' up with the girl who played the bass fiddle. There'd be about eight of us in one five-passenger car, goin' to do these little ol' shows at schoolhouses and courthouses and stuff like that. He'd wait until we'd all go to sleep, and then him and Betsy would get out and go get 'em something to eat. We were about to starve to death." Not only did the boss refuse to pay his hillbilly girls, he expected the three teens to do his cooking, housekeeping, and laundry. "But we couldn't write home and tell Mommy and Poppy about it. See, they'd-a come and got us. And then everybody around there would say, 'Well, they was failures,' you know. So we didn't. We just sat there and starved it out." The Sunshine Sisters, as they were billed, began looking for greener pastures.

"We had heard of Cousin Emmy over at WHAS in Louisville who used a five-string banjo in her act, but we were denting her territory, so she came to Lexington to offer us a job with her group. She painted a beautiful picture of what it would be like and what we would be doing, so we took her up on the offer and went to Louisville. When we got there, we learned that nothing she told us was the truth. She just wanted to get us out of her [central Kentucky touring] territory. So she told us we were too young, she couldn't use us, and sent us back home. But she kept our instruments."

The girls sold chickens to get back on their feet and landed a job at WHIS in Bluefield, West Virginia. In 1940 they moved to Kentucky's "Renfro Valley Barn Dance" to become members of Lily May Ledford's famed Coon Creek Girls string band. "She was just another one of us," Irene says of Lily May, "just a little ol' Kentucky girl. We felt right at home with her."

By the time they arrived at Atlanta's WSB radio in December 1940, the Amburgeys were full-blown country professionals. The station dubbed them "Mattie, Marthie, and Minnie." Lead singer Opal became Mattie. Alto-voiced Irene became Martha. Soprano Bertha was Minnie. They retained their new first names through subsequent solo careers. King Records billed them as Mattie, Marthie, and Minnie in 1951 and 1952. Capitol Records recorded the trio as The Amber Sisters in 1952 and 1953. Atlanta radio listeners knew them as The Hoot Owl Holler Girls throughout the 1940s.

Bertha/Minnie married Ohio musician Charles "Ducky" Woodford in 1941 and the following year moved with him to Ohio when he took a defense plant job. But she returned to the sister trio to write and sing lead on its biggest hit, 1951's "You Can't Live with 'Em (And You Can't Live Without 'Em)." "She was mad at her husband and wrote that one," says Irene/Marthie with a chuckle. "A man's a lot of trouble," the feisty, up-tempo song says. "He'll make your worries double."

Youngest sister Opal/Mattie married harmonica virtuoso and former Prairie Ramblers band member Salty Holmes. They became the popular "Grand Ole Opry" duo Salty Holmes and Mattie O'Neil. Transformed into shapely, platinum blond "Jean Chapel," the same woman became a Sun Records rockabilly artist of the 1950s, then a Music Row songwriter of the 1960s.

Irene/Martha's husband was James Roberts. As James and Martha Carson, The Barn Dance Sweethearts, they became wildly popular on Atlanta radio.

During their heyday in the World War II years in Atlanta, the three sisters popularized the war-themed "I'll Be Back in a Year, Little Darling." This was one of a slew of supportive songs sung by country women during the fight against fascism. Sixteen million men and 350,000 women joined the armed forces during World War II; three of every five women had a husband, son, brother, or father in the war effort.

Patsy Montana altered her repertoire to include "Good Night Soldier" as a salute to her husband in the army. Bonnie Blue Eyes (Loeta Applegate) scored a 1941 hit with "I'm Lending You to Uncle Sammy," and carried on in Chicago as a solo star after her husband and duet partner, Bob Atcher, enlisted. By 1944 a total of forty-nine staffers at WLS/"The National Barn Dance"/"Prairie Farmer" were in the service. Gene Autry, Merle Travis, Grandpa Jones, Doc Williams, The Sons of the Pioneers, Buck Nation, the Maddox brothers, George Gobel, Hank Thompson, Joe Maphis, and dozens of other country stars enlisted. San Antonio Rose (Eva Nichols) quit her job as the female singer in Pee Wee King's hugely successful Golden West Cowboys to sign up for the WAVES. Boston radio cowgirl Betty Lee left WMEX to become a WAC.

On the home front country music women threw themselves into the anti-Nazi cause. At the age of fourteen cowgirl singer Patsy Lee organized her "Victory Round-Up" touring show of 1943 to 1944, featuring her ditty "If Hitler Were My Daddy (And Tojo Was My Son)." Polly Jenkins and Her Plow Boys performed nearly nine hundred USO and military base shows during World War II, singing "They Drafted Zeke from the Mountains" and the sentimental war song "The Kid with the Guitar." In 1944 Polly took out a full page ad in *Billboard* stating that she was "now booking dates to follow Hitler's funeral." Polly and her group were in Gene Autry's 1938 movie *Man from Music Mountain* and on Pennsylvania's Cowboy Records label in 1948.

The Poe Sisters of "Grand Ole Opry" were launched as a country act because of their "Rosie the Riveter" jobs. Nelle Poe (b. 1922) and her sister Ruth (b. 1924) were Mississippi natives who went north for war plant work at General Electric in Connecticut. During weekends they began weaving their close-harmony spell on Bridgeport's WICC and touring with a USO troupe. They auditioned for the "Grand Ole Opry" in 1944 and were hired on the spot.

Country women's wartime efforts were coast to coast. New England's Hickory Sisters, Pat and Lindy, entertained at Red Cross shows for wounded servicemen. The glamour queen brunets were billed as "the most beautiful hillbillies in the East." California singing cowgirl Dixie Darling was cited by the government for her outstanding work in war bond sales. Flaxen-haired St. Louis star Sally Foster (Louise Rautenberg) was a morale booster throughout the war years on KMOX's "Barnyard Follies" as "The Girl with the Smile in Her Voice." As a result of her wartime popularity, Sally scored a Top 10 hit in 1946 with "Someday (You'll Want Me to Want You)." At Chicago's "National Barn Dance" Grace Wilson, Jenny Lou Carson, The DeZurick Sisters, Eva Overstake, and The Sunbonnet Girls (Connie and Bonnie Linder) promoted planting "victory gardens" to ease wartime food shortages.

An upbeat, supportive mood was maintained in country music, despite the real hardships faced by women on the home front. The war brought enormous changes for working-class women, with new jobs, higher pay, and more independence and public roles. But it didn't bring an easy life. Wartime rationing was severe. Sugar, coffee, dairy products, meat, canned foods, and gasoline were doled out via ration coupons because of the shortages caused by disruptions in shipping and the concentrated effort to supply the troops abroad. Malnutrition among poor women and children was common. There were also critical shortages in housing, heating oil, and appliances. Retail prices climbed 27 percent and taxes went up to finance the war machine.

World War II touched and defined all aspects of American life. In the world of fashion, government limits on cloth and work requirements led to simpler and less "feminine" garments, including pantsuits and low-heeled shoes. Skirt lengths shortened considerably. There was even a short "liberty" haircut that was particularly safe for factory workers around machinery.

Several band singers' careers boomed because of their "sweetheart" image with the servicemen, notably those of Dinah Shore, Frances Langford, and "GI Jo" Stafford. Top torch stylist Jane Froman was crippled in a 1943 Lisbon plane crash while en route to entertain the troops. Big-band swing music was the dominant style of the 1940s, and most of the popular orchestras featured beautiful women vocalists swaying in evening gowns. The style's country cousin, western swing music, naturally had cowgirl-attired singers to match.

Laura Lee Owens McBride (1920–1989) joined Bob Wills and The Texas Playboys in 1943, when Bob was discharged from the army, and accompanied him from Oklahoma to the California big time. On Saturday nights wartime factory workers would gather in huge dance auditoriums in the L.A. suburbs or on Pacific Ocean piers. Wills often grossed twenty thousand dollars a night. Laura Lee's first show with his group in California drew eight thousand.

"Bob knew the women would resent a girl singer with the Texas Playboys," Laura Lee recalled in *Music City News* in 1973. "He always said, 'Don't try to sell yourself to these people. You make me like you, and I'll make them like you.' The people—particularly the women—approved of me because they saw that Bob approved of me."

Laura Lee had begun her career as a teenager, singing in a duet with sister Dolpha Jane on their father's Kansas City radio show. He was "Cattle Call" composer Tex Owens and the brother of Texas Ruby, "The Sophie Tucker of the Cowgirls." After high school Laura Lee formed her own KMBC radio group, Laura Lee and Her Ranger Buddies. They moved to Tulsa, where Wills discovered her. Her most popular number with him and the Texas Playboys was "Betcha My Heart I Love You."

After Laura Lee left The Texas Playboys, Wills hired Alabama natives Dean and Evelyn McKinney in 1946 to help him make hay in the Golden State's ballrooms. The sisters wrote or cowrote such 1940s favorites as "A King Without a Queen," "Dusty Plains," and "Bottle Baby Boogie." Carolina Cotton recorded with Wills in 1951, the same year that Ramona Reed (radio's "Martha White" flour girl) became a Texas Playboys member. The next woman to sing with the band was Darla Daret.

The saddest saga of the western-swing singers belongs to Ella Mae Evans (1923–1961). She was a blond teenager straight off the farm when bandleader Spade Cooley hired her as his vocalist and fiddler in 1944. At the time, Cooley was at his peak, drawing eight thousand people weekly to the Venice Pier in L.A. He married Ella Mae in 1945. By 1946 he was the star of the biggest dance hall in California, the Santa Monica Ballroom.

Offstage, Spade Cooley was an insanely possessive, jealous, and abusive man. When singer Ginny Jackson threatened to leave him, he tried to throw her off the Santa Monica pier. The year he married Ella Mae he was tried for rape and acquitted. Throughout the 1950s he kept his wife a virtual prisoner on their ranch near Bakersfield, monitoring her phone calls and sometimes beating her. On April 3, 1961, she told him she wanted a divorce. When fourteen-year-old daughter Melody Faith came home late that day, she found her mother bloody and unconscious in the shower. Cooley grabbed Ella Mae by her hair and dragged his nude wife out of the water. In front of the girl, he burned his wife's breasts with a cigarette, crashed her head to the floor, and stomped on her abdomen. "You're going to watch me kill her," he said. Melody ran screaming from the house. The prosecution called it a "torture murder." During the lurid trial, the bandleader said he killed Ella Mae because she was having an

"IN THE MISTY MOONLIGHT" (Jerry Wallace, revived by Dean Martin)

"JIM, I WORE A TIE TODAY" (Eddy Arnold)

"LORELEI" (Elton Britt)

"MISS MOLLY" (Bob Wills, revived by Riders in the Sky)

"THE NEXT VOICE YOU HEAR" (Hank Snow)

"OKLAHOMA WALTZ" (Johnny Bond)

"TAKE ME IN YOUR ARMS AND HOLD ME" (Eddy Arnold, Les Paul & Mary Ford)

"TRIFLIN' GAL" (Al Dexter)

"TWO GLASSES, JOE" (Ernest Tubb)

"WARM RED WINE" (Ernest Tubb)

"YOU ARE MY TREASURE" (Jack Greene)

LEFT OVER "YOU DON'T KNOW ME" (Eddy Arnold, revived by Ray Charles and Mickey Gilley)

"YOU'RE FROM TEXAS" (Bob Wills)

Tennessee Waltz

By REDD STEWART and PEE WEE KING

RECORDED BY PATTI PAGE FOR MERCURY RECORDS

Featured by
PATTI PAGE

PUBLISHED BY
Acuff-Rose PUBLICATIONS
2510 FRANKLIN ROAD
NASHVILLE 4, TENNESSEE
MADE IN U.S.A.

In 1950 Patti Page turned "The Tennessee Waltz" into one of the biggest country hits in history. Millions of records, as well as pieces of sheet music like this one, have been sold.

affair with Roy Rogers, an outrageous accusation that both Roy and wife Dale Evans vehemently denied. Spade Cooley was sentenced to life in prison and died of a heart attack in 1969.

Becky Barfield, "Miss Movie Teen" Patsy Harding, fiddler Anita Aros, and Soundies video maker Betsy Gay one by one succeeded the homebound Ella Mae in Cooley's band in the late 1940s and early 1950s. At one of Cooley's last Decca recording sessions in the 1950s Betsy warbled a tune he'd written called "You Clobbered Me."

Like vocalist/fiddler Ella Mae Evans, Mary Ford (Coleen Summers, 1928–1977) was both an instrumentalist and a singer in western bands. She played lead guitar in Jimmy Wakely's cowboy band, was a mainstay of The Sunshine Girls western backup group, and sang on Gene Autry's "Melody Ranch" radio show in Los Angeles from 1947 to 1949. That's her singing harmony on Wakely's big 1948 "cheatin'" hit "One Has My Name (The Other Has My Heart)." Discovered by guitarist Les Paul, to whom she was married from 1949 to 1963, Mary became his lead vocalist on a series of startling early 1950s hits. Records such as "How High the Moon" (1951), "Vaya Con Dios" (1953), and "Bye Bye Blues" (1953) had a lush, layered sound achieved via the then-revolutionary technique of multiple tracking "sound on sound," which permitted Mary to harmonize with herself and Les to overdub guitar parts. Enormously successful in pop music, their country backgrounds shone through in songs like "Tennessee Waltz," "I Really Don't Want to Know," and their big 1951 hit "Mockin' Bird Hill." During her heyday, Mary was described as having a "plaintive, folksy, Wisconsin dairy-maid voice."

Les Paul and Mary Ford sold millions with their multiple-track sound, but they weren't the first to use the technique. That honor goes to another country singer turned pop star, Patti Page. Born Clara Ann Fowler in 1927 in Claremont, Oklahoma, Patti was one of eleven children who grew up picking cotton. She first sang in a Tulsa church with seven of her sisters and was on radio in the city before she was out of high school. She took her stage name from Page Milk, her radio sponsor. Her first record was the up-tempo country tune "My Sweet Papa," recorded with Al Clauser and His Oklahomans.

Still struggling in 1947, Patti had no money to pay backup singers during the recording of a song called "Confess." Manager Jack Rael had her double her own voice and put the record out as "Patti Page and Patti Page." The novelty worked, so she recorded four harmony parts and issued 1950's "With My Eyes Wide Open I'm Dreaming" as "The Patti Page Quartet." She also used the technique in 1950 on her immortal "The Tennessee Waltz," one of the biggest-selling records in the history of show business.

Patti's warmth of tone, impressive vocal control, clarity of diction, subtle western accent, and liquid phrasing made her the top female record seller of the 1950s. Her style seems utterly effortless, and it is said that Patti never took a vocal lesson, never practiced, and never had to warm up her voice before performing. Despite painful onstage shyness, she made the transition to TV stardom with three variety series in the 1950s. In 1960 she recalled her gospel roots by playing the evangelist singer in the Oscar-winning film *Elmer Gantry*. Since then, Patti has recorded several country LPs in Nashville, become a regular on the country popularity charts of the mid-1970s, received the 1979 Pioneer Award from the Academy of Country Music in Los Angeles, and costarred with Roy Acuff at the 1983 premiere of The Nashville Network country cable TV channel.

Patti's career closely parallels that of Kay Starr, yet another country diva who successfully crossed over to the pop mainstream. Born Katheryn LaVern Starks on an Oklahoma Indian reservation in 1922, Kay was raised in Dallas. As a nine-year-old with an oversize, bluesy voice, she collected sacks of fan mail as she belted out hillbilly hits on her own fifteen-minute radio show. At twelve the youngster of Iroquois/Cherokee descent graduated to the western swing bands of Bill Boyd's Cowboy Ramblers and the Light Crust Doughboys. The following year her family relocated to Memphis, where she again starred on country radio. Her packed-with-personality, barrelhouse delivery made her a swing band favorite during the war.

Sidelined with severe laryngitis contracted while touring army camps on transport planes, Kay returned after World War II with a throatier, huskier tone and at last hit the charts in 1948. One of her biggest early hits was her 1950 version of the country hit "Bonaparte's Retreat." Kay's Tennessee Ernie Ford duet "I'll Never Be Free" (1950), million-selling

"Wheel of Fortune" (1952), double-tracked "Side by Side" (1953), and topical "Rock and Roll Waltz" (1956) led up to a return to country with 1961's "Foolin' Around," 1962's "Four Walls," and a string of 1970s albums. Later country greats Patsy Cline and K. T. Oslin both cited Starr as a deep influence.

The only other pop music queen of the era who earns such high marks from the critics is Jo Stafford. She, too, has country roots. Born in 1920 in Coalinga, California, Jo learned music at the feet of her mother. A guitarist and banjo player, Mama Stafford taught her family's Tennessee folk songs to Jo and sisters Pauline and Christine. The girls formed a trio in 1935 and became radio regulars on KNX's "Hollywood Barn Dance" in 1936 and 1937. Gene Autry featured the Staffords in his 1938 flicks *The Old Barn Dance* and *Gold Mine in the Sky.* After marriage broke up the trio, Jo joined The Pied Pipers in swing king Tommy Dorsey's troupe in 1941. She went solo in 1944, scoring an immediate hit with the dreamy, languid "Long Ago and Far Away."

By 1955, Jo had racked up eighty-five more, including uptown versions of more than a dozen country classics. No other singer in history brought as many country numbers onto the pop charts as Jo Stafford. She familiarized millions with the sounds of "Tumbling Tumbleweeds" (1944), "I'm My Own Grandmaw" (1948), "If You've Got the Money, I've Got the Time" (1950), and the two-million-selling "You Belong to Me" (1952). Her Frankie Laine duets included the assertive "Gambella (The Gambling Lady)" (1951) and a rendition of Hank Williams's "Hey Good Lookin'." Jo also popularized Hank's "Jambalaya" (1952) and "Tonight We're Setting the Woods on Fire" (1952). She was a huge hit in the Bible Belt with a 1949 Gordon MacRae duet on the 1868 chestnut "Whispering Hope." In 1946 she recorded *Jo Stafford Sings American Folk Songs,* thus becoming one of the first pop acts to record a folk album. Her subsequent rubed-up, yokel-gone-cuckoo workout on "Temptation (Tim-Tayshun)" (1947) as "Cinderella G. Stump" with Red Ingle ranks as the most hilarious hillbilly send-up ever recorded.

Why were so many of the biggest female pop stars of the 1940s from country or southern backgrounds? "Isn't it interesting?" says Dinah Shore when asked. "I've never really thought about it, but it's true: We all were," Kay Starr, Jo Stafford, Patti Page, Mary Ford, The Dinning Sisters. Dinah was from Tennessee; Rosemary Clooney ("Half as Much"/"This Ole House") was from Kentucky; Ella Mae Morse ("Cow Cow Boogie"/"The House of Blue Lights") was from Texas. "Basically, I think all of us were beat singers," Dinah continues. "By that I mean as opposed to people who sang strictly ballad-style. We'd start with a four-beat or a two-beat, and we could sing an 'up' song or any song; and I mean, nobody had to cue us. There's a kind of a sense of meter that comes with country music. You could skip beats, you could do anything and we'd still have that sense of meter. That never failed you." Most of these pop queens were paired with country males for duets. Examples of such pairings included Tennessee Ernie Ford/Kay Starr, Jimmy Wakely/Margaret Whiting, Ernest Tubb/The Andrews Sisters, Gene Autry/ Rosemary Clooney, and George Morgan with Dinah.

Dinah Shore was never a country stylist, but she was certainly well acquainted with the genre. Born in 1917 in Winchester, Tennessee, Frances Rose Shore was the daughter of a small-town Jewish shopkeeper. She recalls her father, Sol, standing her up on the counter as a tot and encouraging her to "Sing, baby. Sing, Fannie Rose," while the farmers gathered around. The Shores moved to Nashville

Dinah Shore cuddles up with bandleader Beasley Smith on the stage of "The Grand Ole Opry." As a servicemen's sweetheart during World War II, Dinah returned to her hometown station, Nashville's WSM.

when she was six years old and struggling with polio. She underwent painful therapy for the potentially crippling muscular illness until she was twelve. By the time she was nineteen and a student at Vanderbilt University, she was on Nashville radio singing "Dinah," which stuck as her stage name. She worked with area dance bands and did guest appearances on WSM's "Grand Ole Opry" as her local fame grew. In 1938 she headed for New York to audition for radio and stage jobs.

"Oh, sure, they made fun of my accent," she says of her still-detectable Tennessee drawl. "But I never would have had a job if I hadn't had that accent. That was the first thing that intrigued 'em. . . . I wasn't pretty. . . . I was a li'l ol' buck-toothed, skinny thing; I was all teeth and eyes. . . . I think that the Southern accent, Southern background, gave people a comfortable feeling. . . . I was always really very proud of it."

Dinah had a soft, soothing, delicate delivery that was not particularly well suited to big-band singing, but her velvety voice worked on radio and records. Because of her sultry, intimate singing quality, Dinah was dubbed "The Nashville Nightingale" and "the girl who starts fires by rubbing two notes together." During World War II she became a jukebox favorite and the GIs' sweetheart. She toured not only to stateside camps, but to the firing lines in the European theater. Dinah settled in Hollywood, where her accent got her cast in film fodder such as *Belle of the Yukon* (1944) and *Aaron Slick from Punkin Crick* (1952). She is not proud of her movies, nor of the lighthearted hokum of her big hits "Doin' What Comes Natur'lly" (1946) and "Buttons and Bows" (1948). Among her eighty-three hits, Dinah's other folksy discs include "Shoo-Fly Pie and Apple Pan Dowdy" (1946), "Lavender Blue" (1949), "Sweet Violets" (1951), and "Dear Hearts and Gentle People" (1949).

She found her true calling—television—in the 1950s. Dinah's gentility, innate graciousness, "me-to-you" informality, and southern warmth made her a TV superstar between 1951 and 1962. Her "See the U.S.A. in your Chevrolet" and "Mmm-wah!" sign-off smooch at the camera became emblems of the Ike-and-Mamie fifties. Beginning with a 1969 TV special, she slowly shed what she called her square, "Alice Blue Gown" image. When her new weekly talk show hit the air in 1970, she emerged as an accomplished tennis player, golfer, and cook. Always politically progressive, Dinah praised feminist leaders, saying she "was always an emancipated woman." And then there was that affair with movie hunk Burt Reynolds, nineteen years her junior, from

1971 to 1977. In 1990 Dinah returned to TV on The Nashville Network with a weekly talk show.

The most unusual act of all the 1940s pop/country women was developed by Dorothy Shay (1921–1978). Glamorous Dorothy was "The Park Avenue Hillbillie," singing amusing rube ditties while wearing designer gowns and evening gloves. She came by her southern accent naturally enough, but Dorothy Nell Sims was trying to leave her Jacksonville, Florida, upbringing behind when she auditioned to become a band vocalist in Pittsburgh in 1938. She'd taken acting lessons to get rid of her drawl and was doing her darnedest to be sophisticated on the road as a singer. Soon after the outbreak of World War II, Dorothy arrived in New York to gain experience on the USO circuit; after the war she became a Manhattan supper-club attraction. One night she encored with the cornball "Uncle Fud," and the crowd went wild. She added a half-forgotten mountaineer show tune called "Feudin' and Fightin'" to her repertoire and recorded it in 1946. By the middle of 1947 the number was a smash.

Dorothy followed it with a string of witty novelties such as "Sagebrush Sadie" (a bearded lady), "Howlinest, Hootinest Gal" (a boasting country amazon), "Joan of Arkansaw" (who matches Joan of Arc's army with an army of hillbilly lovers), and "Mountain Gal" (who turns down an offer to move to the city because she gets all kinds of expensive goodies from traveling salesmen). The cool brunet with the saucy voice contrasted the tunes with an increasingly chic wardrobe, and her career skyrocketed.

By 1951 Dorothy Shay was earning five thousand dollars a night and up, and costarring on the screen with Abbott and Costello in *Comin' 'Round the Mountain*. She was a particular favorite of President Dwight D. Eisenhower and performed at his 1953 inaugural ball. A 1958 marriage to a Los Angeles publicist ended in divorce in 1959, and she never remarried. Dorothy resurfaced as an actress in the 1970s, landing a recurring role as a mountain spinster on the hit CBS television series "The Waltons" before dying of complications of a stroke at age fifty-seven.

"It's funny, isn't it?" the songstress once said. "The Southern accent I worked so hard as an actress to lose turned out to be my bread and butter."

The transformations of female country performers in the 1940s into the biggest stars in the pop music firmament indicates just how influential the country field became during that decade. Wartime population migrations and the intermingling of regional cultures made country music a truly national phenomenon. Gene Autry and his singing-cowboy contemporaries became American icons during World War II. A square-dancing fad erupted. Country music parks attracted huge audiences in New England and in Middle Atlantic states. Western swing ballrooms in

California, Texas, and Oklahoma packed fans in by the tens of thousands.

The New York Times Magazine noted the national trend as early as 1940 with a piece called "Country Dance Goes to Town." *Time* magazine proclaimed a "Bull Market in Corn" in 1943. *The Saturday Evening Post* and *The Christian Science Monitor* called it a "Hillbilly Boom" (1944) and a "Hillbilly Phenomenon" (1948), respectively. As the decade drew to a close, *Newsweek* took note with a 1949 article called "Corn of Plenty."

Country music became big business during the war, with six hundred radio programs playing to a combined audience of forty million. Popular new barn dance shows of the 1940s included the WSB "Barn Dance" (Atlanta), "Big D Jamboree" (Dallas), "Hayloft Jamboree" (Boston), "Louisiana Hayride" (Shreveport), "Hometown Jamboree" (Los Angeles), and "Sleepy Hollow Ranch" (Philadelphia). By 1942 *Billboard* magazine was carrying a music column called "Western and Race," and by 1944 it had weekly "Folk Records" popularity charts. By mid-decade sixty-five record companies offered the style.

Country melodies pervaded the pop mainstream. In 1941 the classic "You Are My Sunshine" was sung by Bing Crosby. The Andrews Sisters joined Crosby to record Al Dexter's country blockbuster "Pistol-Packin' Mama" in 1943. There were five pop hits of "Deep in the Heart of Texas" in 1942. Elton Britt's "There's a Star-Spangled Banner Waving Somewhere" of 1942 sold a million. Phil Harris, Wayne King, Sammy Kaye, Arthur Godfrey, and Marlene Dietrich all recorded country tunes in the forties. The King Sisters ("Divorce Me C.O.D."), Kate Smith ("Foggy River"), and Jo Stafford ("Feudin' and Fightin'") were among the pop lasses who do-si-doed into the country Top 10.

In fact, the first woman to have a Number 1 hit on the newly established country chart was a pop singer, Margaret Whiting. Born in 1924, Margaret was the daughter of Hollywood composer Richard Whiting and the goddaughter of vaudeville superstar Sophie Tucker. Margaret was already big with "Moonlight in Vermont," "It Might as Well Be Spring," "Baby It's Cold Outside," and other forties hits before she teamed with cowboy Jimmy Wakely on country's landmark "cheatin'" hit "Slipping Around" in 1949.

"To my amazement, it was a hit," she recalled in her autobiography. "It started the whole crossover movement of country/pop. I was invited to Nashville to perform on 'The Grand Ole Opry.' For a month I was briefed, as though I were going to a foreign country and should know all the rules of protocol. I was told I was going to meet Little Jimmy Dickens, Roy Acuff, Red Foley, Minnie Pearl, Hank Williams and Ernest Tubb. I kept saying, 'Yes, yes,' and trying to remember their names. To me, it was like trying to remember the names of Lithuanian royalty. I had no idea who anybody was. . . . What a warm welcome they all gave me." Hank pitched her some tunes, and she recognized his genius instantly. Margaret recorded his "Wedding Bells" in 1949 and seven more Williams standards on her LPs of the 1960s.

Her other country hits with Wakely included "I'll Never Slip Around Again," "Let's Go to Church," and "A Bushel and a Peck"; and she scored a solo hit with Cindy Walker's "Dime a Dozen" in 1949. Whiting's reputation as a wide-ranging song interpreter continued to grow in succeeding decades. She also made news with her string of husbands and her long relationship in the 1980s with porn-movie star Jack Wrangler, twenty years her junior.

Margaret Whiting was one of many who were swept along by the craze for country and cowboy music in the forties. On Broadway it was *Oklahoma!* (1943) and *Annie Get Your Gun* (1946). Even urban sophisticate Cole Porter jumped on the bandwagon—er, haywagon—with "Don't Fence Me In" (1944).

During the 1940s the mainstream popular music business turned to the country subculture for the novelty and vitality that had already attracted millions of rural and blue-collar people. And by then country's writers and performers didn't just represent mountain people, or displaced farmers, or miners, or textile workers. They spoke from the common American working-class experiences of dislocation, defense work, war, economic hardships, and painful memories. Country music's women, like women everywhere in America, were becoming independent professionals. At war's end everyone shared a desire to return to normalcy and get on with life. But problems remained, not the least of which was the role of the everyday American woman in peacetime.

"MY COWBOY'S RIDING NOW FOR UNCLE SAM" (Becky Barfield)

"THERE'S A GOLD STAR IN HER WINDOW" (Becky Barfield)

"UNITED WE MARCH" (Marie & Bill Horner and The Nevadians)

"WE'LL WRITE THE LAST PAGE OF MEIN KAMPF" (Marie & Bill Horner and The Nevadians)

"WE'RE LEAVING ONLY THE 'WAS' IN SWASTIKA" (Susie, "The Gal from the Hills"/Mary Louise Wesnitzer)

"WHEN THE BOYS COME MARCHING HOME" (Jenny Lou Carson)

HONKY-TONK GIRL

Kitty Wells and Her Postwar Sisters

Kitty Wells, 1964.

The sun-kissed vision was of a family unblemished by problems with a modern new home in the suburbs, surrounded by an immaculate lawn on a spotless street in a model neighborhood. The reality was an America with a deeply troubled spirit.

The postwar era was a time of tremendous social upheaval in the United States. Country boys by the thousands had faced the grim reality of war, experienced life beyond small-town America, and tasted cosmopolitan culture. Country girls had shucked their aprons and housedresses for slacks and shirts as they entered defense factories, felt social independence, and became economically self-sufficient.

Nineteenth-century moral values faded in this kind of social climate. Immediately after World War II the divorce rate soared. In 1946 a record-setting six hundred thousand U.S. marriages ended. By the late 1940s divorces leveled off, but male-female relationships never returned to their prewar "normalcy."

Female sexuality, more open than ever before in American culture, was both exciting and threatening to men. Half the women in 1953's Kinsey Report admitted to having premarital intercourse. The film noir movies of

the postwar years portrayed sexy women as treacherous and deadly. Marilyn Monroe, Jane Russell, Lana Turner, and Elizabeth Taylor were typical of the voluptuous new movie goddesses. *Playboy* hit the newsstands in 1953. Among its early editorial themes were that married men were slaves and that women were money-hungry manipulators. *Peyton Place,* that potboiler of sexual and social frustration, appeared in 1956.

Popular magazines of the day wrote of women's frustration, restlessness, and discontent. A 1946 poll in *Fortune* found that one-quarter of U.S. females would prefer to have been born males. A poll in 1956 revealed that one-fifth of the couples questioned described themselves as "unhappy."

The simmering battle between the sexes was stoked by the government's sanction of discrimination against women. With men coming home by the millions, women of the late 1940s were encouraged—or forced—to leave their wartime jobs and return to their "proper" sphere of activity, the home. When polled in 1945, 75 percent of women at work said they wanted to keep their jobs, but in some cases women were dismissed from their positions within one week of V-J Day. The aircraft industry laid off eight hundred thousand, mostly women, two months after victory in Japan. Women represented 25 percent of the automobile work force in 1944, but only 8 percent by early 1946. In 1945, one in four women was dropped from her factory job and nine out of every ten women got pay cuts. Female auto workers in Detroit took to the streets with signs reading "Stop discrimination because of sex." The Equal Rights Amendment passed the Senate in both 1950 and 1953, but failed in the House both times.

At the same time as older women were being pushed out of the work force, younger women were being pulled out of the job market by the "baby boom." By 1951 one in three women was married before age nineteen. One-third of all U.S. women had their first child by age twenty during this era. The average family size stopped declining, as it had done ever since the Civil War. In 1941 most women said they wanted two children; by 1950 most said three or more.

When postwar Americans looked for explanations for divorce, juvenile delinquency, truancy, runaway children, and illegitimate births, they pointed their fingers at women. After three million men were deemed unfit for military service by draft boards, a popular 1942 book titled *A Generation of Vipers* attacked "Momism," saying that American mothers were overprotective and raising unmasculine boys. After the war women were criticized for not seeming motherly enough, being away from home in jobs, neglecting their families, or being too permissive and raising irresponsible bobby-soxers and delinquents. *Modern Woman: The Lost Sex,* published in 1947, said that women were disturbed, unhappy, and troubled, and blamed this discontent on emancipation.

So child rearing and housewifery became the renewed focus of women's lives. Social commentators, journalists, and pop psychologists fixated on motherhood. Dr. Spock appeared as a child-rearing guru in 1946. Women's responsibilities as homemakers and wives included being beautiful, gracious hostesses, as well as sexy, alluring partners. Christian Dior introduced the New Look in 1947, featuring small waists, prominent breasts, and high heels.

Rather than building a sense of community and a nation of purpose, the new suburban-living ideal isolated women and families, fueling women's depression. Urban apartment dwelling was replaced by row upon row of prefabricated homes erected on tracts of land on the outskirts of cities. Between 1948 and 1958 eleven million suburban homes were built. Daddy was supposed to commute to work; Mommy was supposed to "keep the home fires burning," presumably around the patio barbecue grill. In the evening, television became the family entertainment. Television ownership grew from one million sets to fifteen million sets in just one year, 1950–1951. Owning an automobile became a necessity, not a luxury.

Psychoanalysis became popular as people groped for understanding in this new age. In 1950 David Riesman wrote *The Lonely Crowd,* a portrait of the conformity, isolation, and alienation of the average American. The 1949 play *Death of a Salesman* also chronicled a social malaise. A mushroom-shaped cloud of anxiety hovered overhead, for this was the first generation to live with the threat of global annihilation in the Atomic Age.

Nowhere were the stress and discontent of postwar life more evident than in the working class. When Professor Eli Chinoy donned the coveralls of an auto worker for research in 1946, he found that most of his coworkers defined work as "a daily imprisonment" with little hope of escape or advancement. More strikes racked the country in 1946 than in any year since the union-organizing days of 1916. Hysteria against "Reds" was stirred in these disputes, and the Korean War, Cold War, and Red Scare were used to suppress workers' demands. "What was good for our country, was good for General Motors and vice versa," claimed the secretary of defense in 1953.

As the voice of blue-collar America, country music responded to the turbulent psyche in the land. Much of prewar country music had drawn its inspiration from Victorian culture. Innocent romance and sentiments of home, family, and religion predominated as country themes. Old-time country music mourned dead children; praised the Lord; revered Mother; waxed nostalgic for the good old days; pitied the poor; idealized rural life; preserved our folk music heritage; and venerated hearts-and-flowers love. World War II and its aftermath changed all of that forever. Country songwriters and performers faced the new, spiritually troubled times head-on. Such previously taboo subjects as infidelity (cheatin'), alcohol, and divorce became common in country songs in the late 1940s and, indeed, became the dominant themes in the country music of the 1950s. The sound changed, too. The intimate, plaintive sound of "The National Barn Dance" harmonizers and the softly mournful style of acts like The Carter Family seemed totally outmoded. Singers became histrionic. Instrumentation thudded with bass and whined with steel guitars.

The change began in the rough roadhouses of the eastern Texas oil fields. There the honky-tonk first assumed its importance as a social gathering place. Oil field laborers who had worked hard all week gravitated to any old dive where they could dance, drink, and raise hell on Saturday nights. The musical accompaniment to this raucous behavior was most often the jukebox. This electronic amplifier of dance records was widely popular between 1938 and 1948. In fact, "juke joint" was a synonym for "honky-tonk." Only the glowing, multicolor jukebox had enough bass and volume to be heard over the din of the smoke-filled barrooms. When live country music was brought into such places, bands had to adjust accordingly.

During the war years western swing was the dominant dance music for country lovers. But a western swing band was usually too large and too expensive for a cheap roadside juke joint of the late 1940s. The band would have to be something new. Something with a slapped stand-up bass for rhythmic punch; an electric guitar for piercing noise; perhaps a small drum kit; and almost certainly a steel guitar for its sustained notes, tortured sound, wide emotional range, and whipped-dog whine. The singer would have to be something new, too. Honky-tonk vocalists went for unabashed theatricality. They wailed; they moaned; they whimpered; they shouted; they pleaded; they cried. With slurred phrases, bent-note effects, vocal breaks, and slippery yodel techniques, they practically wept in tune.

The band and its singer weren't the only things that changed to suit the rise of the unrespectable honky-tonk. Sentimental old-time tunes wouldn't do in an atmosphere of what one songwriter called "Cigareetes, Whuskey and Wild Wild Women." A new type of country song had to be written, and it was. Ted Daffan's "Born to Lose" (1944), Ernest Tubb's "Drivin' Nails in My Coffin" (1946), Lefty Frizzell's "If You've Got the Money I've Got the Time" (1950), and Hank Thompson's "The Wild Side of Life" (1952) all sprang from the Texas honky-tonks. From the social cauldron of postwar California came Merle Travis's "Divorce Me C.O.D." (1946), Tex Williams's "Smoke, Smoke, Smoke (That Cigarette)" (1947), and T. Texas Tyler's "Honky-Tonk Gal" (1948). Alabama's Hank Williams emerged as the definitive honky-tonker during his bright burst of fame, from 1947 to 1953, and he was followed by Louisiana's Webb Pierce and Faron Young, then more Texans, such as George Jones and Johnny Horton, as honky-tonk music rose to dominance.

Eventually, honky-tonk music completely overwhelmed country's other styles. But the wild-side-of-life honesty of the new sound didn't change things much for the women of country music. They still operated as a distinct minority. Fewer than 10 percent of the hit country records between 1945 and 1955 featured women's voices. New female stars were rare; it was all performers such as Lulu Belle, Rosalie Allen, Patsy Montana, and Cousin Emmy could do to hold their own in the busted-beer-bottles-and-busted-hearts climate of honky-tonk mania. The Dinning Sisters, Louise Massey, Louisiana Lou, and Elviry Weaver called it quits. Western stars Gail Davis and Dale Evans stuck to TV.

But as always there were a brave, hardy few who challenged the men on their own turf. Texas Ruby (1908–1963) was a strong, hefty gal with a ranch-life upbringing. She had a vocal bellow that could cut through the rowdiest crowd noise. Her deep, almost masculine alto was equally at home on blue yodels, honky-tonk cheatin' songs, old-time ballads, vaudeville blues, and folk tunes. They billed her as "The Sophie Tucker of the Feminine Folk Singers." Offstage Ruby was a hard-drinking, good-time mama with a cigarette in her red lips, a rowdy laugh, and a heart of pure gold.

Ruby Agnes Owens was belting out songs to the cowboys around the corral by age three in her native Wise County, Texas. The whole family was musical. Her brother Tex composed the cowboy standard "Cattle Call," and her niece Laura Lee Owens McBride gained fame as the female vocalist in Bob Wills's Texas Playboys western swing band. In 1930 Ruby accompanied her father and brothers on a cattle drive to Fort Worth. While their father conducted business, the Owens youngsters sat outside on a buckboard wagon and harmonized. One of the cattle buyers was also a stockholder of Kansas City's KMBC radio station. He offered the husky-voiced brunet a job, beginning a musical journey that took her to Detroit, Philadelphia, and Cincinnati by 1933. In the Ohio River city she hooked up with Zeke Clements and his Bronco Busters band. With Ruby as its powerful new lead singer the act soon rose to fame at "The Grand Ole Opry." Homesick for Texas, Ruby talked Zeke into heading west. En route they heard WHO's well-produced barn dance show from Des Moines, Iowa. They showed up at a rehearsal, sang one song, were hired on the spot, and remained at the show for the next two years. WHO's big star at the time was "The Southern Songbird," Louisiana Lou.

"Texas Ruby was always, I'd say, jealous of any other girl singer," Zeke recalls. "So they didn't have a friendship. Ruby had quite a temper." That's what WHO announcer Ronald "Dutch" Reagan found out. He emceed the Texas Ruby/Zeke Clements radio program until Ruby lit into him one day. "He wasn't real sociable around us," Zeke remembers. "He introduced our programs, but him and Ruby got into a fuss about something. I don't even remember what it was about. And she could be *prolific* with profanity. All I know is one day he wasn't announcing anymore. He refused to emcee. He just *set* there, did the station breaks for the network, and said, 'WHO, Des Moines.' And that's *all* he did." Not long after getting his ears scorched by Ruby's cussing, the future president went west for a screen test.

Ruby and Zeke were booked at New York's famed Village Barn nightclub on Fourteenth Street in 1936. That's where her husky delivery attracted the attention of the owner of Fort Worth's WBAP. He brought the team back to Texas to showcase at the board of directors' meeting of a big oil company that could sponsor their tours and radio shows. "Bless her heart, she got inebriated and *said* some things," says Zeke with a fond grin. "They said, 'You can stay on, but we can't have her.' So we just went on to California."

They paused in Dallas long enough to record for Decca in February 1937. The disc is a fine snapshot of her developing style: Ruby yodels merrily on the cowgirl standard "Pride of the Prairie (Mary)" and gives Jimmie Rodgers's "Blue Yodel No. 1 (T for Texas)" a fine, bluesy workout. Both performers' yodeling skills proved to be timely in Hollywood, for they arrived when Walt Disney was desperately seeking voices to sing the parts of the mining little people in his groundbreaking, full-length cartoon *Snow White and the Seven Dwarfs*. Zeke wound up as the yodeling voice of Bashful; Ruby got loaded and missed the auditions; they split up.

Ruby next teamed up with Tennessee trick fiddler Curly Fox, whom she married in 1939. The low-voiced cowgirl and the dextrous, flashy instrumentalist settled at the Opry from 1944 to 1948. They were among the first Opry stars to get big money on its touring tent shows, asking for and getting five hundred dollars a night. On Ruby's wartime Opry shows she sang "With Jesus on Our Side" and "There's a Star-Spangled Banner Waving Somewhere." During her Cincinnati stint in 1939 she taught

Merle Travis his famous labor song "Nine Pound Hammer." But it was the postwar period that was Ruby's true heyday as a performer. She was not only a "Grand Ole Opry" star, she was a recording star for Columbia (1945–1946) and King (1947). Her songs, many of which she wrote, deal repeatedly with the honky-tonk themes of cheating, betrayal, and recrimination. "Soldier's Return" is about a veteran whose girlfriend has left him for another. "Blue Love in My Heart" and "Ain't You Sorry That You Lied" are classic country postwar problem songs, while "You've Been Cheating on Me," "Have You Got Someone Else on the String," and "Don't Let That Man Get You Down" bring the honky-tonk issues right out in the open.

Ruby's marvelously robust voice was captured on two albums' worth of material before she and Fox relocated to Houston in 1948 to become fifties favorites in Texas. The couple starred on "Town Hall Party" in Los Angeles in 1960, then on Amarillo radio in

Don't Let That Man Get You Down

By FRED ROSE

RECORDED FOR COLUMBIA RECORDS BY TEXAS RUBY AND CURLY FOX

Milene Music

120 CAPITOL BOULEVARD
NASHVILLE 3, TENN.

"The Sophie Tucker of the Cowgirl Singers" poses with husband Curly Fox on the cover of this 1946 piece of sheet music. Deep-voiced Texas Ruby was one of the most assertive women of her era.

1961. In mid-1962 they returned to Nashville. Curly resumed his Opry entertaining, but Ruby made only occasional appearances. In March 1963 Texas Ruby and Curly Fox recorded a comeback album in Music City. On Friday, March 29, he went to the Opry to perform. Curly arrived home that night to find fire fighters battling the flames that engulfed their mobile home. Ruby, fifty-four, perished in the trailer. Most country music insiders believe she passed out holding a cigarette and set her bed on fire. King Records issued Ruby's "Shanty Street" as a posthumous single. It was about a woman from the wrong side of the tracks.

Most of Ruby's records straddle the fence between the prewar and postwar country styles. Her themes are modern, but only occasionally, as on 1946's "Nobody Else but You," was the instrumentation full-blown electrified honky-tonk, complete with drums. Her successors were more aggressive.

California's The Maddox Brothers and Rose plunged into the new style with all the subtlety of a whistle-shrieking locomotive without its brakes. The act was already performing such suggestive fare as "Sally Let Your Bangs Hang Down" when it picked up steam again after World War II. Rose soon added a passel of raucous numbers to fit the mood of California's frenzied country scene—"Hangover Blues," "Honky Tonkin',"

"Ugly and Slouchy," and the like. By this time the former Dust Bowl migrants were resplendent in eye-popping, colorfully embroidered, nouveau-cowboy costumes, and their uproarious honky-tonk showmanship was second to none.

Rose's radio theme song was the up-tempo wail of brokenhearted betrayal "I Couldn't Believe It Was True." She revived Lulu Belle's "I Wish I Was a Single Girl Again," but put a more modern spin on women's issues in the tongue-in-cheek "(Pay Me) Alimony."

"The California scene was completely different," recalls Rose of her honky-tonk heyday. "It's more fun and more raunchy, not quite so professional and after perfection as Nashville. A little more kickin'-ass, let's put it that way."

In 1956 Rose went solo. "It was slowly falling apart anyway. After twenty years together it was just automatically fading. The boys all got married, and their wives was pullin' in another direction, wantin' 'em to stay home and all such as that. I never did agree with them. I was raised in it: Music was just . . . doin' my job. Besides, I didn't know anything different."

She continued her honky-tonking on such 1950s singles as "Hasty Baby" and "Wild, Wild Young Men." She entered the sixties with the biggest hits of her career, "Conscience, I'm Guilty," "Sing a Little Song of Heartache," and "Down to the River." Rose teamed with protégé Buck Owens on four hit duets between 1961 and 1963, "Loose Talk," "Mental Cruelty," "We're the Talk of the Town," and "Sweethearts in Heaven"; then he went on to become a honky-tonk superstar.

"Prairie Home Companion" radio star Garrison Keillor "asked me a few years ago, 'How does it feel to be called Queen of the Honky-Tonks?' I said, 'I didn't know that I was. But I guess it makes me feel all right.' It's better than bein' queen of nothin'. . . . I think I would'a wound up singin', whatever happened in my life. I think I've been singin' for two hundred years, in other lives. I was always a honky-tonk singer."

The dusty soil of the Lone Star State was even more fertile for the growth of the honky-tonk sound than California was in the late 1940s and early 1950s. So it comes as no surprise that the only woman as exuberant and showy as Rose Maddox in the postwar era was Texan Charline Arthur (1929–1987). Charline leaped from stage amplifiers, hollered honky-tonk blues, sang lying down onstage, and cavorted wildly to entertain the tough Texas crowds. Her gutsy, dynamic stage style even endeared her to a young Elvis Presley. "I was the first to break out of the [country female] stereotype and boogie woogie," Charline bragged to journalist Bob Allen in 1985. "I was shakin' that thing on stage long before Elvis even thought about it. I worked harder on stage than he ever worked, and he was not even heard of at the time.

"I was the first woman in country music to wear a slack suit on stage, when all the other women were wearin' those little gingham dresses. . . . Wanda Jackson, Brenda Lee, and Patsy Cline all, in some way, patterned their styles after me. I was a trendsetter. I was a blues singer, and I wanted to sing something different. I wanted to be an original."

She was born Charline Highsmith, in a Texas railroad boxcar, the second of twelve children of an impoverished, harmonica-playing Pentecostal preacher and his guitarist wife. As a kid Charline was enthralled with the sound of honky-tonk star Ernest Tubb. She learned all his songs on a $4.95 guitar she'd bought with money she earned from the deposits on discarded pop bottles she collected along roadsides. She and her sister Dottie formed a duet to sing at churches and community events in their hometown of Paris, Texas. A traveling medicine show came through town in 1945, and the fifteen-year-old got a job in the troupe for twenty-five dollars a week. Despite their religious reservations, her parents let Charline go. She met and married bass player Jack Arthur in 1948 while touring in the show. By 1949 she was hitting the honky-tonks as a solo singer, with him as her manager, and recording a single for Bullet Records. The tune was "I've Got the Boogie Blues," which Charline had written at age twelve.

Charline Arthur, 1954.

In 1950 Charline landed a daily radio job at KERB in Kermit, Texas. She was both a DJ and a singer on the station, broadcasting twice a day, six days a week. Famed music entrepreneur Colonel Tom Parker heard her and brought her to the attention of the Hill and Range song publishing company and of RCA Records in 1952. Both were to discover they had their hands full with the hotheaded, hard-living Texas twister.

In keeping with her bold, pull-out-the-stops singing style, Charline was a scrappy, temperamental woman. She clashed frequently with her music industry bosses, notably producer/guitarist Chet Atkins. "He and I would get up in arms," she recalled. "He always had songs he wanted me to record that I didn't want to record, and I had ones I'd written that he wouldn't let me record." Charline fought for the right to become country's first truly aggressive, independent female of the postwar era. Ultimately she lost.

But not before putting out such feisty country-boogie numbers as "I'm Having a Party All by Myself," "Leave My Man Alone," and "Just Look, Don't Touch, He's Mine." Because of her singles "Welcome to the Club," "Honey Bun," and "Burn That Candle," Charline is often cited as a pioneering rockabilly female. She was capable of such piercing, classic, honky-tonk heartache wailers, yet could romp through something as sprightly and innocent as "Lookin' at the Moon Wishing on a Star" with equal finesse.

She stirred up DJs' attention with several novelty tunes. On "The Good and the Bad" (1954) she argues with herself, using a growling blues tone for sexual aggression and a soft, echo-chamber soprano for "ladylike" behavior. The vamp wins. On "Flash Your Diamonds (Show Your Gold)" (1954) she's a baldly honest golddigger out to take a guy for all he's worth. With its sexy moaning vocal effects, 1955's "Kiss the Baby Goodnight" seems to have raised an eyebrow or two in conservative Nashville.

"[Opry announcer] Grant Turner had to screen my material before they'd let me sing it on the air, because I was so controversial," she recalled with glee. "When I did 'Kiss the Baby Goodnight,' he had to listen to it first and see how dirty it was. They made me leave out some of the real racy parts."

Her RCA contract got her top bookings, including the "Louisiana Hayride," the "Ozark Jubilee," "The Grand Ole Opry," and the "Big D Jamboree" in Dallas. Charline toured with Ray Price, Lefty Frizzell, Webb Pierce, Faron Young, and the other big honky-tonk stars of the day, but lamented, "Most of the time I was the only female singer among the men. . . . That's just how lopsided the music business was in favor of men in those days." In 1955 she finished second to Kitty Wells as Best Female Singer in a country disc jockey poll. But the next year she got into another tiff with Atkins while working in the studio. RCA dropped her, and because of her reputation for being controversial and "difficult," no other major record label took her in. By 1957 she and Jack were living in a mobile home in Dallas. They separated and she began her steady decline into honky-tonk hell, taking jobs for peanuts in dives in "Texas, Minnesota, Montana, Wyoming, California, anywhere I could get a singing job and keep myself alive." She hit bottom in Salt Lake City in January 1960, "so down on my luck I didn't have two nickels to rub together." She got a five-year job in a honky-tonk in Chubbuck, Idaho.

In 1969 Alice M. Michaels found her down and out in neighboring Pocatello. "She was in pretty bad shape at the time," Alice recalls. "She gave up 'til my husband and I took her in and showed her that God's talents were to be used for all the world to enjoy." Alice became her manager and helped Charline get back on her feet with bookings in California and the Rocky Mountain states and with some small-label singles. Charline was a fine lead guitarist and developed into a good stage comedian, but by the late 1970s arthritis had crippled her hands and she was reduced to living on a $335-a-month disability pension. She had no telephone and not even enough money to send out flyers and photos to promote her tattered career.

"Her life story is not pretty," Alice Michaels says. "Twice she climbed from the gutter and went out on top. She wasn't very happy at the end." In later years Charline would sit and watch The Nashville Network on Idaho cable TV and weep at the sight of her former Music City friends and coworkers. The German company Bear Family Records reissued her classic RCA sides of the early 1950s in 1986. "Of course I cried when I heard it," Charline wrote label executive Richard Weize. "It's been 30 years since I recorded the songs, and it opened up a past that I'll never forget. . . . Thank God you had an ear for something no one else seemed to have." Charline died in her sleep at age fifty-eight a year later.

Charline Arthur had a brassy, sassy voice that was packed with personality. Her wide range, ' -your-face wailing, and penetrating barroom quality made her one of the great stylists of the postwar honky-tonk period. She should have been a country queen, but instead wound up bitter, disillusioned, and broke.

There's little doubt that her combative attitude, stick-to-your-guns musical determination, unwillingness to compromise, and outspoken personality were factors in her downfall. A woman who acted like this in the early 1950s was marked as "abnormal" or even "sick" by the army of psychiatrists newly loose on the land. Psychoanalyst Helen Deutsch wrote in 1944 that a "normal" woman "leaves the initiative to the man and out of her own needs, renounces originality." In the era when biology was destiny and a woman's destiny was to be wife and mother, to live through her husband and children, Charline Arthur was swimming against the tide.

Anything that disturbed a woman's adjustment into her postwar role as a housewife was thought to be a problem, said feminist Betty Friedan, who came of age during this era. Having an education, becoming politically active, asserting individuality, and, particularly, working at a career were all unfeminine, she recalled. In the women's magazines, you solved your problems by dyeing your hair blond or having a baby.

So instead of a feisty, saucy shouter, an unassuming southern matron ascended to the throne as the honky-tonk era's Queen of Country Music. Kitty Wells was a thirty-three-year-old wife and mother when she rose to stardom. Into the new world of smoke-filled taverns, thudding jukeboxes, and tears-in-your-beer misery stepped a woman of the old school who bent her traditional country style to suit the temper of the times. Kitty Wells was as much a part of the dying, Victorian, old-time country culture as she was a standard-bearer of the postwar style. Publicly she sang of guilt and remorse, of illicit romance and sin, of betrayal and broken dreams. Privately she was the polite mother of three and a shy, soft-spoken, dutiful housewife. She was steeped in tradition, but became a star as an innovator.

Kitty's tight-lipped intensity, piercing nasality, gospel-touched vocal power, tearful restraint, and pent-up fervor conveyed modern problems so well. She is at once fiercely emotional yet incredibly reserved; it is this tension in her keening, plaintive vibrato that makes her so involving as a stylist. Perhaps not coincidentally, the Opry at first rejected her as a singer because she wasn't exuberant enough, then forbade her to sing "It Wasn't God Who Made Honky-Tonk Angels" on the show because it was too outspoken.

Kitty sang of "honky-tonk angels," but no one would have ever mistaken her for one. She was always proper, always dignified. She dressed in prewar gingham instead of pantsuits, flamboyant western garb, or satin costumes. She was a levelheaded, unpretentious homebody who spun out a doleful catalog of cheatin' songs that spoke directly to women victimized by the honky-tonk life-style.

"I never gave that any thought when I'd listen to a song," Kitty comments. "If I did a song, it wasn't aimed at any certain person. It was just a song I liked and that I hoped other people would like. . . . Country music relates to people because they think that what happened in the songs might have happened to them or to somebody they know."

The lyrics she sang say it all. "You said that you'd be happy / With a baby on your knees," she lamented in 1952's "I Heard the Jukebox Playing," "but here I sit with him in my arms / And you're slipping out on me." When honky-tonker Webb Pierce sang of his "Back Street Affair," Kitty answered with 1953's "I'm Paying for That Back Street Affair." She surrendered to passion but suffered a woman's guilt in 1955's "There's Poison in Your Heart." She took the role of the barroom sinner in 1953's "Honky Tonk Waltz" and "I Don't Claim to Be an Angel." But "She's No Angel" (1957) and "The Life They Live in Songs" (1953) were from the point of view of a woman wise to the ways of the world who keeps her distance from wickedness. She admitted moral weakness in her "One by One" 1954 duet with Red Foley and faced the cheating issue with Roy Acuff in "Goodbye Mr. Brown" in 1955.

She almost always sang weepers like "Amigo's Guitar" and "Searching," for Kitty mined the forsaken territory of losers who moaned of "Jealousy" and "Repenting" on "The Lonely Side of Town." She sang that "Cheatin's a Sin" and wept about being "Mommy for a Day." Hers was a "Wicked World" where she ruled as "Queen of Honky-Tonk Street." Kitty Wells took the woebegone woman's point of view consistently in such honky-tonk monuments as "A Wedding Ring Ago," "After Dark," "Heartbreak

USA," "I Gave My Wedding Dress Away," and "Unloved, Unwanted." Such mournful laments—eighty-one hits in all—made Kitty Wells the biggest female star of her generation.

"Kitty was in the role of the mistreated housewife, and she was very believable," said her producer, Owen Bradley. "People identified with what she was saying. As long as she stuck to that formula, we had a hit."

"Sincerity" is a word often used to describe Kitty's no-frills delivery, and she came by it naturally. Her father was a country guitarist, her uncle a square dance fiddler, and her mother a gospel singer. The whole family sang. Born Muriel Ellen Deason in 1919, Kitty learned folk songs in her Nashville living room, guitar chords from a neighbor, hymns in church, and hillbilly music at "The Grand Ole Opry." But "I never dreamed of makin' a career in music or travelin' like we have. I never thought that one day I would work on 'The Grand Ole Opry.' But I grew up with it." By age fifteen Kitty had dropped out of school and was working at the Washington Manufacturing Company, ironing new shirts for nine dollars a week. Her musical cousin Bessie Choate had moved to Nashville from the country, and Kitty formed an act with her, called The Deason Sisters, sometimes augmented by her real siblings Jewel and Mae. They worked up The Carter Family's "Jealous Hearted Me" and sang it for the men who ran Nashville's WSIX radio station in 1936. "They thought it was a little risqué," Kitty recalls, because of the line "it takes the man I love to satisfy my soul." Station executives cut the teen team off the air in midperformance, but listeners protested. The Deason Sisters wound up with their own fifteen-minute early-morning show.

Cabinetmaker Johnnie Wright had a sister who lived next door to the Deasons. She told him about her musical neighbor, and soon Johnnie and Kitty were swapping songs. Drawn together by their mutual love of country music, the couple married in 1937. Johnnie, Kitty, and his sister Louise were soon singing on the Nashville airwaves as Johnnie Wright and the Harmony Girls. Then he teamed up with Jack Anglin in 1939 to form Johnnie and Jack.

With a newborn daughter, Ruby, Kitty dropped out of any regular radio singing during the early 1940s. She loyally followed the male duo as they trouped from Nashville to a grueling round of second-string hillbilly broadcasting jobs in Greensboro, Charleston, Bluefield, Knoxville, Raleigh, Decatur, and Birmingham. Kitty performed her ballads and gospel songs as the "girl singer" on their show. Second child

Gingham-clad Kitty Wells ponders the mysteries of postwar infidelity on the jacket of this 1958 record.

Bobby was born along the way, as was Muriel's stage name, which Johnnie chose from the old Pickard Family tune "Kitty Wells." Jack Anglin enlisted in the army during World War II; Johnnie took a wartime job north of Nashville at the DuPont chemical factory, and gas rationing put a stop to the radio wanderings.

But after the war Johnnie and Jack were at it again. This time Kitty trailed along to the new "Louisiana Hayride" barn dance on KWKH in Shreveport. She was singing again, and also began spinning records on the air under the moniker "Rag Doll," because she sold quilting supplies on her show. At the Hayride, Kitty and Johnnie became friendly with the tempestuous honky-tonk couple Hank and Audrey Williams.

Kitty recorded some gospel and old-time numbers for RCA in 1949 and 1950, including Rose Maddox's "Gathering Flowers for the Master's Bouquet" and Linda Parker's "I'll Be All Smiles Tonight," but the discs went nowhere. "I don't think they were really promoted that much. . . . I think the record distributors were leery of taking them. . . . I don't know if it really was because I was a woman." In any case she'd pretty much decided to retire when Johnnie and Jack's driving, percussive hit "Poison Love" brought the duo to the Opry cast in 1952. Back in her hometown Kitty was persuaded to record once more when Decca Records brought her an answer song to Hank Thompson's hit indictment of a wayward woman, "The Wild Side of Life."

"I was staying at home quite a bit," Kitty says. "It was just a song to me at the time. . . . I said, 'Well, it probably won't make a hit, but we will at least get a session fee out of it.'" Thinking mostly of the $125 union scale she'd get, Kitty went into Owen Bradley's studio on May 3, 1952, sang "It Wasn't God Who Made Honky-Tonk Angels," the World War II anthem "Searching for a Soldier's Grave," and a pair of other tunes, and forgot about it. Three weeks later she ran into her old friend Audrey Williams, who informed her, "You've got a hit on your hands." "It Wasn't God Who Made Honky-Tonk Angels" was first noted by *Billboard* on June 18, began climbing the charts in July, was a sales sensation by the end of the summer, and was a full-blown phenomenon by the end of the year. "It's a shame that all the blame is on us women," Kitty sang. "Too many times married men think they're still single / That has caused many a good girl to go wrong."

Although the song echoes such venerable sentiments as 1894's "She Is More to Be Pitied Than Censured," its premise that hypocritical, deceitful men are responsible for fallen women was controversial in the conservative climate of the early 1950s. The NBC radio network banned "It Wasn't God Who Made Honky-Tonk Angels" as "suggestive." Kitty wasn't allowed to sing it on Opry broadcasts, either. But Minnie Pearl remembers that audiences adored the number: "Fans went wild over Kitty. When she did 'Honky-Tonk Angels,' they'd scream and holler and carry on. . . . After World War II things began to change. Women began getting fed up with their way of life. They started to push against it, and when they heard songs that reinforced their feelings, or songs of love told from a woman's point of view, they identified with it and they went out and bought the records."

"They didn't seem to write songs for women before then," Kitty recalled to reporter Thomas Goldsmith. "Mostly, [songs] were for men. . . . There weren't a lot of songs to choose from. You had to sing them or not sing at all. . . . ['Honky-Tonk Angels'] was kind of the womenfolk getting back at the men."

She introduced a slew of country standards in its wake, essentially defining the postwar female style. The immortal honky-tonk classics "Release Me" (1954), "Makin' Believe" (1955), and "I Can't Stop Loving You" (1958) were all first brought to the airwaves by Kitty. She warned "Your Wild Life's Gonna Get You Down," moaned "Our Mansion Is a Prison Now," asked "Will Your Lawyer Talk to God?," cautioned "A Woman Never Forgets," and gave a man the kiss-off for his "Broken Marriage Vows." But it was Johnnie who picked the tunes to fit her image and Johnnie who was by her side throughout. He scored a huge 1965 solo hit with "Hello Vietnam," but she remained indisputably the bigger star in their road show. Daughters Ruby and Carol Sue and son Bobby became part of "The Kitty Wells–Johnnie Wright Show," and all three graduated to individual success, Ruby with 1964's "Dern Ya," Bobby on TV's "McHale's Navy" (1964–1966), and Carol Sue as her mother's 1956 duet partner on "How Far Is Heaven."

"We just try to make a family show out of it," Kitty says. "Don't any one tries to outshine the other. We're not jealous of each other. I don't try to push myself out in front of Johnnie. If anything, I'll push him forward rather than to be out front myself. I've always been easygoin'. I don't like to make any enemies. I just like it for everybody to like me, you know?

"It never did bother me about who was Number 1 or who wasn't. In fact, it was kind of embarrassing to go up there year after year, accepting the best-girl-singer award when there were other good singers, such as Goldie Hill, Skeeter Davis, and Jean Shepard." Nevertheless, the music trade magazines named Kitty Wells country's top female stylist every year from 1952 to 1965. She starred in her own syndicated TV show beginning in 1968. One of Nashville's best country chefs, she has published a series of down-home cookbooks. She was elected to the Country

Music Hall of Fame in 1976, opened her own museum in 1983, won the Pioneer Award from the Academy of Country Music in 1986, and was nominated for a 1989 Grammy Award for her "Honky-Tonk Angels Medley" with k.d. lang, Loretta Lynn, and Brenda Lee. During the 1991 Grammy ceremony Kitty was given a Lifetime Achievement Award, along with Bob Dylan, Marian Anderson, and John Lennon.

In her way Kitty stayed contemporary during the decades following her breakthrough hit. She scored a minor hit with Dylan's "Forever Young" as late as 1974 and two years later she commented wryly on a popular TV show with "Mary Hartman, Mary Hartman." She answered a big 1982 David Frizzell hit with "You Don't Have to Hire a Wino (To Decorate Our Home)" and costarred with Tanya Tucker in Gary Morris's humorous 1990 music video "Miles Across the Bedroom." Even into the nineties Kitty worked more than 150 shows a year.

The lonely wail of her voice backed by weeping steel guitar, crying fiddle, thumping bass, throbbing rhythm guitar, and tinny piano can still transport the listener to a crummy, postwar barroom. There, the sorrowful men and women of her songs act out their dramas of passion, regret, anger, joy, and heartbreak. Kitty cried for them and created a spine-chilling body of work that more than earned her the title The Queen of Country Music.

But where were her ladies-in-waiting? Alas, her court was a small one—Kitty Wells came along just as the country music industry was developing a set of business prejudices that would keep female performers down for decades to come. It is a cruel irony for women that this industry settled in Nashville, for no southern city is so hidebound by conservative religion, and no radio barn dance was as resistant to female performers as its Opry. Roy Acuff advised Johnnie Wright not to bill Kitty as a star on their tours, saying, "Don't ever headline a show with a woman. It won't ever work, because people just don't go for women." Music Row's axioms are that country women don't sell records, that fans won't buy tickets for female entertainers' shows, that it's not worth investing in women because they give up their careers for marriages or pregnancies. Up to the 1980s there was an unwritten law at country radio stations that you never played two female records in a row. "It wasn't because they had any prejudice against women," producer Chet Atkins once explained. "They just didn't think they could make any money off them. No one ever had in the past, and in those days women were confined by conformity."

A 1949 *Billboard* magazine story charged that there was discrimination throughout the music world after Jo Stafford's manager complained that women weren't getting a fair shake from concert promoters and radio broadcasters. "A show business battle of the sexes may be shaping up," said the article. "It's necessary for the entire fem contingent to hit the road via theater and concert dates to stimulate their popularity and prove that they are just as sound talent properties as men. If one or several women performers are lax in this respect, the remainder suffer, too."

Kitty Wells's success at least led record companies to experiment with other female country stylists in the early 1950s. Decca Records attempted to duplicate Owen Bradley's golden touch with Kitty by signing Goldie Hill, "The Golden Hillbilly." Good-natured Goldie, born in Karnes City, Texas, in 1933, tagged along with her older brother Tommy to one of his recording sessions in 1952. "A country music bandleader told Tommy he wanted a girl singer who could play bass fiddle," Goldie recalled. "Tommy said he had just the girl, and before I knew it, I was holding a bass fiddle for the first time in my life." Within a year she was a Decca star, a "Louisiana Hayride" headliner, a "Grand Ole Opry" member, and the singer of the chart-topping hit "I Let the Stars Get in My Eyes." The zesty, likable, blue-eyed blonde was heavily promoted by the country fan magazines, winning *Country Song Roundup*'s choice as Best Female Artist of 1953. In 1954 Goldie became the first solo cover girl of the magazine, now country's longest running. Her straightforward alto graced five more hits, and she was scouted by Hollywood. Then she married honky-tonk king Carl Smith.

"Since Goldie's marriage in 1957 to singer Carl, most of her own singing has been as a homemaker indulging in household humming, while hanging up new drapes or a pair of her husband's old jeans in the rambling ranch house," said the liner notes to The Golden Hillbilly's first album. Goldie recorded some more in the late 1950s and late 1960s, but was never consumed with ambition. "I never missed it a bit," she said after her retirement from music. "I was never that hooked on it."

"Kitty and Goldie Start Country-Girl Search" headlined *Billboard* on June 20, 1953. Noting the few country women around, the article said that Kitty's Number 1 hit "It Wasn't God Who Made Honky-Tonk Angels" and Goldie's Number 1 hit "I Let the Stars Get in My Eyes" had music executives "scouring the hinterlands for additional girl country singers." *Billboard*'s scribe continued, "While it is true . . . that girl vocalists in any musical field are never as consistent in sales as are the male singers, the country field has always been a tough one for fem thrushes. . . . While the recording execs are not yet willing to predict a major trend toward girl singers in the country market, they all agree that the spark lit by Misses

In 1954 Goldie Hill became the first solo female star to make the cover of *Country Song Roundup*.

Wells and Hill seems to have fired some additional enthusiasm for the fem singers." Columbia Records had Rose Maddox, Jeanette Hicks, Betty Johnson, Daisy Mae, Molly O'Day, Wilma Lee Cooper, and Polly Possum. King Records signed Ann Jones and Bonnie Lou. MGM signed Rita Faye and Audrey Williams. At RCA Chet Atkins experimented with Charline Arthur, Betty Cody, and The Davis Sisters.

Betty Cody was the closest to Kitty Wells in both plaintive vocal style and heartache lyric content. In answer to Webb Pierce's giant drinking hit "There Stands the Glass," Betty pleaded "Please Throw Away the Glass" in 1953. Betty was born Rita Cote in Quebec in 1921 and moved to northern Maine with her family when she was still a child. Taught music by nuns at her French Catholic school, Betty didn't sing in English until age fourteen. Her brother brought home Patsy Montana's 1935 record of "I Want to Be a Cowboy's Sweetheart" and dared Betty to learn to yodel. She was inspired, as her best-selling "Tom Tom Yodel" of 1952 reveals. Betty began performing on local radio stations at age fifteen and continued to sing semiprofessionally while working in a shoe factory.

In 1940 she married Harold Breau, known as Lone Pine to New England country fans. Joining his act, she adopted her stage name and began to tour the Northeast. They were signed to RCA in 1952 and joined the WWVA "Wheeling Jamboree" barn dance cast the following year. Despite some solid honky-tonk heartbreak tunes and a Top 10 hit with the catchy answer song "I Found Out More Than You'll Ever Know" (1953), Betty's recording career never really took off. She retired to raise her three sons, one of whom became the jazz guitar great Lenny Breau.

Woman after woman tried and failed to duplicate Kitty Wells's success in solo singing careers during the hard-hitting honky-tonk era. Georgia's Ginny Wright was billed as having "the voice that Hank Williams would have had if he'd been a girl," but her Abbott records stiffed. Her sixteen-year-old labelmate Carolyn Bradshaw managed one Top 10 hit by answering Jim Reeves's "Mexican Joe" with 1953's "The Marriage of Mexican Joe," then disappeared from the charts. WWVA's Mabelle Seiger, WLS's Phyllis Brown, and WRVA's Arline Wiltshire all attempted unsuccessfully to capture the national audience. A flurry of promotion for kiddie acts didn't work, either. The only one who made any radio noise was RCA's Sunshine Ruby (Bateman), with her husky, castanet-propelled "Too Young to Tango" hit of 1953.

Sister duos proliferated, but few scored big hits. Jean and Jane Leeper, known as The Oklahoma Sweethearts, got noticed with their Korean War tune "Don't Steal Daddy's Medal" in 1951. Chicago's Miccolis Sisters kept up with the times with "Boogie Woogie Yodel" and "Truck Driver's

Blues" in 1948. The Morgan Sisters tried the same with "Mambo Honky-Tonk" and "Low Down Hoe Down" in 1953 and 1954. The saucy-voiced Marlin Sisters, Trudy and Gloria, got the biggest hits of the postwar sister duos by teaming with polka king Frankie Yankovic on 1949's "Charlie Was a Boxer" and "Blue Skirt Waltz."

Country music women continued to seek safety in numbers—several all-girl bands formed. The Westernettes worked out of Norwalk, California, in the mid-fifties as a western-swing ensemble. During the late forties The Saddle Sweethearts were active in Philadelphia, and the all-girl gospel band The Crusaders serenaded Detroit. Former circus trapeze artist Ardis Arlee Wells assembled her Rhythm Ranch Girls in Minneapolis/St. Paul in 1956 and 1957.

Ann Jones and Her Western Sweethearts got together in 1955. A hefty alto, Jones was billed as "The Kate Smith of the West" as she rose to fame in California. Born in Kansas around 1925, Ann was the youngest of fourteen children who moved west with their parents during the 1930s. A brief attempt at a radio career with her sister ended with both women's marrying; Ann wed her manager, Huey Jones, in 1937. She was quite active in sports, becoming a star in a wartime all-girl softball team. But she returned to music in 1947. In 1949 she hit the country charts with the self-composed "Give Me a Hundred Reasons," her biggest hit. Her other Capitol Records honky-tonkers included "Bloodshot Eyes," "You've Gotta See Mama," "Post Office," and "Baby Sitter's Blues." An article in the 1952 *Scrapbook of Hillbilly Western Stars* explained her dedication to songwriting: "Like most gal singers, Ann has found it a problem to find songs for girls, since most are written for men. She solved this by writing many of her own tunes." Her output from 1951 to 1955 included "Hi-Ballin' Daddy," "A Little Bit of Nylon," "I've Had It," and "Knockin' Blues." Ann is the only female country star of the era who wrote all her own material; she also provided songs for other stars. As a bandleader, she kept her all-female Western Sweethearts lineup together for more than a decade.

With the exception of Lily May Ledford and The Coon Creek Girls, only one other woman enjoyed more longevity as an "all-girl band" leader. Abbie Neal's first experience in an all-female lineup was in 1940; more than twenty years later she was still sharing songs with sisters-in-harmony. Abbie was born around 1920 in the Pennsylvania Appalachians, an area most Keystone State residents call "Pennsyltucky." At age six she was playing organ in Brookville, Pennsylvania. She picked up the violin at age eight, taught herself guitar at twelve, and by seventeen had mastered banjo, mandolin, piano, accordion, and ukulele.

In the wake of World War II, the "all-girl band" concept was kept alive by Ann Jones and Her Western Sweethearts, pictured here on an LP jacket of the mid-1950s.

After winning several fiddle contests, she organized her first band in 1936. Four years later she became the lead instrumentalist in Cowboy Phil's Golden West Girls band in Greensburg. This all-girl combo entertained at bases in the South Pacific on a USO tour in 1945 and 1946, then took up residence at KQV radio in Pittsburgh. Stints at the WWVA "Wheeling Jamboree" in West Virginia and WHO "Barn Dance Frolic" in Iowa followed.

Abbie formed her own Ranch Girls band in 1949. A Pittsburgh jewelry company sponsored the women, and they became stars of their own daily TV show on the then-new medium. "Everything stops at our house when it's time for 'our' gals to visit with us at seven o'clock," wrote one Steel City fan. The women became regulars on Wheeling's "Jamboree," commuting back to Pittsburgh for weekly TV broadcasts in the mid-1950s. Abbie married WWVA executive Gene Johnson in 1953. Two years later Abbie Neal & The Ranch Girls won on "Arthur Godfrey's Talent Scouts" and were showcased nationally on CBS. In sporty petite cowgirl hats, crisp white western boots, elaborate white-fringed outfits, and stylish hairdos, The Ranch Girls graduated to supper clubs, international air force tours, recording, and Las Vegas show rooms in the late 1950s. Their longevity was at least partly due to their versatility, for the women could breeze through western swing, polkas, close-harmony numbers, gospel, and even rock 'n' roll with aplomb.

Banjo-playing songwriter Betty Amos carried the "all-girl band" tradition into the 1960s. The Virginia native first gained fame when she joined her cousins The Carlisles from 1950 to 1954 on such raucous hits as "No Help Wanted," "Shake a Leg," and "Iz Zat You, Myrtle?" Betty formed her all-girl band when she joined the Starday label in the 1960s. During this period she wrote and sang an indictment of country-star parenting called "If Mommy Didn't Sing." Betty found that songwriting was her true niche by penning Jean Shepard's "Second Fiddle" and "Franklin County Moonshine" of 1964.

Audrey Williams (1923–1975) was another who took the all-girl concept into the sixties. After dreadful solo records on Decca and MGM in the 1950s Audrey slowly slid into the same abyss of drugs and alcohol that killed her legendary husband, Hank. Painfully ungifted, but beautiful and fiercely ambitious, the blond entrepreneur became a country music movie mogul, song publisher, and booking agent before forming a miniskirted, all-brunets band to back her in a comeback attempt. They were called The Cold, Cold Hearts. Like all her other singing attempts, this effort was doomed. In addition to being practically tone deaf, Audrey was hampered by her reputation for out-of-control emotions and substance abuse. After The Cold, Cold Hearts called it quits in 1970, so did she. The faded honky-tonk consort attempted suicide, was arrested for drunk driving, and staged a chemical-crazed Hank Williams garage sale in Nashville that turned into an embarrassing media spectacle. Her extravagant life-style and openhearted generosity devastated her finances. The day before the IRS came to take away the home that she and Hank had shared, Audrey died in bed.

When Hank and Audrey were in their prime in the early fifties, all-girl acts were common. One of the most significant was The Melody Ranch Girls, for it launched the greatest female honky-tonk stylist of all, Jean Shepard. Born one of ten Oklahoma sharecropper children in 1933, Jean moved with her family to California in 1943. "We were so poor that when there was a Depression we didn't even know it," Jean recalls. "I know Loretta Lynn was poor, but compared to us she couldn't even *spell* it.

"My mother and daddy hocked every stick of furniture in their house to a finance company to buy me a big upright bass. They were very supportive of me. You see, me and a bunch of girls who went to high school together formed an all-girl band. We called it The Melody Ranch Girls." At age fifteen Jean was singing virtually every weekend. She remained with The Melody Ranch Girls throughout her early career, 1951 through 1954. "We weren't really that good, but we had a lot of fun. We played for dances and everything, and we done pretty good. We averaged playin' about three nights a week and went out to Oregon, Washington, and up the West Coast a lot. One night I had the pleasure of gettin' up and singing with Hank Thompson. Hank had out 'The Wild Side of Life' and was just really great. He asked me if I had a recording contract. And I said, 'No, sir.' And he said, 'Well, you will have soon.'" Six months later the seventeen-year-old was signed to Capitol Records.

"Producers didn't believe in female singers," Jean recalls. "They said they just couldn't imagine country girl singers ever making it. . . . In fact, [Capitol producer] Ken Nelson told Hank, 'Female singers just really won't sell.' Hank said, 'Well, but every band needs one.' Hank just insisted." Thompson's faith was rewarded. Jean's Okie twang and piercing vocal penetration hit the hillbilly airwaves in 1952's "Cryin' Steel Guitar Waltz," the first of dozens of superb honky-tonk performances that characterize the first phase of her long recording career. Jean first hit Number 1 in 1953 by teaming with Ferlin Husky on the Korean War weeper "A Dear John Letter."

In 1954 Jean released country music's first female concept album, a brilliant tapestry of distaff emotions called *Songs of a Love Affair.* She hit the road, arriving at the "Ozark Jubilee" in Springfield, Missouri, in

1955, when she was scoring hit after hit with "A Satisfied Mind," "Beautiful Lies," "I Thought of You," and other singles. "It was scary, because I'd never been out on my own, to go rent my own little apartment. It was adventuresome. . . . Women just weren't headliners; they just were not."

Jean also joined "The Grand Ole Opry" in 1955, a time when the only other female cast members were comedian Minnie Pearl, piano player Del Wood, and superstar Kitty Wells. In time, Jean became the show's most outspoken and fiery female personality. The Opry's tall, handsome Hawkshaw Hawkins fell for the petite firecracker. During a 1960 road show in Wichita, Kansas, they were married in front of four thousand delighted fans. Jean was eight months pregnant with their second son when he perished in the 1963 plane crash that also took the lives of Patsy Cline and Cowboy Copas. In the middle of the night on March 5, 1963, Kitty Wilson, Minnie Pearl, and Jan Howard rushed to Jean's side. Although Patsy's death dominated media reports, country fans supported bereaved Jean by buying her next hit in huge quantities. It was her feisty 1964 masterpiece "Second Fiddle." On the flip side was a touching ballad that Marty Robbins wrote for the widowed mother, "Two Little Boys."

Jean Shepard dealt with her grief by throwing herself into her work. She had to; she now had two sons to support on her own. "At first I always had Ferlin there. Then Hawk was there to take care of the business and everything, and back then I was very meek and mild. After his death I became a little hardened, I think. I really had to become hard-nosed, I really did. . . . I've always been sassy to a certain extent. But I've had to be to survive." Drawing on her courage and the support of her Opry friends, three months after the tragedy she bravely sang on the same Wichita stage where she'd married. "It was rough at first, getting back into the swing," she said, "but after so many years in show business it becomes . . . natural. . . . It doesn't leave me much time to think. . . . And I've always enjoyed singing."

In 1966, the year she crowed "Many Happy Hangovers to You," Jean married Nashville cop Archie Summers. "I think it was maybe out of loneliness, and I felt my two young children needed a father image. It was just a very bad mistake." Jean got a divorce in 1968 and married Roy Orbison's gentle-natured guitarist and road manager, Benny Birchfield.

Jean's triumphant yodels, to-the-point women's lyrics, honky-tonk honesty, and pure-country attitude brought her more than forty-five hits in a career that spans five decades. But she worked in the long shadow of Kitty Wells throughout her early career; then Loretta Lynn, Dolly Parton, and Tammy Wynette outshone Jean's hit-making of the 1970s.

"As the Lord is my witness, if I have ever resented any woman in this business, I couldn't tell you who it was. Kitty was the Queen, but I didn't resent her. She made her place, and she deserved it. I don't think anybody could ever truthfully say that I have ever said anything derogatory about any female in this business, because I never have. Here's the way I feel about it: When I can't hold my own, it's time for me to get out." Singer Jan Howard testifies that Jean Shepard was the first Opry woman to befriend her when she arrived in Music City. When Skeeter Davis was suspended from the Opry for supporting "Jesus freak" hippies in the sixties, Jean went to bat for her with the show's management.

Jean's blunt honesty, no-nonsense style, and shoot-from-the-hip manner have frequently ruffled feathers in Nashville. In the 1960s she agitated for better union scale for her band members. After pop star Olivia Newton-John won top country awards in 1974, Jean took part in the protest and championed a back-to-country movement. Red-faced DJs she sassed stopped playing her records. Her embarrassed record company dropped her. In 1982 she and Benny rededicated their lives to Christ; as a result she asked not to be booked in drinking places. In the late eighties Jean was one of the few celebrities to take up the cause of the forgotten and ignored Vietnam vets. In 1988 she and Benny organized Roy Orbison's Nashville memorial service.

The tough little sparrow who braved the macho honky-tonk climate of the early fifties is now the Opry's matriarch. Still blessed with a resonant silver bugle of a voice, Jean has good-ol'-gal warmth and earthy common sense that have served as touchstones for two generations of female stars. And in the final roll call of the great female honky-tonk tunes are scores of Jean Shepard performances. There are few women's country discs that have stood the test of time as well as "Sad Singin', Slow Ridin'," "Seven Lonely Days," "Girls in Disgrace," "It's a Man Every Time," "The Root of All Evil," "Don't Fall in Love with a Married Man," and "I Want to Go Where No One Knows Me."

Jean Shepard's achievement is all the more remarkable because she was the only early-fifties country music woman who made it on her own.

Kitty Wells had Johnnie Wright and Texas Ruby had Curly Fox, but for most of her career Jean had no husband/protector as part of her traveling show. The country couples' route was far, far more common than Jean's independent road. Virtually all the other women remembered as outstanding performers from this period were part of husband-wife teams.

In the late 1940s and early 1950s, the happy-couple image took hold to an unprecedented degree in country music. More than forty spouse teams were active during the postwar era. Country fan magazines launched columns with titles like "His'n, Her'n" (*Hoedown*) and "Meet the Mrs." (*Country Song Roundup*). Again country culture mirrored the times: This was the era of domestic TV comedy shows like "The Life of Riley" (1949–1958), "I Love Lucy" (1951–1961), "The Adventures of Ozzie and Harriet" (1952–1966), "The Trouble with Father" (1950–1955), "Life with Father" (1953–1955), "Father Knows Best" (1954–1963), "Make Room for Daddy" (1953–1956), and "My Favorite Husband" (1953–1957).

Country music's couples put a distinctly working-class spin on the domestic duet. Before the war couples had the sweet, sentimental repertoires common to most female acts of the period. But a hit duet of 1949 by pop singer Margaret Whiting and cowboy crooner Jimmy Wakely changed everything. It was "Slipping Around," the first big country song to openly confront modern infidelity. Male-female duets were never the same afterward. Few went in for out-and-out honky-tonk wailing, but several husband-and-wife teams accepted country's new realism.

Joe and Rose Lee Maphis souped up their sound and proved that they could raise a ruckus as good as any honky-tonker's. Baltimore native Rose Schetrompf (b. 1922) was a radio star in her own right before she met Joe Maphis. As "Rose of the Mountains" she had her own program in Hagerstown, Maryland, at age fifteen. She was in the all-girl western band The Saddle Sweethearts and came to Virginia's "Old Dominion Barn Dance" as a duet with Mary Klick under that same billing in 1948. At the show Rose Lee fell in love with World War II veteran Joe Maphis, a multi-instrumental wizard who is remembered as one of the greatest guitar pickers in country music history. She followed him west to California in 1951. They married in 1952 and were soon dubbed "Mr. and Mrs. Country Music."

They became favorites on Los Angeles radio and TV shows. Joe's flashy guitar work as "King of the Strings" made him an in-demand studio musician on hundreds of recording sessions. With his showmanship and her singing, the Maphises themselves were soon recording. Mr. and Mrs. Country Music created the California honky-tonk classic "Dim Lights,

Thick Smoke (And Loud, Loud Music)" in 1952.

The hit led to a dozen albums over the years that fused bluegrass wailing, honky-tonk energy, and instrumental excitement. Although truly at home in traditional music, Joe and Rose Lee Maphis returned to honky-tonk themes in such performances as "Whiskey Is the Devil in Liquid Form" and "Where Honky-Tonk Angels Spread Their Wings." Rose Lee's solo album of 1960 was typical of their dual repertoire, containing both "Bury Me Beneath the Willow" and "You Can't Divorce My Heart." In later years the Maphises lived in a mobile home in Nashville, and that is where Joe died in 1986. With the wolf at her door, Rose Lee put her seamstress skills to work in the costume department of the Opryland theme park.

"I don't miss singing," she says. "The only thing I miss is the traveling. I probably wouldn't have gone on with it as long as I did, except it was in Joe's blood. We were a couple."

Like Joe and Rose Lee Maphis, Mattie O'Neill sensed the change in the air. The formerly old-timey Opal Amburgey shifted gears in the early fifties to address modern problems. "My Little Son's Plea" (1951) was "Mommy, please stop drinking / Throw your cigarettes away / It would make me feel much better / To see my mommy kneel and pray." She wrote and sang one of the era's best-known antialcohol songs, "Don't Sell Daddy Any More Whiskey" (1950). In "Divorces" (1951) Mattie sang, "Courtrooms are crowded wherever you go. . . . / If you are a victim, my heart aches for you / Only God knows what divorces can do." All of these discs featured the expressive harmonica playing of her husband, Salty Holmes, and tunes such as "My Worst Mistake" added modern steel guitar to her sound.

Other spouses who experimented with contemporary lyrics included Marilyn and Wesley Tuttle ("Our Love Isn't Legal"), Herb and Kay (Adams) ("Juke Box Jig"), Smiley and Kitty Wilson ("Red Silk Stockings and Green Perfume"), Annie Lou and Danny Dill ("Dime a Dozen"), Biff Collie and Little Marge ("If I Loved a Liar"), Indian Bill and Little Montana (Evalina) Stallard ("Goodbye Booze"), and Radio Dot and Smokey Swan ("You're No Good"). The "Sunshine Pals" Jane and Carl (Swanson) were singing "Goodbye Little Sweetheart Goodbye" in 1941,

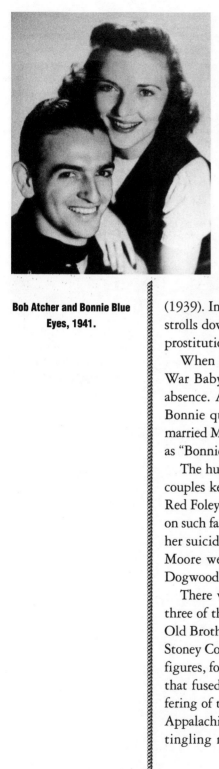

Bob Atcher and Bonnie Blue Eyes, 1941.

but after the honky-tonk era they addressed such topics as "Marijuana." The Collies, Dills, and Stallards all broke up because of divorces, as did such popular teams as Buck and Tex Ann Nation, Joe and "Little Shirley" Barker, and Bob Atcher and Bonnie Blue Eyes.

Atcher and his "Bonnie" (Loeta Applegate) were among many country couples who sang both sweet, old-fashioned numbers and modern cheatin' and drinkin' songs. Their lives mirrored the tension between old-timey values and postwar turmoil, as well. She married him in 1935, and they rapidly became huge favorites at "The National Barn Dance" in Chicago. The couple popularized "You Are My Sunshine" as a duet. He sang "I Dream of Your Bonnie Blue Eyes" to her, and fans thrilled to their radio romance. Bonnie's solos tended to be old-timey, but she could be tart as well as sweet, notably with a wry "weeper" delivery on "I'm Going Home to Mother" (1939). In the humorous "Seven Beers with the Wrong Man" (1940) she strolls down to the neighborhood tavern and winds up being busted for prostitution.

When Bob went to war, Bonnie carried on as a solo, singing "The War Baby's Prayer" and "I'm Lending You to Uncle Sammy" in his absence. Almost immediately after his return in 1945, they divorced. Bonnie quit recording, left Chicago, and moved to Hollywood. Bob married Maggie Whitehill in 1947 and by the early 1950s was billing *her* as "Bonnie Blue Eyes" on WLS.

The husband-wife image was so important that several other country couples kept up a facade even when things were far from rosy at home. Red Foley and his wife, Judy Martin (Eva Overstake), were harmonizing on such fare as "Our Christmas Waltz" practically right up to the time of her suicide over his extramarital affair. West Virginia's Lee and Juanita Moore were popularizing the religious parable "The Legend of the Dogwood Tree" while their marriage was disintegrating.

There were many husband-wife teams active in West Virginia, and three of them helped redefine country female singing—Daisy Mae and Old Brother Charlie, Molly O'Day and Lynn Davis, and Wilma Lee and Stoney Cooper. The women in these three acts are pivotal country music figures, for all sang in an openly emotional, mournful mountain manner that fused the "heart" in old-time country music with the naked suffering of the honky-tonk style. Daisy Mae, Molly, and Wilma Lee took Appalachian vocal fervor and threw it into overdrive, creating a spine-tingling new female country sound, a throbbing, sobbing, thrilling, chilling delivery that would influence stylists for years to come. And although nominally members of duos, all three women were unmistakably the stars.

Daisy Mae was the most restrained of the three stylists, but her pure soprano was an arrow of emotional truth that never missed the bull's-eye on her Mercury and Columbia sides of 1948 to 1954. Born Ethel Irene Reddy, the St. Louis native took her stage name from the buxom blond character in the wildly popular *Li'l Abner* comic strip. She met Charles Arnett in 1944 when both were performing at the "Renfro Valley Barn Dance" in Kentucky, and they married six months later while on tour in Texas. He wrote their radio scripts, played piano, and did sentimental recitations. Daisy Mae composed most of the songs and, despite the billing, sang nearly all of them as solos. Her specialties were tender salutes to Mother, such as "I Had a Visit from Heaven" and "Sweeter Than the Flowers." But Daisy Mae could also kick up her heels, as on 1952's "The Boy Across the Street" and "Cotton Lisle Stockings and a Two-Dollar Dress." Her sassiest performance was unquestionably her 1953 hillbilly golddigger romp "I'd Rather Be an Old Man's Darlin' (Than Be a Young Man's Slave)." Its sentiment was exactly echoed in the hit movie comedy *How to Marry a Millionaire* that same year.

Like most country radio folks, Daisy Mae and Old Brother Charlie were quite nomadic. In addition to starring in Charlie's native West Virginia from 1945 to 1947, they worked at stations in Indiana, Ohio, Kentucky, North Carolina, and Florida. Daisy Mae and Old Brother Charlie had their own Country Barn Record Shop in downtown Tampa in the fifties.

Daisy Mae paved the way for Molly O'Day (1923–1987), a mountain wailer who took the drive and urgency of the honky-tonk style and applied it to acoustic music, creating a sort of barroom-bluegrass sound. "Molly was, without a doubt, the female Hank Williams," says bluegrass great Mac Wiseman. Molly was the first major artist to record Hank's songs. She discovered Wiseman and honky-tonk hero Carl Smith, immortalized the country standard "Tramp on the Street," and was poised to become a female country superstar when she quit show business abruptly to devote herself to evangelism in 1952. Columbia Records executive Art Satherley called her the greatest female country singer of all time. Dolly Parton cited her as an influence, and bluegrass great Earl Scruggs admitted he stood in awe of Molly's spine-tingling singing and banjo-picking talents. She even inspired her cousin, Fannie Belle Fleming, to take up country singing. Fannie Belle's vocal career was brief, however; the West Virginian found far wider renown as stripper and Earl Long consort Blaze Starr.

Molly's own hero was Lulu Belle. As a Kentucky tot, LaVerne Williamson was devoted to the "National Barn Dance" broadcasts, since they featured more women singers than "The Grand Ole Opry" radio shows her brothers preferred. Patsy Montana and Texas Ruby were among Molly's other influences. Molly and her brothers all picked up instruments because of their fondness for the country radio shows of the 1930s. Rather than follow in his father's footsteps into the coal mines, Skeets Williamson landed a job on West Virginia radio in 1939. He sent for his sixteen-year-old singing sister, dubbed her Mountain Fern, and put her on the air in Charleston. During a subsequent Beckley radio stint she became Dixie Lee. After her brother's group broke up, Molly struck out on her own and joined Lynn Davis's group, The Forty-Niners. She and Davis married in 1941. During World War II, Molly's repertoire was laced with songs like "Boys, Don't Let Them Take Away Our Bible," "Waiting for the Boys," and the anti-Japanese "Rising Sun." During this time the couple left West Virginia for radio jobs in Alabama and Kentucky. In Montgomery she met the then-unknown Hank Williams. In Louisville she acquired her final stage name, Molly O'Day.

In 1945 Molly and Lynn moved to Knoxville and WNOX. This is where she achieved her greatest popularity, selling songbooks and mailing fans photos as fast as they could be printed. Satherley offered her a Columbia contract in 1946. She remembered Hank's Alabama tunes and recorded five of them, including that timeless honky-tonk moan "I Don't Care If Tomorrow Never Comes." These, as well as her fondly remembered "Tramp on the Street," "The Drunken Driver," and "Matthew Twenty-Four," were delivered with Pentecostal fervor and sobbing conviction.

Her popularity skyrocketed. During the late 1940s Molly O'Day and Lynn Davis toured throughout the South and penetrated such northern markets as Michigan, Illinois, Ohio, and Pennsylvania. Columbia arranged numerous promotional appearances, everything from record-store autograph parties in Kentucky to a stunt boxing match in St. Louis. She guested on "The Grand Ole Opry" and "National Barn Dance," recorded prolifically, and broadcast daily.

Initially quite vivacious and enthusiastic about her career, Molly began to question the entertainment life-style. She recorded more and more religious material, much of it morbid and darkly contemplative. "I almost couldn't sing that song; it made me want to cry," she recalled of one of her graveyard meditations. "Crying does wonders for you," she added. "There'd be a whole lot less need for psychiatrists if people would cry more."

In late 1949 she apparently suffered a nervous breakdown. An item in the December 31 issue of *Billboard* noted that she'd been hospitalized. Three months later she and Lynn joined the Church of God. In 1950–1951 they went to the province of Saskatchewan in Canada to attend Bible school. Molly did two final recording sessions for Columbia in 1950 and 1951, but by early 1952 she'd completely turned her back on show business. In the fall of that year Molly was stricken with tuberculosis and had a portion of a lung removed. In 1954–1955 Lynn became an ordained minister.

Molly used to joke that she was born so far back in a Kentucky hollow that "you had to break daylight with a sledgehammer, and the groundhogs carried the mail." The dark hollows and dingy coal-mining towns of Appalachia are where she and Lynn returned as evangelists. Refusing offers from the country recording industry, they preached in a succession of small West Virginia communities for the next thirty years. Molly recorded religious albums in 1961 and 1968, but never returned to the breakneck pace that nearly ruined her health. She died of cancer at age sixty-four in 1987.

Molly O'Day had just one simple explanation for the riveting emotionalism in her performances: "I sing from the heart," she said. "I always have. I don't think they're doing that enough these days."

"I've always looked for a song that tells a story," explains Molly's fellow West Virginia stylist Wilma Lee Cooper. "And if the record company insisted I sing something that wasn't a story song, it never amounted to anything. Because I couldn't put no feeling into it.

"I like to keep some of the old folk songs in there, because that's my background. That's what I was raised on. And I don't ever want to forget where I came from. . . . I'm just a plain ol' country singer."

Wilma Lee was the finest fusion artist of her day, able to wail the murder ballad "Poor Ellen Smith" or the honky-tonkin' "Don't Play That Song (On the Jukebox Tonight)." She brought bluesman Leadbelly's "Big Midnight Special" into country music. She could infuse a gospel tune like "Thirty Pieces of Silver" with hair-raising conviction or belt out a Cousin Emmy banjo-rouser like "Stoney (Are You Mad at Your Gal)."

Wilma Lee Cooper took such sturdy songs into the modern country music world, maintaining a simple mountain dignity in an increasingly spangled and flamboyant country climate. "I've Been Cheated Too" she sang as she walked the dimly lit "Heartbreak Street." But even after spitting "You Tried to Ruin My Name" at a faithless lover, Wilma Lee could pour her heart out for "Willie Roy, the Crippled Boy," ache on "I Dreamed About Mom Last Night," lift spirits with "The Sunny Side of the Mountain," frolic to the innocent "West Virginia Polka," or clap hands to the gospel of "There's a Big Wheel."

Born Wilma Leigh Leary in 1921, she was the oldest of three gospel-singing daughters of a West Virginia coal miner and his musical wife. "There was train tracks that went through where we lived," Wilma Lee recalled, "and there was an eight-fifteen train that would go through at night, every evening. . . . Hearing that train blow its whistle . . . well, it was just haunting. You'd hear it way off in the distance, that lonesome sound, and you'd think, 'Well, one of these days I'm going to be going somewhere. I'm not gonna be here. I'm gonna be out seeing the world.' I guess I was always a dreamer.

"We had a battery radio, but nobody turned it on but my dad, and nobody dialed it but my dad. It was only turned on during the week when the news was on; and on Saturday nights he'd turn it on and we'd listen to Lulu Belle on 'The National Barn Dance.' After she was done, he'd turn to Nashville to hear Fiddlin' Arthur Smith and The Delmore Brothers. And that was it. After they'd played, it went off.

"My mother was the one who really knew music. She played the pump organ . . . that was a treasured possession, a luxury item. . . . We all learned music together. After the family started singing together, we sang in all the churches in our part of the country. People would come from sixty miles away to have us sing their funerals. We weren't frowned upon as women going into music and entertainment, because we were a family."

The act featured Wilma Lee and her sisters, Gerry and Peggy, with their parents providing soprano and bass harmonies. As the result of a statewide contest the Learys were chosen to represent West Virginia at the National Folk Festival in Washington, D.C., in 1938. They were also recorded by the Library of Congress as part of its American song preservation efforts. During this period Wilma Lee says she taught Roy Acuff "The Hills of Roane County," which he used as the basis for his hit "The Precious Jewel." The Learys added a fiddler named Dale Troy "Stoney" Cooper to their act in late 1938. One of the reasons he decided to join, he later confessed, was that he was quite taken with the pretty Leary daughters.

The parents stuck to gospel tunes, but the girls began to incorporate secular songs into the family repertoire. Wilma Lee and Stoney courted on stage to the verses of the Appalachian play-party ditty "Paper of Pins." They married in 1939. After their daughter Carol Lee was born in 1942, they decided to quit country music in order to be proper parents.

"One of the hardest decisions we ever made was when we quit the business when Carol Lee was born. We felt you couldn't raise a kid . . . going out every night, playing show dates. . . . Stoney got a job. He drove a delivery truck for the Vaughn Beverage Company in Wheeling. Squirt was their big brand. . . . It was awful hard to settle down that way. I wasn't happy. I'd go and put Carol in that stroller and just walk and walk and walk. I was goin' nuts at home." Delivering soda pop wasn't exactly Stoney's cup of tea, either.

"They offered us seventy dollars a week to go to Nebraska and have a regular radio show—forty-five dollars for him and twenty-five dollars for me—so we took off across the country in this Studebaker roadster we had with patched tires. What an adventure! I wasn't scared. I had a lot of trust in Stoney. He knew how to take care of himself, you know. He was a boxer and a baseball pitcher. And he was a fine talker, a good emcee, and one of the best salesmen in the business."

The duo moved from Nebraska to Indiana. Bob Atcher heard them there in 1943 and recommended them to Chicago's WJJD to take over his and Bonnie Blue Eyes' duet slot when he was called for military service. Wilma Lee auditioned with "Cowards over Pearl Harbor" and was welcomed to the Windy City as "the she–Roy Acuff." Stoney took a defense plant job in Gary, Indiana, for a time, then the couple returned to their native West Virginia for a barn dance slot on WMMN's "Sagebrush Roundup." At her urging they formed The Clinch Mountain Clan and developed a full-blown touring show. By 1947 they had a recording contract with Rich-R-Tone and were creating a sensation on WWVA's fifty-thousand-watt "Jamboree." "Everything was an encore," Stoney recalled. "It was either they'd never heard anything like that before or I don't know what. Just thunderous applause. . . . We just rocked that place."

At WWVA the performers were paid according to how much mail for sponsors was addressed to them. Acts sold nylon hose, insurance, burial monuments, cosmetics, baby chicks, garden seeds, nostrums, kitchen knives, and other products. The Coopers landed the top-dollar sponsorship of Carter's Pills and soon had a syndicated three-day-a-week show on twenty big stations. Columbia Records offered a contract in 1949. Wilma Lee recalls recording duets with Hank Williams in 1951, but these have never surfaced.

Following a decade at the "Jamboree" the Coopers were offered cast membership on "The Grand Ole Opry." They arrived in Music City in 1957 and enjoyed a steady string of hits on Hickory Records into the early 1960s. Daughter Carol Lee Cooper began singing with them regularly as a teenager. Today the statuesque brunet leads the Opry's backup vocal group The Carol Lee Singers.

Wilma Lee and Stoney Cooper, c. 1945.

WILMA LEE COOPER'S FEMALE REPERTOIRE

Mountain stylist Wilma Lee Cooper was one of the first big women stars to emphasize the songs of country's emerging female songwriting community. Among her favorites were these:

JUANITA MOORE'S
"Legend of the Dogwood Tree"

ELEANOR PARKER'S
"Moonlight on West Virginia"

MOLLY O'DAY'S
"When My Time Comes to Go"

OLA BELLE REED'S
"All on Account of You"

RUBY MOODY'S
"Walking My Lord up Calvary's Hill"

LORENE ROSE'S "At the First Fall of Snow"

MARTHA CARSON'S
"You Can't Take It with You (When You Go)"

JEAN CHAPEL'S
"Rachel's Guitar"

Stoney developed a heart condition in the 1970s. "Stoney wasn't well for a long time," Wilma Lee recalls sadly. "He would just stay home and do the office and put me out there and let me work. His health had gotten to where he just couldn't take the traveling." Their long and happy duet ended when he died of a heart attack in 1977. They were truly partners. "You see, Stoney and I had worked together all those years. We'd been man and wife; we worked together; we traveled together; and when we were home, we were home together. We were never apart. . . . We worked fifty-fifty together. If something came up, why we'd sit down and figure out what to do, the best direction to go. One didn't make the decision; we were both involved in the decisions. . . . And then, all at once, you find yourself alone. . . . It was an awful lot to think about."

In the 1980s she rebuilt The Clinch Mountain Clan, began a new recording career, became a favorite on the bluegrass and folk festival circuit, earned a degree in theology, and carried on as the Opry's mountain music matriarch.

"Mountain. That's what we are, mountain music," says the woman who wedded Appalachian soul with honky-tonk urgency. "We're country, you know, with a little beat to it."

Wilma Lee, Molly, and Daisy Mae all survived the honky-tonk onslaught because they were able to straddle the fence between old and new. All three were superb traditional singers who embraced the modern sound. Mattie O'Neill, Texas Ruby, and Rose Lee Maphis made the transition, too. If a singer couldn't, chances are she went under.

Sunshine Sue (1912–1979) was probably the biggest female star torpedoed by country's new barroom style. She was the monarch of WRVA's "Old Dominion Barn Dance," country radio's only woman barn dance host. Beloved by millions for her soft vocals, homey manner, and smiling warmth, Sue decided she'd had enough in 1957. By then Nashville's wailing honky-tonk sounds had been joined by the beat of country's teen-delinquent offshoot, rockabilly music, and Sue's smooth serenading seemed totally out of date.

"Sometimes I am surprised when riding along in the car, listening to a country station, at some of the subjects that are being exploited in song," Sue once said. "I guess my generation gap is showing."

Her retirement marked the end of a long career. Sunshine Sue was born Mary Arlene Higdon in Keosauqua, Iowa, the youngest of six farm children. She married her high school sweetheart, John Workman, at age seventeen and worked the Midwest barn dance circuit with him throughout the Depression. Sunshine Sue and her troupe debuted on WRVA in January 1940.

A ukulele, guitar, piano, and accordion player, Sue performed in The

Happy Valley Girls all-female band at WLW in Cincinnati from 1942 to 1943. After the war the Workmans took up permanent radio residence in Richmond. By 1946 she was the unquestioned ruler of "The Old Dominion Barn Dance," billed as "radio's only femcee." She was much more. Sue chose the performers; planned the shows; organized the touring groups; rehearsed; did a daily morning broadcast; ran her own office; did commercials; and still found time to cook, sew, do needlework, raise two children, manage 196 acres, restore a two-hundred-year-old colonial Virginia home, go fishing, be the organist at her Presbyterian church, tend a half-acre garden, and can three hundred quarts of fruits and vegetables a season. Her soft, easygoing style of showmanship masked a keen business sense, organizational ability, and impressive financial skills. Sue used her radio charm to bring WRVA's show to premier status among the barn dances. The "Old Dominion Barn Dance" cast was nationally heard on the CBS radio network and even made it to the Great White Way as part of a 1954 musical called *Hayride.*

Sunshine Sue, 1946.

"Kick off your shoes, let 'em roll down the aisle," she'd coo to her barn dance audiences. "We'll sort 'em out later: You might even get a better pair." Sue's signature song on radio was "You Are My Sunshine." Always more of a personality than a great singer, Sue recorded very little. Her biggest record was probably 1954's "Blackberry Winter," but most fans remember an oft-sung radio favorite called "My Mother's Mansions Are Higher Than Mine," Sue's touching country salute to mother love.

Sue and John handled their money wisely. She was able to leave the airwaves at age forty-five, and they retired comfortably in Savannah, Georgia. When their son Billy was on the road with them hamming it up as a five-year-old, they put a third of his earnings away in a trust fund to pay for his education. "He actually worked his way through college before he was in kindergarten," she quipped. Daughter Ginger became host of "The Old Dominion Barn Dance" after her mother left in 1957. Sue made personal appearances until 1963, then quit for good except for a 1975 reunion show in Richmond, which she referred to as her "firm and final curtain call." And it was.

"I think [country music] has changed a great deal . . . some maybe not for the better," she said. "I don't believe there are as many actual folk songs being done today. They are more current with the trend of the thinking."

The "trend of the thinking," as Sue put it, swept aside old-time country music and replaced it with the newfangled honky-tonk style. But the old-timers didn't go down without a fight. As the 1940s eased into the 1950s, Pentecostal religion rose to smite the barroom infidels. The southern gospel music industry was born.

ALL-DAY SING

Women and Southern Gospel Music

The Carter Sisters and Mother Maybelle went gospel with this 1949 songbook.

In 1801 more than twenty thousand people converged on little Cane Ridge, Kentucky, for a six-day marathon of preaching, singing, praying, and feasting. That's when the old-time southern camp meeting was born. Ever since, religious revivals have swept across Dixie. Hundreds of songs were left in their wake, creating a body of country music standards.

Religious song publishing firms thrived in the early decades of the twentieth century, notably Nashville's Benson Company, Dallas's Stamps-Baxter firm, Missouri's Albert E. Brumley & Sons, and Tennessee's James D. Vaughan Music Company. Male quartets toured to promote their songbooks. By the 1920s and 1930s several of these touring promotion groups were popular in their own rights, independent of the publishers. In the late 1940s and early 1950s some became national attractions, including The Speer Family.

At a time when white gospel acts in the South were almost exclusively male, the Speers starred women. The Speer Family was organized in Cullman County, Alabama, in 1920, when George Thomas "Dad" Speer married Lena Brock "Mom" Speer (1900–1967). The original Speer Family was Mom as lead singer and pianist, Dad's

The Carter Sisters and Mother Maybelle
Song Folio No. 1

Acuff-Rose
PUBLICATIONS
2510 FRANKLIN ROAD
NASHVILLE 4, TENNESSEE

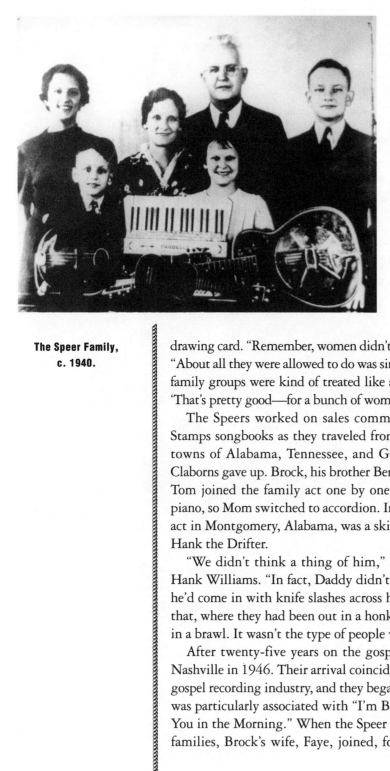

The Speer Family, c. 1940.

sister Pearl as alto, her husband, Logan Claborn, as tenor, and Dad as bass.

"Mom had an outstandingly beautiful soprano voice, a floating type of voice," recalls son Brock Speer. "And my Aunt Pearl had the strongest, most robust voice you ever heard on a woman. Oh, she was so loud that her voice would really carry. If we got there after the singing started, we could drive up to the church and could tell if Aunt Pearl was in there, 'cause you could hear her voice above everybody."

From the start, the novelty of the female voices was the act's drawing card. "Remember, women didn't even vote back then," says Brock. "About all they were allowed to do was sing in the church choirs. . . . Mixed family groups were kind of treated like amateurs. They'd say things like, 'That's pretty good—for a bunch of women.'"

The Speers worked on sales commissions peddling Vaughan and Stamps songbooks as they traveled from church to church in the small towns of Alabama, Tennessee, and Georgia. Weary from travel, the Claborns gave up. Brock, his brother Ben, and sisters Rosa Nell and Mary Tom joined the family act one by one after 1925. Rosa Nell took up piano, so Mom switched to accordion. In 1941 the Speers' radio opening act in Montgomery, Alabama, was a skinny teenager who called himself Hank the Drifter.

"We didn't think a thing of him," Brock recalled of the legendary Hank Williams. "In fact, Daddy didn't like his singing at all. . . . Plus, he'd come in with knife slashes across his leather jacket and things like that, where they had been out in a honky-tonk the night before and got in a brawl. It wasn't the type of people we associated with."

After twenty-five years on the gospel circuit, the Speers moved to Nashville in 1946. Their arrival coincided with the birth of the southern gospel recording industry, and they began making records in 1947. Mom was particularly associated with "I'm Building a Bridge" and "I'll Meet You in the Morning." When the Speer daughters left to start their own families, Brock's wife, Faye, joined, followed by a long succession of "adopted Speer" daughters, notably three-time Gospel Music Association Female Vocalist of the Year Sue Chenault. Mom maintained an astonishing clarity of tone and syncopated sense of rhythm in her lead vocals well into her fifties and sixties.

In 1954 the act became a gospel TV pioneer with its own daily broadcasts in Music City, and the exposure magnified its popularity enormously. The Speers have recorded more than sixty albums, won ten Dove Awards from the Gospel Music Association, and been nominated for five Grammy Awards. The matriarch lived to see her family rule the gospel-singing field, but died four years before she and Dad were placed in the Gospel Music Hall of Fame in 1971.

Women may have been rare when Lena Brock Speer began singing, but by the late 1920s record companies were finding them in gospel acts every now and then. The most common style featuring women's voices was the shape-note, Sacred Harp gospel tradition. Mamie Ruth Denson Edwards is the most important force in keeping this aged music alive. Women were also the sidekicks of a number of singing evangelists recorded early in country music history. Gospel is where we find most of country's first all-female acts: The Giddins Sisters, Ruth Donaldson & Helen Jepsen, The Tietge Sisters, The Southland Ladies Quartette, The Palmer Sisters, The Forman Sisters, and The Wisdom Sisters all recorded from 1926 to 1930.

By the 1930s a few country groups were making a living with religious songs, and these acts lit the fuse for the gospel explosion of 1945 to 1955. Along with the Speers, the outstanding such act featuring women was The Chuck Wagon Gang. D. P. "Dad" Carter met his wife, Carrie, at a singing school, and as west Texas sharecroppers they entertained neighbors with their family's front-porch singing. Dad formed a singing group with the three oldest of the nine children, Rose, Anna, and Jim. The quartet's first paying job was on the radio in Lubbock in 1935. Bewley Mills of Fort Worth became the group's sponsor in 1936 and dubbed it The Chuck Wagon Gang.

In the beginning the Carters' repertoire was mostly cowgirl; they featured only one gospel song per program. Mail response to the sacred selections was so overwhelming, though, that The Chuck Wagon Gang adopted an all-gospel format by 1938. Bewley Mills offered a free photo of the act via coupons in its flour sacks and was stunned when more than one hundred thousand were mailed. Columbia began recording The Chuck Wagon Gang in 1936, and the act stayed on its roster for the next forty years. Roy replaced brother Jim in 1954.

Led by the voices of Rose and Anna, the group wove a magical spell on disc. The Chuck Wagon Gang's sound is an intricate pattern of call and response, bright bursts of phrasing and crest-and-ebb harmonies. "I'll Fly Away," "We Are Climbing," "The Church in the Wildwood," and "I'll Shout and Shine" were among the hundreds of enormously popular Chuck Wagon Gang performances. The Gang's "He Set Me Free" of 1941 became the melody for Hank Williams's immortal "I Saw the Light," and the *Chuck Wagon Gang Favorites* songbook was a big influence on the emerging southern gospel style in the late forties. As gospel fervor swept through Dixie after the war, The Chuck Wagon Gang began to tour for the first time in its career.

But traveling was hard for the Carter daughters, who were trying to raise families. Rose retired in 1965. Anna's husband Howard Gordon was the group's guitarist, but after he died in 1967, she married country/gospel star and former Louisiana governor Jimmie Davis and went into semiretirement. Younger sister Ruth Ellen Carter Yates took Anna's slot, and Roy's daughter Shirley Carter Coers eventually took Rose's part. Since 1989 non-Carter women have kept the act's style alive. With the voices of Debby Trusty and Alynn Bilodeau, The Chuck Wagon Gang was voted Gospel Group of the Year by fans at the TNN/Music City News Awards in 1990.

The Chuck Wagon Gang's leap from regional radio favorite to national touring attraction and The Speer Family's transition from Deep South harmonizers to recording stars were made possible by a dramatic updating of gospel's image after World War II. Groups became more exuberant, injecting a boogie-woogie beat into the music. They adopted slick matching suits and pomaded hairdos. They clapped their hands, beat tambourines, and hammed it up. They became fervent salesmen of the gospel message. Old-time fundamentalists railed against charging money to hear the Word, against the "worldly" clothes and makeup, against the secular new rhythms. It was too late. Gospel music had entered show business.

Singing conventions drew bigger and bigger crowds. In 1948 promoter Wally Fowler staged gospel's first All-Night Sing. It took place in Nashville, and the concept soon spread to other cities—Atlanta, Memphis, Charlotte, Birmingham, Knoxville, Winston-Salem, Spartanburg. A regular touring circuit developed, and gospel groups became professionals who charged admission and sold records at shows. The days of the quartet's asking for a "love offering" and hawking a company's songbooks came to an end. Radio shows and record companies picked up on the emerging trend. Established stars such as Rose Maddox, Molly O'Day, Kitty Wells, and Martha Carson issued records in the new style, beginning a tradition of country entertainers' issuing gospel LPs.

This gospel boom was related to a larger postwar religious movement. In the wake of World War II and its morality-loosening aftermath came an uprising of charismatic Christianity. The terrifying new nuclear age drove many to search for solace and security. The social climate of honky-tonks, illicit sex, and divorce drew a powerful reaction from the nation's pulpits.

The Pentecostal movement came mainly from the Churches of God and Assemblies of God groups. Beginning in 1946 these sects developed their own Bible schools. Their philosophy was puritanical and austere—no dancing, no drinking, no tobacco use, and no suggestive dressing. Pentecostalism was a many-sided protest against modernity. Against science. Against technology. Against industrialization. Against urbanization and the moral decay that accompanied it. Anthropologists analyzed the Pentecostal movement as "the vision of the disinherited," for its adherents were the poor, the unschooled, the rural, the left-behind.

Music was central to any typical charismatic service. Mournful "Old Rugged Cross"–type standards were sung, as well as joyful "Give Me That Old-Time Religion"–type songs, accompanied by guitar, piano, tambourine, and banjo. These tunes were rhythmic warm-ups to the ecstasy that followed. The excitement of the congregation increased as the singing proceeded, with interjections of "Hallelujah!" and "Thank you, Jesus!" and "Glory!" amid the tambourine thumping and shouted verses. Some folks would "get the Spirit" during the music and begin to tremble, laugh wildly, jerk violently around, and speak incoherently. Then came the "testimonies" of the faithful. Sinners were called to the altar, while shouting and singing urged them into the flock.

Talking in tongues was also part of the holiness revival, evidence of the Holy Spirit's presence. In the wilder denominations, the devout held their hands over kerosene-lamp flames. Foot washing was practiced. Demon possession was feared. Another hallmark of the movement was faith healers such as Oral Roberts, who rose to fame between 1947 and 1958. The practice of snake handling made headlines throughout this era in Tennessee, West Virginia, Kentucky, and North Carolina. From 1940 to 1955 at least fourteen people died as a

The Chuck Wagon Gang recorded for the Columbia label for more than forty years. This is a 1960 record jacket.

result of this religious phenomenon, several of them female evangelists.

Almost all the outside observers who witnessed Pentecostal services during their heyday commented on their erotic undertones as participants "let go" to experience the pulsating music and the emotional abandon in the services. Women were central in Pentecostalism. At least 65 percent of those attending these services in the forties were women, according to sociologist Liston Pope, and they were the most given to talking in tongues and being healed. In addition, women were permitted to preach because the devoted believed that anyone was capable of receiving the Holy Ghost.

The outstanding female evangelist of the period was Kathryn Kuhlman (1907–1976). She was raised in rural Missouri, quit school at sixteen to become an itinerant soul saver in the Midwest, and settled in Pittsburgh as a faith healer in 1947. Kathryn dressed in flowing white chiffon, gestured with her large expressive hands, and spoke with folksy charisma. Tens of thousands attended her services to hear her "rebuke" illnesses and handicaps. Journalists dubbed her "The Miracle Woman," "the most celebrated Christian charismatic in America," "Queen of the Faith Healers," "the most famous woman preacher in the world," and a "one-woman shrine of Lourdes." At her peak Kathryn syndicated a daily half-hour radio show and a weekly TV show nationally, wrote a series of books, made a record album called *I Believe in Miracles,* and published a songbook titled *The People Sing with Kathryn Kuhlman.* "Isssssn't it wunnnnnnnnderful?" she sighed beatifically, even beyond the grave, as her taped broadcasts continued on radio until 1982.

Among Kathryn's best friends in the gospel community were Rex Humbard and his wife, Maude Aimee Humbard (1922–1984), the pioneers of TV evangelism. Rex was the son of a husband-wife preaching team in Arkansas. Maude Aimee was a Texas gospel singer. They met in 1939, married in 1942, and became popular radio and recording artists during the southern gospel boom. The Humbards recorded for more than a half dozen labels and were aired worldwide on the Armed Forces Radio Network. One day in 1952 the backwoodsy preacher noticed a crowd watching the new TV invention in an Akron, Ohio, store window and was inspired. By 1973 Rex and Maude Aimee's TV show was the biggest religious program on earth and the cornerstone of their multimillion-dollar Cathedral of Tomorrow empire. Rex's sister Leona and daughter Liz also became prominent female vocalists in The Humbard Family, which eventually included fourteen members of the clan. "Throughout the world there's a moral breakdown, which started with the home and family," Rex believed. "That's the basic unit of society, the church, even the economy.

The Singers, together on stage as a family, make an impression."

"The family" was the focus of much Pentecostal preaching in the late 1940s and early 1950s. And almost all the great female country-gospel singers of the time performed in family groups. Eva Mae LeFevre rose to prominence in the 1940s as the diva of her dynasty. Born Eva Mae Whittington in 1917, she played piano and sang at her father's revivals from the age of four. She married gospel singer Urias LeFevre in 1934, and with his brother Alphus formed a trio. They landed a daily radio show in Atlanta in 1940. Eva Mae ran the show and produced LeFevre records while the men were at war, and after it she led them to gospel stardom. Variously known to fans as "The Queen of Gospel," "Miss Gospel Singer," "Mama," and "The Fabulous Eva Mae," she became the first living woman inducted into the Gospel Music Hall of Fame (1977).

The Johnson Family Singers emerged from North Carolina with a sound built around the piano playing and singing of daughter Betty. Born in 1932, she was on the road with her parents at age five, and by 1940 the six-member Johnson Family was starring on "Carolina Calling" on WBT radio in Charlotte. The act began recording its straightforward gospel harmony style in 1946 and was nationally known by the early fifties. Betty's sweet soprano was virtually free of country inflections, and her wholesome blond good looks eased her transition to pop stardom. While on a family trip to New York in 1952 Betty won a talent contest that netted her an engagement at The Copacabana. She was soon singing ad jingles and making TV appearances, notably on NBC's soap opera "Modern Romances" and on the syndicated country-pop show "Eddy Arnold Time." Her pop hits of 1956 through 1959 included "Little White Lies," "I Dreamed," and "The Little Blue Man." She was a regular on "The Jack Paar Show" in 1957 and 1958, but also periodically returned to Nashville to record gospel with her family.

If the Johnsons were the pop end of the southern gospel spectrum, The Lewis Family was the hillbilly sound *in excelsis deo.* Billed as "The Singing Sensations from Dixie," the Georgia-bred Lewis clan fused virtuoso bluegrass picking, electrifying stage showmanship, uproarious humor, hand-clapping fervor, and joyous, scintillating female harmony to create the greatest troupe on the gospel road. Roy "Pop" Lewis and his wife, Pauline, trained their six kids to pick and sing, and they set out from Lincolnton, Georgia, in 1949 to entertain in the small churches of northeastern Georgia and western South Carolina. Miggie, born in 1926, handled the low harmonies. Polly, born in 1937, sang lead, emceed, and played piano. Janis, born in 1939, was the high harmony voice and played upright bass. When the raven-haired trio clapped hands, raised their voices,

The Lewis Family, 1983.

and marched forward in barn-raising enthusiasm while brothers Talmadge, Little Roy, and Wallace burned up the strings behind them, audiences went wild. The Lewis Family landed a weekly TV show on Augusta's WJBF in 1954; it is still on today, perhaps the longest-running television show on earth.

"We had to plan our marriages, honeymoons, and pregnancies around the show day," says Polly with a chuckle. She and her sisters have shouted the "good news" on such memorable records as "They're Holding Up the Ladder," "There Is Power in the Blood," and "Keep on the Sunny Side." On their fifty-some LPs Miggie Lewis, Polly Lewis Williamson, and Janis Lewis Phillips have the thunderclap impact of triple-powered Molly O'Day. "We give the people a lot of entertainment . . . play a lot of up-tempo things . . . and respond to each other on stage," Polly says. "And the people seem to enjoy it. We've been blessed."

Sister Vestal Goodman has a similar let-'er-rip delivery. Her belting distinguishes the sound of The Happy Goodman Family. Born in 1930, Vestal started harmonizing with Howard Goodman and his sisters and brothers in 1949. The act achieved some notoriety at the All-Night Sings; but this edition of the Goodmans sputtered to a halt in 1956. A reconstituted Happy Goodman Family emerged in 1963, starring Vestal with husband, Howard, and his brothers Rusty and Sam.

Armed with Vestal's lung power and Rusty's songs, the quartet was soon bringing down the house with such rousers as "When It All Starts Happening," "I Wouldn't Take Nothing for My Journey Now," "The Lighthouse," and "Had It Not Been." The group is also noted as the first in its field to incorporate steel guitar, drums, and other instruments into its sound during an era when most acts used simple piano accompaniment. The Goodmans demanded decent pay from show promoters when most of their peers were still meek and mild. "Rebels? Sort of, we were," Vestal said during an Associated Press interview. "If we felt like it would make it better, we weren't afraid to try it. I guess we were pioneers in a lot of things. We opened doors for others to do things that were not the norm." Between 1965 and 1971 The Happy Goodmans had their own syndicated TV show, "Gospel Singing Jubilee." They won Grammy Awards in 1968 and 1978, and when the Gospel Music Association began handing out its Dove Awards in 1970, Vestal Goodman was the first woman chosen Female Vocalist of the Year.

Women like Lena Brock Speer, Eva Mae LeFevre, and Vestal Goodman laid the foundation for dozens to follow. Among the most prominent have been Labreeska Hemphill, whose Singing Hemphills developed the custom tour bus business in Nashville; Gloria Gaither, the prolific gospel composer of The Bill Gaither Trio; native American Lillian Klaudt, who sang with her four sons as the colorfully costumed Klaudt Indian Family; rotund "Hee Haw" comic Lulu Roman; and the sublimely countrified Peg McKamey of The McKameys, who waves her arms, mugs delightfully, and kicks off her shoes when she's "in the spirit" in song.

Of all the women who emerged from the culture that developed and defined the modern gospel industry, none was more prodigiously creative than Kentucky's Dottie Rambo. This remarkable craftsman was a musical fountain from whom poured more than seven hundred gospel compositions. Dottie is one of eleven children of a blind Pentecostal minister and his wife, and seems to have always had a mystic streak. As a nine-year-old she was sitting on a creek bank in the country when she started humming a tune and singing lyrics she'd never heard before. She ran home to her mother in wonder and confusion. Recalled Dottie, "I started crying, it scared me so bad." When she was ten in 1945, Dottie Luttrell joined her mother and uncles in a singing group. She listened to "The Grand Ole Opry" on the family radio and by age eleven had taught herself to play guitar along with the bands. By the time she married Buck Rambo at age sixteen, she was an accomplished lead guitarist. When they formed their Gospel Echoes group, he played rhythm to her lead. Both are outstanding country singers, but The Gospel Echoes operated on a regional, semiprofessional level until after daughter Reba Rambo (b. 1951) was old enough to take part.

Rechristened The Singing Rambos, the trio developed an unusual sound that caught record companies' ears in the early sixties. Dottie's moaning, yearning alto, Reba's piercing soprano, and Buck's sturdy, sincere leads were quite a combination. When the trio shouted in harmony with the throttle wide open, the effect was stirring. Following the lead of the Goodmans, the Rambos backed their vocals

The Happy Goodman Family, c. 1965.

with modern, Nashville Sound instrumentation, eventually incorporating steel guitar, drums, and even small string sections. "I'm not a great singer; I'm a communicator," says Dottie, yet she numbered among her fans entertainers ranging from Elvis Presley to The Allman Brothers. Among those who have recorded her songs are Bill Monroe, Dottie West, Jimmie Davis, Pat Boone, and Jerry Lee Lewis. "Sometimes when I have finished a song, I sit back and look at it and think, 'I didn't write this. I couldn't have.' So often I just say that I take dictation from the Lord."

"I consider gospel music to be anything about Mom, Dad, home, country, or Jesus," says Dottie. "I'll never run out of something to write about as long as I remember that."

To fundamentalist Christians, the soaring divorce rate of the postwar era was one of the great evils of modern life. So when Lucille and Johnny Masters split up, it was kept quiet. The Masters Family, after all, had been a fixture of country-gospel recording since 1946 and had originated the classic "Gloryland March."

Martha Carson's divorce, on the other hand, was painfully public. After her apprenticeship in The Amburgey Sisters and Coon Creek Girls, Martha joined the southern gospel movement in a duet with husband James billed as "The Dixie Sweethearts." Her driving guitar and his staccato mandolin bursts backed wonderfully inventive harmony work on "He Will Set Your Fields on Fire," "Salvation Has Been Brought Down," and other discs of 1947 to 1950. But their family-gospel image on the radio barn dance shows of Atlanta and Knoxville was a sham. "He started goin' out with women, hangin' out in bars, got stinkin' drunk, and these types of things," Martha recalls. "It just got to the point where I couldn't live with it anymore. . . . If I didn't get away from him, I was gonna have a nervous breakdown. . . . But I was so loyal to the fans out there, because they had named their children James and Martha. . . . You talk about suffering: After we'd sing, he'd sit down and tell me what thing he'd been out with the night before. . . . He was cruel. . . . He always tried to make me feel inferior or half a woman 'cause I couldn't get pregnant." He also expected her to let his pregnant girlfriend move in with them and refused to let Martha break up the act with a divorce. She finally got him to sign the papers in 1951.

A woman castigated Martha at the radio station, saying that audiences wouldn't want "people like her" as their entertainers. She said that fans were furious that a divorced woman was singing spiritual songs. Martha felt that the stigma would destroy her career as she rode out of Knoxville with Bill Carlisle en route to her first solo show. "It was the awfullest hurt I ever had in my life. I never was a crybaby, but buckets wouldn't have held the tears I cried on the way across the Smoky Mountains to do that show. I felt like, 'I don't have an act; I can't sing by myself; now I don't have any fans; I have nothing.' All of a sudden it just seemed like I heard a voice that said, 'What are you crying for? I'm satisfied, and you're satisfied.' And the words to that song just almost split me open. I'm in the backseat of Bill Carlisle's car, looking for a paper to write this down on . . . and I saw an old blank check of Bill's laying on the floorboard facedown. It had a bunch of shoe prints all over it. They were dry. I dusted the dirt off and turned it lengthwise, and that's where I wrote 'Satisfied.'"

"Satisfied" became a huge hit. Martha's subsequent songs include the standards "I Can't Stand Up Alone," "I'm Gonna Walk and Talk with My Lord," "Let the Light Shine on Me," and "Rock-a My Soul." Martha Carson became "The Rockin' Queen of Happy Spirituals." She cracked the supper club circuit and starred on the TV shows of Steve Allen, Ray Bolger, Tennessee Ernie Ford, Arlene Francis, and Arthur Godfrey with her whoop-it-up gospel style.

Mother Maybelle and The Carter Sisters turned to gospel during this period, too. In fact, almost all the songs that Maybelle composed for their first songbook (1949) were religious numbers. She brought her brood to Nashville and "The Grand Ole Opry" in 1950, just in time to catch the wave of gospel fervor that was sweeping through the country music community. The Carters performed gospel throughout their careers, and the early songs Maybelle and her cousin Sara sang in The Carter Family became southern gospel cornerstones ("Will the Circle Be Unbroken," etc.). But the divorces of Anita and June perhaps discouraged them from pursuing full-time gospel stardom. Anita married fiddler Dale Potter; married, divorced, remarried, and redivorced steel player Don Davis; and married and divorced guitarist Bob Wooten. June wed honky-tonk star Carl Smith (1952), contractor Rip Nix (1960), and superstar Johnny Cash (1968).

Maybelle, Helen, June, and Anita maintained the old-fashioned country sweetheart image throughout the postwar period, for despite the thumping tambourines of gospel and the newly frank lyrics of honky-tonk music, most female acts were expected to have

Martha Carson's career-making song "Satisfied" was included in this 1954 songbook in Nashville.

wholesome looks. "Sex and glamour can be poison for the girl who wants to get ahead in the hillbilly field," observed reporter H. B. Teeter after attending the 1954 Disc Jockey Convention in Nashville. Washington DJ Ann Jones told him that a female country singer should "stick to ginghams and buckskin. She should steer clear of fancy hairdos, figure-revealing clothes and uplifts." North Carolina DJ Mozelle Phillips advised Teeter that "there is no place in country music for the slick and polished dames of screen and popular music. . . . Our fans want us to be natural, normal people like themselves." Both Mozelle and Ann were singers as well as announcers.

The country music women of West Virginia steadfastly clung to the old images. Evangelists Grandad and Grandma Hite and gospel couples such as Rex and Eleanor Parker and Buddy and Marion Durham reigned on the Mountain State's hillbilly airwaves in the postwar era, as did the old-timey Scotty and Tar Heel Ruby (Perry and Ruby Scott), Ted and Wanda (Henderson), and vaudeville vets Salt and Peanuts (Frank Kurtz and Margaret McConnell).

None were more popular than Doc and Chickie Williams. Chickie, born Jesse Wanda Crupe in 1919, became a West Virginia institution at WWVA in Wheeling as "The Girl with the Lullabye Voice." In 1946 she took a sentimental poem by Pittsburgh Pirates sportscaster Rosy Roswell called "Should You Go First and I Remain" and combined it with the 1936 Blanche and Virgil Brock hymn "Beyond the Sunset." She made a recording of it to give to husband Doc as an anniversary present. He decided to share it with the world on his Wheeling label. Chickie's gift was soon a country religious standard recorded by Ernest Tubb, Hank Williams, and many other stars.

Chickie Williams's backing musicians on that touching 1947 ballad "Beyond the Sunset/Should You Go First and I Remain" were two sisters known as "Radio's Only Blind Twins." Born in 1925, Maxine and Eileen Newcomer were educated at the Western Pennsylvania School for the Blind in Pittsburgh. Both were accomplished on piano, guitar, mandolin, and violin. The Newcomer Twins joined WWVA in 1941 and rapidly became GIs' listening favorites and correspondents. After the war nobody expected these sweet blind sisters with their girlish dresses, pet canaries, and crochet skills to engage in honky-tonk histrionics. They reminded listeners of an earlier era as "The Girls with a Song in Their Hearts."

In fact, there was an entire barn dance show of the forties devoted explicitly to preserving gingham-and-sunbonnet innocence, the vision so devoutly cherished by the southern gospel acts. This was Kentucky's "Renfro Valley Barn Dance," located in "the valley where time stands still." There were no barroom lyrics and no honky-tonk angels in Renfro Valley. Just the echoes of Sunday camp-meetings, Saturday square dances, pie socials, barn raisings, and corn huskings. Here you would find the sunny Swiss yodel of Judy Dell and the calico-clad Doyle, Dickerson, Bullock, Flye, and Travers sisters. Dulcimer damsels such as Elsie Behrens, sentimental stylists like Miss Fredericks, and such duos as The Pleasant Valley Sweethearts and The Blue Ridge Mountain Girls populated Renfro Valley.

After an incubation period in Cincinnati and Dayton, promoter John Lair brought his dream show to a picturesque spot sixty miles south of Lexington in late 1939. He wanted to "make it a spot where future generations could come for a glimpse of the Pioneer America that was." Lair built a thousand-seat barn for the shows and eventually added rustic tourist cabins, craft shops, restaurants, a mill, a pioneer museum, a post office, and a lodge. The whole enterprise was promoted on radio via Saturday night's "Renfro Valley Barn Dance," the "Sunday Mornin' Gatherin'" gospel show, and Monday's "Redbud Schoolhouse" show. "Tune in for a glimpse of the America which the patriotism of our Founding Fathers fashioned for us and the faith of our Mothers bids us cherish and preserve," went one radio promotion.

Chickie Williams, 1947.

Renfro Valley had a number of national stars in the forties. Chief among the women were the members of the trailblazing Coon Creek Girls string band. The durable vaudeville trouper A'nt Idy (Margaret Lilly) also became a Renfro attraction. Superstar Red Foley was a Renfro Valley investor, and his oldest daughter Betty (1933–1991) became a regular there—Betty Foley Cummins served stints as her father's duet partner and in The Coon Creek Girls before achieving a Top 10 solo hit with "Old Moon" in 1959.

The show also gave us two of the last great female country novelty acts, Granny Harper and Little Eller Long. Granny's real name was Elora Williams (1870–1961). During the Depression she was a street performer in Lexington who found radio success on Asa Martin's "Morning Roundup" on WLAP. She was a four-foot-nine-inch mountain sprite who smoked a pipe, played harmonica and fiddle, sang in a gravelly voice, and did "the fastest jig in seven counties." The tiny Granny danced vigorously until her retirement from the barn dance at age eighty-five. Little Eller

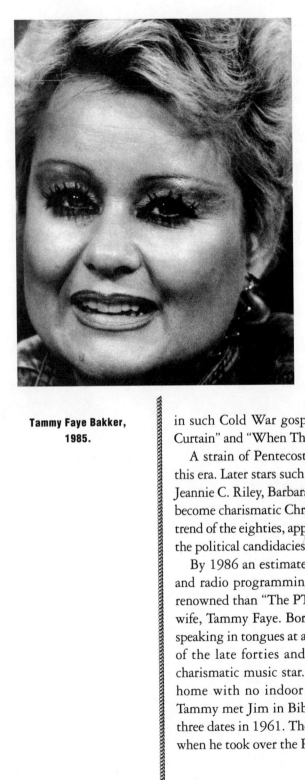

Tammy Faye Bakker, 1985.

was Ellen Mayhew (b. 1920), a six-foot-four-inch stringbean of a comic who won a 1939 amateur contest in her native Detroit, made her radio debut on Chicago's "National Barn Dance," and was paired on the "Renfro Valley Barn Dance" with the diminutive Shorty Hobbs in 1940. After achieving stardom there, Eller married Luther "Smokey" Ward, and the couple relocated to WNAX in Yankton, South Dakota, in 1948. Eller was a regular on Pee Wee King's ABC-TV series of 1955 and later appeared on TV's "Ozark Jubilee."

Renfro Valley's gospel program went on NBC's radio network in 1942 and remained in national syndication well into the seventies. For decades the "Sunday Mornin' Gatherin'" stars were Bess Farmer and The Farmer Sisters. In addition, the show featured gospel singer Flossie Thomas, who came to the barn dance as a member of The Crusaders Quartet in the 1940s. Jack Holden was trained in Renfro Valley fundamentals, then formed a duet with wife Frances Kay to specialize in such Cold War gospel fare as "They Locked God Outside the Iron Curtain" and "When That Hell-Bomb Falls" from 1950 to 1952.

A strain of Pentecostalism has remained in country music ever since this era. Later stars such as Skeeter Davis, Wanda Jackson, Connie Smith, Jeannie C. Riley, Barbara Fairchild, The Whites, and The Judds would all become charismatic Christians. Several became part of the TV evangelism trend of the eighties, appearing on shows to give their testimonies, support the political candidacies of conservatives, or promote their gospel records.

By 1986 an estimated $1.5 billion was being spent for religious TV and radio programming in the United States, and no show was more renowned than "The PTL Club," costarring Jim Bakker and his singing wife, Tammy Faye. Born in 1941, Tammy Faye LaValley Bakker began speaking in tongues at age ten. She rose from kiddie performer in revivals of the late forties and early fifties to become the apotheosis of the charismatic music star. She was the oldest of eight children raised in a home with no indoor plumbing in International Falls, Minnesota. Tammy met Jim in Bible college in Minneapolis and married him after three dates in 1961. They worked their way up as evangelists until 1974, when he took over the PTL (Praise the Lord) ministry in North Carolina.

On the widely seen PTL television broadcasts she could burst into wild laughter, shouts of ecstasy, and sobs of remorse. Tammy conveyed a certain childlike joie de vivre. The overall message of her wacky yet endearing manner was to trust in God for miracles both spiritual and financial—all she ever wanted was for everything to be pretty. Tammy took the glitzy style of the southern gospel movement to its extreme with her elaborate outfits, expensive jewelry, and over-the-top cosmetics flair. In performance Tammy favored a kind of fevered flamboyance that disguised her limited vocal range. On her many Nashville-recorded LPs of 1975 through 1985 her country-girl alto was surrounded by choirs and elaborate pop productions.

Tammy is said to have had affairs with her record producers Gary Paxton and Thurlow Spurr, but it was husband Jim's dalliance with a church secretary that brought down their one-hundred-million-dollar-per-year Heritage USA empire/Christian theme park in 1987. A media spectacle erupted. Tammy released "The Ballad of Jim & Tammy" to the tune of "Harper Valley P.T.A." to sing their side of the story. She admitted to a seventeen-year addiction to prescription drugs. Jim went to prison for fraud in 1988. NBC aired *Fall from Grace*, the TV movie of their lives, in 1990. Tammy Faye filed to divorce Jim in 1992. Daughter Tammy Sue, also a gospel recording artist, took over the Bakkers' struggling New Covenant ministry in Florida.

In 1984, at the height of Jim and Tammy Faye's success on "The PTL Club," the University of Pennsylvania and the Gallup polling organization found that "dissatisfaction with the prevailing moral climate may be one of the most distinctive bonds between religious programs and their viewers." You could have said the same during the southern gospel explosion of 1945 to 1955.

ROCKABILLY WOMEN

9

Let's Have a Party

Janis Martin, 1957.

"It's the beat, the beat, the beat," chanted the Reverend Jimmy Snow rhythmically from his revival pulpit in 1961. Captured forever in a CBS News film clip, Snow clenched his fists and pressed them to his chest as he railed against the teen music that had nearly obliterated both creamy-voiced pop singers and raw country honky-tonkers on the radio. "I know how it feels when you sing it," Snow said. "I know what it does to ya. I know the evil feeling that you feel when you sing it. I know the *lost* position that you get into, and the *beat."* His voice climbed in pitch as Snow reached the fervent core of his argument. "Well, if you talk to the average teenager of today and you ask them what it is about rock 'n' roll music that they like, the first thing they'll say is, 'the beat, the beat, the beat.'"

At the time, the Reverend Snow was married to Wilma Lee and Stoney Cooper's beautiful and curvaceous daughter Carol Lee Cooper. The evangelist was the son of "Grand Ole Opry" superstar Hank Snow. He'd toured with Elvis Presley, boozed it up with Gene Vincent and Wanda Jackson, slept around Nashville, and popped pep pills in the mid-1950s. But now he was saved, and "called" to testify. "Rock 'n' roll primarily appeals to the sensual

nature," he asserted in his most popular pulpit diatribe. "It produces sexual hysteria in crowds and leads young people to surrender to the passions of the lower nature. It takes control of the mind and opens the door to drugs and illicit sex. Don't try to tell me it doesn't. I know. I've been there."

Snow toured the South as a tent show revivalist. The raven-haired Carol Lee led the singing as the two country offspring took their message from town to town. In Plant City, Florida, Jimmy mopped his sweating brow with a handerchief and suggested, "If you want to be set free tonight to serve God with a pure mind . . . get rid of your records and sheet music." The stirred listeners suggested a bonfire of rock 'n' roll music. The next evening, flames towered treetop tall as hundreds of records, posters, and books were tossed onto the blaze. The event made national headlines.

The Reverend Snow was right. Rock 'n' roll music was about sex and rebellion. The long hair of performers was like a proud badge of delinquency. It was about loosening morals. Its stars violated standards of behavior with wild emotionalism, pelvic dance movements, and, yes, the beat, the beat, the infernal beat. It brought the races together. It promoted ecstasy and celebration and abandon. It created a cultural revolution.

"Elvis was the pioneer of the rock-and-roll craze," Snow recalled in his autobiography. "Before he came on the scene, country was country, pop was pop and rhythm-and-blues was rhythm-and-blues. Elvis ran them all together with a fast beat and set a style."

Up north they called the flamboyant r&b of Chuck Berry and Little Richard rock 'n' roll. Down in the South they named it rockabilly when country acts began adding extra octane to their "jump" tunes, singing with bopping hiccups and "cries," using studio echo chamber effects, and adopting rhythm-and-blues mannerisms. An amalgam of country, swing, r&b, and gospel, rockabilly flowered between 1953 and 1963. It was so popular that dozens of country heroes altered their styles to experiment with it.

But rockabilly was also performed by country music women. Its pubescent excitement and uninhibited expressiveness were attractive to young females, too. Most women who recorded this teen sound, in fact, *were* teenagers, whereas their male counterparts were almost all twenty-one or older. Rockabilly threatened the social order when men adopted slithering wiggles and emotional sobbing, previously female-identified behavior; likewise, women challenged the status quo when they took on sassy manners and musical aggression, or male-identified behavior. The descendants of feisty "banjo-pickin' girls" traded their ginghams for dungarees or tight sheaths.

"The beat, the beat, the beat" was heard by Rose Maddox and her brothers in California. Just as they had pioneered the honky-tonk style after World War II, the act seized on the emerging teen style in the early 1950s. Their crazed anarchy on stage, predilection for r&b tunes, and hard-driving energy translated easily into rockabilly terms, notably on "Wild Wild Young Men" (1955) and "Hey Little Dreamboat" (1954). The Maddoxes' raucous, country-boogie arrangement of "New Mule-skinner Blues" (1949) was aped by The Fendermen in a big rock 'n' roll novelty hit of 1960.

"When I was doin' what they're callin' rockabilly now, I thought it was hillbilly music," says Rose. "I had got my songs and stuff in rhythm and blues, you know, from the colored people's records. But I turned 'em around and did 'em my way. . . . In order to work the big dance halls, you had to get a certain beat to your music. And we just automatically did it. We didn't have no better sense than to do it," adds Rose with a loud burst of laughter.

The souped-up hillbilly boogie of Rose Maddox was characteristic of other proto-rockabilly females. The uninhibited stage antics and recorded energy of Charline Arthur are also cited as milestones on the road to female rockabilly. Texan Ella Mae Morse is sometimes given a nod as a rockabilly precursor, too, because of her smoldering "House of Blue Lights," "40 Cups of Coffee," "Buzz Me," "Patty Cake Man," and "Cow Cow Boogie" discs of the 1940s.

Rockabilly music's incubator is generally regarded as 706 Union Street in Memphis, the address of the Sun Records studio. That's where Elvis Presley, Roy Orbison, Conway Twitty, Carl Perkins, and Jerry Lee Lewis experimented. Sun's owner, Sam Phillips, thought the novelty of women recording rockabilly might be lucrative. He had particularly high hopes for a teen duo from Elvis's hometown of Tupelo, Mississippi, The Miller Sisters. Phillips evidently signed on these sisters-in-law, Elsie Jo Miller and Mildred Wages, as competition for Nashville's Davis Sisters, whose peppy "Rock-a-Bye Boogie" of 1953 was one of the earliest rockabilly discs. But The Miller Sisters' "Ten Cats Down" of 1955 failed to catch on, despite its rhythmic drive and unerring harmonies. "Maybe they were just too perfect," lamented Phillips.

The executive's favorite female was the husky-voiced and generously endowed Barbara Pittman, whose stormy up-tempo numbers and sultry ballads better suited the urgency of the emerging rockabilly style. Her recording output for the company was larger than any other female artist's and included such rockabilly tunes as "I Need a Man" (1956), "I'm Getting Better All the Time" (1957), and "Handsome Man" (1960).

DADDY-O

Words and Music by BUFORD ABNER, CHARLIE GORE and LOUIS INNIS

AS RECORDED BY BONNIE LOU FOR KING RECORDS

BONNIE LOU

MAR-KAY PUBLISHING CO.

Sole Selling Agent: KEYS MUSIC, INC.   146 West 54th Street, New York 19, N. Y.

Country yodeler Bonnie Lou was transformed into a teen-appeal singer with numbers like the bouncy "Daddy-O" of 1955. The sheet music photo combines Bonnie's off-the-shoulder blouse with a straw hat, perhaps to appeal to both rocka-billies and traditionalists.

"But recording for Sun in the fifties was, for a woman, being part of a man's world," Barbara reflects. "It was tough just to get heard then by the label, and I guess I was one of the lucky few. My records were not promoted, though. Not like the men's. They didn't think they should spend any money on a girl's records. . . . When somebody suggested that I could have a hit if I went on Dick Clark's show, the people at my label sat back and did nothing. Sam Phillips once said he didn't know exactly what to do with Barbara Pittman.

"I was just a young girl then, you know. . . . At eleven I looked eighteen. My mother said I came into the world with a training bra on. I've always been built like an adult, even as a little girl. . . . I thought that [singing rock-abilly] was just the most tremendous thing. Well, it was. It was just fantastic. . . . My mother used to tell me . . . 'You were born singing.' Either singing or cussin'! I can't remember which one, 'cause I really never stopped doing either!" Salty, sassy Barbara still sings now and then in Memphis and on overseas tours.

Maggie Sue Wimberly was the third principal female act on Sam Phillips's roster. Born in Muscle Shoals, Alabama, in 1941, Maggie Sue was raised singing in her parents' harmonizing Wimberly Family and was discovered in an all-girl gospel group called The Harmonettes. She first recorded for Sun at age thirteen.

She stayed closer to country than rockabilly at Sun, leaning toward the teen style only on 1955's "Daydreams Come True" and the unissued "Rock 'n' Roll Cinnamon Tree." Maggie Sue returned to country music as singer/songwriter Sue Richards in the seventies. The former teenage Sun stylist hit the country charts with her sexy "Sweet Sensuous Feelings" in 1976. She's still singing today, harmonizing alongside Tammy Wynette in the country star's road show.

The finest rockabilly performance by a woman at Sun Records was unquestionably "Welcome to the Club" by Jean Chapel. Of all the females at the company, Jean had been in country music the longest and in the greatest variety of roles. The former Opal Amburgey of Neon, Kentucky, had worked with her sisters as The Hoot Owl Holler Girls in the forties and become Mattie O'Neill to sing with husband Salty Holmes in the early fifties.

What brought a country music woman just past her thirtieth birthday to Sun in 1956 to attempt the new rockabilly style? "I was into that kind of music," Jean said later. "Anything that *moved*. Even today, let me rock. I love it. I used to sit on the steps at home and sing for hours as a kid. I had rhythm." To go with her new "rhythm routine," Jean became a platinum blonde in form-fitting outfits. Phillips sold her Sun recording contract to RCA, just as he had done with Elvis, so Jean was marketed as "The Female Elvis Presley." RCA issued another strong Jean Chapel rockabilly effort, "Oo-ba-la Baby," and she hit the road in the summer of 1956 on a rock 'n' roll tour. The key concert was New York, where she stopped the show at the Brooklyn Paramount with "Roll Over Beethoven" during one of the famed Alan Freed rock 'n' roll revues.

Jean Chapel might have been the best of Sun's rockabilly women, but she didn't lack competition. More than a dozen other Memphis belles experimented with the emerging genre. Sun superstar Jerry Lee Lewis had a sister twelve years his junior who inherited both his rockabilly style and his flamboyant personality. Born in 1947, Linda Gail Lewis had married twice by age sixteen—another four husbands have followed— and was in the Sun studio with her celebrated brother even earlier. After her country and rockabilly flings, she retired to raise children, but reemerged as a rockabilly revivalist in 1987.

Rockabilly became popular with American young people of Linda Gail Lewis's generation with breathtaking speed. Literally within months of Elvis Presley's 1956 breakthrough there were dozens of pouting, pompadoured, pelvis-thrusting imitators recording. Seeing the success that an independent company like Sun Records could have, small record labels sprouted throughout the land, all eager to find their version of the King of Rock 'n' Roll. Or the Queen.

"The beat, the beat, the beat" was heard in every American community. The folks at King Records heard the siren call of rockabilly in Cincinnati. They took WLW "Midwestern Hayride" yodeler Bonnie Lou (Kath) and retooled her for the teen market with 1955's "Daddy-O" and other bouncy novelty ditties. "When the rockabilly thing got popular . . . King directed me that way," Bonnie Lou says. "The people at King always got the songs for the artists. They told us what to record. King had a lot of country and rhythm-and-blues artists then, you see; and sometimes both black and white would play on the sessions." Born near Bloomington, Illinois, in 1926, Bonnie Lou began entertaining on the radio barn dance circuit as Sally Carson while still a teen. She landed in Cincinnati in 1945 and scored Top 10 country hits with 1953's "Seven Lonely Days" and "Tennessee Wig Walk." Bonnie's finest rockabilly performance was 1958's "Friction Heat," issued by Cincinnati's Fraternity label. After her teen-tune days ended, Bonnie Lou remained a beloved fixture of Cincinnati TV into the 1980s.

"The beat, the beat, the beat" was in the air of the Southwest, too. In Phoenix, Arizona, in 1961 Mirriam Johnson (b. 1943) sang the folk tune "Lonesome Road" accompanied by the same raucous sax used on her husband Duane Eddy's "twangy guitar" hits. Mirriam divorced Eddy in 1968, married Waylon Jennings in 1969, and became country "outlaw" queen Jessi Colter.

Vivacious Jo-Ann Campbell heard "the beat, the beat, the beat" as a teen in Florida. Born in 1938, Jo-Ann was a Jacksonville drum majorette who loved to dance. Her parents moved with the Florida State Twirling Champion to New York in 1954. The idea was to get her on Broadway, but the pert jitterbugger became enthralled with rock 'n' roll instead. "If I wasn't out dancing somewhere, I was in my bedroom with the door shut, listening to Alan Freed," she recalled. "When he had a stage show at the Brooklyn Paramount, I went and stood in line with a couple of my friends, and finally we got in." On the bill were lady truck driver Lillian Briggs, belting "I

Jo-Ann Campbell, 1958.

Want You to Be My Baby" in gold lamé, and peroxided Jean Chapel, a vision in white romping through "Welcome to the Club." Jo-Ann experienced an epiphany. "I said to myself, 'This is it, I've got to be a singer; I've got to sing rock 'n' roll; and I've got to be on an Alan Freed show someday.'"

Jo-Ann began recording in 1957, contributing the frantic "Come on Baby," "Wait a Minute," and "Nervous" to the emerging rock 'n' roll repertoire. "You're Driving Me Mad" and "Rock and Roll Show" are particularly prized by rockabilly collectors today. The former was banned because of its "drive on, baby" line, which censors evidently thought was too raunchy for a five-foot, nineteen-year-old blonde to be singing.

When she delivered these tunes onstage, Jo-Ann was a wiggling wildcat. One Connecticut fan remembers her gyrating in an ultratight slit skirt. "At the end of her act, the slit had progressed all the way up to her hip. As she was twisting and bumping on stage, all the stitches were coming out! To this day, I believe those stitches were purposely designed to break, and what a show she performed that day!"

No wonder they billed her as "The Blonde Bombshell." Alan Freed hired her to be on his fateful all-star rock 'n' roll tour of 1958. When the two Greyhounds full of rockers hit Boston, trouble was in the air. "We had to stop the show several times for roughhousing in the balcony," Jo-Ann recalls, "and Alan came out and tried to quiet everybody down. Finally we were able to get it in." The agitated crowd milled around the stage door afterward as the performers pulled out of Beantown. The next morning's newspapers carried the headlines of a postconcert teenage riot. "The insinuation, of course, was that it had happened during the performance or because of the performance," Jo-Ann told *When Rock Was Young* author Bruce Pollock when recalling the incident. "Then the news just spread from city to city: 'Oh dear, there were some people knifed in Boston; the Alan Freed show caused a horrible riot. Cancel them out.'" Freed was indicted for the Boston incident. His tour faced cancellations and finally limped back to New York two weeks ahead of schedule. Mutual Radio and NBC banned rock 'n' roll. The 1960 payola investigations in Washington targeted Freed for destruction.

Jo-Ann kept rocking. By this time she was an "American Bandstand" TV favorite. She sang in the 1958 rock 'n' roll movie *Go, Johnny ,Go!* and returned to the recording studio for more teen tunes in 1960. As the sixties dawned, Jo-Ann and her roommate, Loretta Martin (soon to become the second of the three Mrs. Dick Clarks), were frequenting a dive on West Forty-fifth Street in New York called The Peppermint Lounge. There they began promoting a new dance called the twist. Jo-Ann took fellow rockers to the club; other celebrities followed, and soon the gossip columns got wind of a chic new nightlife trend. In 1961 The Blonde Bombshell starred in *Hey, Let's Twist!,* the film that immortalized the Peppermint Lounge phenomenon.

But Jo-Ann Campbell scored her biggest hit when she answered country star Claude King's "Wolverton Mountain" with "I'm the Girl from Wolverton Mountain" in 1962. She posed as a blue-jeaned, pigtailed country cutie on the subsequent LP cover and did only one rocker on it, a kittenish rendition of Tommy Roe's "Sheila." "You know the old saying— when you get married, it's all over," she says wryly. Jo-Ann wed

The Davis Sisters, 1953.

singer/songwriter Troy Seals. As Jo-Ann and Troy they recorded 1964's "I Found a Love, Oh What a Love," and by the time the disc was steaming up the charts, Jo-Ann was pregnant. After the birth of their son, Jo-Ann appeared for a while on Dick Clark's 1965 rock 'n' roll TV show "Where the Action Is," but eventually, Jo-Ann Campbell quit entertaining. The family moved to Nashville in 1979. Troy is now one of Music Row's most successful songwriters, and Jo-Ann campaigns in Music City for the Humane Association and against the wearing of furs.

Nashville kept its ear on the rockabilly phenomenon as the nation went wild for the records that Elvis Presley, Gene Vincent, Conway Twitty, and The Everly Brothers were recording in its studios in the late 1950s. And the Reverend Snow wasn't the only one listening. RCA executive Steve Sholes, in particular, was keen to find these men's female equivalents. The company's Davis Sisters certainly had the head start with "Rock-a-Bye Boogie," but a 1953 car crash killed Betty Jack Davis and left partner Skeeter Davis (Mary Frances Penick) a physical and emotional wreck. RCA's Chet Atkins tried to mold Charline Arthur into a rockabilly, but the chemistry between the singer and producer was all wrong. The label's Jean Chapel pulled back from rockabilly to nurse her ailing husband and raise her daughter. RCA persevered with a 1957 disc called "Rocky Rolly Lover Boy" by Judy Faye.

'Nita, Rita, and Ruby were groomed for the teen market with a number of RCA singles from 1955 to 1957. The three singers were Maybelle's daughter Anita Carter, Kitty Wells's daughter Ruby Wright (b. 1939), and yodeler Don Winters's daughter Rita Robbins (b. 1932). But the trio dissolved because, as Ruby recalls, "'Nita traveled with her sisters. When I traveled, it was with Mom and Dad. Also, I was a cheerleader in school and wasn't really serious about a music career. . . . We were just havin' fun. . . . Finally everybody went their separate ways. . . . I got married."

Elvis Presley's label still didn't give up. Finally Sholes and Atkins seized on a southern teenager named Janis Martin, the first rockabilly female to be given a major-label promotional buildup. Janis Darlene

Martin was born in Virginia in 1940. She had her own radio show by age thirteen and a year later was invited to join the cast of "The Old Dominion Barn Dance" in Richmond. Like many teens of the time, Janis was attracted by the new rock 'n' roll sounds of rhythm-and-blues acts, particularly LaVern Baker and Ruth Brown, whose hits she performed in her country shows. In early 1956 Janis made a tape of "Will You Willyum"; Sholes heard the fifteen-year-old's throaty delivery, recognized her teen appeal, and brought her to Nashville to record for RCA with Atkins. In addition to "Will You Willyum," Janis tore into "Drugstore Rock 'n' Roll" and "Let's Elope Baby." Billed as "The Gal with the Elvis Presley Voice," Janis hit the promotional circuit with her blond ponytail bouncing. Before the year was out, she was in Nashville again to record the rollicking "Ooby Dooby," "My Boy Elvis," and "Little Bit."

She appeared on "American Bandstand," "The Tonight Show," "The Today Show," "The Grand Ole Opry," and "The Ozark Jubilee" in 1956 and 1957. RCA kept the promotional machinery working by getting Janis a screen test at MGM, bringing her to New York for another round of appearances, and booking her on country star Jim Reeves's European tour. "Billy Boy Billy Boy" (1957), "Cracker Jack" (1957), and the percussive "Bang Bang" (1958) kept her rockabilly flame burning brightly.

But in 1958 eighteen-year-old Janis had a baby boy. She'd been secretly married since age fifteen. RCA probably saw the handwriting on the wall for her teen image and cooled toward the once heavily promoted "Rockin' Country Gal." Janis got a divorce around 1960 and attempted to start over on the small Palette label, but before her resuscitated career could get any momentum, she remarried. Her second husband could not accept the idea of his wife's working as a rockabilly entertainer and gave her an ultimatum of marriage or career. She retired again.

"You cannot change a person's entire life and all they have known," Janis said years later. "I tried, but the music was too strong inside." In 1970 she formed a new band, and three years later got her second divorce. She was touring again as "The Female Elvis" when Presley died in 1977. "I just lost interest in the whole idea after that. I felt a part of me had died, too."

RCA kept trying. In 1957 the company pushed Jean Chapel's energetic gospel-singing sister Martha Carson in an Elvis direction by having her record "Now Stop," "Just Whistle or Call," and "Music Drives Me Crazy (Especially Rock 'n' Roll)" in New York. But it continued to pin its rockabilly hopes on the country talent pool in Nashville.

Music City's rockabilly queen was in town, all right. But Decca found her, not RCA. Brenda Mae Tarpley is one of those extraordinary, once-in-a-generation creatures, a prodigy so gifted that melody is as natural as

breath. She came into this world in an Atlanta hospital charity ward in December 1944 and was singing by the time she was toddling. Not little-kid, wobbly-pitch, wispy-thin attempts. *Singing.*

"She liked music even when she was a baby," recalled Mama Grace Tarpley. "When she was eight months old, she loved to listen to music on the radio." By age three little Brenda could hear a song twice and then skip around the house singing it. "It was amazing," said Mama. "She did it so easily, I am sure it was a god-given talent." At age five the child took first prize in a talent contest in Conyers, Georgia, singing "Take Me Out to the Ball Game." A few weeks later she auditioned successfully as a regular on an Atlanta radio show called "Star-makers Revue" by singing "Too Young." At age six she belted out the Hank Williams hit "Hey Good Lookin'" to win a slot in the cast of the new "TV Ranch" show on Atlanta's WAGA-TV. In May 1953 Brenda's father was killed in a construction site accident, and the family became destitute. Brenda's singing became more than a youthful pastime; it became an economic necessity. She was just shy of her eighth birthday.

"I can't ever remember a time when I *wanted* to become a singer, because I've always been one," Brenda says, looking back. "After my father died, it became necessary for me to work . . . because I was the only one making any money. . . . It was no great amount or anything, but it was better than my mother working eighteen hours in a cotton mill every day.

"I was singing . . . because we were poor. You spell that with four *o*'s, p-o-o-o-o-r. We knew what it was like to be hungry."

So Brenda Mae Tarpley became professional singer Brenda Lee. "I was working every weekend, making a living for my mother, two sisters, and a brother. I'd leave Atlanta on a bus on Friday for . . . Ohio . . . and return on Sunday night. I'd be so tired Monday morning . . . Miss Norton, my third-grade teacher . . . would let me put my head down on the desk and sleep until about one o'clock." The hardworking ten-year-old soon became a "little girl with grown-up reactions," as country star Red Foley once described her. Foley discovered Brenda Lee in Augusta in early 1956. He brought her to Springfield, Missouri, and starred her on his ABC-TV network show "Ozark Jubilee." She debuted with the Hank Williams Cajun rave-up "Jambalaya."

"I had a lot of influences from my mother because she used to sing me a lot of Hank Williams, Sr., songs. That was the first kind of music I ever heard, other than gospel. A lot of people don't know it, but a lot of my background is made up of gospel influence. Mahalia Jackson was an idol of mine."

Armed with the heart of Hank and the booming power of Mahalia, little Brenda stormed the national TV scene on the network shows of Perry Como, Steve Allen, and Ed Sullivan. Decca Records signed her in 1956 and brought her to Nashville to record. She was only eleven, but refused to be treated like a child. "I think I was kind of outspoken as a youngster about how I wanted to sound and how I wanted things done when I was singing. It might have come off just a little bit bratty, I'm sure. In the first session that I did, we had finished and were listening to the cuts, and I said, 'The bass player hit a wrong note.' [Producer] Owen Bradley said, 'What do you mean?' And I said, 'Play it back and hear the wrong note.' Nobody believed me. But we played it back, and he did." Bradley wasn't the only one who got a comeuppance from the self-assertive tyke. Later in the session Decca executive Paul Cohen began using baby talk to try to explain something to the child. "Suddenly," Bradley recalls, "Brenda cocked her head back, looked him straight in the eyes, and said, 'Well, goo-goo.' Everybody in the studio cracked up."

Brenda Lee's first single was "Jambalaya," backed with what many believe to be her best rockabilly performance, "Bigelow 6-200." One side took off in America; the other became a hit in England. She followed it with 1957–1959 boppers including "Rock the Bop," "Ring-a-My-Phone," "Let's Jump the Broomstick," "One Teenager to Another," "One Step at a Time," and "Dynamite," from which she acquired her billing as "Little Miss Dynamite." In 1958 she recorded one of rockabilly music's most enduring singles, "Rockin' Around the Christmas Tree."

Her big, mature voice and explosive stage presence made her a fixture on early rock 'n' roll touring shows, even though she was considerably younger than the others on the bills. "Sometimes I feel sorry for the artists that are in rock today. I don't think they are having near the fun that we did. I toured with all the people that were there at the time—Carl Perkins, Chuck Berry, Fats Domino, Elvis, The Big Bopper—it was so much fun because there was a camaraderie between the acts then. We were all sort of working as a unit. We had these huge package tours where everybody and their brother was on them, and the show went on *forever,* for hours. You got to travel with each other; you got to know each other, and you got to be friends.

"I was very young, touring with a lot of adults, and I was very insulated because my mother traveled with me. I mean, I *wanted* to get into trouble, but there was no way. . . . I wasn't allowed to date until I was sixteen. . . . I can remember I did a tour with Fabian and he asked me for a date . . . in San Antonio, and we were going to go down by the Riverwalk. Oh, I was so excited, and I got dressed. It was our night off, and we didn't have to do a show. . . . Well, at every bush and every building behind us there was one of my band members or my mother or my manager all peeking . . . to make sure of what Fabian and I were doing. Needless to say, it ruined my night."

Although Brenda sang rockabilly with a distinctly sexy and powerful growl, her mother refused to grant her permission to tour with Jerry Lee Lewis, claiming that he was "an animal." And country music fan magazines questioned the propriety of the child star's performing at all. Opined *Country & Western Jamboree,* "We cannot possibly understand why a nightclub would book a 12-year-old girl, or why anyone in charge of the child's schedule would permit such a booking. . . . We paused to wonder when we saw Brenda booked for eight straight days around Minneapolis during the first of May, right before normal school examinations." Levelheaded Brenda did just fine in school, thank you. She even found time to be a high school cheerleader, school newspaper worker, and debating team member in Nashville alongside her classmate and future pop singer Rita Coolidge.

"Nobody told me I was a star. Nobody told me I was any different from anybody else. When you're little, you believe what you're told. I wasn't rebellious. When I listen to the rock songs I sang, not knowing what in the world the lyrics must've meant, I was singing them like I knew. . . . I don't know how, I have just always known . . . what's best for me."

On her 1959 hit "Sweet Nothin's," for instance, the then-fourteen-year-old Brenda shouts, pouts, and purrs over a steady beat in a way that can only be described as "adult." A similar effect is achieved on 1961's "Dum Dum" and 1960's "That's All You Gotta Do." Whether preteen or sweet sixteen, whenever Brenda Lee opened her mouth to sing, she was a woman. The reserved, normal American kid became a tornado of emotion behind a microphone. There were some who refused to believe that vocal firestorm came from such a young girl. "In 1959, when I first went to France, the French people had heard my voice, but had never seen me. . . . So we sent photos of me as I looked at fourteen years of age. Well, they didn't believe it. They didn't think that voice should come out of a fourteen-year-old, especially one that looked like she was six. So they planted a story that I was actually a forty-year-old midget . . . which certainly helped sell tickets. We couldn't have asked for a better publicity campaign.

"I was a name over there [in Europe] before I was here. . . . I really got my first big break in England. I started touring over there and cultivating that audience, working with Cliff Richard and Dusty Springfield and all the groups. The Beatles used to open shows for me [in Germany] before they made it in the United States—when I came back to the States, I tried to get Decca to sign them, but the company wasn't interested." She also became a sensation in Latin America before rising to superstardom in America. By the mid-sixties Brenda Lee was a major headliner in Japan. Her gravel-voiced, hiccuping rockabilly stylings also drove them wild in Australia. In 1961 five hundred shrieking Aussie teens besieged her hotel room.

"I think I helped pioneer, a little bit, what's happening in music today," says the former rockabilly star. "I think I helped lay the foundation for what women are doing in the rock field, and it always makes me extremely elated that I may have been influential in another woman's career. . . . Dolly Parton has talked to me about how influential I was in her music; and Cyndi Lauper and Stevie Nicks and a lot of the British woman artists have, too. In the country field, Barbara Mandrell. . . . It's a thrill when they tell me that."

In the 1960s Brenda took the ferocious conviction and commanding technique she developed as a rockabilly singer and applied them to a series of throbbing, torn-from-the-chest ballads that made her the biggest female record seller in history. She starred in the movie comedy *The Two Little Bears* in 1961 and toured in summer stock in the teen-themed musical *Bye Bye Birdie* in 1962. In 1963 she eloped with Ronnie Shacklett, whom she'd met at a Jackie Wilson concert in Nashville. Her mom disapproved of the match. Brenda was a mother by age twenty-one, and thereafter she concentrated on torchy trademark tunes like "I'm Sorry." In the 1970s and 1980s she reverted to country music and earned four Grammy nominations.

Nashville had other female rockabillys. Like their male counterparts, several established country women jumped on the rockabilly bandwagon. In addition to Jean Chapel and Martha Carson, these included Jean Dinning, Boots Collins, and Sue Thompson. Particularly good at the new style was Decca's Barbara Allen (Peggy Joye Tunnell), who had a rockabilly fling with "Sweet Willie" (1958) before retreating to conventional country stylings at "The New Dominion Barn Dance" and WWVA's "Jamboree." The durable all-female band Abbie Neal & The Ranch Girls turned up the heat with "I'll Take Back the Heartache" and "Hillbilly Beat" on West Virginia's Admiral label (c. 1958). But for the really wild women of the rockabilly era, you had to look west.

"The beat, the beat, the beat." It came crashing into California with the power of the Pacific surf. The continually growing working-class suburbs of Los Angeles were the most fertile areas for the growth of rock 'n' roll culture. Indeed, by the 1960s California was in the vanguard of almost all teen fads, fashion developments, and musical innovations. The state came to symbolize the farthest-out expressions of American pop culture and to serve as a barometer of the nation's social trends. As early as 1947 California reported the first juvenile delinquent motorcycle gangs, later immortalized in the 1954 film *The Wild One.*

California was the capital for nonconformity and the site of the earliest rebellions against the "gray flannel" corporate world. It was the cradle of the Beats, with author Jack Kerouac, comedian Lenny Bruce, and poet Allen Ginsberg creating a circle of social protesters to bomb-shelter culture. In a society on the verge of self-destruction, antiheroes emerged. *Rebel Without a Cause* movie star James Dean would die in 1954 from a fast life and fast cars, becoming an instant teen icon. More than a hundred Hollywood releases capitalized on teen alienation between 1954 and 1962. Some titles say it all—*High School Hellcats, Girls in Prison, The Delinquents, Runaway Daughters, Untamed Youth, Unwed Mother, Teenage Doll, Girls on the Loose, Girls Town, Rebel Angel, Live Fast Die Young, High School Confidential, Date Bait, The Wayward Girl, Dragstrip Girl, Beat Girl, Hot Car Girl, Sorority Girl, Reform School Girl, Hot-Rod Girl.*

Rockabilly's raw energy, restless feeling, blunt attack, and rhythmic power were in the discs of dozens of West Coast women. Rose Maddox's many rocking daughters included Liberty Records singer Laura Lee Perkins, with her string of raspy-voiced singles, including "Kiss Me Baby," "Don't Wait Up," and "Oh La Baby." Era Records' entry was Phoenix native Alis Lesley, with her "He Will Come Back to Me" and "Heartbreak Harry" single. Alis was yet another billed as "The Female Elvis"; she even shaped pieces of her hair to look like sideburns.

Canadians Lucille Starr and Bob Regan headed to southern California to record for Hollywood's Ditto Records in 1959. The resulting "Eeny-Meeny-Miney-Moe" and its successors "What's the Password," "The Flirting Kind," and "The Big Kiss" were superb, imaginative rockabilly records, distinguished by Lucille's bopping hillbilly vocal with high hiccup effects and Bob's biting guitar breaks. Lucille Saboie began her career in an all-female French-singing Canadian folk group called Les Hirondelles (The Swallows). She and Bob Frederickson (Regan) met and married as country performers in Vancouver, British Columbia; but by the mid-fifties they'd adopted a snappy, youth-oriented style. She came from a strict French Catholic upbringing, but says that never bothered her as a rocker.

"I was doing what came naturally," says Lucille. "I didn't know what I was not supposed to do, so I always danced around; I was doing what was later called the twist. It was just a natural thing; I always loved to move around a lot, and I still do. One of my records was very risqué for the time. My mother said, 'I can't possibly play this for the parish priest!' It was called 'Demon Lover.' *That* was a no-no."

The team starred for seven years on Los Angeles television, and eventually Lucille became the singing voice of Bea Benaderet's "Cousin Pearl Bodine" character on "The Beverly Hillbillies" TV show from 1962 to 1963. North of the border Bob and Lucille became superstars of the sixties as The Canadian Sweethearts, but Regan's envy of her solo work caused a rift between them. Lucille Starr scored a major international hit with "The French Song" in 1964, increasing the marital friction. "I was so sad when I recorded that. It was one of the lowest times of my life. My personal life was such a disaster. When I sang 'I'm alone,' I really meant it." She increasingly recorded country songs in Nashville without Regan. In 1967 Lucille introduced the female country standard "Too Far Gone." After going through a bitter 1977 divorce, she moved to Music City and resumed her recording career.

The Collins Kids, 1957.

The junior version of the Bob and Lucille rockabilly team on Los Angeles TV was The Collins Kids. Lorrie Collins (b. 1942) and her little brother Larry were raised on an Oklahoma dairy farm and attended a one-room schoolhouse. When she was eight, Lorrie won a Tulsa talent contest, and her parents were urged to take her to Los Angeles. In 1953, when she was eleven and Larry was nine, the gifted siblings began commuting for Saturday night appearances as regulars on the popular "Town Hall Party" country TV series in L.A. They were irrepressible scene stealers who rapidly ascended to stardom on the show. Each week The Collins Kids got their own spot as "something for the youngsters." Lorrie and Larry's "hopped-up hillbilly" style predated Presley and virtually all the other teen rages of the day. Lorrie was the anchor, belting the songs with confidence, turning heads with her teen-queen looks, and playing socko rhythm guitar, while crew-cutted little Larry impishly bopped around her, playing electric lead guitar.

Two years after their TV debut, the rockabilly juveniles began recording for Columbia. The Collins Kids sound was built around Lorrie's buoyant, exuberant vocals, supported by Larry's high harmonies and stinging guitar work, the latter a product of hot picker Joe Maphis's tutelage. Both sides of their debut disc, "Beetle Bug Bop" and "Hush Money," are real toe-tappers. These and the rest of their hot rockabilly sides on Columbia from 1955 to 1959 showcase a bursting-with-energy team. "Rockaway Rock," "Whistle Bait," "Mama Worries," "Hoy Hoy," and "Rock and Roll Polka" practically twitch with excitement. All the rockabillys spoke directly to the teen generation of the fifties, but Lorrie and Larry had especially gum-snapping material—"Hot Rod," "Soda Poppin' Around," "In My Teens," and "Party," for instance.

By age fifteen Lorrie was an adorable blue-eyed brunet. A regular "Town Hall Party" TV viewer and on-set visitor was the shy, seventeen-year-old teen heartthrob Ricky Nelson. "Nobody took him serious about his music," Lorrie recalls. "It was like, 'Okay, he's a good-looking guy and a popular TV artist, and everybody cuts a record now and then, and you never hear from them again.' But he was dead serious about his music. . . . And I think that was one of the things that was appealing to him about me . . . because my life was music.

"Rick Nelson was like the heartthrob of the world. Poor me. I just adored him." He was smitten, too. Biographer Joel Selvin refers to Lorrie as "the first real love in his life." Lorrie and Ricky both knew the loneliness of being a child star. Both longed for a normal teenage life. Both were shy, soft-spoken, and tentative. Both were musical. They spent hours together picking and singing, and cowrote his first composing attempt, "My Gal." He gave her his ring to be his "steady." Lorrie appeared on "The Adventures of Ozzie and Harriet" as Ricky's girlfriend, and the couple sang The Collins Kids' version of "Just Because" on one episode. The relationship became more serious. Neither set of parents especially approved when the two teens began talking of marriage. Lorrie's folks sent little Larry along on dates to keep an eye on things. "There were so many people around all the time," Lorrie says. "There were times when we would just ride around in the car and not even talk, just hold hands and be happy to be alone and be with each other. It was like being a normal girlfriend and boyfriend. I think we both yearned for that. . . . I guess we really loved each other a lot."

Inevitably their ardor cooled. Then, abruptly, the romance was killed.

"It was pretty awful, and it was my fault," Lorrie admits. While The Collins Kids were on tour with Johnny Cash, the rockabilly princess was romanced by Cash's manager, Stu Carnall, nineteen years her senior. They got married in Las Vegas. Nelson read about it in a gossip column and was crushed. Lorrie withdrew from The Collins Kids duo to raise a family. She and brother Larry reunited for some TV appearances in the 1960s and some Nevada casino shows in the 1970s.

The Los Angeles rockabilly scene that included Lorrie Collins and Ricky Nelson revolved around songwriter Sharon Sheeley's apartment. She was the girlfriend of rockabilly great Eddie Cochran and cowrote his pile-driving "Somethin' Else," as well as Nelson's 1958 hit "Poor Little Fool" and other teen tunes. In one of rock's most famous tragedies, Cochran was killed and Gene Vincent partially crippled in a 1960 taxi crash in England. Sharon, also badly injured, returned to Los Angeles barely able to walk. Though she and Cochran had planned marriage, she set about rebuilding her life by writing songs with Sharon Lee Myers, a teenager recently arrived from the South. Miss Myers was to become far better known as pop princess Jackie DeShannon.

Jackie DeShannon, 1966.

Born in Hazel, Kentucky, in 1944, Jackie was the daughter of a country musician father and a blues singer mother. Her grandmother sang and played Irish folk songs, and several aunts and uncles were also involved in music. Jackie was a country radio performer in Kentucky and Illinois by age eleven. She first recorded in 1957. Unfortunately, the company "didn't believe that girls sold as well as boys," so her debut disc wasn't widely promoted. Gone Records billed her as "Jackie Dee," perhaps to disguise her sex. By age fifteen she was trying her luck in Music City. "I was going to Nashville and recording and promoting myself," she recalls. "I was very young, but my parents were encouraging. Either my mother or my father would accompany me on these trips." She issued her purest rockabilly single, "Buddy," in 1958, then the bopping "Just Another Lie" as "Jacquie Shannon & The Cajuns."

A reporter for *Folk and Country Songs* magazine went gaga over the rockabilly youngster in early 1959 after stumbling on a Nashville rehearsal session: "In my opinion Jackie Dee is one of the greatest new finds since the inimitable Elvis Presley. Electro-magnetic power— jet-propelled action and a voice to match—that's the Jackie Dee story in a nutshell." Also supportive during her Nashville days were Opry stars Homer & Jethro. But at a show in Chicago, Jackie met Eddie Cochran, then a rockabilly king with his huge "Summertime Blues." "He was very, very encouraging. He reminded me a lot of James Dean. He said, 'If you really want to get somewhere, you've got to come to California.'" Jackie arrived in 1960 and promptly tore into a ferocious female reworking of Elvis's *King Creole* movie tune "Trouble."

The record is one of a handful of rockabilly singles where females express the kind of anger and antisocial tendencies that marked males' rock 'n' roll rebellion. Jackie was joined as a rockabilly "tough gal" by Jane Bowman, whose "Mad Mama" dealt with an overly jealous mate. "Let me tell you, honey, this mama is mad," Jane sang. "I'm gonna bash in your head." Using the musical setting of Dave Dudley's "Six Days on the Road," West Virginian Boots Collins contributed "Mean" to the era's "tough-gal" trend. Her disc featured threats to her man with a shotgun. Angriest of all was Arkansan Joyce Green. In her echoey, sinister "Black Cadillac" she vows to bury her man. It has become one of the most collectible of all rockabilly singles, selling for hundreds of dollars on the rare-records market.

None of these records became hits. It was okay for Elvis to snarl, "don't you mess around with me," but not lithesome, flaxen-tressed, teenage Jackie DeShannon. But Jackie kept trying. She issued four songs, including the aggressive "Put My Baby Down," in 1960 and was then signed by Liberty Records. Six successive singles stiffed in 1961, and even startlingly soulful renditions of Ray Charles's "I'll Drown in My Own Tears" and her own "The Prince" the next year didn't turn the tide. Blessed with a gripping growl, a dark alto dip, and a country-gospel wail in her voice, Jackie was certain she had what it took as a singer. But it was her songwriting that sustained her.

She met Sharon Sheeley at Liberty, and the two became a hit factory for Brenda Lee, The Fleetwoods, Troy Shondell, Dodie Stevens, Peggy March, Bobby Vee, and other teen idols.

"I loved having other people do my material. The thing was that I wanted to do some, too." Convincing the record label of the value in her distinctive, hoarse, emotion-packed delivery was another matter. Jackie finally made the national charts in 1963 with a soul-drenched reworking of the Bob Wills country classic "Faded Love." Then she found a Sonny Bono/Jack Nitzsche song called "Needles and Pins." "Everything I presented to the label, they hated." During the subsequent British Invasion, The Searchers copied her record and created a classic. The group did the same with the impassioned DeShannon original "When You Walk in the Room."

Jackie's collaborator Sheeley married "Shindig" TV host Jimmy O'Neill, and he began featuring the headstrong, rocking singer/songwriter on his TV show and in his club, Chez Paree. The press labeled Jackie "the new Red Hot Mama with a rock beat." Things began looking up. After filming the 1964 teen flick *Surf Party,* Jackie headed to England to capitalize on her Searchers successes and her notoriety as an opening act for The Beatles on their debut U.S. tour. She appeared on Britain's "Ready, Steady, Go!" teen TV show, was the songwriter of Marianne Faithfull's "Come and Stay with Me" and "In My Time of Sorrow," and had a romance with future Led Zeppelin guitarist Jimmy Page. Back in the United States, Jackie recorded versions of Buddy Holly's "Oh Boy" and "Maybe Baby." She was on the bill of the show he was en route to when he died in 1959, and she'd never forgotten Buddy.

Jackie became increasingly outspoken at her record label. "When I would . . . go in and ask about the sales of my record, they would call me a pushy broad. Or, because I'm small, they'd treat me like a child. I still have hang-ups about those days." She scored a major international hit with "What the World Needs Now Is Love" in 1965 and had her biggest success in 1969, with the million-seller "Put a Little Love in Your Heart," which she'd penned. Dolly Parton brought it into the country fold with a 1993 rendition.

On her later albums Jackie leaned toward country-pop on songs. In 1975 Kim Carnes scored a giant hit with the Jackie DeShannon–cowritten "Bette Davis Eyes."

Jackie has recorded with lush orchestras, as well as raw rockabilly bands. She has sung soul and country and folk and some of the most melodic, shimmering pop ever recorded. Although hugely successful as a songwriter, she never got the success she deserved as a singer. Was it her attitude? "I saw *Rebel Without a Cause* and never got over it," she says with a laugh. "I never made it out of that fan club."

West Coast rockabilly found its fullest female expression in Wanda Jackson. Her rockabilly singles from 1956 to 1961 are without parallel in the history of rock 'n' roll. With her snarling, powerhouse singing, Wanda Jackson captured the elemental, low-class wildness of this music better than any other female of her day. She wrote her own rockabilly classics "Mean Mean Man," "Baby Loves Him," and "Rock Your Baby." She attacked The Coasters' "Riot in Cell Block #9" and Little Richard's "Rip It Up" with almost frightening savagery. Some listeners consider her incendiary "Funnel of Love" and "Fujiyama Mama" sexually suggestive. Her "Honey Bop" has been cited as the greatest of all female rockabilly records. And her jubilant "party" trilogy—"Let's Have a Party," "There's a

Party Goin' On," and "Man We Had a Party"—extended rockabilly's life into the early 1960s, when most of the music's male stars were in eclipse, embroiled in moral scandals, or dead.

The most assertive woman rocker of her era was a bewitching, black-haired beauty who kicked off her country cowgirl boots to slither in gold lamé or shimmer in sequins. She had fire, energy, and uninhibited verve that doubtless shocked conservatives. Although frequently compared to Gene Vincent, of "Be Bop a Lula" fame, Wanda was tutored as a rocker by none other than the King himself. According to her, rockabilly was just "doin' what comes naturally."

"I was innovative in my time," she says. "But in retrospect, I was just bein' me. . . . I do different interviews now, and they talk about how I was quite—what's the word for the new feminist movement?—yeah, 'liberated.' Well, I didn't realize it at the time, but that's just it. My folks had raised me to think for myself."

Tom and Nellie Jackson had their only child in October 1937 in his hometown of Maud, Oklahoma. It was the Depression, so few people were paying to hear Tom's hillbilly band. "Hearing of the good wages being paid in California, the three of us moved to California in 1942. It was in Los Angeles that I was introduced to western swing music. . . . As I watched the female singers in their shiny clothes, I knew at the age of six that I was going to be 'a girl singer.' My daddy began to teach me to play the guitar, and we sang around the house all the time. . . . After the war ended, the three of us moved back home to Oklahoma." Wanda began singing in the Baptist church in Oklahoma City. By age thirteen she had her own daily radio show over KPLR and became ever more dedicated to music. "Wanda wasn't like other children after the guitar came into her life," recalled her mother. "Our problem was never to get her to practice—it was getting her to stop. She never wanted to quit." Said a high school classmate, Wanda "never had time for dates, nothing like that. Just that guitar—that's all she thought about."

Through her radio program she came to the attention of Hank Thompson, who recorded the teenager with his group in 1954. Band member Billy Gray and Wanda had a hit duet with "You Can't Have My Love" that year, and she had several other releases while she was still in high school. Capitol Records signed her to a solo contract as soon as she graduated. In 1955 the young country stylist was put on tour with Elvis Presley, and they began dating.

"When I worked with Elvis, he said, 'Now you really should start doin' the kind of music I'm doin'. You can see how they like it and how

Wanda Jackson, the greatest of the rockabilly women, put some of her finest performances on this 1960 collection.

the young kids buy those records. And you've got the voice for it.' He really talked it up to me. . . . He took me to his house, and we went through records, old black blues stuff he had. I listened to a bunch of 'em, but told him, 'Nah. I can't do it.' And I just kinda forgot it."

Red Foley starred the teenage Wanda on his ABC network TV show "Ozark Jubilee" from 1954 to 1957. The glamorous and poised Wanda was one of the early country stars to book into the Vegas and Reno show rooms. She hired the then-unknown Roy Clark as a member of her Party Timers band, as well as black country keyboardist Big Al Downing.

By the time she began recording in Hollywood in 1956, Wanda had taken Presley's advice to heart. She took to rockabilly like a bee to a flower. With the always-hot Joe Maphis on guitar, the eighteen-year-old vocalist growled her way through "Hot Dog! That Made Him Mad," "Honey Bop," "Cool Love," and her first rockabilly hit, "I Gotta Know." In 1957 she returned to L.A. to record "Let's Have a Party," "Fujiyama Mama," and other rockabilly numbers.

"I didn't know if the fans were going to accept it. At the time, country music was really takin' a backseat to this then-new music called rock 'n' roll and rockabilly. . . . We were there in that period when all the country stars were tryin' to rock. . . . As far as I know, I was the first woman to do the growlin' and the hollerin' and stuff like that. That's what the guys were doin.' And I liked it. I think the reason I didn't think about it being unladylike is because I've always been very feminine.

"My mother and I designed a tight-fitting sheath with rhinestone spaghetti straps and a little short silk fringe. My mother's a fantastic seamstress; she made all my stage clothes. I was wearin' that before go-go girls ever did. I dreamed it up because I said that way I don't have to wiggle. I can just pat my foot, and the fringe will shake. I didn't want to look vulgar; I wanted to look sexy. I wanted to look like a lady, but I wanted to cause a little stir, too." Wanda also had a low-cut "fishtail" gown and a gold lamé number that transformed her into a teen femme fatale.

A disc jockey in Des Moines, Iowa, discovered "Let's Have a Party" on a Wanda album

Wanda Jackson, c. 1960

in 1960 and began playing it. Public response was enthusiastic, Capitol put it out as a single, and by that summer Wanda had her first major national smash. She responded with the torrid LPs *Rockin' with Wanda* and *There's a Party Goin' On* and her "split" albums with country on one side and rockabilly on the other, *Two Sides of Wanda* and *Right or Wrong*. These 1960–1962 collections included her oft-imitated rock 'n' roll stutterer "Tongue Tied," as well as versions of teen favorites of the day.

"I love to sing the rock songs. I really had fun with 'em. I think you can tell by the way I sing 'em that it just was natural. But I didn't like that rock 'n' roll scene that all of a sudden I was thrown into workin' with. That whole scene—those little teenyboppers . . . the bubble-gum set—of course I wasn't much older myself, but I thought I was grown up. And I just didn't like all that screamin' and hollerin'. Course now I do.

"Then country music began comin' back, and I had written a ballad called 'Right or Wrong' and it became a big hit. . . . I think that when I went back to country, I lost my rock 'n' roll fans." She made the country Top 10 again with 1961's "In the Middle of a Heartache," wrote the 1962 Buck Owens hit "Kickin' Our Hearts Around," scored a big European success with 1965's "Santo Domingo," and issued a fine album of orchestrated standards called *Love Me Forever* to complete her transition.

Of Wanda's many country hits of 1961 to 1972, none recaptured her rockabilly zing, although several stressed women's issues. These included the temperance tune "A Girl Don't Have to Drink to Have Fun"; a female "answer" song called "By the Time You Get to Phoenix"; the threatening number "My Big Iron Skillet"; and even a women's penitentiary song, "Tennessee Women's Prison." Wanda also introduced the social justice ode "If I Had a Hammer" as a country music single.

Her resonant, compellingly throaty voice won her two Grammy nominations, and she was at her peak with hits like "A Woman Lives for Love" when she reached her personal crossroads in 1971. She'd married Wendell Goodman in 1961 and had two children, but was unhappy and unfulfilled. "My husband and I were living a life-style that I knew was not the best. . . . I had become a problem drinker . . . and our marriage was in trouble, to say the least."

He was boozing, too. "I had sworn years before that would never happen to me," Goodman recalled in 1990. "You see, my father . . . was a bad drinker and brawler. He was very abusive to my mother . . . and us kids. I swore then to myself that I would never drink or abuse my own wife. Yet here I was, thirty years later, a problem drinker and abusive to my wife. When I was drinking, I was extremely jealous, possessive, and distrusting. I was a mean drunk. . . . I do not know why Wanda stayed with me, other than the fact that she really loved me."

At their children's urging the couple went back to church one Sunday. "To this day, I cannot remember what that young preacher preached about," Wanda reflects, "but I do remember that . . . the choir began to sing . . . [Fanny Crosby's] invitation hymn called 'Pass Me Not, O Gentle Savior.'" She left the pew, headed for the altar, and Goodman followed. "God spoke to me that Sunday," she says, "because my heart just broke, and I said, 'Do somethin' with my life. I've gotta have some help. I've gotta have a happy life, or there's no point in going on.' . . . God delivered me from the drinking." With five years to run on her Capitol contract, Wanda asked to be let go to sign with Word Records as a gospel artist. She and her husband/manager spent the next decade giving their testimonies in churches.

European interest in her classic rockabilly records continued to climb. So in the 1980s she put together the "Happy Wanda Jackson Country Gospel Rockabilly Show," which went over like gangbusters in Scandinavia, France, Germany, and England. In 1986 Wanda rekindled her rockabilly fire with an LP called *Rock 'n' Roll Away Your Blues.* Then, in 1990, California country newcomer Jann Browne paid homage to her idol by asking Wanda to record "I Forgot More" with her as a duet; the resulting performance revealed that The Queen of Rockabilly's vocal powers were undimmed by time.

"We sure had a lot of fun in those days," she says of her rip-roaring rockabilly years, "and I miss that now. . . . But anyway it's been a wonderful life. I wouldn't trade it."

It *was* fun. It was a heady time in American culture, full of the optimism, experimentation, energy, and innocence that come with the birth of a musical movement. Rockabilly could be goofy, menacing, frenzied, or bouncy. It could be screaming, hiccuping, yodel-y, raspy, whining, barking, or slurred. There were no real rules.

In retrospect, the entire female rockabilly trend might seem like just one big nutty country experiment that took place in this freewheeling teen environment. After all, only Wanda Jackson and Brenda Lee emerged with big national hits in the style. Maybe people dismissed rockabilly women because of their youth. Adults could shrug off such girls as being just "wild kids" who'd soon meet the mates who would tame them. "Nobody took us seriously in the mid-fifties," says Sun Records stylist Barbara Pittman. "We had to make our own way as best we could."

These performers all see themselves as rock 'n' roll pioneers. They enjoyed driving audiences wild and appearing (or being) bad. They were investigating new musical expressions, blazing trails of independence and individuality. Most of all, they were young professionals, defying, for a flashing moment in the spotlight, the 1950s' conformist expectations of marriage and motherhood.

"Back then, women were expected to get married and have children," observed Rose Maddox. "That's *all*. Well, I just wasn't made that way. . . . Music was all I thought about in life. So I plunged into it. The whole thing was such a terrific challenge. You had to give yourself support every day, because nobody else was going to do it."

Nearly all of them have scrapbooks and photos and fond memories of their rockabilly years. And somewhere there is footage of quite a few of them in action. These women were in the first generation of country stars entertaining on the most revolutionary innovation of the era, television. Wanda Jackson and Brenda Lee on "Ozark Jubilee," Lorrie Collins and Lucille Starr on "Town Hall Party," Bonnie Lou on "Midwestern Hayride," and Jo-Ann Campbell and Janis Martin on "American Bandstand" all point to the increasing importance and influence of television in the fifties.

In the minds of the evangelists, TV was almost as evil as rock 'n' roll, alcohol, tobacco, and lust. It was "worldly." It pictured frivolity, dancing, and other secular delights. "I was automatically suspect because I had been in show business," recalled the Reverend Jimmy Snow. "Some preachers checked on my worldliness quotient with . . . 'Does he watch TV?' 'Does he go to the movies?'" He and Carol Lee Cooper divorced in 1972, and the evangelist married Radio Dot and Smokey's daughter Dottie Swan. Snow eventually survived "a music culture where sexual indiscretions are sung about, stimulated, and glorified" to become a successful Nashville preacher, often on the airwaves of his "Gospel Country" and "Grand Ole Gospel shows."

Despite revival-tent fears, television maintained a fairly conservative agenda. Prime-time TV shied away from rockabilly music, even though Elvis's 1956 appearance on "Ed Sullivan" had captured about 83 percent of the viewing audience. The style could be heard on daytime shows like "American Bandstand," but the big variety series shunned country's brash new rockabilly stepchildren. Alan Freed's ABC show "The Big Beat" lasted all of four episodes in 1957. Dozens of half-forgotten pop crooners hosted their own programs, yet despite massive youth appeal, none of the young rockabilly stars did. To find the rockabillys, you turned to country shows. The then-infant networks offered roughly twenty country series between 1946 and 1960, including video versions of the "National Barn Dance," "Grand Ole Opry," "Midwestern Hayride," and other radio barn dances.

As TV stations sprouted in towns all over America, and households with televisions grew from 10,000 in 1947 to 40 million in 1957, dozens of locally popular country music women got their own programs. The sometimes rocking Abbie Neal and Her Ranch Girls were superstars in Pittsburgh. In the Philadelphia area Sally Starr became a TV celebrity doing rockabilly for tots. Her repertoire included "TV Pal." In what must be the earliest expression of boob-tube as baby-sitter, Sally chirped, "You've got a friend in the living room," so "Turn your TV on when things go wrong." Sally was rockabilly superstar Bill Haley's collaborator, and she also performed kooky examples of kindergarten rockabilly like "Rockin' in the Nursery" and "A.B.C. Rock" to her toddler audience.

The Number 1 show in America in the 1950s was "Arthur Godfrey's Talent Scouts." Pop ladies like The Chordettes and The McGuire Sisters had the mainstream, suburban appeal the show wanted. So did Pat Boone, another "Talent Scouts" winner. Rocking Elvis Presley flunked his audition (1955), and so did Buddy Holly (1956). But in 1957 the avuncular, whiskey-soaked Godfrey couldn't deny the fire and passion of a Virginia woman who captivated his viewing audience. His Monday-night network TV series introduced the nation to Patsy Cline.

10

THE NASHVILLE SOUND

Patsy Cline and "The Grand Ole Opry"

Patsy Cline looks the part of a pop-crossover queen in the contemporary garb of this 1960 record jacket.

Back in the middle fifties when you were touring, sometimes you played places with promoters that were a little suspect," Brenda Lee remembers. "We always used to say that you needed to get a 'first count,' to get to the box office before the show went on and get paid, or perhaps the promoter would go out the back door with the money and you wouldn't get paid at all. Well, we were doing a tour with Patsy Cline and it was the first time I had ever met her. I was about eleven or twelve, and it was one of those dates where the promoter took the money; and my mother and I were left stranded in Texas. We had no money, and we had nobody to send us any money. We had no way to get back home.

"Patsy was traveling in a big Cadillac limousine. She just took us under her wing—put us in the car, fed us, gave us money, and took care of us for a week or so until we could work a few more dates and get enough money to get home.

"Patsy was like a big sister to me. She sat me down and she'd say, 'You know, things are tough and hard, but you're gonna be all right. So hang in there, because you're talented.' And I appreciated that. We came to be very close, and I loved her dearly. . . . She was wonderful."

Dottie West was trying like the devil to make it in Music City when Patsy was a country superstar. "At one time or another, she must have helped all of us girl singers who were starting out," Dottie wrote in 1981. "Patsy was always giving her friends things. . . . [like] the scrapbook of clippings and mementos Patsy gave me weeks before she was killed. . . . When I got home I was leafing through it and there was a check for $75 with a note saying, 'I know you been having a hard time.' It was the money . . . I needed to pay the rent. . . . There'll never be another like Patsy Cline. She was the consummate singer, the consummate human being. . . . Let me tell you, I miss her."

A shy and stage-terrified Jan Howard met Patsy in an Opry dressing room shortly after moving to Music City. "Well, you're a conceited little son of a bitch," bellowed Patsy. "Who do you think you are, anyway? You just waltz in here . . . and leave without saying hello, kiss my ass, or anything!" Replied Jan, "Now wait a damned minute. . . . Where I come from, it's the people's responsibility who live in a town to welcome a newcomer. And not one person welcomed me here."

"Anyone a block away could have heard her laugh," Jan recalled in her autobiography. "You're all right, honey," Patsy said. "Anyone that'll talk back to the Cline is all right. We're gonna be good friends."

"I can't stand phonies," Jan says. "I can pick 'em out a mile away. Patsy Cline was real."

Barbara Mandrell was on the road as a thirteen-year-old steel guitar prodigy when she was befriended by bighearted Patsy. "We were introduced as the two-week tour began. We checked into our separate motel rooms and went out for a bite to eat. Then she insisted, absolutely insisted, that I room with her. She would not hear of me staying alone in my room. . . . I was officially her roommate for the rest of the trip. . . For all her bluster and sense of humor, there was a fragile side to her." In her best-selling autobiography, *Get to the Heart,* Barbara recalled Patsy as "a model of a country singer who could cross over toward pop music, touch anybody. . . . I got the feeling a woman could be a star, just like a man."

"She taught me a lot about show business," recalled Loretta Lynn in *Coal Miner's Daughter,* "like how to go on a stage and how to get off. She even bought me a lot of clothes. Many times when she bought something for herself, she would buy me the same thing. She gave me rhinestones— I thought they were real diamonds, and I still have the dresses she bought me, hanging in my closet. . . . She even bought curtains and drapes for my house because I was too broke to buy them. . . . She was a great human being and a great friend."

Brenda, Dottie, Jan, Barbara, and Loretta all became stars in their own rights. But these five, like all Nashville female singers since, measured themselves against the standard—the magnetic personality, charismatic stage presence, and stunning voice of Patsy Cline. Three decades after her death, Patsy remains the ultimate gauge. The almost-agonizing emotionalism in her voice, the exquisite tension and release of her phrasing, the heart-plucking "cry" in her notes, have reached through the decades to make generations of younger singers quake.

To this day Patsy sells more records than any other country artist on MCA Records. Her life and music have provided the raw material for a Hollywood film, a video documentary, two books, two stage productions, and several tribute albums. She was still making the country charts in 1981. Actress Jessica Lange garnered a 1985 Oscar nomination for bringing Patsy's personality to life on screen. In 1988 and 1989 two new Patsy Cline albums of live performances were successfully marketed. A seven-hour radio documentary on Patsy's life aired in Canada in 1990. In 1991 she sold millions via a TV record offer and was saluted with a lavish CD boxed set reprising four hours of her music. In 1992 her *Greatest Hits* album passed the four-million mark in sales and was the only album from the 1960s still on the charts. Other country stars have come and gone. Patsy Cline endures.

"Patsy, I think, opened the door for all the girls," says Loretta. Added Dottie, "She was really proving to the world, and especially the world of country music, that a *woman* could close the show and that she could sell tickets and that she could sell records. . . . In the era of country music we came up through, women didn't have the clout they have today. There was Kitty Wells and Jean Shepard—they were big in country—but Patsy crossed over and had massive pop appeal when this was virtually unheard of. . . . More than anyone, Patsy opened the door for us. . . . Before that, we'd only been used as window dressing."

To understand the significance of Patsy Cline, you have to understand Nashville. Just as New York's intellectual cauldron defined magazine and book publishing, just as Hollywood's free-spiritedness defined motion picture production, so Nashville's conservatism shaped the country music industry. Tennessee's capital is also the headquarters of the Southern Baptist Convention; the Methodist Publishing House; the Nazarene Church; and Thomas Nelson, the world's largest publisher of Bibles. It is an aggressively middlebrow town whose culture revolves around churchgoing. You could not buy liquor by the drink in Nashville until 1967. It is a community run by wealthy good ol' boys, not the type of place that nourished professional women. Other early country music centers, like Atlanta, Chicago, Dallas, and Los

THE ONLY MAGAZINE PUBLISHED EXCLUSIVELY FOR RURAL LISTENERS!

Vol. 1. No. 1.   FEBRUARY, 1938   Ten Cents

CRAMMED FULL OF PICTURES, GOSSIP AND NEWS OF RURAL RADIO PERSONALITIES.

"THE *New* PARTY LINE"

This *Rural Radio* magazine cover of 1938 deftly illustrates the appeal of the "Grand Ole Opry"'s comedy team Sarie and Sallie. The sisters were reportedly even funnier off the air.

Angeles, produced female stars. Music City did not.

In 1925 Nashville's radio station WSM, owned by the National Life and Accident insurance company, put on a weekly country music barn dance show. It was designed to attract farmers and poor folks to its policies—its slogan was *We Shield Millions.* The first performer was old-time fiddler Uncle Jimmy Thompson, accompanied by the piano playing of his niece, Eva Thompson Jones (c. 1895–1973). Eva also sang sentimental Stephen Foster numbers on the air, setting the pattern for "Grand Ole Opry" women. For decades, most were instrumental accompanists, backup singers, comics, and "parlor song" or religious singers in between male headliners' performances.

The most durable of the Opry's 1920s women was Alcyone Bate Beasley (1912–1982). She was a pianist and ukulele player in her father's WSM string band, Dr. Humphrey Bate's Possum Hunters. Billed as "the little girl with the great big voice" as a teen, Alcyone favored sentimental chestnuts like 1873's "Silver Threads Among the Gold." Between 1936 and 1954 Alcyone was in Betty & The Dixie Dons, Nashville's first professional background singers. She was the Opry's longest continuous member and unofficial historian when she died in 1982.

The "family harmony" tradition of The Carter Family and its imitators, which influenced so many of country music's earliest women, seems to have bypassed Nashville completely. There were even fewer women on the Opry in the thirties than there had been in the twenties. Nevertheless, the period did produce the Opry's first major female attraction, the remarkable sister act Sarie and Sallie. They were the first comedy stars, male or female, on the Opry. Remembered by Opry old-timers as side-splittingly funny both offstage and on, the team specialized in a drawling, gossipy, over-the-back-fence style of repartee. Sallie (Margaret Waters) was rotund, smiling, and lovably scatterbrained. Her sister Sarie (Edna Wilson, b. 1896) was gaunt, deadpan, and sharply witty. Sarie and Sallie guest-starred on "The National Barn Dance" in 1937, were cover girls of *Rural Radio* magazine in 1938, and appeared in Gene Autry's movie *In Old Monterey* in 1939. After 1940 Sarie continued alone with a comedy character called Aunt Bunie.

WSM had become a fifty-thousand-watt radio titan in 1932, and "The Grand Ole Opry"'s broadcasting clout increased when it got a weekly NBC national network slot in 1940. This coincided with the war era, when more women than ever before entered public life in America. Among the show's women during the period were the cowgirl-garbed Lakeland Sisters, Ann and Mary. Boisterous, big-voiced Texas Ruby returned to the Opry for a wartime stint. Roy Acuff's new band included banjo player Rachel Veach (1921–1980) and bassist Velma Williams. Rachel was billed as dobro player Bashful Brother Oswald's sister in order to avoid the scandal of an unchaperoned woman on the road with a group of men. Opry star Pee Wee King hired The Hoosier Maids, Little Texas Daisy (Rhodes), San Antonio Rose (Eva Nichols), Becky Barfield, and Minnie Pearl to tour with his Golden West Cowboys in the forties.

"HowDEEEE! I'm jest so proud to be hyere!" hollered Minnie with her best, aimin'-to-please smile on her face. Arms flung wide and her straw hat's price tag ($1.98) bobbing up and down in the spotlight, the skinny comic with the tales of her neighbors and relations in Grinders Switch, Tennessee, walked to the Opry's center-stage microphone with hope in her heart and laughter on her lips for fifty years. Her well-worn "Mary Jane" shoes, white cotton stockings, and gingham dresses would become familiar to millions. But in 1940 she didn't know that.

No, in 1940 Minnie Pearl was just a broken-down thespian limping back home to Nashville with only the faintest glimmer of a theatrical career and only the vaguest notion of how to entertain. She was from a "good" family. Yet here she was, reduced to playing for yokels and hayseeds from the stage of that low-class embarrassment to polite society, "The Grand Ole Opry."

"I won't pretend . . . that I wanted to be on 'The Grand Ole Opry' because I had been a fan all my life," Minnie recalled in her 1980 autobiography. "I never thought about it one way or the other, except that I didn't particularly like the music. . . . I had never even gone to see an Opry broadcast, much less felt a desire to be on the show."

But times were tough and she was desperate for any kind of show-biz job. Minnie was the daughter of a well-to-do Centerville,

Tennessee, sawmill owner. Born Sarah Ophelia Colley in 1912, she never lacked for toys or clothes as a child. Her mother would take her the fifty miles into Nashville for shopping trips, which is where Minnie unwittingly witnessed her future.

"I used to go to the Princess Theater. Elviry Weaver used to come there and do her act with her two 'brothers.' Back then, you could put a child in a theater and leave 'em there while Mama did her shopping. I sat there and learned every one of Elviry's lines." Minnie says she was also exposed to the radio shows and early films of Judy Canova.

All of the five Colley daughters were well educated, but when it came time for the family's spoiled, playacting baby to go to school, the Depression had ruined her father's business. There was just enough money to send Minnie to the Ward-Belmont ladies' finishing school in Nashville for two years. After graduating in 1932, she went to work teaching drama, piano, and dancing in Centerville. In 1934 the small-town aspiring actress with the "drawing-room" upbringing joined The Sewell Company. She toured the South on its behalf organizing penny-ante musicals for local Lions Clubs and civic organizations using amateur talent. In the winter of 1936 she arrived in the mountains of northeastern Alabama to mount a production of *Flapper Grandmother*. The school principal who hired her sent her to board for ten days with a mountain woman and her family. There Minnie got to know her first real hillbillies.

"At night I'd go back to this woman's house. I enjoyed talking with her and her family. They fascinated me. They were funny people, witty people, who didn't know they were being funny and didn't try to be. . . . I just loved it. The whole scene reminded me of *Sergeant York*. . . . The way these people expressed themselves had an innocence and a wit about it that just charmed me." The food was meager and the house heat was minimal. Even though the poor seventy-year-old woman was open-hearted and generous, the experience was "roughing it" for the young actress. "I thought I'd never get outta there; and it turned out to be the biggest influence on my life.

"When I got to the next place, I got to tellin' people about this woman. By 1938 I was 'doing' her, but I hadn't named her. So I just picked out two nice women's country names"—Minnie and Pearl. "I began using the character when I had to go into new towns to solicit ads for the play or urge groups to sell tickets to get a big turnout. Minnie Pearl would come out and say 'Howdy' . . . then tell a few stories about her family." One of her fellow Sewell thespians coached her in hillbilly dialect. One of Minnie's drama students showed her a funny way of singing purposefully loud and off-key, like a hick Edith Bunker doing the opening of TV's "All in the Family" forty years later. Minnie learned to bray "Careless Love," "Jealous Hearted Me," "Maple on the Hill," and other old-time country tunes at the top of her lungs while flailing away at the piano. The Minnie Pearl costume came next: Most of it was the result of ten dollars spent in a thrift store in Aiken, South Carolina. "On one of the racks I spotted a pale yellow dress made of sleazy organdy. . . . I was as thin as a rail then and the dress made me look like Olive Oyl in the *Popeye* cartoon series. I found some white cotton stockings . . . and a tacky straw hat. . . . I bought some flowers to plop on that." She added the price tag and shoes during her early years on the Opry.

By 1939 the Sewell road work was beginning to dry up. The company's creaky, corny old plays were worn out. More and more people in small towns had radios and movie theaters entertaining them. "In the spring of 1940, I returned to Centerville, not in the triumph I had always envisaged, but in utter defeat. I was 28 years old; I was broke; I had no job, and no promise of one. I wasn't married, and I didn't have a career. I wasn't even qualified to do anything, except teach dancing or dramatics. . . . I had left home in a burst of optimism, and returned broke, an old maid, a *failure.*" She got work running Centerville's children's recreation center to support herself and her widowed mother. That fall she auditioned at WSM for a guest spot on the Opry. The show's executives were reluctant about the comedy character. They were afraid country fans might think she was mocking them, or think she was a phony. They put her on at 11:05 P.M., long after the network portion of the show was over, after many listeners had gone to bed and when most audience members in the hall were weary. Minnie did her hillbilly one-liners for about three minutes. After it was over, she asked her mother how it had gone. "Several people woke up," said Mama encouragingly. But more than three hundred pieces of mail from listeners arrived at WSM during the next week. She was asked to join the cast at ten dollars a week.

"As far as the audience was concerned, I was one of them. And, as the weeks went by, I felt more and more at home. There were about 50 other members of the Opry cast. They were all very friendly to me, very supportive, and accepted me into the 'family' immediately. I might add that I represented no threat to any of them. I didn't sing and I was a woman. Men, at that time, *never* figured a woman to be a threat."

As a member of Pee Wee King's troupe, she shot to fame during the war, entertaining the troops. On the road Minnie Pearl became a little more racy, a little less inhibited, and a lot more fun. She got sillier; she got louder. National radio familiarized millions with her aggressive friendliness and lovable foolishness on the Opry.

The character of Minnie Pearl is a blend of brash and bashful. She's the man-hungry old maid with a coy demeanor and a glint in her eye. She's the homely wallflower with just enough pluck and grit to keep her chin up. She's a small-town gossip without malice, bubbling with the news of Uncle Nabob, Aunt Ambrosy, Brother, Lizzie Tinkum, and the other characters who inhabit her fictional Grinders Switch neighborhood.

Old maid Lizzie, said Minnie, called the fire department when a man tried to crawl in her bedroom window. "They said, 'Miss Lizzie, you don't need the Fire Department; you need the Police Department.' She said, 'No I don't: He needs a longer ladder!'" One of Minnie's favorites was: "The robber said, 'Gimme your money.' I said, 'But I haven't got any money,' so he frisked me and said, 'Are you sure you ain't got any money.' I said, 'Nossir, but if you'll do that again I'll write you a check.'" And then there was the woman who made out her will stipulating only female pallbearers at her funeral: "If those ol' boys won't take me out when I'm-a livin', I sure don't want 'em takin' me out when I'm dead."

Minnie Pearl, 1969.

Minnie said that her neighbor Mrs. Orson Tugwell "has had so many young'uns she's run outta names . . . to call Orson."

Minnie's well-bred graciousness and genuine affection for her raw, less-schooled hillbilly costars made her the Opry's mother confessor, chaperon, and goodwill ambassador. She married pilot Henry Cannon in 1947, eventually moved into a home next to the Governor's Mansion, and became the country world's go-between to Nashville society. By the 1950s she was appearing on the network TV shows of Dinah Shore, Tennessee Ernie Ford, and Jack Paar. She recorded her routines and novelty songs for RCA, Starday, Decca, King, Bullet, Everest, and other labels.

She became a "Hee Haw" national TV star in the seventies and a "Nashville Now" cable TV celebrity in the eighties. With the cream of the comedy world she starred in Comic Relief to raise money for the homeless in 1987. By age sixty-five she had become one of the most beloved entertainers in America, a 1975 inductee into the Country Music Hall of Fame, and the star of her own museum.

The gentle, kindhearted Minnie also became known for her involvement in numerous charities. In 1985 she had a double mastectomy for breast cancer, and she was soon spreading the word to women about the importance of checkups as a spokeswoman for the American Cancer Society. She also recuperated from a 1989 fall at home and a 1990 heart pacemaker operation. Minnie suffered a debilitating stroke in 1991 at age seventy-nine.

When Minnie Pearl joined "The Grand Ole Opry" in 1940, she was the show's only female cast member. Or as she later put it, "the first woman to scramble with my fingernails up the side of a wall to try to get some recognition in a man's world." And she was the one female star whose popularity never dimmed throughout the city's rise from medium-size southern poultry-and-publishing center to international show-biz mecca.

Minnie Pearl's arrival in the forties coincided with the emergence of "The Grand Ole Opry" as a national attraction and of Nashville as country music's capital city. The Opry's aggressive talent drive during the honky-tonk era lifted it to the front ranks of radio barn dances in the late 1940s, and from it spun an entire entertainment industry. By the end of the next decade Nashville was the undisputed headquarters of country music, with record labels, recording studios, talent agencies, and song publishing companies all sprouting in the west-side neighborhood that became known as Music Row.

Throughout the 1950s "The Grand Ole Opry" remained the focus of Nashville's country music business. More women began making the pilgrimage to its stage as the show entered the modern era—Mother Maybelle & The Carter Sisters (1950), Kitty Wells (1952), Jean Shepard (1955), Wilma Lee Cooper (1957).

This era also produced "The Grand Ole Opry"'s first million-selling woman, pianist Del Wood (1920–1990). In fact, Del Wood is the only female instrumentalist in history, in any field of music, to have a single that sold so well. Born Polly Adelaide Hendricks on her family's farm just north of Music City, Del was raised in working-class east Nashville. She was a gifted pianist by the time she was in high school, so she went to work in dime stores' music departments selling records and sheet music. In the

Del Wood, 1955.

1940s she took a job with the Tennessee Public Health Department. "And I hated it," she stated flatly. "I like *action*." In 1951 her rollicking, barrelhouse treatment of the 1921 ragtime tune "Down Yonder" "liberated me from the typewriter keys to the eighty-eights. Actually, it was a bigger hit on the pop charts than it was in country." But Del always yearned for hometown, country music acceptance, and got it when the Opry asked her to join in 1953.

Her stage name was calculated so that radio programmers wouldn't know she was female. "Back then women weren't accepted too well. 'Del' [from Adelaide] could be either one, male or female." The "Wood" came from a contraction of Hazelwood, the name of the husband she divorced and always referred to as "my one big mistake." Del's honky-tonk piano pounding was a fixture at the Opry for four decades. "The Queen of the Ivories" recorded more than twenty albums and sixty singles, including "Piano Roll Blues," "Muskrat Ramble," and "Johnson's Rag." She was cited as an inspiration by rockabilly wildman Jerry Lee Lewis, hired by folk star John Prine to back him on his 1981 single "I Saw Mommy Kissing Santa Claus," and tapped by Dolly Parton to portray a hillbilly band member in the 1984 movie *Rhinestone*.

Behind the scenes Del was a longtime union activist. She was a board member of the Nashville chapter of AFTRA (American Federation of Television and Radio Artists) and the only woman to have served on the board of the American Federation of Musicians. She was also active in ROPE (Reunion of Professional Entertainers), a Nashville group raising funds to build a retirement home for country performers. She was preparing for the "Legendary Ladies of Country Music" ROPE benefit concert when she suffered a fatal stroke in 1990.

This 1950s influx of female stars into "The Grand Ole Opry" came as the radio show's popularity was threatened by television and rock 'n' roll. This, plus the rise of non-Opry music businesses in Nashville, seems to have created a climate for experimentation. In 1956 the Opry hired Dee Kilpatrick as its first and only manager who did not come up through the ranks of the show or its parent life insurance company. Kilpatrick, a former Capitol and Mercury executive, argued that the Opry badly needed to attract a younger audience and adopt a more stylish image. "The hillbilly record business has been too long dominated by men," Kilpatrick reasoned. "If you got just *one* girl singer really started, look at the business she'd do, just because there wouldn't be any competition. . . . There's just as many boy hillbilly fans as there are girl hillbilly fans. It used to be that the old girl would say to her old man, 'Let's go to the Opry,' and he'd go reluctantly, because all he was going to get to listen to was old hairy-legged Ray Price, Roy Acuff, Marty Robbins, and so on. But when it got to where these boy fans could . . . hear Kitty sing a love ballad, and Jean Shepard, why, naturally they were a lot more eager to go." Kilpatrick only lasted three years as a force for change, but his ideas remained with his successor, Ott Devine, the man who brought an entire generation of female stars into the Opry cast in the decade to come.

The first and foremost of these was 1960 Opry inductee Patsy Cline. She did more than usher in a new decade—she transformed what it meant to be a female country star. "The Opry is the epitome of country music, and we are all very much aware of that," observed Del Wood. "Patsy wanted to be a part of it. . . . She wanted to be Number One." And what Patsy wanted, Patsy fought for. She was aggressive and ambitious and self-assertive. "You wouldn't have to tell Patsy anything about this women's lib business," observed her record producer, Owen Bradley. "I do believe she could have taught them a thing or two." In her day they called her "brassy," "cocky," "brash," "hard," and "rough." She carried a pint of whiskey in her purse and could swear like a sailor. But she cried as easily as she laughed and had the proverbial heart of pure gold. She was salty and sentimental, tough and tender. And she knocked conservative Nashville on its ear.

Born Virginia Patterson Hensley in the mountains of Virginia in 1932, Patsy was obsessed with the Opry broadcasts. "From the time she was about ten, Patsy was living, eating, and sleeping country music," said Mama Hilda Hensley. "I know she never wanted anything so badly as to be a star on 'The Grand Ole Opry.' . . . Everybody she spoke to about becoming a singer told her how tough it would be for a woman to go into country music. But that didn't faze Patsy. Knowing her, it probably made her all the more determined."

By age fourteen she was pestering the radio station and clubs in her hometown of Winchester, Virginia, to let her sing. Her father deserted the family when she was fifteen, so she quit school and went to work clerking in a Winchester drugstore by day and singing with area bands by night. In 1948 she boldly wrote the Opry asking for an audition. The show wrote back asking for a tape and photo. When Wally Fowler and his Oak Ridge Quartet came to Winchester for a gospel concert, Patsy talked her way backstage, sang for Fowler, got on the show, and persuaded him to use his influence in Nashville to get her that audition. Nothing came of the subsequent trip to the country capital, but Patsy didn't give up. In 1952 she joined Bill Peer's Melody Boys and Girls, a fairly well known regional attraction. Peer and the hot-blooded twenty-year-old apparently carried on an affair while he helped promote her singing career. He complained that Virginia wasn't a suitable stage name, so she started calling herself "Patsy," adapting it from Patterson, her middle name.

In 1953 she married small-town playboy Gerald Cline. Later that year Peer took her again to Nashville, where she sang on Ernest Tubb's "Midnight Jamboree" radio show. Peer also helped her make a tape that won her a 1954 contract with Four-Star Records. During the next five years, Patsy groped for her own sound on the label, recording everything from traditional gospel ("Life's Railway to Heaven") to rockabilly ("Gotta Lot of Rhythm"), from all-out pop ("Too Many Secrets") to straight country ("I Love You Honey," "Honky-Tonk Merry Go Round," "There He Goes"). Her singing idol was pop star Kay Starr, but she also favored yodeling and honky-tonk vocal effects. Much of the material Four-Star forced her to sing was mediocre, but several signature songs emerged from this period, notably, "Three Cigarettes in an Ashtray," "I've Loved and Lost Again," and her lifetime show opener, "Come On In."

In 1955 Patsy returned to Nashville and at last got a guest spot on the Opry. Later that year she talked herself onstage with Jimmy Dean in a Washington, D.C., nightclub and landed a job on his TV show "Town and Country Time." She used this as a stepping-stone to Arthur Godfrey's top-rated national "Talent Scouts" program, on which she triumphed in January 1957, singing "Walkin' After Midnight" and Hank Williams's "Your Cheating Heart." The bluesy "Walkin'" was issued in February and became a national hit that led to an appearance on one of Alan Freed's rock 'n' roll shows in New York. The record's B side was a torchy "heart" number called "A Poor Man's Roses," and in years to come this type of tune would become her forte.

In March the philandering Patsy divorced the philandering Cline; seven months later she married the original "Good Time Charlie," Charlie Dick. Their tempestuous relationship—fueled by alcohol, argument, pills, passion, jealousy, success, tears, and laughter—

formed the basis for the 1985 film and book *Sweet Dreams.*

By the close of 1957, Patsy Cline seemed to be on her way. Her "Arthur Godfrey" win and her hit record garnered her *Billboard* magazine's Most Promising award during that year's fifth annual country convention in Nashville. After guesting on TV's "Ozark Jubilee," Patsy paused during 1958 while Charlie finished his army hitch and she delivered daughter Julie. The family moved to Music City in 1959. In January 1960 she joined the Opry cast, instantly charming the show's established female stars.

"I loved Patsy," Jean Shepard recalled in Ellis Nassour's *Patsy Cline* biography of 1981. "I got along well with her because, just like me, she was quite plain spoken. She had a great sense of humor and was on the brassy side. I don't think, though some might disagree, that I was quite as brassy as she. But that was Patsy and I liked her as she was. . . . There weren't too many people that met Patsy who didn't like her. She could be mean as hell, but she could also be as adorable as they come."

"We laughed a lot together," June Carter recalled in her book *From the Heart.* "She stayed with me at my house when she first came to Nashville. . . . We talked all night a few times. We shared a lot of secrets. I knew all about her—she knew all about me. Sometimes she'd call late at night and just say, 'Pray with me, June.' I did that several times." June also recalls that Patsy once gave her a "green speckled capsule" that not only got her through a show, but kept her up for three days.

"There was thirteen years' difference in our ages," said "Queen of the Ivories" Del Wood, "but that didn't stop Patsy and me from being good buddies." Backstage the two Opry stars swapped "man trouble" tales. "Maybe in a way, she looked on me as a big sister." Del and Patsy came up with these words to live by for women in country music: "Just keep your chin up and your skirt down."

Gossip has circulated in Nashville for years about Patsy's sexual appetite. In addition to Bill Peer, among those she is alleged to have "rolled in the hay" with were Faron Young, Jimmy Dean, and Randy Hughes. Her battles with Charlie intensified the rumors, but most insiders agree that they remained bonded to each other despite their domestic disputes. She complained to her girlfriends about him and even had him arrested once.

"Well, there was only one actual fight [where] I smacked the hell out of her because she was hysterical one night," says Charlie Dick. "I'm sure, physically, I could have knocked the hell out of Patsy Cline. But if I'd have hit her a couple of times, she'd of picked up a damned chair or something and let me have it. You know, you're not gonna run over Patsy. Not me or anybody else. . . . She could handle things. She'd been out supportin' herself since she was sixteen, workin' in joints. She had street smarts."

GROUP IN YEARS TO COME INCLUDED RACHEL VEACH, VELMA WILLIAMS, JERRY JOHNSON, JUNE STEARNS, THE LACROIX SISTERS, AND JUNE WEBB.)
11. SALLY ANN FORRESTER IN BILL MONROE'S BLUE GRASS BOYS (AT VARIOUS TIMES, GLADYS "BOBBIE JEAN" FLATT AND MELISSA MONROE WERE ALSO IN THE GROUP.)
12. THE HOOSIER MAIDS IN PEE WEE KING'S GOLDEN WEST COWBOYS
13. LITTLE TEXAS DAISY (RHODES) IN PEE WEE KING'S GOLDEN WEST COWBOYS
14. SAN ANTONIO ROSE (EVA NICHOLS) IN PEE WEE KING'S GOLDEN WEST COWBOYS
15. BECKY BARFIELD IN PEE WEE KING'S GOLDEN WEST COWBOYS
16. MINNIE PEARL
17. MOTHER MAYBELLE AND THE CARTER SISTERS
18. KITTY WELLS
19. GOLDIE HILL
20. ANNIE LOU DILL
21. MARTHA CARSON

Throughout 1960 Patsy stayed busy with Opry performances and appearances on the "Town Hall Party" and "Ozark Jubilee" TV shows. She got free of her old contract and signed with Decca Records. In January 1961 baby Randy was born and "I Fall to Pieces" was released as a single. The record was a landmark in the development of The Nashville Sound.

Rock 'n' roll had knocked the stuffing out of country music in the mid-1950s. Television had co-opted much of radio's content and popularity, so radio dropped live entertainment, including most of the barn dances, and concentrated on playing records. Radio developed "formats," station identities centered on one musical style or another. Working-class country wasn't at the top of anybody's list. In Chicago even pioneering WLS dropped "The National Barn Dance" and switched to teen music in 1960. By 1961 there were just eighty-one full-time country radio stations in the United States.

The threatened country subculture battled back. A country DJ association to defend the music grew out of the annual "Grand Ole Opry" birthday celebrations begun in 1952. That organization evolved into the Country Music Association in 1958. The Opry's birthday party evolved into the annual Country Music Week business convention, confirming Nashville as the world's country capital.

Around the same time, the record producers on Music Row began to update the country sound. Hoping to attract pop consumers alienated by rock, they married the warm "heart" in country singing to cool, elegant orchestral effects and sighing background choruses. They smoothed country's rougher emotional edges with sophisticated arrangements and new studio technology. A typical Nashville Sound record features strumming acoustic guitar rhythm, a slight echo effect on the lead vocal, creamy "ooooh"s from backup singers, rippling piano work, and a soaring string section.

The four architects of this new sound were Chet Atkins (RCA), Don Law (Columbia), Owen Bradley (Decca), and free-lance arranger Anita Kerr. "Anita deserves so much more credit than she gets," says Atkins. The Anita Kerr Singers "gave a sophistication and a smoothness to country music that made it so much more palatable to audiences all over the world."

Born Anita Grilli in Memphis in 1927, Anita was playing organ in Catholic church and writing arrangements for the choir by age ten. Her skill led to her move to Nashville in 1950 to lead the gospel group on WSM's "Sunday Down South" radio show. The Anita Kerr Singers were soon doing radio jingles for other stations and taking part in Nashville's emerging recording-studio scene. They also commuted to New York as regulars on Arthur Godfrey's TV show. In addition to vocal backups, Anita began providing charts for the string sections that were incorporated into The Nashville Sound. By the mid-fifties her stamp was on the city's music.

She can be heard on such early Patsy Cline efforts as "In Care of the Blues," "Stop the World and Let Me Off," "Just Out of Reach," and "Let the Teardrops Fall." Those are Anita's vocal arrangements on the classic Nashville Sound hits "My Special Angel" by Bobby Helms (1957), "He'll Have to Go" by Jim Reeves (1959), "The Three Bells" by The Browns (1959), and "Detroit City" by Bobby Bare (1963). Anita Kerr arranged both orchestra and chorus for such blockbuster records as Skeeter Davis's "The End of the World" (1962), Floyd Cramer's "Last Date" (1960), Dottie West's "Here Comes My Baby" (1964), and Roy Orbison's monumental "Only the Lonely" and "Running Scared" (1960 and 1961). She sang on "I'm Sorry" and most of Brenda Lee's other top-selling pop ballads of the early sixties. No other woman and few other men had as powerful an impact on Nashville music production.

Anita won a gospel Grammy Award in 1965 for an album called *Southland Favorites,* and she won pop Grammys in 1965 and 1966. She moved to Los Angeles and teamed with poet Rod McKuen on the 1967–1968 "mood music" albums *The Sea, The Earth*, and *The Sky.* These million-sellers, which Anita composed and conducted, were the earliest harbingers of "new age" music. In the 1970s Anita moved to Europe with her Swiss-born husband/manager Alex Grob and began composing film scores.

The Nashville Sound is now regarded as the style that "saved" country music during its darkest hour. But Patsy Cline initially wanted no part of it. In her live shows she displayed remarkable yodeling ability, and she always thought of herself as an up-tempo honky-tonker rather than a heartache balladeer. But Nashville Sound architect Owen Bradley heard something else in her voice—the bitterness, yearning, and sadness accumulated over years of rough living, hard struggling, and broken dreams. He gently but firmly pushed her toward the new style.

He was a former pop pianist. She was a gut-bucket hillbilly. The tension between them produced a brilliantly emotional string of records. At one of their early sessions together, Patsy was persistently difficult. Finally Bradley turned to her and said, "You're the meanest bitch I ever met." Patsy roared that big, chesty laugh she had. "From then on, everything was fine."

Jan Howard, then married to "I Fall to Pieces" cowriter Harlan Howard, sang the demo (demonstration tape) of the song that Patsy learned from. Jan recalls, "They took it to Owen to get Brenda Lee to cut it, but Brenda didn't like it. Then Owen tried to get Roy [Drusky] to do it. And finally Owen made Patsy record it, 'cause she didn't like it, either. Let me be more definite. . . . 'I hate that damn song!' she told me, knowing full well I was Harlan's wife. She said, 'I'm never gonna sing that thing.'" But she did, to the soft vocal accompaniment of The Jordanaires quartet and the distinctive bell-like tones of Grady Martin's new guitar device. By mid-1961 it was a Number 1 country hit and a top pop smash.

"When 'I Fall to Pieces' was pressed . . . and had gone into the charts, the first thing Owen Bradley did was give Patsy an advance," recalls Jordanaires bass singer Ray Walker. "And she came in that studio and she said, 'Boys, they can't take that refrigerator now. They'll never get my car now. 'Cause I paid cash for it and it's mine and I'm a-keepin' it.' I said, 'Well, where'd you get the money?' She said, 'Owen gave it to me, 'cause, baby, I got a hit record!'"

But her career momentum was stopped cold that spring when Patsy was nearly killed in a gory Nashville car crash. She suffered a dislocated hip, a fractured arm, multiple contusions, and a horrible gash that began at her right eyebrow, ran across the bridge of her nose, extended completely across her left brow, turned upward across her forehead, and ended in the top of her skull. Her face looked like raw hamburger when Dottie West arrived on the scene. "When I got there, she was still on the side of the road. She was so concerned about the others that were hurt, she insisted they be taken to the hospital first. . . . I went in the ambulance to Madison Hospital with her, and on the way I was picking a lot of the glass from the windshield out of her hair. She was a bloody mess. I was trying not to look at her because I didn't want her to see me crying."

"I never lost consciousness from the time it happened," said Patsy, "through the sewing up of my head—saw the other lady die—and until they gave me gas to set my hip. I cut an artery and I lost lots of blood. They thought I was gone twice during the sewing up and had to give me three pints of blood. I don't think I'll ever be able to ride in a car again." Loretta Lynn dedicated "I Fall to Pieces" to the hospitalized Patsy on "The Midnight Jamboree" radio show, launching their friendship.

Wearing the heavy, scar-hiding makeup that she used for the rest of her life, Patsy returned to the Opry stage in a wheelchair. "You're wonderful," she told the country fans following their thunderous ovation. "I'll tell you one thing: The greatest gift, I think, that you folks coulda given me was the encouragement that you gave me. Right at the very time I needed you the most, you came through with the flying-est colors. And I just want to say, you'll just never know how happy you made this ol' country gal." In August she returned to the recording studio on crutches to record Willie Nelson's "Crazy" as the follow-up to "I Fall to Pieces." Despite the still-searing pain in her ribs, she taped one of the greatest vocal performances in country music history. Like its predecessor, "Crazy" became a major pop and country smash. "She had a great way of introducing her newest hit," remembers Barbara Mandrell. "She would tell the audience, 'I recorded a song called "I Fall to Pieces," and I was in a car wreck. Now I'm really worried, because I have a brand-new record, and it's called "Crazy."'"

Patsy finished 1961 as the Number 1 female vocalist of the trade publications during the Country Music Week festivities in Nashville, then triumphed at Carnegie Hall in a country showcase that costarred Minnie Pearl and other Opry greats. She also starred on TV's "American Bandstand" and "Tennessee Ernie Ford Show." "She was steamrolling the business like no one we'd ever seen," remarked top country broadcaster Ralph Emery.

As 1962 dawned, Patsy scored her fourth major pop-country heartache success, "She's Got You." By this time she'd long since abandoned the cowgirl duds of her early career in favor of elegant gowns. Another thing that set Patsy apart was that she moved sensuously around the stage as she performed. In the decades since her death, Patsy Cline aficionados have pointed repeatedly to her enormous vocal talent as the explanation for her superstardom. What's often forgotten is that Patsy was electrifying in concert, a breakthrough country female as an *entertainer.* "In one word, Patsy Cline's brought something new to hillbilly singing—oomph!" wrote *Washington Star* reporter Meredith S. Buel. Country promoter and TV mogul Connie B. Gay concurred: "Patsy has brought out a brand of showmanship and rhythm to hillbilly music that's as welcome as a cool country breeze in springtime," he said. "We call her a country music choreographer. She creates the mood through movements of her hands and body. . . . Most female country music vocalists stand motionless, sing with a monotonous high-pitched nasal twang. Patsy's come up with a throaty style loaded with motion and E-motion." Commented one fan, "That's the first woman who could make me feel like crying out of one eye and winking out of the other!"

As she rode ever higher on Bradley's cool zephyrs of arrangement and production, Patsy began to embrace The Nashville Sound with more conviction and enthusiasm, recording pop standards such as "Heartaches," "The Wayward Wind," and "Love Letters in the Sand." Her thrilling voice invariably invested these with new depth. Patsy's dramatic control of volume , stretched-note effects, sobs, pauses, and unique way of holding back and then bursting into full-throated phrases also breathed new life into country chestnuts like "San Antonio Rose," "Blue Moon of Kentucky," and "Half as Much." Observed Bradley succinctly, "Patsy put in the passion."

She starred with Johnny Cash and the Carters at The Hollywood Bowl in mid-1962 while "When I Get Through with You" was becoming her fifth Top 10 hit. "Imagine That" and "So Wrong," both among her most expressive performances, filled out the year on the radio. She bought her dream house and proudly showed it off to buddies Loretta, Brenda, and Dottie. But there was an undercurrent of sadness about Patsy during this time. Several people say she had a premonition of death. "I . . . wonder sometimes if it's really worth what we go through, what we put up with," she confided to Dottie one night. She gave Dottie her scrapbook, saying, "I want you to have it. . . . it ain't gonna do me no good 'cause I'll never live to see thirty." Patsy even dictated her funeral wishes to June Carter, who dutifully jotted them down one night when they were driving between shows in California. But Patsy did turn thirty, and right after that she was named Most Programmed Artist by radio DJs at the 1962 country convention. A month later she was headlining in Las Vegas.

"Leavin' on Your Mind" was headed for the Top 10 in February 1963 when Patsy recorded for the last time. After hearing Jackie DeShannon's version of "Faded Love" on the radio, Patsy had bragged to Charlie that she could hit the highest notes in its chorus without lowering the key, as Jackie had done. He dared her. She not only hit the notes, she raised the key. The next day she recorded her immortal "Sweet Dreams," and the day after that, "He Called Me Baby." All three heart-stopping performances would become posthumous hits. Patsy called Jan and Dottie to come hear the playbacks when she was finished singing. "She never seemed happy with what she'd just done," Dottie recalled. "Yet it was so-o-o-o fantastic." Said Jan, "'Sweet Dreams'—who can listen to that without getting cold chills? 'Faded Love' is another. . . . I was in awe of Patsy. You know, afterward you're supposed to say something nice. I couldn't talk. I was dumbfounded."

In March both Patsy and Dottie went to Kansas City to sing at a benefit concert. Dottie and her husband, Bill, drove. Patsy flew with Hawkshaw Hawkins and Cowboy Copas in a private plane piloted by Randy Hughes.

"She did close the show," said Dottie. "She *was* the star. I walked out and watched. . . . And I will never forget that white chiffon dress. As I watched her, I thought, 'My God. She sings like an angel, and she looks like one.' She was in this draped chiffon dress, and she was just beautiful.

"She almost rode back in the car with Bill and I, rather than flying, because . . . there was no clearance for the plane. There were no flights. It was a really bad, foggy rain. Anyway, the last thing that I said to Patsy was, 'I'm really going to be worried about you flying in this weather.' She said, 'Don't worry 'bout me. When it's my time to go, it's my time.'"

Hughes lost his bearings in the fog. The plane crashed in some woods near Camden, Tennessee, ninety miles east of home. Jean Shepard lost her husband, Hawkshaw. Kathy Copas Hughes lost both her father, Cowboy, and her husband, Randy. Charlie Dick and the world lost the woman that many still consider to be the greatest female country singer in history.

They laid her out in the living room of her dream house while the country community mourned the quadruple tragedy. June Carter kept the children while Charlie took Patsy back home to Winchester to bury her. There was talk of canceling the Opry that weekend. Instead there was a tribute and a gospel song from Patsy's loving backup singers, The Jordanaires. The Opry audience was sniffling and holding hankerchiefs when Minnie Pearl bravely went out to do her comedy routines. Despite an aching heart, she got them laughing. Announcer Ralph Emery remembers that Minnie had tears streaming down her face when she came off.

In the weeks that followed, Jan Howard was approached to record an album of Patsy's songs. She indignantly refused to capitalize on her friend's death. For years afterward, so did every other female singer in Nashville. Finally Loretta released her touching *I Remember Patsy* collection in 1976 and brought "She's Got You" and "Why Can't He Be You" back to the charts. That opened the door. Since then a host of singers have saluted their idol. Reba McEntire ("Sweet Dreams"), k.d. lang ("Three Cigarettes in an Ashtray"), Emmylou Harris ("Back in Baby's Arms"), and Linda Ronstadt ("Crazy") are just a few who have acknowledged Patsy Cline's overwhelming influence.

Of the Nashville Sound singers who followed immediately in Patsy's wake, her confidant Dottie West was the most profoundly affected. "I think I was most influenced by Patsy Cline," Dottie candidly admitted. "She *said* things for people. There was so much feeling there. In fact, she told me, 'Hoss, if you can't do it with feeling, *don't*.'" Dottie got her first hit as a songwriter the month Patsy died, and before the year was out, she was on the charts as a singer. For the next three decades Dottie "did it with feeling."

Like her idol, Dottie knew hard times, hard work, and hard knocks. And like Patsy, she was no overnight success. Born Dorothy Marie Marsh in 1932 to a farm family in the Frog Pond community outside McMinnville, Tennessee, Dottie was the oldest of ten children who learned to accept work and responsibility at an early age. She used to say she was "raised on corn bread, butter beans, and fiddles," for her father was a musician who placed a guitar in his baby daughter's hands as soon as she could hold one. But her mother, Pelina Marsh, gave Dottie the resolve she would need in the years to come. "My dad was a mean drunk. I mean, when he was drinking, he would beat us, and that's just inhuman. I try to forget about that part of my life." The alcoholic abandoned the family, and Pelina moved her kids to McMinnville to open a restaurant. "I think my strength came from my mother. She was very determined . . . and I've always had this determination. I mean, I knew that we were poor. There were times when I was even embarrassed. But I had too much pride to ask for a handout."

Dottie made her singing debut at age twelve on local radio. She worked her way through high school waitressing in her mother's restaurant. She worked her way through Tennessee Tech in Cookeville, too. During the day she clerked in a florist shop, and at night she waited tables. Every Saturday morning she sang on the radio, and every other Friday she performed at the student square dances. At her side was steel guitarist Bill West. They met as freshmen, got married in 1953, and had two sons by graduation day. "It's true: I married the first man who ever kissed me," Dottie admitted.

Bill took a job at a steel company in Cleveland. Dottie won a five-year slot on the TV show "Landmark Jamboree," which aired in Cleveland, Columbus, Toledo, Dayton, and several other Ohio towns. Nashville stars made guest appearances on the program; Dottie listened and learned while singing in a duo called The Kay-Dots with Kathy Dee (Kathy Dearth, 1933–1968). Among her most important female role models were Mother Maybelle Carter & The Carter Sisters, with whom she later toured. "I really watched Mama Maybelle and those girls. Mama Maybelle was really a strong person. I can remember one cold winter tour that we did together. And I rode right in the car with her. She always insisted on driving, no matter how long or miserable the trip. She was driving the Cadillac, and there were four of us girls with her. She was very dedicated to her career, but she was also a very good mama. She really took care of those girls. I watched how she handled the business part, the stage, the performance, the traveling. I learned how to be a mother in show business from her." In 1958 Dottie had another baby, her daughter Shelly, but kept working. On weekends the Wests would drive to Nashville to try to make music-business contacts.

"In 1959 Bill and I were heading back to Cleveland, going north on Dickerson Road [in Nashville]. I said when we got to the Starday Records building, 'Just pull in right here. I'm going in there, and I hope they'll listen to me.' I walked in and said, 'I really am going to make hit records. I am gonna be a singer in Nashville. Here's a scrapbook of the TV show I do.' And then I auditioned live with my guitar. . . . It worked. It's funny: Looking back, I don't even think I realized how tough it might be. When you're that young, you're not afraid. I had absolutely no doubt that I could be a top singer. I was just 'goin' for it,' that's all."

She and Bill moved to Nashville in 1961, and once they were settled, Dottie began hanging out with the "Young Turk" songwriter crowd that included Willie Nelson, Hank Cochran, Roger Miller, Justin Tubb, and her frequent collaborator Red Lane. A second recording contract, with Atlantic, fared no better than her hitless one at Starday. But in 1963 she struck pay dirt as a writer when Jim Reeves sang her "Is This Me?" and took it to the top of the country charts. Reeves brought Dottie to the attention of Chet Atkins, who signed her to RCA and produced her self-composed "Here Comes My Baby." In 1964 the

Dottie West, 1967.

ballad became Dottie West's first major hit, earned her "Grand Ole Opry" cast membership, and won her the first Grammy Award ever given to a country music woman. She followed it with such definitive Nashville Sound hits as "Would You Hold It Against Me?" (1966) and "Paper Mansions" (1967). The stylish up-and-comer appeared in the low-budget country films *Second Fiddle to a Steel Guitar* and *There's a Still on the Hill* during this decade.

Dottie's most moving performances were recorded in the early 1970s. From the beginning she had a voice that was "born to cry." She'd even done a 1966 theme LP called *Suffer Time* so listeners could "taste the unhappiness of the eternal loser," as the liner notes put it. By the time of "Forever Yours" in 1970 her singing had acquired a broken, moaning quality that she began using to great emotional effect. She seemed almost on the verge of sobbing on "Careless Hands" (1971), "I'm Only a Woman" (1972), "Lonely Is" (1971), and her compositions "Clinging to My Baby's Hand" (1969) and "The Cold Hand of Fate" (1970). She actually was

Dottie West, 1966.

weeping when she recorded the single-parent guilt song "Six Weeks Every Summer" (1971). "You can tell I was crying, I think, on the record. I sang it through just one time . . . and we really got into the song. About halfway into it I started the recitation part, and the whole band stopped. [Guitar player] Grady Martin was going through a divorce, and he wept and wiped his eyes. . . . We spliced it together, and that's the way the song was done." Dottie mentioned her Shelly by name on the record, for she felt especially guilty about being away from her daughter so much. She also dedicated her 1968 *Country Girl* LP to Shelly and used the child's photo for the album jacket.

Dottie's greatest experimentation with The Nashville Sound also occurred during this period, notably on her agony-and-ecstasy delivery of the sophisticated "If You Go Away" (1968) and "Once You Were Mine" (1971). She hit new peaks as a writer, too. Dottie was hired to compose a series of twelve ad jingles for Coca-Cola. One of them, "Country Sunshine," won the ad world's top Clio Award honor and became a big hit single in 1973.

She gave other female writers a break, as well. Dottie was among the first Nashvillians to record the songs of Jessi Colter, Sandy Mason, Toni Wine, and Jeannie Seely. She discovered Larry Gatlin, paid for his plane fare to Music City, recorded his songs, and got him session work as a backup singer. She found teenager Steve Wariner in Indiana and launched his career by hiring him for her band. Daughter Shelly got her introduction to the big time in the Dottie West road show, too, as did Capitol Records artist Tony Toliver. Dottie was particularly fond of feeding needy songwriters hearty, home-cooked meals and hosting women's quilting bees.

"I think I feel especially close to all the girls in the business; we have a lot in common," she said. "I can honestly say I've never felt jealous of any other female entertainer. That's just not the way with me.

"The position of women has changed a *lot* in country music. . . . I remember one night at the Opry in sixty-two or sixty-three when Patsy Cline showed up in this gorgeous . . . Nudie-designed pantsuit and [Opry manager] Ott Devine told her she couldn't wear it! You *had* to wear a dress back then. I'm still pretty shy about wearing pants on the Opry for that reason," said Dottie in 1983. She was ultrafeminine, yet strong-willed in her career. "It's hard for a man to accept an independent woman. I am not really into women's lib, but at the same time, I know I am very independent."

Dottie's marriage to Bill broke up. She said years later that her pride was wounded badly when she found out he was cheating on her. When she went to the altar again in 1972, she changed "'til death do us part" to "as long as love shall last" in the ceremony. The groom was drummer Byron Metcalf; he was twenty-nine, and she was forty-one. "Older men have been chasing young girls for years," she said, "so it should be okay for women to be involved with younger guys. Why should I go around with some old fuddy-duddy if I don't want to? I'm attracted to younger men, and I'm not afraid to admit it. . . . I don't mind saying it. I have nothing to hide." She was afraid her fans would disapprove, but instead Dottie acquired a sexy new image and became more popular than ever before. Her career boomed.

From 1978 to 1981 she topped the charts repeatedly as the duet partner of Kenny Rogers. Just ten years earlier she'd declined to record Kris Kristofferson's "Help Me Make It Through the Night" because she thought it was too suggestive. In 1978's "Anyone Who Isn't Me Tonight" she trumpeted to Rogers, "When you made love to me tonight, I felt as if I'd died and gone to heaven / And if that's how it feels to die, then baby in your arms I'm through with livin'," while he growled back, "You've got the kind of body that was made to give a man a lot of pleasure. . . . Every inch of you that's woman makes me that much more a man." Dottie also dueted with Jimmy Dean (1971), John Schneider (1983), Jim Reeves (1964), and, unforgettably, Don Gibson (1969). But with Rogers she had her biggest commercial success, winning back-to-back Duo of the Year awards from the Country Music Association in 1978 and 1979, and getting pop radio airplay with "What Are We Doin' in Love" and "Every Time Two Fools Collide."

As a solo, Dottie got the first Number 1 record of her career with the spitting, sassy "Lesson in Leavin'" in 1980. Among its follow-up hits was the equally feisty "(I'm Gonna) Put You Back on the Rack." She adopted a glamorous new image to go with her newfound fame. She got a face-lift. She restyled her cascading mane of titian red waves. She posed in skintight white satin pants with her blouse unbuttoned, titled an album *Wild West,* and did a peekaboo photo spread in the men's magazine *Oui.* "I just don't feel my age, so don't expect me to act it," said the fifty-year-old vamp. "And now a girl can be more open. . . . I have a healthy attitude about sex, about the body. . . . I want to be 'doing it' when I'm eighty-three. Really. And you can quote me on that. It's part of life. . . . If God made anything better, he kept it for Himself." Again her fans accepted the change. "You know what? I never had one bad letter about it. Not one. In fact, now I get all these love letters."

Metcalf's drinking ended their marriage in 1980. He asked for fifty thousand dollars a year in alimony (but didn't get it). "It blew my mind," said Dottie, "but I'll tell you one thing: My heart quit hurtin'. I wasn't broken-hearted anymore." In 1983 she wed her twenty-eight-year-old concert sound technician, Al Winters. She installed a mirror over her brass bed and cruised around Nashville in flashy cars. Dottie did scads of interviews during this period, appeared on a myriad of television shows, and continued to do more than three hundred concerts a year. Daughter Shelly also rose to stardom, winning CMA Duet of the Year trophies in 1981 and 1982 with David Frizzell and graduating to solo success in 1983.

Dottie's recording and concert offers became sparse after 1986. But the proud redhead held her head high throughout the tough final years of her life. She divorced Winters in January 1990. In March her Los Angeles manager sued her. In June the bank foreclosed on her spacious home and auctioned it off. Dottie wept in front of the "Entertainment Tonight" cameras as she packed a lifetime of treasures to move. Her Corvette was taken next. Kenny Rogers lent her one of his cars. "I'm a survivor," she said bravely. "You can knock me down, but you better have a big rock to keep me there. . . . I know how to make money, and I'll make it. . . . So many of my friends have called and offered to help. I have too much pride for that. . . . I am going to be fine." She filed for bankruptcy in August, citing a decade of poor investments by her business manager. To satisfy her million-dollar tax bill, IRS agents confiscated her career mementos, dolls, guitars, and sentimental souvenirs, and staged a humiliating public auction in June 1991. Dottie tearfully bid on some of her own things. A month later she was banged up in a car wreck. With buddies like Roger Miller, Kenny Rogers, Willie Nelson, and Steve Wariner she intended a comeback album of duets. Tammy Wynette and Tanya Tucker planned a trio with her for the project. She started an autobiography. But in September Dottie was late for an Opry show and asked a neighbor to drive her there. He lost control of his car approaching the Opry House from the highway. She died of her injuries five days later at age fifty-eight.

Wariner stood alone and sang a lonesome, sad "Amazing Grace" at the Nashville funeral, which hundreds attended. Said Rogers in his eulogy, "When she sang about pain, she felt pain; when she sang about love, she felt love; and when she sang about beauty, she felt that beauty. While some performers sang words, she sang emotions."

She "did it with feeling." Patsy would have been proud.

Jan Howard graduated to stardom, too. After Patsy's death she belted out more than twenty-five Nashville Sound hits. Jan's brassy, sassy delivery seemed so self-assured, so downright gutsy, that the torments revealed in her candid, compelling autobiography, *Sunshine and Shadow,* came as startling revelations when the book was published in 1987.

"For years people who thought they knew me said, 'You ought to write a book.' I always said, 'Yeah, it would make a great soap opera,'" Jan says with a throaty laugh. She finally wrote it because she became suicidal in 1979. "It was a very bad time in my life. I was in Florida, and I didn't know whether I was going to walk into the ocean or not. And I can't swim. I went back into the house that I was visiting. I sat down on the floor and wrote this song called 'My Story,' which turned out to be the outline for the book.

"When I started, I wrote all of the hate and bitterness. That was therapeutic, because later I threw it away. It was better than going to a psychiatrist, and a lot cheaper. Once I started again, it was just like rolling back the years."

Jan had a lot of wounds to cleanse. Her saga includes rape, wife beating, bigamy, poverty, war, teen suicide, cheating, divorce, thievery, and mental collapse. "Mine is a story that could be any woman's story. . . . It's the story of a hard, real life. It isn't sugar-coated. It's not a fairy tale."

She was born Lula Grace Johnson in 1930, the eighth of eleven children of an impoverished farm couple near West Plains, Missouri. She attended a one-room schoolhouse wearing the rags of a rural Depression-era child. "The first time I heard the Opry I was eight or nine years old. My dad used to tune it in on the radio on Saturday nights, but he only listened long enough to hear Texas Ruby. She was his favorite." Jan and her older sister played make-believe country radio stars. But the child hid a dark secret from her playmates. She was raped at the age of eight by one of her father's friends.

As a teenager she worked in West Plains at the Model Drugs and the Cinderella Confectionary. Chronically truant and never much of a student, Jan dropped out of school to marry at age sixteen. During the next four years she had three sons, while her husband turned her life into a living hell. He beat her viciously. One night he held a butcher knife to her throat, but as he was about to kill her, a friend stopped by. She fled, then had a nervous breakdown. She fell in love with a military man and married him after her divorce in 1953. Their first baby died in infancy, and she miscarried the second when she found out he was a bigamist. This time, she got on a Greyhound Bus bound for Los Angeles. "I probably had thirty jobs in thirty days when I first got there. . . . I worked as a waitress in a lot of different places. . . . Eventually I got a job as a secretary, which was quite a deal because I didn't type or take shorthand. But I got by . . . on nerve, I guess."

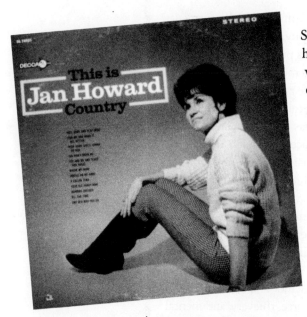

A friend was dating country singer Wynn Stewart. Jan started going to clubs with her to hear him. At one, she met a kindhearted factory worker named Harlan Howard, who dreamed of writing country hits. Thirty days later they got married in Las Vegas. After miscarrying again, Jan had complications from surgery and had to have a hysterectomy at age twenty-seven. She was washing dishes during her recovery when Harlan came in unexpectedly and heard her singing as she worked. "I didn't know you could sing," he said. Few did. "I always loved to sing, but I was really shy about it. I never sang in front of anybody, not even my family, when I was a child." Harlan practically dragged her into the living room and taught her his song

"I'm not the ginghams-and-ruffles type," said West Coast immigrant Jan Howard when she arrived in Music City. This LP cover of 1967 was more her style.

"Mommy for a Day" on the spot. He took her to a studio, where they made a demo tape of the tune and sent it to Nashville. Kitty Wells had a hit record with it in 1958. "After that, every spare minute and dime was spent at the studio."

Harlan decided Jan could make hit records, too. Backed by Wynn Stewart's band, she released Harlan's "Pick Me Up on Your Way Down" and "I Wish I Could Fall in Love Again" in 1959. The record company changed "Lula Grace" to "Jan." She and Wynn did some duets, then Jan Howard got her first solo hit in 1960 with Harlan's song "The One You Slip Around With." The only problem was, she was still painfully shy. "For a long time, I had such severe stage fright, I would literally get physically ill at the thought of going onstage. . . . Even with hits and everything, I still didn't have the confidence."

In 1960 the Howards quit their jobs and moved to Nashville. Jan's troubles were far from over. The psychological scars from her youth were deep, and the anxiety of beginning a new adventure preyed on her mind: "Many nights, after the kids were in bed, I'd pace the floor. I had horrible fears that something bad was going to happen; it possessed my mind and wouldn't let go. I knew it was ridiculous, but I couldn't shake it. I was afraid of being closed in. I was frightened of open places, of heights and of the dark . . . my nerves were shot." When her weight dropped below ninety-seven pounds, Harlan institutionalized her. She subsequently went into therapy.

Because of the 1960 radio success of "The One You Slip Around

With," Jan got called for guest spots on the Opry. "Jean Shepard was really one of the first ones to be really nice to me. She's honest, and she's a real person. Skeeter Davis and Patsy—the majority [of the women] were nice; the minority were hateful. I got anonymous phone calls: 'Go back to where you came from'; 'We don't need you here.' Well, I didn't want to be here in the first place, at that time. And I didn't want to be in show business, at that time. I had so little self-confidence." The transplanted Californian also felt out of sync with the Opry's expectations for female acts. "I didn't know where I fit in. I tried to take people's advice at the time—what to wear, what to say, what not to say, where to be. Like they told me to wear ginghams and ruffles. Well, I'm not the ginghams-and-ruffles type and I was very uncomfortable in it. But I wore it because I thought that was what I was supposed to do. Until I realized I had to be myself." Fans found her blunt, no-nonsense manner and stylish, no-frills look appealing. Jan won the Most Promising Country Female award from *Billboard* magazine in 1960, then landed a 1963 hit with a new version of Lulu Belle's "I Wish I Was a Single Girl Again." Unlike her contemporaries Patsy Cline and Dottie West, Jan specialized in up-tempo tunes, usually with feisty female lyrics provided by Harlan or her other steady source of material, Bill Anderson. She brought feminine spunk to The Nashville Sound.

Examples of Jan's sass include "What Makes a Man Wander" (1965), "Evil on Your Mind" (1966), "Bad Seed" (1966), "Roll Over and Play Dead" (1967), "Count Your Blessings, Woman" (1968), and "Let Him Have It" (1972). Between 1965 and 1972 she and Anderson were one of country's hottest duos on the road, on his syndicated TV show, and on record, with hits from 1966's "I Know You're Married (But I Love You Still)" to 1972's "Dis-Satisfied." She was made a "Grand Ole Opry" member in 1971.

Yet the misery of her private life continued. She caught Harlan with another woman, and says he duped her out of half of their song publishing business before their divorce in 1967. When Mr. and Mrs. Howard separated, life became even more difficult. "Friends started dropping by the wayside. People who had been to the house, some of whom I thought would be friends for life, suddenly stopped calling. I felt like a leper." With Harlan gone, Jan's singing became an economic necessity for the first time in her life.

Although not a hit factory like Harlan Howard or Bill Anderson, Jan wrote songs, too. She penned the 1966 Kitty Wells hit "It's All Over but the Crying" and Anderson's "Love Is a Sometimes Thing" of 1970, as well as her own singles "Marriage Has Ruined More Good Love Affairs"

(1971) and "The Life of a Country Girl Singer" (1981). She also wrote 1968's "My Son," a moving recitation that began as a letter to her son in Vietnam. Anderson heard it and insisted she record it. "I tried to put it down on tape, but I couldn't get through it without crying; it just destroyed me. They finally put several takes of it together to get the recording that was released. I consented to the record being released when I realized the song could be about anybody's son, any boy who was over there." The mother's plea for the safe return of her son had been out two weeks when Jan's boy Jimmy was killed in the war. Listening to it became almost unbearably painful, and performing it became impossible. But Jan got more than five thousand letters from soldiers and their parents. "They said they felt like it was for them."

Four years later David, her high-strung, theatrical youngest son, committed suicide. June Carter and Johnny Cash helped Jan put her life back together by hiring her to tour with them. Then she became a part of Tammy Wynette's show. By the mid-1980s Jan had a real estate license and was working on her first novel. In 1990 she married Dr. Maurice M. Acree, Jr.

"One thing I want to make really clear is that I'm not a martyr. I can't stand self-pity. I don't deserve and don't want any kind of pity. . . . There are a lot of people who have gone through worse things than I have. . . . [I'm] a girl/wife/mother who happens to be an entertainer. . . . It almost seems like an accident that I became a singer. And I'm so thankful for it."

Patsy, Dottie, and Jan opened the door for many more Nashville Sound stylists. Marion Worth, Margie Bowes, Connie Smith, Jeannie Seely, and Connie Hall climbed the charts. Virtually all of the female country stylists of the day tried on Nashville Sound clothes, sometimes wearing them comfortably (Jean Shepard, Wanda Jackson) and sometimes seeming like matrons in prom formals (Kitty Wells, Rose Maddox, Wilma Lee Cooper).

One of the best of the post-Patsy Nashville Sound stylists was Wilma Burgess. She had a warmth of tone in her yearning soprano that Owen Bradley put in lovely instrumental settings on such hits as "Baby" (1965), "Tear Time" (1967), and the enduring classic "Misty Blue" (1966). Wilma was born in Orlando, Florida, in 1939 and was a physical education major in college. Inspired to sing by the sweet sound of Jo Stafford, she starred on local TV in the Sunshine State before moving to Nashville in 1963. Wilma continued to record into the 1970s, and in the late 1980s she opened Nashville's first women's bar.

During its heyday The Nashville Sound dominated the charts and permeated the whole hillbilly music world. Its influence was felt even by women in the previously raucous West Coast country scene. The queen of the Las Vegas country showrooms was Judy Lynn, who recorded prolifically in the style throughout the sixties. Born Judy Voiten in 1936 in Boise, the golden-haired singer/songwriter was Miss Idaho in the 1955 Miss America pageant. Judy was an able yodeler, but her hits were mainly Nashville Sound ballads such as 1962's "Footsteps of a Fool." In her day she was the flashiest of all country music women: Judy boasted eye-popping, form-hugging cowgirl outfits encrusted with rhinestones, sequins, and embroidery. Dripping in silver and gold fringe, she was a vision in neon-hued spandex stretch pants, elaborately tooled western boots, and jeweled cowgirl hats. She retired from music in 1980 to become a minister.

After Joe and Rose Lee Maphis moved to Nashville, Johnny and Jonie Mosby (Janice Irene Shields, b. 1940) became California country's leading husband-wife team. Jonie met Johnny in 1958 when he hired her to sing with his band, and they married later that year. Despite their honky-tonk lyrics, 1963–1964 singles like "How the Other Half Lives," "Make a Left and Then a Right," and "Don't Call Me from a Honky-Tonk" were sung by the attractive couple in a smooth style that was doubtless influenced by the polished Nashville Sound. The Mosbys ran their own country music nightclub, starred on a weekly California TV show, were active in the formation of California's Academy of Country Music, and in their cute matching outfits remained fixtures of the West Coast country scene for two decades.

Johnny and Jonie had four children between 1959 and 1971. After their divorce Jonie married a man named Donnie Mitchell in 1977. She made headlines in 1992 when she gave birth at age fifty-two to a test-tube baby in Los Angeles. Her seven-pound son was conceived with an egg donated by a thirty-year-old woman fertilized by her husband's sperm that was then transferred to Jonie's uterus. Interviewed by *People* magazine as the oldest woman in the United States known to have given birth this way, Jonie said, "I'd do it over in a minute." To those who disapproved of her postmenopausal motherhood, she merely shrugged. "I've always done things differently," she said. "If Social Security picks up the tab," she added with a good-natured jab at her age, "I just might do it again."

Bonnie Guitar was unquestionably the female leader of California country. She was a session guitarist, a record label owner, a producer, and a songwriter, as well as the singer of such hits as "Dark Moon" (1957) and "A Woman in Love" (1967). The combination of her caressing vocals,

There were many female contributors to the development of The Nashville Sound. Among some of the lesser-known hit makers were these:

MARGIE BOWES (B. 1941)—"Poor Old Heartsick Me" (1959), "Understand Your Gal" (1964)

SHIRLEY COLLIE (B. SHIRLEY CADDELL, 1931)—"Willingly" (with Willie Nelson, 1962)

DOTTIE DILLARD OF THE DOTTIE DEE SINGERS

CONNIE HALL (B. 1929)—"The Bottle or Me," "Poison in Your Hand" (1960)

BILLIE JEAN HORTON—"Ocean of Tears" (1960)

MILLIE KIRKHAM, BACKUP SINGER

PRISCILLA MITCHELL (B. 1941)—"Yes Mr. Peters" (with Roy Drusky, 1965)

THE NASHVILLE EDITION WOMEN

MARION WORTH (B. MARY ANN WARD, c. 1930)—"Shake Me I Rattle (Squeeze Me I Cry)" (1963)

top-notch musicianship, and executive ability was unmatched by any other woman at that time. Bonnie Buckingham was born in 1923 in Seattle, the daughter of a fiddler, and she was on the road with her own western band by age seventeen. Dubbed "Guitar" when she moved to Los Angeles, she was hired as a studio instrumentalist on records by Ferlin Husky, Jim Reeves, and other stars. "I was one of the first women doing that, when that was a man's world . . . but I never thought of it at the time," Bonnie says. As a singer, she turned out more than a dozen hits in the 1960s. "The Tallest Tree" created some controversy in 1966, for it was about a mother mourning the death of her son in Vietnam. Bonnie says she was forbidden to sing it on network TV. Although she had several Top 10 successes and was named Female Vocalist of the Year by the Academy of Country Music in 1966, she retained the laid-back, contemplative personality of a picker.

"If my [singing] careeer was messed up, I did it. . . . I did not dedicate myself to it. I had many calls to do 'The Grand Ole Opry,' and I refused all the time. I turned down Las Vegas time after time because I don't feel that I'm that dynamic. . . . I was into the studio. I was learning to produce [records]. I was learning to run the equipment. And that's what I wanted to do. As an artist, I spread myself in too many directions. My head was in production. . . . I was just consumed with the things that the equipment could do, so I was constantly trying new things, new sounds."

In 1958 she found a group in her home state called The Fleetwoods and recorded them on her own Dolton label. The teen trio scored massive pop hits with the sighing, close-harmony ballads "Mr. Blue" and "Come Softly to Me." Bonnie's ear for the new and different won her a six-year stint as the country music A&R (artist and repertoire) director for the Dot and ABC-Paramount labels on the West Coast in the sixties. She also found time to write "The Cheating Game" as a 1973 hit for Susan Raye. Bonnie married her third husband, Mario Depiano, in 1967 and by the close of the decade was spending more time in Washington than Hollywood. She raises and races quarter horses and still periodically returns to recording and performing.

"I'm not a [women's] liberation soul, but whether you are or not that's cool. Because I have never felt that I was treated as less than an equal. . . . I was always treated as a *musician.*"

At one point, Bonnie was offered an executive job in Music City, but she turned it down to stay in the Northwest. By the late sixties Nashville had completely taken over as country's capital. The West Coast dried up as a country center, and only Buck Owens, Susan Raye, Merle Haggard, and Bonnie Owens kept Bakersfield alive as a challenge to The Nashville Sound.

Everyone from Ann-Margret and Teresa Brewer to Carol Channing and Rosemary Clooney came to Nashville hoping that some Music City gold dust would rub off on them. Hollywood's Connie Stevens attempted *The Hank Williams Songbook* LP in 1962. Connie Francis began recording in Nashville in 1959. She had major hits with the country songs "Everybody's Somebody's Fool," "My Heart Has a Mind of Its Own," and "Breakin' in a Brand New Broken Heart" in 1960 and 1961, and recorded duets with Hank Williams, Jr., in 1964.

But Nashville didn't need to import ladies to record for the mainstream music market. It created its own pop princesses, transforming a trio of country gals and taking The Nashville Sound to its logical conclusion. What Patsy Cline began, Sue Thompson, Skeeter Davis, and Brenda Lee finished.

Sue was the veteran. She was in her mid-thirties when she purred "Paper Tiger," chirped "Norman," and whimpered "Sad Movies (Make Me Cry)" on the pop charts from 1961 to 1965. But there was something in her coquettish delivery that made her sound like a thirteen-year-old, and something in her vivacious style that inspired charming audio gimmicks from the Nashville Sound pickers. Whether boop-boop-a-dooping the bouncy "James (Hold the Ladder Steady)" or sniffling a ballad like "Have a Good Time," Sue sounded like the quintessential teen queen.

Born Eva Sue McKee in 1926, she was the only child of farmers forced off the land near Nevada, Missouri, during the Great Depression. Captivated by singing cowboy movies, Sue decided at an early age that she wanted to become the female Gene Autry. She got a guitar when she was seven. In 1937 her parents migrated to central California to work as fruit pickers. The McKees eventually settled in San Jose. During World War II Sue worked in a defense plant near Oakland. She married in 1942, had a daughter in 1946, and divorced in 1949. By then she was working days as a theater box office cashier and nights as a club singer in the Bay Area. Discovered by western swing bandleader Dude Martin, she began singing on his San Francisco TV show. He also became her second husband. They moved to Hollywood in 1951 and proved to be just as popular on TV with southern California viewers. Signed to Mercury, she issued a string of mildly popular singles, including the first version of the standard "You Belong to Me."

The contentious Hank Penny joined the Martins' troupe in Hollywood, and he romanced her despite the gossip columnists' tongue

The pert, "itty bitty" sound of Sue Thompson made her a teen star, although she was thirty-six years old by the time this first LP appeared in 1962.

wagging. Sue divorced Martin in 1953 and married Penny. In 1955 she gave birth to a son, and a few months later the Pennys moved to Las Vegas to work the casino lounge circuit. Penny got his pert wife recording contracts with Decca and Columbia, but she still didn't click in either country or pop musical settings.

But in Nashville at Hickory Records in the 1960s, she found her niche with teen-themed novelty tunes. She had a sweetness and innocence in her voice that seemed to especially inspire John D. Loudermilk, the composer of all her pop hits. Both "Sad Movies" and "Norman" hit the teen Top 10, propelling the petite strawberry blonde onto "Hullabaloo," "Shindig," "American Bandstand," Where the Action Is," and "Hollywood A-Go-Go." Her almost-cartoonish, youth-oriented voice was dubbed "itty bitty" by publicists. She and Penny divorced in 1963.

She returned to country music with an unsuccessful string of singles between 1971 and 1976, then went back to the Nevada casinos and to radio as the host of a show from North Hollywood's country nightclub, The Palomino.

Skeeter Davis had better luck switching back and forth between pop and country. Her wistful, plaintive "The End of the World" (1963) was one of the biggest pop hits of the Nashville Sound era, and she toured with rock 'n' rollers ranging from Elvis Presley to The Rolling Stones. Yet she retained her "Grand Ole Opry" membership and repeatedly made the Top 10 on country charts during this period.

At least part of Skeeter's appeal was her unmistakably hillbilly personality. Producers could dress her up in the citified arrangements of Carole King's "I Can't Stay Mad at You" (1963) and "Let Me Get Close to You" (1964), but they couldn't take the "country" out of her charmingly rattled conversational style. Her breathless delivery, run-on sentences, stream-of-consciousness manner, and flitting energy gave her her nickname, "Skeeter."

She was born Mary Frances Penick in Dry Ridge, Kentucky, in 1931. Skeeter grew up a country music fan but had no professional aspirations before she teamed up with her high school friend Betty Jack Davis (1932–1953) to form The Davis Sisters. Betty Jack carried the melody and played guitar, and Skeeter provided the high harmonies. The girls performed in the Cincinnati and Lexington areas in 1949 and 1950, then devoted 1951 to earning enough money from cafeteria waitressing so they could buy a car. A year later they were offered a job on Detroit's WJR radio singing on its "Barnyard Frolics" show. After recording for the Motor City's Fortune Records label, The Davis Sisters were signed by RCA in Nashville. "I Forgot More Than You'll Ever Know," backed by the rockabilly classic "Rock-a-Bye Boogie," became a Number 1 country record in 1953. But the week it was at the top of the charts Betty Jack was killed in a car crash en route home with Skeeter to Kentucky from an appearance on the WWVA "Wheeling Jamboree." Skeeter teamed with Betty Jack's sister Georgia for a while, then went solo in 1956.

Skeeter was a gifted harmony singer with a thin, delicate delivery that wasn't particularly potent in solo performance. But producer Chet Atkins "double-tracked" all of her vocals, fleshed out her sound with echo, provided her with the velvet cushion of Anita Kerr's arrangements, and had her sing harmony with herself, creating a clever, distinctive Skeeter Davis sound. She hit the country Top 10 in 1959 with "Set Him Free" and was made an Opry member. Most of Skeeter's early country successes were "answer" songs to men's hits such as "(I Can't Help You) I'm Falling Too" (1960), "Lost to a Geisha Girl" (1958), and "My Last Date (With You)" (1961). She even recorded an album called *Here's the Answer* that featured her responses to RCA hits by Jim Reeves, Eddy Arnold, Don Gibson, and other stars.

She was married to top radio DJ Ralph Emery from 1960 to 1964. They broke up bitterly and rarely spoke of their union for the next twenty-five years. He is now the premier talk show host on The Nashville Network cable TV channel.

She was a teen sensation in the early sixties, but when the pop hits stopped, Skeeter skipped back to country with a 1966 version of Dolly Parton's "Fuel to the Flame." She subsequently became the first to devote an entire LP to Dolly's songs. Another "theme" collection was 1967's *Skeeter Davis Sings Buddy Holly.* She solidified her country standing by recording duets with Bobby Bare, Porter Wagoner, George Hamilton IV, and Don Bowman.

But Skeeter never conformed to the Nashville Sound era's expectations of country music women. She is a true individualist, an authentic free spirit. As the sixties drew to a close, she became the nearest thing to a flower child the Opry ever had. She let her hair down, took off the heavy makeup, and put on granny dresses and blue jeans. She adopted twelve dogs, two cats, an ocelot, a dove, and many other creatures. The living room walls of her home were scrawled with mottoes and graffiti. Her 1970 LP *It's Hard to Be a Woman* was a landmark with her Vietnam protest "When You Gonna Bring Our Soldiers Home," a country version of "Bridge over Troubled Water," and the evangelistic "We Need a Whole Lot More Jesus (And a Lot Less Rock 'n' Roll)." She also released country singles of the hippie odes "Let's Get Together" (1970) and "One Tin Soldier" (1972).

"It was a period of time in my life I was making this transition [from]

Skeeter Davis's transition from Nashville Sound pop star to "Grand Ole Opry" hippie is illustrated in these photos from 1960, left, and 1972.

trying to live the life that somebody wanted me to live," she later recalled. "I wanted to be myself. . . . When people come up to me and say, 'Well, you look like a hippie,' I tell them I'm right back where I was born. . . . My mother laughs at me and says, 'Skeeter, you're right back to wearing the things I used to make for you.' I love to wear my jeans." The Opry management became increasingly unhappy with the looks of her scruffy, long-haired band. She displeased booking agents by refusing to sing in clubs where alcohol was served. The last straw was when she spoke out in 1973 on a live Opry broadcast. A group of fifteen hippie "Jesus freaks" had been arrested in Nashville for allegedly bothering shoppers. After Skeeter spoke out on the air defending them, the Opry suspended her for more than a year. The police demanded an apology. "I said I wouldn't apologize because I only made a statement," Skeeter said. She went on tour with charismatic Christians, was dropped by her manager, and lost her contract with RCA.

Outspoken Opry matriarch Jean Shepard finally went to bat for Skeeter. "It was all blown out of proportion," Jean recalls. "It really was. A couple of policemen overreacted. I said [to the Opry manager], 'Some people have been asking about Skeeter and when she's gonna be let back on the Opry. I just think it's a dirty piece of laundry that needs to be washed out and hung out to dry. If you're gonna fire the girl, fire her. But if you're gonna hire her back, for God's sake, somebody needs to do it.'"

"I felt so unloved when I got kicked off the Opry," Skeeter recalled. "I'm childlike in many ways. It seems to me like I've been a rebel all my life, too. . . . I feel like my spirit is really free now. . . . I feel like an old tree that got shook by the wind and blew over, and then sprang back up. I'm a survivor."

She maintains enormous popularity overseas and spent part of the 1980s touring to such locales as Singapore, Jamaica, Africa, Hong Kong, and Scandinavia. In 1985 she staged a remarkable recording comeback by teaming with the cult rock band NRBQ on the acclaimed Rounder Records LP *She Sings, They Play.* Two years later she married the group's gentle-natured bassist Joey Spampinato, fifteen years her junior. Since the late 1970s she's been telling people she's writing an autobiography.

Brenda Lee has no intention of writing hers. Still in her forties, still singing powerfully, and still making the charts as the 1990s dawned, Brenda has no time to pen any memoirs. This astonishingly durable and gifted vocalist has been an audio inspiration through five decades. Brenda worshiped Sophie Tucker and Judy Garland, but also counts herself a Cyndi Lauper and Madonna fan. She started in rockabilly in the 1950s, became the planet's top-selling female pop balladeer in the 1960s, achieved country stardom in the 1970s, got Grammy Award nominations in the 1980s, and entered the 1990s as a bona fide music legend still at the peak of her vocal powers.

If Brenda's rockabilly work was exciting, her Nashville Sound performances were simply thrilling. The transition began with 1960's "I'm Sorry" and ran through a string of more than a dozen torrid torch tunes in the sixties. Backed by Music Row's string section crescendos and subtle vocal backups, she gave throbbing passion to heart-stirring melodies and lyrics of abject pain. Even today her pop performances sound so immediate, so smoldering with embers of emotion, so downright electrifying that it seems impossible that they came from a mere teenager. She could have been Edith Piaf emoting in a darkened Left Bank café on "All Alone Am I" (1962) or a female Frank Sinatra sauntering in a smoky show room on "We Three" (1960). Although just a kid, Brenda enacted an aging blues chanteuse in "Emotions" (1961) and "You Can Depend on Me" (1961), and a brokenhearted country woman from Anytown, U.S.A., in "Fool #1" (1961) and "As Usual" (1964). She was a pleading, groveling, desperate diva in "Break It to Me Gently" (1962). She was a sassy teen popster in "Thanks a Lot" (1964) and "Coming On Strong" (1966). Her settings ranged from the almost Motown-ish "My

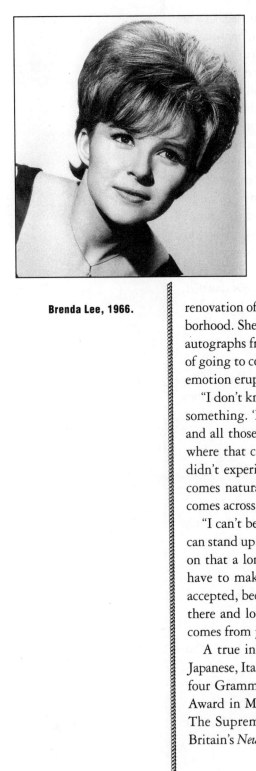

Brenda Lee, 1966.

Whole World Is Falling Down" (1963) to the tropical pulse of "He's Sure to Remember Me" (1964), yet in the throes of a ballad she could stop your heart with the fevered desire of "I Want to Be Wanted" (1960) or the magnificent desolation of "Losing You" (1963).

There was no more compelling Nashville Sound pop vocalist. Indeed, there were few singers in any era, in any field of music, who could grab you by your shirt collar and *demand* that you listen the way Brenda Lee could. By the late eighties she had sold more than ninety million records worldwide, more than any other woman singer in history.

There was torment in her voice, but contentment in her life. Still happily married to Ronnie Shacklett, the boy she defied her mother to elope with in 1963, Brenda has experienced none of the agony of which her vocal performances tell. She has raised two lovely daughters and dotes on the renovation of her modest antique home in a blue-collar Nashville neighborhood. She collects doll houses and miniature furniture, loves getting autographs from other celebrities, and is an avid reader who still dreams of going to college someday. Where on earth did that volcano of musical emotion erupt from?

"I don't know how I get inside those songs and do those lyrics. It's just something. 'Break It to Me Gently' and 'All Alone Am I' and 'Fool #1' and all those kinds of songs that were so gut-wrenching, I don't know where that came from that I could do that kind of material. Because I didn't experience that in my own life. I think it's something that just comes naturally. I'm basically an emotional person, and that emotion comes across in my songs.

"I can't be pretty and sing. You know, I'm not one of those girls who can stand up there and not sweat and look beautiful. I made up my mind on that a long time ago. I mean, I'm not very feminine. . . . But you have to make up your mind and say, 'This is how I am going to be accepted, because this other role doesn't fit me.' I could never just stand there and look good. It's hard when you're four foot nine. What I do comes from just the love of singing. All of the other is secondary."

A true international celebrity, Brenda has recorded hits in Spanish, Japanese, Italian, German, French, and English. She's been nominated for four Grammy Awards and given the Recording Academy's Governor's Award in Music City. She ranks fourth behind The Beatles, Elvis, and The Supremes as America's most successful chart act of the 1960s. Britain's *New Music Express* voted her the world's top female vocalist every year from 1961 through 1965. But the titan-voiced Brenda Lee has never thought of herself as a queen.

"Well, I was . . . a world star in that time period," she reflects. "I feel like being from Nashville and my values and what I was raised with probably kept me from obtaining the heights that someone like Judy Garland did. But they also kept me from going into the depths, too. So you have to weigh one against the other. In a way Nashville saved me. I could come back here and just be who I am."

Even today Brenda doesn't seem to realize she's achieved the artistic stature and surpassed the sales of her heroines Judy, Sophie, and Patsy. "I'm basically a pretty even-tempered person, and I am very comfortable with myself. . . . I don't know that I've ever thought of myself as being famous. As trite as that sounds, I really mean that. I'm very proud of my accomplishments and what I've been able to do. But words like 'star' and 'superstar' and all that, I think they're just words.

"I was given the opportunity to have a key role in the development of Nashville as a recording industry center. The hits that Owen and I were having in the early sixties were sort of a magnet that drew national attention to Nashville. I've always been very proud that I was in on the ground level of what later became a worldwide success story."

This Nashville Sound era was a time when a community of female country singers coalesced. Bonds of sisterhood were forged in an environment where women were striving for stardom in greater numbers than ever before. Because this took place at the barn dance and in the city that had been most resistant to females, these women supported one another personally and professionally. They understood one another's ambitions and pains. As Nashville, the Opry, and Music Row were transformed by the economic success of The Nashville Sound, so was women's position in country music.

In a broad sense The Nashville Sound can be seen as a return to country music's "feminine" side. Women are the bearers of the "heart" tradition. In folk times, mothers' songs were romance ballads, while men were associated with fiddle and drinking tunes. The Carter Family's gentle home-and-hearth repertoire of the 1920s contrasts with Jimmie Rodgers's "Rough and Rowdy Ways." The gentleness of the 1930s' "National Barn Dance" women gave way to the harsher, male-dominated sounds of honky-tonk rockabilly. But with the creamy Nashville Sound style came a resurgence of the ballad tradition, slow songs sung with intense feeling and emotional conviction.

This era, this style, brought female country music into the commercial mainstream to stay.

THE FOLK REVIVAL

Come All Ye Fair and Tender Maidens

Maybelle Carter, 1964.

Those bouffant hairdos. Those rhinestones. Those wounded, self-pitying, weepy voices. Those nakedly sentimental sagas of poverty, broken romance, barroom indiscretions, blue-collar work, and abandoned dreams.

By the 1960s country music was openly mocked by "sophisticates." Its honky-tonk histrionics were embarrassing to suburbanites, and dressed up in its slick, "respectable" Nashville Sound arrangements, modern country offended purists who preferred its raw roots and folk traditions.

A movement of young urban dwellers—increasingly educated, and increasingly alienated—went in search of authentic musical expression and rediscovered country music's folk traditions. These musicians heard authenticity and truth in the voices of Texas and Appalachia, voices that gave expression to their feelings, validity to their social concerns, and a framework to their own songs. These performers transformed folk music into American pop of the 1960s. The new troubadours began by singing the folk standards and pieces of Americana that had long been in the country repertoire, but within a very short time these folkies were imitating hillbilly and folk tunes with original compositions.

The simmering movement boiled over in late 1958 when The Kingston Trio hit Number 1 with the venerable Appalachian murder ballad "Tom Dooley." The Brothers Four ("Greenfields," 1960), The Highwaymen ("Michael Row the Boat Ashore" and "Cotton Fields," 1961), and other groups cashed in. Soon the Chad Mitchell Trio, Journeymen, Limeliters, Serendipity Singers, Smothers Brothers, Four Preps, New Christy Minstrels, and dozens of other acts made it a full-blown craze.

Nashville instantly seized on the trend. The boom brought new profits to country music as folk stars flocked to Music Row's studios to record. Promoters booked country artists onto folk festival and college campus stages, and folk songwriters provided cashbox-jingling country hits.

Another of the folk revival's contributions was a revival of interest in the bluegrass and old-time music styles that were being pushed aside by The Nashville Sound. "In those days," Emmylou Harris recalls, "you'd hear a contemporary artist like Joan Baez . . . do some of the old Carter Family songs, and then you'd go get the original stuff. God, the first time I heard the Carters sing 'Gold Watch and Chain,' I thought about my grandparents and I cried." In sending young collegiate performers back to old-time sounds, the folk revival movement reeducated America about its country music heritage.

In so doing, it gave veteran country entertainers new careers. The movement repopularized women such as Maybelle Carter, Samantha Bumgarner, Ramona Jones, and Cousin Emmy. These and other barn dance vets found a new audience by playing at folk festivals and on college campuses.

The folk revival is strongly identified with female performers. By 1962 Mary Travers's ringing alto was leading Peter, Paul and Mary into the pop Top 10. Lynne Taylor's soprano led The Rooftop Singers to the top of the charts on 1963's "Walk Right In." Beverly Bivens's rousing lead vocal propelled We Five's "You Were on My Mind" into the pop stratosphere two years later. Gale Garnett's "We'll Sing in the Sunshine" of 1964, The Singing Nun's "Dominique" of 1963, Norma Tanega's "Walkin' My Cat Named Dog" of 1966, Merilee Rush's "Angel of the Morning" of 1968, and Janis Ian's "Society's Child" of 1967 also built folk music's new popularity.

Although the movement produced many male stars (Bob Dylan, Gordon Lightfoot, Donovan, John Denver, and the like), it was the first pop music trend that numbered a nearly equal number of women among its superstars—Joan Baez, Judy Collins, Buffy Sainte-Marie, Janis Ian, Joni Mitchell, Melanie, and Odetta. And from its ranks graduated such stellar successors as Bonnie Raitt, Linda Ronstadt, Mama Cass Elliot, Emmylou Harris, and Anne Murray.

In fact, the folk revival women served as role models for an entire generation of female musicians. When you talk to female country performers of the nineties, many cite the folk movement women as their inspiration, rather than the honky-tonk heroines of the same era. Kathy Mattea, Mary-Chapin Carpenter, K.T. Oslin, Wynonna Judd, and Lacy J. Dalton are just a few of the female contemporary-country hit makers inspired by their folk revival forerunners. The women of the folk era also gave birth to "women's music" of the seventies and eighties, exemplified by acts such as Holly Near, Ginni Clemmens, Meg Christian, Teresa Trull, Chris Williamson, Willie Tyson, Lavender Jane, and Margie Adam. Several of these feminist acts turned in country music albums, notably The Deadly Nightshade and Casse Culver.

That women took part so vigorously in the folk revival movement is probably the result of several factors. American women of this era were better educated than ever before. Just one and a half million women were in college in 1940; thirty years later, seven million women were. College gave increasingly large numbers of women an experience outside of the family mold and created a culture of its own. With education came jobs and increasing independence. By the end of the sixties, 43 percent of U.S. women were in the labor force, representing a third of all workers.

More and more young women remained single, despite the still pervasive cultural ideal of marriage and family. By 1971 more than half of all women twenty years old were single, in contrast to only one-third in 1960. Women were forming new types of interpersonal relationships. Student surveys of the mid-sixties found increasing acceptance of premarital sex. And the famed "sexual revolution" of the 1960s was just one of many sociopolitical developments of the folk revival era.

Virtually all of America's contemporary political issues were identified in movements forged during this period—the environmental movement, the civil rights movement, the antiwar movement, and the women's movement. And women had central roles in all of them. Activism on these issues blossomed on college campuses between 1958 and 1969.

The American college campus was the center for the folk music revival, as well as the new politics, and the two developed hand in hand. The folk movement of the forties had emphasized unionism and welded country music to old-left politics. Musicians such as Woody Guthrie, Pete Seeger, and Sis Cunningham had used songs as weapons on behalf of coal miners, dust bowl migrants, and other oppressed working-class groups. The collegiate singers of the sixties inherited this association with progressive causes.

The first folk revival's origins lie in Bascom Lamar Lunsford's 1928

Joan Baez, 1965.

launching of the Mountain Dance and Folk Festival at Asheville, North Carolina, and in Sarah Gertrude Knott's 1934 creation of the National Folk Festival in St. Louis. Jean Thomas's American Folksong Festival was an annual event near Ashland, Kentucky, from 1932 to 1972. By the late forties and early fifties folk music was entering the U.S. cultural mainstream, aided by radio and recitals star Cynthia Gooding, by *Sing Out, Sweet Land* thespian Alma Kaye, and by such popular nightclub chanteuses as Evelyn Knight ("The Lass with the Delicate Air") and Terrea Lea ("The Gal with the Folksy Air").

Biggest of all were The Weavers, who popularized "Goodnight Irene," "Sloop John B," "Down in the Valley," "On Top of Old Smokey," and other folk favorites between 1949 and 1955. The Weavers featured the stirring lead alto of Ronnie Gilbert. This first folk revival also brought to prominence such authentic country women as Aunt Molly Jackson, Sarah Ogun Gunning, and Jean Ritchie.

Variously known as "folkniks" and "city-billies," the folk revival singers of the 1960s found their central cause in the civil rights movement. They got their rallying cry from the folk collecting of another woman. Zilphia Horton was musical director for the Highlander Folk School in Monteagle, Tennessee, from 1935 to 1956. Among her songs was an old gospel number called "I'll Overcome," which she learned in 1947 from striking North Carolina tobacco workers. Zilphia turned it into "I Will Overcome" and taught it to Pete Seeger, who modified it into "We Shall Overcome." Among the others who learned the song at Highlander was Rosa Parks, who in 1955 refused to move to the back of a bus in Montgomery, Alabama, igniting the contemporary civil rights struggle. Guy Carawan popularized "We Shall Overcome" when he participated in the 1959 Nashville sit-ins protesting segregation.

But the song's finest hour came at the 1963 Freedom March on Washington when the voice of Joan Baez led 350,000 others through its verses. That was the same occasion when Dr. Martin Luther King gave his immortal "I Have a Dream" speech. "It was a mighty day," Joan recalled in her 1987 autobiography, *And a Voice to Sing With.* "One of the medals which hangs over my own heart I awarded to myself for having been asked to sing that day. . . . I was near my beloved Dr. King when he put aside his prepared speech and let the breath of God thunder through him, and up over my head I saw freedom and all around me I heard it ring." Joan was identified with "We Shall Overcome" from then on. She became the symbol of the entire folk revival, the Joan of Arc of its politics, the conscience of the music world.

Joan Baez (b. 1941) is the daughter of a Quaker physicist of Mexican descent. Alienated from the sun-and-fun shallowness of her California high school peers and bored with formal education, Joan began playing guitar and singing folk songs as a teenager. "I was looking for something real," she said, "and those old songs seemed very pure and very real, as opposed to rock 'n' roll. . . . The music that lifted up my teenage soul was folk music." Joan enrolled at Boston University and became fascinated by the emerging coffeehouse folk scene of the Cambridge-Boston area. Roommate Debbie Green, later the wife of folk star Eric Andersen, became her folk tutor.

"Debbie taught me new songs and how to really play the guitar," Joan noted. "And we practiced duets, 'Fair and Tender Maidens' appropriately being our finest offering. . . . Debbie . . . to my constant envy and frustration, had waist-length hair. I had cut mine short just before leaving California, and now waited impatiently for it to grow out into tresses so that I could be like . . . all the fair and tender maidens in all of the long and tragic ballads."

After becoming an attraction around the Boston area, Joan made her big-time debut at the first Newport Folk Festival, the 1959 event that signaled the arrival and overwhelming popular acceptance of the new folk scene. She recorded versions of "Banks of the Ohio," "Careless Love," and other traditional tunes for a small Boston company in 1959. Her first solo album appeared in late 1960; it included "Silver Dagger," "House of the Rising Sun," and the Carter Family standards "Wildwood Flower" and "Little Moses." The Carter repertoire also aided her second effort, which included "Engine 143" as well as "Wagoner's Lad" and "Barbara Allen."

Joan was a major star by 1962 when she appeared at Carnegie Hall and made the cover of *Time* magazine. Critics raved about her "achingly pure" soprano and exotic raven-haired beauty. On her *In Concert* albums Joan maintained her Appalachian musical explorations of the early 1960s, but her performances now also included "We Shall Overcome" and Julia Ward Howe's anthem "The Battle Hymn of the Republic." And by 1964 Joan was recording contemporary country songs such as "Long Black Veil," "Satisfied Mind," and "I Still Miss Someone." Inevitably, it seems, she began recording regularly in Nashville in 1968. Her first Music City albums were her million-selling Dylan song compendium *Any Day Now;* her country offering *One Day at a Time*; and a collection called *David's Album,* dedicated to her draft-resisting husband of 1968 to 1973, David Harris.

The Queen of Folk's madonnalike singing in the rain became an indelible image of the 1969 Woodstock Festival. Joan's subsequent *Blessed Are* and *Come from the Shadows* collections were also recorded in Nashville. She finally got her Nashville hit in 1971 when the Civil War saga "The Night They Drove Old Dixie Down" scaled the charts.

Joan remained committed to social justice issues, pacifism, and political activism throughout the seventies. She opened the landmark Live Aid concert for African famine relief with "Amazing Grace" in 1985. She reemerged in Nashville in 1991 to work on a comeback album. During the sessions, protests in the disintegrating Soviet Union spurred her to broadcast to Radio Free Europe, and she sang her enduring "We Shall Overcome" for the faraway demonstrators.

Joan Baez is the most outspoken of the "fair and tender maidens." But she is by no means alone. Her confederate Judy Collins has also had a lifelong commitment to social justice. Like Joan, Judy began her career by reviving aged Appalachian ballads. Among those associated with Judy are "Maid of Constant Sorrow," "House Carpenter," and "Pretty Polly." Like Baez, she comes from an educated, middle-class family.

Born in 1939, Judy was fifteen when she heard Jo Stafford's record of "Barbara Allen" playing on the radio in Denver. "The song took my breath away," Judy wrote in her autobiography, *Trust Your Heart.* "I had to sing 'Barbara Allen.' I felt it belonged to me. . . . I got the record and learned it, accompanying myself on the piano." She was performing as a folkie by the time she married Peter Taylor and had a baby in 1958. They were the quintessential beatnik couple, she with her aquiline features, azure eyes, and ever-present guitar, he with his literature studies and philosophical bent.

"I always loved the saddest songs, and as young as I was, I already had a sense of loss in my life. I couldn't have told you what I had lost, but I knew that whatever it was, it was irreplaceable." Judy initially sang her mournful, traditional tunes to support her baby and student husband. But soon coffeehouse audiences in Denver, Chicago, Boston, and New York were clamoring to hear her. She recorded her first album in 1961. "As I listen to the songs on the album, there is an almost painful quality of nostalgia to it all," Judy wrote in a *Ms.* magazine article. "It makes me almost physically unhappy, almost as if music were the only way I could get those feelings out; the longings and dreams I had in those days." She *was* unhappy. Her career was pulling her one way, her marriage another.

She divorced in 1963 and lost custody of her son for a time because she was in psychoanalysis.

By 1963 she was adding protest songs to her repertoire—Woody Guthrie's "Deportees," Bob Dylan's "Masters of War" and "Lonesome Death of Hattie Carroll," Pete Seeger's "Turn! Turn! Turn!," and Malvina Reynolds and Barbara Dane's "It Isn't Nice," as well as the coal-mining songs of country composer Billy Edd Wheeler, "Coal Tattoo," "Red Winged Blackbird," and "The Coming of the Roads."

In those days, simply to *be* a folksinger meant you were political. The movement had its own life-style, the beginnings of the youth culture that would revolutionize American life for decades to come. Folk music was first popularized in coffeehouses, dingy, dimly lit rooms where intellectuals and alienated youths gathered to read poetry and strum guitars by the light of candles stuck in Chianti bottles. The new female style favored simplicity, a rejection of the coiffures, hair spray, and elaborate makeup that characterized mainstream fashion. To paraphrase a folk favorite of the time, black was the color of my true love's clothes. The folkies were protesting the conformity and restrictiveness of 1950s America, and the music bonded them together. Its simplicity encouraged

Judy Collins, 1966.

group participation: Everybody could and did pick up a guitar; everybody could and did sing along with the words. The sing-along get-together was called a "hootenanny," a term popularized by The Almanac Singers. The atmosphere was spiritual and communal in the midst of a Cold War climate of nuclear fear, gray-flannel-suit rigidity, and capitalist competition. This was the birth of an era of trust and love: You could recognize a fellow traveler by her clothes or her long hair. And the new community was strengthened as the folk movement became aligned with the civil rights struggle. People held hands as they sang the songs of blue-collar workers and poor people's religions. The music made you feel you could change the world.

In 1964 Judy Collins went to Mississippi to help with voter registration, beginning a life of political involvement. One memorable effort was coproducing a 1967 LP called *Save the Children* that rounded up the cream of the crop of female folkies. Janis Ian, Joan Baez, Mimi Fariña, The Pennywhistlers, Odetta, Barbara Dane, Hedy West, Malvina Reynolds, and Buffy Sainte-Marie joined Judy in peace songs against the Vietnam War on this Women's Strike for Peace effort.

In 1972, Judy Collins joined a group of women who told their stories of illegal abortions in *Ms.* magazine. "We had to speak out so that we might give women who are not as visible the courage to choose. . . . It is a question of choice, a personal matter each woman must decide for herself," she said later. "The choice for motherhood is never painless, and the choice for abortion is never easy. Like many women, I have made both." So have many, many other female entertainers, including country stars. But few have told their tales as movingly as Judy did in *Trust Your Heart.* The book also recounts her 1978 treatment for alcoholism and is candid about her drug experimentation, that other hallmark of sixties youth culture. Judy's life also reflected the era's more open sexuality. Among Judy's lovers have been actor Stacy Keach, rock star Steve Stills (who wrote "Suite: Judy Blue Eyes" about her), cinematographer Coulter Watt, and designer Louis Nelson.

Her bonds with women were equally important. Judy joined a consciousness-raising group in the early 1970s, and from it grew her award-winning, Oscar-nominated 1974 documentary *Antonia: Portrait of a Woman.* It was about Antonia Brico, the pianist/conductor who had trained her.

"My friendships with women began to fill the gap of loneliness in my life," Judy recalled, "and the political work I did eased my own sense of isolation. . . . The impact of women singers made up an enormous part of the popular folk music in the early sixties. As I look back, I can count fifteen women folksingers, and have probably forgotten a dozen more. . . . One of these women who had a great impact on my writing and my musical sensibilities was Joni Mitchell. . . . Her experience as a woman came through in her writing, and this autobiographical form . . . served as a catalyst for my own work."

Judy introduced Joni's "Michael from Mountains" and "Both Sides Now" on the landmark LP *Wildflowers,* leading to a successful recording career for the songwriter. Besides "Both Sides Now" (1968), Judy's major hits have included Ian Tyson's western tune "Someday Soon" (1969) and the sturdy 1799 country hymn "Amazing Grace" (1971). Both entered the modern country repertoire, as Judy herself attempted to do with a 1984 duet with Nashville star T. G. Sheppard called "Home Again."

As for Joni Mitchell, her songs have often entered the country field. In fact, Opry star George Hamilton IV scored a Top 10 success with Joni's "Urge for

Going" a full year before Judy Collins won a Best Folk Record Grammy Award with "Both Sides Now." Boots Randolph, Johnny Cash, and others took up Joni's tunes in the late sixties and early seventies. In 1982 Gail Davies had a big country hit with Joni's "You Turn Me On I'm a Radio."

Joni Mitchell was born Roberta Joan Anderson in the Canadian province of Alberta in 1943. She jettisoned her art studies to plunge into the Yorktown folk scene in Toronto in 1964, where she was tutored in "damsel-in-distress" ballads, as she put it: "The guy rides off and leaves her, and she throws herself into the lake."

Of all the folk revival acts, the closest to true country music performers were Ian and Sylvia. The music the Canadian team made from 1968 to 1972 in Nashville was brilliant—four LPs of shimmering harmonies, top-flight songs, and virtuoso instrumental work. But the country establishment was more than a little ambivalent about folkies. For years Nashville had endured insults and denigration from pop music sophisticates, and now pop fugitives like Ian and Sylvia, Bob Dylan, Joan Baez, The Byrds, Neil Young, and Buffy Sainte-Marie were recording in its midst, saying how much they respected country culture. Music Row took the compliments, the folkies' songs, and the recording-studio money, but closed its radio charts to the outsiders.

"It appears in retrospect that we were ahead of our time," Sylvia once observed in *Rolling Stone,* "but that doesn't make any difference when you don't sell records." Ian's "Four Strong Winds" became a 1965 country smash for Bobby Bare, and "Someday Soon" hit the country Top 10 for Suzy Bogguss in 1991. Sylvia's "You Were on My Mind" was a 1965 We Five pop hit and a 1971 Bobby Penn country single. Crystal Gayle popularized her "River Road" in 1980.

They were quite a team. Ian Tyson, born in 1933, was a for-real rodeo rider, migrant worker, and lumberjack from British Columbia. Sylvia Fricker, born in 1940, was from the small farm town of Chatham, Ontario, where her mother was the church organist and choir leader. Sylvia was a bookish, quiet girl who memorized folk songs and dreamed of escaping rural life.

"It's a lousy place to be an adolescent in. I wanted to be a folksinger from the time I was about fifteen," Sylvia recalls. After high school she moved to Toronto and spent her days clerking in a clothing store and her nights singing in folk clubs. At one of them the willowy brunet met the handsome cowboy. They began harmonizing in 1959.

The Canadian folk duo Ian and Sylvia was the most countrified of all the folk-revival acts of the 1960s. This LP appeared in 1965.

In 1961 they booked their first U.S. concert, a cotillion ball in South Carolina. "They didn't dig us," recalled Sylvia. "They found us a little raw. They wanted The Kingston Trio. Our music had a mountain flavor to it. They said, 'I don't want to hear that stuff. My grandmother sings it. That's not folk music.'" Heading for New York, Ian and Sylvia landed a recording contract and issued their debut LP in 1962. It was laced with traditional material like "Handsome Molly" and "Down by the Willow Garden." By the time of their second album, in 1964, they were married and writing songs.

Ian and Sylvia incorporated bluegrass, French Canadian, traditional ballad, cowboy, and pop material into their songbag, mixing together everything from their own compositions to Johnny Cash's "Come In Stranger" and Gene Pitney's "24 Hours from Tulsa." By 1966 they were major folk celebrities, inspiring a similar team, Jim and Jean (Glover).

The raw feeling in their delivery, evocative nasality, and untutored vocal honesty led Ian and Sylvia inexorably toward country music as the decade wore on. They arrived in Music City for 1968's LP *Nashville*. "Actually, I think the pickers were a little disappointed that some of our material was so country, because they were looking forward to playing some really far-out stuff," she recalls. "We were looking for country music."

The succeeding LPs *Full Circle, Great Speckled Bird,* and *Ian and Sylvia* remain their country masterpieces. Ian provided stirring western-themed material such as "Rio Grande," "Summer Wages," and "Some Kind of Fool." Sylvia blossomed as a country composer with "Smiling Wine," "Woman's World," "Shinbone Alley," and the inspirational "We Sail." Together, they penned stunning heartache material like "I Learned from Leah." They hit the road with a fine country-rock band called Great Speckled Bird. But country audiences ignored the outfit, and folk fans rejected the new style. "People even got up and walked out," Sylvia recalled ruefully. "They would have a violent reaction to the steel guitar. They'd walk out on the first bars that the steel player would hit." Dispirited, they returned to Toronto. Ian was busted for marijuana possession in 1972, effectively preventing the team from staging any further forays into the United States.

They did a popular Canadian TV show for several years called "Nashville North," then grew apart in the late 1970s. Sylvia hosted the "Touch the Earth" folk music radio series on Canada's national CBC network from 1977 to 1982, did a TV series from 1983 to 1984 called "Country in My Soul," formed her own Salt Records label, and organized the 1984 "Classic Country" Canadian network TV special, performing with Emmylou Harris, the Whites, and Shelly West. Ian and Sylvia were amicably divorced by the mid-eighties, but reunited for a Toronto concert in 1986 with admirers Emmylou, Linda Ronstadt, and Judy Collins.

Sylvia Tyson's Nashville experience was echoed by Buffy Sainte-Marie, who both lived and recorded in the country capital in the late sixties and early seventies. Along with Joan Baez's *One Day at a Time,* Bob Dylan's *Nashville Skyline,* and the Ian and Sylvia albums, Buffy's 1968 LP *I'm Gonna Be a Country Girl Again* ranks as one of the finest country records ever produced by a folkie. Like the others, it was rejected by the commercial country music community, which simultaneously embraced her as a songwriter.

She was born in 1941 of Cree Indian parents on a reservation in Saskatchewan, Canada, and raised in New England by the family who adopted her. After college Buffy Sainte-Marie was captivated by the bohemian coffeehouse scene of Greenwich Village. Her debut LP, *It's My Way!,* appeared in 1964, and Buffy's striking looks, use of the native American mouth-bow, penetrating vocal vibrato, and strong protest material attracted immediate national attention. The fiercely antiwar "Universal Soldier" emerged as the biggest song from that first LP.

Although it is strongly identified with her work, protest material represents only a small part of Buffy's song output. Her achingly wistful love ballad "Until It's Time for You to Go" became a big number for Elvis Presley, Cher, Neil Diamond, and many others. In the country field, Bobby Bare popularized Buffy's "The Piney Wood Hills" (1967), George Hamilton IV recorded "Take My Hand for Awhile" (1968), and Glen Campbell sang "Universal Soldier" (1965).

Buffy arrived in Nashville in 1968, crafting

WOMEN'S WORK (1988)—Linda Allen (includes "Rosie the Riveter Revisited," "After School," "Night Charge Nurse")

Buffy Sainte-Marie, 1967.

I'm Gonna Be a Country Girl Again there, as well as her next six LPs. The disc contained a clutch of heart-stopping female country songs, including "A Soulful Shade of Blue," "Take My Hand for Awhile," "He's a Pretty Good Man If You Ask Me," and "Gonna Feel Much Better When You're Gone." She moved to Music City in 1975 and set her sights on pop stardom. Her Nashville-recorded rocker "Mister Can't You See" was a Top 40 hit. Buffy's stock as a songwriter continued to rise, culminating with a 1982 Academy Award for the song she cowrote for *An Officer and a Gentleman*, "Up Where We Belong."

Buffy Sainte-Marie's fame also rose as a result of television. She spent five years as a regular on the famed children's TV show "Sesame Street." The exposure allowed her to introduce native American culture to toddlers.

Children's music became a big outlet for many of the folk revival women. Jean Ritchie, Peggy Seeger, Maria Muldaur, and Malvina Reynolds are just four of the many who have marketed kiddie tunes.

Janis Ian was practically a kid herself when thrust into the folk-star limelight with her 1967 saga of interracial love, "Society's Child." Born Janis Eddy Fink in 1951, she was a child prodigy in New Jersey who played piano at age three, picked up guitar at age eleven, wrote songs at twelve, and performed professionally at thirteen. "Society's Child" created a furor when it was originally released in the politically charged climate of 1966. Controversy swirled around the cocky teenager.

"It was pretty traumatic all around," Janis recalls. "I did a lot of dope, said a lot of tearful good-byes." By age nineteen she was a has-been. But in 1973 she wrote the hit "Jesse" for Roberta Flack. It entered the country field in versions by Dottie West, Margo Smith, and Diana Trask. The title tune of 1974's *Stars* was picked up by Glen Campbell, Cher, and several others. Then Janis capped her Grammy Award–winning comeback with "At Seventeen," popularized in Nashville by Anita Kerr. This massively popular, "everyteen" ugly-duckling saga signaled her feminist awakening. "It never occurred to me as a kid that there was anything I couldn't be—an astronaut, the president, whatever—I somehow avoided the message that a woman couldn't do this or that," Janis recalls. "I only started running into the 'female' stuff when I hit my twenties and started working with a lot more musicians, mediocre players who had problems working with a woman who was as good as they were and better." Her instrumental abilities are every bit as strong as her singing and songwriting. "I get told a lot, 'You play like a guy.' I'm never quite sure I know what they're talking about. . . . I write, score, arrange, play, and lead a band. How many other women do you see doing that?"

In 1982 Janis won another Grammy as part of the all-star children's album *In Harmony II*. But again she hit rough waters. Her 1978–1988 marriage to Portuguese writer/producer Tino Sargo ended in a mess when he sued for support. Bad business management left her deeply in debt to the IRS, which seized all her property and sold it. Her recording career foundered anew. Desperate for funds, she attempted a comeback tour in 1986. "I managed to do New York and L.A. and then wound up in a hospital in Miami with a burst intestine. Oh, it was awful. I was lying there with five strangers saying they were gonna operate on me. . . . They said, 'You have forty-five minutes and then you're dead.'" She came to Nashville to convalesce under the care of songwriter Kye Fleming and other women.

Alone among the folk revival's female superstars, Janis Ian chose to settle in Music City; and her songs have been recorded by the community's Amy Grant, Kathy Mattea, and Chet Atkins, among others. Janis embarked on another comeback as the eighties drew to a close. She became an AIDS activist, raising more than forty-five thousand dollars in 1989 for research. Her health intervened again when she was diagnosed with Epstein-Barr, a debilitating mono-type virus, but she resumed singing and writing, appearing on the soundtrack of the 1992 John Mellencamp country movie *Falling from Grace*.

During its heyday, the folk revival was full of maidens of song. The long-haired, unadorned, but captivating young women of the folk revival projected that innocence with strength and beauty. Rebels, yes, but alluringly feminine. And audiences, male and female, idolized the young women performers. These were the first female role models in youth culture who projected intelligence and independence. Carolyn Hester, Melanie, Judy Henske, Jeanie West, and Mary McCaslin were just a few who flowered between 1960 and 1975. There were even a number of all-female acts, The Womenfolk, The Pennywhistlers, and Charley's Aunts among them.

The new image for music women spread to England, too. Marianne Faithfull exemplified the folk revival there with her 1964–1965 performances of "As Tears Go By," "Come and Stay with Me," and "This Little Bird." Judith Durham's robust delivery of "A World of Our Own" and "I'll Never Find Another You" brought The Seekers fame on both sides of the Atlantic in 1965. Dusty Springfield began her hit-making career by leading The Springfields on the female-country classic "Silver Threads and Golden Needles" in 1962; and her group traveled across the ocean to Nashville to record its *Folk Songs from the Hills* LP the following year. Mary Hopkin's "Those Were the Days" and "Goodbye" of 1968 and 1969 were also in the British folk revival mode. One of Olivia Newton-John's first

GINNI CLEMMENS

CATHY FINK

"UNCLE RUTHIE" BUELL

MALVINA REYNOLDS

The folk revival not only
thrust dozens of women
forward as stars, it
created the first large
group of female music
entrepreneurs and bus-
iness figures. Among the
notable:

MALVINA
REYNOLDS—Cas-
sandra Records

BARBARA DANE—
Paredon Records

MARIAN LEIGHTON—
Rounder Records

CAROLYN PATON—
Folk-Legacy Records

AGNES "SIS" CUN-
NINGHAM—
Broadside magazine

ALICE GERRARD—Old
Time Herald magazine

MARSHA
NECHELES—
Folkscene magazine

GERRY ARM-
STRONG—The Old
Town School of Folk
Music

LENA SPENCER—
Caffé Lena

JEAN COSTNER
SCHILLING—The
Folk Life Center of
the Smokies, The Folk
Festival of the
Smokies

MAUD GODSHALL—
The Philadelphia Folk
Festival

English hits was the American murder ballad "Banks of the Ohio" in 1971.

Back in the United States, The Simon Sisters introduced alto Carly Simon, later a seventies star and, from 1972 to 1981, wife of troubadour James Taylor. The rollicking Even Dozen Jug Band introduced the petite, vivacious warbler Maria Muldaur in 1963. A year later she joined the Jim Kweskin Jug Band and began stealing its shows with her sprightly fiddling, gypsy image, and saucy rendition of "I'm a Woman." "I was singing along with Kitty Wells and Hank Williams when I was five years old," says the New York native born in 1942. "I learned to play country fiddle and to frail a banjo. But that was just one stop in my odyssey through American music."

Maria's eclectic repertoire was characteristic of several other folk revival women, notably Tracy Nelson, Odetta, and Barbara Dane. Odetta Holmes Felious, known throughout her life simply by her first name, was born in Birmingham, Alabama, in 1930. She emerged on the California folk scene of the 1950s. Her powerful dignity of tone, warmth of presentation, and deep contralto range were first heard on disc in 1956. Easily the most important black female star of the folk movement, she recorded Appalachian material on such albums as *Odetta Sings Folk Songs* (1963) and *Ballad for Americans* (1965). Her lumberjack-mule song "Timber" has long been a staple in the concerts of country star Kathy Mattea; country stylist Rattlesnake Annie McGowan has sung with her; and Odetta turned to country recording, herself, with Nashville sessions in 1984 and 1986.

The trailblazer to Music City was blues mama Tracy Nelson, the first pop star of the sixties to relocate to the country capital. Although initially rejected like most of her folk peers, she eventually achieved Nashville fame. Her 1974 "After the Fire Is Gone" duet with Willie Nelson (no relation) got a Grammy nomination; Bonnie Raitt recorded her song "I Could Have Been Your Best Friend"; Linda Ronstadt popularized her signature tune "Down So Low"; and numerous Nashvillians hired her as a session singer.

Born in 1944, Tracy was a student and coffeehouse singer at the University of Wisconsin when she made her 1965 record debut with the folk-blues collection *Deep Are the Roots.* Tracy made the pilgrimage to San Francisco during the peak of the hippie era, 1966 to 1968. "I thought the whole situation out there then was just appalling," recalled the blunt, outspoken singer. "It was sick and weird and stupid, and the people were arrogant. I didn't like anything about it." She formed the rock band Mother Earth there, then set out to tour in support of its 1968 debut LP. A stopover in Nashville became permanent when she bought a farm outside town. *Mother Earth Presents Tracy Nelson Country* appeared in 1971. "Stand by Your Man," "I Fall to Pieces," and its other country standards were revolutionized by her flamethrower delivery. Her collections of 1973 to 1976 included such country fare as "I'll Be Your Baby Tonight," "Can You Fool," and "Couldn't Do Nothing Right."

Like the other folk revival graduates of her generation, Tracy Nelson was perceived as a hippie outsider by the conservative country community of the day. And her aggression and independence were in distinct contrast to the demure "country sweetheart" image that was expected. She was a fearsome presence in concert, with a tigress temper that matched her torrid vocals. But she mellowed in the eighties, gaining new popularity with club tours, jingles, albums, and appearances on The Nashville Network cable TV channel. Tracy's thunderous alto can be heard above the all-star country chorus on The Nitty Gritty Dirt Band's *Will the Circle Be Unbroken Vol. 2* of 1989.

Barbara Dane is just as fiercely independent as Tracy Nelson or Odetta, and a good deal more politically radical. Barbara turned her back on the commercial folk stardom that almost certainly would have been hers to sing in Cuba and North Vietnam, battle on union picket lines, work in the GI resistance movement, and make leftist music for people's liberation. "You can't make revolutions without songs," she said.

Barbara's parents were Arkansas natives who participated in the great migration of Southerners to the North between the world wars. Born Barbara Spillman in 1927, she went to work in Detroit factories as a teenager and learned her first folk songs during an auto workers' strike in 1946. She moved to San Francisco in 1949, supporting three children with department store and door-to-door sales jobs. Around 1955 she worked up a jazz nightclub act, opened for hipster comics Lenny Bruce and Mort Sahl, and recorded for such mainstream companies as Dot and Capitol.

Barbara Dane left pop to return to folksinging, becoming a regular at San Francisco's then-new Ash Grove in 1958. She started KGO-TV's "Folksville U.S.A.," America's first folk TV series, and starred on KPFA radio. In 1959 she recorded a collection of such female folk favorites as "Single Girl," "Little Maggie," and "Who's Gonna Shoe Your Pretty Little Foot." Barbara starred at the first Newport Folk Festival in 1959, a blond fair-young-damsel vision, complete with full skirt and guitar.

Like Joan Baez, Carolyn Hester, and others, Barbara Dane rejected the national "Hootenanny" ABC TV show because it blacklisted Pete Seeger.

Anne Romaine—Tennessee Grassroots Days

Louise Scruggs—management, booking, publishing, and financial magnate for Flatt & Scruggs

Nancy Talbott—The Boston Friends of Bluegrass and Old-Time Country Music, The Berkshire Mountain Festival

Margaret Winters Moore—*How to Play the Dulcimer* instructional book

Seen here at the start of her career in 1959, Barbara Dane eventually became the most politically radical of the folk females.

By the mid-sixties she'd dropped out of commercial music completely to tour Mississippi during Freedom Summer, sing at Berkeley during the Free Speech Movement, and organize the 1965 Sing-In for Peace at Carnegie Hall. Thereafter she devoted her full energies to the antiwar effort. Barbara formed her Paredon Records label to distribute political music such as Beverly Grant's *Working People Gonna Rise!* LP of 1975 and Barbara's own *FTA/Songs of the G.I. Resistance* (1973) and *I Hate the Capitalist System* (1974). The latter contained Sarah Ogun Gunning's title tune, The Carter Family's "Single Girl," and Barbara's own "Working Class Woman."

The folk revival era was full of distinctive, compelling female personalities like Barbara Dane. Icily beautiful Nancy Ames was a TV star from 1964 to 1965 as the dry, biting folkie who introduced the sharp-pointed songs of Tom Lehrer on "That Was the Week That Was," television's pioneering political satire show. Gutsy, independent Rosalie Sorrels began her career singing *Folk Songs of Idaho and Utah* in 1961, but didn't hit her stride until after her divorce in 1966. Alice Stuart trod a similar path, first recording as a folkie on 1964's *All the Good Times,* but blossoming musically after her divorce about four years later. Both women evolved into strongly assertive female songwriting voices, Rosalie remaining in the folk tradition as "The Travelin' Lady," and wild-haired Alice entering the rock world.

One of the most unforgettable personalities of all was grandmotherly Malvina Reynolds (1901–1978). She was a late-blooming California mother, steelworker, newspaperwoman, teacher, and social worker who left behind a potent group of topical songs, among them "What Have They Done to the Rain," "Little Boxes," and "God Bless the Grass." They called her "Mama Lion," for she was the matriarch of the whole folk revival brood.

Malvina was in her sixties when she began to perform. Folk superstar Pete Seeger's sole appearance on the pop charts was with Malvina's "Little Boxes" (1964), a song criticizing suburbia that made the expression "ticky tacky" part of the language. The Seekers scored a British hit with her "Morningtown Ride" in 1966. Dick and Dee Dee popularized "Turn Around" in 1963, and the song went on to serve as a sweetly sentimental Kodak camera jingle. The antinuclear/environmental "What Have They Done to the Rain" became the most widespread of Malvina's songs among folkies, entering the repertoires of Joan Baez, Marianne Faithfull, Judy Collins, and legions of others. Malvina probably wrote the first modern feminist anthem with 1956's "We Don't Need the Men." At any rate, the consciousness-raising women of the seventies enthusiastically embraced the number.

Like Malvina, many of the folk boom's female performers became feminists, and some began to emphasize women's cultural history. Peggy

Seeger, born in 1935, recorded *Folk Songs of Courting and Complaint* in 1955, one of the earliest compilations of women's traditional songs. In 1976 she contributed another landmark, *Penelope Isn't Waiting Anymore: An Album of Women's Songs.* Katie Lee (Vozack), born in 1919, compiled the 1975 *Love's Little Sisters* LP of folk songs about prostitutes.

Hedy West's work chronicles the songs of the "lower class," as she puts it, "specifically from and about farm workers, mill hands, and miners." She is the folk revivalist who has sung most about blue-collar women. Running throughout her recorded work is the theme of working-class protest, as expressed in "Come All Ye Lewiston Factory Girls," "Whore's Lament," "Pity Me All Day," "The Coal Miner's Child," "Cotton Mill Girls," and many other songs in her repertoire. Unlike most of her peers, Hedy West is authentically "country." Born in 1938, she is the daughter of a Georgia union organizer and the granddaughter of a mountain balladeer. Hedy went to New York to go to college in 1959, but her ballad singing, banjo playing, and natural southern ways charmed the folkies, who began to record her in 1961. Hedy cowrote Bobby Bare's giant 1963 country and pop hit "500 Miles Away from Home."

Hedy West says she sings the songs of the "lower class." The Georgia native is pictured here in 1967.

Kathy Kahn's *The Working Girl: Women's Songs from the Mountains, Mines and Mills* echoed Hedy West's and Peggy Seeger's work. It accompanied Kathy's eloquent 1972 book of Appalachian heroines, *Hillbilly Women.* "One promoter called me . . . and told me he could get me a recording contract if I'd just keep my political messages to myself and let him 'sell' me as a 'girl singer,'" Kathy related in a *Country Music* magazine article of 1974. "Well, I'm a singer, and I'm a woman, and I'm political. It's part of who I am. . . . I never perform a song unless I believe in its message."

Thanks to the folk revival, a whole string of albums has documented the history of women's music. In addition to these building blocks of women's history, the folk movement left other lasting impressions on the female music scene. A side effect of its festivals, coffeehouses, publications, and record companies was a certain song-poet climate that nurtured such later performers as Suzanne Vega, Tracy Chapman, The Roches, Kate and Anna McGarrigle, The Indigo Girls, Shawn Colvin, and Christine Lavin. Female troubadours appeared in

OUR FAVORITE FOLK SONGS
RCA VICTOR
THE BROWNS
FEATURING JIM EDWARD BROWN

From left are Bonnie, Jim Ed, and Maxine Brown, Nashville's most successful folk-revival stars. The Browns issued this collection of folk standards in 1961.

popular music throughout the succeeding decades.

The impact of the folk revival wasn't a bit lost on the country community, which soon encouraged a group of young women to explore the market. Marijohn Wilkin, the Nashville composer of the folk standard "Long Black Veil," recorded a 1960 collection of Civil War songs called *Ballads of the Blue and Gray.* Rose Lee Maphis posed as a folkie on her debut LP in 1960, and Jody Miller was introduced as one on her 1963 debut. Anita Kerr Singers member Winifred Smith entered the ranks of the "fair and tender maidens" with three LPs of southern folk songs. Starday Records signed Kentucky's A. L. Phipps Family to re-create the folk Carter Family sound in 1962. Teen folkie Cathie Taylor was rewarded for her 1965 folk LP with the Most Promising Female Vocalist award from the Academy of Country Music in Los Angeles. Sometime Nashville recording artist Connie Francis donned denims and a bandanna for *Connie Sings Folk Favorites.* Melba Montgomery and George Jones's splendid 1964 duet LP was *Bluegrass Hootenanny.*

The artistic triumph of country folk was scored by Anita Carter. Maybelle's youngest daughter brought The Carter Family tradition up to date with the albums *Anita Carter* and *Anita Carter Sings Folk Songs* in 1963 and 1964. They are the equal of anything Joan Baez or Judy Collins did during the same period, featuring Anita's yearning, mountain-air soprano on "I Never Will Marry," "Fair and Tender Ladies," and some of the loveliest songs of the Carter heritage.

The commercial triumph belonged to Maxine and Bonnie Brown. As the sighing, pitch-perfect harmony behind their lead vocalist brother Jim Ed, they made The Browns Nashville's top folk revival act. The Browns were Arkansas natives, a saw mill owner's children who'd sung together since childhood. Maxine (b. 1932) and her younger brother initially worked together as a duet. Little sister Bonnie (b. 1937) joined to fill out the group's liquid harmony in 1955.

Huge hit singles like "The Three Bells," "Scarlet Ribbons," and "The Old Lamplighter" made the trio one of the most successful folk acts in America in 1959 and 1960. They continued to mine the style by recording popular versions of "Shenandoah," "You Can't Grow Peaches on a Cherry Tree," and other folk melodies in the sixties, as well as such albums as *Our Favorite Folk Songs* (1961). Their lovely trio harmonies also graced revivals of "Wildwood Flower," "My Adobe Hacienda," and "Down in the Valley." The Browns moved from the "Louisiana Hayride" and "Ozark Jubilee" to the network TV shows of Ed Sullivan, Perry Como, and Dick Clark, then graduated to "The Grand Ole Opry" in 1963. But they stunned the crowd at the 1967 Opry Birthday Celebration when Bonnie tearfully announced that it would be their last show together. She and Maxine wanted to get off the road and raise their families. Maxine occasionally recorded solo in the 1970s. The salty, good-humored alto announced in 1990 that she's writing her memoirs.

The folk spotlight also shone on The Stonemans in Nashville. Ernest "Pop" Stoneman was a country recording pioneer of the early 1920s. He and his wife, Hattie, raised fifteen children, all of them musical. Ground into poverty during the Depression, the family staged a comeback in the 1950s as folk stars. Daughters Patsy (autoharp, b. 1925), Donna (mandolin, b. 1934), and Roni (banjo, b. 1935) and sons Scotty, Van, and Jimmy emerged as the Stoneman clan's second-generation stars. In 1956 they were winners on "Arthur Godfrey's Talent Scouts." Folk revivalist Mike Seeger produced their comeback LP in 1957. With Donna's sprightly country dancing, Roni's madcap comedy, Pop's storehouse of traditional music, and the whole clan's instrumental abilities, The Stonemans wowed 'em on the folk circuit. They played everywhere from the Monterey Folk Festival to the Smithsonian Institution. Usually recording in a souped-up bluegrassy style, the increasingly female-led family band turned out a plethora of albums.

Anita Carter, 1966.

They settled in Nashville in 1966, began placing singles on the country charts, and had their own syndicated TV show, "Those Stonemans," from 1966 to 1967. The Stoneman Family was named Vocal Group of the Year by the Country Music Association in 1967. The act's records combined traditional folk material, new folkies' songs, bluegrass numbers, and modern Nashville compositions, effectively summarizing the whole folk revival era.

Roni and Donna initially performed alongside Pop, while Patsy led her own band. After Pop's death in 1968 Patsy joined her sisters. Roni became a comedy/banjo star on TV's "Hee Haw," withdrawing from the act in 1973 to portray the gap-toothed hillbilly harridan "Ida Lee" on the long-running show. "Marjorie Main, who played Ma Kettle, was my

favorite actress when I was growing up," Roni says. "Most girls my age liked Esther Williams and glamorous stars like that. But I liked Marjorie Main because she reminded me of the Stonemans. I learned to talk like Marjorie Main. I learned every inflection of her voice." A 1981 double LP called *The First Family of Country Music* reunited nine of the children and their off-spring and received wide acclaim for its old-time repertoire.

"I just don't want people to forget us," Patsy says. "The history of The Stonemans and our music should not be forgotten. I am not ready to hang up our instruments yet. We have too much to offer to just throw up our hands. Besides, we have been in this business longer than anyone else; and it just wouldn't be fair to Daddy to stop."

As the folk revival movement gained momentum, more and more country music women began appearing at festivals. During the late 1950s and early 1960s, collegiate folk fans embraced the historic country sounds of Samantha Bumgarner, Lily May Ledford, Cousin Emmy, and Wilma Lee Cooper, as well as the traditional ballads of such matriarchs as Almeda Riddle, Sara Cleveland, Aunt Ollie Gilbert, and Jean Ritchie.

Jean Ritchie, in particular, was a folk revival touchstone, for she understood the world of the academics, as well as the world of the mountains. Born in 1922, Jean is the youngest of the fourteen Ritchie children of Viper, Kentucky. She learned dulcimer playing and traditional ballads in her mountain home before attending Cumberland College and the University of Kentucky. With a degree in social work, Jean moved to New York in 1946, and by 1949 she was a folk music favorite there and a regular on the WNYC radio show "Folksong Festival."

She made her professional recording debut in 1952 and began publishing her series of folk music books three years later. She starred at the Newport Folk Festival in 1959 and four years after that joined its board of directors. After a string of more than thirty LPs, she had a burst of renewed creativity on 1977's *None but One.* Recorded with country instrumentation, it included harmonies by Janis Ian and Mary Travers, as well as such original compositions as the protest "Black Waters" and the gentle ballad "Sweet Sorrow in the Wind," which was later recorded by

Emmylou Harris. On the famed *Trio* LP, Emmylou, Dolly Parton, and Linda Ronstadt sang Jean's "My Dear Companion." Jean Ritchie continues to record on her own Greenhays label, and she played Patrick Swayze's aunt in the 1991 movie *Next of Kin.*

"I was never on top of the [folk revival] boom," Jean once reflected. "I really detest the star system. I didn't want to be a star. . . . One great thing about the folk music field is that the older you get, the more admired and revered you are, instead of having to keep young and beautiful. . . . People such as Lily May Ledford and myself can grow older and become grand old dames, and it's great!"

Several of the country music women adopted by folkies actually became bigger stars among collegiates than they'd ever been on the hillbilly circuit. That was particularly true of Ola Belle Reed, Ina Patterson, Janette Carter, and Hazel Dickens. And Patsy Stoneman and Ramona Jones were at least as big among folkies as they were among country fans.

Mountain singer Ola Belle Reed, born in North Carolina in 1916, had knocked around the Maryland/Pennsylvania countryside for years before her elevation to folk-star stature. After beginning her banjo-playing career in the late 1940s, she formed The New River Boys with her brother Alec. West Virginia's fifty-thousand-watt WWVA began broadcasting Ola Belle's performances in the sixties, and that's how the folk revivalists heard her. Ola Belle's later records were on such folk labels as Folkways and Rounder. They are the best known of her career and expressed her strong feelings for the poor and downtrodden. In 1993 Marty Stuart turned Ola Belle's "High on a Mountain Top" into a major country hit.

"I got my education mostly out of life," she says. "I think that's why people took so to my music. It's straight out of life." The folk revival was about "people recognizing that the hillbilly way of life is respectable. I like to believe they're saying to us . . . that we're part of humanity, too."

Ina Patterson, born in 1929, and her husband, Ray, are natives of the Southwest, but their charming duet sound recalls the soft family-harmony ambience of the southeastern mountain acts of the thirties such as The Delmore Brothers and The Blue Sky Boys. Folk

Jean Ritchie pauses during Oscar Brand's radio show in 1948 with her fellow folk-revival founders Woody Guthrie, left, Fred Hellerman, and Pete Seeger.

revivalists flipped when they heard the couple's preserved-in-amber renditions of antique parlor songs and southern gospel favorites of days gone by. The Pattersons were captured on a series of popular folk LPs beginning in 1966 and showcased at the San Diego Folk Festival, the Colorado Rocky Mountain Bluegrass Festival, and other events.

"It is hard for us to put into words the way we feel about these old-time songs," Ina says, "for they seem to cover the past, present, and future, and describe the feelings of the common person of past generations. Folk songs tell of individual feelings that cannot be found in history books."

Hazel Dickens subscribes to this "common person" philosophy, as well. And like Ina Patterson, she steadfastly refused to alter her old-time, backwoods delivery to suit modern country tastes. She, too, kicked around on the small-potatoes country circuit before finding folk fame.

Hazel attended the school of hard knocks growing up one of eleven children in the coal camps in the West Virginia hollows. Born during the Great Depression, she left home at sixteen and cleaned houses until she was old enough to go to work in a textile mill, tin can factory, electric-iron plant, paper cup factory, restaurant, and department store in the early 1950s. Inspired by a burgeoning bluegrass scene, she began to sing in the country bars and bluegrass clubs of Baltimore and Washington, D.C. When she married and divorced, she made the choice that would change her life. "The first thing my father said when I got married was, 'Well, I don't guess you'll be playing anymore now.' That was a very hard thing for me to cope with, to still continue with the music and be what I thought was a good wife. . . . I feel that women have been really repressed. . . . This role of being the chief cook and bottle washer, have the kids and stay at home—I think it's just too much to expect of a human being. I didn't know exactly what I wanted to do, but I knew that I wanted to do something, have more of an identity."

Folk revivalists Alice Gerrard and Mike Seeger were infatuated with old-time country sounds. When they heard Hazel singing in 1955, the music they'd heard on old 78s and Library of Congress tapes "was brought to life," as Alice later put it. Hazel and Alice began to sing together in 1962. Mountaineer Hazel and college-educated Alice made an odd pair, but the music they created together was extraordinary.

They first recorded in 1967, but the duo's most influential recordings appeared on Rounder Records in 1973 and 1975. By then, they'd honed their rustic, spine-tingling delivery to a sharp emotional point. Alice moaned the melodies, while Hazel wailed above in bluegrass harmony. On the early albums, they'd concentrated on old-timey fare. Now they augmented Wilma Lee Cooper's "Tomorrow I'll Be Gone," The Coon Creek Girls' "Banjo Picking Girl," and The Carter Family's "Hello Stranger" with their nervy original tunes, notably Alice's "Custom Made Woman's Blues" and Hazel's "Don't Put Her Down, You Helped Put Her There" and "Working Girl Blues."

Their sound electrified the folk world, and women, in particular, were inspired by their example. Somewhat reluctantly, Hazel and Alice were elevated to cult figures by women's-music exponents in the seventies. Their sound even created ripples in mainstream country music. Emmylou Harris picked up their arrangement of "Hello Stranger." The New Riders of the Purple Sage recorded "Don't Put Her Down." Exene Cervenka, generally associated with rock, turned in a countrified rendition of Hazel's "Will Jesus Wash the Bloodstains from Your Hand." And Naomi Judd was inspired by Hazel and Alice's version of "The Sweetest Gift (A Mother's Smile)" to begin harmonizing with her daughter Wynonna.

Hazel was recruited for the soundtrack of Barbara Koppel's Oscar-winning 1976 documentary *Harlan County U.S.A.*, contributing "Black Lung" and "They'll Never Keep Us Down" to the film. In the 1987 movie *Matewan*, Hazel appeared as a singing evangelist. Her piercing, craggy, stark, and utterly compelling voice has also been showcased on a series of solo albums. She feels the folk revivalists validated her culture and gave her a respect that was denied by mainstream America. "When I met a lot of these people who didn't look down on what I came from and musically what I was trying to do, I think that really sustained me," Hazel told one interviewer.

While not as obscure as Hazel Dickens prior to the folk revival, Ramona Jones was chiefly known as a backing musician until the folkies applauded her old-time fiddling skills. She entered the world as Ramona Riggins in 1925 in rural Indiana and was certain by the time she was a teenager that she wanted to be a professional musician. She first attracted attention in 1942 as a member of Sunshine Sue's band at WRVA in Richmond, Virginia, then in the all-female group The Harmony Girls at

Hazel Dickens, 1980.

WLW in Cincinnati. Female band members were rare then, but Ramona's skills kept her working steadily. She joined The Bailes Brothers troupe and relocated to the Opry in Nashville.

"People would comment on the fact that I was a woman fiddler," Ramona once recalled to scholar Charles K. Wolfe. "I always heard, 'Boy, she's good for a girl.' . . . Back then, when I was starting, The Coon Creek Girls were the only other girls well known that played instruments much like I did. . . . I really think people frowned on you playing. . . . You'd get on a bus with a fiddle, and they'd sort of stand back and size you up. . . . And I sort of resented that. . . . They couldn't hardly accept a girl traveling around playing an instrument."

She married Grandpa Jones in 1946 and was soon recording as his bassist, mandolinist, fiddler, and duet partner on such early 1950s records as "Dark as a Dungeon," "Mountain Laurel," and "Keep on the Sunny Side." Her exposure as Grandpa's musical sidekick on TV's "Hee Haw" and her deep knowledge of traditional music gradually attracted folklorists' attention. Festival appearances led to her series of fiddle albums in the seventies and eighties.

Janette Carter's Carter Family Fold in Appalachia has been a bastion of old-time music. Her mother, Sara Carter, had set out from there in 1927 to become country music's first star female voice, and Janette has always felt that her wing of the Carter dynasty is a little underappreciated. Born to Sara and A.P. Carter in 1923, she accompanied the clan to Texas to broadcast on the continent-blanketing border radio stations of the late 1930s. But after her parents' divorce, Janette returned home to the Smokies to live with her father. Inspired by the success of her Aunt Maybelle and cousins Anita, June, and Helen on the folk festival circuit, Janette and her brother Joe began recording for the folk revival label County in 1966. Around 1969 Janette began making college appearances.

She transformed her late father's general store into the Fold in 1974, and the place soon became a mecca for young folkies in search of mountain-music inspiration. She admits that some neighbors looked askance at her ambition: "People criticized me. I think a lot of it was because I was a woman a-doin' a man's job." Sara was a regular visitor to her daughter's enterprise. Maybelle came, too, and by then she was a folk superstar.

Of all country's pioneering women, Maybelle Carter got the warmest welcome from the folkies of the sixties. In retrospect it seems unlikely that the Carters' music would have endured without the folk revival, for most of their contemporaries have been swept under the rug by modern Nashvillians. The respect conferred on Mother Maybelle by college students, not Music Row businessmen, is what made her an American music idol.

"I appreciate the interest all of 'em have taken in our music," Maybelle said. "There are quite a few folksingers that I love to hear, too, like Joan Baez. I have always loved her singing. And I've met others at folk festivals, and I appreciate their music very much." Spurred by folk interest, a string of Carter Family reissue albums began appearing in 1961. Maybelle was invited to the Newport Folk Festival in 1963. Matriarchs Maybelle and Sara recorded the landmark *An Historic Reunion* LP in Nashville in 1966 and triumphed at Newport together in 1967.

Throughout the sixties and seventies Maybelle Carter issued solo albums that reestablished her musical reputation. Already a guitar legend, Maybelle revolutionized autoharp playing during the folk revival. The instrument was merely chorded and strummed by most players up to that time, but Maybelle stunned audiences by plucking out intricate melodies on the multistringed autoharp; her prowess was captured on more than ten LPs between 1960 and 1975. She also performed on the all-star *Will the Circle Be Unbroken* collection of 1973, Flatt & Scruggs's *Songs of the Famous Carter Family* tribute LP of 1961, and numerous records by son-in-law Johnny Cash. Maybelle and her daughters were also regulars on Cash's network TV series and road tours.

Music City News crowned Maybelle the "Mother of Country Music" in 1968, and in 1970 the original Carter Family was inducted into the Country Music Hall of Fame. In 1974 Mother Maybelle and The Carter Sisters won an American Music Award as that year's favorite country group.

But by the late 1970s her health was failing. According to daughter June, Maybelle hit a wrong note on her autoharp during a 1976 TV taping and never picked it up again: "Mother was a perfectionist." She took her final bow with Sara at the 1976 Carter Family Reunion at Janette's Fold, then retired. Maybelle was afflicted with arthritis, then with a form of Parkinson's disease that killed her in October 1978. Sara died three months later.

"Seems like the folk people like our songs," Maybelle said simply. "I've had a lot of people tell me that my guitar playing has influenced them to play guitar, and if they hadn't heard the records, they probably would never have played. . . . I'm proud and happy that they like the style we started. I think that folk music will never die because there are a lot of people in the world that like it, and they will keep it alive. . . . If I had it to do over, I'd do the same thing. . . . I was brought up on folk and country music . . . it's all I've ever known."

YOU'RE LOOKIN' AT COUNTRY

12

Loretta Lynn and Working-Class Pride

In lyrics like "Fist City," "Your Squaw Is on the Warpath," "Rated X," and "Don't Come Home A-Drinkin'" feisty Loretta Lynn refused to be stepped on by a man, by a rival, or by society at large. In "Coal Miner's Daughter" and "You're Lookin' at Country" she stuck out her chin to defend poor folks' culture. Like the lady herself, Loretta's songs shoot from the hip. Her secret is in her honesty. Her strength is in her womanhood. Her pride is in her working-class background.

Loretta Lynn is paramount among the blue-collar heroines of country music, promoting a positive, self-assertive style for women and taking the side of underdogs everywhere. Her sassy point of view transformed female country music in the 1960s with its earthy humor, warmth, and sensitivity. Her from-pitiful-shack-to-ante-bellum-mansion life story transfixed millions in a best-selling autobiography in the 1970s and Oscar-winning film of the 1980s. She had seventy-five hit records between 1960 and 1988, when she was inducted into the Country Music Hall of Fame. Simply put, she is a living legend.

She's been showered with accolades and praised by presidents, yet has clung to the source of her art, her experience as an Appalachian woman. "I've got a roomful of

awards now," reflects Loretta. "And as I go back and look at 'em, I know what I achieved to get each one. . . . When young people ask me how I got where I'm at, I say, 'It's absolutely hard work.' There ain't nobody gonna wave a magic wand. . . . You pay for what success you get. . . . All you have to do is open up your life to the people.

"You know, I don't even like to be high up on a stage, really. I like to be where I can look at ya. I don't want to sing down to you. I want you to sing with me. . . . I ain't no star. A star is something up in the night sky. People say to me, 'You're a legend.' I'm not a legend. I'm just a woman."

She carried that message to America from the darkest shadow of mountain poverty. Just as she sings, Loretta is a "Coal Miner's Daughter." She was born Loretta Webb in 1935 in Butcher Hollow, Kentucky, and raised in a mountain cabin with seven brothers and sisters. "Mommy and Daddy built this little shack and papered it with movie magazines. I was named after Loretta Young. . . . I always thought she was so beautiful. . . . One of the things I thought of the other day was, 'from a tin plate to fine white china.' . . . I remember eatin' offa tin plates as a little girl. And Mommy had these old kegs, barrels that you get nails in and stuff. That's what I'd eat off of, settin' on the floor."

That was a scene almost unimaginable to the suburbanites who learned to love her. But in the underbelly of America's prosperity is a burning ulcer of poverty. In 1959, the year Loretta began her career, there were an estimated fifty million citizens living below the poverty line, 22 percent of the population. During Loretta's girlhood in the 1940s, it was even worse.

"There were a lot of things we left out [of the film *Coal Miner's Daughter*] on purpose. We didn't want to make it too bad because we didn't want nobody to be depressed when they watched the movie. It was a lot sadder than what it looked like on film. And a lot sadder for me, 'cause I know the depth of what was goin' down. . . . We're talkin' POOR. . . . I never was ashamed of not having an education. There was nothin' I could do about it. If there'd a-been something I coulda done about it, then I'd-a been ashamed.

"Course I lived in a shack, too, where I lived when I got married. I didn't have a washing machine. I washed on a board. . . . Before I was singing, I cleaned house, I took in laundry, I picked berries. I worked seven days a week. I was a housewife and mother for fifteen years before I was an entertainer. And it wasn't like being a housewife today. I mean, it was hand laundry and cooking on an old coal stove. . . . I've grown and canned things almost every year since I started. When I slow down, I'll do it again. . . . *That's* what's real. . . . I know how to survive. Who knows? Tomorrow I may have to. . . . If anything ever happened, I'd go back to that."

In one of the most compelling tales in American popular culture, Loretta married Oliver Mooney Lynn when she was a barely schooled hillbilly girl of thirteen. Known as "Doo," the twenty-one-year-old war veteran with a hell-raising reputation moved the innocent mountain child across the continent to Custer, Washington. Doo became her second father and is as much responsible for raising her as her true parents. She bore four children by age eighteen. "After we had kids of our own, Doo would take a belt to me as quick as he would to one of them," she told interviewer Joan Dew. "It's funny how it's the old hurts that never heal." Isolated from her native culture, tied to endless domestic work, and desperately lonely, Loretta turned to the gift of music she inherited from her mother, Clara Butcher Webb.

"Mommy taught me a song called 'The Great Titanic,'" Loretta recalled in her book *Coal Miner's Daughter*, "and she taught me how to make motions with my hands in telling the story. . . . Most of our songs told a story. You could tell me that's the old-fashioned way people had of telling news, before newspapers and radio. All I know is, most country songs are ballads. . . . We didn't have a radio until I was 11." Young Loretta had a voice that pealed like a village church chime, as well as a native mountain wit that charmed everyone who met her. Mooney heard talent in his wife, and bought her a seventeen-dollar guitar at Sears. She taught herself to play it and started writing songs. In 1959 Mooney began taking Loretta to sing in local honky-tonks and grange halls. He pushed her into a Tacoma talent contest, which she won. A Vancouver lumberman liked what he heard when she subsequently appeared on local TV. He financed a recording trip to Los Angeles and put out "I'm a Honky-Tonk Girl" on his little Zero Records label.

The 1960 single reveals that Loretta was patterning herself after Kitty Wells, then the dominant female country star. Her vocal is very much in the weepy Wells style, and the number is in the seduced-and-abandoned mode that Kitty popularized in hits like "It Wasn't God Who Made Honky-Tonk Angels." "That song told me there was a woman out there kinda takin' up for herself," Loretta recalled. "I'd always tried to write songs before that. . . . So when Kitty Wells came out with 'Honky-Tonk Angels,' I thought, 'Hmmm: what about "Honky-Tonk Girl?"'" Mooney took a photo of Loretta in a cowgirl outfit and mailed it out to 3,500 radio stations with the record. "Annie Oakley couldn't a-held a candle to me," Loretta recalled, laughing. "I'm tellin' you, I thought I was the prettiest thing that ever hit the streets.

"We set out in our old Mercury to promote the record. We were pitiful. . . . Because we were too poor to stay in hotels, we slept in the car and ate bologna and cheese sandwiches in the parks. When we were driving, I'd just wear jeans or something. When we got near a radio station, I would jump in the backseat and change into my only good dress, cowboy hat, and boots. Then we'd go into the radio station and pester the DJ to play my record. We didn't care if it was a five-hundred-watt local station or a fifty-thousand-watt clear-channel station. We'd hit them all. We were on the road three months."

Astonishingly, it worked. "I'm a Honky-Tonk Girl" hit the charts in the summer of 1960 and brought Loretta to Music City. She was instantly smitten with the music of Nashville's rising star Patsy Cline, who was sidelined by a car accident in 1961 shortly after Loretta's arrival. Loretta dedicated "I Fall to Pieces" to Patsy on the "Ernest Tubb Midnight Jamboree" radio show and the touched country diva invited the new-comer to her hospital bedside. After recuperating, Patsy gave the still-naive Loretta tips on clothes and hair. "You know, for years my husband wouldn't let me wear makeup or cut my hair," Loretta said years later. "To shave my legs, I had the children watch at the doors and windows in case he came home. He didn't want it, wouldn't allow it. But I wanted to do just like Patsy Cline did, to be as pretty as her." Loretta was teaching herself to use an eyelash curler one day at the Opry when Dottie West came into the dressing room. "I turned to say hello to Dottie when she walked in. I ripped all the eyelashes offa one of my eyes. Walked around bald-eyed for a while then!" On one of her early tours, a booking agent updated her image by buying a sheath, hiding Loretta's cowboy boots, and making her practice walking in her first pair of high heels. "I'll bet you I fell fifty times. . . . it embarrassed me to death." Frustrated by her balance problems during the concert, Loretta kicked off the heels and broke into a Kentucky buck dance in her stockings. The spontaneous hillbilly gesture remained in her show for years afterward.

As she gained confidence, Loretta's vocals became exultant bugle trills, whoops of defiance, honky-tonk moans of pain, and soulful wails of passion. She mingled Kitty's tense, pent-up quality with Patsy's more exuberant belting and came up with her own style. After Patsy's death, Opry stars Ernest Tubb and The Wilburn Brothers took Loretta under their wings. Teddy Wilburn molded Loretta's natural songwriting gift into something refreshingly frank and startlingly original, and his brother Doyle pressured Decca Records producer Owen Bradley into signing her. Owen and Loretta's first hit together was 1962's "Success," a song with the theme that a woman's happiness doesn't lie in material things. "Wine, Women and Song" (1964) and "Happy Birthday" (1965) were sassy, don't-step-on-me numbers. Loretta hit her stride from 1966 to 1968 with the country-gal spunk of "You Ain't Woman Enough," "Don't Come Home A-Drinkin'," "Fist City," and "Your Squaw Is on the Warpath."

"From then on, it all sort of fell in place," Bradley recalled. "I've said it many times—I think she's the female Hank Williams. . . . She's the spokesman for the ladies. . . . Kitty Wells was the mistreated woman whose man is out drinking and cheating. . . . Loretta had a lot of different ideas, and they were very fresh. . . . All of a sudden, it was just the other side. And the women's lib also was coming on at that time. . . . You have to be in the right place at the right time. And I think Loretta was standing right there."

True enough. Just as Loretta was coming out with her feisty, country-gal statements, the leaders of America's feminist movement were stirring. The year after "Honky-Tonk Girl" introduced her, President Kennedy established the Commission on the Status of Women to express his concern for working women's lives. While Loretta was having her first major-label hits in 1963, Betty Friedan's ground-breaking *The Feminine Mystique* and the commission's findings were rallying women to action. Loretta rose to the top of the charts in 1966, the year the National Organization of Women was formed.

In 1968, a group of protesters visited the Miss America Pageant and tossed girdles, false eyelashes, and bras into a "freedom trash can." Media attention to the new movement erupted. By 1972, when *Ms.* magazine appeared, Loretta was taking humorous note of the women's movement in "One's On the Way." The landmark anthology of women's writings *Sisterhood Is Powerful* documented the inequality experienced by everyone from secretaries to welfare moms, from female prisoners to women in universities. Contrary to its later characterization as an elitist movement for college and professional women, these early writings demonstrated the women's liberationists' deep concern with the problems of working women and homemakers. They called for equal pay for equal work, day care, wages for housework, and men's involvement in domestic duties. The book appeared in 1973, the same year that Loretta hit the top with "Coal Miner's Daughter."

"Most of my songs were from the women's point of view," Loretta wrote in her own best-seller. "There's plenty of songs about how women should stand by their men and give them plenty of loving when they walk through the door, and that's fine. But what about the man's responsibility? . . . I feel there's better ways to handle a woman than whipping her into line. And I make that point clear in my songs. . . . I'm not a big fan of Women's Liberation, but maybe it will help women stand up for the respect they're due. . . . The men have enough things going for 'em in this life. We women have got to stick together. My shows are really geared to women fans . . . to the hard-working housewife who's afraid some girl down at the factory is going to steal her husband, or wishing she could bust out of her shell a little bit. . . . That's who I'm singing about and singing to during my shows. And the girls know it. . . . Most of my fan club is women, which is how I want it."

She rose to fame on The Wilburn Brothers' syndicated TV series. In those days, Opry stars taped weekly programs that were sent out for weekend broadcasts by stations in towns from Akron to Wichita Falls. The general format was simple—the star on a single hay-bales-type set introducing his big hits, instrumental numbers from band members, a guest star, the resident comic, "and now something from our pretty miss" or "and now here's a religious number from our girl singer." No women hosted these shows.

Similarly, women did not headline their own concert tours. Apart from Patsy Cline, none had the box office power to command top billing. Reeling from the impact of rock 'n' roll, the field had few stars of either sex with enough clout to sell tickets on their own. In general, country acts toured in "package shows," groups of touring entertainers who found strength in numbers. A package show might include a star honky-tonker, a bluegrass band, a novelty act, a handsome balladeer, and *one* woman singer. Records by women were treated gingerly. A record label would rarely release two female singers' singles at the same time, since there were so few radio slots available to women. It was assumed that women bought the show tickets and records of the rhinestone-studded men who were fantasy lovers or country dream dates. Loretta poked a big hole in this assumption by appealing directly to women. Audience response was volcanic.

"It was a man's world when I came here fifty years ago, and it was still a man's world when Miss Kitty and Loretta came in," said Minnie Pearl. "But Loretta battered down all those barriers."

Loretta's revolutionary approach to songwriting created a whole new subgenre of country song. Soon both men and women composers on Music Row were creating material customized to her country-feminist point of view. Tucked away on her albums are many such striking songs. "Two Mules Pull This Wagon" argues for equality in marriage. "Old Rooster" pokes fun at male vanity. "Pregnant Again" is the lament of a woman in the family way who's too poor to afford groceries, never mind another child. In "Night Girl" she rejects the advances of a rich man who thinks he can make a working-class gal his mistress. Even radical temperance activist Carry Nation would find "I Burnt the Little Roadside Tavern

Down" extreme. "Wanted Woman" is a startling number about a mentally disturbed murderess. On "Then You'll Be Free" a wife bides her time for divorce until her children are grown. "I Can't Say It on the Radio," "Married Ladies," and "Adam's Rib (To Women's Lib)" took Loretta's spunky attitudes into the eighties.

She ruffled some feathers along the way. Her single "Wings upon Your Horns" was considered a little dirty and stalled just outside the country Top 10 in 1969. She got by with "Rated X" (1973), which condemned people who look on divorced women as used goods and sexually easy, but her birth control celebration "The Pill" (1975) created a furor.

"When we released it, the people loved it. I mean the *women* loved it. But the men who run the radio stations were scared to death. It's like a challenge to the man's way of thinking. See, they'll play a song about making love in a field because they think that's sexy, from a man's point of view. But something that's really important to women, like birth control, they don't want no part of, leastways not on the air. Well, my fans . . . forced most of the radio stations to play it. Some preachers criticized it in church.

"I'm glad I had six kids, because I couldn't imagine my life without 'em. But I think a woman needs control over her own life, and the pill is what helps her do it. . . . I don't think I could have an abortion. It would be wrong for me. But I'm thinking of all the poor girls who get pregnant when they don't want to be, and how they should have a choice instead of leaving it up to some politician or doctor who don't have to raise the baby. I believe they should be able to have an abortion."

Among Loretta's finest moments on disc are such strong female statements as 1970's "You Wanna Give Me a Lift (But This Gal Ain't A-Goin' That Far)"; 1971's "I Wanna Be Free"; 1978's "We've Come a Long Way Baby"; 1973's "Love Is the Foundation"; 1975's "When the Tingle Becomes a Chill"; and 1973's "Hey Loretta," the song of a runaway housewife who crows, "This woman's liberation, honey, is a-gonna start right now." Wittiest of all is "One's On the Way" (1972), which contrasts "the girls in New York City" who "march for Women's Lib" with a Topeka housewife who's swamped in domestic problems.

By the mid-seventies Loretta was an absolute superstar, one of the handful of country celebrities whose names were known throughout the music world. With her guileless, open, unpretentious manner, she became a TV talk show favorite of Johnny Carson, Dinah Shore, Mike Douglas, David Frost, and David Letterman. She was featured on the cover of *Newsweek* (1973), *Redbook* (1974), and other national periodicals. She starred in a high-profile series of commercials for Crisco shortening, campaigned for literacy, and even became the subject of a fancy collector's doll.

Loretta's rise coincided with the increasing professionalism of country music, which by the 1960s was beginning to view itself as a distinct American industry. Evening gowns and rhinestone-studded stage attire had replaced the ginghams and ruffles of an earlier era. Gone were the caravans of Cadillacs, replaced by gleaming tour buses customized with bunks, kitchenettes, and carpeted living quarters. Booking agencies, record labels, management offices, and song publishing firms had sprung up in the houses along Music Row, forging a business center for the culture. A weeklong annual October business convention evolved into a focal point for the emerging industry. The Country Music Association formed in 1958; Country Music Hall of Fame inductions began in 1961; the Country Radio Seminar convention was launched in 1969.

The Grammy Awards, begun in 1958, included the Best Country & Western Performance category from the start; Loretta got her Grammy in 1971. Gold Record awards were also instituted in 1958, and Loretta had four such plaques by 1983. California's Academy of Country Music began handing out statuettes in 1965. The Nashville industry followed suit in 1967 with its national CMA awards. Its first Female Vocalist of the Year was Loretta Lynn. She duplicated the feat in 1972 and 1973, and in 1972 became the first woman honored by the CMA as Entertainer of the Year. In 1966 *Music City News* began polling its subscribers for their favorites; between then and 1992 Loretta won fourteen of its fan-voted awards. The Loretta Fan Club—headed by Colorado-bred sisters Loudilla, Loretta, and Kay Johnson—led the way for all others by spawning the umbrella International Fan Club Organization (IFCO) and backing the 1973 inauguration of Nashville's wildly successful annual Fan Fair festival. Loretta Lynn formed her own booking agency, song publishing company, western-wear clothing store chain, and Tennessee dude ranch.

Despite the industry's new professionalism and despite the truckloads of accolades, Loretta stayed close to her roots. Her shows became country gal therapy sessions.

"Most of the women liked me. . . . They could see I was Loretta Lynn, a mother and a wife and a daughter, who had feelings just like other women. Sure, I wanted men to like me, but the women were something special. They'd come around to the bus after the show, and they'd ask to talk to me. They felt I had the answer to their problems because my life was just like theirs. . . . I ain't Dear Abby. . . . I had a few problems maybe *they* could have solved for me."

Her devotion to her fans became legendary, but it wore her down. She tried to be everybody's friend and wound up being a lonely symbol, doing more than 200 concerts a year. The bus became her home. The pressures of constant travel, smiling, and chatting began to show as stardom took an increasing toll on her mental and physical health. In 1976 she suffered a complete breakdown onstage in Illinois. She developed migraine headaches and ulcers, and she was hospitalized several times for exhaustion.

Life at home was no happier. Conflicts with Mooney increased as she gained fame and self-confidence. None of her children went on to the higher education she'd dreamed of for them. Twins Patsy and Peggy, the two born after her career began, married young and sporadically attempted singing careers of their own. Cissie developed her own road show; Ernest Ray is a member of his mother's troupe when he's not in trouble with the law; Betty Sue, who also married as a teenager, writes songs for Loretta's albums as "Tracey Lee." Jack Benny, her oldest boy, drowned in 1984. Loretta was badly shaken, too, when her mother died in 1981.

Her problems, her collapses, her tragedies, and her weaknesses only endeared her all the more to her fans. And she never stopped giving and giving to them. Loretta can't say no and continually pitches in for the less fortunate. She is antiracist and proworker and has repeatedly expressed her pride in her Cherokee Indian heritage. "When I die, I want God to put me in charge of all the people that nobody loves. They can even put it on my tombstone," she once said.

"I'm proud and I've got my own ideas, but I ain't no better than nobody else. I've often wondered why I became so popular, and maybe that's the reason. I think I reach people because I'm with 'em, not apart from 'em."

The essence of Loretta Lynn's enormous working-class popularity lies in her proud-to-be-country attitude and her assertive woman's stance. Both were tremendously appealing to a blue-collar America that was feeling embattled and embittered in the sixties and seventies. Loretta Lynn wasn't ashamed of being a woman. And she wasn't ashamed of having come from the poor.

Pride in your culture and pride in who you are became a hallmark of the era's social dialogue. White working-class citizens felt like minorities felt—used, ridiculed, exploited, and overlooked. Caricatured as redneck, bigoted, conformist, and stupid, they found self-esteem and a defensive voice in country music. Loretta and her peers created a new kind of Nashville song.

Country music of the period reasserted working-class dignity and self-worth. It celebrated their life-style in sharp, proud contrast to that of the dominant, Madison Avenue culture. What became central to the defi-

nition of "country" was to be poor, simple, or a laborer. In song, country people don't have and don't value material things. They have love rather than riches and would choose it over wealth anytime. In fact, wealth is often defined as a cause of misery.

Country radio listeners have become well acquainted with these themes over the past three decades. The goodness of country people is the subject of "Po' Folks" (Bill Anderson), "Common Man" (John Conlee), "Rednecks, White Socks and Blue-Ribbon Beer" (Johnny Russell), "I'm Just a Country Boy" (Don Williams), "All I Have to Offer You Is Me" (Charley Pride), and "Poor Folks Stick Together" (Stoney Edwards).

Country music women added their own dimension. Like men, they sang of preferring a life of love in blue-collar bungalows over that of loveless mansions. But while men resisted being stepped on by bosses, women took resistance into the house. There were women's hits about secretaries, waitresses, prostitutes, and truckers, but the major battleground was domestic. Jean Shepard, for instance, in her housewife hit of 1968, asked how you can expect "A Real Good Woman" "to stay with a no-good man." And always, always, there were lyrics of poverty, a staple of country songwriting since the 1920s. The country stars sang of an America that the mainstream media ignored.

Throughout the 1970s the most critical issue in all industries was the mechanization and accelerated pace of work that improved production and profits but worsened workers' lives. When Loretta was singing how proud she was to be a "Coal Miner's Daughter," miners were being laid off while those remaining had their workloads tripled. In 1965 protests and wildcat strikes erupted in mining areas throughout Appalachia. Spontaneous strikes in the textile, steel, and auto industries were also launched by rank-and-file unions.

Increasingly, women felt the problems of work as intensely as men. "Pink-collar" secretarial workers unionized and demanded living wages. By 1975 nearly half of all married women were in the labor force, the most significant influx consisting of mothers. In 1950, 28 percent of women with school-aged children held jobs; by 1970 that proportion had doubled. An even greater growth rate was in the mothers with children under six in the work force: By 1970, 30 percent of them were working, triple the proportion of twenty years earlier. And with the divorce rate escalating and a dramatic increase in female-headed households, work became ever more essential to women. In 1960, roughly 70 percent of households conformed to the ideal of daddy-at-work and mommy-at-home-with-children; but by 1980 only 14 percent did.

Poverty was never far from every working woman's door. Most women found themselves in low-paying, dead-end jobs. Female wages were generally inadequate for raising a family, and female jobs were usually lower in prestige and status. Seventy percent of women were largely sex-segregated in a pink-collar occupational ghetto. Many college-educated women were equally segregated working as nurses, elementary school teachers, librarians, and social workers. The average working woman in 1975 earned sixty cents for every dollar earned by a man.

Women's awareness of their situation grew rapidly. In 1962 less than one in three polled felt discriminated against. But by 1970 half said they did; four years later two out of every three American women surveyed said they had experienced discrimination.

Country music's women chronicled the times in several notable songs of the era. A diminutive honky-tonker named Billie Jo Spears lifted her voice for the new secretarial army in 1969's "Mr. Walker It's All Over." Billie Jo marched into the office and onto the Top 10 of the country hit parade when she mouthed off to the boss in this number. Sung in a Texas accent as thick as salsa and twice as tangy, the tune told of a secretary's woes on the job, as well as of her misery living in Manhattan. Billie Jo Spears followed "Mr. Walker It's All Over" with "Pittsburgh General," a similarly assertive song that spoke up for nurses.

Billie Jo knew a working girl's problems firsthand. She was a tough Texan who'd worked as a drive-in carhop and as a secretary. Born in the east Texas oil town of Beaumont in 1937, she had a father who was a truck driver and a mother who was a shipyard welder, as well as a guitarist in the Light Crust Doughboys western-swing band. Billie Jo was singing in clubs by age thirteen and continued to do so during her tenure as a clerical worker at the Beaumont Bag and Burlap Company. She arrived in Music City in the early 1960s and applied a seasoned, earthy style to a series of hard-hitting singles. In addition to her working-girl tunes, Billie Jo found success with "Stepchild" (1969), the saga of an abused boy who kills his mean stepfather, and "Marty Gray" (1970), a number about teen pregnancy.

Her "Mr. Walker It's All Over" and "Pittsburgh General" were part of a

trend of working-woman country songs. The long-haul trucker became a hero in country songs of the sixties, a restless interstate cowboy with a vital job and a heart of gold. Country music women reflected a rise in female truck drivers with a number of tunes, notably Kay Adams's 1966 hit "Little Pink Mack." Sang Kay, "In my truck-driving boots, I stand about five-foot-three / But don't let the size fool you, man, I can take care of me."

Kay was born Princetta Kay Adams in 1941 in Knox City, Texas. She was named the Most Promising Vocalist of 1965 by the Academy of Country Music. During her heyday she was notable for her country concept albums. "Little Pink Mack" appeared on a trucker collection called *Wheels and Tears.* A 1968 LP was titled *Alcohol and Tears.* "You'll find her in any town, in any bar on any stool," wrote producer Cliffie Stone in its liner notes. "She will have a drink in her hand and a smile on her too heavily made up face. You may have seen a thousand like her. She is someone's daughter, someone's wife or someone's mother. How did she come to be in that bar? . . . In this album . . . you will find the answer as Kay Adams sings the songs of the forgotten woman. . . . the gal who probably started out on the right road but, somewhere along the way, got detoured into the Land of Alcohol and Tears." Kay's last notable single was a version of Carolyn Hester's humorous topical tune of 1974, "Henry in the Centerfold."

"Little Pink Mack" was just one of dozens of women's country songs spawned by the trucker culture of the 1960s and 1970s. Maggie Owens's "Peterbilt Mama" and Stella Parton's "Truck Driving Mother" were among the most assertive. Country singers Judy Pannell, Kay Shannon, and Lisa Worley actually worked as long-haul drivers.

A variety of other working women appeared in songs of the folk and country women of the time. Linda Gail Lewis faced life as a secretary in "(I'm a) Working Girl." Anne Romaine dreamed of going back to her country home and leaving her "Indiana Factory Job." Melba Montgomery was a merry short-order cook in "Something to Brag About." Sandy Posey's touching "Single Girl" made her own way and paid the bills but yearned for "a sweet lovin' man to lean on." Tammy Wynette was a barmaid sick of dirty jokes and lewd passes who begged for escape in "Take Me to Your World." Wanda Jackson was an inmate in the "Tennessee Women's Prison." Arlene Harden was a proud stripteaser in "Ruby Gentry's Daughter." Sylvia Tyson was a waitress in a "Trucker's Cafe," as was Minnie Pearl in "Giddyup-Go Answer."

Besides Loretta Lynn, the most consistent performer of working-class women's material was Norma Jean. Between 1964 and 1971 she hit the charts with a string of singles enlarging the working-girl song tradition. "It started out not intentional, but I like that kind of thing, and I like songs like that," says Norma Jean (Beasler). "It was kind of take a stand or something. They were just good country songs.

"It used to be that people used to look down on you because you were in country music. I'd go into a store, and if they found out I was a singer, they'd ask, 'What kind?' When I said, 'Country,' they'd turn their noses up. Really, it was that bad.

"I was born January 30, 1938, in a little farmhouse. . . . I guess we lived about as far out in the country as you can live and were about as poor as you can be, money wise. . . . We never had many treats or toys when I was small, but I was never without love.

"Kitty Wells was just my idol when I was just a kid. I would listen to her every Saturday night on 'The Grand Ole Opry' and think, 'Someday that's what I want to do.' . . . I started traveling when I was fifteen or sixteen, working with different western-swing bands. . . . I was unchaperoned. That was my first big experience," she says with a chuckle. She'd been on radio with her own show since age thirteen and was a divorced mother singing full-time by age twenty-one. "I guess you could say it was tough, but I was enjoying it so much, it didn't seem that terrible at the time. Because when you want to do something more than anything else, you don't mind. . . . When I came to Nashville, there just weren't that many female singers at all, about a half a dozen. . . . There really weren't many opportunities for girl singers. We were few and far between." In 1960 she became "Pretty Miss Norma Jean," the "girl singer" on the Porter Wagoner show. It was the rhinestone-spangled Opry star who helped fashion her blue-collar image, intentionally cultivating her as a singer of down-to-earth songs about poor folks' lives and values.

"I left the Porter show in sixty-seven. When I left,

Norma Jean, 1964.

uh, it was not real cordial. Porter and I were more than friends: We had a relationship, and, well, I was very much in love with Porter. Anyway, we had a long-term relationship. . . . He was married—but separated—at the time." Norma Jean married a childhood sweetheart and left the music business in 1974 to move back home to Oklahoma with him. After another divorce she returned to Nashville in 1984, resumed singing, marketed a TV package of her favorite hits, and married country entertainer George Riddle. She hasn't recorded any new hits, but she's already left a collection of country classics.

Her first hit was the eyebrow-raising proposition "Let's Go All the Way" (1964). During the next few months, she gave her guy the gate in "Go Cat Go," suggested, "Don't Let That Doorknob Hit You," and declared, "I Wouldn't Buy a Used Car from Him." Norma Jean's Okie drawl fit such plainspoken lyrics perfectly. One of her biggest numbers was 1967's "Heaven Help the Working Girl (In a World That's Run by Men)," a look at the life of a café waitress. Norma Jean followed that hit with the assertive "Truck Drivin' Woman" (1968). The next year's "Dusty Road" was a depiction of poverty as seen through the eyes of a child. Her finest concept LP was 1972's *I Guess That Comes from Being Poor.* In addition to the title tune, it included such vivid songs as "Hundred Dollar Funeral," "There Won't Be Any Patches in Heaven," and "The Lord Must Have Loved the Poor Folks (He Made So Many of Them)."

The attention Norma Jean, Billie Jo Spears, Kay Adams, and others paid to working women was matched by a wave of self-assertive housewife songs. Ann J. Morton, an Oklahoman of native American descent, suggested a "Housewife's Union" in 1972. Dolly Parton became a homemaker spokeswoman with 1972's "Washday Blues." Alabama singer-songwriter Ava Aldridge recorded an entire concept album of such material in 1975, *Frustrated Housewife.* Jody Miller won a 1965 Grammy Award by answering Roger Miller's "King of the Road" with "Queen of the House."

"Answer" records were a prime vehicle for women's points of view during this period. One of Roger Miller's other big songs was "Dang Me," the humorous saga of an irresponsible lug. Ruby Wright agreed with that assessment and answered with the even stronger "Dern Ya" (1964). Ruby is the daughter of Kitty Wells, who'd previously recorded during the rockabilly era as one-third of 'Nita, Rita, and Ruby.

Besides "Dern Ya," other feisty-female "answers" of the era included Margie Bowes's turning the tables on Johnny Cash's "Understand Your Man" with "Understand Your Gal" (1964); Lois Williams's response to Cash's "A Boy Named Sue" with "A Girl Named Sam" (1969); and Wanda Jackson's retort to Glen Campbell's "By the Time I Get to Phoenix," "By the Time You Get to Phoenix" (1968). Former rockabilly

Wanda also contributed "My Big Iron Skillet" (1969) to the spunky-housewife statements of the post-Loretta era. Another pioneer who slipped easily into the feisty-female mode was Rose Maddox, who entered the 1960s on such sassy tunes as "Baby You Should Live So Long" and "That'll Learn Ya, Dern Ya." Joyce Paul sang of her no-good man, "Mama's Gonna Fix the Baby's Wagon" in 1968. Marti Brown became the first country music woman to embrace the then-new title encouraged by the women's movement by calling her 1973 LP *Ms. Marti Brown.*

Peggy Sue picked up the assertive attitude displayed on her hits "I'm Gettin' Tired of Babyin' You" (1969) and "Apron Strings" (1970) firsthand. Born Peggy Sue Webb, she is Loretta Lynn's younger sister and her cowriter on "Don't Come Home A-Drinkin'." After her recording career waned, Peggy Sue became a backup singer for baby sister Crystal Gayle. In 1991 Peggy Sue endured a personal tragedy when her twenty-three-year-old only child, Doyletta Wells McCanless, was shot and killed by husband Kevin McCanless.

Loretta Lynn was an inspiration to many of her fellow female performers, and she gave a helping hand to several. In addition to Peggy Sue, Crystal Gayle, and her daughters, she boosted singer-songwriter Leona Williams, whom she hired as her band's bassist.

Leona grew up the ninth of twelve children born to a Missouri road construction worker and his wife in the foothills of the Ozarks in 1943. Little Leona Belle Helton didn't have electricity until she was twelve and didn't have any education beyond the eighth grade, but she had plenty of music. Papa Helton was a fiddler; Mama played the banjo. Leona, her four brothers, and her seven sisters all learned to pick and sing. The Helton family began entertaining locally, and Leona was offered her own radio show at age fifteen, launching her career. She had a streak of country-gal independence and shed her first husband by age sixteen. With second husband Ron Williams, a drummer, Leona headed for St. Louis to go to beauty school and work the clubs. Loretta Lynn hired the couple for her band in 1966. She recalls that Ron was jealous of Leona's talent and tried to keep the two women apart.

Leona Williams rapidly attracted attention in Music City because of her abilities on guitar, bass, fiddle, drums, and mandolin, not to mention her talent as a singer and songwriter. Loretta recorded Leona's "Get What 'Cha Got and Go" in 1967, and Tammy Wynette did Leona's "Broad-minded" the next year. Connie Smith had a hit with Leona's tune "Dallas" in 1974. By then the songwriter was making records herself. Her kickoff performances included a barmaid's lament called "A Gentleman on My Mind," a plea for understanding called "Yes Ma'm (He Found Me in a

MINNIE PEARL'S "GIDDYUP-GO ANSWER"

KAY ADAMS'S "LITTLE PINK MACK"

NORMA JEAN'S "TRUCK DRIVIN' WOMAN"

Leona Williams, 1976.

Honky-Tonk)," and her first hit, the frisky "Country Girl with Hot Pants On" (1971). "Your Shoeshine Girl" (1973) was about a wife who does all the household work, right up to the day she walks out.

Superstar Merle Haggard met the newly divorced mother of two in 1974 and was smitten. In 1976 he accompanied Leona on *San Quentin's First Lady,* the first prison LP ever made by a woman. It included "Working Girl Blues," as well as such penitentiary songs as "Prisons Aren't Only for Men," "I'm Here to Get My Baby Out of Jail," and "San Quentin." The country-singing couple married in 1978 and released their 1981 hit trucker duet "The Bull and the Beaver" the same month. Both were respected performers, both were as country as grits, and both had wills of iron. They fought and loved with equal fire right from the start. In his autobiography Haggard alternately curses her independence and determination and praises her spunk, spirit, and soul. "She had more talent than any 10 women I'd met," he wrote. The divorce proceedings revealed the brutality and humiliation of her married life, with Leona charging him with physical abuse and alcohol and drug addiction. "I had to leave; I actually got run off," she said. "It's the hardest thing I've ever done, just to make up my mind and leave. I had circles under my eyes, and I was so nervous. In fact, I was scared to death. You know, you live like that for years, it's hard to get over it, I guess." Ironically, their *Heart to Heart* duet LP appeared in 1983 just as their marriage ended.

Haggard's subsequent Number 1 hits included "You Take Me for Granted" and "Some Day When Things Are Good," both written by Leona. Her versions appeared on her 1984 solo LP. She married Nashville songwriter Dave Kirby in 1985, and since then her songs have been recorded by George Jones, Willie Nelson, and others. The Leona Williams/Merle Haggard song "We're Strangers Again" became a Tammy Wynette/Randy Travis duet single in 1991.

In addition to doing assertive domestic and working-girl songs, a good many country stars of the late 1960s and early 1970s sang proudly of the enduring strength of womanhood. They portrayed the country woman as the powerful life force, the resilient mother, the source of love, and the rock of support. Sometimes the theme was combined with antimateri-alistic, poor-but-happy lyrics where a working man could look to his woman for comfort and their relationship was a shield against life's hardships. Examples of this strongly profemale song style include Jean Shepard's "My Name Is Woman" (1971) and "A Woman's Hand" (1970), Andra Willis's "Down Home Lovin' Woman" (1973), and Diana Trask's "Lean It All on Me" (1974).

"Bobbie Roy sings about all kinds of woman—the woman in love, the knowing woman, the doggedly faithful woman, the vulnerable woman . . . the sensuous woman . . . all kinds of woman," read the liner notes to the 1972 LP *I'm Your Woman*. Bobbie also sang the country version of Helen Reddy's women's lib anthem "I Am Woman."

Melba Montgomery, best known for her duet work with others, recorded country's all-time motherhood song. "No Charge" is the story of a little boy who presents his mother with a bill for his chores. She responds with a litany of motherly selflessness. With a tremor and a moan in her throat, Melba began to sing, "For the nine months I carried you growing inside me, no charge." While instruments swelled behind her, she added, "For the nights I sat up with you, doctored you, prayed for you, no charge." By the time she got to "the price of real love is no charge," her voice was audibly faltering, and as soon as the tape stopped rolling at the recording session, she wept openly. "No Change" hit Number 1 on Mother's Day 1974.

Supreme among all the "womanhood" singers was Jeanne Pruett, who specialized in the theme throughout the sev-enties. Jeanne's belief that happiness lies in the heart, not in material possessions, expressed itself in such hits as "Satin Sheets" (1973), "Back to Back" (1979), and "A Poor Man's Woman" (1975). She sang stirring paeans to fidelity such as "Hold to My Unchanging Love" (1971) and "I'm Your Woman" (1973), then combined the two themes on 1974's superb "You Don't Need to Move a Mountain." Beginning in her resonant hillbilly alto, Jeanne built the number into a gospel shout of enduring, tender passion. She asks her man for nothing other than to "lay your head on my breast" and accept her love. The wise and accepting lover builds a bulwark around her man and herself, and as a couple they face a harsh world.

Melba Montgomery had an uptown look on this 1966 album cover, but on the disc "the female George Jones" was country through and through.

In 1978's "I'm a Woman" Jeanne Pruett declared that she was "proud and equal . . . unbroken and free," but had chosen to be a wife and mother. By 1983's "Lady of the Eighties," Jeanne had adopted a more independent tone. But whether pleading "Love Me," bemoaning the

JEANNE PRUETT
Feedin' Friends Cookbook II

The greatest of country's "womanhood" singers of the seventies has a second career today as the author of a strong-selling series of down-home cookbooks. Jeanne Pruett published this one in 1988.

"Honey on His Hands," cheating in "Temporarily Yours," swearing unquestioning devotion with "Call on Me," leaving her man in "Count Me Out," or quietly musing "It's Too Late," Jeanne Pruett always communicated womanly strength, backwoods country honesty, and intense emotional conviction.

She came by that hillbilly fervor naturally. Born Norma Jean Bowman on a farm outside Pell City, Alabama, in 1937, Jeanne was raised in a family of twelve that got by on red-clay vegetables and cotton mill jobs. The Bowmans spent summer evenings harmonizing on the front porch, and she picked up piano and guitar skills. In 1956 she moved to Nashville with her husband, Jack Pruett, and he got the job as guitarist for Marty Robbins. She held things together on the home front. "I wasn't singing yet; I was still staying home," she recalls. "Jack and I had two children together, and I was a mother and a housewife. It [music] all started out as a hobby that I loved dearly, and eventually it became a way of life."

Jeanne began writing tunes, and boss Robbins expressed his approval by recording several. So did Conway Twitty, Tammy Wynette, Nat Stuckey, Bill Phillips, and other Nashville stars. Her own first attempt at recording was in 1963 to 1964 for RCA, but the singing housewife didn't strike pay dirt until she signed with Decca/MCA in 1969 and was turned loose on some hard-core country tunes. "I'm basically a country gal, a country songwriter, and a country singer," she said. "I could probably sing 'Stardust,' but it ain't nearly as pretty to me as 'Wild Side of Life.'" With her simple rhythm guitar, rolling bass lines, and pure, keening, double-tracked harmonies, Jeanne Pruett sounded like springtime down south. The label thought "Satin Sheets" was "too country," so Jeanne promoted and publicized it herself by cutting up squares of satin with her pinking shears and mailing them to every country DJ in the nation. It was named 1973's Song of the Year by the Country Music Association, and she became a "Grand Ole Opry" member.

Jeanne is one of the warmest, funniest, earthiest female personalities in the Opry cast. Her dressing room backstage at the Opry is always a female gathering spot. "We are a pretty close-knit bunch," Jeanne says, "and have shared a lot of love, hurt, pain, good times and bad, and a lot of colds and coughs. We've enjoyed each other's loves, husbands, children and grandchildren, hit records, flops, misfortunes, and fortunes. . . . We've offered each other love and friendship, we've helped each other every now and then. We've borrowed belts, buckles, shoes, jewelry, makeup, mirrors, underslips, hair spray, perfume, powder, and shoes from each other. We've watched each other grow up, grow older. . . . People think the girl singers fight and pull each other's hair, and that's not true at all . . . I still love . . . my Opry Sisters."

After a 1985 TV special saluting the Opry's sixtieth anniversary showed a segment about female Opry stars, Jeanne got a brainstorm. She went to Opry matriarch Jean Shepard, urging her to approach the show's management about doing an "all-girl" segment on the radio barn dance. Shepard hosted it in February 1986, with Jeanne Pruett, Connie Smith, Jan Howard, and Jeannie Seely as her guests. It was the first time in the show's long history that women had been given their own block of time. "This is something I've been trying to get together for a long time in Nashville," said Jeanne afterward. "And not only on the Opry; I'd like to have an all-girl road show. . . . You know what? If we got together Jean Shepard, Jeannie Seely . . . and Jeannie C. Riley and me, we could have an 'I Dream of Jeannie' segment on the Opry."

Jeannie C. Riley had the biggest hit of all the feisty-female singers. Her hard-driving delivery of "Harper Valley P.T.A." not only topped the country charts, it crossed over to Number 1 on mainstream pop radio, eventually selling more than five million copies, earning a Grammy Award, and winning country's 1968 Single of the Year. Jeannie became the very image of the sassy new country gal with her miniskirts, boots, cascading auburn tresses, sultry pouts, and "sock-it-to-'em" stage attitude.

In reality she was a small-town innocent from a deeply religious background who'd been sexually exploited, introduced to booze, and generally taken into the fast lane by the smooth talkers of Music Row. Born Jeanne Stephenson in 1945, she is from Anson, Texas, which is in approximately the middle of nowhere north of Abilene. Daddy was an auto mechanic, and Mama was a fundamentalist Christian housewife. Jeannie C. Riley spent her teen years daydreaming about the country stars she saw on TV and in the pages of *Country Song Roundup.* She sang at a local barn dance and learned shorthand just so she could transcribe song lyrics from the radio. The high school majorette married gas station attendant Mickey Riley at seventeen. They had a baby, then headed for Nashville in 1966 to make Jeannie's country-star dreams come true. During her first two years in Music City, the curvy beauty with the creamy complexion and small-town naivete was seduced by a sleazy record executive, pawed

Jeannie C. Riley, 1968.

over by DJs, and exposed to the seamy side of show biz.

By 1968 she felt like a cheap floozy. And that's when she recorded "Harper Valley P.T.A." The song tells the story of a widowed mother who is criticized for loose morals by the town PTA members. In retaliation the woman faces her accusers and exposes *their* secret vices. "The lyrics reflected the mood of the nation," Jeannie recalled in her autobiography. "The Vietnam War, with all its hypocrisy, had stirred the anger of the youth of America. People were confused. The nation was frustrated. . . . I was mad at the whole world. . . . I stood close to the mike and let it all pour out, sassing everything I hated . . . I really didn't care that much about the national situation nor about small-town hypocrisy. I was just angry at the people around me, angry at myself for being the kind of woman I was . . . I was ready to sock it to the entire world, which is what I did."

Jeannie was typecast as the sassy country hussy, a role that allowed her to issue some of the most outspoken women's songs of 1968 to 1973. In "The Girl Most Likely" she was the sexy poor girl everyone thought would wind up "in trouble," who wound up laughing at the popular rich girl who got knocked up instead. She murdered a rival and went to prison in "The Ballad of Louise." In "Good Enough to Be Your Wife" she refused to become a suitor's mistress. In one of her most darkly compelling singles, she told of a pill-popping prostitute on "The Back Side of Dallas," "where every taxi driver knows her name." The hard-hitting songs on her *Harper Valley P.T.A.* album addressed sex, alcoholism, and poverty.

But even at the height of her brassy, miniskirted "Harper Valley" days, Jeannie C. Riley was ill at ease. Like a puppet, she appeared on TV variety shows and Vegas stages doing scripted patter and showing off her high school baton-twirling skills. Her handlers insisted she maintain the sexpot image, despite her increasing objections to their manipulation. The conflict reached a crescendo the night Jeannie won the Single of the Year award at the nationally televised "CMA Awards" in 1968. She had planned to wear a dress with tiers of organza down to the floor; but when record executive Shelby Singleton learned of this, he had the skirt cut off to mini length. Jeannie C. Riley spent the biggest night of her life looking like a humiliated flamingo in silver go-go boots. Her sense of self-worth eroded; her marriage dissolved; the demands of her career ran away with her life. The ravishing beauty with the hot country hits and the shady-lady image was still essentially an unsophisticated girl from Texas. "People told me I was at the top—I thought so, myself—and I had everything I ever dreamed of. But really, I guess I was at the bottom."

She and Mickey split up in 1970. Jeannie had an affair with a manager, then another with a musician, this time accompanied by marijuana smoking and hippie astrology. "You think you're runnin' free, Jeannie, but you ain't," her mother warned. "Like a heifer on a rope, one day you'll take off a-runnin' and almost break your neck, because that rope's tied to God's tree." Encouraged by singer Connie Smith and other Nashville music women, Jeannie turned to Jesus, remarried Mickey in 1975, and tried to move her career in a religious direction.

Loretta Lynn, 1974.

Prophetically, her 1969 single "The Rib" had translated feminism into biblical terms. In it, she is the spirit of Everywoman, the phone operator, the secretary, the clerk, the housewife. She is made by God as "The Rib," to be "side by side . . . not lesser than, not greater than," and most definitely not "a foot bone to be stepped on . . . a leg bone to be walked on [or] . . . a hip bone to be sat on."

Loretta Lynn, Jeannie C. Riley, Melba Montgomery, Norma Jean, Leona Williams, Jeanne Pruett, and their proud-to-be-country peers drew their women's material from the lives they lived and the lives they saw around them. None of them would ever call themselves "feminist," but all of them reflected working-class women in song. They couldn't relate to the middle-class women's movement of the time, but they could relate to The People.

As usual, Loretta summed it up best: "The best thing for all of 'em to think of, while they're drivin' around Nashville in their Mercedes-Benzes, is if they don't remember where they came from, how are they gonna know where they're goin'? The public is where it's at. They're the ones that feeds us."

13

THE HEROINES OF HEARTBREAK

Tammy Wynette and Traditional Values

If you were to ask the average person to describe a country star, one adjective that would almost certainly come up is "conservative." Ever since the political upheavals of the 1960s, country music has been aligned in the popular imagination with patriotism and religious fundamentalism.

As the nation grappled with civil rights, the Vietnam War, feminism, and the social-justice movements of the 1960s and 1970s, Nashville's stars sometimes reacted with fear and intolerance. Many country songs stressed moral, upright, family-oriented values that were a contrast to the much-publicized sexually free, dope-smoking, "anti-American" hippies. Country stars' own sexcapades and drug experimentation were concealed, and the country culture's tradition of rebellion was forgotten. Merle Haggard's conservative anthem "Okie from Muskogee" of 1969 came to symbolize country's reactionary bent.

During the height of the antiwar protests, Haggard condemned them in "The Fightin' Side of Me" (1970). Dave Dudley spoke out with "What We're Fighting For" (1966). Sergeant Barry Sadler had a massive national hit with his Nashville-recorded song of patriotism, "Ballad

of the Green Berets" (1966), and Music City also provided the controversial "Battle Hymn of Lt. Calley" (1971). Ernest Tubb sang "It's America (Love It or Leave It)" and "It's for God, and Country and You, Mom (That's Why I'm Fighting in Vietnam)." Johnny Sea answered Barry McGuire's apocalyptic 1966 pop hit "Eve of Destruction" with country's conservative response "Day for Decision." Leroy Van Dyke's "Mr. Professor" of 1970 blamed liberal college teachers for draft dodging, atheism, protest marches, and even arson.

Dixie fertilized "three R's"—the right, racism, and religion. Images of a reactionary South were not hard to find. Local governments turned a blind eye to bombing, murdering, and intimidation by antiintegrationists. By 1975 the Ku Klux Klan claimed organized and functioning klaverns in Texas, Arkansas, Louisiana, Mississippi, Alabama, Virginia, Georgia, Florida, and the Carolinas. The American Nazi Party has its headquarters in Virginia.

Country music reflected racism. A Louisiana singer called Johnny Rebel issued a string of singles during the civil rights period with titles like "Move Them Niggers North" and "Nigger Hatin' Me." These were distributed via mail-order ads in the Klan publication *The Fiery Cross.*

Country superstar Marty Robbins supported the right-wing presidential candidacies of George Wallace and Barry Goldwater. Under the pseudonym "Johnny Freedom," Marty recorded songs for the Wallace campaign. Autry Inman, Hank Snow, Billy Grammer, and The Wilburn Brothers also actively campaigned for Alabama's conservative governor.

Country music women became almost as active conservatives as their male counterparts. Tammy Wynette was a big Wallace supporter. Barbara Mandrell, Reba McEntire, and others have aligned themselves with the Republican Party. Anita Bryant became a champion of God-and-country patriotism. Sharon White supported right-wing evangelist Pat Robertson for president in 1988. Richard Nixon arrived in Nashville for the grand opening of the new Opry House in 1974. "I want to say a word about what country music has meant to America," he said. "First, it comes from the heart of America. It talks about family. It talks about religion. And it radiates a love of this nation—a patriotism. Country music makes America a better country." Since that time, country music's conservative image has been reinforced by the community's close ties to country fan George Bush.

"Behind the country music sound there is a 'grassroots gospel,'" explained country star Bobby Lord in his 1969 book, *Hit the Glory Road.* "Right is right and wrong is wrong." The Southern Baptist Convention, headquartered in Nashville, dominates the religious culture of every state from North Carolina to Texas. Almost half of Dixie's church members are Southern Baptists, and the Convention's influential beliefs dovetail with conservative politics.

Religion and morals color all aspects of southern life. Nightclubbing, theatergoing, and even fancy restaurant dining carry the taint of immorality. Many southern towns and counties are dry. You could not buy alcohol by the drink in Nashville until 1967, and as recently as 1991 the city threatened to withdraw the beer permit of its concert amphitheater. Tennessee and other southern states still frown on gambling, horse racing, public lotteries, and even bingo.

Women's issues have evolved into southern conservatives' hottest political battleground. After the Senate approved the Equal Rights Amendment for women in 1972, only two of the thirty-four states that ratified it by 1973 were southern, Texas and Tennessee—and the latter later tried to rescind its approval.

Although racism and anticommunism were central to the initial emergence and coherence of the New Right, the movement became quickly defined by its antifeminist beliefs and conservative sexual views. The communist threat weakened, and racism became socially unacceptable, but feminism's threat to traditional family values could still stir right-wing passions. But that outlook was not phrased as antiwoman; it was "profamily."

This profamily ideology first emerged around 1968 in the movement to oppose sex education in schools. But the two issues that crystallized and defined the New Right's agenda were the Equal Rights Amendment and abortion. Phyllis Schlafly's 1972 STOP-ERA movement built its case on fears that women would have combat roles in the military and would not have access to separate public bathrooms. "The claim that American women are downtrodden and unfairly treated is the fraud of the century," said Schlafly in a 1974 interview. "The truth is that American women have never had it so good. Why should we lower ourselves to 'equal rights' when we already have the status of special privilege?" Opposition to abortion reached a fever pitch in the fifteen years following the 1973 Supreme Court decision that restrained states from restricting women's rights to abortions. The movement unquestionably drew its strength from religious zealots.

Underlying both of these efforts to restrict the lives and choices of women was a philosophy best expressed by Mirabel Morgan in her popular 1973 book, *The Total Woman*. She used the Bible to support her theory of marital relations in which the man was king and the woman his queen. Morgan asked, "Are you guilty of that heinous act ingratitude? . . . a wife cannot be grateful if she's grasping for her rights." She recommended that a woman be prepared for sexual intercourse each night, particularly a working woman. Her husband would be threatened by her paycheck and need this reassurance and appreciation.

Morgan's book was one of many reacting to the threat of feminism. In fact, the production of such publications became a veritable cottage industry in the late sixties and early seventies. Most of them were by female fundamentalists reasserting Christian teachings along the lines of "ye wives be in subjection to your own husbands" (1 Peter 3:1) or "the husband is the head of the wife, even as Christ is the head of the church" (Ephesians 5:23). Eugenia Price's *Woman to Woman* and *The Unique World of Women* were prominent and pioneering titles. But literally dozens of others set forth elements of the philosophy—including *The Way Home: Beyond Feminism and Back to Reality* (1984) by Mary Pride, *You Can Be the Wife of a Happy Husband* (1974) by Darien B. Cooper, *Beyond Our Selves* (1968) and the other works by Catherine Marshall, *The Joy of Being Woman* (1975) by Ingrid Trobisch, *Let Me Be a Woman* (1976) and more by the prolific Elisabeth Elliot, and *The Power of a Woman's Love* (1983) by Barbara Rice. Beverly LaHaye not only published *The Spirit-Controlled Woman* (1976), she organized Concerned Women of America to defeat the ERA and fight Planned Parenthood. "The woman who is truly Spirit-filled will want to be totally submissive to her husband," LaHaye wrote. "This is a truly liberated woman. Submission is God's design for women."

Typical of these Christian books was Shirley Boone's *One Woman's Liberation,* published in 1972. "I'm convinced that submission is the key to freedom," wrote Pat Boone's singing wife. "The Bible charges wives to be submissive to their husbands. So, when Pat and I disagree completely about a point, I tell him how I feel. But, after I've done that, I whole-heartedly back his final decision. That is the crux of my new attitude."

Nashvillians Pat and Shirley recorded the duet LP *Side by Side* in 1959, but she didn't become an active entertainer until they incorporated daughters Cherry, Lindy, Laury, and Debby into the act on records and in a series of national TV appearances in the mid-1970s. Pat and his quintet of singing women were nominated for a gospel Grammy Award in 1971.

Shirley, born in 1935, pointed out in her book that she was the daughter of "National Barn Dance" headliner Eva Overstake (of Three Little Maids fame) and country superstar Red Foley. But she did not mention either the former's suicide or the latter's drinking. After the girls grew up and Debby became a solo singing star, Shirley remained active in Pat's campaign for virtue, godliness, and wholesome family values. They cowrote a marriage-advice book called *The Honeymoon Is Over,* continued to appear on religious broadcasts, and starred in their own Nashville Network cable TV show.

More prolific as an author was Anita Bryant, who published nine inspirational volumes in the 1970s, four in collaboration with then-husband Bob Green. "Bob wasn't about to let me walk over him," Anita wrote of their marital difficulties in *Mine Eyes Have Seen the Glory* (1970). "I realized I'd better . . . really turn it over to him. . . . And the only way I knew how to do that was to turn my bossy nature over to God. When I accepted Christ, He helped me relinquish authority so my husband could assume proper control."

Anita was a kiddie country singer who became a beauty queen, pop star, and gospel diva. She was born in rural Oklahoma in 1940, became a professional at age eight, and had her own Tulsa TV show at twelve. "I would sing mainly country music, because I used to live out in the sticks. And we were very poor. We used to listen to 'The Grand Ole Opry' on Saturday night and that's how I learned songs. My favorite was Little Jimmy Dickens—'A-Sleepin' at the Foot of the Bed,' 'Take an Old Cold Tater and Wait' and those kinds of things." In 1957 she won on "Arthur Godfrey's Talent Scouts." A year later she was named Miss Tulsa, then Miss Oklahoma. Her looks and talent carried her to the 1959 Miss America Pageant.

Anita sang her way up the pop charts in 1960 with "Paper Roses" and "My Little Corner of the World," both of which later became country hits for Mormon chanteuse Marie Osmond. In the mid-sixties she began emphasizing religious and patriotic themes in her Nashville recordings. Her gospel LPs earned Grammy nominations in 1968, 1971, and 1973. She sang on the Billy Graham Crusades and was a seven-year regular on Bob Hope's Christmas tours of Vietnam. She felt the American fighting men "wanted good, wholesome entertainment, not just cheap laughs. They wanted to look at a real woman from back home, not just what Bob Hope called the 'sexpot type.' And Bob and I learned that these men . . . very much cared about God."

She sang at both national political conventions in 1968, winning standing ovations from both Republicans and Democrats with her trademark, emotion-packed rendition of "The Battle Hymn of the Republic." But pressures from singing, book writing, TV appearances, recording, and family problems mounted. Anita suffered what was reported as a "near nervous breakdown" in 1974 and kicked a Valium habit two years later.

In 1977 an ordinance was introduced in Miami to prevent job dis-

Anita Bryant, 1966.

crimination against homosexuals. When she testified against it, she became too controversial and lost show-business jobs because of her vehemently antigay views. "I don't regret that, because I feel like what I did was right," she maintained in 1990. "The good news is that a lot has come out since about that particular life-style, and we now know that when you choose it, the ramifications are very destructive," she added, referring to AIDS.

A browse through a country record store in 1972 would have turned up such typical items as Jan Howard's fervent blend of religion and patriotism *For God and Country* or Loretta Lynn's *God Bless America Again* collection. Yet neither Anita Bryant nor Shirley Boone became a mainstream country star, despite their Nashville connections, fervent fundamentalism, and strong patriotism. Perhaps they were too outspoken. Significantly, most of the popular records by country music women concerning these turbulent times were nowhere near as pointed as the men's. The Vietnam conflict, for instance, was generally addressed in such tragedy-of-war records as Wanda Jackson's "Little Boy Soldier" (1968), Arlene Harden's "Congratulations (You Sure Made a Man Out of Him)" (1971), and Loretta Lynn's "Dear Uncle Sam" (1966). Country's female stars couched their political views in personal terms, usually using heartache lyrics to state their views.

That's not to say that right-leaning messages didn't emerge in female country music. In fact, country queen Tammy Wynette rose as one of country music's most famous conservative spokespeople. And her renown rests on a testimony in song that Phyllis Schlafly, Mirabel Morgan, Beverly LaHaye, Shirley Boone, and Anita Bryant would all applaud, "Stand by Your Man."

It might have lacked the religious dimension found in the antifeminist dialogue of her contemporaries, but with Tammy's soul-piercing delivery, "Stand by Your Man" sounded like it came from a whitewashed holy-roller church in the full heat of Pentecostal fervor. "Stand by Your Man" went to Number 1 on the country charts like an Atlas missile in 1968. It crossed over and became a Top 20 pop hit. It entered the movies as the keynote song in Jack Nicholson's *Five Easy Pieces* of 1970. It traveled to England to become a disc sensation of 1975. It became the title of Tammy's 1979 autobiography and the 1981 TV movie based on her life. "Stand by Your Man" is said to be the largest-selling single by a woman in the history of country music.

The song typecast Tammy as the long-suffering housewife, forlornly putting up with abuse for the sake of love. Her gripping, teardrop-in-every-note vocal style seemed to weep for every working-class woman who'd ever tolerated a beer-swilling, unfaithful slob; who'd ever slaved for a pack of ungrateful brats; who'd ever endured neglect and abuse. She was the choked-with-heartbreak victim, a doormat for her man and society.

"I'll See Him Through," "My Man (Understands)," "He Loves Me All the Way," "The Ways to Love a Man," and many other songs from her early days, 1966 through 1972, seem to justify feminists' branding her as the quintessential country-female victim. The gist of these works is that suffering ennobles a woman, acceptance is a woman's lot in life, and a woman's identity is defined through her man. "Good Lovin' (Makes It Right)" from 1971 sounds like it came straight from the pages of *The Total Woman*. In "(You Make Me Want to Be) A Mother" (1975) Tammy wanted to "walk around with pride with your child inside." And her supplicant position was refined in such LP tunes as "Make Me Your Kind of Woman" and, more explicitly, "Don't Liberate Me (Love Me)."

Yes, Tammy was a conservative, but there is much more to her music and her image than the stereotype pinned on her. Tammy's much-discussed doormat/victim material was tempered by many other female points of view. "Your Good Girl's Gonna Go Bad" (1967), for instance, is a classic feisty-female country number of the "turnabout-is-fair-play" variety. In "Woman to Woman" (1974) she warns the innocent country housewife of the wiles of painted hussies. "I Don't Wanna Play House" (1967), "D-I-V-O-R-C-E" (1968), "Bedtime Story" (1972), and "Kids Say the Darndest Things" (1973) creatively express the ways disintegrating marriages affect children. The wistful "We Sure Can Love Each Other" (1971) and "'Til I Get It Right" (1973) are sad contemplations of love gone wrong. In the pulsating "Womanhood" (1978) and "They Call It Making Love" (1979) Tammy took a candid look at modern sexuality.

In 1983's "Unwed Fathers" she criticized irresponsible men who leave the consequences of sex to women. She recorded Loretta Lynn's "Don't Come Home A-Drinkin'" and added "Stayin' Home Woman (Gettin' Tired of This Stayin' Out Man)," "You Can't Hang On," and other titles to the feisty-female country songbag. In 1982 Tammy scored a Top 10 hit with "Another Chance," the triumphant song of a victim who turns into a self-sufficient winner.

Tammy Wynette feels she has been misunderstood. The stirring "Singing My Song" (1969), for instance, is about being selfless and giving, but doesn't suggest being a victim. Even "Stand by Your Man" may have been misjudged.

"I have had so much criticism from that song," Tammy says. "But the line that they complained about the most, the feminists, was, 'If you love him, you'll forgive him. After all, he's just a man.' Well, hey, I'd like for a man to say, 'If you love her, you'll forgive her. After all, she's just a woman.' The first 'bra burning,' as they called it, was in September of sixty-eight, and 'Stand by Your Man' came out in August of [that year]. So it was perfect timing to be really, really scrutinized by the feminists."

"They took it the wrong way," Tammy told interviewer Joan Dew. "I didn't sing the song to say, 'You women stay home and stay pregnant and don't do anything to help yourselves. Be there waiting when he comes home, because a woman needs a man at any cost.' No, that's not what I was saying at all. . . . All I wanted to say in the song was, 'Be understanding. Be supportive.'"

Not all her peers heard it that way. "The line, 'If you love him, you'll forgive him'—that bothers me," said the sassy "Harper Valley P.T.A." gal Jeannie C. Riley. "It sounds like you should take anything he dishes out. . . . That's one of my pet peeves, songs that say you should belittle yourself for a man." Loretta Lynn recorded Tammy's tune, but cautioned, "I think you ought to stand by your man if he's standin' by you. If he ain't standin' by you, why, move over! I think if your man's doin' you right, fantastic. But how many men treat their wives right? Think about it."

But move over to *where*? As Tammy explained to writer Peter Guralnick, "If I was back home in Mississippi, being a Mississippi farmer's wife, you'd stand by a man regardless of what happened because you wouldn't have any reason or hope to do anything better. Because you have no education, you work in a shirt factory or something, and there's no way that you could better yourself if you wanted to."

Tammy is no farm wife. She is a star who has changed husbands like costumes. "I guess I've proven that I don't believe in staying with a man you no longer love." As virtually any country fan can tell you, Tammy

Wynette has "Stood by Her Man" at the altar five times. "I don't believe in staying married any longer than you stay in love," she says. And no matter what she sings, that is a code she has lived by.

Her image is ultrafeminine, but Tammy is quick to clarify it: "*Fragile?* Good Lord! Fragile I am not. I've been through an awful lot. . . . And I'm hangin' in there." While working the grueling, one-night-stand grind of country stardom for the past twenty-five years, she has gone through an appendectomy, a hysterectomy, a gallbladder operation, four surgeries for abdominal adhesions, two bladder suspensions, electroshock therapy, and drug dependency. She has suffered everything from pancreatitis to fever blisters. She has been kidnapped, shot at, harassed, bankrupted, and beset by family woes. She could write a guidebook to American hospitals and divorce courts. Tammy Wynette insists she's a lot gutsier than people think she is. She says she's a survivor, a fighter.

"My daddy's mother, my grandmother, was an inspiration to me. She was four foot eleven, weighed about a hundred and five pounds, and had nine kids. On her eighty-fifth birthday she went bowlin' and bowled one-sixty-eight! She lived to be ninety-two. When I'd talk about going to Nashville to make it in music, everybody would say, 'No, no, no!' And she'd say, 'Go on!' She kept saying, 'You sing as well as anybody I hear on the radio. Why don't you go on up there? I'll keep the kids.' She was very, very supportive. But she was the only one. . . . My mother did not want to see me leave the farm and Mississippi and head off with three kids and divorced with no job, no husband, no money. . . . I've sat and thought about that and thought, 'What if one of my kids came up to me and told me they had three kids and said, "Mama, I'm going to L.A. and I'm going to be a movie star."' I'd say, 'You've lost your mind.'"

Tammy was born in 1942. Her father died of a brain tumor when she was nine months old, and her mother went to work in a Memphis defense plant during World War II, leaving baby Virginia Wynette Pugh with cotton-farming grandparents. "I hated every minute I spent picking cotton," Tammy recalled in her autobiography. "I had made up my mind that I'd do anything before I'd go back to that life. . . . There *had* to be more to life than picking cotton and doing housework. Even when I was a little kid who'd never been off the farm, I knew that." She still keeps a copper dish on her living room mantel, full of cotton she picked on her grandfather's farm. "I keep it there to remind me, to make me humble."

Tammy was enthralled with the gospel quartets who traveled through Mississippi and Alabama during the southern gospel explosion in the late 1940s and early 1950s. The music and its conservative Pentecostal politics had a profound effect on her. She formed a singing trio called

"Wynette, Linda, and Imogene" with two friends to perform on a local gospel radio show.

Tammy was seventeen when she married Euple Byrd in 1959 a month before her high school graduation. Her mother was furious. Tammy's first child, Gwen, was born in 1961. A year later came Jackie. Euple couldn't keep a steady job, so Tammy enrolled in beauticians' school in Tupelo, Mississippi. During a brief stint in Memphis, she worked as a barmaid in a honky-tonk and sang country songs to the customers. The young family moved from place to place during the next five years, always one step ahead of destitution. In 1965 she asked Euple to leave and had their third child, Tina, while waiting for her divorce. Her family considered her exodus from marriage so radical that Euple and her mother tried to institutionalize her as insane. By age twenty-three the bedraggled young mother of three was in Birmingham, singing on a local TV show from 6 to 8 A.M., then working at Midfield Beauty Salon until 7 P.M. every day. She made forty-five dollars a week and lived in a government housing project. In October she accompanied a songwriter friend to Nashville for the annual Country Music Week convention and became hooked on the fantasy of becoming a country queen. That winter she moved to Music City and started knocking on doors.

One day in 1966 Tammy walked into the office of producer/songwriter Billy Sherrill, blurting, "My name is Wynette Byrd, and I've recently moved here from Birmingham. . . . I want a recording contract." Amazingly, he listened. Despite her inexperience, he recognized her natural vocal gift, one of the most dynamic emotional instruments in the annals of country music. The sharp, penetrating chills of her keening upper register and the soulful warmth in her lower tones affected millions the way they affected him that day. Two weeks later he altered her name to Tammy Wynette and recorded her singing Johnny Paycheck's country weeper "Apartment #9." It was the beginning of a long and profitable collaboration. Sometimes Sherrill wrote the songs; sometimes she did; sometimes they wrote together, as on "Stand by Your Man." Tammy's compositions are indistinguishable from those written for her by Sherrill or by such songwriters as Glenn Sutton, George Richey, and Norro Wilson. "There was no conscious decision to make an image," Richey later recalled. "It's just that we were all so close; we were all thinking alike." Just as Loretta Lynn's own songs blend seamlessly with those tailored to her image by Music Row professionals, so Tammy's hits form a cohesive musical statement whether they come from her pen or not.

When "Apartment #9" climbed onto the lower end of the charts at the end of 1966 Tammy thought her troubles were over. She desperately needed money from live shows to feed her three children; but even though she had a record out, she found that most country booking agents wouldn't work with female singers because of the "trouble" caused by their conflicting duties as wives and mothers.

"I had begun to realize I was working in a man's world, and most of them looked down on women in the business," Tammy reflected in her autobiography. "The same men who treated wives and girl friends with respect and consideration treated girl singers like a piece of merchandise. . . . Everybody joked about what the 'boys' did, but if a woman stepped out of line her reputation was ruined, and she could kiss her career good-bye. We had to be professional, dignified, prompt and always ladylike. But we also had to be tough enough to stand up for ourselves. . . . Every career woman knows the fine line you walk to succeed."

The contrast between this demure, pliant public self and the guts and will she needed in her professional life characterized Tammy's entire career. It's a phenomenon that writers have dubbed "steel magnolia" or "iron butterfly," and it informs the personalities of Tammy, Dolly Parton, Barbara Mandrell, Donna Fargo, and innumerable other country women who broke through in the macho country climate of the 1960s and 1970s.

"In those years, there weren't more than a half-dozen women head-lining their own shows in country music, and every time one of us stood up for our rights she made a point for us all. We had our own 'liberation movement' going, but I don't think any of us were aware of it. I know I wasn't. All I wanted was the right to work in my chosen field and be treated with as much respect as the men who did the same job.

"Professionally, I was learning to stand alone, but personally I still needed a partner," Tammy recalled. In 1967 she married songwriter Don Chapel, the younger brother of the 1940s Amburgey sisters trio Mattie, Marthie, and Minnie. Mattie was Jean Chapel, Tammy's neighbor in a Nashville trailer park, and she encouraged Tammy and Don's courtship. Don shared billing with his new wife. But Tammy's star rose ever higher during 1967 with the Top 10 success of "Your Good Girl's Gonna Go Bad" and the Number 1 hit "I Don't Wanna Play House." Professional jealousy soon consumed her relationship with Don. In addition, Tammy's idol George Jones was paying increasing attention to her. The country superstar was at her house one day in 1968 when a fight erupted between the Chapels. At Jones's invitation, Tammy and her daughters piled into his Cadillac Eldorado and drove away. He became her third husband in early 1969. Her fourth daughter, Georgette, was born in 1970.

Jones was an undisputed country king, and during her six-year marriage to him, Tammy rose to superstardom, as well. During their union she ruled the charts with her heartache singles and swept awards shows clean. The couple toured together as country's "President and First Lady" and recorded a series of hit duets chronicling their romance, marriage, breakup, reconciliation, disillusion, and divorce. During Jones's legendary rampages on cocaine and alcohol, he could strike her or shoot at her. Tammy never drank, but she experimented with marijuana and became dependent on pain pills as her medical problems proliferated. Country fans became fascinated by both stars' stormy personal lives, and Tammy became a staple of the tabloid newspapers. Each surgery, each divorce, each heartache, became a public debacle eagerly consumed by gossips. After divorcing Jones, she had affairs with New England Patriots pro football star Tommy Neville, Vanderbilt University coach Len Hughes, Gatlin Brothers tenor Rudy Gatlin, and movie star Burt Reynolds.

The separation from Jones was her trial by fire as a country star. For the first time in her life, Tammy was the sole headliner. Night after night fans yelled to the stage, "Where's George?" "I didn't realize just how much I had depended on him on stage until after we divorced. I did no talking. He carried the whole show. . . . Even though I'd been on stage for eight years, I didn't know how to communicate with the people."

But Tammy put together a startlingly good road show. She'd rouse the crowd using hand-clapping gospel harmony tunes with Sue Richards and her other backup singers. She'd romp through sassy numbers, then pour her guts out in a sad song. At one point Tammy would invariably sit alone on a stool and tell the fans about her life. It was like sharing her diary in song, an extraordinarily intimate moment. She'd softly sing "I'll just keep on fallin' in love 'til I get it right," and everyone in the audience felt they understood. The heart-tugging recitation "Dear Daughters" chronicled the pain country music's women feel about constant life on the road away from their growing children. It invariably reduced her working-women listeners to guilty tears. Tammy Wynette concerts became must-see events for even noncountry fans, for they were startlingly emotional experiences of shared insight, touching frankness, and simple-hearted vulnerability.

Her fame was brighter than ever, but Tammy's private life became ever darker. Her home was burglarized fifteen times; there were threats on the lives of her children; mysterious fires were set on her tour bus and in her house. A take-charge Nashville real estate personality named Michael Tomlin entered her life, driving a Mercedes, drinking Dom Perignon, and renting Learjets to fly to her concerts. Within weeks of meeting her, he proposed. He became her fourth husband in 1976. The marriage lasted six weeks. Then the bills for his extravagances all came to her.

The hospitalizations continued—for cystic mastitis, vocal cord nodes, inner ear infections, kidney problems, stomach ailments. In 1978 she was abducted from a Nashville shopping center, driven eighty miles, beaten by her kidnapper, and dumped on a rural highway. The case was never solved. As her girls entered their teens, some inevitable mother-daughter conflicts began to simmer. Tina was cut from the same willful cloth as her mother; she ran away from home at sixteen. By this time, Tammy was hooked on pain pills.

She married her fifth husband in 1978. Actually, he'd been there all along. George Richey had cowritten "You and Me," "(Let's Get Together) One Last Time," and other hits for her, and he and Tammy had collaborated on her 1976 signature song "'Til I Can Make It On My Own." She'd often relied on his judgment, business sense, and strong musicianship. Now, for the first time in her life, she fell in love with a friend. Richey became the rock she'd been looking for, taking the burden of career management from her shoulders, leading her band, producing some of her albums, and in general "standing by his woman." They have weathered some storms together—deaths in their families, her 1986 treatment for addiction at the Betty Ford Center, a 1988 bankruptcy filing in the wake of some failed Florida investments, and his 1991 heart attack. But there has been sunshine, too. In 1986 Tammy joined the cast of the CBS TV soap opera "Capitol," portraying waitress Darlene Stankowski. Old friend Burt Reynolds cast her in his 1985 movie *Stick* and directed her 1990 music video "Let's Call It a Day Today." By the end of the 1980s she had scored twenty Number 1 singles and eleven Number 1 albums, won two Grammys and three CMA awards, and sold more than thirty million records. She was given the Living Legend honor at the 1991 TNN/Music City News Awards.

Musicians from all over the musical map have lined up to sing with her. She numbers Tom Petty, Elvis Costello, Jeff Lynne, Elton John, Melissa Etheridge, James Taylor, and Patty Smyth among her noncountry fans and was cited as a major influence by the crop of new-traditionalists who reinvigorated the country sound in the late 1980s and early 1990s. Soulful Mark Gray teamed up with her for the 1985 Top 10 hit "Sometimes When We Touch." Emmylou Harris, Vince Gill, Ricky Van Shelton, Rodney Crowell, and a raft of other young stars sang on her landmark 1987 LP *Higher Ground.* In 1990 she hit the charts with Randy Travis, singing "We're Strangers Again." She and close friend Loretta Lynn began collaborating as songwriters in the late 1980s, and Tammy began cowriting with Dolly Parton in 1992. But her unlikeliest collaboration was with the enigmatic British duo The KLF. Tammy created a 1992 international hit sensation singing their dance-pop number called

"Justified and Ancient." The woman who'd once campaigned for segregationist George Wallace cavorted in the KLF video with half-nude black dancers and roared to Number 1 on pop charts throughout the world. "I did it because it was so much fun to do, something different. I have such a square image. Heartbreak-and-hurt. The songs that were big records for me were sad, hurtin' songs. So I think people think of me as being a sad person. But I'm not."

Tammy Wynette is an extraordinarily charismatic woman, one of the most compelling female personalities in country music. It's easy to get lost in her honeyed Alabama flatland drawl, the soft-yet-firm candor of her speech, her natural gift of conversation. She simultaneously projects gentility and earthiness. She has the same kind of intense character beauty as movie great Barbara Stanwyck had, and there's that same smoldering emotionalism beneath her ladylike demeanor. She has tried to be honest with herself and honest to her audience.

And Tammy knows that audience is female. "I never want to go out there and be a threat to any woman. I think about how many times I sat where they were sitting, watching someone else on stage. If you were too sexual, you were a threat to them. I make two clothes changes in my show because I think the women really appreciate fashion and like to see different outfits. . . . I think I dressed classy, but conservatively classy. . . . I have always wanted to look like a lady on stage. . . . I had rather they know me, the truthful woman, than for me to be put on a pedestal, where I don't belong. I'd rather they know that I'm just a plain human being. I may be a singer, but I'm just a plain human being. . . . The only thing different between me and you is my job and your job. I travel and I sing and you don't. But you work someplace else.

"When I started, and even through the years when Jones and I were married, I was very, very conservative. . . . I've tried to explain to people that that was the way I was born. At home in Mississippi and Alabama where I grew up, the man's word in the house was God."

Tammy has often been billed as "The Heroine of Heartbreak," but she hasn't suffered alone in song. Several of the most towering country voices of the sixties and seventies sang from the depths of despair. Many, like Tammy, spoke for conservative Middle America in both music and life.

The most volcanic-voiced of them was Connie Smith, whose pillar-of-fire delivery sobbed with desolation. The ecstatic pain in Connie's hair-raising vocal power poured from a truly tortured soul. She was a reluctant star. Between 1966 and 1976, when she routinely topped the charts, Connie was a deeply troubled woman who couldn't reconcile her profession with her religious beliefs, her marriage, and her motherhood.

Connie's rise to stardom from small-town Indiana is the stuff of which music legends are made. She was born Constance June Meador in 1941, and her father was an alcoholic who sometimes beat, but more often neglected, her and her thirteen siblings. She says she "was the shy, quiet one, the one who just watched everyone else." The emotional scars of her childhood led to a nervous breakdown at age eighteen. As a young housewife in 1963 she was talked into entering a talent contest in Ohio. She won it by singing Jean Shepard's "I Thought of You" and was spotted by Opry star Bill Anderson, who invited her to Nashville. Chet Atkins signed her to RCA. In July 1964 she recorded Anderson's heartache song "Once a Day." By the time of that year's Country Music Week festivities, she was the Cinderella of country music.

Connie Smith, 1971.

The lovely, fawnlike young woman with golden-blond hair and glacier blue eyes recalls with some horror the drunken conventioneering disc jockeys' pawing her. "I was terrified; I was miserable," she says of those days. "I was so unready to be here. I didn't know what I was doing. I kind of had the reputation of being snotty or stuck up, I guess. But it wasn't that. I was just plain scared to death. . . . I was real ignorant and real gullible.

"I used to work clubs, and often the attitude was that if they booked you, they owned you as a woman. They bought you to play the club. They bought you, period. It didn't take that much to set them straight, but it hurt just the same. And it was an insult."

Her power and her victory were in her voice. Wherever Connie Smith opened her mouth to sing, she electrified listeners with her searing emotionalism and heart-in-throat conviction. At her best, Connie expressed a deep yearning for love and pleaded for understanding in her music.

She says now that the aching lyrics of "Where Is My Castle?" (1971), "Ribbon of Darkness" (1969), "Burning a Hole in My Mind" (1967), "The Hurtin's All Over (Me)" (1966), and "Just for What I Am" (1972) were chillingly autobiographical.

Unhappiness enveloped her. Connie's first marriage, to Ohio steelworker Jerry Smith, had been shaky even before the couple arrived in Nashville. Under the pressure of show business it disintegrated, and Connie was left alone with son Darren in a world that seemed false and shallow. A marriage to guitarist Jack Watkins survived just over a year and left her with a second son, Kerry. Her career accelerated dramatically as she was showcased in the country movies *Road to Nashville* (1966), *Las Vegas Hillbillies* (1966), and *Second Fiddle to a Steel Guitar* (1965). The titanically gifted vocalist was marketed with the trivial slogans "Cute 'n' Country" and "Sweetheart of 'The Grand Ole Opry.'" The unsophisticated Nashville newcomer says she was shocked and disillusioned by the backstage sexuality, drinking, and partying she found among the country stars she'd idolized. By 1968 small-town Connie had big-city problems. She was contemplating suicide and seeing a psychiatrist when she found Jesus.

Her faith has sustained her ever since. When she signed with Columbia Records, she insisted that she be allowed to record at least one gospel album a year, and in 1974 *Connie Smith Sings Hank Williams Gospel* became one of her greatest moments on disc. Secular success continued, as well. "Just One Time" (1971), "If It Ain't Love" (1972), "I Never Knew" (1974), "Why Don't You Love Me" (1975), and the fed-up "I Don't Wanna Talk It Over Anymore" (1976) stand the test of time as among the most powerful country female vocal performances of the seventies.

But while she was dominating the radio airwaves, her dissatisfaction was building. "I never could get used to the idea that you're a 'product' that's to be sold. I took it all so personally. And you can't take the music business personally, because then you get hurt, and then you get bitter. That's what happened to me. . . . But sometimes when you're the most unhappy, the music is at its peak. That was the only way I could release what I was feeling. Singing was like therapy for me." Her performances swelled with almost unbearable vocal intensity as she struggled to find personal peace. During the 1972 country convention she married telephone installer Marshall Haynes. They began doing evangelistic work together and now have three daughters. In 1978 Connie stopped touring. When the fans voted her Gospel Act of the Year at the 1979 *Music City News* awards show, she announced that she was forsaking country music for religious singing. Shortly afterward Connie withdrew completely from the Music Row whirl, performing only on "The Grand Ole Opry" stage for years to come.

"I have never regretted that decision," she says. "I was sick and tired of it all. There just wasn't enough of me to go around. I nursed all three of my girls on the road. I couldn't keep doing what I was doing in church and with the family and the career. I couldn't afford someone to clean my house and do all that stuff. So the only thing I could give up was the singing. And I never really thought I'd go back to it." Her talent was too mighty to lie still. Connie was lured back onto country labels in the mid-1980s, although she never regained her career momentum.

Connie Smith still pours out her soul each weekend on the Opry. She is a woman who found a balm in religion and traditional values. As for women's liberation, she says, "That's for unhappy women." She once told interviewer Mary Ellen Moore, "There's a lot of thinking you do about your husband when you iron his shirts. I'd rather hear him say, 'That's a good supper' than 'That was a good recording.' . . . I'd rather quit what I'm doing than have him quit what he's doing. I like the feeling of knowing my husband makes enough money to take care of me and my kids and that it's not me making the living. I know most men like that, but I like it too."

She goes to her little corner of the music world on "The Grand Ole Opry" each weekend to share her gift. And that's enough for her. "Singing on the Opry has always been a joy. It's like going back to home, to a family reunion. Some of my favorite times have been just backstage at the Opry with the girls."

Record producer Fred Foster calls Connie Smith "the essence of country music. . . . the epitome of country singers." Dolly Parton adds an amen to that. "There's really only three female singers in the world," says Dolly, "Streisand, Ronstadt, and Connie Smith. The rest of us are only pretending."

Heartache stylist Barbara Fairchild followed the same path as Connie. She, too, was brought to Nashville as an innocent and achieved prodigious success. She, too, faced disillusion and confusion before turning to the Lord.

Like her idol Brenda Lee, Barbara was a child performer. The daughter of a long-haul trucker and farmer, Barbara was born in 1950 in Knobel, Arkansas. As a tot she sang gospel in a trio with two aunts, and her father took her to clubs to sing with bands. The Fairchilds moved to St. Louis when she was twelve, and she made her first record at fifteen for the tiny Norman label. When she was seventeen, her dad drove Barbara and her songwriting friend Ruby Van Noy to Nashville to audition. Signed to Kapp Records, Barbara issued "Remember the Alamo-ny" and "Breaking in a Brand New

Man" in 1968 before moving to the star-making CBS corporation.

In 1972 Barbara issued her LP *A Sweeter Love*. The title tune was a cheating number, but late that year DJs began playing a different song from the collection, an odd, seemingly fluffy little ditty called the "Teddy Bear Song." By 1973 it was a Number 1 smash, a pop crossover success, and a Grammy nominee. It was sung from the point of view of a bruised young romantic who wishes she was a child's teddy bear with no feelings to get hurt. Barbara returned to the theme of yearning for childhood innocence in "Kid Stuff" and "Baby Doll," both of which also vaulted into the Top 10.

"I waited so long for a hit record," she later recalled. "When it came, I wanted to be ready. When I finally got it, I still wasn't ready. . . . At that point in my life, I'm not sure who I was." Barbara was typecast as the kiddie-theme singer, "and that's the type of bag . . . that you can't stay in eternally. . . . After 'Teddy Bear,' we got songs sent to us like 'Boo Boo' and 'Yogi Bear,' I mean *everything* to do with that kind of thing." She spent 1974 through 1978 in a frustrating quest for an adult image, creating the most powerful music of her career but stalling ever lower on the charts.

She issued three richly textured explorations of female emotions, 1974's *Standing in Your Line*, 1976's *Mississippi*, and 1977's *Free and Easy*. "Let Me Love You Once Before You Go" (1977) and "Cheatin' Is" (1976) were brilliantly performed songs of marital infidelity. "She Can't Give It Away" (1978) was the stark portrait of an aging prostitute. In the searing "Standing in Your Line" (1974) she was helplessly drawn into a destructive relationship. "This Stranger, My Little Girl" (1974) concerned the mother of a troubled teen. "Lonely Old Man" (1974) was a bitter indictment of males. "I'm Not Weak, I'm a Woman" (1974) explained tears. Barbara's big antiliberation number was "I Just Love Being a Woman" (1975).

But none of these later songs cracked the Top 10. People didn't seem to want to listen when she wasn't warbling kiddie-theme material. "Our records just slipped and slipped, and I was doin' less and less," Barbara recalls. "And at that point . . . I had a lot of trauma in my personal life, had a really rocky marriage." Two of them, actually. She divorced first husband Mike Haines and married jazz pianist Randy Reinhard, under whose sway she recorded the pop-oriented *This Is Me!* (1978). "Musically, it was *not* me. If you listen to the songs in that album, you can hear how rocky our marriage was. Remember 'It's Sad to Go to the Funeral (Of a Good Love That Has Died)'? I was tryin' to make my marriage work, tryin' everything I knew. Sometimes you can be a puppet and not realize it."

When CBS dropped her contract, she moved to Texas for seven years. She wasn't even thirty, and she was a miserable has-been.

In the Lone Star State she divorced Reinhard, found Jesus, and married reformed Texas honky-tonker Milton Carroll. She recorded some 1980 duets with Opry star Billy Walker, then a 1982 solo single about abortion, "The Biggest Hurt." "It deals with the subject gently," Barbara said. She decided to proceed. "I knew that I didn't believe in it [abortion], but I thought there were extenuating circumstances, and I can understand a woman being in a position where she feels like she has to have one. . . . most people making that decision don't really know what all it involves. I don't want to be mean and hateful to anybody. I think we're here to love one another."

Although blazing with religious zeal, Barbara doesn't preach hellfire or damn the world around her. Hers is the gospel of love and Christian charity. She's a truly gentle spirit with a zesty, madcap sense of humor, a cockeyed-optimist outlook, and a merry charm. She goes to Mexico every year with Christmas presents for the poor, is the spokesperson for Caring for Children, and is an enthusiastic charity worker.

When she and her family moved back to Music City in 1984, Barbara went to work as a waitress. By 1986 she was on her feet again. In 1990 she teamed up with Happy Goodman Family daughter Tanya and Hemphills dynasty member Candy Hemphill Christmas in a gospel trio called Heirloom. The act's delicious harmony blend captivated the religious-singing world, and Heirloom won a Dove Award from the Gospel Music Association. Barbara's solo gospel debut, *The Light,* appeared in 1991. Its theme song was "Turn Right and Then Go Straight."

Midwestern housewife Eleanor Johnston Stoller built her entire career

around themes of patriotism, God, and heartache. As Cristy Lane she revolutionized country music marketing by appealing directly to TV viewers through a series of widely seen record ads. Her cornerstone performance, "One Day at a Time," resonated through alcohol rehabilitation programs, religious revivals, and self-help centers. She was one of the most visible country entertainers among the troops in Vietnam. At a time when international corporations were taking over the country business, she succeeded with her own record company. Cristy also pioneered the country migration from Nashville to Branson, Missouri.

Perhaps no other country music female is as unlikely a standard-bearer. Cristy was a shy personality with a wispy, private little singing voice that she was happy using as accompaniment to dishwashing, child rearing, and housework. It was her hustling, marketing-genius husband, Lee Stoller, who pushed her into the role of a family values spokeswoman and made her the centerpiece of a small music empire.

Cristy Lane's 1983 book became a best-seller, thanks to an ingenious TV marketing campaign.

"I do everything for Cristy's career but sing the songs," Stoller said. "I'm her manager, producer, record promoter, and . . . I okay everything concerning her public appearances. I even drive the bus, emcee our shows, and hawk the merchandise after the show." He even wrote her book, *Cristy Lane: One Day at a Time. Tennessean* newspaper reporter Sandy Neese was startled when he volunteered to do the talking for a Cristy Lane feature article while his wife sat silently by his side.

Cristy was born in 1940, the shy one among the twelve children in her Peoria, Illinois, family. She married Stoller in 1959, and they had three toddlers by 1964. He sold Pepperidge Farm baked goods. She worked for a printing company. But one day Stoller overheard her singing "The Tennessee Waltz" in their kitchen and got the brainstorm that she could be a star. He changed her name from Ellie Stoller to Cristy Lane. He had her dye her hair. He pushed her into singing "Paper Roses" at a local club in 1966, pushed her into writing a song, pushed her into recording a small-label single, pushed her into touring regionally, and pushed her into a 1968 guest shot on Chicago's dying "National Barn Dance." Cristy was petrified. "I tried to please him," she recalled. "He wanted me to sing so bad, and when I didn't, I caught hell." When she balked at becoming an entertainer, he sent her to a psychiatrist who put her on tranquilizers, then got her stacks of self-help books to read. She amended his reading list with her Bible. He billed her as "The Sweetest Voice This Side of Heaven." She described her early singing as "awful."

By 1968 she was a wreck. Stoller had her performing in their own Peoria nightclub and was pushing harder than ever. She overdosed on pills. "I just feel like I have no control over my life," Cristy reports telling her Mayo Clinic psychiatrist, "that no matter what I do, it's not good enough. If I say something wrong, Lee gets upset. If I pick out a dress he doesn't like, it goes back to the store. He even tells me what and how to eat sometimes. . . . He's so sure of himself, so positive, so outgoing. I'm none of those things. . . . I feel so insignificant next to him. I'd never go out and push myself the way he does. And I certainly would never go after a singing career on my own."

In 1969 Stoller booked her to tour army outposts in Vietnam. It wasn't a USO-sponsored trip or a Bob Hope junket. This was a ragtag string of 120 show dates that took them to the front lines. Unlike many Vietnam entertainers, Cristy Lane saw combat death firsthand and nearly lost her own life. Despite her fragility, she persevered in the jungles. The Stollers wound up losing $12,500. After they got home, Cristy overdosed again.

His business skills got them back on their feet financially, and in 1972 they moved to Nashville. After Cristy's tapes were turned down by the major record companies on Music Row, Stoller formed their own LS Records label and began issuing Cristy Lane singles. By the mid-seventies her whispery voice was on the airwaves with whimpering heartache material such as "I'm Gonna Love You Anyway" and "Let Me Down Easy." Many of her biggest records had simple, almost nursery-rhyme melodies—1978's "Penny Arcade" and 1979's "Simple Little Words," for instance. Even her one assertive lyric, "I Just Can't Stay Married to You," came out sounding like a merry-go-round ditty. Fittingly, she revived Marion Worth's 1963 kiddie tune "Shake Me I Rattle."

The Stollers' persistence and hard work began to pay off when she won the Academy of Country Music's Top New Female Vocalist award of 1979. A year later she sang her career-defining record, dusting off a 1974 Marilyn Sellers hit, "One Day at a Time." The Marijohn Wilkin/Kris Kristofferson lyric and Cristy's feathery, intimate, average-folks delivery struck a chord with listeners; the disc became a Number 1 hit, and Stoller used its success to build a mini–mail-order empire. "One Day at a Time" became the centerpiece of a gospel album and the title of Cristy's book, both of which are said to have sold a million, thanks to Stoller's marketing them on TV and in ads placed everywhere from *The National Enquirer* to *TV Guide.* Succeeding LPs emphasized the religious side of her repertoire, while *Cristy Lane Salutes the G.I.'s of Vietnam* mined patriotism. There were T-shirts, souvenir photos, and even a fourteen-inch-tall Cristy Lane doll. By the early 1980s Cristy Lane TV products seemed to be everywhere.

But in 1982 Stoller was convicted under federal racketeering statutes and sentenced to a prison term. After he got out, the sharp-thinking Stoller continued to market his wife's soft, gentle singing. He was one of the first in Nashville to see the potential of Branson, Missouri, the country tourism center in the Ozarks. Cristy Lane's blend of gospel music, singsong heartache tunes, and patriotic numbers made her a major attraction there.

Through it all, Cristy preferred to watch TV soap operas and do needlepoint. "I like staying home," she said. "I like working around the house, baking, taking care of the kids."

Cristy's passivity was a feminine ideal that many other stars of her era aspired to. Pennsylvania native Lynda K. Lance (b. 1949) made her biggest splash on the charts with the unfeminist "A Woman's Side of Love," and her 1969 LP of the same title contained the equally pliant "The Weakness of a Woman," as well as a remake of Sandy Posey's 1966 hit "Born a Woman."

"A woman's place in this ol' world is under some man's thumb," sang Sandy in this riveting song. "If you're born a woman, you're born to be . . . treated like dirt." What's more, "I was born a woman; I'm glad it happened that way." "Born a Woman" was written by future Warner Bros. Records Vice President Martha Sharp. Although a far bigger pop hit than "Stand by Your Man," as well as a more masochistic song, it oddly never received the feminist bashing that "Stand by Your Man" got. It appeared two years earlier—before the women's liberation movement crystallized—and that may be one reason why. Another might be that its singer avoided the limelight. Reticent and unaggressive by nature, Sandy Posey gave few interviews during the

height of her stardom and never became a
touring star.

In addition to Sandy Posey and Lynda K.
Lance, "Born a Woman" was recorded by
country singers Alice Creech, Connie Smith,
Patti Michaels, Jean Shepard, and Jan
Howard. And by the early 1970s it had
several imitators. "God Made Me a Woman"
was released by both Sharon Forrest and
Tracy Miller. Similarly, Karen Wheeler was
"Born to Love and Satisfy" and was a worshipful "Woman in Love." Dorothy Jean
sang "Your Love Made Me a Woman."
Torchy Florida stylist Brenda Kaye Perry
sang, "When I feel your child inside, then
I know 'I Am a Woman'" and added the
pliant "Make Me Your Woman" to the
antilib repertoire. Teresa Brewer made one of her occasional recording trips to Nashville to do her 1975 LP *Unliberated Woman*.
Sunday Sharpe answered Paul Anka's "Having My Baby" pop hit with
the country single "I'm Having Your Baby" (1974). "Make him your
reason for living," advised Baltimore-bred Bobbi Martin in her big 1970
hit "For the Love of Him." Is it any wonder that women's liberationists
looked at their country music sisters as antifeminist reactionaries?

"I'm no women's libber," said "Grand Ole Opry" star Jeannie Seely in
1973, "but I do think that it's great that the world is giving the female
entertainer the chance to prove what she can do."

Torch-singing Jeannie smoldered with throaty emotion when she
sang. One of the finest heartache/victim singers of the late sixties and
early seventies, she suffered mightily on disc with such performances as
"Don't Touch Me," "Little Things," and "It's Only Love." But no one
who encountered Jeannie Seely in real life would ever mistake her for a
shrinking violet. Rather than the conservative meekness of Connie Smith
or Cristy Lane, Jeannie Seely inherited the salty, bawdy, good-time-gal
style of her heartache-music foremother Patsy Cline. She might have
enacted the lovelorn victim onstage, but back in her dressing room you'd
find Jeannie puffing on a cigarette, sipping booze, and sharing a dirty
joke. The bighearted blonde's wisecracks and witticisms are legendary in
Nashville. Her smoky speaking voice and robust laughter have enlivened
many a country gathering.

"Oh, Lord, I'm always sayin' something," she says. One Seely-ism

Shy studio singer Sandy
Posey rocketed to pop
fame with this 1966
record. "Born a Woman"
was subsequently sung by
a host of country female
performers.

goes, "Of course I want you for your body. I've got a mind of my own." Another is, "I woke up on the right side of the wrong bed this morning." Women loved her when she sassed, "An ex-husband is one mistake you don't have to live with"; and everyone can relate to her one-liner, "You knock me to my knees, but you cannot make me crawl while I'm down there." "Actually," she confides, "the way I really wrote it was, 'They can knock me to my knees, but they cannot make me give head while I'm down there.' But I cleaned it up."

Jeannie's frank talk, striking intelligence, free-spirited life-style, and deeply moving vocals have long set her apart from most female country stars. When she arrived in Nashville in 1965, women were still expected to portray the submissive country sweetheart. Jeannie blazed a nonconformist trail from the moment she hit the Opry stage in her miniskirt.

Jeannie Seely, 1970.

She'd learned to be independent as the child of a poor Pennsylvania farmer and steelworker. Born in 1940 in tiny Townville, Jeannie was singing on local radio by age eleven and was a regular on an Erie TV station by age sixteen. "They all made fun of me because I sang country," she recalls of her teenage years. "I grew up poor, and in those days calling somebody 'country' was a put-down." The cheerleader and majorette took a secretarial job after graduation, enrolling in classes at night school in banking and law. But she and three girlfriends decided they wanted to see the country. They saved their money and took off in their sports cars in 1961. Jeannie had a job for a year in a Beverly Hills bank, but quit it to take a secretarial job for half the money at Liberty Records because she wanted to learn the music business. Meanwhile, she began singing on an L.A. country TV show, writing songs for Four Star Music, working as a DJ for the Armed Forces Radio Network, and recording for Challenge Records. Soul singer Irma Thomas recorded Jeannie's "Anyone Who Knows What Love Is," scoring a hit with it in 1964. Country stars Dottie West, Norma Jean, and Connie Smith also did her early tunes.

Songwriter Hank Cochran took a shine to the petite blonde and encouraged her to move to

Music City. "Well, I'm here!" she announced to him after turning up unexpectedly at the 1965 DJ Convention with fifty dollars and a Ford Falcon to her name. "Do you still want to work with me?" He answered, "Yes, if you're going to let *me* make the decisions and do what I know is best for you." Cochran wrote a throbbing song of unfulfilled passion called "Don't Touch Me," which Jeannie sang with aching conviction. It shot up the charts in 1966 and won a Grammy Award. She joined "The Grand Ole Opry" and married Cochran, who provided several of her subsequent successes.

A string of hits from 1966 to 1969 solidified her reputation as a country torch singer. Jeannie's husky, cigarette-stained voice moaned with such agony that she was dubbed "Miss Country Soul."

"Back in those days, you couldn't even mention sex. I didn't know there were such rules. I never went to 'The Grand Ole Opry' until I was on it. Ott Devine called me into his office and said, 'Honey, you're not allowed to wear a miniskirt on the Opry.' I thought he was joking at first. I said, 'I never heard that rule.' Finally I made a deal with him. I said, 'Okay: If you don't let anybody in the front door with a miniskirt on, I won't come in the back door with one on.'" She continued to mirror the times rather than don an old-fashioned "sweetheart" uniform. If go-go boots were in, she wore them; if it was pantsuits, Jeannie sported a stylish one. When jeans were fashionable "outlaw" wear, she donned denims. Her music was contemporary, too. Jeannie's "Who Needs You?" is almost certainly the only lyric sung on the Opry's hallowed stage to this day that mentions smoking dope.

"I never planned to set any sort of trend," said the woman who broke the Opry's "gingham curtain." "I'm about like any other normal American girl my age. I think I dress and act pretty much the way she does. . . . A lot of my fans have always been women because my songs said what they really felt."

During the seventies, Jeannie palled around with the Willie Nelson "outlaw" crowd. She continued to be a regular presence on the charts, scoring hits in 1973 and 1974 by reworking the hobo lament "Can I Sleep in Your Barn Tonight Mister?" into "Can I Sleep in Your Arms?" and adapting the Appalachian ballad "Come All You Fair and Tender Ladies" into "Lucky Ladies." Jeannie became franker as the decade progressed, trading in heartache tunes for the spicy "Take Me to Bed" (1978) and the autobiographical "We're Still Hanging In There Ain't We Jessi?" (1977), which chronicled the marital ups and downs of Jan Howard, Dottie West, Tammy Wynette, Jessi Colter, Sammi Smith, and herself.

But life as a country music woman had its downside, too. Jeannie's marriage broke up. She hit the booze for a time, and concert bookings became scarcer. After she was involved in a near-fatal car accident in 1977, Dottie West helped her get back on her feet. Jeannie opened her own Nashville nightclub in 1985, but it failed within a year. "The only bright spot in my life right now is a flashing neon sign . . . and even that comes and goes," she wisecracked. She believed her independent spirit had cost her much personal happiness: "There's a catch-22 that goes with being free—you want it, but there's a loneliness that comes with it, too."

Toward the end of the 1980s plucky Jeannie parlayed her personality into a budding theatrical career. Teaming with veteran Jean Shepard and newcomer Lorrie Morgan, she costarred in a three-ages-of-women country musical called *Takin' It Home* in 1986. In 1988 she played "Miss Mona" in a Nashville production of *The Best Little Whorehouse in Texas,* and in 1989 she took a nonmusical role as the bag-lady title character of *Everybody Loves Opal.* She published *Pieces of a Puzzled Mind,* a book of witticisms, in 1988 and in 1989 starred at the unveiling of the forty-foot statue of the goddess Athena in Nashville's Parthenon.

With her chin-out, tough/tender, heart-of-gold manner Jeannie Seely remains one of country's most completely modern female personalities. "They always used to tell me if I had a brain, I'd be dangerous. Well, I wonder if they know by now that I do. . . . and I am."

Like nearly all the women of her country generation, Jeannie teamed with a powerful male star for duets. In her case it was multiple-award-winning Opry great Jack Greene. The fiery Jeannie and the laid-back Jack were a potent harmony team from 1969 to 1972, and their touring show was one of country's best. Most male stars of the sixties and seventies wanted women in their acts to dress up the stage and provide both visual and vocal contrast. Jack was the seasoned vet, and Jeannie was the up-and-comer. This was a typical pattern and a standard strategy for women trying to break into the business. Since it was so difficult for women as soloists, many hoped that being a star's duet partner would launch them as stars in their own right. But Sherry Bryce, Lois Johnson, Mary Lou Turner, and a large number of others never got beyond the second-class "duet partner" status.

Gifted Bonnie Owens has spent her entire career obscured by male superstars. Born in Oklahoma in 1932, Bonnie Campbell initially performed with husband Buck Owens, achieving a little solo fame for her Patsy Cline tribute single, "Missing on a Mountain." Then she married Merle Haggard and sang as his duet partner. The charismatic Haggard soon eclipsed her singing, yodeling, songwriting, and business management talents. Despite five fine albums for Capitol in the 1960s, her solo career dried up. Surprisingly, Bonnie remained as a backup singer in Haggard's road show throughout his two successive marriages. She even served as bridesmaid to Leona Williams when she replaced Bonnie as Mrs. Merle Haggard in 1978.

The gigantic talent of honky-tonk superstar George Jones has dwarfed many a female partner. His first harmonizer was Virginia Spurlock, followed by the almost-as-obscure Jeanette Hicks and Brenda Carter. Margie Singleton's twin-harmony work with him on 1962's "Waltz of the Angels" is one of his best early duets.

But the most influential Jones pairings were his efforts with Melba Montgomery from 1963 through 1968. The George-and-Melba lyrics set the tone for an entire generation of "dialogue" discs, for they specialized in both the "we're cheatin'" songs that let sexual sparks fly and the "funny fight" songs that allow country boys and girls to air their differences in harmony. The latter were musical domestic skits with echoes of vaudeville-stage comedy, as well as of the question-and-response courtship folk tunes of Appalachia. George and Melba's alternating male and female verses generally cast the singers as a blue-collar couple with opposing views of romance.

In "Party Pickin'" George and Melba enacted the familiar scene of a couple bickering after a party. In "Feudin' and Fightin'" she's complaining shrilly about being trapped raising the kids while he says she's let her looks go to pot. In "Let's Invite Them Over" they're each in love with a partner of the couple who are their best friends. In "Now Tell Me" she complains about housework and he complains about debts.

Melba wrote or cowrote some of their finest numbers, including "Simply Divine," "Until Then," and "Livin' on Easy Street," which portrays a hillbilly couple on welfare. She also wrote their biggest hit, 1963's "We Must Have Been Out of Our Minds." Melba's mournful moan was the perfect vocal foil for George's bent-note phrasing. "Flame in My Heart," "Close Together," and the entire contents of their *Bluegrass Hootenanny* LP of 1964 are the evidence.

She went on to record dynamite duets with pop star Gene Pitney (1966's "Baby Ain't That Fine") and Opry star Charlie Louvin (1970's delightful blue-collar romance "Something to Brag About"). Melba also recorded more than fifteen solo LPs, although her only major solo hit was 1974's motherhood ode "No Charge." Melba Montgomery (b. 1938) realized too late that she was typecast: "I guess I just couldn't get away from the duets. I believe, to a certain extent, that duets did overshadow my work as a solo artist."

George Jones's most famous duet partner was, of course, Tammy

Wynette. She'd previously sung "My Elusive Dreams" as David Houston's foil. But with Jones, Tammy achieved hillbilly duet nirvana. From 1971 to 1980 they chronicled their courtship, marriage, and divorce in "Take Me," "The Ceremony," "Let's Build a World Together," "We're Gonna Hold On," "We Loved It Away," and "Two Story House." The Tammy-and-George records endure as the perfect examples of the genre. Their splendid marriage chronicle "Golden Ring" and magnificently humorous, poor-but-proud "(We're Not) The Jet Set" will be played as long as people love classic country duet harmonies.

Tammy was a newcomer when she teamed with George. Likewise, young Loretta Lynn was boosted by superstar Ernest Tubb in duets. The rumbling honky-tonk bass and the clear mountain soprano enacted domestic problems in several of their tunes, including 1964's "Mr. and Mrs. Used to Be." Loretta definitely had the "funny-fight" upper hand in 1967's "Sweet Thang" and 1969's "Who's Gonna Take the Garbage Out."

Her second duet partner was Conway Twitty. They did some funny-fight material, notably "You're the Reason Our Kids Are Ugly." But

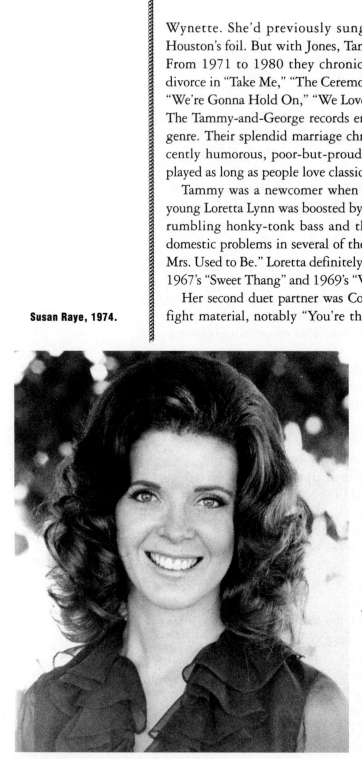

Conway and Loretta were generally a more sensual team, seething with emotions in a spectacular duet series from 1971 to 1981 that included "Lead Me On," "Louisiana Woman, Mississippi Man," "Feelin's," and "After the Fire Is Gone."

June Carter and Johnny Cash won the only funny-fight duet Grammy Award when they teamed up for the memorable 1967 spat "Jackson." In it, he's sick of their small-town marriage and wants to head for the bright lights of sin city. June hollers after him, "Well, go on down to Jackson . . . make a big fool of yourself. . . . See if I care."

"I'll Take the Dog" was the funny-fight duet saga of a divorcing couple who argue so strongly over which one gets the family pet that they decide to stay together. It was sung by Jean Shepard and Ray Pillow, the only notable team of the era composed of a star woman with a less-famous male. In fact, their 1966 and 1967 duets were the biggest hits Pillow ever had.

More typical was passive, pretty Susan Raye, who rode in on the coattails of skyrocketing star Buck Owens in 1970. Born in Oregon in 1944, Susan had a sweet, suburban brunet loveliness and an attractive, pop-tinged voice. Perhaps because her duets from 1970 to 1975 were abetted by "Hee Haw" TV stardom, Susan joined Tammy and Loretta as one of the few to graduate from duet singing to solo success. She scored more than twenty hits in the seventies. But Susan retired in 1978 because of religious convictions and a desire to raise her six children. "I have learned never to sacrifice my children or my husband for music," she said. Susan Raye went back to college to get a psychology degree, taught Bible-study classes, and became active in the PTA before recording again in 1985.

"I just kind of did what I was told," is how Susan described her tenure with Buck Owens. "I don't take too much credit, because Buck handled the business. . . . I'm not really pushy. I just don't do that sort of thing well, so I've been very lucky. I have someone else who does that for me, and who gets the material for me and says, 'This is what you sing.' So all I have to do is sing."

Like Buck Owens, rhinestone-bedecked "Grand Ole Opry" great Porter Wagoner was a savvy pro who knew his way around show business. The veteran's highly entertaining road show of the 1960s included a sizzling fiddler, a gap-toothed rube comedian, gospel homilies, honky-tonk tunes, rousing up-tempo fare, just-folks appeal, humble sincerity, and eye-popping costumes. It also included the requisite female singer. Norma Jean's working-girl tunes and clear-eyed beauty were enormously popular with Wagoner's fans. When their affair ended and she left his troupe, the superstar began looking for someone to replace her who wouldn't remind audiences of Norma Jean's absence. He first hired Tammy Wynette, then took Jeannie Seely on the road. But in a bubbly mountain girl named Dolly Parton, Wagoner found not only the decorative element he wanted, but a duet partner who could match him lick for lick in funny-fight songs, as well as conjure up passion in "cheatin'" numbers.

The Porter-and-Dolly discs from 1967 to 1980 contrasted his hound-dog baritone with her mountain-songbird soprano. The couple glowed in rural romance, pledging eternal devotion in "Lost Forever in Your Kiss," "Is Forever Longer Than Always," "Tomorrow Is Forever," and "Say Forever You'll Be Mine," as well as a string of titles featuring the word "always." They suffered broken hearts in the hits "Making Plans," "Just Someone I Used to Know," and "The Last Thing on My Mind." They recorded a striking amount of material that luxuriated in the guilt and

The ploy of pairing two independent stars in a duet arose from the cheating-song successes of Margaret Whiting & Jimmy Wakely ("Slipping Around") and Elton Britt & Rosalie Allen ("Quicksilver") in 1949 and 1950. Thereafter this kind of singing was institutionalized in country music:

KITTY WELLS & ROY ACUFF . . . KITTY WELLS & RED FOLEY

ANITA CARTER & HANK SNOW . . . ANITA CARTER & WAYLON JENNINGS . . . ANITA CARTER & JOHNNY DARRELL

DOTTIE WEST & JIM REEVES . . . DOTTIE WEST & DON GIBSON . . . DOTTIE WEST & JIMMY DEAN . . . DOTTIE WEST & KENNY ROGERS

SKEETER DAVIS & BOBBY BARE . . . SKEETER DAVIS & PORTER WAGONER . . . SKEETER DAVIS & DON BOWMAN . . . SKEETER DAVIS & GEORGE HAMILTON IV

ROSE MADDOX & BUCK OWENS

GOLDIE HILL & RED SOVINE . . . GOLDIE HILL & JUSTIN TUBB

LORENE MANN & JUSTIN TUBB . . .

shame of illicit love. These torture-of-temptation songs included "This Time Has Gotta Be Our Last Time," "Slip Away Today," "Before Our Weakness Gets Too Strong," and "Burning the Midnight Oil." Another recurring theme was the poor-but-happy idea of "The House Where Love Lives" and "Poor Folks Town."

But what stood out on every album was the funny-fight number where Porter and Dolly spatted, sassed, and traded quips. In "We'll Get Ahead Someday," "Run That by Me One More Time," and "Fight and Scratch," they portray blue-collar couples bickering over money. In "Better Move It On Home" she steams on the homefront while he's out in a barroom. In "Her and the Car and the Mobile Home" she gets fed up with him and leaves, taking everything. In "I've Been Married Just as Long as You Have" she wants to go out partying, too, instead of being left at home. Dolly wrote most of these domestic disturbances, which generally ended with Porter and her ad-libbing insulting wisecracks in the studio.

It wasn't all fun and games. Porter was hopelessly in love with her, but Dolly resisted his advances. She began to assert her independence, and that made things even more complicated. He bullied and battled his protégée when she tried to go beyond the innocent mountain girl he'd molded into a star. The possessive Porter kept acting like Dolly's mentor and boss while she was outgrowing him. He didn't like her talking to reporters without him. She sat silently while he did all the talking on "The Tonight Show." He produced her records and instructed her performances and reportedly used threats and intimidation to control her. By 1972 his hit-making days were fading, while her career was rising faster than a baking biscuit. When she finally announced in 1974 that she was leaving his troupe to try her wings as a solo act, the news hit the country community like a warhead.

"Porter knew I was plannin' to leave, and he didn't like it one bit," Dolly told one interviewer. "I tried explainin' things to him, hopin' we could work it out between us, but he wasn't of a mind to listen. . . . and when I saw I wasn't getting through to him, I just made up my mind that I was goin' to go the best way I knew how. He wasn't ever gonna give me his permission, so I just took it and left."

Porter said, "We were gonna do things my way. Because that's the kind of person I am. Dolly Parton's career up until she left me was done my way. That's the only way it could be successful operating with me. . . . I signed the checks . . . so we did things my way, and that was the way I was born and reared to do—that if you paid a man to work for you . . . he didn't tell you what to do." To one interviewer he suggested that Dolly had used her wiles on him to get where she wanted to go. She called it "putting legs on my dreams."

Although the male ususally got top billing, the female voice typically carried the melody in the classic duos. Jim Ed Brown and Helen Cornelius emulated the pattern and took this classic duo sound into the late seventies. After his sisters Bonnie and Maxine left him to raise their families, Jim Ed had an up-and-down career as a solo act. By the mid-1970s the executives at RCA decided that what he needed was another partner in harmony.

Up in the Mississippi River town of Hannibal, Missouri, Helen Cornelius was in training for country stardom. Born in 1941, she became a songwriting housewife. Her husband saw her potential. "Lewis would come home at night and ask me what I had written," Helen recalled. "When he found out I hadn't, he would almost order me to. He said he didn't care if the house was clean or not. He just wanted me to write songs."

With the husband and three children in tow, she moved to Music City and met her singing partner. Helen was vivacious and ambitious; Jim Ed Brown was placid and famous. Their roller-coaster ride together was five years of hits and heartaches.

Not long after being introduced by RCA producer Bob Ferguson, Jim Ed and Helen were creating controversy with their debut duet, "I Don't Want to Have to Marry You." Many country radio stations took one look at the title and refused to play it, although the lyrics were actually against premarital sex. Jim Ed's butter-melting vocal warmth and Helen's bright-sunbeam delivery eventually won everyone over, propelling the song to Number 1 and sweeping the team to victory as the Country Music Association's 1977 Vocal Duo of the Year. They stoked the fires of passion on several sexy follow-ups—"Lying in Love with You," "Fools," "Morning Comes Too Early," and "The Bedroom." The hot new duo costarred for four years on the popular syndicated TV show "Nashville on the Road" and became the toast of Music Row.

"When I came here from Hannibal, Missouri, I was very sheltered, very prudish, and very green," Helen told reporter Bob Millard. "I was introduced to the fast lane of life very quickly with a Number 1 record, traveling, and being taken away from my family. But you cannot work that closely with someone on the road like that and not be emotionally involved in some way."

The former Baptist Sunday school teacher found herself living out the cheating song lyrics. Jim Ed's wife, Becky, filed for divorce in 1979, citing his "questionable relationship" with Helen. In early 1980 Helen divorced Lewis. By this time her dream of solo stardom had been crumpled and tossed aside. RCA never gave her her own album. She was

LORENE MANN &
ARCHIE CAMPBELL

CARL & PEARL
BUTLER

KAY ADAMS & DICK
CURLESS

JAN HOWARD & WYNN
STEWART . . . JAN
HOWARD & BILL
ANDERSON

SUE THOMPSON & DON
GIBSON

PATTI PAGE & TOM T.
HALL

WILMA BURGESS &
BUD LOGAN

CONNIE SMITH & NAT
STUCKEY

MARION WORTH &
GEORGE MORGAN

JUNE CARTER &
JOHNNY CASH

JEAN SHEPARD &
FERLIN HUSKY . . .
JEAN SHEPARD &
RAY PILLOW

WANDA JACKSON &
BILLY GRAY

SHERRY BRYCE & MEL
TILLIS

LOIS JOHNSON & HANK
WILLIAMS, JR.

MARY LOU TURNER &
BILL ANDERSON

LINDA GAIL LEWIS &
JERRY LEE LEWIS

PENNY DEHAVEN &
DEL REEVES

BILLIE JO SPEARS &
DEL REEVES

JUNE STEARNS &
LEFTY FRIZZELL (AS
"AGNES &
ORVILLE") . . . JUNE
STEARNS & JOHNNY
DUNCAN

BARBARA MANDRELL
& DAVID HOUSTON
. . . BARBARA
MANDRELL & LEE
GREENWOOD

Helen Cornelius, 1976.

hopelessly tied professionally and personally to Jim Ed Brown. He reportedly proposed. She turned him down. Enraged, he fired her from his show, threw her costumes off the tour bus onto her front yard, and told her he'd never set foot onstage with her again. The breakup became an embarrassing public spectacle when Jim Ed begged his wife to take him back during a live Opry broadcast and Helen called a press conference to tell her side of the story. At the event she nestled against hunky South Carolina nightclub owner Jerry Garren, whom she married in 1981. RCA dropped both her and Jim Ed. He went back to Becky and the security of Opry cast membership. But Helen was treated like used goods by the music business. She slipped practically unnoticed through contracts with Elektra and Dot, then fell off the charts.

Helen explained to interviewer Bill Littleton, "In the duo, my ideas and sometimes my capabilities didn't matter because there was a set pattern of what I had to do or could do. . . . I felt very stifled and very limited. . . . It was made plain to me that Jim Ed Brown was the quarterback on the team and that I was not. . . . and it *was* his show, his band, his bus." After eight years apart the team reconciled for a tour in 1988.

As a solo act Helen strongly emphasized religion, patriotism, and ladylike conservatism. Her performances were laced with gospel songs and ended with throbbing versions of "America" and "God Bless the U.S.A." that brought state fair audiences to their feet. "I'm still a very basic, down-to-earth country girl," Helen said. "I'm not a liberated woman. I'm not free. I feel I need to be there when there's a scraped knee, to do the cooking for my children and my husband. I feel guilty when I know there's something at school involving my children. I need to be there. When these things crop up on me when we're on the road . . . I have guilt feelings. . . . Sometimes I cry.

"Women are pursuing their own careers, and that's beautiful. That's great. They should be successful, they should be proud. But at the same time, we all learn from each other's mistakes. . . . Many marriages are failing because women are going out and working."

Many of the country heartache heroines of the 1960s and 1970s shared Helen's belief that feminism meant work and career and that nonfeminists valued motherhood and family.

"I guess I believe in a double standard," said Connie Smith. "I feel that the man is over the woman. I want my husband to be over me. He can shut me up, y'know. He might not shut me up inside, but he'll shut me up on the outside, and I'm glad he can. I respect him for that. As a woman, I like to be able to lean. I don't want the whole responsibility."

"I think women country entertainers have a tendency to let the man wear the pants," observed Jean Shepard. "'Cause most of them are country girls and this is the way they were raised. I don't think the men give the women enough credit for having real good sense. . . . it's hard to deal with them because you are a woman. . . . [But] the women's lib thing doesn't turn me on. I can't stand for a woman to stand up and say, 'I can do anything a man can do.' Maybe mentally she can. But I think it's still kind of a man's world, and to be frank, I kind of like it that way."

The antilib heartache sufferers wore their submissiveness as a badge of honor, a sign of their strength. Yet while singing of dependence and passivity, all of them pursued independent careers in the male-dominated country music industry. Despite their antifeminist rhetoric, they broke down barriers in their profession and drove female country music forward. Regardless of their comments or their lyrics, women like Jean Shepard, Helen Cornelius, Barbara Fairchild, and Tammy Wynette were what women's liberation was all about. They never accepted the label of feminism, yet they lived its goals.

"I won't go out and work for women's liberation because I believe I *am* free," said Tammy Wynette. "But I will teach my children, in my home, that they're equal to any man, because that's how I feel."

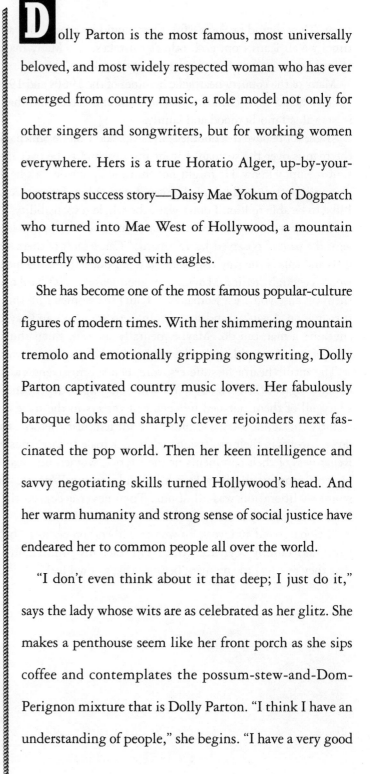

14

JUST BECAUSE I'M A WOMAN

Dolly Parton and Her Savvy Sisters

Dolly Parton, 1973.

Dolly Parton is the most famous, most universally beloved, and most widely respected woman who has ever emerged from country music, a role model not only for other singers and songwriters, but for working women everywhere. Hers is a true Horatio Alger, up-by-your-bootstraps success story—Daisy Mae Yokum of Dogpatch who turned into Mae West of Hollywood, a mountain butterfly who soared with eagles.

She has become one of the most famous popular-culture figures of modern times. With her shimmering mountain tremolo and emotionally gripping songwriting, Dolly Parton captivated country music lovers. Her fabulously baroque looks and sharply clever rejoinders next fascinated the pop world. Then her keen intelligence and savvy negotiating skills turned Hollywood's head. And her warm humanity and strong sense of social justice have endeared her to common people all over the world.

"I don't even think about it that deep; I just do it," says the lady whose wits are as celebrated as her glitz. She makes a penthouse seem like her front porch as she sips coffee and contemplates the possum-stew-and-Dom-Perignon mixture that is Dolly Parton. "I think I have an understanding of people," she begins. "I have a very good

sense of humor. . . . I'm a very honest, open person. I think one of the reasons I am a good boss is because you will always know what I'm a-thinkin'. I won't pout at you or treat you bad. I'll just say, 'Hey, Joe, there's somethin' that's really been buggin' the shit outta me.' . . . Anybody that works with me will tell you that."

She is worth, they say, two hundred million dollars. "Big business is not as scary as it seems," says the platinum powerhouse. "I find my common sense and the fact that I was born and raised in the country are the greatest gifts that I possess. Just havin' good ol' horse sense, you can make more money and get more done than all the people that have gotta fumble through their books to try to find an answer to somethin'."

You get the impression that the hardest part about working with Dolly Parton would be simply keeping up pace with her. Her empire extends from eastern Tennessee to Hawaii and includes everything from real estate to restaurants, from a theme park to her own movie production company. She contemplates creating a cosmetics line, composing Broadway shows, writing self-help books, and marketing diet foods.

"I figure if God gave me this talent, he also meant for me to use good sense with it. And that means good business sense. The way I look at it, this is my life, this is my livelihood. . . . If I'm gonna spend my life doin' something . . . I'm the one who has to be responsible. . . . I have made some real smart moves."

"I'll never have too much money," she states bluntly. "I'm from a very poor family. There's no such thing as too much money for somebody that's as poor as we were. . . . But money is not what motivates me. . . . the opportunity to achieve is even more important to me.

"I'm proud of the humble beginnings, the fact that dreams can come true for just simple people, ordinary people. I was blessed to come from those humble beginnings. . . . I hope that I'm an inspiration to people and to women."

Dolly Rebecca Parton was born in a one-room cabin in the mountains of eastern Tennessee in Sevier County. It was the cold winter of 1946. She was the fourth of twelve children born to sharecropper/moonshiner Lee Parton and his wife Avie Lee Owens Parton. Dr. Robert F. Thomas rode his horse up a dirt path to attend to the birth and was paid with a sack of cornmeal.

No electricity. No running water. No telephone. No indoor plumbing. The whole mountain-poverty works. Both sides of the family were highly musical, especially the women. Great-grandma Cassie Ann Rayfield was remembered as the "prayingest, singingest, shoutingest" woman in Tater

Ridge, Tennessee. Grandma Lindy Owens played harmonica and sang the sad old ballads like "Barbara Allen" and "The Letter Edged in Black." It was from her that Avie Lee learned "Two Little Babes," "Letter to Heaven," and the rest of her tragic songs of doomed, dying, blind, and orphaned children.

"Mama sings real good. She's the one that taught us all," says Dolly. "I'm gonna do an album sometime called *Songs My Mama Taught Me.* Mama always sang those old songs, those cryin', hurtin' songs. . . . I have such a feeling for those songs, 'Little Rosewood Casket' and all of those old-time numbers."

The children were all creative personalities, inventing their own amusements and gathering together for family sing-alongs. "My family is still the closest thing to me. We help each other a lot. . . . We all have great senses of humor, and we make each other laugh so much, it hurts. All musical, too." Five of the kids eventually became professional musicians, but Dolly was something special, a true visionary.

"I had a lot of big dreams. I always thought that I would do a lot of things. . . . I was just born a dreamer. . . . Both sides of my family are very creative people . . . and I just believed that I can do it, and I wanted to see the world outside the Smoky Mountains.

"I was always impressed with Cinderella and Mother Goose and all those things when I was a kid, because we didn't have television or movies then. I kinda patterned my look after Cinderella and Mother Goose—and the local hooker."

"I was thinkin' I was gonna be a star. I thought I was singin' to a lot of people when I was singin' to my brothers and sisters and the chickens and the dogs with a tin can as a make-believe microphone." Dolly was composing songs before she could read and write, the earliest being an ode to her corncob doll she called "Little Tiny Tasseltop." Avie Lee wrote it down for her. Dolly's teachers observed that she had an uncanny gift of memory, an ability to absorb information at an astounding rate.

The child had several professional role models among her mountain kinfolk. While Dolly was growing up, Avie Lee's sister Dorothy Jo Hope became a gospel songwriter and evangelist. Songs by Aunt Dorothy Jo, as well as by grandpa Jake Owens, later surfaced on Dolly's *Golden Streets of Glory* LP of 1971. Dolly's uncles Bill, Robert, and Louis Owens tasted success as local country entertainers. Uncle Bill gave Dolly her first guitar. The child had been singing in churches and local theaters for a couple of years when Knoxville entrepreneur Cas Walker invited her to become a regular on his "Farm and Home Hour" broadcasts. Her Aunt Estelle began driving determined Dolly the forty miles to Knoxville on weekends, and the child lived with Estelle during summers to do the show daily.

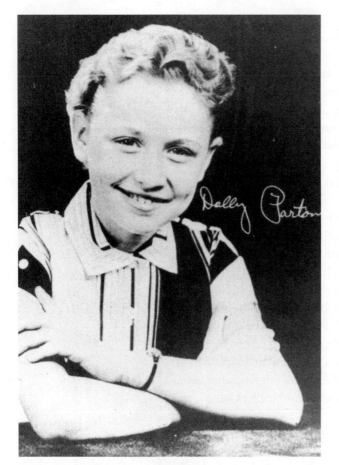

As a singing tot in 1959, Dolly Parton already looks ready for stardom in her first publicity photo.

"I was ten years old. My Uncle Bill Owens took me up to Knoxville to meet Cas Walker to be on his radio and television show that promoted his grocery stores. I wanted to go. I thought it was exciting. . . . The audience responded more to my being small, I think, than to me being good. But I just loved it. In a big family, you don't always get lots of attention. This way I did. I decided I wanted more of that. 'Stand there and follow the red light on the cameras,' they told me. So I did. It's funny: I was on TV before we *owned* one." She made twenty dollars a week and continued with the show throughout her junior high and high school years, ignoring the teasing of her rock-'n'-rolling classmates who were doing the twist.

Dolly began to make tapes in the studios of WIVK in Knoxville and WSEV in Sevierville. She liked bouncy songs back then, favoring the up-tempo efforts of Brenda Lee or tunes like Connie Francis's "Everybody's Somebody's Fool." "I don't believe I've ever told George Jones that my big number was his 'You Gotta Be My Baby.' That one and the old Rose Maddox song 'I Love a Tall Man' were my two biggies. Everybody around eastern Tennessee's heard me sing those things a billion times. They're probably still sick of them to this day."

Dolly's disc debut was also in the rockabilly mode. In 1960 Louisiana's Goldband Records issued the fourteen-year-old's peppy "Puppy Love," and the youngster parlayed it into a one-shot appearance on the Opry in Nashville. Next Dolly took her radio station tapes to song publisher Buddy Killen, who signed her to a Music Row songwriting contract and arranged for her Nashville recording debut. Mercury Records issued Dolly singing "(It May Not Kill Me But) It's Sure Gonna Hurt" when she was sixteen. Again, it was in the hopped-up Brenda Lee rockabilly style.

Kitty Wells was also an inspiration to Dolly, as she was to virtually every other country-singing woman of the time. The youngster recorded six songs in tribute to the Queen of Country Music, including "It Wasn't

God Who Made Honky-Tonk Angels," "Making Believe," and "Release Me." "Well, I'll tell you how that happened. I was in school at the time. I was probably a freshman or a sophomore. I was a young girl. And I used to make all these trips to Nashville whenever I could to try and push songs, try to get a record deal, whatever. . . . Remember when they used to do all those sound-alike records? They had a big thing in Nashville where people would go in and sing [others' hit] songs and then you'd get just a flat fee. I think I got two hundred and forty dollars. We needed gas money." Dolly's six songs were combined with five Faye Tucker performances in tribute to Patsy Cline and issued as the "supermarket" package *Hits Made Famous by Country Queens* in 1963 by Somerset Records.

In 1964 Dolly became the first member of her family to graduate from high school. The ceremony was on a Friday night. On Saturday morning she boarded a bus bound for Nashville, carrying a cardboard suitcase full of dirty clothes and bright dreams. On her first day in town she went to a Wishy Washy. Handsome Nashville native Carl Dean drove by and honked his horn at the pretty blonde. Just as she would have back home in the country, she cheerfully waved back. He stopped. They chatted, began dating, and fell in love. When he got out of the army two years later, they wed. The two are still married today, but Carl has been a shadowy presence in Dolly's public life. His total avoidance of the limelight has led to much media speculation about their marriage.

"Even if I wasn't married to him, he'd be one of my favorite people in the world," she says. "We have wonderful times together. He's the funniest, wittiest man I've ever met. He don't give a damn for show business or this Dolly Parton business. . . . He's got tremendous pride and integrity. . . . Carl and I are very independent people. . . . We don't want to own each other and change things that made us fall in love in the first place. . . . Believe me, nobody will ever take Carl's place. . . . See, I really like that guy in addition to lovin' him." She calls him "Daddy"; he calls her "Princess." Publicity-shy Carl, by the way, appears on the cover of her 1969 LP *My Blue Ridge Mountain Boy*.

There was a period when the aspiring Dolly was down to relish and mustard in her refrigerator in those early Nashville days. Her weight dropped to ninety pounds. Motherly honky-tonk singer Pearl Butler (1929–1989) sometimes fed her and lent her stage clothes. Dolly took part-time jobs as a receptionist at a neon-sign company, a waitress in a family restaurant, and a singer on the local early-morning TV program "The Eddie Hill Show." Dolly says, "When I came to Nashville, I went through a lot of heartache and I had a lot to learn." But things actually happened fairly quickly for her. She was signed to a songwriting contract by Combine Music, cowrote the 1966 Bill Phillips hit "Put It Off Until Tomorrow," and she can be clearly heard singing harmony on its chorus. Within months Skeeter Davis had success with Dolly's "Fuel to the Flame," and Hank Williams, Jr., was on the charts with her "I'm in No Condition." The Combine connection also led to a record contract. Dolly's deceptively titled "Dumb Blonde" and her novelty composition "Something Fishy" made the Top 25 in early 1967.

She began to tour, learning firsthand how tough the country business was for a woman alone. "I was always scared in honky-tonks and dives and chicken-wire places when I played them. One time, one girl in a honky-tonk got real mad that her drunk husband was gettin' carried away. I guess she'd had some to drink, too. She yelled out, 'Let me at that bitch! I'll get that wig offa her!' And the band was gathering around to protect me. But bein' a country girl, I'd have taken her on if she'd got to me. We would have probably had a brawl right there." For years Dolly packed a pistol in her purse.

She and Carl Dean got married on Memorial Day 1966 in the no-waiting southern marriage capital Ringgold, Georgia, but Dolly kept the news quiet. Her distinctive vocal on "Put It Off Until Tomorrow" and her successful solo singles were creating a buzz. Fan magazines and trade publications were beginning to write about her. Monument Records, her label, thought it best that she appear to be unmarried. Meanwhile Porter Wagoner caught wind of the vivacious country newcomer and offered her the job vacated by Norma Jean in his road show and widely seen syndicated TV show. By then Wagoner was a bona fide star with more than twenty major hits, two Grammy Awards, "Grand Ole Opry" membership, a TV show in eighty-six markets, and a state-of-the-art touring troupe that played 230 dates a year to packed houses. It was a stupendous opportunity for the still-green Dolly.

Her infectious personality and effervescent disposition suited Wagoner's down-home presentation perfectly. He oozed with professional hillbilly sincerity, and she had it naturally. He was a spangled country king who believed in giving the people flash and outrageously colorful visuals, as well as music. She loved to play dress-up and look her best, too.

Dolly says her makeup style came from her childlike fascination with the trashy town "'strollops,' as my mother called them—strumpets and trollops. . . . They had blond hair and wore nail polish and tight clothes. I thought they were beautiful." And then there's that staggering figure.

"I always had them," she told *Cosmopolitan* about her celebrated breasts, "and as a young girl I had to deal with them. I took a lot of teasin', but I had a very nice shape and I always enjoyed the attention. . . . I was boy crazy. I loved knowin' boys were watchin' me sashayin' down the hall. Still do. I'm full of mischief that way. Love to flirt.

"Did I ever use silicone? They ain't got that much plastic.

"I'm a real character. I'm exaggerated in every way. I catch your attention with my big wigs and big boobs and my big rear end, too. . . . I want my looks to match what I feel like inside, and I want it to be overwhelming."

Within months of joining Wagoner, Dolly was churning out powerfully emotional songs. Wagoner orchestrated a move from little Monument to the mighty RCA, introduced her to his audiences with the Top 10 hit duet "The Last Thing on My Mind," wrote the liner notes for her debut RCA LP, then stood back as she hit 'em with the wallop of its title tune, "Just Because I'm a Woman." Dolly's breakthrough single of 1968 is a country female classic that condemns the double standard. In it she must confess to her fiancé that she's not a virgin. "Just Because I'm a Woman" is a striking performance, alternating her trembling mountain vibrato with a tense, to-the-point tone that is direct and uncompromising. She seems to both beg for understanding and demand it.

"I had my own opinion long before women's liberation," she told *Country Music* magazine. "I figure, what's fair for the goose is fair for the gander."

Dolly says, "I believe in rights for all people. I think there are many women that are qualified for many jobs; and everybody should be paid well for what they're qualified to do. . . . I think children and blacks and reds and all people should have an equal shot. I just think we're all God's children and should be treated with respect."

Her women's songs of the late sixties and early seventies cover many issues. "Mama Say a Prayer" and her 1969 hit "My Blue Ridge Mountain Boy" are moving prostitute sagas. "More Than Their Share" addresses a woman's emotional inequalities in a relationship. She enacts a rough-and-tumble "lady muleskinner" by feminizing Jimmie Rodgers's 1930 classic "Muleskinner Blues" in a 1970 hit. She deals with the way insanity is used against women in her asylum song "Daddy Come and Get Me." She is pregnant and abandoned in "Down from Dover" and "The Bridge," yet an independent, ramblin'-on lady lover in "When Possession Gets Too Strong." In 1972's "Touch Your Woman" she asks her man for strength and reassurance. Dolly sings for the working girl whose bills are overwhelming in "A Little at a Time." In a version of Shirl Milete's "Baby Sister" Dolly rescues her sister from barroom dissipation. She pleads with a beautiful temptress to leave her man alone in "Jolene," which launched her string of Number 1 hits in 1973.

Like Loretta Lynn, Dolly brought an enormous sense of working-class dignity to her songs. By the dawn of the 1970s she'd joined the Coal Miner's Daughter as a true blue-collar heroine, as well as a common-folks feminist. Dolly's "In the Good Old Days (When Times Were Bad)," "We'll Get Ahead Someday," and the deeply touching recollection of her childhood poverty "Coat of Many Colors" rank as some of country music's finest poor-but-proud songs. She also recorded others' songs in this vein, including Charlie and Betty Craig's "Chicken Every Sunday" and Wagoner's housewife protest "Washday Blues." Dolly's 1969 single of Mac Davis's "In the Ghetto" finds her expressing sympathy for inner-city poor people.

There isn't much she won't tackle as a tunesmith. Sunny Dolly has a somber, melodramatic, sentimental side that comes out in her music. Doubtless influenced by her mother's ballads of death and tragedy, she has sung of suicide, adultery, insanity, drugs, illegitimacy, and other dark topics. "Evening Shade" is about children burning down their hated orphanage. "Curse of the Wild Weed Flower" is about marijuana. "Jeannie's Afraid of the Dark" is about a dead child. "Joshua" portrays a mountain hermit. She compared her body to used goods in 1975's "The Bargain Store," incurring rejection from some conservative country stations. The bitter alcohol indictment "Daddy's Moonshine Still" seems to spring from personal experience, as does a 1969 single wherein Dolly pleads on behalf of her aging mother with her "Daddy" who wants to leave for a younger woman. Despite the upbeat lyrics of "My Tennessee Mountain Home," everything was not always "peaceful as a baby's sigh" during her childhood. "We had our problems. Daddy, he often ran around, and he had some children outside of us. But he was a good father and a good husband. He always came home. He was just a little wild."

Towering above all her compositions are her immensely tender love songs, several of which have been recorded by other stars. "I Will Always Love You," "My Blue Tears," and "The Last One to Touch Me" are lump-in-throat emotional jewels. As her fame increased, men everywhere lost their hearts to her disarming style. Wagoner admits he was deeply in love with her, as does superstar Merle Haggard, who wrote his 1975 Number 1 hit "Always Wanting You" about his unrequited passion for her. Dolly wasn't above flirting and temptation, but she always maintained the upper hand. "I never sold myself out. I never went to bed with anybody unless I wanted to, never for business reasons. . . . I've always been proud that I've had my own success, that I've never had to depend on a man for it."

Although Wagoner was her country music mentor, she began to chafe at his domination. Dolly had become an Opry cast member in 1969, fulfilling a childhood dream. Her songwriting had earned wide respect throughout the country community, and by the mid-1970s even pop-music critics were beginning to recognize the brilliance of Dolly LPs like *My Tennessee Mountain Home* (1973), *Coat of Many Colors* (1971), *The Fairest of Them All* (1970), and *Jolene* (1974). Linda Ronstadt recorded Dolly's "I Will Always Love You," Maria Muldaur worked up "My Tennessee Mountain Home," and Emmylou Harris did "My Blue Tears." Between 1971 and 1975 Dolly Parton had five solo Number 1 hits; Porter Wagoner had none. She cut the ties, endured his lawsuits, and headed out on her own. It was around this time that writers started referring to the gutsy trouper as the "Iron Butterfly."

The vibrantly inspirational "The Seeker" and zesty "All I Can Do" of 1975 and 1976 showed that the fans were with her when both romped into the Top 10. The Country Music Association named Dolly Parton its Female Vocalist of the Year in 1975 and again in 1976. She launched her syndicated TV show "Dolly!" in 1976.

She'd maintained ties to Wagoner as her record producer, but in 1977 declared her complete independence by producing her own *New Harvest, First Gathering* LP. Sweeping and ambitious, it showcased her on the soul song "Higher and Higher"; reaffirmed her songwriting gift with "Light of a Clear Blue Morning"; and paid homage to her Appalachian heritage in "Applejack," which featured backup singing by country legends including such female forerunners as Kitty Wells, Rose Lee Maphis, and Wilma Lee Cooper. The album bombed, as did The Traveling Family Band, which Dolly put together with her kinfolks.

Undeterred, Dolly announced she was staging an assault on big-time show biz with the hot young Los Angeles manager Sandy Gallin as her battle strategist. The cliquish, suspicious Nashville community reacted with resentment. No country "girl singer" had ever been so nervy.

"When I left to try and expand, when I was one of the *big* country women, I wasn't makin' any money," Dolly explained. "I couldn't even clothe my band and pay for my bus. I was making three thousand dollars a night, and that was with all my expenses coming out of that. I'd be clearing a couple of hundred dollars a show if I was lucky. . . . That's not enough money to buy toothpaste. . . . I thought, 'Well, shit, this is the music business—why not think of the business end of the business?'"

"I'm not leaving country," she protested to her narrow-minded Nashville critics. "I'm taking it with me." Dolly Parton paved the way for other Nashville singers to expand their careers. And while she was at it, she brought country music new validity and respectability as an art form.

Pop composers Barry Mann and Cynthia Weil penned the jaunty

"Here You Come Again," which Dolly warbled to the top of both pop and country charts in 1977. "Heartbreaker," "You're the Only One," and "Starting Over Again" were glossily produced ballads that all became sizable pop/country hits, as well. Dolly began appearing in the pages of *People, Time, Rolling Stone,* and *Good Housekeeping.* She made the cover of *Playboy* in 1978, leading Porter Wagoner to grouse, "You'd never catch Kitty Wells doing that." "Well I guess not," responded Dolly in *Vanity Fair* later. "I don't think *Playboy* would want Kitty Wells on the cover. But it was that kind of mentality: Kitty Wells wouldn't do that, Loretta Lynn wouldn't do that. Well, I'm *not* Loretta Lynn. I'm *not* Kitty Wells." She appeared in all the prestigious pop show rooms, and musicians such as Jerry Garcia, Z. Z. Top, and The Eagles proclaimed themselves fans. She formed her own publishing company and marketed an immensely successful Dolly doll, complete with boobs and a red-and-silver jumpsuit. She became one of Johnny Carson's favorite "Tonight Show" guests. In 1978 Dolly won a long-overdue Grammy Award and was named Entertainer of the Year by the CMA. Two years later she staged one of the splashiest show room debuts in Las Vegas history. She was only beginning.

Hollywood movie star Jane Fonda met Dolly by chance on a plane to New York. Jane recalls, "We talked for a while, and I thought, 'That's it—that's Doralee!' I went to see Dolly perform in concert, and I was knocked over." Jane's production company was planning a working-woman film called *9 to 5.* She recruited the country personality to costar as Doralee alongside her and top comic Lily Tomlin. They portrayed a trio of secretaries who battle sex discrimination, corporate greed, sexual harassment, and job degradation.

Diamond Dolly's silver screen debut became a career triumph in 1980. The film was a major box office success. Her title tune, complete with clacking typewriter keys, became a gargantuan pop and country smash and was nominated for an Academy Award. Its strikingly class-conscious lyrics stated, "It's a rich man's game, no matter what they call it / And you spend your life puttin' money in his wallet." "9 to 5" touched on worker solidarity, wage slavery, and visions of empowerment. "You're just a step on the boss man's ladder," she sang, "but you've got dreams they'll never take away." The number became the centerpiece of a concept LP devoted to working people's songs titled *9 to 5 and Other Odd Jobs.* In it Dolly sang of rural poverty in "Hush-a-Bye Hard Times," miners in "Dark as a Dungeon," migrant workers in "Deportee," and prostitutes in "The House of the Rising Sun." Sister Freida Parton provided the thematic "Sing for the Common Man," and Dolly herself penned the proud "Working Girl."

Her subsequent film career surprised some traditional country fans. But it shouldn't have, since Dolly Parton is the first country superstar who developed in front of the cameras of television. From Cas Walker's "Farm and Home Hour" in Knoxville to Nashville's early-morning "Eddie Hill Show" and through stints on the national "Dolly!" and "Porter Wagoner Show," she has been almost as active on screens as she is on radio and records.

Her breakthrough as TV's first big country female star was timed perfectly. By the 1960s, 90 percent of America's homes had a television set. Country and TV had grown up together. Country had been on the tube regularly since the 1948 inauguration of hillbilly music TV shows in Cincinnati, Louisville, New York, Philadelphia, Los Angeles, and Washington, D.C. *Billboard* magazine reported in 1956 that there were eighty-nine local country shows airing in thirty-one states.

During the 1950s the national networks had built an audience for country stars by airing the "Ozark Jubilee" (1955–1960), "Grand Ole Opry" (1955–1956), and "Midwestern Hayride" (1951–1959) barn dances and had presented Jimmy Dean (1957–1966), Eddy Arnold (1952–1956), Pee Wee King (1955), and Tennessee Ernie Ford (1956–1961) in their own series. During the same period, television syndicators were beginning to experiment, sending out programs such as "Old American Barn Dance," "Town and Country Time," "Stars of the Grand Ole Opry," and "Western Ranch Party."

But the explosion of country culture on TV came in the sixties when CBS launched the ratings bonanzas "Hee Haw," "Petticoat Junction," "Green Acres," "Gomer Pyle," and "The Andy Griffith Show." The trend reached its zenith with the gigantically popular "Beverly Hillbillies," which ran from 1962 to 1971. Vaudeville, radio, and movie veteran Irene Ryan (1902–1973) was the show's Granny, the matriarch of an Ozarks family named Clampett who struck it rich in oil and moved to a Beverly Hills mansion. Miss New Orleans of 1957, Donna Douglas, got the Daisy Mae Yokum part of Elly May, a blond, curvaceous mountain innocent who loved her "critters." "The Beverly Hillbillies" was a show-biz sensation, the Number 1 TV series in America during its first two seasons and one of the ten highest rated programs of the decade. Bea Benaderet (1906–1968) portrayed the show's scene-stealing Cousin Pearl Bodine and was given her own "Petticoat Junction" spin-off series from 1963 to 1970. "Petticoat" country cuties Jeannine Riley and Gunilla Hutton became "honeys" on "Hee Haw," which went on the air in 1969.

It featured corny one-liners in a cornfield and a lineup of scantily clad characters patterned after *Tobacco Road* slatterns or Daisy Mae, Moonbeam McSwine, and the other bodacious babes of Al Capp's *Li'l Abner* comic strip.

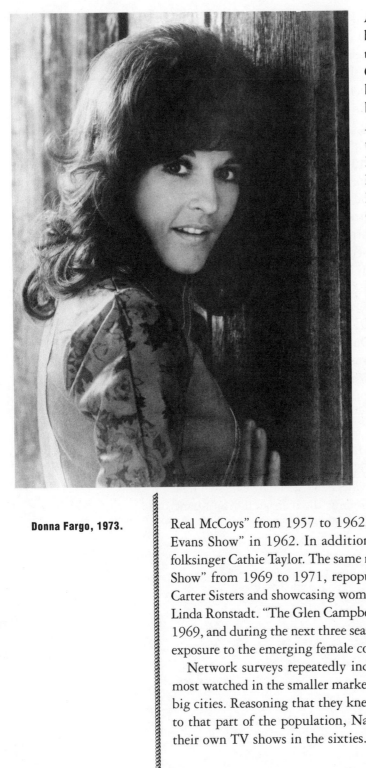

Donna Fargo, 1973.

Among the most memorable have been Lisa Todd's sultry "Advice-to-the-Loveworn" brunet, Marianne Gordon's molasses-accented southern belle, Misty Rowe's ditzy hillbilly bimbo, Cathy Baker's cheerful "That's All!" girl, and Irlene Mandrell's scatterbrained dummy. *Playboy* playmate Barbi Benton, former Elvis girlfriend Linda Thompson, and future Nashville candy magnate Mackenzie Colt all also served time as "Hee Haw" honeys. Not all the women connected with country music's longest running television show have been "honeys." Minnie Pearl became a regular in 1970. Jumbo-size Lulu Roman provided both comedy and gospel songs. Banjo player Roni Stoneman's hillbilly harridan "Ida Lee" shrieked weekly insults at her shiftless drunk of a husband. Although dropped by CBS in 1971, "Hee Haw" went on to become the most successful syndicated program in history.

Other shows picked up the torch. ABC, which had presented "The Real McCoys" from 1957 to 1962, offered "The Roy Rogers and Dale Evans Show" in 1962. In addition to Dale, it featured the talents of folksinger Cathie Taylor. The same network presented "The Johnny Cash Show" from 1969 to 1971, repopularizing Mother Maybelle and The Carter Sisters and showcasing women ranging from Tammy Wynette to Linda Ronstadt. "The Glen Campbell Goodtime Hour" began on CBS in 1969, and during the next three seasons Campbell, like Cash, gave ample exposure to the emerging female country stars of the day.

Network surveys repeatedly indicated that the country shows were most watched in the smaller markets of Middle America rather than the big cities. Reasoning that they knew best how to market entertainment to that part of the population, Nashville executives began developing their own TV shows in the sixties. These were produced in Music City studios, copied, and sold to local stations, generally to fill in nonnetwork weekend time slots.

Porter Wagoner launched his in 1960. It lasted for twenty years and while Dolly Parton was its costar was seen in more than a hundred markets. More than twenty-five other Nashville stars have also starred on weekly syndicated shows. Dolly believes that television is what lifted country out of its blue-collar ghetto: "When country music started gettin' on TV, people realized that we are not just hillbillies and hicks." When she put her show into syndication during the 1976–1977 TV season, Dolly became the first country music woman with her own television program.

From 1978 to 1979 Donna Fargo stepped into Dolly's role as country's female TV representative. The "Donna Fargo Show" was produced by Utah's famed Osmond brothers, who'd seen her perform at Carnegie Hall and invited her to do a pilot. Like Dolly, Donna did only a year's worth of programs. But both women's series were important milestones en route to the TV stardom later achieved by women such as Barbara Mandrell and Anne Murray.

The way to Donna Fargo's TV stardom was paved just as Dolly Parton's had been, with a string of country classics that she'd penned and that earned her enormous respect as a composer as well as a performer. She is generally associated with lighthearted, positive-think songs such as "The Happiest Girl in the Whole U.S.A." and "Funny Face." But Donna's work is deeper than that.

"I think the songwriter has a great responsibility to humanity because people are influenced so much by music," Donna says. Her hallmark as a personality as well as a composer is a frank, plainspoken folksiness mixed with a certain spiritual quality. She is a product of the North Carolina mountains, born Yvonne Vaughan in 1940 in Mount Airy. The daughter of a successful tobacco farmer, Donna attended High Point College, then headed to California to become an English teacher in the Los Angeles suburb of Covina. She sang, but had no professional-music aspirations.

"My goals weren't clear enough back then," she confesses. "I wish I'd developed my musicianship earlier." All she had going for her at first were sheer guts and a restless creative spirit. She met former rock-'n'-roll singer Stan Silver in L.A. He taught her to play guitar and encouraged her to write country songs. He also married her and became her record producer and manager. Around 1967 she adopted Donna Fargo as her stage name and went to Phoenix to record her first single for the small Ramco label. A year later she recorded for the larger Challenge Records. Her first Nashville session was for "Who's Been Sleeping on My Side of the Bed," which country radio stations thought too suggestive. All the while Donna continued to teach.

"It was like living two different lives or something. I was slow to begin performing live. I was really shy. I just didn't know if I could do it." Her small-label singles sank without so much as a ripple on the national charts. But in 1971 her upbeat "Happiest Girl in the Whole U.S.A." was picked up by Dot Records. It hit both country and pop charts in early 1972. Donna gave her final exams three weeks early that year and jetted off for her Las Vegas show debut. By the time the song was at Number 1 that summer, Donna was on her way to Nashville. "Happiest Girl" won her a Grammy, an Academy of Country Music honor as Female Vocalist of the Year, BMI's Most Performed Country Song award, a gold album, and 1972's Song of the Year and Single of the Year awards from the CMA.

"Funny Face" was an even bigger hit with both country and pop listeners, giving her a second million-seller. Donna was stereotyped as the "skippetydoodah" singer of cheerful domestic ditties. But the rocking "Superman" kicked off 1973, showing a sassier side of the pert newcomer. "You do your thing and I'll do mine," she snapped to a critical lover in the tune. "And if it ain't good enough for Superman, he ain't good enough for me."

"It doesn't matter what sex you are," Donna says when questioned about being a woman in country music. "I've tried never to see things like class and race and sex as barriers. I guess that's because that's what I practice." Fellow humanist Dolly Parton campaigned for Jimmy Carter in 1976. Donna's candidate, Hubert Humphrey, was a liberal, too.

Like Dolly, Donna formed her own song publishing company and developed one of country's most appealing touring units. Between 1972 and 1979 she scaled the country Top 10 sixteen times. She sold more than six million dollars' worth of records during the first four years of her career, and Warner Bros. reportedly lured her away from Dot in 1976 by offering her a million-dollar contract.

As she gained clout and confidence, her recorded performances gained increasing emotional depth. "Forever Is as Far as I Could Go" (1973) is a chilling account of a woman writing a suicide note to her unloving husband. "A Song with No Music" (1976) is about an embittered, unfulfilled woman. In love songs like "I've Loved You All the Way" (1976) and "Do I Love You (Yes in Every Way)" (1978) Donna seemed to vibrate with conviction. "You Were Always There" (1973) eulogized her mother. "Sign of the Times" (1983) was the story of a working man who lost his house and job. "Honeychild" (1974) was a touching plea for interracial harmony. "There's a merging of different kinds of people going on in America today . . . through integration," Donna told the *Chicago Tribune.* "In the long run, integration still is going to be good, whether it's forced or whatever." Although never a powerhouse singer, she proved to be an able reinterpreter of such country classics as "Mockin' Bird Hill," "Don't Be Angry," and "Walk On By" in the late seventies.

Donna Fargo was taping her new TV show for the Osmonds in 1978 when she felt a recurrence of a strange numbness she'd first experienced two years earlier. After extensive tests that summer, doctors diagnosed multiple sclerosis, an incurable, degenerative nerve disease. Despite MS, she completed her TV tapings and by year's end was doing concerts again. "I dug into my joke books and asked the writers for my TV show to come up with some hospital things." She'd tell her fans, "The doctors and nurses were all so good to me. As I was leaving, I asked, 'Oh, how in the world will I ever be able to repay you all?' And they told me: 'By check, money order, or cash.'"

The dewy brunet found strength, faith, and guts she never knew she had as she battled the disease during the next decade. She refused to write songs about her problem or accept pity and sympathy. "Oh, I *hate* that. Don't pity me. . . . I don't expect any special treatment because of it. . . . It's burdensome on you . . . to have to talk about your health condition all the time. I'm out there on the road earning my livelihood, practicing my trade. . . . You learn something about yourself. That's what's important. . . . In dealing with any kind of illness or crisis, you try to learn from it. I think that's what our obligation is . . . to have a deeper awareness."

She kept the disease at bay through most of the eighties, continuing to make the charts as recently as 1987 with her Billy Joe Royal duet "Members Only." In 1986 she issued her most feminist number, "Woman

Bobbie Gentry, 1971.

of the '80s." "Obviously, the woman's role in society has changed, and it was time to do a salute that people could sing along with." "Woman of the '80s" chronicles the experiences of a single girl, a divorced mom, a housewife, a female Wall Street executive, and a stewardess. Like so many of her best songs, it swelled with optimism. "I've always tried to take anything negative and turn it around into something positive," Donna once said. "I will always try to uphold that 'Happiest Girl' type of attitude, 'cause I've always believed it. And it's really helped me get through this easier."

This was an era when many female composers were making their marks in country music. As they're fond of saying in Nashville's song-publishing community, "A hit song don't care who wrote it."

Bobbie Gentry wrote one of the biggest of all, a huge country-pop smash of 1967 called "Ode to Billie Joe." For years afterward her haunting, mysterious saga had people wondering, "Why *did* Billie Joe McAllister jump off the Tallahatchie Bridge?" Bobbie isn't telling.

Roberta Streeter was born in Chickasaw County, Mississippi, in 1944. Raised in Greenwood, she taught herself to play piano on an upright her grandmother got in a trade for a milk cow. Bobbie composed her first ditties at age seven, notably "My Dog Sergeant Is a Good Dog," which later became an amusing part of her nightclub act. The family moved to California when she was thirteen; she graduated from high school in Palm Springs, then studied philosophy at UCLA and music at the Los Angeles Conservatory. A statuesque beauty with a thick mane of long black hair, Bobbie worked as a secretary, nightclub singer, and Las Vegas showgirl before recording "Ode to Billie Joe" as her debut disc. Its strikingly sparse sound—Bobbie's bluesy voice and guitar backed by the sighing of six violins and two cellos—was a revelation on the psychedelic airwaves of 1967. The disc sold three million copies and won three Grammy Awards. The Academy of Country Music named Bobbie Gentry its Most Promising Female Singer of 1967. Nashville's Country Music Association chose her to cohost its first awards show.

Most of Bobbie's other songs similarly evoked her Mississippi memories. Her drawling phrasing, delta-tinged melodies, grits-and-gravy accent, and vivid imagery characterized southern atmosphere.

Later Bobbie Gentry songs explored the seamy side of life and were perhaps influenced by her long tenure as a Vegas headliner. "The Girl from Cincinnati" (1972) was a tarnished starlet who "played the backseat heroine in a thousand different cars," "Belinda" (1971) was a burlesque queen, and "Fancy" (1970) was a prostitute.

By the dawn of the seventies Bobbie was the star of a $150,000 nightclub revue with a million-dollar Vegas contract. "I write and arrange all the music, design the costumes, do the choreography, the whole thing," she reported. "I'm completely responsible for it. It's totally my own from inception to the performance. . . . Besides that, I produce my own records. I originally produced 'Ode to Billie Joe' and most of the others—but a woman doesn't stand much chance in a recording studio. A staff producer's name was nearly always put on the records."

Like Dolly Parton and Donna Fargo, she graduated to television stardom in the 1970s, landing her own series on BBC-TV in London. It was later widely shown in Germany, Holland, Australia, and elsewhere around the world. In the summer of 1974 CBS aired four episodes of "The Bobbie Gentry Happiness Hour," but did not develop it into a series. "Ode to Billie Joe" became a TV movie in 1976, offering the controversial suggestion that its hero killed himself because he was homosexual. In 1978 Bobbie wed entertainer Jim Stafford. But she divorced him after eleven months, a few weeks after having their baby. Not much was heard from the sultry-voiced singer in the 1980s, but in 1991 her writing came back into the spotlight when Reba McEntire had a major hit single and video with a dramatic remake of "Fancy."

Singer/songwriter Linda Hargrove was billed as the "Blue Jean Country Queen" for a series of five albums in the mid-1970s. This gifted composer, session musician, producer, and performer developed one of the strongest musical reputations in Music City before contracting cancer and turning to gospel in the eighties. The Florida native, born in 1951, was the teenage veteran of several rock and soul bands when she arrived in Nashville in 1970. Sandy Posey was the first to record one of Linda's songs. Steel guitarist/producer Pete Drake was playing on the session. He signed Linda to a songwriting contract and began using her as a studio guitarist on discs by Waylon Jennings, Mac Davis, and other stars.

Jan Howard sang Linda's "New York City Song"; Johnny Rodriguez hit Number 1 with Linda's "Just Get Up and Close the Door"; Lynn Anderson scored big with Linda's "I've Never Loved Anyone More"; and Ernest Tubb did her "Half My Heart's in Texas." Olivia Newton-John's "Let It Shine" and George Jones's "Tennessee Whiskey" are other Hargrove-penned hits.

Beginning in 1973, Linda won critical applause for her own performances. She is a superb crafter of love songs, but her albums always covered broader topics. Linda's female songs generally dealt with the themes of lost virginity, soiled innocence, and the degradation of the fast-lane life-style of drugs and alcohol. She could also be feisty and

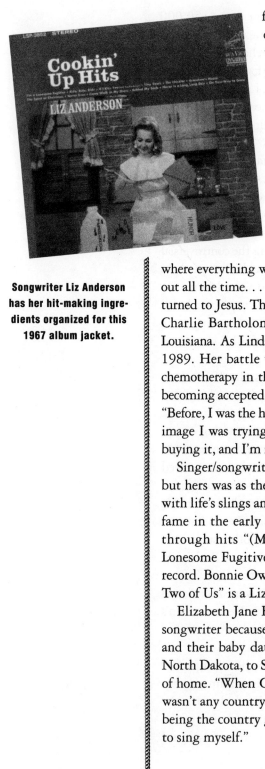

feminist. Linda made the lower ends of the country charts eight times between 1974 and 1978. Despite her wide acceptance on Music Row as a songwriter and instrumentalist, the Blue Jean Country Queen was not embraced by radio. This was an era of evening-gown glamour in Nashville, and Linda wore no makeup, had long unstyled hair, and dressed in denims. Behind the scenes Linda became a producer as well as a singer, songwriter, and instrumentalist, notably of ad jingles for Plymouth, Frito-Lay, and Dodge trucks.

"At one point in my life, to be successful in the music business was all that I was living for," Linda recalls. "The music business nearly killed me. . . . I had a terrible cocaine habit. . . . It got to the point where everything was wrong with my career, and I was getting so burned out all the time. . . . I had a gun. I was going to blow my brains out." She turned to Jesus. Then she married a gentle Christian businessman named Charlie Bartholomew, became a traveling evangelist, and moved to Louisiana. As Linda Bartholomew she recorded gospel LPs in 1981 and 1989. Her battle with leukemia began in 1986, and she was still in chemotherapy in the early nineties. The irony of her old, casual image's becoming accepted in modern country music isn't lost on Linda Hargrove: "Before, I was the hard-living, hard-drinking country queen. That was the image I was trying to project, and they weren't buying it. Now they're buying it, and I'm not selling."

Singer/songwriter Liz Anderson also adopted an unglamorous image, but hers was as the humorous housewife, a matronly blonde who dealt with life's slings and arrows with a smile and a wink. Liz initially rose to fame in the early sixties as the composer of Merle Haggard's breakthrough hits "(My Friends Are Gonna Be) Strangers" and "I'm a Lonesome Fugitive." Her "Be Quiet Mind" was Del Reeves's first big record. Bonnie Owens and Merle Haggard's hit duet "Just Between the Two of Us" is a Liz Anderson song.

Elizabeth Jane Haaby Anderson (b. 1930) says she became a country songwriter because she missed the country. Husband Casey moved her and their baby daughter Lynn from their hometown of Grand Forks, North Dakota, to Sacramento, California, and Liz yearned for the sounds of home. "When Casey and I moved to Sacramento in 1957, there just wasn't any country stations around. I wasn't hearing any new songs, and being the country girl that I am, I just started writing, so I'd have some to sing myself."

Liz Anderson's songwriting prowess brought her to the attention of RCA, which signed her to a recording contract. The Andersons moved to Nashville in 1966. A year later Liz was in the Top 10 with "Mama Spank," her biggest hit. It was a characteristically witty performance, dealing with an errant spouse as though he were a naughty child who had to be threatened with punishment to behave. In another funny number, she referred to her old man as "Ekcedrin Headache #99." Her "Husband Hunting" hit of 1970 found her scouring the taverns for him on payday. She confronted a rival in 1967's "The Wife of the Party" and threatened her in 1969's "Stand Back (There's Gonna Be a Fight)." In the turnabout-is-fair-play mode was 1971's "It Don't Do No Good to Be a Good Girl." Wittiest of all were her runaround-gal song "Me, Me, Me, Me, Me" and the kiss-off number "Did You Have to Bring That Up (While I Was Eating?)," both of which were embellished with zany studio sound effects in 1968 to complement her coquettish vocals.

During Liz's heyday as a recording act, between 1966 and 1973, she wrote and sang some of country's finest female material. Her divorce/breakup songs were almost all sung from the point of view of the hardy survivor—"Go Now, Pay Later," "So Much for Me, So Much for You," "Thanks but No Thanks." Daughter Lynn Anderson began her career by singing her mother's spirited songs of independence "No Another Time" and "If I Kiss You (Will You Go Away)." In the eighties Liz and Casey Anderson resurfaced as the cohosts of a Nashville Network cable TV travel show called "Side by Side."

Running parallel to Liz at RCA as a singer/songwriter was Lorene Mann. Her initial renown came as the writer of such early-sixties hits as Kitty Wells's "Left to Right," Rex Allen's "Don't Go Near the Indians," and Skeeter Davis's "Something Precious." Unlike many of her contemporaries, Lorene's dream was to make it as a professional writer, not a singer. She was the youngest of ten kids in the Mann family of tiny Huntland, Tennessee, near the Alabama state line. Born in 1937, she learned guitar

Linda Hargrove, 1975.

from her brothers at age twelve, graduated as the valedictorian of her high school class, and moved to Nashville to pursue her songwriting ambition in 1956. After her initial successes, from 1960 to 1962, musicians started urging her to perform, as well as write.

Lorene's first singing hits were her cheatin' duets with Justin Tubb in 1965 and 1966, and with Archie Campbell, in 1968 and 1969. But she supplemented these with some strikingly original solo songs. In "Don't Put Your Hands on Me" Lorene spurns a two-timer's advances. "Tell It All" speaks out against the double standard, saying that if you criticize an unwed mother, you should criticize the unwed father, too. In 1970's "The Apron Tree," Lorene is a female ex-con who wants to go home—in a plot identical to that of the massive hit "Tie a Yellow Ribbon" of three years later, she asks her mother to tie an apron to a tree if she's still welcome and finds a whole "apron tree" waiting in the front yard. Most striking of all was Lorene Mann's "Hide My Sin" of 1972. While The Jordanaires spell out "A-B-O-R-T-I-O-N, N-E-W Y-O-R-K" in the background, Lorene sings the saga of a seduced-and-abandoned pregnant girl. At the conclusion of her abortion she pleads, "God be kind to me on Judgment Day."

The woman who ignited the explosion of female songwriters on Music Row was Felice Bryant. When she and her husband, Boudleaux, moved to Nashville in 1950, they became the city's first full-time songwriting professionals.

Felice Scaduto was a merry girl who played and sang Italian folk songs with her family in her hometown of Milwaukee. "I was singing 'O Sole Mio' when they cut the umbilical cord," she says with a laugh. Born in 1925, Felice was a vivacious, nineteen-year-old elevator operator and soda jerk in 1945 when she experienced love at first sight. He was a professional violinist named Boudleaux Bryant, who was performing in a local hotel. She offered to buy him a drink. Three weeks later they were married, and forty years later they were still holding hands whenever they walked together. They were a remarkable team, bound to each other with immense warmth, ready wit, deep love, and tremendous talent.

Boudleaux took her back to his home state of Georgia. Big-city Felice was bored to death in Moultrie. "We tried the two movie theaters that ran the same movie for a week, so there was two days shot," she recalled. "Next we tried the pool hall. The next day there was a sign on the pool hall door barring me from coming in." She began spending her time at home making up poetry and song lyrics, as she had often done as a kid. Her example inspired Boudleaux, who was soon coming home from work eager to see what she'd come up with each day. "I'd still be playing the fiddle if it hadn't been for my wife," he once recalled. "Without Felice I'd be a complete nothing." They got a *Billboard* magazine, copied every address they could find in it, and embarked on a mail campaign to get their collaborations published. Meantime they hit the road as a vaudeville act, a nightclub singing duo, and even a Green Bay, Wisconsin, disc jockey team.

The breakthrough came in 1949 when "Grand Ole Opry" star Little Jimmy Dickens recorded their "Country Boy." They got a song publisher to pay them thirty-five dollars a week for their services and moved to Nashville to get other country singers interested in their works. "Everybody thought we were crazy, but we saw the far vision," Felice says.

In 1952 they briefly signed with MGM and recorded as "Bud and Betty Bryant," but after they scored big hits with honky-tonking Carl Smith's versions of "Hey Joe" and "Just Wait Till I Get You Alone" in 1953, they concentrated on songwriting exclusively. They signed with the big Acuff-Rose song publishing firm in 1956. The Bryants recorded most of their demo tapes as a duo, so it was natural to provide Acuff-Rose newcomers The Everly Brothers with tunes. The Everlys transformed twelve Bryant songs into all-time pop classics, among them "Bye Bye Love," "Wake Up Little Susie," and "Take a Message to Mary." Buddy Holly recorded "Raining in My Heart," creating another teen standard.

By 1985 the Bryants had more than fifteen hundred songs recorded and were responsible for some $250 million in record sales. "Our life," Felice said, "has been like Santa Claus coming to our house—and staying."

She was the more disciplined of the two, seldom letting a day go by that she didn't jot down a lyric idea. When she came up with melodies, she hummed or sang them for Boudleaux to transcribe. Both wrote tunes; both wrote words; their communication was almost mystical. Occasionally Felice wrote alone. As a birthday gift to Boudleaux she came up with the tender love song "We Could," and it was subsequently

"BLUE BOY"—Jim Reeves

"FALL AWAY"—Tex Ritter

"I CAN HEAR KENTUCKY CALLING ME"— Chet Atkins

"I'VE GOT A HOLE IN MY POCKET"— Ricky Van Shelton

"SLEEPLESS NIGHTS"—Emmylou Harris

"WE COULD"— Charley Pride

Boudleaux and Felice Bryant, 1956.

Marijohn Wilkin, c. 1975.

recorded by Jim Reeves, Jimmy Dickens, and, definitively, Charley Pride.

Felice and Boudleaux were inducted into the Nashville Songwriters Hall of Fame in 1972, into the National Songwriters Hall of Fame in 1986, and into the Country Music Hall of Fame in 1991. One of the warmest love stories of popular music ended when Boudleaux died in 1987. Felice, as vibrant and charming as ever, still appears at music industry functions, often on the arms of sons Del and Dane, both of whom are Nashville music business executives.

Felice's followers were many. Professional women songwriters became a permanent part of the Nashville scene in her wake. Among the earliest to arrive were Mae Boren Axton, who cowrote Elvis Presley's first national hit, "Heartbreak Hotel," and Marijohn Wilkin, a former schoolteacher who cowrote such hits as "Long Black Veil," "Waterloo," "Cut Across Shorty," "Fallen Angel," and "One Day at a Time." "I never had a desire to be a star," said Marijohn. "Songwriting was what I wanted."

Born in 1918, she was raised Marijohn Melson in Sanger, Texas, north of Dallas. She moved to Nashville in 1958, taking a piano bar job at the Voo-Doo Room in Printer's Alley and signing on as a fifty-dollar-a-month songwriter at Cedarwood Music.

Stonewall Jackson's "Waterloo" and Lefty Frizzell's "Long Black Veil" vaulted her into the songwriting big time in 1959. Within a year more than fifteen country stars had recorded her works. By 1961 national pop figures such as Teresa Brewer, Ann-Margret, Gene McDaniels, and Eddie Cochran were singing her songs. In 1962 Jimmy Dean's version of her John F. Kennedy salute "P.T. 109" became a major hit and Patsy Cline recorded "Tra Le La Le La Triangle." By the end of 1963 she was getting a song recorded every week. Marijohn left Cedarwood in 1964 to blaze a trail with her own company, Buckhorn Music.

She was the "den mother" counselor to Nashville's songwriters, but the new Music Row mogul had troubles of her own. She was drinking heavily, and her marriage was disintegrating. She attempted suicide twice and delved into spiritualism and the supernatural. Meanwhile Buckhorn became a haven for the maverick left field of the songwriting community, notably the poetic Kris Kristofferson. Marijohn returned from a European vacation in 1970 to find Kris's "For the Good Times" raking in money for her company.

Still troubled, she wrote "One Day at a Time" as a prayer for help. Kris helped her finish it, and in 1974 it was recorded by Marilyn Sellars and more than two hundred other stars. It opened a floodgate of creativity in Marijohn, launching her into a new career as a gospel composer. "The songs had been given to me for a purpose," she said. "I still didn't want to be into recording, except I knew the Lord wanted me to." Her 1974 LP *I Have Returned* was the first of several gospel recording efforts. The pioneering female composer/publisher entered the Nashville Songwriters Hall of Fame in 1975.

Inevitably, more women joined Marijohn Wilkin, Felice Bryant, Donna Fargo, and Dolly Parton in forming song publishing businesses. By the end of the decade women were making inroads at record labels and in management companies, as well. Tootsie's Orchid Lounge owner Hettie Louise Bess (1915–1978) got female company in the nightclub business. The developing ad jingle and syndicated TV businesses in Music City also got female executives. And virtually every trade association, industry organization, and professional society in Nashville's music business was headed by a female executive director.

Dolly Parton, 1977.

These developments mirrored a societywide trend. One of the most radical and visible social shifts of the late sixties and early seventies was the increased participation of women in occupations and professions that had previously been almost the exclusive domain of men. Approximately 80 percent of employed women remained in "female" occupations such as nursing, secretarial jobs, domestic work, and waitressing. But women began to make inroads as airline pilots, auto mechanics, carpenters, television and film producers, fire fighters, engineers, and welders, too.

Women also became increasingly active as business owners. By 1982 women owned 25 percent of the nation's twelve million business companies, the result of a record-setting influx of female entrepreneurs during the previous decade.

This societywide shift was very much in evidence on Music Row as the seventies progressed; and the influx of women into the country music business accelerated even more in the 1980s. Some of country music's largest and most important tourism businesses, video companies, booking agencies, song publishers, management offices, and public relations firms are now either owned or run by female executives.

Again mirroring American business as a whole, entertainment corporations promoted many female executives during the 1970s and 1980s. Women rose to the vice presidential level in the Nashville record company offices of MCA and Warner Bros., and Paige Levy was placed in charge of Warners' cowboy and Latin specialty labels. Donna Hilley began as a radio station secretary and wound up the vice president and chief executive officer of Sony Tree Publishing. Celia Froehlig rose through the ranks to head the Nashville office of Screen Gems–EMI. These are two of the three largest song publishers in Nashville.

The glue that holds the Nashville music scene together is provided by a cluster of trade associations, all headed by women. The Country Music Association is by far the most important of these. It has been called "the world's most active trade organization," and there's plenty to back up that claim. When the newly formed group hired Jo Walker-Meador in 1958, country was a backwater style being programmed by fewer than one hundred radio stations. Thirty-three years later, when Jo retired, one-fourth of America's eight thousand stations were country, and the $735 in the CMA bank account had swollen to $2 million. From a one-woman office with borrowed equipment, the organization grew to a staff of eighteen in its own Music Row palace.

"They didn't really have a clear definition of my job," she says in her slow, soothing drawl as she recalls the organization's infancy. "They were looking for someone with organizational skills and who had stenographic skills, someone who could type, could do the bookkeeping, a general person who could do everything. Their plan was to hire a man as executive director." There was just one problem. No man would work for the pitiful salary the CMA could pay. So the farm girl from Orlinda, Tennessee, who had dreams of becoming a girls' basketball coach stayed on alone.

In 1959 she organized a unifying banquet that became an annual event. The CMA invented the Country Music Hall of Fame in 1961 and marketed a then-revolutionary TV package of country hits in 1963. The record sold a million copies and put the organization on its financial feet. Jo and her board of directors did a fund-raising drive among Music Row's record labels, song publishers, and booking agencies to build the

Country Music Hall of Fame & Museum building in 1966. The organization launched its annual awards in 1967, and a year later the event graduated to national TV. In conjunction with "The Grand Ole Opry"in 1971 the CMA inaugurated the Fan Fair, which during the next decade evolved into a giddy celebration of country love, a crazed fiesta of the proletariat that draws twenty-five thousand to Nashville each year for concerts, star autographs, snapshots, and fan club fun.

At Jo's retirement dinner in 1991 Emmylou Harris said to her, "Whether you realize it or not, you are one of the biggest stars of country music." Added Brenda Lee, "Even though she's never sung a note, she's blessed us with harmony."

The "banks" of the music business are the performance rights organizations ASCAP, SESAC, and BMI. Every songwriter belongs to one of these firms because they issue licenses to radio stations, nightclubs, TV broadcasters, jukebox operators, and other businesses that make money from the public performance of music. The fees collected are then distributed as royalties to the songwriters and publishers.

These three agencies control hundreds of millions of dollars in royalty money annually, and all three of them have been guided by females. The head of the Music Row outpost of the American Society of Composers, Authors and Publishers (ASCAP) is Connie Bradley. The daughter-in-law of Music Row founder Owen Bradley and the wife of Opryland Music Group chief Jerry Bradley, Connie is a blond sparkler of wit and energy. Deliciously unpretentious, uproariously funny, and as twangy as a tobacco field hand, Connie can charm even the most cold-blooded music business lawyer. Her parties and receptions are justly famed for their style and pizzazz. Over at SESAC, tall and glamorous Vice President C. Dianne Petty enjoys the reputation as the most music-loving of all the performance rights executives.

The world's largest performance rights organization is Broadcast Music Inc. (BMI), which distributes five hundred million dollars annually to its music makers. BMI was also the first to reach out to the Nashville industry.

In 1950 Nashville native Frances Williams

Billboard took note of the female songwriter trend with its 1969 headline "Gal Writers Click," citing more than fifty professional women composers on Music Row at the time. Betty Jean Robinson, Naomi Martin, Sharon Higgins, Becki Bluefield, Peggy Forman, Audrey Allison, Margaret Cobb, and Vivian Keith were just a few who had come up with hits by then.

Jo Walker-Meador, 1991.

RECORDING STUDIO WOMEN

Despite the inroads made by Linda Hargrove and Anita Kerr, country recording session work has remained very male-dominated. Among those who have contributed nevertheless are the following:

MADGE SUTTEE—barrelhouse pianist on the Texas-recorded honky-tonk masterpieces of Lefty Frizzell

VELMA WILLIAMS SMITH—Nashville Sound–era guitarist

LILLIAN VANN HUNT—the pioneer in assembling string sections for the Nashville Sound sessions

MARIAN HALL—California studio steel guitarist

JANA JAE (GREIF)—California fiddler

THE CATES SISTERS—fiddlers and backup singers on Music Row

ALCYONE BATE BEASLEY—The Dixie Dons backup group

ANITA KERR—arranger and Anita Kerr Singers leader

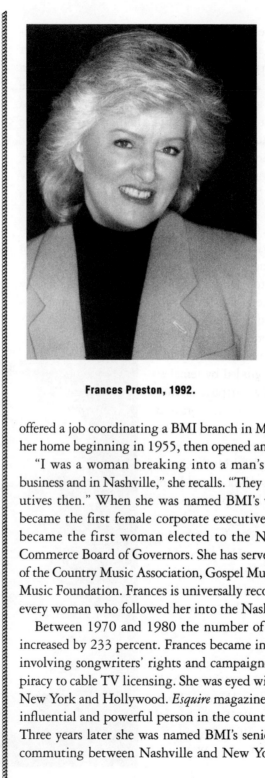

Frances Preston, 1992.

Preston was working as a receptionist at WSM, opening fan mail for Hank Williams and other Opry stars. The station came up with the idea of inviting other country broadcasters to Nashville to celebrate the Opry's birthday in 1952, beginning the tradition of Country Music Week. The next year, BMI's New York office decided it would be a nice idea to give awards to its country songwriters at the convention. Frances's congeniality, intelligence, and easygoing way with the then-young country music community impressed the New Yorkers, and she was offered a job coordinating a BMI branch in Music City. She worked out of her home beginning in 1955, then opened an official BMI office in 1958.

"I was a woman breaking into a man's world, both in the music business and in Nashville," she recalls. "They just didn't *have* women executives then." When she was named BMI's vice president in 1965, she became the first female corporate executive in Tennessee. In 1968 she became the first woman elected to the Nashville Area Chamber of Commerce Board of Governors. She has served as president of the boards of the Country Music Association, Gospel Music Association, and Country Music Foundation. Frances is universally recognized as the role model for every woman who followed her into the Nashville music business.

Between 1970 and 1980 the number of BMI-affiliated songwriters increased by 233 percent. Frances became involved in federal legislation involving songwriters' rights and campaigned hard on issues from tape piracy to cable TV licensing. She was eyed with increasing admiration by New York and Hollywood. *Esquire* magazine referred to her as "the most influential and powerful person in the country music business" in 1982. Three years later she was named BMI's senior vice president and began commuting between Nashville and New York. "I can't even type," she quipped. In 1986 she was elevated to the presidency of the worldwide BMI empire. "This is getting embarrassing, one promotion after another," the gracious executive responded. "I want to share my honor with everyone in Nashville, because we all did it together," added the woman being elevated to the most pivotal position in the entire music world. *Fortune* profiled Frances in 1987 as one of "the year's 50 most fascinating business people." *Savvy* dubbed her "St. Frances of Nashville" in a 1989 feature. In 1990 *Ladies' Home Journal* selected Frances Preston as one of the fifty most powerful women in America.

Frances has championed the songwriting careers of Willie Nelson, Dolly Parton, Alabama, Kris Kristofferson, Roger Miller, Rosanne Cash, and thousands of others. She is knitting together performance rights organizations in countries all over the world in an attempt to bring global fairness and uniformity to music business practices. This charismatic business leader describes herself simply as a "people person," yet knows how to apply her considerable interpersonal skills in the toughest business negotiations. A confessed workaholic, Frances pursues her job with rigorous, unflagging energy and with such attention to detail that she'll stoop to pick up debris outside BMI's sleek Music Row office building.

"Just forget you're a woman and go to work," she advised one interviewer. "Think of yourself as a businessperson, not as a woman. Think of yourself as an equal."

Dynamic Dolly Parton would agree. "Being a star just means that you just find your own special place and that you shine where you are," Dolly told Andy Warhol for his *Interview* magazine. "If I was a waitress, I'd be Flo [of TV's "Alice"]. I would own my own club. If I was a barmaid, I'd be Miss Kitty [of "Gunsmoke"]. I would tell the worst jokes. I would make everybody happy. I would loan everybody money. I would have a good time. If I worked in a factory, I'd be the one making cookies for everybody at Christmas. I would always make a living. . . . I would be a star wherever I was."

CAROL LEE COOPER AND NORA LEE ALLEN—"Grand Ole Opry" backup vocalists

THE NASHVILLE EDITION—"Hee Haw" backup vocalists

PHASE II—studio backup vocalists (all three members—Janie Fricke, Judy Rodman, and Karen Taylor-Good—graduated from studio work to record as solos)

DELORES DINNING, WINIFRED BREAST SMITH, MILLIE KIRKHAM, SHIRLEY BOONE, MARIJOHN WILKIN, LAVERNA MOORE, SANDY POSEY, PRISCILLA MITCHELL, LEA JANE BERINATI, DIANE TIDWELL, LISA SILVER, SHERRY KRAMER, AND FLORENCE WARNER—studio backup singers (Lea Jane subsequently became a national officer of the American Federation of Television & Radio Artists)

15

HOLLYWOOD TENNESSEE

*Barbara Mandrell
and the Show Queens of
Country Music*

O n April 26, 1980, records by women on *Billboard*'s country music chart occupied the positions 1, 2, 3, 4, 5, 8, 10, and 11. This was an astonishing event, so unprecedented that the magazine even pointed it out in a little box on the page headlined "Females Rule 45s." Barbara Mandrell, Lynn Anderson, Dolly Parton, Tammy Wynette, Dottie West, and Crystal Gayle hits dominated the country radio airwaves. Their glittering shows were booked into the finest Vegas casinos, as well as the biggest state fairs. They were full-blown American media stars in network TV shows and national magazines. This explosion of popularity for country music women capped a decade of female achievement in Nashville. Never before or since has there been as big an era of growth for women in country music as the 1970s.

There was something in the air as early as 1970, when *Music City News* proposed that radio stations celebrate "Country Girl U.S.A. Day" by playing nothing but female records on June 18. The magazine further suggested that local broadcasters throughout the land solicit all-female advertising for that day, plugging women's clothing, cosmetics, flowers, beauty salons, and grocery stores. In February 1971 *Billboard* pointed out that

women had recorded a quarter of the popular country records out at the time and a third of the records played in some markets. In 1974 *Country Music* magazine devoted its July issue to women performers. *Stereo Review, Redbook,* and *Newsweek* followed with female-country articles from 1974 through 1978.

By the time the historic *Billboard* chart appeared in 1980, women had been making their voices heard loudly for a full decade. Women sang on eighty Number 1 country records during the 1970s, up dramatically from twelve during the 1960s and up astronomically from just five Number 1 records in the 1950s. Prior to the 1970s female country music never accounted for more than 5 to 10 percent of the marketplace. But thanks to breakthrough women such as Loretta, Dolly, and Tammy, during the 1970s women doubled their share of the country music marketplace from roughly 10 percent to approximately 20 percent. In the early 1980s their share of the charts rose to nearly a third.

"It's now quite obvious that female artists can, and will, handle the show just as well as a man," commented Opry torch singer Jeannie Seely. "Women's liberation may have something to do with it. . . . women are now playing a more important role in all fields than they were a few years ago."

"I think a career is just as important to a woman," added Dottie West in *Country Music's* all-female issue of 1974. "I'm sure there's fewer and fewer housewives today. . . . That is just not enough to keep a woman happy. She has got to have something of her own—I don't care what it is."

"When I got to Nashville in 1961 there weren't hardly any women in country music," recalled Loretta Lynn. "Things aren't as hard for a woman now. I think women's lib got a lot to do with it."

"Maybe it *was* the women's lib thing," agreed Lynn Anderson, "the fact that women started enforcing their opinions, buying records. . . . It's just not workable anymore for the women in the business to be dependent on men."

Lynn Anderson was among the creators of a new breed of female country performer, the flashy, glamorous show queen who was as at home on the pop music charts as in the country field. Her "Rose Garden" of 1970 ushered in a decade of "crossover" country women whose music reached out to the broader pop marketplace and dramatically expanded country music's national popularity. Along with her show queen contemporaries Barbara Mandrell, Crystal Gayle, and Anne Murray, Lynn Anderson led the way into a new era and made the seventies a landmark decade for female country.

Lynn was eighteen when she came to Nashville in 1966. She'd been born in North Dakota in 1947, but raised in Sacramento, California, as the headstrong only child of Liz and Casey Anderson. Mama Liz's songwriting prominence won her the RCA Records contract that brought the family to Music Row.

"When we came to Nashville, we came specifically for Mother to get a record contract with RCA," Lynn recalls. "But they started letting me sing [backup] on her sessions. In effect, they heard me and said, 'Would you like a contract, too?' I did feel guilty about it for a while, because it was so easy for me, when in fact it had taken Mother years to get to that point."

So while Liz's "Mama Spank" and "Game of Triangles" singles were hitting the Top 10 in the late 1960s, her daughter's debut discs were also creating a stir. The two became a mother-daughter team on 1968's "Mother, May I"; Lynn saluted her mother with the 1970 LP *Songs My Mother Wrote*, and Liz composed five of her daughter's biggest early singles. But Lynn was very much a celebrity in her own right. She costarred on Chicago's "American Swing Around" TV show and became a network TV regular on "The Lawrence Welk Show" in 1967 and 1968. In 1970 she had a hit with Boudleaux and Felice Bryant's "Rocky Top"; the number later became the Tennessee state song.

Lynn married songwriter/producer Glenn Sutton in 1968. He was renowned on Music Row for his zany antics and wild carousing. Their life together was sometimes a battle royal and sometimes a laugh riot. They rose like twin stars in the country firmament at CBS Records. He cowrote the Grammy-winning "Almost Persuaded" and produced his wife's hit records. She got her Grammy for 1970's "Rose Garden," a Joe South song inspired by the popular novel of female mental illness *I Never Promised You a Rose Garden.* The number's enormous success on both pop and country stations won Lynn Anderson the Country Music Association Female Vocalist of the Year award and more than twenty-five other music industry accolades.

In subsequent singles Lynn was stereotyped as the sunny-voiced blonde who belted out joyous, exultant, upbeat fare like "Wrap Your Love All Around Your Man," "He Turns It into Love Again," and "What a Man My Man Is." But that image wasn't completely accurate. In 1975 and 1976 Lynn proved she could be poignant with "I've Never Loved Anyone More," downhearted with the divorce saga "All the King's Horses," and socially conscious with the strip-mining song "Paradise." She also recorded one of the first albums chronicling the history of women in country music, 1969's *Songs That Made Country Girls Famous.*

Lynn became a major superstar of the seventies, hitting the charts with thirty-five singles and starring in her own 1977 CBS TV special.

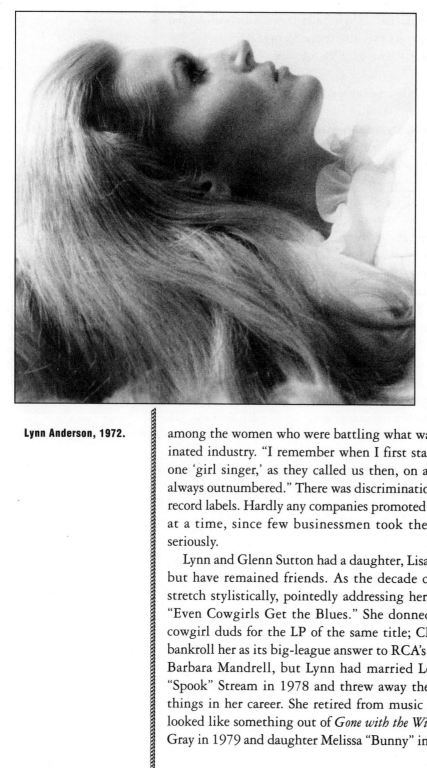

Her chiseled features and long, flaxen hair were highly photogenic, and she was often pictured in designer gowns. Lynn's stage shows were high-energy events showcasing her dazzling zip through the tongue-twisting "I've Been Everywhere," her hit rendition of Loggins & Messina's "Listen to a Country Song," her version of Karla Bonoff's "Isn't It Always Love," and country oldies from "Sea of Heartbreak" to "It Wasn't God Who Made Honky-Tonk Angels."

Lynn was a high-strung star, known for her temper and demanding ways. She was among the women who were battling what was then a very male-dominated industry. "I remember when I first started that there'd only be one 'girl singer,' as they called us then, on a concert bill. . . . We're always outnumbered." There was discrimination from radio stations and record labels. Hardly any companies promoted more than one female act at a time, since few businessmen took the emerging female stars seriously.

Lynn and Glenn Sutton had a daughter, Lisa. They divorced in 1977, but have remained friends. As the decade closed, she continued to stretch stylistically, pointedly addressing her happy image on 1980's "Even Cowgirls Get the Blues." She donned skintight, white satin cowgirl duds for the LP of the same title; CBS was reportedly set to bankroll her as its big-league answer to RCA's Dolly Parton and MCA's Barbara Mandrell, but Lynn had married Louisiana oilman Harold "Spook" Stream in 1978 and threw away the opportunity for bigger things in her career. She retired from music to a baronial estate that looked like something out of *Gone with the Wind.* She had son William Gray in 1979 and daughter Melissa "Bunny" in 1980. But in 1981 Lynn filed for divorce, citing physical abuse. Battered but determined to rebuild her life, she returned to Nashville in 1982.

Music Row's record companies didn't exactly welcome the prodigal daughter back with open arms. None would sign her. "I can't blame them," she said. "I turned my back on my career. I walked away from it all when I was successful." She signed with the Dallas-based Permian Records and issued the finest album of her career, *Back,* in 1983. "That was the way I felt at the time," she says of the disc's collection of emotional, bruised numbers like "What I Learned from Loving You." She performed a riveting version of the LP's "This Time the Heartache Wins" at a 1984 benefit concert for Nashville's shelter for battered women and narrated a documentary video on the topic for the YWCA. "You're Welcome to Tonight," her duet with Gary Morris, returned Lynn to the Top 10, but the label went bankrupt.

Stream followed her to Nashville, and for the next seven years Lynn's life became a nightmare of litigation as he sought custody of Gray and Bunny. As their fights continued to make newspaper headlines, she lost custody of her two youngest children in 1991.

The negative publicity destroyed her career. She issued a flurry of fine singles between 1986 and 1988, including the Ed Bruce duet "Fools for Each Other" and the old-folks love song "Read Between the Lines," but by 1990 most of Lynn's public appearances were as a horsewoman rather than a singer.

"I still enjoy all my hits," says Lynn Anderson. "Whenever I'm asked what my favorite is, I say 'Rocky Top.' Some people are surprised by that because 'Rose Garden' was a bigger hit for me. But 'Rocky Top' has brought so much happiness to so many people. They want me to be up-tempo and positive. Which is good, because that's how I feel usually," adds the woman who has experienced so much personal turmoil. "I have my down days just like anybody else, but basically my outlook is cheerful and positive."

The willful quality characteristic of Lynn Anderson during her heyday could also describe Barbara Mandrell. Like Lynn, Barbara had widespread pop appeal, and like Lynn, she had to endure spirit-breaking unhappiness. Barbara's best-selling 1990 autobiography, *Get to the Heart,* revolved around the 1984 automobile accident that nearly crippled her and profoundly altered her go-getter personality.

"There's a strong side to me that I'm only still discovering," Barbara wrote, "the kind of business and military instincts we call 'masculine,' for lack of a better word. I've asked questions about my business with a hard-headedness some people might call 'masculine.' . . . When the feminist

"The Princess of
the Steel" comes to
Nashville in 1968.
Barbara Mandrell
was ready to give up
show business to be
a housewife before her
fateful move to
Music City.

movement began in the Sixties, I was shocked to find it was such a big issue." Perhaps the toughest soldier in the female army that invaded the country charts in the seventies, Barbara could outwork, outperform, outtalk, and outsmile virtually anyone in show business.

All in all, she's quite an entertainment package. Barbara was "The Princess of the Steel," a child prodigy who excelled as an instrumentalist for a decade before she turned to singing. Her ash blond hair and ocean-blue eyes could have earned her a career as a model. She's a good enough public speaker to have become a minister. As a competitive tomboy teenager she won enough sports honors to consider a career as an athlete.

But music was her destiny. Born in Houston on Christmas Day 1948, Barbara grew up in southern California in a house full of melody. Father Irby was a singer and guitarist. Mother Mary was a pianist and music teacher. Mary gave her oldest daughter lessons on the accordion when the tot was barely big enough to hold it. Barbara could read music before she could read and write. At age five she made her performing debut with "Gospel Boogie" in her parents' church. At eleven she made her professional debut on steel guitar when her father took her to a Chicago music convention to demonstrate the Standel amplifiers he was selling. Country guitarist Joe Maphis was at the convention. Recognizing her potential, he hired "The Princess of the Steel" for his Vegas show, and for the cast of L.A.'s "Town Hall Party" TV show. By 1962 she was touring with such stars as Johnny Cash and Patsy Cline.

"Men dominated the world of country music," she recalled in *Get to the Heart,* "but I looked around and discovered there were more women than you might have thought. Marian Hall was an inspiration, playing the steel guitar. Rose Maphis could keep pace with Uncle Joe onstage. Of course, on 'The Grand Ole Opry' there was the immortal Minnie Pearl. . . . I became aware of Martha Carson . . . who had great showmanship and energy. And there was Rose Maddox. . . . I learned a lot from watching her on television and in person. She wasn't just a woman sitting up there sweet and pretty. She took charge."

By her midteens the diminutive starlet had added banjo to her instrumental arsenal. "Folk music was popular then, and the theme from 'The Beverly Hillbillies,'" she recalls. "My dad owned a music store . . . so it was easy to walk in and pick up a banjo and learn to play it." Barbara also picked up bass guitar and mandolin. Her sister Louise became a proficient bassist and fiddler, while Irlene, the baby of the family, took up drums.

Even though she was working in the music business, Barbara made the high school track team, was in the marching band, joined the school choir, made the honor roll, served on the student council, and was named Miss Oceanside, California, at age sixteen. Irby and Mary were strict with her; there was a solidly religious Pentecostal Mandrell family background.

Irby formed The Mandrells with steel guitarist Barbara, Mama Mary on keyboards, and himself on guitar. By the time Barbara was twenty-one, she'd played Vegas six times, as well as numerous military bases. The drummer in the family band was Ken Dudney, and he and Barbara fell in love. "I'd dated him since I was 14, and I just couldn't wait to graduate high school so I could be Mrs. Ken Dudney. We married 10 days before I graduated so that we could be together two weeks before I left for four months to Vietnam . . . with my father to entertain. Now, that was going to be my last performance. My parents were moving to Tennessee and I was moving to Washington State where Ken was stationed. And that was it with music. But once I saw the Opry, I wanted it all."

She was visiting her parents in 1968 when her father took her to the world's most famous country show. "I wasn't cut out to be in the audience," she realized. Barbara took her instruments to Nashville's Printer's Alley nightclub district, where people like Brenda Lee and steel guitarist Lloyd Green began dropping by to marvel at the multi-instrumental wonder woman. Within weeks six record companies offered contracts. Good-hearted Ken gave up his career as a navy pilot so that his wife could reenter the show business she loved so much. By 1969 her singles were beginning to make the charts.

Barbara is a heavy smoker, and this gives her vocals a hoarse, urgent quality that she put to good use on "blue-eyed soul" versions of r&b songs such as 1971's "Do Right Woman, Do Right Man" and "Treat Him Right." But her breakthrough was a 1973 cheating song called "The Midnight Oil." It told the tale of a woman lying to her husband about working late. "And tonight I'll cheat again, and tomorrow I'll be sorry," she sang. "And I'll feel a little dirty, 'cause I'll have that midnight oil all over me." Because of its frankness, the single is regarded as a breakthrough female disc. "Until then, only men were singing outspoken songs about [cheating]. . . . Women were recording songs that only delicately hinted at love affairs. But with 'The Midnight Oil,' I created a whole new precedent. I felt it was an important step forward for women singers."

Barbara continued to smolder in sin after moving to the ABC/MCA Records fold in 1975, scoring cheating hits with 1977's "Married but Not to Each Other" and "Midnight Angel," and 1979's "(If Loving You Is Wrong) I Don't Want to Be Right," which crossed over from country to pop charts. "I've recorded a lot of cheating songs, but there were a lot of cheating songs I turned down," says the model Christian wife and mother. "It depends on the lyrics. . . . God loves prostitutes, too."

She enacted the angry wife in "Standing Room Only" (1976); the heartbroken loser in "The Best of Strangers" (1980); and a sultry chanteuse on the well-crafted ballads "Hold Me" (1977), "Tonight" (1978), and "Years" (1980). By the close of 1980 she had a dozen Top 10 hits.

"Even with all the records female artists are selling . . . the feeling still seems to be that women can't draw on a show," Barbara complained. "I don't know why, but I definitely think it's much more difficult for a woman to be a headline act. I think Loretta Lynn made a tremendous breakthrough for women by being the first to win Entertainer of the Year [in 1972]. I did a show in Norwalk, Connecticut, and the promoter booked myself and Jeannie C. Riley on the package—just us, no men. Everybody said, 'It won't work. You can't have two girls on a show.' They had to turn people away."

Barbara accepted immediately when she was invited to become an Opry cast member in 1972, but "being the assertive, ambitious person that I am," she asked the management, "What do you have to do to be a host of a segment?" In her autobiography Barbara recalls, "Somebody said you had to gain enough national stature, which sounded fair to me. Oh, yes, and you had to be a man. I bit my tongue, but in the back of my mind, I knew I would change that someday. I do not consider myself to be a feminist— I hate labels—but I wanted to do it for myself, and for all women."

She had son Matthew in 1970 and daughter Jaime in 1976, never missing a beat in her career. In fact, "I booked my second child. I'm a great planner."

As her record success increased in the seventies, Barbara developed one of country music's flashiest shows. Customers got the hits, plus a spunky trouper who bounded around the stage from instrument to instrument. She tossed some gospel, some rockers, and some weepers. The whole effect was dazzling, though country purists complained that she was supper-club slick.

In 1979 Barbara Mandrell was named Female Vocalist of the Year by the Country Music Association. In 1980 and 1981 she won back-to-back Entertainer of the Year honors. Since then she has won more than fifty other major show-business accolades. NBC signed her to do a national TV variety series, where Barbara had to battle not only stereotypes against country music, but prejudice against variety entertainment, which at the time was dying on network television. "They expect you to be barefoot and ignorant," she remarks about the L.A. and New York attitudes she's encountered. "They were shocked when our show made it." In her book Barbara candidly explained her attitude toward her elevation to network stardom: "I went to Hollywood at a time in my life when I was ready to assert myself. Sure, I was confident from winning the top awards in my business, but it was more than that. I had been paying attention to my elders in show business for a quarter of a century. I was the least political woman you could imagine. Feminism, women's liberation, equal rights, they were just words to me. I was too busy working. But some part of it must have sunk in, because when I got to Hollywood. . . . I wanted control." Observed a *TV Guide* reporter on the set, "She throws herself into it as if it were a competition she had to win." Barbara and her beautiful sisters Louise and Irlene learned to dance and do comedy sketches, and Barbara cheerfully became the butt of most of the jokes. More than forty million people tuned in each Saturday night.

But the grueling weekly production schedules of songs, dances, and sketches ground down even the boundless energy of Barbara Mandrell. In 1982 she announced she was quitting to save her voice and her sanity. "I quit for my health. . . . They threatened me with you-name-it when I said I was quitting. I'm the only person that I know of that has ever left a television series with a five-year contract." "Barbara Mandrell & The Mandrell Sisters" was the last successful variety series on network television.

In 1983 she returned to Las Vegas in triumph with her stage extravaganza "The Lady Is a Champ." It incorporated her TV choreography, multiple-instruments showpiece, and a stirring rendition of her favorite song, "The Battle Hymn of the Republic." The "human dynamos'" disc success continued, as well. In 1983 Barbara issued "In Times Like These," a song of lovers enduring financial hardship together. Her 1981 single "I Was Country When Country Wasn't Cool" became her proud-to-be-country anthem. "Only a Lonely Heart Knows" (1984) and "There's No Love in Tennessee" (1985) were powerful heartache songs.

Crystal Gayle, 1980.

She won Grammy Awards for gospel performances in 1982 and 1983 and teamed with Lee Greenwood for potent love duets.

Her career built to a crescendo in 1984 when Barbara starred in the made-for-TV movie *Burning Rage,* taped her first network special, and built her career museum. Her charity work, notably an annual celebrity softball game to raise money for Vanderbilt Hospital, made her one of Nashville's most beloved public figures. She was the Golden Girl of Music City, U.S.A.

But it all came to a screeching halt in a tangled mess of glass and steel in September 1984 when a teenage driver hit Barbara's silver Jaguar head-on. He was killed instantly. She suffered a broken right femur, a shattered right ankle, a nearly destroyed right knee, and a severe concussion that left her disoriented for months. The suburban California princess, the beauty queen, the perfect wife and mother, and the beloved superstar had conducted her career with a self-discipline that seems to have precluded self-doubt and serious introspection. Now, in physical agony, it was as though Barbara Mandrell came to really know herself for the first time. The accident forced her to "stop and take some stock of things," she says.

During her recuperation she had third child Nathan, campaigned for seat belt use and organ donation, became an arthritis spokeswoman, marketed a gospel album, and began work on her remarkably candid autobiography. "The whole book was a difficult project for me. I've always pushed and tried to do my very best . . . and I cried buckets doing that book." *Get to the Heart* joined Loretta Lynn's *Coal Miner's Daughter* as one of the few country music tomes to make the *New York Times* best-seller lists.

With her buddy Dolly Parton as her opening act, Barbara Mandrell returned to the stage at the Universal Amphitheater in Los Angeles in 1986. She had a pin in her leg and an ankle brace hidden in her cowgirl boot, but the pain didn't show. In 1988 the Mandrells moved into a four-million-dollar, twenty-thousand-square-foot palace in the woods north of Nashville. Said to be the largest home in the county, the log mansion contains an indoor swimming pool, a forty-eight-foot-square living room, thirty-foot ceilings, multiple indoor balconies, a portrait of "Battle Hymn of the Republic" composer Julia Ward Howe, and the hide of one of circus star Gunther Gebel-Williams's deceased Bengal tigers.

Barbara Mandrell signed with Capitol Records in 1987 and has since recorded some strong-female lyrics such as "Child Support," "I'm Not Your Superwoman," and "This Rock." Her 1990 CD was *No Nonsense,* and she signed a commercial tie-in with the company that produces panty hose of the same name to sponsor her concerts. She also remains extremely popular on the corporate convention show circuit.

"I'm not a quitter, and I'm not a loser," says the tough-minded lady who fought for female respect in country music. Barbara's battles against prejudice toward women in the seventies were real. "There is more pressure on a female artist," said booking agent Virginia Rutledge to *Billboard* magazine in 1974. "A man is allowed to age. If a male singer gains a bit of weight, starts to lose his hair, the hotel bookers don't threaten to drop the contract. The male star can be seen in the same tux, and nobody complains. The female has got to spend money for the gowns. She must keep her figure looking good, and she can't get older." In sum, "It is a tougher field for a woman than a man."

Despite the obstacles, female country acts became more and more numerous as the seventies wore on. They brought in new, contemporary images that rejected the old cowgirl and sweetheart styles. In both looks and music these women showed that country music could be as sophisticated and polished as pop. They gave country glamour and mainstream appeal.

No one exemplified the new, smooth stylishness more than Crystal Gayle. Her sleek fashions, brunet elegance, and soft-spoken grace bore no traces of hillbilly culture. Her gentle, folkish sound with just the tiniest "cry" in her voice went down easily with pop music listeners.

Crystal floated through an astoundingly successful career as if in a dream, as though touched by some magic wand of fame. She did, in fact, title a 1977 LP *We Must Believe in Magic.* It contained a languid, bluesy tune called "Don't It Make My Brown Eyes Blue," which topped both country and pop hit parades, won her a Grammy, and sold a million copies. The "magic" was hers on seventeen other Number 1 records and thirty-four Top 10 hits in all.

In 1987 the singer opened the elegant Crystal's, a Nashville shop con-

A host of lovelies were signed to country contracts in the wake of breakthroughs by the glamorous show queens. Among them were the following:

SUSIE ALLANSON ("Baby Last Night Made My Day," "Maybe Baby," and "Two Steps Foward and Three Steps Back")

CONNIE EATON (formerly Miss Nashville) ("Angel of the Morning")

BARBI BENTON (a former *Playboy* Playmate) ("Brass Buckles")

KATHY BARNES ("Body Talkin'")

STEPHANIE WINSLOW ("Say You Love Me," "Crying," and "Baby I'm-a Want You")

PENNY DEHAVEN ("Down in the Boondocks," "I Feel Fine," and "I'll Be Doggone")

SHERRI JERRICO ("Thanks for Leaving, Lucille")

SUNDAY SHARPE ("I'm Having Your Baby")

DAWN CHASTAIN (a Neiman-Marcus fashion model)

---

taining the jewelry, gifts, and creations of Baccarat, Lalique, Orrefors, Fabergé, and other European artisans. Her west Nashville home is full of such museum-quality pieces, as well as rock crystal specimens. And she is a walking encyclopedia of crystal and semiprecious stone lore.

"They do have powers," she says softly. "Some have healing power. Some give you greater awareness. . . . They use quartz crystals in watches and in computers; they must have something. I always carry a crystal onstage with me. I wear various ones, like tourmaline, rubelite. Amethyst is the healing stone. I'm particularly fond of malachite and lapis lazuli because they were used by the Egyptians. I've collected every book ever written about crystals. . . . You read studies that there's no proof of this. But I can feel a difference from them. And if you believe something is beneficial to you and it works, then it does have power. I know that music does."

If all that new age lingo sounds a long way from the Kentucky coal fields, well, so is Crystal. By the time Brenda Gail Webb was born in Paintsville, Kentucky, in 1951, her oldest sister, Loretta Lynn, was already married with babies of her own, and Papa Ted Webb was disabled by black lung. When Crystal/Brenda was four, Mama Clara Butcher Webb moved the family to the rather more cosmopolitan town of Wabash, Indiana. Clara worked in nursing homes to support the brood; Ted died in 1959. "My mother really believed in me," says Crystal. "Anytime someone would come over to the house, she'd make me sing. I took to hiding because I was so shy, but she always found me and pushed me out in front of whatever audience there was. Once I started singing, though, I was fine. . . . I grew up knowing I was going to be a singer. There was never any doubt about that.

"I was influenced by all types of music when I was growing up," Crystal continues. "I've always enjoyed folk, pop, rock, gospel, country, everything. I was singing along with Lesley Gore, Brenda Lee, and Patsy Cline when I was tiny. Then along came Peter, Paul and Mary, and of course The Beatles. Having Loretta as my sister was a big influence, too."

Loretta got Crystal a contract at Decca and wrote her first single, 1970's "I Cried the Blue Right Out of My Eyes." She also picked her sister's stage name. The label already had Brenda Lee and didn't want another Brenda, so as Loretta drove by a Krystal hamburger stand one day, she was inspired. "Changing it to Crystal—I felt like, well . . . I'm a star or something. It *is* a pretty name, and one of the reasons my sister picked it out was because she thought it was bright and shiny, and she thought that's what I was."

Crystal languished at Decca, probably stigmatized by being the sister of the company's biggest star. But the success of "I've Cried the Blue Right Out of My Eyes" was enough to pique interest elsewhere. In 1974 she signed with United Artists and issued the assertive, sexy "Restless." During the next three years she rose to stardom by singing similarly modern romance lyrics—the divorce ode "This Is My Year for Mexico"; the survival numbers "I'll Get Over You" and "I'll Do It All Over Again"; the lost-love lament "You Never Miss a Real Good Thing"; and the seduction song "Wrong Road Again." All were backed by the catchy, gently rhythmic productions of Allen Reynolds, who encouraged Crystal to expand her musical horizons.

After "Don't It Make My Brown Eyes Blue" became the disc sensation of 1977, Crystal began reaching beyond modern Music Row for her material. She revived Gogi Grant's "The Wayward Wind," Billie Holiday's "God Bless the Child," Jimmie Rodgers's "Miss the Mississippi and You," and Bill Withers's "Lean on Me." Critics praised her versatility. She made the pop charts a dozen times, and perhaps symbolized her uptown aspirations by titling her 1981 LP *Hollywood, Tennessee.* As her stack of gold and platinum albums grew, Crystal won dozens more show-biz accolades. She starred in five network specials between 1979 and 1982; toured the world; and headlined in the casinos of Las Vegas, Reno, Atlantic City, and Tahoe.

Amazingly, she and her lawyer husband, Bill Gatzimos, did it all without a manager. Publicity-shy, woman-of-few-words Crystal Gayle made all her own decisions. Her obsession with controlling her own destiny became legendary on Music Row. She asked for and got the title of "director" on her recordings. "I don't want someone else telling me what to do," she explained to Chet Flippo in *Playboy.* "I like to be in control. . . . I fought for my own identity." It was Crystal who selected "Don't It Make My Brown Eyes Blue" as a single when the record label was against it. "What is readily apparent is that *no one* tells Crystal Gayle what to do," observed Flippo.

She moved from United Artists through contracts with Columbia, Elektra/Warner Bros., and Capitol/Liberty, all the while maintaining consistently high professional standards. "Ready for the Times to Get Better" (1978) and "Livin' in These Troubled Times" (1982) took a hard look at life and love. She applied her liquid alto to such lushly melodic ballads as "Talking in Your Sleep" (1978), "Til I Gain Control Again" (1982), and "When I Dream" (1979). But she could also swing smartly on upbeat tunes such as "Why Have You Left the One You Left Me For?" (1979), "Too Many Lovers" (1981), and "The Sound of Goodbye" (1983). Her best female-oriented performance of the period was 1981's "The

DIXIE HARRISON (a Miss Indiana contestant)

HELEN HUDSON (a New York teen model)

STEPHANY SAMONE (formerly Miss Texas)

LIZ LYNDELL (a Miss Tennessee contestant)

JOANN BON & THE COQUETTES

IDELA "THE HILLBILLY SEX POT" & COUNTRY CREAM

CONNIE CATO ("Super Kitten" and "Super Skirt")

CAROL CHASE ("Sexy Song" and "This Must Be My Ship")

MARY K. MILLER, KELLY FOXTON, JOYCE PAUL, CHERYL POOLE, MARIE OWENS, RITA REMINGTON, BRENDA KAY PERRY, JERIS ROSS, AND MARY KAY JAMES

OPRYLAND
GRADUATES

Opryland U.S.A. turned
out to be a great training
ground for show people.
Among its graduates are
the following:

CYNTHIA RHODES—
noted for movie roles
in *Dirty Dancing,
Flashdance,* and
Staying Alive; for
singing lead in Ani-
motion; and for
marrying pop prince
Richard Marx

DENISE DiRENZO—of
Broadway's *Cats* and
A Chorus Line

DEBORAH ALLEN—
country-pop star

MARY ELIZABETH
MASTRANTONIO—
Robin Hood and
Scarface movie star

CINDY SMITH AND
LISA ALVEY—of
Dave Rowland and
Sugar

LORRIE MORGAN—
country star

Woman in Me." "I like that," she says. "'You'll never break the woman in me, but you might hurt the child.' . . . I think a good many women can relate to that. A lot of women stand up under a lot of pressure." Her 1992 single "Three Good Reasons" told of a divorced single mother's will to survive.

Crystal and Bill had daughter Catherine Claire in 1983 and son Christos James in 1986. She said that motherhood transformed her outlook. Except for parenting and collecting beautiful things, her interests outside her career seem to be few. Crystal reads palms and says she thinks she might have the same psychic gift that her mother and oldest sister have.

She remained at the top through most of the eighties, finding particular success with TV and movie music.

But her enduring image isn't in a song. Crystal Gayle will be forever recalled by music fans for the sexy toss of her head that sent waves of motion through her Godiva-like brunet tresses. By the late eighties the singer with the cobalt blue eyes, high cheekbones, uptown image, and cool demeanor had hair that nearly reached the floor.

The stardom achieved by the beautiful pop crossover singers Crystal Gayle, Barbara Mandrell, and Lynn Anderson was all the men of Music Row needed to see. In the 1970s the executives promoted a stampede of glamorous women onto the country hit parade, few of whom attracted record buyers. Ex-*Playboy* playmate Barbi Benton, Miss Nashville runner-up Connie Eaton, Neiman-Marcus fashion model Dawn Chastain, Miss Indiana contestant Dixie Harrison, and a long line of other stunning beauties filed onto the country hit parade. Among the most successful were Minnesota's Susie Allanson, South Dakota's Stephanie Winslow, Illinois's "Super Kitten" Connie Cato, and North Dakota's "Sexy Song" singer Carol Chase.

Pretty Charlotte Denise McClain went for a polished, cosmopolitan look, because "to say that all country-lovin' people live on farms or wear blue jeans misrepresents an awful lot of us. . . . You don't have to have wagon wheels and hay behind you just because you're a country singer." As Charly McClain, the singer evolved into a pert, doe-eyed brunet with a chic hairstyle and stylish clothes to match. Born in 1956, Charly was a professional at the "Mid-South Jamboree" in Memphis by 1973. Her kittenish phrasing and southern-belle charm won her a recording contract, and she bowed on the country charts in 1976 with a torn-between-two-lovers ditty called "Lay Down." The practically worshipful "Men" became a notable hit, but Charly's stardom rested on her utterance of one word in 1980. The word was "git-tar," which she growled in

"Who's Cheatin' Who?" just before the churning rockabilly guitar break. The single became her first Number 1 hit. She enjoyed ten more Top 10 tunes in the eighties, including the sexy up-tempo duet with Mickey Gilley "Paradise Tonight" (1983) and her sweet working-girl tune "Radio Heart" (1985). The Memphis belle graduated to TV in "Hart to Hart," "CHiPS," and other series and married actor Wayne Massey in 1984.

Charly was one of the first to speak out about sexual harassment on Music Row. In 1982 she protested that "the producers and stars in Nashville expected sexual favors from me. . . . So many men in the business want you to sleep with them in order to get a record out, to be on a show or anything else. . . . I've had to slap big men here in Nashville in the face; ninety-eight percent of them will try to take advantage of you." Charly was solicited by both *Playboy* and *Penthouse* to pose nude. "I just feel that I'm too intelligent to have to take my clothes off to get somebody's attention," she said indignantly. Ten years later women at record labels and song publishing firms filed Music Row's first formal sexual harassment complaints.

Marketing music using sex appeal destroyed some women's careers. Beautiful Sami Jo Cole, a native of Arkansas, had a spectacularly evocative delivery, full of smoky drama, raspy soul, and dark emotion. Her "Tell Me a Lie" and "It Could Have Been Me" of 1974 were promising beginnings. But her raven-haired looks were all that mattered to the men around her. Sami's producer, Sonny Limbo, told her, "Do everything I tell you, and I'll make you a star." In the 1977 book *Rock 'n' Roll Is Here to Pay* he bragged, "She did. . . . That kind of attitude, an outasight voice and a motherfucker song—to break a chick that's all it takes. Then if she looks good and has big tits, she just might make it." By the dawn of the eighties Sami's career was kaput.

The female rock duo Toni Brown and Terry Garthwaite went country with a 1973 album called *Cross-Country.* They had been informed by a producer that they needed to be sexier. "He told Terry and me . . . that we'd better wear low-cut gowns," Toni recalled. "And why didn't we get out there and try to turn people on? That . . . made it impossible for us to work with him."

It was all apparently too much for petite Ohio blonde Sheila Andrews. She was a startling powerful alto who displayed pile-driving conviction on the 1978 and 1979 singles "Too Fast for Rapid City" and "Love Me Like a Woman." But after two excellent LPs she reportedly got sick of being treated like country merchandise and went back home with her family.

Sylvia Kirby moved to Nashville from her native Kokomo, Indiana, in

1976. Producer Tom Collins told her to lose weight and learn to use makeup, and when she did, he gave her a recording studio break in 1979. Born in 1956, she was a Hoosier singer with stars in her eyes who initially worked as Collins's receptionist. Using the moniker Sylvia, she was soon turning out Top 10 country hits like "Tumbleweed," "Drifter," and "The Matador" in an attractive, airy style she called "prairie music." She scored a major pop crossover hit with 1982's "Nobody."

"Golden Tears" described a country girl who traded her jeans for designer dresses in a climb to riches that made her miserable. That 1979 chart-topping smash seemed to sum up the lives of the women who sang it. "Golden Tears" was one of a string of huge harmony hits by the trio Dave & Sugar. The glamorous women of Sugar wore fancy gowns. They sparkled in the spotlights of the finest country nightclubs. They glowed in the stardom of ten consecutive Top 10 hits from 1975 to 1980. Just like the lady in the song, they climbed the ladder from obscurity to celebrity. And like the lady in the song, they were miserable.

Former Stamps Quartet and Four Guys member Dave Rowland was down on his luck in 1975 when he hit on the idea of framing himself with a beautiful woman on either side. He called the harmony singers "Sugar" and dubbed their uptown trio sound "tuxedo country." It was a class act. The ladies were lovely, and the full-throated singing was thrilling on hits like "Queen of the Silver Dollar," "The Door Is Always Open," "Tear Time," and "Don't Throw It All Away." But the Sugar women with the glorious golden voices wept "Golden Tears" of anonymity. They had no billing as individuals. And as the hit catalog grew, so did Dave's ego. Although the women often sang lead, he did the interviews; he took the credit; he owned the act. So on stage and TV the Sugars glided through their routines, smiled, sang their hearts out, looked great, and had no names. And as if being just "Sugar" wasn't enough, by 1980 it was "Dave Rowland and Sugar." The females in the famed trio began quitting with such frequency that Dave could have installed a revolving door to the audition studio.

Today Nashville is full of ex-Sugars, gifted singers who sang some of the biggest hits of the seventies and starred in the snazziest show rooms of Las Vegas and Lake Tahoe. But they are practically unknown. Vickie Baker, Jackie Frantz, Sue Powell, and Melissa Prewitt sang on the biggest Dave and Sugar hits, and they have been succeeded by more than a dozen other Sugars.

"When the name changed, I started realizing what direction it was going in," Sue recalled. "RCA offered to record me, but Dave got real upset if I was going to record on my own. . . . So I stayed for about another year so I wouldn't cause a hassle." In 1982 Dave titled his debut solo album *Sugar Free* and described its sound as "country elegance."

The idea was to make country music palatable to the pop mainstream, to shed its low-class image and make it the music of all Americans. By adopting the trappings of television variety entertainment—the costumes, stage patter, and dancing—country entertainers hoped to gain fans beyond the truckers, factory laborers, waitresses, farmers, and domestic workers of its bedrock audience. Perhaps not coincidentally, such folks had completely abandoned the term "working class" by this time. Everyone called themselves "middle class," and during the 1970s the U.S. middle class made significant economic strides forward. All of this era's show-queen acts downplayed regional accents and the grittier, blue-collar aspects of country songwriting in favor of positive lyrics and high style.

When the executives of WSM created a musical theme park in 1972, this was the type of entertainment they installed. The park grew from the notion that "The Grand Ole Opry" was badly in need of a new concert hall, so on 110 landscaped acres along the Cumberland River they build that hall, a hotel, a TV production facility, a showboat, gardens, museums, amusement rides, and stages for music, music, music. Opryland U.S.A. features clean-cut, attractive youngsters doing Broadway-style interpretations of Dixieland, blues, gospel, rockabilly, country, and other American music genres. The theme park has been a first-rate training ground for show people. Among its graduates are film actresses and Broadway stars, as well as some of Dave's Sugars and country divas Deborah Allen and Lorrie Morgan.

More than a million people went through Opryland's turnstiles during its first season. In 1976, 1977, and 1978 attendance topped two million, and it remained at that level or higher throughout the 1980s. These figures parallel country music's growth. When Nashville assumed its preeminence as country's recording capital around 1960, the country record business was worth around thirty million dollars. As the 1970s dawned, country discs sold one hundred million dollars, roughly 10 percent of the billion-dollar U.S. record business. By 1975 country records were at the two-hundred-fifty-million-dollar sales level, and by 1980 more than half a billion dollars from record sales rolled down the streets of Music Row.

By broadening the definition of country, emphasizing acts like the show queens, adopting more contemporary images, and downplaying the hayseed factor, Nashville was learning how to compete in the big-time pop arena. The community was heady with monetary success and alive with experimentation in the 1970s. The rush to sign female talent reached in all directions. Teenage girls, black women, TV and movie stars, foreign-born singers, and country-star kinfolks were all signed, recorded, and promoted.

Tanya Tucker led the teen charge with a string of then-shocking performances. Her hits had themes no girl singer her age had ever tackled before. She was only thirteen when "Delta Dawn," a saga of female insanity, made her a star in 1972. By the time she was sweet sixteen, Tanya had sung of illegitimacy, murder, sex, and more in such singles of 1973 to 1975 as "What's Your Mama's Name," "Blood Red and Goin' Down," and "Would You Lay with Me."

Floridian LaWanda Lindsey recorded when she was fourteen. Wendy Holcombe was a popular teen fiddler/banjoist on country TV shows of the seventies. Sandy Croft came to Nashville after winning the International Miss Cinderella Pageant. Kippi Brannon was fourteen when she arrived in 1980.

Debby Boone was just twelve when she began touring with her famous father, Pat, and only twenty when she recorded the yearning "You Light Up My Life." Debby (b. 1956) and her sisters, Cherry (b. 1954), Lindy (b. 1955), and Laury (b. 1959), were wholesome, all-American girls who toured as the distaff counterparts to The Osmond Brothers. Mama Shirley and her girls began to record "Pat Boone Family" gospel albums in 1971. Cherry was the lead singer in the early days, but Debby's purity of tone gradually replaced her. "You Light Up My Life" sold four and a half million copies and won its singer a Grammy Award. But while Debby soared in solo stardom in 1977, sister Cherry was hospitalized as an eighty-pound skeleton suffering from anorexia and other eating disorders. Cherry survived to publish *Starving for Attention* in 1982; she and the book received a lot of attention in the wake of singer Karen Carpenter's death from the disorder in February 1983.

Meanwhile, fresh-faced, honey-haired Debby was on her way to country fame. She followed "You Light Up My Life" with a number of hits, among them her 1979 revivals of the Connie Francis songs "My Heart Has a Mind of Its Own," "Breakin' In a Brand New Broken Heart," and "Everybody's Somebody's Fool." She hit Number 1 on the country charts with 1980's "Are You on the Road to Lovin' Me Again," then became an award-winning gospel star. Her 1989 *Home for Christmas* album featured "White Christmas" as a duet with her mother-in-law, Rosemary Clooney.

Other stars' relatives who entered the ranks of female country performers of the 1970s included Tanya Tucker's sister LaCosta, Barbara Mandrell's sister Louise, Dolly Parton's sis Stella, Onie Wheeler's daughter Karen, and Conway Twitty's daughters Joni Lee and Kathy (aka Jessica James).

For a while it seemed as if it was "anything goes" for female country acts. Debbie Dawn's "Hands" was the first disc about massage parlors. Zella Lehr, who made the Top 10 with Dolly Parton's "Two Doors Down" in 1978, was a unicyclist and former bullwhip vaudeville act. Brenda Joyce was wheelchair-bound. Terri Gibbs was blind. Hilka (Cornelius) was German. Philomena Begley was Irish. Tina Rainford was British.

The first African-American female country acts were promoted during this period. Esther Phillips (1935–1984) was the pioneer with her "Release Me" of 1962. In the wake of country successes by Charley Pride, O. B. McClinton, and Stoney Edwards, the record companies went looking for their female equivalents. Ruby Falls (1946–1986), Linda Martel, Sarge and Shirley West, Virginia Kirby, and Joanne Neel ("Daddy Was a Preacher but Mama Was a Go-Go Girl") were all promoted this way. The Pointer Sisters won a Grammy Award for their 1974 country tune "Fairytale," and Anita Pointer had a major 1986 country hit as Earl Thomas Conley's duet partner on "Too Many Times." Tina Turner recorded country LPs in 1974 (*Tina Turns the Country On*) and 1979 (*Good Hearted Woman*). Millie Jackson tried her luck with 1981's *Just a Li'l Bit Country.* No black women have had sustained country success, but singers like Frankie Staton, Donza Payne, and Nisha Jackson have persevered in the eighties and nineties.

Canadian country also laid siege to the country charts in the seventies. There is a strong north-of-the-border country tradition, whose female exponents of the fifties included such stars as Myrna Lorrie and Lucille Starr. In the seventies Canadians Carroll Baker, Iris Larratt, Debbie Lori Kaye, and The Family Brown were all welcomed to Nashville. And Anne Murray was elevated to superstardom.

Anne's "Snowbird" was the first Top 10 hit in a country career that has included more than twenty. Her impeccable vocal taste, dry wit,

The Pointer Sisters introduce their Grammy-winning country hit "Fairytale" on the Grand Ole Opry stage, 1974.

cool demeanor, and flawless talent for song selection made Anne the equal of her pop crossover American counterparts. Like them, she became just as at home in a Las Vegas show room as she was on the Opry House stage.

And like the others, her music is not easily categorized. She prefers to think of herself as simply a "singer," rather than a "country singer." Anne Murray (b. 1945) is the daughter of a small-town doctor from the mining town of Spring Hill, Nova Scotia. She sang folk music and majored in physical education in college, then became a gym teacher on Prince Edward Island. But in 1966 Anne became a member of the cast of the Canadian hootenanny TV series "Singalong Jubilee." Her folkie first LP appeared in 1968. "Snowbird" made her a U.S. star two years later.

The step from coffeehouse to concert hall was difficult: "When the hit records started to come and I started playing in places where it was really important to play, I was a wreck. I was so nervous going out onstage that I would freeze right up." Her metamorphosis into a show queen is ironic, since the flashy trappings of show business made her so uncomfortable in this period.

She married TV producer Bill Langstroth in 1975 and went into semi-retirement to raise children in Toronto. Anne's home life remains more important to her than performing, so she restricts her concert appearances to just eighty per year. She began her career's second phase with 1978's "You Needed Me," and followed that million-seller with "I Just Fall in Love Again," "Broken Hearted Me," and other country-pop ballads. In 1980 she sang "Could I Have This Dance," the love theme from the movie blockbuster *Urban Cowboy.*

Success agreed with her. Anne shed her girl-next-door image in favor of a more sensuous, womanly look. She developed a casual yet showy concert style that featured choreography, audience participation, costume changes, chatty dialogue, and self-mocking humor. "I learned to relax," she says. "I learned to say, 'To hell with it. I really don't have a whole lot to prove.'"

"I've never been obsessed with this, ever," she says of her remarkable career. "Not to get any highfalutin' ideas about my contribution or anything, but . . . I know I'm some kind of role model." Her exquisite taste in songs and beautiful, stars-at-midnight alto have brought Anne Murray more simultaneous success on pop and country charts than any other singer in history. To date she has sold more than twenty million albums and won four Grammy Awards. In 1985 she was given the Companion of the Order of Canada, the highest honor awarded a citizen there.

Australia and New Zealand also have a long country music heritage.

"Down Under" cowgirls were particularly gifted, and discs by such yodeling stars of the 1940s and 1950s as June Holmes, Shirley Thoms, and The McKean Sisters are highly sought after by collectors today. Power-voiced Diana Trask, born in the little Victoria town of Warburton in 1940, brought Aussie music stateside in the seventies. She caught fire in 1972 with "It Meant Nothing to Me," one of the angriest female vocals of its era. She didn't whimper about being cheated on, she lashed out: "I've had enough! And, God, I can't stand it when you say, 'It meant nothing to me.'" Diana Trask continued to stun listeners with her fiery technique in mid-1970s performances such as "Say When," "It's a Man's World," and the strong womanhood song "Lean It All on Me." Boasted booking agent Buddy Lee, "In person, Diana is a . . . flame-haired, electrifying performer, so capable a stylist that she can sing pop, jazz, and country all in one show. . . . The modern country sound is her specialty."

Anne Murray, 1981.

Jewel Blanch came to town to stay. She was an Aussie child star who performed in her father's family act in the fifties and sixties. Signed to RCA in Nashville, Jewel made the country charts with a handful of singles, including "Can I See You Tonight" in 1979.

Australian, Canadian, European, whatever—the country-female possibilities seemed limitless. They came scampering onto the charts from New York and Hollywood, too. "Carol Burnett Show" star Vicki Lawrence (1973's "The Night the Lights Went Out in Georgia"), "Lawrence Welk" singer Ava Barber (1978's "Bucket to the South"), and "Mike Douglas Show" regular Peggy Little (1970's "Mama, I Won't Be Wearing a Ring") all tasted country success. *W.W. and the Dixie Dancekings* movie starlet Conny Van Dyke, "Dean Martin Show" "Gold Digger" Jimmi Cannon, and "Laugh-In" comedian Ruth Buzzi got country contracts, too. "Ray Anthony Show" TV regular and supper-club headliner Vikki Carr trekked south for her LP *Nashville by Carr*.

Hollywood actress Sissy Spacek grew up surrounded by country sounds in Quitman, Texas, where she was born Mary Elizabeth Spacek in 1949. Sissy performed as a folkie early in her career and spent the late 1970s preparing for the role of her life, portraying Loretta Lynn in *Coal*

Donny and Marie Osmond, 1979.

Miner's Daughter. The film won Sissy a 1980 Best Actress Oscar, and her soundtrack won a Gold Record. Sissy then unveiled her own style with a 1983 LP that yielded the hit "Lonely but Only for You." "There's reality there, real human emotion," says Sissy. "I think that's what makes country music, country music."

"I'm a little bit country," chirped toothsome, teenage Marie Osmond on TV's "Donny and Marie," which ran from 1976 to 1979, while her brother responded, "I'm a little bit rock 'n' roll." But after big success in her teens with oldie remakes of Connie Francis's "Who's Sorry Now?" and Anita Bryant's "Paper Roses" and "In My Little Corner of the World," TV star Marie languished in the bottom reaches of the country charts. Born in Ogden, Utah, in 1959, the Mormon princess was still a young woman when she returned to the Top 10 in splendid duets with Dan Seals ("Meet Me in Montana") and Paul Davis ("You're Still New to Me"), and the 1986 and 1987 solos "There's No Stopping Your Heart" and "Read My Lips."

Like Debby Boone, Marie was a devout Christian with a wholesome, girl-next-door image. And like Barbara Mandrell, she was a child star who evolved into a hardworking, driven perfectionist. Marie says being raised the only girl among the eight Osmond brothers made her spunky, and she always includes a tribute to the women of country music in her stage show. "I like the fact that women can be successful in country music and that there's some longevity to a country singer's career," she says. And like the other country-pop crossover queens of her era, Marie had a patriotic, high-energy, fashion-conscious concert act that matched her upbeat, pop-flavored tunes. "I don't think I'd be legitimate in traditional country music," she explains. "Who would believe that coming from me?"

Easily the most delightful import from television-land was Mary Kay Place. This brilliant madcap portrayed aspiring country starlet "Loretta Haggers" on TV's cockeyed soap opera satire "Mary Hartman, Mary Hartman." Mary Kay's Tulsa twang was authentic, and so was her country music ability. Comedy producer Norman Lear initially put her on his "All in the Family" sitcom to sing her hilarious composition "If Communism Comes Knocking at Your Door, Don't Answer It."

Mary Kay's wicked wit, twinkling eyes, and devilish grin were perfect for "Mary Hartman, Mary Hartman," and as soon as she started singing on the show, she began to get recording offers. She debuted on the country charts in 1976 and 1977 with the zesty songs she wrote for TV, "Baby Boy" and "Vitamin L." She posed in front of a bowling alley for the tongue-in-cheek cover of her LP *Tonight! At the Capri Lounge: Loretta Haggers,* but the performances inside were sincere. Dolly Parton, Emmylou Harris, and Anne Murray pitched in on backup vocals. The second LP, 1977's *Aimin' to Please,* was even better and sported a hit Mary Kay Place/Willie Nelson duet revival of the blue-collar classic "Something to Brag About." Mary Kay adopted country's feisty-female attitude on the LP's "Don't Make Love to a Country Music Singer," "Marlboro Man," and "Cattle Kate."

"I don't feel I need a man in order to survive," Mary Kay said at the time. "I come from a family of very strong, independent, secure women who are aware of their self-worth."

The enormous explosion of female talent in country music of the 1970s directly paralleled women's achievements in other areas of American life previously dominated by men. Breakthroughs into "male" occupations were everywhere. In 1972 came the first woman admitted into the U.S. Navy, the first woman to run in the Boston Marathon, the first woman rabbi, and the first woman to sit on the New York Stock Exchange board of directors. Shirley Chisholm announced her bid for the Democratic presidential nomination in 1972 and got more than 28 percent of the votes during her primary campaigns. The first female commercial airline pilot took off in 1973. Girls entered Little League in 1974. In 1976, Barbara Walters became the first female network news anchor. The Susan B. Anthony silver dollar saluted America's best-known suffragist in 1978; that was the same year that female sportswriters invaded locker rooms and that the first female astronauts were named.

In the 1970s women entered the ranks of professionals in ever-growing numbers. There were enormous increases in the number of female doctors, architects, dentists, lawyers, and judges, as well as country singers. The profound shift in country music culture created more than just a few superstar figures. In previous decades only the most outstanding female personalities got onto the charts. Now not only were they at the top, they populated the middle and bottom levels, as well. Because the field was so fertile, a variety of "outsiders" tried carpet-

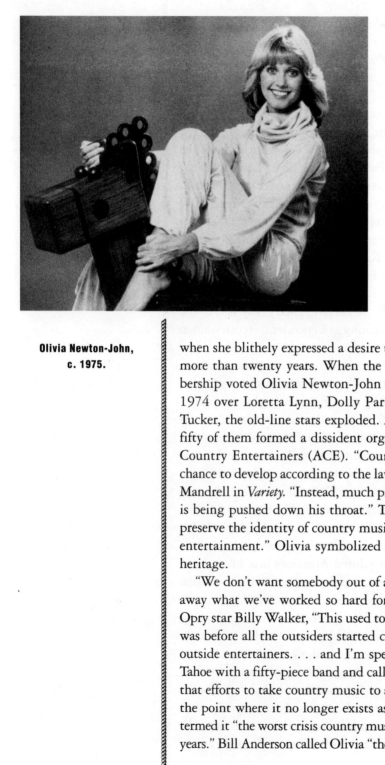

**Olivia Newton-John,
c. 1975.**

bagging as country acts. Music Row bristled when women from the mainstream pop world proclaimed themselves "country." At various times during the seventies, Cher, Maureen McGovern, Helen Reddy, Mary MacGregor, Bonnie Tyler, and Pia Zadora all made the country charts. Peroxided lounge singers who couldn't rock decided that country was the best marketplace for their efforts. The traditionalists at "The Grand Ole Opry" seethed.

The resentment boiled over into outright anger when Olivia Newton-John became a country star. Olivia fueled the grumbling when she blithely expressed a desire to meet Hank Williams, then dead more than twenty years. When the Country Music Association membership voted Olivia Newton-John its Female Vocalist of the Year in 1974 over Loretta Lynn, Dolly Parton, Tammy Wynette, and Tanya Tucker, the old-line stars exploded. After a meeting at Tammy's house fifty of them formed a dissident organization called the Association of Country Entertainers (ACE). "Country music is not being given its chance to develop according to the laws of the free market," said Barbara Mandrell in *Variety.* "Instead, much product not wanted by the consumer is being pushed down his throat." The stated purpose of ACE was "to preserve the identity of country music as a separate and distinct form of entertainment." Olivia symbolized how country had drifted from its heritage.

"We don't want somebody out of another field coming in and taking away what we've worked so hard for," groused Johnny Paycheck. Said Opry star Billy Walker, "This used to be a trustworthy industry, but that was before all the outsiders started coming in. . . . I'm speaking of the outside entertainers. . . . and I'm speaking of the artists who play Lake Tahoe with a fifty-piece band and call themselves 'country.'" Walker said that efforts to take country music to a wider audience would dilute it to the point where it no longer exists as a distinct style. Barbara Mandrell termed it "the worst crisis country music as an art form has faced in twenty years." Bill Anderson called Olivia "the straw that broke the camel's back," complaining, "Olivia Newton-John has gone on national television denying she is a country singer. This upsets us. We would rather see a Tammy Wynette or a Loretta Lynn or somebody who will say 'Yes, I am country' win [awards]."

Poor Olivia. It wasn't her fault. She never had country stars in her eyes. She was the victim of sophisticated music marketing—a coalition of music publishing and record label executives who decided she could make them lots of money if she were promoted simultaneously to both pop and country listeners. "My producers said they were releasing it country, and I didn't even know what they were talking about," she later confessed. Born in England in 1948 and raised in Australia, the wide-eyed blonde was initially a folk fan who recorded things like "Banks of the Ohio" and "If Not for You" as early singles. From 1973 to 1976 Olivia bombarded the U.S. charts with bright, up-tempo fare like "Let Me Be There" and "If You Love Me Let Me Know," as well as mooning, whispery-voiced ballads such as "I Honestly Love You" and "Have You Never Been Mellow." These numbers were synthesizer concoctions recorded in England. Nary a steel guitar was heard.

Jack Blanchard and Misty Morgan, 1974.

At this same time, country music was at the peak of its glitzy, show-queen era, and Nashville was making its own brand of pop crossover, style-bending music. Why shouldn't Olivia's buoyant British sound be played beside Lynn Anderson's rendition of The Carpenters' pop bauble "Top of the World" or Crystal Gayle's show tune "One More Time/ Karneval" or Barbara Mandrell's soul song "Show Me"? Apparently it was okay for Nashville to cook up such confections, but not a foreigner. Despite Olivia's attempts to reach out to the country audience with "Please Mr. Please" and "Every Face Tells a Story" and to mollify the industry by recording part of her 1976 LP on Music Row, the furor over her award never died down. Only Stella Parton came to her defense with "Ode to Olivia" ("We ain't got the right to say you're not country").

Misty Morgan was just about as unlikely as a country star. But she and her husband, Jack Blanchard, were so different that nobody ever figured out exactly *what* they were. Born in

Buffalo, New York, in 1945, Misty was a piano prodigy who entered professional music in pop combos of the fifties. In 1963 she married Jack, a wonderfully off-center songwriter, and they teamed up in Florida to perform jazz, rock, Dixieland, or anything else it took to put bread on the table. Misty hooked up all kinds of electronic devices to her piano, so the two never needed more band members.

Jack and Misty developed a quirky, "stoned" sound, something like Sonny and Cher lost in a poppy field in South Carolina. His "velvet saw" bass voice cut across her warm, dreamy alto, while underneath pulsed a steady shuffle beat dotted with harmonica and steel guitar bubbles of sound. Jack's lyrics alternated between totally bizarre novelty nonsense and deeply felt social commentary. They called their distinctive creations "Jack and Misty Productions," so she can be credited as country's trailblazing female record producer. When the wacky "Tennessee Bird Walk" topped the country charts in 1970, Misty Morgan became the first woman in music history to have coproduced a Number 1 hit. The record crossed over to become a sizable pop hit, as well. The twosome followed this with the equally kookie "Humphrey the Camel," "Fire Hydrant #79," and "Legendary Chicken Fairy."

But there was more to the beautiful brunet and her mod-costumed, long-haired husband than that. "There Must Be More to Life (Than Growing Old)" and "Poor Jody" ruminated on aging. "Bethlehem Steel" was about a discouraged, homesick factory worker. "Big Black Bird" and "The Shadows of the Leaves" had mystical love lyrics. "Changin' Times" lamented the commercialization of modern life. The compelling "Somewhere in Virginia in the Rain" told the story of a working-class pair's breakup and reconciliation. Jack's groaning rasp oozed with soul, while Misty's delectable, behind-the-beat phrasing anticipated the popularity of stylists such as Willie Nelson.

Given the pop-oriented trend in country music of the seventies, it was almost inevitable that Music Row would turn back to its original pop crossover stylists. Singers from the Nashville Sound era of ten years earlier got a new lease on life. Both Brenda Lee and Dottie West staged highly successful comebacks in the seventies. And the mass immigration of women onto the country charts made it possible for veterans Jean Shepard, June Carter, and Billie Jo Spears to return, as well. All had the biggest solo hits of their careers.

"I don't really think I started doing country," Brenda says. "I just think that the music changed so much that the music I was doing in the seventies had become what was called country." Brenda Lee had thirty-two country hits in the seventies and early eighties. The Recording Academy saluted her with its Governors Award in 1984; she costarred in the 1987 Cinemax cable TV special "The Legendary Ladies of Rock 'n' Roll"; she did two seasons headlining at Opryland in 1988 and 1989; and she was nominated for the Rock 'n' Roll Hall of Fame in 1989.

Nashville Sound stylist Dottie West took on a glamorous new image during the 1970s country show-queen era and also enjoyed a huge resurgence in popularity. She took lovers twenty years her junior, got a face-lift, outfitted herself in some eye-popping costumes, and became a major arena headliner. Her concerts were big-production events, full of high style and glamour. Dottie traded in her country frocks for a hundred-thousand-dollar show-queen wardrobe by Cher's designer Bob Mackie.

Dottie's producer, Larry Butler, was also behind the career resurgence of Opry star Jean Shepard, who blasted back to the top in 1973 with the rhythmic "Slippin' Away." A year later she planted tongue firmly in cheek for the hillbilly whoop-it-up "At the Time." It was an enormously clever song, contrasting blue-collar images with high-class references to flatter a lover. It was written by the prolific Bill Anderson, to whom Jean turned again for the ballad "The Tip of My Fingers" in 1975. Jean's trademark in the seventies was the hand-clapping, gospel-flavored, up-tempo romance celebration. But in 1974 and 1975 she also introduced a frank sexuality in ballads such as "Poor Sweet Baby" ("You're too big a boy to go to bed hungry") and "Another Neon Night" ("There's someone lying next to me and I don't even know his name").

Dottie, right, with her daughter Shelly West, 1986.

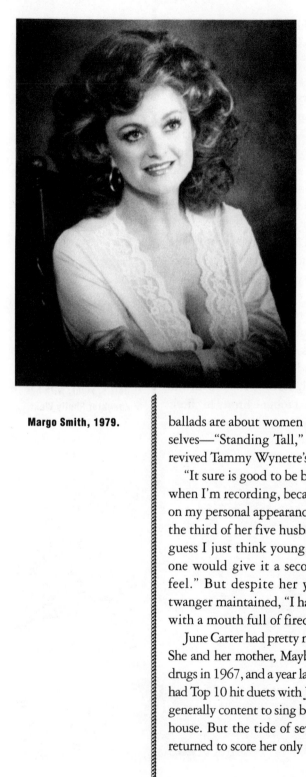

Margo Smith, 1979.

These performances represented a personal breakthrough for Jean, who'd long wanted to express frank emotions. "Ken Nelson, my ex-producer, would never let me record a 'triangle' song unless I was on the right side of the fence. He'd always say, 'Oh, no, they just don't expect that of you. You're such a sweet little country girl.' I could never convince him."

Butler's third major female client of the time was Billie Jo Spears, for whom he fashioned a country-disco style. After her working-girl songs of the sixties Billie Jo had faded from popularity. But with the toe-tapping "Blanket on the Ground," "What I've Got in Mind," and "If You Want Me" of 1975 through 1979, she sang some of the most distinctive pop-country fusion discs of the day. She even turned Gloria Gaynor's strong-woman disco song "I Will Survive" into a country hit. Billie Jo was unusual for a country female of the period in that she recorded hardly any "victim" material. Almost all the star's hit ballads are about women leaving, surviving, or otherwise asserting themselves—"Standing Tall," "I'm Not Easy," "I've Got to Go." In 1981 she revived Tammy Wynette's sassy classic "Your Good Girl's Gonna Go Bad."

"It sure is good to be back," Billie Jo said. "I'm a different person now when I'm recording, because I'm also able to present a much better show on my personal appearances," added the show-queen convert. She married the third of her five husbands, a man fifteen years her junior, in 1975. "I guess I just think young," she said. "If it was the other way around, no one would give it a second thought. . . . You're only as young as you feel." But despite her youthful, disco-influenced sound, the Texas twanger maintained, "I have no desire to be a pop artist. I couldn't go pop with a mouth full of firecrackers."

June Carter had pretty much given up any dreams of a solo career by 1970. She and her mother, Maybelle, had joined together to get Johnny Cash off drugs in 1967, and a year later the superstar became June's third husband. She had Top 10 hit duets with John in the sixties, but after they wed, June seemed generally content to sing backup with The Carter Sisters, raise kids, and keep house. But the tide of seventies female country swept her up, too. June returned to score her only solo hit with 1971's "A Good Man," and in 1975

Johnny produced her excellent, mountain-flavored LP *Appalachian Pride.*

One of the most striking facts about the revivals of these careers is that all of these women were entering middle age at the time. Dottie West was forty-four when producer Butler gave her a new sound in 1976. Jean Shepard was forty in 1973 when he brought new sparkle to her discs. Billie Jo Spears was forty-two when she stirred a disco stew with "I Will Survive." June Carter was forty-six when she issued *Appalachian Pride.*

Former Ohio kindergarten teacher Margo Smith was thirty-seven in 1979 when she wrote and sang a theme song for these stars and millions of other women, "Still a Woman." The song is country music's biggest all-time hit asserting the dignity and sexuality of the middle-aged woman. It led to a sexy new image for Margo, a new love life, duets with young Rex Allen, Jr., an intensely loyal female fan club, and one of the era's flashiest show-queen stage routines.

"Sex is a part of every woman," said Margo in 1980. "And if she says it ain't, she's a liar. That's the way I feel." Margo felt the time was right in country music to begin dealing openly with it. "This is a great time for a woman to live," she said. "Now the trend is, some younger men are beginning to like older women. . . . I have grown. I used to think I belonged back in New Carlisle, Ohio, baking them chocolate chip cookies. I'm more confident now."

Margo was considerably different when she was Mary Lou Miller. Born in 1942 and raised on a farm near Dayton, she was captivated as a teenager by the yodeling of "Midwestern Hayride" star Bonnie Lou. Margo learned to yodel, but her first career was as a schoolteacher. She married small-town banker Ken Smith, had kids, and puttered around with songwriting. Margo first hit the charts using her new stage name with her 1975 compositions "There I Said It" and "Paper Lovin'." Signed by Warner Bros. in 1976, she had hits with three more of her own songs, "Love's Explosion," "Take My Breath Away," and "My Weakness," the last two of which contained quasi-yodel vocal "breaks." All this while she had a housewife image with long brown hair, large Bette Davis eyes, and a Jean Arthur purr in her voice.

But things began changing after "Still a Woman." On her 1979 *Just Margo* album cover she posed in a white satin robe open to the waist. On 1980's *Diamonds and Chills* she was radically transformed into a slinky blond siren with a dangerously plunging neckline. Margo added spandex and satin costumes, risqué jokes, and energetic choreography to her stage show. "I believe in style," she said. "Women like style." She separated from her husband and reportedly had an affair with manager Bob Fry. The hunk filed suit against her after he was fired in 1981, saying she dis-

missed him because he stopped having sexual relations with her. In 1982 Margo married businessman Richard Cammeron, who took over the management of her career.

During the next few years she returned to her homey image. Margo capitalized on her show-stopping yodeling ability by issuing 1983's *The Best of the Tennessee Yodeler* and successfully marketing it via direct-response TV ads. She eventually formed a gospel duet with daughter Holly. "The sexy image, sexy song album was a mistake on my part," she later reflected. "I had an image for singing sweet ballads, and I should'a stuck with it. I hired a choreographer and spent a fortune, and you know what? I wound up changing everything anyway and doing it all myself. . . . We wanted to give it class. . . . I wore sparkly dresses cut up the side . . . saloon-type dresses." But when all was said and done, she was back to being friendly country lady Margo Smith.

Janie Fricke went through a similar metamorphosis and got the same results. Janie was the sweet, smiley-voiced singer of likable radio hits who tried to vamp up her image with flashy costumes and bouncy choreography. When the dust settled, she was still a sweet singer of likable radio hits.

Born in rural Indiana in 1947, Janie was inspired by the examples of Joan Baez and Judy Collins to pick up a guitar and begin singing in coffeehouses. In the early seventies Janie became a wildly successful backup singer and ad-jingle vocalist in Memphis and Nashville, earning a reported hundred thousand dollars a year by harmonizing in the background on more than five thousand records. "I never dreamed of trying to be a star," she said. "I guess most people would want that. But it just isn't that important to me." After getting her own recording contract in 1977, she then did remakes of Hank Locklin's "Please Help Me I'm Falling" (1978) and Johnny Rodriguez's "Pass Me By (If You're Only Passing Through)" (1980), then entered what she called her "two-step, country dance period" with "Down to My Last Broken Heart" and "I'll Need Someone to Hold Me" in 1981 and 1982. Then she surprised listeners by shedding her image as a buoyant balladeer for a tougher, huskier style on hard-edged material such as "It Ain't Easy Bein' Easy," "Tell Me a Lie," "You Don't Know Love," and "He's a Heartache." The performances, the finest of her career, earned Janie accolades as Female Vocalist of the Year and coincided with her show-queen evolution.

"Now that's class," marveled a Canadian reviewer who caught Janie's polished concert presentation in 1985. "As she bounced forward from the intro in a sizzling gold lamé jumpsuit, she radiated healthy energy and pure enjoyment. There were a number of moments when it seemed she was about to break into aerobics." Janie buckdanced, wailed gospel, played guitar and mandolin, chatted amiably, and swiveled around in outfits she designed herself.

The country show queens of the seventies left an indelible mark on the culture. To this day many female stars in the field work with high-fashion designers, image creators, stylists, choreographers, and stage consultants. These superstars of the seventies brought big business to Nashville and broke down the community's parochial mentality. They overcame the prejudices that said women couldn't headline shows or sell records. They forced labels to sign women in greater numbers. They broadened country music's audience. And they were role models to hundreds of performers who followed.

Watching and studying throughout the late seventies was a wide-eyed Oklahoma rodeo rider who was serving an apprenticeship in the lower half of the country charts. "We're not where we want to be yet," said Reba McEntire. "I want a better stage show. . . . When people come to see Reba McEntire . . . I want to be able to really dazzle them, to give them their hard-earned money's worth." She added, "I want to get in the big leagues. . . . I think country music is gettin' out of the cornfield, which is what I want to do." Within a decade Reba McEntire would become the biggest show queen of them all.

16

BACK TO COUNTRY

Emmylou Harris and the Country-Rock Fusion

Emmylou Harris, c. 1977.

420

Songwriter Linda Hargrove raised her voice in protest with a 1977 cautionary ode called "Nashville, You Ain't Hollywood." In it the "Blue Jean Country Queen" spoke for an increasing group of young artists who despised the pop dilution of the rootsy culture they loved. "When they've watered down all the truth," she sang, "they'll have the gall to call it country music."

What is country music? That was a question being asked by a lot of people by the mid-1970s. Was it Dolly Parton's Appalachian "Coat of Many Colors" or Barbara Mandrell's version of the soul song "Do Right Woman, Do Right Man"? Both, after all, were major hits of 1971. Was it Loretta Lynn's sassy "Rated X" or Lynn Anderson's sunny pop tune "Top of the World"? Both were popular in 1973. In 1975 Jeanne Pruett was proudly proclaiming herself "A Poor Man's Woman" while Olivia Newton-John was mewing "Have You Never Been Mellow," both on MCA Records. Crystal Gayle's cocktail lounge staple "Don't It Make My Brown Eyes Blue" and Emmylou Harris's revival of Kitty Wells's "Making Believe" were on the charts at the same time in the summer of 1977 when Linda Hargrove sang her anger and frustration.

Country music was in the middle of the biggest

identity crisis of its existence. It had dramatically expanded its audience by adopting the trappings of mainstream pop show business. Now it was the music of suburbia, as well as of Alabama cotton farmers, Texas ranchers, Kentucky coal miners, and Pennsylvania factory workers.

Critics charged that country music was losing its conscience. Country's inspiration and creativity had historically sprung from a hard way of life shared by its performers and its audience. Increasingly, it seemed to be following marketing fads and commercial whims. It had no touchstone. It was a culture cut adrift. Was it losing its soul?

To some, country's pop crossover mentality was a violation of its heritage, a capitulation to everything in popular culture that country music had historically opposed—artificiality, rich-folks "airs," big-city ways, and Hollywood phoniness. Others were proud of the genre's newfound respectability, uptown image, and widespread appeal. They pointed to the mass-media inroads that traditional country music made when pop crossover acts attracted new converts.

Writer Everett J. Corbin called the whole identity crisis a "Storm Over Nashville." His book by that title called the pop crossover sound "Nash Trash."

For a time, there was talk of getting rid of the term "country" because marketing executives thought it alienated pop music consumers. The phrase "American music" was suggested as a replacement. Back in the 1920s and 1930s the music had been called "hillbilly," "old-time," and "mountain." With the popularity of moviedom's singing cowboys, the term "western" came into vogue. By the time the first country popularity charts were introduced in the 1940s, the music marketers were using the term "folk" both on record labels and in trade magazines. "Country & western," or "c&w" for short, was the accepted description of the sound between 1950 and 1962. But the then-new CMA felt the general term "country" was classier and argued correctly that "country & western" was no more descriptive of the music than "country & bluegrass," "country & Cajun," "country & rockabilly," or "country" coupled with any of its other substyles. Now, at the height of the pop crossover era, even "country" seemed antique to some.

Country's identity crisis spawned records like Jimmie Helms's "The Death of Country Music," Justin Tubb's "What's Wrong with the Way We're Doing It Now?," and Jean Shepard's "The Real Thing." It led to the formation of an alternative organization to the CMA. The Association of Country Entertainers (ACE) was composed largely of hard-core country acts who were being pushed into the background by the Vegas-bound newcomers.

Traditional country lover Ralph Compton suggested, "The country fan and the country artist are at the mercy of an industry concerned only with quick money. . . . 'broadening' the appeal simply means destroying its true identity." ACE supporter Grandpa Jones lamented, "I feel most of the writers are writing only for the charts, with no feeling at all." Lamented Hank Snow, "Crossover music, pop music, or middle-of-the-road or whatever you want to call it has come in and drowned the basic country artist."

Although dismissed by many at the time as being the voice of reactionary crackpots, embittered has-beens, and cranky old fogies, ACE served an important function in trying to define the qualities that needed to be preserved in country music. No ACE members ever asserted that country was either rural or southern in its essence. They were trying to get at its heart, not its symbols. ACE leader Jean Shepard was astounded to hear the likes of Donny and Marie Osmond on country radio in 1977. "Now they're beautiful children, and they're very talented," she said, "but they wouldn't know a country song if it hit 'em in the hind end with a broom handle!"

"I wish that something could happen to turn it around in a different direction than it is going today," said Roy Acuff at the time. Something did. Ironically, it came from outside the traditional country fold. It came from the folk-rock community of California, the rowdy beer halls of Texas, and the dope-smoking back rooms of Music City. They called it "country-rock" and "outlaw music." And it kicked Nashville in her sequined behind.

The woman who carried its beacon was a soft-spoken former folkie with a passionate interest in pure, old-time sounds. With a gentle touch, a punchy backbeat, a historian's reverence, and a radical's fiery vision, Emmylou Harris did the unthinkable. She united old-line country conservatives and rock-loving liberals in a common cause and a common sound. She gave country music back its pride in its heritage. She took country music to pop fans and taught them to love it on its own terms, not those of the Vegas show room, the TV variety show, or the Broadway stage. She showed Nashville that country music could succeed uncompromised with dignity intact. She made country music hip.

"We had high musical standards," Emmylou said, "and we were playing real aggressive country music. . . . hard-core country music with a rock-'n'-roll attitude."

She wasn't a coal miner's daughter, a sharecropper's wife, an Appalachian waif, or a cotton mill girl. She was a middle-class music enthusiast who found purpose and meaning in the classic country sounds. They gave her a

Emmylou Harris, 1981.

sense of cultural rootedness and a mission in life.

By all accounts, Emmy's childhood was fairly ordinary. Born in 1947 in Birmingham, she is the daughter of a career Marine Corps officer who became a POW during the Korean War. The family moved around from base to base after his return home, and Emmy spent her childhood in Alabama, North Carolina, and Virginia. She was a straight-A student, a cheerleader, a saxophonist in the marching band, and the 1965 class valedictorian of her Woodbridge, Virginia, high school. She also won the Miss Woodbridge beauty title. Emmy got a drama scholarship to the University of North Carolina, but her stints there and at Boston University were brief. The coffeehouse was her education, not the classroom.

Emmy was so swept up in the sixties folk revival that she quit college to go to New York with her guitar in 1967. There, she landed occasional jobs at clubs like The Bitter End and eventually found her way to little Jubilee Records. The company issued her folkie LP called *Gliding Bird* in 1969. The title tune was by Tom Slocum, her first husband. The couple moved to Nashville with baby daughter Hallie in 1970, but the local music industry took little notice of the long-haired hippie. Her marriage disintegrated. Emmy eked out a living as a waitress. She was on food stamps and Medicaid.

"My life, I suppose, has been a feminist one," Emmy reflected in a *Nashville* magazine article. "I've dealt with all the problems that the movement deals with. And I think of myself as being pretty aware. Like in my very early days when I was a working single mother and found that two girls, each with a child, couldn't share a house and each get food stamps at the same address. There needed to be and there still needs to be a lot of consciousness-raising. Just to know what the issues are, what a woman has to deal with, how to make it easier for her to just live a normal life."

With poverty snapping at her heels, Emmy limped out of Music City around Christmastime in 1970. She and her baby went back to suburban Washington, D.C., to live with her parents. Emmy eventually found work as a hostess at a model home in a Columbia, Maryland, housing development.

"At that point, I'd retired forever from the music business. I was so tired and disillusioned that I felt like an old woman at age twenty-three," Emmy recalled. "I tried to put it out of my mind that I was a musician. It was too painful. I wanted so much to do it, and I knew that probably my life as a musician was over because I had to raise a child."

Emmy started singing at The Red Fox Inn in Bethesda, Maryland. After a 1971 show at a night spot called Clyde's she met the California country-rock group The Flying Burrito Brothers. Burrito member Chris Hillman, later the leader of The Desert Rose Band, told his ex-partner Gram Parsons about the remarkable female singing talent he'd discovered. Parsons came to see Emmy and was properly smitten. A year later he sent her a plane ticket to L.A. to come sing on his debut solo album *GP.*

Parsons, regarded as the godfather of California's country-rock movement, lived like a wild rock 'n' roller but had a deep feeling for authentic country music. His passion rubbed off on his protégée: Emmy was soon singing Tammy Wynette to Gram's George Jones, notably on a sizzling remake of the Carl and Pearl Butler honky-tonker "We'll Sweep Out the Ashes in the Morning." In years to come she would maintain that Gram Parsons was the person who gave her musical direction, who taught her the beauty of country music. But their work together aroused little interest in the mainstream country community. On the road Parsons and his Fallen Angels band were the picture of rock-n' roll-decadence.

Emmylou was even more prominent on the second Parsons LP, *Grievous Angel,* delivering fine duet performances on such Nashville fare as "I Can't Dance" and "Love Hurts," as well as the Parsons classics "In My Hour of Darkness," "Las Vegas," and "Hickory Wind." But Emmy's mentor died of alcohol and drug abuse in 1973 before the album even saw the light of day. She was devastated with grief.

Parsons's record company offered her a solo contract. She spent part of 1974 preparing *Pieces of the Sky* as a continuation of his artistic vision. The album included "Boulder to Birmingham" as her elegy to Parsons. It included nods to her country heroes Merle Haggard ("The Bottle Let Me Down") and Dolly Parton ("Coat of Many Colors"). Nashville hits such as Dave and Sugar's "Queen of the Silver Dollar" and Lucille Starr's "Too Far Gone" were also given the Emmylou treatment. In the summer of 1975 her LP's reworking of the Louvin Brothers classic "If I Could Only Win Your Love" with future Desert Rose man Herb Pedersen as her harmony foil sailed into the country Top 10. The single was like a splash of mountain spring water on the Pan-Cake-makeup face of Music City.

"I do best when I have a crusade," says Emmylou. "I don't see why on the Country Music Association awards show we can't see people like Kitty Wells performing. . . . I think country music should take pride in its roots."

"Amen!" shouted a chorus of Nashville traditionalists. The Opry's Jeanne Pruett was one of many who welcomed Emmy's arrival. "She came onto the scene a little bit different, because she came in kinda from the underground side," said Jeanne. "But . . . she's as country as a can o' kraut."

"When I first started coming to Nashville," Emmy recalls, "I did find that everyone seemed to be delighted with my success, delighted with the records. I think it brought out the love of traditional music: Everybody was happy about it because everybody was basically on that side. But everybody had just sort of assumed that it wouldn't work commercially. And when they found out that it did, we all sort of shared in the excitement of it.

"Here was this music that I loved from afar and embraced, but to be standing on the same stage with Tammy Wynette was being catapulted into a whole different world. You have to understand how thrilling that was for me. . . . When I started doing this music, it never concerned me how popular it was going to be. . . . I've always sort of done what I want to do, without thinking too much about that. . . . But there is the pulse of the people and what they want. I trust the people; I really do. I think if good music is made available to them, they will be drawn to it. . . . I thought I was coming totally from out of left field with this 'If I Could Only Win Your Love' record. And it became a success. . . . I was surprised to find an audience for my music, because I thought it was too 'precious' or perhaps too narrow for the masses. . . . Now I believe there will always be an audience for pure country music. Uh, and even if there isn't, I'll still be singing it."

Sing it, she did. In 1976 Emmylou brought back Buck Owens's "Together Again," George Jones's "One of These Days," and Patsy Cline's "Sweet Dreams." She kicked up her heels by countrifying Chuck Berry's "You Never Can Tell" in 1977, then ached on the Kitty Wells ballad "Making Believe." *Elite Hotel* (1976), *Luxury Liner* (1977), and *Quarter Moon in a Ten Cent Town* (1978) all became gold records. She won country Grammy Awards in 1976, 1979, and 1980, and with the two more she collected in 1984 and 1987, Emmylou Harris became the Recording Academy's most honored female country star in history. She was named Country Music Association Female Vocalist of the Year in 1980.

Her record label thought the time might be right to turn her into a pop crossover star, but Emmy confounded them by turning in the even more country-purist *Blue Kentucky Girl* in 1979 and an outright bluegrass effort called *Roses in the Snow* in 1980. To almost everyone's surprise, they, too, sold a million. "Wayfaring Stranger," "Beneath Still Waters," and "Two More Bottles of Wine" all became Top 10 hits between 1978 and 1980. Her albums resonated with a sense of history and heritage. Emmy sang Loretta Lynn's "Blue Kentucky Girl," The Carter Family's "Gold Watch and Chain" and "Hello Stranger," Jean Ritchie's "Sorrow in the Wind," and Patti Page's "Tennessee Waltz." Her version of Dolly Parton's "To Daddy" remains one of Emmy's strongest performances, for Dolly's song is about a wife and mother who exits a loveless marriage to find a new life.

"Once I found country music, or country music found me, I just found so many wonderful places to explore within that medium that I have no desire to go off and try any other kind of music. I have occasionally done a pop song or this and that. But I'm just very happy being where I am. It's like you've got everything you want at home. You can probably find all of life in even the smallest town. To me, there's just so much . . . in country music."

Emmylou Harris reinvigorated the country sound in a profound way. Not only did she teach it new respect for its traditions, she introduced it to songwriting that existed off the beaten path of Music Row by bringing the work of poetic spirits such as Townes Van Zandt, Jesse Winchester, Delbert McClinton, Carlene Carter, and Rodney Crowell to the forefront. Her version of Utah Phillips's "Green Rolling Hills of West Virginia" gave the folk star's number the authenticity of a Wilma Lee Cooper tune. In her hands Bruce Springsteen's "Racing in the Streets" became a dirt-road showdown. She made rocker Robbie Robertson's "Evangeline" steam with bayou atmosphere. When she sang James Taylor's "Millworker," Emmy's voice resonated back 150 years to the earliest laments of the New England factory girls.

Emmylou became the touchstone for a generation of young female stylists as well as the spiritual mother of the entire "neotraditionalist" movement that swept through the country music world in the late 1980s and early 1990s. Her repertoire influenced the direction of contemporary country, and so did her band. From Emmy's ranks Ricky Skaggs, Pam Rose and Mary Ann Kennedy, Rodney Crowell, and The Whites all graduated to their own stardom. Star singers Vince Gill and Rosanne Cash, MCA Records producer Tony Brown, steel guitar great Hank DeVito, and top producer Brian Ahern were also part of her musical circle.

She was married to Ahern between 1977 and 1984, and they have a daughter named Meghann. During the divorce Emmy moved from Los Angeles to Nashville and began collaborating with songwriter Paul Kennerley, who became her third husband in 1985. She'd met the British-

born Kennerley when he recruited her for his 1980 concept LP *The Legend of Jesse James,* and he subsequently penned her hits "Born to Run" (1982) and "In My Dreams" (1984). They crafted one of Emmy's most ambitious works, the enigmatic, autobiographical concept album *The Ballad of Sally Rose* (1985). Although not a commercial success, it is her finest showcase as a songwriter.

Emmy is known as a willing collaborator and has harmonized on hits with Roy Orbison, Don Williams, Earl Thomas Conley, John Denver, Vern Gosdin, and Buck Owens, among others. She has often appeared with other women on disc, including Kathy Mattea, Rosanne Cash, Gail Davies, Trisha Yearwood, and Tammy Wynette. This sharing spirit led to one of her most acclaimed projects. In 1987 Emmylou Harris participated in a landmark event in female music history. With longtime friends Linda Ronstadt and Dolly Parton she released the massively successful *Trio* album. The LP triumphed at the Grammy and CMA awards, sold a million copies, and bore four major hits, "To Know Him Is to Love Him," "Telling Me Lies," "Those Memories," and "Wildflowers."

"I sense that certain songs are just very feminine," says Emmy of the prizewinning collection's heirloom-lace tone. "They don't necessarily have to be written by women. But a lot of times they are. I mean, Kate and Anna McGarrigle's work is incredibly feminine. There's a certain elegance about the way a woman writes.

"Dolly represents the finest of women's traditional music. Linda and I are in mutual admiration of Dolly as our favorite singer. Dolly's voice is almost the focal point of this record, in a way."

Trio had an unmistakably feminine feeling, an Appalachian quilt of colors that all three participants say was quite intentional. In addition to

Dolly's compositions, it featured works by Jean Ritchie ("My Dear Companion"), Linda Thompson ("Telling Me Lies"), and Kate McGarrigle ("I've Had Enough"), as well as "Rosewood Casket," learned from Dolly's mother, and "Farther Along," drawn from Emmylou's traditional repertoire. The project's strength and delicacy are unquestionably the result of female participation. Is there such a thing as "women's music"?

"Hmmm: That's a tough one," says Linda Ronstadt. "It's hard to say, exactly. I have a hard time with that question. . . . I think that in history there is a female point of view. I wouldn't call it the feminist point of view, because that's something different altogether. But I do think that there's a female point of view. That wasn't what we were sitting down to do; but we didn't mind it when it was that way. We'd even laugh and say to each other, 'Well, that's a real *girl* thing.' I mean, 'Dear Companion' is very female somehow. But . . . it's awfully hard to separate these things.

"This album was done because of our shared love. That's what I felt. We each have our individual voices, and then the trio has its own voice, the fourth voice. . . . We were really always in control. We were always the ones making the decisions, saying, 'We want to do this and we want to do that.' There wasn't anybody standing with an ax over our heads.

"Emmy is a great guitar player. . . . So she would be the groove. And usually each girl would sort of improvise the harmony. But if we got stuck and it really came down to the crunch, I'd usually sort out the harmony parts." And then there was Dolly, the pulse of the trio. "What's thrilling to us about Dolly's music is that she's really an authentic," says Linda. "She's the genuine article. Emmy and I came to this music later in our lives. We heard it on the radio when we were kids and really focused on it when we were teenagers, through the folk music revival. We'd go nuts listening to recordings of Smoky Mountain music. And Dolly was the real thing: She'd lived that life. She crawled out of her cradle singing that music.

"I think Dolly is a girl who was born with an amazing amount of insight into people. It's like an intelligence of compassion. Shakespeare really understood human behavior. Tolstoy could write the greatest novel ever because he really understood what makes people tick. And I think Dolly Parton is one of those kinds of people. She has that kind of intelligence; she is amazingly perceptive; she's scary." The lovingly hand-stitched sampler *Trio* remains Linda's favorite album because "No one got in the way. What we did was exactly what we planned to do when the three of us were sitting in Dolly's living room and singing with our hair in curlers."

For Linda Ronstadt *Trio* was a reaffirmation of her love of country. During her journeys through various musical styles, she has frequently

Linda Ronstadt plays make-believe as Dogpatch denizen Moonbeam McSwine on this 1970 LP jacket. The Nashville-recorded album contained "Long Long Time," her first solo hit.

"touched home" in country music. This many-faceted interpreter has successfully sung cabaret standards, soul songs, rock, operetta, Mexican mariachi music, Broadway show tunes, punk, and even opera. But like her confederate Emmylou, her roots are in the country-connected folk revival.

Linda was born in Tucson, Arizona, in 1946, the daughter of a Mexican-German hardware merchant. Papa Gilbert played guitar and sang, Mama Ruthmary played banjo, and Linda grew up surrounded by all the music styles she would later embrace as a professional. Her destiny was clear to her from the start: "When I was in the first grade I flunked arithmetic. . . . I remember looking at my report card and thinking, 'It doesn't matter. I'm going to be a singer.'" At age eighteen she quit college and left home with thirty dollars, her parents' blessing, and shoot-for-the-stars optimism. "When I left Tucson, I thought it would be a big deal to have your name on the marquee of a club. That was the pinnacle of success. I never dreamed I'd have a Number 1 record."

Linda landed in L.A. in late 1964 and hooked up with folkies Bob Kimmel and Kenny Edwards to form The Stone Poneys. The trio found work at The Troubadour and was signed by Capitol Records in 1966 as a West Coast answer to Peter, Paul and Mary. With her big brown eyes, long brunet hair, miniskirts, and bare feet, Linda was the focus. She was painfully timid and peered shyly from beneath her curtainlike bangs onstage. But when she sang, there was a gripping, heart-tugging yearning. That quality leaped from radio speakers in the winter of 1967 when she transformed Michael Nesmith's "Different Drum" into a female cry of independence. The group got back on the charts in 1968 with the country-flavored "Up to My Neck in High Muddy Water," but it soon dissolved, leaving its lead singer to fulfill the recording contract on her own. Linda's resulting solo album was a textbook example of the country-rock fusion style then emerging in California, featuring her wailing versions of "Silver Threads and Golden Needles," "Break My Mind," "The Only Mama That'll Walk the Line," and "We Need a Whole Lot More Jesus." Despite its many merits, it bombed.

Linda headed for Nashville. She played "The Grand Ole Opry," showcased on TV's "Johnny Cash Show," and recorded a Music Row LP called *Silk Purse*. It included "Long Long Time," which in 1970 became her first solo hit. Confident that country-rock was her mission, Linda returned to California, hired the future Eagles as her backing band, and released a pair of California LPs that explored the style in 1972 and 1973 with tunes like "Love Has No Pride," "I Fall to Pieces," "I Still Miss Someone," and "Desperado." She found the magic touch in 1974 with *Heart Like a Wheel.* Its Betty Everett soul revival "You're No Good" went to Number 1 on the pop charts; her Hank Williams remake "I Can't Help It (If I'm Still in Love with You)" became a massive country hit; and her Everly Brothers number "When Will I Be Loved" became a Top 10 tune on *both* charts. "I Can't Help It," which won a Grammy, featured the harmony vocals of Emmylou Harris, then simultaneously emerging as a country-rock performer. "Everyone was telling me for two years that there was this girl who was doing everything that I was doing, and they were raving about her," Linda recalled. "I saw Emmy, and I died. Here was someone doing what I was doing, only, in my opinion, better." After Gram Parsons died, it was Linda who went to bat for Emmy to get her a solo recording contract.

Prisoner in Disguise (1975) repeated the Linda Ronstadt formula with its soul hit "Heat Wave" and its country smash "Love Is a Rose." It also featured Linda singing Dolly Parton's "I Will Always Love You" and a duet with Emmy on "The Sweetest Gift (A Mother's Smile)." *Hasten Down the Wind* (1976) yielded country hits with remakes of Patsy Cline's "Crazy" and Buddy Holly's "That'll Be the Day." *Simple Dreams* (1977) dipped into the folk tradition. Linda did the cowboy standard "Old Paint" and teamed with Dolly to sing The Carter Family classic "I Never Will Marry." The album yielded "Blue Bayou" as a major pop and country smash, and the star rerecorded it for the Latin American market as "Lago Azul." The up-tempo "Poor Poor Pitiful Me," "It's So Easy," and "Tumbling Dice" made *Simple Dreams* her turning point: Her next three collections (*Living in the U.S.A., Mad Love,* and *Get Closer*) would find Linda exploring rock.

But throughout this period, Linda quietly maintained her country ties. She and Emmy had appeared on Dolly Parton's syndicated TV show "Dolly!" in 1976, and the following year began recording songs for their trio project. These early collaborations mostly found their way onto assorted Emmylou albums, although the trio version of Dolly's "My Blue Tears" was the finale number on Linda's *Get Closer* collection of 1982. Linda and Emmy also staged a surprise appearance at Dolly's L.A. concert in 1979, and all three women can be heard on Emmy's *Roses in the Snow* and *Ballad of Sally Rose* LPs.

Of the three, Linda has the most frivolous image. She has a nervous giggle in conversation that masks a keen intelligence. Her sex-kitten photos and

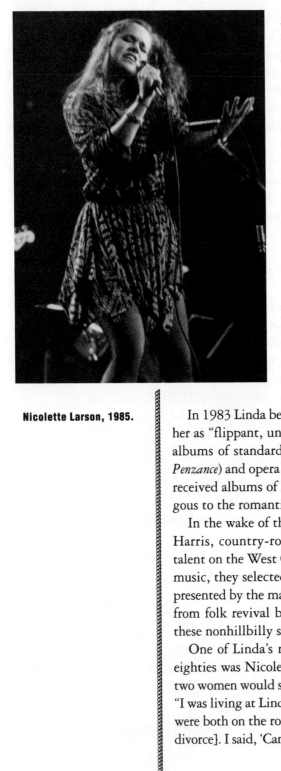

girlish stage manner also undercut what is essentially a very thoughtful, serious nature. Despite her cutie-pie image, Linda Ronstadt has never married. Her name has been linked with politician Jerry Brown, rocker Mick Jagger, singer/songwriter J. D. Souther, writer Pete Hamill, movie mogul George Lucas, comedian Steve Martin, producer John Boylan, New Orleans impresario Quint Davis, and many others. "Staying single is not a crime," Linda told *USA Today* in 1986. "I wish people would stop planning a family for me." *People* magazine once called her an "old maid." *Redbook* pictured her on its cover in 1979 as "The Queen of Lonely," but inside she said, "When I began to realize I might never get married, I thought maybe I didn't need it. In a sense, I know it's better for me not to be married. . . . A woman who can do all it involves and have a career is really the exception." In a 1981 interview she added, "I wouldn't have any desire to be a traditional wife, and frankly I don't know what man would want to put up with me." Later that year she moved to the San Francisco area and adopted a baby daughter she named Mary.

In 1983 Linda became disenchanted with rock, saying its lyrics struck her as "flippant, unemotional." She embarked on a trio of orchestrated albums of standards and went to Broadway to do operetta (*Pirates of Penzance*) and opera (*La Bohème*). In 1987 and 1991 Linda released well-received albums of Mexican mariachi and ranchera music, styles analogous to the romantic cowboy songs of the 1920s and 1930s.

In the wake of the breakthroughs by Linda Ronstadt and Emmylou Harris, country-rock became a dominant style for emerging female talent on the West Coast. These performers did not grow up in country music, they selected it from the vast menu of American musical styles presented by the mass media. Like Linda and Emmy, most of them came from folk revival backgrounds. And like Linda and Emmy, several of these nonhillbilly singers found acceptance in the country community.

One of Linda's roommates in her Malibu beach house in the early eighties was Nicolette Larson. When they weren't on concert tours, the two women would sit around and harmonize on country tunes they loved. "I was living at Linda's house for a couple of years," Nicolette recalls. "We were both on the road, and I was in between places [and going through a divorce]. I said, 'Can I stay for a couple of weeks?' And I wound up leaving a year and a half later: 'The Thing That Wouldn't Leave!' It was like a sorority, borrowing shoes and loaning a scarf. And we're both chronic singers, addicted singers. So we'd . . . sit in front of the fire and . . . sing in crummy little terrycloth robes."

Pert, coquettish Nicolette initially aimed for a career behind the scenes in show business. Born in 1952 in Montana, she was raised in Kansas City and dropped out of the University of Missouri to board a Greyhound for San Francisco in 1974. "I had been working as a waitress and a Kelly Girl, and I thought even if I could just be a secretary at a record company, that would be nicer." She got a job as the production secretary for the Golden State Bluegrass Festival and spent her free time jamming backstage with the pickers. Encouraged by the country musicians who heard her, she took an opening-act slot at an Eric Andersen concert in Vancouver. "I did a Poco tune. I did 'Silver Threads and Golden Needles,' like every other girl in the history of girl singing. I did a blues number, a Jamaican song. Just me and guitar. I wasn't that good, but I did it." Her boyfriend and later husband Hank DeVito was the steel player in Emmylou Harris's band, so Nicolette moved to L.A. She sang backup on Emmy's albums *Luxury Liner* and *Quarter Moon in a Ten Cent Town*, then took jobs on the road with Hoyt Axton and as a member of the country-boogie act The Commander Cody Band.

Nicolette was signed as a country act by Warner Bros. in 1977. Her debut on the label was a Ronstadt-style mixed bag, rather than the purer approach of her mentor Emmylou. Neil Young's "Lotta Love" and Jesse Winchester's "Rhumba Girl" became Nicolette pop hits in 1978 and 1979. The collection also contained The Louvin Brothers' "Angels Rejoiced" and her version of the Don Williams country hit "Come Early Mornin'." In 1983 she hit the road in the touring company of the country musical *Pump Boys and Dinettes,* and a year later she followed Emmylou Harris to Nashville.

"It's not just a country album; it's a commitment," she said when her Nashville-recorded LP *Say When* appeared in 1985. "With this record, there's no doubt. People can say they don't want to play it for a lot of reasons, but they can't say it's because it's not country." The collection won her the Top New Female Vocalist award from California's Academy of Country Music. Nicolette returned to Nashville for *Rose of My Heart* in 1986. It included Linda Ronstadt re-creating their "kitchen duet" sound on the Louvins' "You're Running Wild," as well as a Top 10 hit duo with Steve Wariner called "That's How You Know When Love's Right." Now remarried and a mother, Nicolette still sometimes performs, calling what she does a "variety pack" of music.

California produced a number of such "variety pack" female singers. Los Angeles native Kim Carnes (b. 1946) broke into music in the sixties as a member of the folk troupe The New Christy Minstrels. The raspy-voiced stylist hit both country and pop charts as Nashvillian Gene Cotton's duet partner on 1978's "You're a Part of Me." She duplicated the feat with Kenny Rogers on her 1980 ballad "Don't Fall in Love with a Dreamer." Kim achieved rock stardom by singing Jackie DeShannon's "Bette Davis Eyes" in 1981, yet her 1987 song "Make No Mistake She's Mine" was a country hit for Ronnie Milsap and Rogers. So by 1988 Kim was back in Nashville to record the country-folk LP *View from the House.* "I've gone full circle," she said.

During rock queen Bonnie Raitt's long, ten-album climb to stardom, she also dabbled in several styles. This native of Los Angeles (b. 1949) is primarily known as a blues interpreter, but her biggest hit prior to her 1989 pop breakthrough was in fact on the country charts. Bonnie's hit "Don't It Make You Wanna Dance" was recorded for the watershed soundtrack of the 1980 country music film *Urban Cowboy.*

Languid-voiced soul stylist Rita Coolidge made the country charts ten times in the late 1970s, usually as the duet partner of then-husband Kris Kristofferson. Although a Californian since the late sixties, Rita was born in Nashville in 1944 and was a high school cheerleader alongside Brenda Lee.

Canadian Colleen Peterson, born in 1950, served a folk apprenticeship before coming to Nashville to make her country-rock bow with *Beginning to Feel Like Home* in 1976. *Colleen Peterson* (1977) and *Takin' My Boots Off* (1978) put Colleen into the swim of the California country-rock scene, but by 1980 she'd moved back to Nashville. She became a backup singer for Charlie Daniels, J. J. Cale, and others; ran Daniels's song publishing company; signed as a staff writer for Warner Bros. Music; and evolved into one of Music City's most respected club and session vocalists.

Jennifer Warnes possesses perhaps the purest voice of all the "variety pack" females. Her country-pop masterpieces remain her big hits of 1977 and 1979, "Right Time of the Night" and "I Know a Heartache When I See One," both of which are still country oldie airplay staples. "My mother raised me on records that had some country music in them," says Jennifer, who was born in Seattle in 1947 but raised in southern California. "Hank Williams and old Patti Page stuff, the Everly Brothers, and Brenda Lee is the music I was sorta raised on. So that's in my music without trying."

One of the most haunting vocals of her career was the movie theme song for Sally Field's Oscar-winning turn as a southern textile worker in

Norma Rae (1979). "It Goes Like It Goes" was never released as a single, but it still won the Best Song Academy Award. This led to interest from Hollywood. With Joe Cocker as her duet partner she repeated the movie theme triumph with Buffy Sainte-Marie's cowritten "Up Where We Belong" from 1982's *An Officer and a Gentleman.* It, too, won an Oscar.

Despite mainstream success, Jennifer remained resolutely unconventional. The L.A. pop scene didn't know what to do with her, so "MCA Records sent me to Nashville. They spent a week or so with me. . . . Among the songs that I submitted were things that I had worked on with . . . African rhythms. . . . That's the kind of stuff I was bringing to them, plus Leonard Cohen stuff. And they were going, 'Get out of my office' and 'What do we do with her?' They gave my contract to Nicolette Larson instead." After signing with the Cypress label in 1986, Jennifer finally got to make her album of Leonard Cohen songs, *Famous Blue Raincoat,* which she produced. Ironically, its "Ain't No Cure for Love" made the country charts, not the pop hit parade, and Jennifer wound up showcasing the album on The Nashville Network.

"I finally became myself," she said. "Every time I would go into a recording contract I would say, 'I want to produce or coproduce my own albums.' And in every possible situation and in every possible way, they would say, 'No.'" Women who want to produce their own records are tagged as "difficult" by record label executives, she added.

She took another lefthand turn in 1987 to harmonize with Bill Medley on "(I've Had) The Time of My Life" from the movie *Dirty Dancing.* It topped the pop charts, giving Jennifer Warnes the distinction of becoming the only person in history to originate three Oscar-winning songs.

Artists like Jennifer Warnes, Nicolette Larson, Colleen Peterson, and Linda Ronstadt had an elemental country "cry" in their voices. All were products of the folk revival, and all were country-pop fusion stars. Yet all proved they were able interpreters in many other musical styles. The first woman to become a country star with this "variety pack" approach was Jody Miller (b. 1941). This fiddler's daughter was raised in Arizona and Oklahoma. After high school she headed for L.A., where she landed a contract with Capitol Records. The label introduced Jody with the 1963 folk revival collection *Wednesday's Child Is Full of Woe,* and she became a regular on Tom Paxton's folk TV show. But she first attracted attention with the pop tune "He Walks Like a Man." She flipped over to country with "Queen of the House" and "Silver Threads and Golden Needles" in 1964 and 1965, but then issued the pulse-pounding hippie protest song "Home of the Brave." It was back to country for *Jody Miller Sings the Great Hits of Buck Owens* in 1966.

Jody eventually fused the two styles in the late sixties on performances like "It's My Time" and "Long Black Limousine." Her best late-period LP was 1977's Ronstadt-influenced *Here's Jody Miller.* In the 1980s Jody retired from music to raise quarter horses on her Oklahoma ranch.

The country-pop approach Jody pioneered was a profitable one for many successors. Among those active on the California scene in years to come were Tret Fure, Katy Moffatt, Patricia Hardin (of Hardin & Russell), and Lucinda Williams. Los Angelino Renee Armand cowrote the big 1974 country hit "Boney Fingers" and sang it as a duet with Hoyt Axton.

One of the biggest stars the scene produced was Juice Newton, who blazed brightly in the country firmament from 1979 to 1988. "I was never pushed into country music or raised on it," Juice told interviewer Toby Goldstein, "but it seems to be a natural kind of music for me.

"I like good French food, but I also eat hot dogs from a street vendor. . . . I dress this way [in jeans and cowboy boots], I dress other ways. I wear my hair up. I wear it down. I have an eclectic approach to living and to music, and I think it's a healthy way to be. . . . I sing folk music, rock 'n' roll and rhythm-and-blues. . . . but country-rock, rockabilly, just seem to come out right. . . . It's very good . . . to become more aware of America's true music."

Juice began playing guitar at age thirteen. The daughter of a navy officer and his wife, Judy Kay Newton was born in 1952 in Virginia Beach, Virginia. Her two older brothers gave her her nickname. She says her early interest in music stemmed from her desire to "break the ice" with her classmates as the Newtons moved from base to base. She blossomed as a folksinger while attending college in northern California, where she met handsome, strapping blond songwriter Otha Young. The two began performing in bars in 1970. "Club owners would say, 'You have an accent. You must be a country singer.'" Eventually, Juice and Otha formed a band called Silver Spur, issuing three excellent samplers of California country-rock from 1975 to 1977.

The band broke up in 1978, but the couple persevered. Billed as a solo, Juice began making the country charts in 1979 and 1980 with "Let's Keep It That Way," "Lay Back in the Arms of Someone," and the like. The fact that she and Otha were live-in lovers for thirteen years certainly didn't fit the conservative country mold, and she talked candidly about considering children out of wedlock. But it didn't seem to affect her climb, and perhaps even more amazing, neither did the relationship's eventual dissolution. "Otha and I were together for years and years and years as a couple. As my career progressed—and we always talked about this—we agreed that this is a mutual career. . . . As we grew up, our emotional side wasn't probably why we were together. We had a mutual dream."

Juice finally broke through on both country and pop charts in 1981 with "Angel of the Morning" and "Queen of Hearts." Otha's ballad "The Sweetest Thing" became her first Number 1 hit late that year, and for the rest of the decade she was a regular in the country hit parade. She revived slow songs like Brenda Lee's "Break It to Me Gently" (1982) and "Emotions" (1987), but was also successful with country-rockers like "Love's Been a Little Bit Hard on Me" (1982) and "Cheap Love" (1986). Initially reserved and uncomfortable as a country star, the Californian soon relaxed with a frolicking, easygoing stage style and a dry wit in interviews. In 1986 Juice Newton married polo player Tom Goodspeed; after they had children, Juice toured and recorded less.

Gail Davies, trained on the West Coast, walked more in Emmylou Harris's purist shoes than in those of Juice, Linda, Nicolette, and the other style-hopping women. Although Gail, too, experimented outside the country mainstream, her pop, jazz, and rock forays all paled next to the half dozen extraordinary female-country LPs she recorded in Nashville between 1977 and 1987.

Gail Davies's story is one of exceptional grit and determination. On the outside, she seemed like a typical middle-class, country-rock princess of the day, but beneath the surface were boiling psychological turmoil and as much heartache as had been suffered by any poverty-bred country music woman who'd gone before her. She was born Patricia Gail Dickerson in Broken Bow, Oklahoma, in 1948. Gail's childhood was peppered with incidents of domestic violence fueled by her father's alcoholism. She has a lot of ambivalence about her memory of him because he was also the parent who introduced her to country music. When she was five, her parents split up and her mother moved to Seattle and married a man named Darby Alan Davies. Gail began singing in clubs at age fourteen with her brother Ron. When she was nineteen the siblings signed a recording contract in Los Angeles, but their album was never issued. A short-lived marriage to a jazz musician in L.A. introduced the aspiring performer to that genre. Gail toured with a rock band, then took backup singing jobs with country-rock acts.

Struck by the lovely simplicity of her songs, Gail's Los Angeles song publisher sent her to Nashville. Richard Allen, who worked in the publisher's Music Row office, spent a week working with her. At the end of the week, he asked her to marry him. She did. They divorced five years later, in 1981.

"When I got the divorce, I really started searching for myself," she recalls.

Juice Newton, 1984.

"Not as I had done in the past and not as most women do, which is searching for yourself in another person. That doesn't work. I hate to say I was 'finding out who I was,' but that was it. Because your life gets so tied up with another person that there is an identity crisis." Her search would soon make her one of country music's most outspoken female personalities.

Gail first made her mark in Nashville as a songwriter, providing Ava Barber with the hit "Bucket to the South" in early 1978. *Gail Davies* appeared as her debut LP later that year. It was a stunning effort, easily the equal of anything Emmylou Harris and the other country-rock women were recording at the time. One track featured Gail's mother, Jewell, on guitar, backing her Grandma Whitten singing the folk tune "Come-a-lou, Come-a-hi-lo." From this emerged Gail's immensely evocative "Grandma's Song." Elsewhere on the album Gail saluted country music history with spine-tingling versions of "Poison Love," "Are You Teasing Me?," and "No Love Have I." The collection spotlighted her as the writer of "Someone Is Looking for Someone Like You," one of the great anthems of charity and giving. The album was a triumph, but Gail recalls it with bitterness. She fought constantly for control in the studio and says she was reduced to tears trying to get her own way with her music. In 1979 she changed record companies and won the right to produce her own records.

"When I first came to Nashville," she said, "the industry was not open to a woman . . . having much to say about the production. . . . But I feel strongly about my music, and I don't believe being firm about my convictions and standing up for them is in conflict with my femininity."

Her catalog of hits began with 1979's "Blue Heartache." While Nashville's homegrown sequined chanteuses were trying out pop tunes, Gail aligned herself with the California crowd by recording simple, sincere salutes to country's heritage like "It's a Lovely, Lovely World," "I'll Be There," and "Singing the Blues," all of which became hits. Her albums pictured her as a fresh, natural beauty in jeans and sport jackets and included nods to tradition like "No One to Welcome Me Home" and "Kentucky." By 1984 she had had ten Top 20 country music chart successes.

But her personal life remained in upheaval. She dated songwriter Gary Scruggs and discovered she was pregnant by him as the relationship was cooling. Gail decided not to marry him and had son Christopher on her own in late 1982. "During the pregnancy I discovered a whole side of society that bothered me very much. And that was an attitude toward women that I had never really confronted before. Being pregnant and unmarried, I found so many people going, 'Oh, poor Gail: She got pregnant, and this guy wouldn't marry her.' I'd go, 'No, that wasn't it.' And then I started seeing how women are looked at, like my behavior was bad, yet nothing was said about the man. And so I started reading a lot of books on women and our self-image. . . . During that time I found a lot of strength."

She released two feminist-oriented collections, *Givin' Herself Away* (1982) and *Where Is a Woman to Go?* (1984). From the first one came her hit treatments of K. T. Oslin's self-assertive "Round the Clock Lovin'" and Joni Mitchell's "You Turn Me On I'm a Radio." In addition to Oslin's title tune, *Where Is a Woman to Go?* included strong-female material such as "Nothing Can Hurt Me Now," "Break Away," and Gail's version of "Unwed Fathers," a song that questions the double standard that the singer faced in real life. "Boys Like You (Give Love a Bad Name)" and "You're a Hard Dog (To Keep Under the Porch)," from *What Can I Say* (1983), also had a country-feminist tone.

"I guess what the ladies in these songs are saying is that they can use all the love and affection they can get. . . . but a lot of women are finding out that they can supply the other things themselves. They can put bread on their own tables. The image of women in country music has changed. Country music has always been a reflection of what's going on in society. Now the new independence that women have found and the confidence that women are finding in themselves are going to be reflected in the music."

The hypnotically arranged "Jagged Edge of a Broken Heart" pointed the way toward a new direction in 1984. Two years later Gail Davies formed a band called Wild Choir. This adventurous outfit combined a British-rock spirit with country harmonies to forge a fresh but decidedly left-of-center sound. It didn't sell. She returned to solo work on albums for MCA and Capitol, then got hired as a producer by Nashville's Liberty Records office.

Gail has no regrets: "Lately I see a lot of women in country who are getting involved in the making of their albums, so I feel like it's all been worthwhile. I may not get any awards for melting away old prejudices, but I do have the personal satisfaction of knowing I broke up the ice a little bit."

Lacy J. Dalton was yet another who migrated from the coffeehouses to the honky-tonks. She, too, took a stand for musical quality and independence in Music City. Lacy was born Jill Byrem in 1948 in the Appalachian town of Bloomsburg, Pennsylvania. She grew up surrounded by the sounds of her beautician/waitress mother and her mechanic/hunting guide father, both of whom played in a country band.

But the youngster turned her back on her parents' style in favor of folk revival acts like Joan Baez and Bob Dylan. After a year at Brigham Young University, Lacy quit college and hit the road with a fiddle-playing Mormon girlfriend. They sang folk tunes in Salt Lake City, then moved to Brainerd, Minnesota, "where I dyed my hair black and sang protest songs and played terrible guitar, drank beer and got fat, and took birth control pills." Her mother hauled her back to Pennsylvania. Then Lacy ran off to California with a hippie who was selling psychedelic posters at a crafts fair.

"Even today, if I won the Pennsylvania lottery, I'd probably go somewhere up in the mountains of Wyoming with my dogs and horses and grow an organic garden. I would. I'm just a hippie. I think the reason I got into show business was I thought it would be the easiest way to buy a farm."

In Los Angeles she met and married musician John Croston. She formed her own band and began making a little headway as a live attraction, but in 1971 John was paralyzed from the neck down in a freak swimming accident. A week later Lacy discovered she was pregnant. Son Adam was born in the charity ward of an L.A. hospital. She moved the family to a cabin in the Santa Cruz Mountains in northern California; applied for food stamps; and began eking out a living as a waitress, topless dancer, cook, and part-time singer. Croston's health gradually deteriorated. He died in 1974, leaving her a widowed mother at age twenty-seven. As Jill Croston, she issued several small-label records. One of them, *Nashville Lady Singer,* was a portent of things to come. Lacy sent a copy of her 1978 EP to an old friend who was a show-business lawyer. He sent a tape to CBS in Nashville. The company signed her instantly, but insisted she change her name. She selected "Lacy" because it sounded pretty, "J" so she could hold on to Jill, and "Dalton" from a troubadour she admired named Karen Dalton. Lacy J. Dalton burst upon the country scene in a firestorm of press attention in 1979. "Crazy Blue Eyes" became her first hit and won her the Top New Female Vocalist award from the Academy of Country Music. On its memorable chorus Lacy sang, "I never could stand the touch of a man / Who'd brand me to keep me around."

In 1980 she followed it with a remake of "Tennessee Waltz" and her first Top 10 success, "Hard Times." The latter was the first of many records that emphasized her working-class commitment. Lacy landed a role in the 1980 movie *Take This Job and Shove It*; then "Takin' It Easy," "Everybody Makes Mistakes," and her female-country anthem "Hillbilly Girl with the Blues" were issued to Top 10 radio acclaim. The California lady with the Janis Joplin delivery was given a major promotional buildup.

Lacy recalls, "I was a woman working in a man's world. And, truly, country music is a man's world. . . . I think that I am sometimes perceived as difficult. . . . I know people consider Gail Davies to be extremely difficult, but I have immense respect for her. She's one of the women in country that I really will listen to."

As she progressed, Lacy looked increasingly for material that made a statement. "I would just like to see a little more consciousness in my music and in country music in general," she explained. "Music is supposed to uplift, inform, move you. . . . I don't want to end up being a smile that somebody remembers. I want to have said something to people." In 1982 she sang the man-sassing "Wild Turkey" and a number that became the theme song for the entire Nashville music community, "16th Avenue." After successful singles with "Dream Baby" (1983) and "Size Seven Round" (a 1985 duet with George Jones), Lacy issued a blue-collar concept LP called *Highway Diner* in 1986.

"I've been touring all over this country, and I've seen how hard the working-class person has been hit," she told the *Washington Post.* "A lot of people who want to work can't find jobs. People who have done everything possible to hang on to their farms are losing them through no fault of their own. I come from a working-class background; it wasn't so long ago that I was waiting on tables for a living. I think people need courage and inspiration right now, and I'd like to do what I can." The album's "Working Class Man" became a hit, but by this time Lacy's stock was slipping. She was overcoming a drinking problem, had broken up with her guitarist/lover, and was unhappy at CBS.

She staged her comeback with 1989's *Survivor,* another "theme" collection. Its songs "The Heart," "Hard Luck Ace," and "I'm a Survivor" concerned the human spirit's ability to triumph over adversity, as Lacy had done. "All I could think of was that I'm not the only person," she told interviewer Marjie McGraw. "Half of the people in Watts are single women supporting families—so many single mothers are out there hanging on for dear life through real difficult job conditions, inadequate care for their kids, or some guy at work bothering them, but they can't do anything about it because they need the job so desperately. I thought a lot about women during this time. I thought about how hard it is for anybody who is hanging in there. I hope the album gives people strength."

Her personal life went into an upswing, too. In 1989 Lacy married Aaron Anderson, then moved from California to Nashville. "I met him in 1985 when he filled in for our sound engineer on tour. I don't think it was a week before I knew I was in love with Aaron. But I'm so much older [she is thirteen years his senior], that I really didn't want to make a move. He began to spend more and more time with me. We became very, very close on the tour together. By that time, we were sharing a room. He said, 'Let's get married,' and I said no because I was very concerned about the differences in our ages. Finally I became convinced that he really did love me."

She became increasingly active as a concerned citizen and was the only country act to raise her voice with rock stars on a record to raise consciousness about the earth's vanishing rain forests. She also raised funds for hunger organizations and women's groups. "Black Coffee" became a major Lacy J. Dalton hit in 1990, kicking off a new era for the "survivor." "Wouldn't it be great to be a woman and be just like Willie Nelson? I've often thought, 'God, would that be great, to be the first woman out there with wrinkles and not trying to cover it up.' Wouldn't that be a wonderful thing?"

In addition to injecting new purity and integrity into the country sound, all of these California folkies-gone-country brought a new image. Women such as Lacy J. Dalton, Nicolette Larson, Juice Newton, and Gail Davies were unadorned and natural in appearance. Emmylou Harris let her hair go prematurely gray and wore the result proudly. Linda Ronstadt performed in bare feet during her early country-rock days. Jennifer Warnes steadfastly wore her wire-rim spectacles. All of these women dressed casually. They rejected heavy makeup and fancy hairdos. "Grand Ole Opry" stars saw them as hippies, but the wholesome, fresh-air appearance of these West Coast ladies was actually more "country" than the prevailing style in Nashville.

This image reflected a broader trend in American life. The late 1970s and early 1980s was a period of health food, environmental awareness, personal fitness, and natural fibers. The trappings of the hippie movement of the 1960s moved into the mainstream. It was the "organic era."

No big political movement emerged during this period, but a major revolution in life-styles was under way. The number of people living alone doubled during the 1970s, reaching 23 percent of the adult population, and a "singles" culture emerged. Pundits called it "the Me Decade." In addition to a variety of psychological therapy trends, people became involved in all kinds of self-improvement programs. The popularity of things like granola, bottled water, vitamins, homemade bread, backyard gardening, health food stores, weight-loss programs, and food processors signified a new interest in diet. Aerobics, jogging, health clubs, and a sports boom reflected Americans' search for self-fulfillment, too.

Women were at the forefront of many of the "natural" trends. *Our Bodies, Ourselves* was published in 1973 as a landmark of female self-help. It contained medical information that showed women they could know as much about their bodies as doctors, that they could take control of their physical health. Breastfeeding babies was promoted. More than one hundred freestanding birth centers developed between 1974 and 1984. Using nurse-midwives, they emphasized childbirth as a natural process not requiring the usual impersonal medical technology of a hospital setting. Fathers and entire families became involved in the birth experience. By 1976 there were over four hundred rape crisis centers, most started and staffed by female volunteers. Battered-women shelters, child-care centers, consciousness-raising groups, and health collectives sprang up as other components of this movement.

There was a whole movement of art, music, film, and literature produced by women during this time, which was given serious consideration in the mass media. Just as Lacy, Gail, and Emmylou demanded to be taken seriously as musicians, so did women in other arts. A whole new body of criticism grew up, analyzing women's art according to whether or not it was "feminist" or "liberated." Personal choices in fashion, hair, and makeup became political statements. If you were too dolled up, you were making yourself an object for men. Being principled and having independent convictions became more important to this new generation than "finding the right man" or starting a family.

Inevitably, the country music performers who embodied these values of integrity, purpose, and power were branded "lady renegades," "new-breed women," and "female outlaws." The "outlaws" term was particularly reserved for the rebels in Nashville. Beginning in the mid-1970s, groups of musicians gathered in the studios of Jack Clement, Pete Drake, and Tompall Glaser. They were opposed to the slicked-up Nashville style and the cliquish, political nature of the country music business establishment. They grew their hair long, experimented with drugs, and stripped away what they thought was artificial and phony about country music. Glaser Studios manager and *Country Music* columnist Hazel Smith started using the term "outlaw" to describe the scene. By 1975 acts like Waylon Jennings and Willie Nelson were scoring major hits in the rootsy style, defying Nashville's supper-club aspirations. RCA Records executive Jerry Bradley took note and assembled an album called *Wanted: The Outlaws.* In 1976 it became the first country LP in history to be certified a platinum record for one million sales. The album contained big hits by Nelson and Jennings, plus Glaser's humorous women's-lib song "Put Another Log on the Fire."

There was one woman on that landmark collection. Her name was Jessi Colter. The "outlaw" scene, like almost everything else in Nashville, was a boys' club. But Jessi and a few other females fit into its do-your-own-thing atmosphere, take-a-stand attitude, and alternative–life-style philosophy.

Jessi's real name was Mirriam Johnson. She took her stage moniker from her great-great-great-uncle Jesse Colter, an 1870s Wild West train robber, a *real* outlaw. She was the daughter of a mining engineer father and an evangelist mother, born in 1947 and raised in Phoenix. Her mother was unquestionably the major force in Jessi's development. Helen Johnson had sold cosmetics and run a hotel before being gripped by the spirit and called to the ministry. She held tent revivals that featured faith healing and talking in tongues. Jessi was her pianist. Although the girl was brought up strictly, she had a wild streak. At age fifteen she began sneaking out of the house to play in bars, and at sixteen she ran off with rock-'n'-roll star Duane Eddy. He produced her early singles, took her on tour, and married her.

After the couple divorced in 1968, Jessi and her daughter, Jennifer, left Hollywood and returned to Phoenix. She was writing songs by this time, and Dottie West had scored a moderate hit with Jessi's "No Sign of Living" in 1965. Jessi was thinking increasingly of a career in music when she fell in love with handsome, dangerous-looking, honky-tonk hot shot Waylon Jennings. Mama Helen strongly disapproved. Jessi got a recording contract with RCA, and during the production in Nashville of her debut LP, *A Country Star Is Born*, her relationship with Jennings deepened. He wound up singing on some of the album, writing its liner notes, and coproducing it. The two were married by her mother in 1969, and her record appeared the following year.

"I'm Not Lisa" became her first hit record when she signed with Capitol Records in 1975. It shot to the top of both country and pop charts. "'Lisa' is a very female song," Jessi says of her tale of a woman whose husband calls her by his first wife's name. "Girls understand what I'm saying in that song." Her big-selling LPs *I'm Jessi Colter* (1975) and *Jessi* (1976) were at their best when the emphasis was on her stark, piano-and-voice ballads. "What's Happened to Blue Eyes," "Storms Never Last," "It's Morning," and "You Ain't Never Been Loved" were eloquent evidence of her unique composing and performing skills. When *Wanted: The Outlaws* became a phenomenon, Jessi and Waylon's duet "Suspicious Minds" became a major 1976 hit, and they embarked on an extensive tour with Willie Nelson.

"An outlaw is someone who is outside a working system," she said. "In my own work, being an outlaw means that when I sit down to write a song, I don't have any form that I follow, nor do I have to write at a mental level for any one type of brain or person. There are really no creative boundaries to what I can do on record. . . . It means a lot of creative freedom."

"It is not primarily the artists who control what kind of music is being made today," Jessi told the *Kansas City Star.* "Most of the decisions are made by businessmen who see the record industry as primarily a money-making enterprise. There's a lot of politics involved, and a lot of artists get destroyed along the way." Few better explanations for the outlaw movement were ever given.

The daughter of a female Pentecostal preacher, Jessie Colter rode alongside the men in country's "outlaw" movement. This LP jacket dates from 1978.

"Marshall's a good ol' boy: She can come on the bus," decreed Waylon after encountering six-foot Vanderbilt University coed Marshall Chapman (b. 1949). Marshall was the privileged daughter of a South Carolina textile magnate who bolted to run with the outlaw crowd in Music City. This witty Thoroughbred had the most magnetic stage personality of all the female outlaws and became their most celebrated songwriter.

Me, I'm Feelin' Free emerged as her debut LP in 1977. It contained the gripping southern-poverty saga "Somewhere South of Macon," as well as the hell-raiser "Rode Hard and Put Up Wet," which became an *Urban Cowboy* movie soundtrack standout by Johnny Lee. Jessi Colter recorded Marshall's "A Woman's Heart (Is a Handy Place to Be)." Marshall evolved into a bluesy rocker, applying her drawling, Lauren Bacall–like alto to five subsequent albums from 1978 to 1992. "I'm a marketing man's nightmare," she said. "Rock 'n' roll is really my body. My heart's country, and my soul is r&b. . . . I'm just trying to figure out how to make a living in this business." The long, lean blonde dubbed one of her groups Marshall Chapman and Her All-Boy Band and another Marshall Chapman and The Love Slaves as she experimented with her blues-country-rock fusion. "I guess I am tough, in a way; I take care of myself," she said of her distinctive appeal. "I also think being a woman and playing electric guitar with a band attracts a lot of attention; though that's not why I do it. It's just right for me."

Besides Jessi Colter's "I'm Not Lisa," the biggest hit by an outlaw woman was Sammi Smith's extraordinarily sexual performance of "Help Me Make It Through the Night," Kris Kristofferson's celebrated ballad of midnight need, aching loneliness, and smoldering desire. Her sultry single went to the top of the country and pop charts in 1971 and won Grammy, Country Music Association, Academy of Country Music, and

gold record awards. Sammi shucked her chanteuse evening gowns in favor of T-shirts and jeans to sing it for Willie Nelson's long-haired audience with her band, The Knee-Walking, Commode-Hugging, Lady-Kicking Cowboys.

"I never did see anything scandalous about that song," Sammi says. "I never knew it was until I read the remarks from some of the other girl singers in publications. For me it was just a very tender song. I honestly don't see anything distasteful about the song, now or then. . . . I don't think I'm an outlaw or a rebel woman. I think that outlaw term was just stuck on anybody who didn't do things the usual Nashville way."

Sammi was born in southern California in 1943, but grew up in Oklahoma, Texas, Arizona, and Colorado as her family moved around. She dropped out of school at age eleven and was singing professionally in bars by twelve. Marriage at fifteen and three babies in succession didn't slow her down. She continued to sing with her husband's bar bands. "My marriage blew up after six years, and I decided that I would go on with my singing alone," Sammi recalled. "It wasn't easy during those years that I was trying to get along . . . but I kept plugging along, sometimes singing only for my meals or a few dollars a night." She developed a smoky, bitter-sounding style that reflected life's hardships and broken dreams.

After "Help Me Make It Through the Night." Sammi moved into the outlaw era with the prostitute sagas "Girl in New Orleans" (1972) and "Sunday School to Broadway" (1976); the illicit-love hit "Cheatin's a Two-Way Street" (1981); a country version of Three Dog Night's rock song "Never Been to Spain" (1974); the seduced-and-abandoned "What a Lie" (1979); and definitive versions of the standards "Today I Started Loving You Again," "City of New Orleans," and "My Window Faces the South." Sammi toured with Waylon Jennings, appeared at Willie Nelson's Fourth of July Picnics, and became a fixture on the "outlaw" scene. "Waylon gave me the nickname 'Girl Hero.' I guess they figured that anybody that could travel with Waylon was a hero or somethin'."

In 1975 she moved to the San Carlos Apache Reservation in Arizona and adopted three native American children. Sammi's mother was Apache, and the singer became increasingly involved in Indian causes.

Sammi's affiliation with the Southwest was crucial to her outlaw identification, because much of the musical experimentation of this era took place outside Nashville. In Georgia and other southeastern states, country boys with blues influences were developing a raucous hybrid style called southern rock. Among the red-hot mamas who roared with them were Ruby Starr of Black Oak Arkansas, Dale Krantz of The Rossington-Collins Band, Miki Hunnicutt of A-Train, and Brenda Patterson of The Coon Elder Band.

Texas, in particular, was an epicenter for anti-Nashville country music. The thriving collegiate bar scene of Austin spawned many long-haired country "outlaw" stars of the day. Particularly associated with the Austin sound was the western-swing band Asleep at the Wheel. Just as the western-swing groups of the 1940s had featured cowgirl-clad singers and yodelers, this revival group was fronted by a blue jean–clad female vocalist. Asleep at the Wheel's Chris O'Connell sang lead on its hits "The Letter That Johnny Walker Read" (1975), "Nothin' Takes the Place of You" (1976), and "The Trouble with Lovin' Today" (1977).

The most popular female Austin singer during the outlaw era was probably "long, tall Marcia Ball," a leggy brunet who fused r&b, western, rock, country, and Cajun elements into her style. Marcia repopularized "I Want to Be a Cowboy's Sweetheart" in her live shows, did a Capitol Records Nashville LP in 1977, and made the country charts with "I'm a Fool to Care" before settling into a soul groove on Rounder Records LPs of the 1980s.

Rattlesnake Annie McGowan was billed as "the female Willie Nelson" because of her bluesy tone, behind-the-beat phrasing, stripped-down musical settings, guitar work, and unconventional life-style. A product of the West Tennessee farms, Rose Ann Gallimore first came to Nashville as part of the contest-winning Gallimore Sisters trio at age thirteen in 1954. They got a guest appearance on the Opry and had lunch at Mother Maybelle Carter's. When she was sixteen, Annie went to Memphis to sing the blues on Beale Street. Then came a two-year stint as a cocktail lounge singer near the space center in Huntsville, Alabama. As the divorced mother of two in the 1960s, she moved to Texas, where she married Ed McGowan, settled on a ranch on the Brazos River, and adopted a bohemian style that rejected fancy fashion and included her trademark rattler earring. Rattlesnake Annie met Willie Nelson in 1972 and began to blossom as an Austin-style singer-songwriter shortly thereafter. She formed her own Rattlesnake Records and issued "Texas Lullaby" as her debut single in 1974. Her song was later recorded by outlaw biker star David Allan Coe. In 1980 she produced, manufactured, and marketed her debut LP, *Rattlesnakes & Rusty Water*, which included her ecology song "Goodbye to a River." The LP attracted attention overseas, so she embarked on a four-year, eighteen-nation European sojourn. She became the first female country act to appear in East Germany, Poland, and Czechoslovakia, and the first to record an LP for the Czech market.

"You can make a lot more money off of your records if you do 'em yourself," says Rattlesnake Annie. "You can sell them yourself and have a lot closer relationship with your fans. . . . And I like being in control. I like being my own master."

Annie's second homemade U.S. LP appeared in 1986. Titled *Country Livin',* it included her American Indian lament "Comanche Tears" and a duet with Willie on "Long Black Limousine." CBS took note of this self-promoted, self-published, self-booked, and self-managed success story, and signed her to make *Rattlesnake Annie* in 1987. It included her remake of Marshall Chapman's "Somewhere South of Macon" and a stark rendition of "16 Tons." Like many women going back to country basics during this time, Annie sought out her musical ancestors. She befriended Patsy Montana and recorded a duet of "Cowboy's Sweetheart" with the country legend.

In the 1990s Rattlesnake Annie expanded her popularity to Japan. "The fact that we raise tobacco and cotton is exotic to them. They don't have that there. Hell, I spent my life tryin' to get out of choppin' that stuff. Maybe another reason I've had some success overseas is because I'm not real flashy. They have so much of that in their own pop music. And so do we. . . . A lot of what we've got on country radio is pop music. It's ruining the business, putting it in a tailspin."

Most of Rattlesnake Annie's Texas colleagues agreed. Rejecting Nashville Sound arrangements and formulaic songwriting, the Texas tunesmiths prided themselves on being more poetic than their Nashville counterparts, just as the unfrilly Lone Star State performers believed they were more "real" than the radio stars produced by Music City.

The finest female composing talents who emerged from this Texas scene were probably Cass County native Susanna Clark and Dallas-bred Karen Brooks. Susanna's works include Kathy Mattea's "Come from the Heart," Dottsy's "I'll Be Your San Antone Rose," Gail Davies's "You're a Hard Dog (To Keep Under the Porch)," and Emmylou Harris's "Easy from Now On." There's a strong-female strain in Susanna's writing that's evident in such numbers as "Oh Yes I Can" (sung by Rosanne Cash) and "This Time I'm Gonna Beat You to the Truck" (Sissy Spacek, Live & Kickin'). She is also an accomplished visual artist. Susanna's atmospheric oil paintings appear on the covers of LPs by Willie Nelson (*Stardust*), Emmylou Harris (*Quarter Moon in a*

Ten-Cent Town), and husband Guy Clark (*Old Number One*).

During her Texas days Karen Brooks (b. 1954) lived with Austin musician Gary P. Nunn, with whom she had a son. Then she moved to Nashville to room with frisky country-rocker Carlene Carter. Karen's good-time cowgirl personality, off-center sense of humor, and feisty charm dazzled many a beau in those barhopping days. After a stint in a California band with Rodney Crowell, Karen rose to writing fame as the composer of Emmylou Harris's hit "Tennessee Rose" and of the Rosanne Cash/Tracy Nelson favorite "Couldn't Do Nothing Right." This led to her own record contract.

Karen moved back to Nashville in 1980, and two years later *Walk On* appeared, to a chorus of critics' hosannas. The LP's "Every Beat of My Heart" and title tune were structured like shimmering Roy Orbison creations, full of drama, pounding excitement, and wailing crescendos. "Shores of White Sand," "If That's What You're Thinking," and "New Way Out," her first hit single, were stately, melodic ballads. Shortly after the album appeared, Karen sang "Faking Love" as a duet with T. G. Sheppard. It went to Number 1 in 1983 and cinched her Academy of Country Music win as Top New Female Vocalist of the Year.

During the late 1980s Karen kicked a substance abuse problem and went through a divorce from cowboy husband Jack Lawrence. A ride-'em-cowgirl fixture of the rodeo circuit for more than a decade, she reemerged on the music scene in 1992 in a duo with songwriter Randy Sharp. "Baby I'm the One," her single from their album, contained country's first female rap.

If you had to pick "alpha and omega" female personalities bred on the rollicking Texas music scene, they would have to be Tanya Tucker and Dottsy. Working-class Tanya could raise hell with the best of 'em. Middle-class Dottsy was the sweet, wide-eyed, innocent, blond girl-next-door, but her contribution to the scene was bringing outlaw songs onto the national radio airwaves in gentle, folkie arrangements. Born Dottsy Brodt in 1954, she was a twenty-one-year-old University of Texas coed in Austin when she landed a contract with RCA. This Junior Miss Pageant winner who looked like she'd stepped out of an Ivory soap commercial became an unlikely outlaw ally when her version of Jessi Colter's "Storms Never Last" swept up the charts in 1975. She followed it with Susanna Clark's "I'll Be Your San Antone Rose" and Waylon Jennings's "Tryin' to Satisfy You." Dottsy's biggest hit was the 1977 jukebox classic "(After 'Sweet Memories') Play 'Born to Lose' Again." When her contract with

"Rattlesnake Annie" McGowan, 1979.

RCA ran out, she married her high school sweetheart.

Torrid Tanya Tucker lived it up as country's "wild child" during this period of country-rock experimentation, back-to-basics commitment, and outlaw rebellion. Along the way she sang such era-defining songs as "Texas (When I Die)," "San Antonio Stroll," "It's a Cowboy Lovin' Night," "Don't Believe My Heart Can Stand Another You," and "Pecos Promenade."

The tabloid newspapers dubbed her "tempestuous Tanya" and "The Texas Tornado," and she roared all night with her songwriter buddies. Tanya developed the image of the naughty Nashville gal with a rollicking reputation, the jezebel with a string of love affairs, the mother of out-of-wedlock kids, the sexy dresser, and the free-spirited party girl with a saucy outlook and a sassy mouth. And to almost all the Music Row conservatives' surprise, she became enormously popular with fans, adored by the press, and celebrated for her heart-of-gold generosity. More than any other woman, Tanya Tucker shattered the old country-sweetheart stereotype. She was the field's first female superstar with an open, free sexual image. And along with Gail Davies, Tanya broke ground as a star publicly facing motherhood without matrimony.

Despite her fifty-plus hit songs, Tanya Tucker remains a star who is known more for her offstage escapades than her music. She's one of the greatest country vocalists alive, but is often trivialized as gossip fodder. "I have a whole audience that really doesn't know my music," she observes candidly. "They know me as a celebrity, so to speak, a tabloid queen." Is she as wild as they say? "I've settled down some . . . but I still like to rock," she says with a mischievous grin. That dazzling, flashbulb-intense smile, and a hearty, earthy laugh are devastatingly disarming in conversation. Her throaty guffaw is somewhere between healthy, outdoorsy cowgirl and cigarettes-and-whiskey barroom buddy. Tanya on a tear is a formidable presence indeed, capable of dancing on tabletops and vamping every man in sight. But there's a sweet homebody in there, too, a doting mama and kitchen magician who loves to swap recipes and stories with her girlfriends.

Her image, her life-style, and her behavior reflect country's acknowledgment of the dramatic shift in social conventions that was taking place. American women of the seventies and eighties were more independent than ever; taboos and restrictions were defied. Premarital sex, couples' living together, divorce, and single parenthood became the accepted norm, rather than the scandalous exception. Sure, Tanya lives it up. But so do many of the Saturday-night, kick-up-your-heels honky-tonk gals in her audience.

Sure, she defies the demure country-sweetheart stereotype. But so do most American working women. When she was finally named country's Female Vocalist of the Year in 1991, young country fans felt the honor was long overdue. But the conservative old guard was rather outraged.

"I don't think about what people might say behind my back," she responds. "Not really. If I thought about it at all, it was very fleeting. My fans have been so supportive. And you can't look at those kids and say that was a mistake. I think, too, that I'm probably making a statement for the single mothers out there. There are a lot of them, and unfortunately a lot of them are in real financial trouble taking care of their kids. They're busting their butts working nine to five. I really have a lot of respect for those women. 'Cause I don't think I could do it on my own."

Her two children's father is a struggling Los Angeles actor named Ben Reed. Tucker fell in love with him while costarring with him in her "Strong Enough to Bend" video. But they broke up while she was pregnant with daughter Presley Tanita Tucker. After Presley was born in 1989, Ben and Tanya grew close again, and again she became pregnant. "Then it didn't work out for real," she confesses. "I'm not ashamed of it," she said backstage after hosting the TNN Music City News awards on TV while visibly expecting in the summer of 1991. "To me it's a very joyful thing." Son Beau Grayson Tucker was born the night she triumphed at the CMA Awards that October.

"I don't make a conscious effort to be anything particularly different. It's just 'Hey, here I am.' This is me." Tanya's striking individuality is all the more impressive because she was a child star who grew up in the public eye. Born in 1958 in Seminole, Texas, Tanya was a talented nine-year-old when her construction worker father asked her which she'd rather do—go to school and live a normal life or become a professional singer. "I want to be a star," she replied. "I came to Nashville when I was nine in 1968, and we went to every record company, everybody in town. Everybody turned me down." When she was twelve, Beau moved wife Juanita, daughters Tanya and LaCosta, and son Don into a trailer in Henderson, Nevada, hoping to get his singing kid a job in a club along the nearby Las Vegas Strip. A year later producer Billy Sherrill discovered Tanya in Vegas, brought her to Nashville, and made her a sensation. "There I was, a little kid sitting in this big chair in Billy Sherrill's office. The first song they played for me was 'The Happiest Girl in the Whole U.S.A.' I said, 'I don't like it.' They all looked at each other. Here was this girl with an opinion. They could'a said, 'You: Outta here, back to Vegas.' But they didn't. They let me have my say. I'll always be grateful for that. The next day they played me 'Delta Dawn,' and I said, 'That's the one.'

It's pretty unusual to be thirteen years old and have a Number 1 record the first time out, on the first label you've ever been on."

"Delta Dawn" was no fluke. From 1972 to 1978, while still a teenager, Tanya had a dozen Top 10 hits, including the womanly "You've Got Me to Hold Onto" and "Here's Some Love." She dropped out of school in the ninth grade to devote herself full-time to her music. Even her earliest image seethed with pubescent sexuality, and Tanya often cited Elvis and his rockabilly brethren as her inspirations. Beginning with 1978's *TNT* album, she began getting more musically rambunctious, restlessly pushing at country's borders and restrictions. It contained rock 'n' rollers like Buddy Holly's "Not Fade Away," Elvis Presley's "Heartbreak Hotel," and Chuck Berry's "Brown Eyed Handsome Man," as well as folk star John Prine's "Angel from Montgomery." The LP jacket featured her snaking a microphone cord between her leather-sheathed legs, and it opened to a full-length shot of Tanya in a second-skin red spandex jumpsuit licking her lips lasciviously. Her wanton rocker image continued with 1979's *Tear Me Apart* collection. It was produced by British rock mogul Mike Chapman, with whom she had an affair. She prefigured Madonna with 1981's *Should I Do It* by posing and performing in lacy Victorian undergarments.

As the high-spirited cowgirl spread her wings musically, she sowed her wild oats socially. Tanya moved to L.A. in 1978 and began hanging out with the "fast lane" crowd of movie stars and pop celebrities. When her parents tried to rein her in, she ran off with Merle Haggard, who was forty-four, twenty-three years her senior. In the 1979 movie *Amateur Night at the Dixie Bar and Grill* she costarred and carried on with Don Johnson, later famed for TV's "Miami Vice." Her most famous liaison was with Glen Campbell. When they became lovers in 1980, she was twenty-two and he was twice that. She called him "the horniest man I ever met," and they snuggled together in photos, planned a 1982 Valentine's Day wedding, and sang love duets on Tanya's LP *Dreamgirls*. Amid rumors of booze and cocaine abuse, the passionate couple brawled publicly in restaurants and hotels. The tabloids had a field day. She sued him for assault and breach of promise. He got religion and married someone else. Tanya thinks the main problem was that Glen was from an older generation and couldn't accept her modern-woman independence, career dedication, and sexual image. She found new boyfriends on the Manhattan party circuit, doomed pop star Andy Gibb and boxer Jerry Cooney. Along the way there was also a European skier, a Texas cowboy, and a Tennessee musician or two. "Do I have to have a man in my life? No, I guess not. That's obvious. Falling in love isn't my big problem.

Staying in love is. . . . I don't know if I'll ever be married."

She has been forthright and candid about her mistakes, as well as her triumphs, and the fans love that. Good-hearted Tanya has a splendid sense of humor, an appealing earthiness, and a likable no-bull attitude that add a lot to her undeniable charisma. Becoming a single parent seems to have endeared her all the more to female fans.

These rebels, these outlaws, these back-to-basics female stars all defied country music conventions by creating not only a new kind of country music, but a new kind of country music woman. They were not driven by Music Row's commercial, pop music aspirations or manipulated by marketers, producers, or music executives. They had musical purpose and determination. They had integrity.

These women led; they didn't follow. Their creativity, honesty, and imagination created a new country aesthetic that struck a responsive chord in an audience, an audience that Nashville neither expected nor understood. Emmylou Harris and her sisters were the first wave of a monsoon of youth-appeal country stars. They were among the first to get middle-class "baby-boomers" to listen to country sounds. And by the 1990s the fruits of their labors were abundant.

"All of us who became hooked on music, these children of the sixties that we are, are rootless children," says Emmylou Harris. "We have to make our own roots. It's real important that we have authentic music, and that's why it's so important to preserve this [country] music. . . . Because I think that the lack of roots is a big problem that people have. There's all this psychosis and stuff. Yet nobody's going to move back to Appalachia and pretend they were raised in a log cabin with twelve children. We are what we are. But roots are universal, music is universal. And I think it feeds us in a way that we desperately need. . . . I believe that music is a real, positive, life-changing thing that is as necessary to . . . the quality of life as things like food and shelter. We need those intangibles like love and a good relationship, but we also need things to help us along the way, and I think music is a really powerful part of that."

Tanya Tucker, 1982.

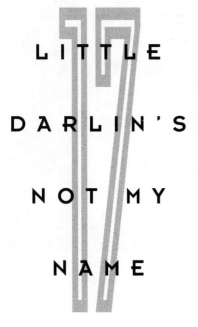

LITTLE DARLIN'S NOT MY NAME

Women in Bluegrass

In 1989 Tanya Tucker scored a major hit by reviving the 1928 Jimmie Rodgers classic "Daddy and Home," one of several old-time music revivals that occurred in mainstream country music as a result of the outlaw, folk revival, and country-rock movements. Like Tanya, many country music women who came of age during the late 1970s were interested in stripping country of its showy, choreographed excesses and reconnecting it with its roots. So in addition to giving The Nashville Sound a country-rock kick, female performers of the day dug into its history and heritage. Linda Ronstadt had a Top 10 hit in 1978 with the Appalachian chestnut "I Never Will Marry." Dolly Parton did "Muleskinner Blues" (1970), and Crystal Gayle recorded "Miss the Mississippi" (1979), both Jimmie Rodgers numbers.

The role model was Emmylou Harris, whose repertoire included The Carter Family's "Hello Stranger," The Louvin Brothers' "If I Could Only Win Your Love," and entire albums devoted to old-time gospel and bluegrass. Emmy's explorations of antique country sounds were an outgrowth of a widespread old-time music revival movement spurred by the folk revival.

A striking number of old-time revival bands of the

1970s showcased female singers and musicians. Even more revolutionary was women's full-scale invasion of the closely related bluegrass world. Created in the mid-1940s by adding hot picking, hard-edged singing, and overdrive tempo to the string band tradition, bluegrass music remained an almost completely male domain during its first twenty-five years. Its emphasis on instrumental flash, aggressive vocals, and conservative social structure made it the most male-defined of all country's styles. But as in so many other aspects of American life, that began to change in the seventies. Suddenly, as if from nowhere, there were women fiddlers, singers, banjo pickers, guitarists, and bandleaders at bluegrass festivals, on bluegrass albums, and in bluegrass clubs.

Bluegrass men responded to the invasion by shouting derisively at female pickers, making sexual overtures backstage, or snickering behind their backs. "She picks pretty good, for a girl," was a typical backhanded compliment. As women began participating in greater numbers, their presence became "a divisive topic of conversation among men," recalls folklorist Thomas A. Adler. "Many men resisted and continue to resist the very idea of women's participation in bluegrass. Some flatly assert that women can't pick bluegrass, can't sing bluegrass, and don't belong in bluegrass."

"It is a fact that bluegrass music has traditionally been a man's world," noted a *Bluegrass Unlimited* reviewer in 1979. "At one time, if women were found in bluegrass bands at all . . . it was in minor roles such as bass player, and they hardly ever sang."

Bluegrass music's earliest women were relatives of its male stars—Bill Monroe's daughter Melissa and girlfriend Bessie Lee Mauldin; Lester Flatt's wife, Gladys; Howdy Forrester's wife, Sally Ann. This heritage continued into the fifties and sixties with such talented wives as Carl Tipton's Sophie and Hubert Davis's Ruby working in their husbands' shadows. Family groups and male-female duet teams—often working in the bluegrass-gospel idiom—were the most common entry points for women. John and Margie Cook, Rex and Eleanor Parker, Bill and Mary Reid, and Benny and Vallie Cain became active in the late 1940s and persevered as teams into the 1970s. But although cast in a bluegrass setting, most of these women were closer to the parlor-song style of The Carter Family than to the hair-raising "high lonesome sound" of Bill Monroe.

A surge in popularity for bluegrass music occurred as a direct result of the folk festivals of the sixties. Country veteran Barbara Allen performed at what is regarded as the first bluegrass festival, in Luray, Virginia, in 1965. Mother Maybelle Carter was another early participant, both at festivals and on a Flatt & Scruggs LP of 1961 called *Songs of the Famous Carter Family.* Roni Stoneman was among those recorded on the 1957 Folkways LP *American Banjo Scruggs Style,* which historian Neil V. Rosenberg cites as the first bluegrass album. Her sister Donna contributed mandolin to the 1962 LP *Rose Maddox Sings Bluegrass.* "Bluegrass has been almost exclusively man's music," said Ken Nelson in its liner notes. "Now, just as if to prove that it's a man's world only till a woman decides she wants some of it for herself, along comes the wonderful Rose Maddox with a bluegrass album." Cousin Emmy also became part of bluegrass history when The Osborne Brothers transformed her "Ruby" into a bluegrass standard in 1970.

Perhaps not surprisingly, several of the female bluegrass pioneers came from collegiate, folk revival backgrounds, rather than from more repressive rural roots. Joan Baez performed and recorded with The Greenbriar Boys in the 1960s, collaborated often with Earl Scruggs, and promoted the music of the bluegrass world throughout her career. New York–born, Hollywood-raised Dian James recorded a bluegrass LP backed by the Greenbriars in 1963.

But for over-the-top performance passion in women's early days in bluegrass, you have to look to gospel. Mountain wailers such as Wilma Lee Cooper and Molly O'Day were the overwhelming influences, and their fervor was carried on by the seminal bluegrass-gospel act The Lewis Family. With its trio of lead-singing sisters, this gifted Georgia clan has epitomized bluegrass showmanship on the festival circuit for thirty years. In the wake of the spectacular Lewis Family came Alabama's two Sullivan Family acts, the first featuring the fervent, husky belting of Margie Sullivan, and the second starring the hard-driving style of her cousin Tammy Sullivan. Of Ohio's gospel-singing Marshall Family, *Bluegrass Unlimited* opined, "If you don't like the Marshalls' music you've got stone ears and a lead heart." The Marshalls began performing in 1967; guitarist/songwriter/vocalist Judy Marshall was the leader. Born in 1951, she was deeply influenced by the religious sincerity and musical skills of Kentucky gospel great Dottie Rambo.

Bluegrass families, usually singing gospel, were launchpads for women in the field. But as bluegrass instrumentalists, lead singers, and bandleaders, women were rare. Among the earliest to shine as pickers were the Stoneman women, who began performing in their father's Bluegrass Champs band around 1956. Patsy, the oldest Stoneman daughter, led her own group in the Washington, D.C., area shortly afterward. Pennsylvania's Gloria Belle (Flickinger) was probably the first female lead singer in bluegrass. She was active as early as 1957.

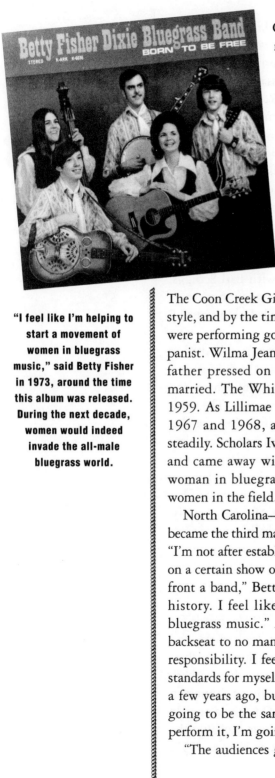

Gloria led her own Green Mountain Travelers, recorded solo LPs, and served a long stint as a singer and bass player with Jimmy Martin. "She's been taking Jimmy's on-stage insults since 1968," observed writer Bob Artis in 1974. "She breaks into a rousing song while Jimmy makes faces at her, holds his nose in a gesture of blunt criticism, and encourages the audience to boo, which it is too polite to do. Gloria Belle, like most women bluegrass singers, leans toward that belt-'em-out Molly O'Day style."

Lillimae was another Molly O'Day/Wilma Lee Cooper disciple. Born near Roundhead, Ohio, in 1940, Lillimae Haney was named after Lily May Ledford, of the famed all-girl 1930s string band The Coon Creek Girls. Her father played guitar in the Maybelle Carter style, and by the time Lillimae was eight, she and her sister Wilma Jean were performing gospel as The Haney Sisters, with him as their accompanist. Wilma Jean got married and quit the act, but Lillimae and her father pressed on with mandolinist Charles Whitaker, whom she married. The Whitakers formed their own group, first recording in 1959. As Lillimae & The Dixie Gospel-Aires, they recorded again in 1967 and 1968, and throughout the 1970s the group performed steadily. Scholars Ivan and Deanna Tribe got to know Lillimae in 1976 and came away with this impression: "She feels it is tough being a woman in bluegrass and would welcome more ready acceptance of women in the field."

North Carolina–bred Betty Fisher would echo that sentiment. Betty became the third major female bluegrass bandleader of the early seventies. "I'm not after establishing records like being the only woman performer on a certain show or being one of the few women in bluegrass music to front a band," Betty told writer Don Rhodes. "But I do feel a part of history. I feel like I'm helping to start a movement of women in bluegrass music." Although never a spectacular singer, Betty took a backseat to no man as a guitarist, songwriter, and bandleader. "I feel a responsibility. I feel people are looking at me, and I have to set high standards for myself. . . . There were not many women in country music a few years ago, but now there are a lot. I believe bluegrass music is going to be the same way. And if women love the music and want to perform it, I'm going to help them all I can."

"The audiences generally have over 50 percent women," said Betty, "and I think they like to see another woman on the stage. I have as many women fans as men. We talk about soap operas and swap recipes. The reason I think there are not many women in bluegrass . . . is because the men [in bluegrass] tend to be more old-line in their thinking about the role of women. . . . Men in bluegrass music feel differently about women, partly because so many of them come from the sticks and were raised in a traditional way and on old-fashioned beliefs. A woman in the old days used to walk in back of her man. Now the woman is walking with him, but she is still not walking ahead of him."

By the 1970s bluegrass music had drifted outside the country mainstream to occupy its own cultural niche. Bluegrass created its own publications, popularity charts, record labels, and touring circuits. Its fans are not nearly so numerous as those of mainstream country music, but they are fanatical devotees. Artists measure success in the size of outdoor festivals, rather than in record sales; yet hundreds also record profitably by selling their wares at live shows. Specialty labels, rather than international conglomerates, tend to market the style. Bluegrass developed a strong us-against-them attitude toward the rest of the music world, with rigid musical definitions, an almost vicious internal gossip network, and a highly self-critical nature. Change was threatening, and innovation was difficult.

By 1975 this climate was changing. Several writers noted that the number of females performing bluegrass seemed to be increasing. In addition to Betty Fisher, the women who were recording included Texan Holly Bond; North Carolinian Arlene Kesterson; Georgia's "Queen of Bluegrass" Mary Padgett; Washington, D.C.'s, Liz Meyer; New Hampshire's Judy Carrier; and Kentuckians Audrey Barger and Emma Smith.

The finest of them was Oklahoma's Delia Bell. "If Hank Williams and Kitty Wells had married and had a daughter, she would have sounded like Delia Bell," raved Emmylou Harris after her first experience with the mournful, lonesome sound of Delia's voice. Emmy brought Delia to national prominence in 1983, but the bluegrass diva's saga starts long before that.

Delia Nowell Bell is a product of the Depression, a sharecropper's daughter and an ironworker's wife who began singing in a fundamentalist church in her hometown of Hugo, Oklahoma, when she was in her teens. After marrying Bobby Bell, she met his boyhood friend, mandolinist Bill Grant. Bill and Delia formed a singing team in 1959 and began appearing on Hugo's KIHN "Little Dixie Hayride" radio show. By the late 1960s they'd gathered their Kiamichi Mountain Boys band and were recording. Delia became the talk of the bluegrass festival circuit

Ginger Boatwright, 1973.

during the 1970s. She, Bill, and the band made more than a dozen albums locally and toured England and Ireland eleven times.

"I used to be so shy," Delia recalls. "When I met Bill, I couldn't hardly get up in front of people and open my mouth. He just kept pushing me out there. If it hadn't been for him, I never would have done it publicly like I have. . . . Our parents liked to hear us sing, and friends and family. But I never thought about singing anywhere else. I just liked to sing. I knew I could sing, but that's as far as I thought."

Delia Bell's first solo LP, *Bluer Than Midnight,* appeared in 1978. It included "Roses in the Snow," the song that became the centerpiece and title tune of Emmylou Harris's bluegrass album two years later. Emmy was so smitten with Delia's singing that she produced, arranged, and sang harmony on 1983's *Delia Bell,* released nationally by the big-time Warner Bros. label. That collection revived The Davis Sisters' classic "I Forgot More (Than You'll Ever Know)," Kitty Wells's timeless "Back Street Affair," and The Carter Family chestnuts "Wildwood Flower" and "Will You Miss Me." Using country star John Anderson as her duet foil, Delia made the charts with the LP's George Jones oldie "Flame in My Heart."

Critics began praising her as "the female Ricky Skaggs"; Music Row agencies vied to book her; Warners urged her to pursue mainstream country stardom. "All of this scared me to death," Delia recalls. "I didn't know what was happening. . . . I'd be so depressed. It scared me to death if the record went up the charts, and it scared me if it didn't!" The big-label LP elevated her stature enormously in the bluegrass world, but the company dropped its confused and reluctant female bluegrass star. Delia and Bill began appearing as an old-timey mandolin/guitar duo in the mid-1980s, sometimes with Delia's beautician sister Mona on bass. But on Rounder Records albums, they continued to perform with bluegrass backing.

"Women haven't had the opportunity men do," says the breakthrough bluegrass woman. "Men can just pick up and stay out a week, go to a festival, while women stay at home, take care of the kids, keep house, and all of that. They don't have the opportunity to get out and learn. . . . When I started, there weren't any women in bluegrass, at least around where we lived."

More and more women were. Ginger Hammond Boatwright was another pioneer, with her Red, White and Blue (Grass) group. "I'm probably one of the longest-running and original women in bluegrass," says the guitarist/songwriter/singer. Raised in Pickens County, Alabama, Ginger learned bluegrass from her father and put together Red, White and Blue (Grass) in Birmingham when she was a college student in 1966.

Red, White and Blue (Grass) was probably the most eclectic bluegrass act of the time and was often criticized by purists for its fancy production touches, off-the-wall antics, and pop influences. But Ginger's band won a Grammy nomination with its 1972 LP, made the country charts in 1973, and won Most Promising Vocal Group from *Billboard* in 1974. Still, "the acceptance of their album will depend largely on how one feels about the role of the female voice in bluegrass," cautioned a reviewer in 1975.

Ginger moved to Nashville in 1974 and opened her Old Time Pickin' Parlor nightclub. She disbanded Red, White and Blue (Grass) in 1979. "I stayed off the road for two and a half years, and nearly went nuts." She began fronting The Doug Dillard Band in 1981 and recorded *Fertile Ground* as her first solo CD with backing by Dillard and other star pickers in 1991. "If the money were there, there'd be more women in bluegrass," Ginger believes. "In country music, women can have a bus or fly; and the work is just on weekends or in the summer. In bluegrass you have to stay out on the road a good long while. It's really hard to leave your family and go on the road. But I made a decision in 1967 that I would do whatever it took."

Little by little, band by band, women infiltrated the male bluegrass domain. South Carolina native Martha Hearon Adcock plays guitar and sings lead in Talk of the Town, the band led by her banjo/guitar virtuoso husband, Eddie Adcock. Active on the bluegrass scene since the late 1970s, Martha has a pure, folk-country contralto that she generally applies to songs with old-timey sentiments on the group's albums.

Sweet-voiced Cincinnatian Katie Laur used Alabama-bred charm in fronting her popular 1970s band. A highlight of each show was a witty medley of fifties teen golden oldies, performed by the Katie Laur Band in bluegrass style with doo-wop vocals. The group also did a takeoff on "The Flintstones" TV theme titled "Bedrock Breakdown." And Katie gave the feminist movement a wink by titling a 1979 LP *Msbehavin'*.

Elmo and Patsy (Shropshire) brought chuckles to bluegrass fans, too.

They were San Franciscans with their own radio show, "Bluegrass Experience." Patsy was an accomplished guitar picker who joined Elmo's Turkey River Band in 1971. In 1979 the couple recorded their famous country Christmas novelty "Grandma Got Run Over by a Reindeer." By 1983 it was a national hit on Epic Records, and it continues to sell.

Women trickled into bluegrass bands as "sidemen" throughout the seventies, and by 1980 there were at least a dozen who were raising eyebrows with their picking skills. It wasn't easy for them. Most had to endure taunting from men or stand their ground in male-dominated competitions. The bluegrass "boys club" was often openly and unapologetically sexist. There was even a bumper sticker of the early seventies that read, "Bluegrass Is Man's Music."

In response, some female pickers turned to all-women bands for support and self-defense. Kentucky's all-female act The Woodetts featured Joyce, Shirley, Willie, and Mary Woods. Their bluegrass-gospel album appeared in 1973, the same year that Washington, D.C.'s, Williams Sisters, Gracie and Eileen, titled their debut LP *The New Female Voices of Bluegrass*. And that's about when the floodgates opened. During the next ten years a plethora of all-female bluegrass acts developed—Feminine Grass, Sweet Dixie, Cherokee Rose, Ladies Fancy, Sugar in the Gourd, The Happy Hollow String Band, Mountain Lace, Petticoat Junction, Sassygrass, and more.

The Buffalo Gals were apparently first. Composed of Syracuse University coeds, the band originally got together for a lark, not as a political statement. "At the time, in the early seventies, women were mainly like lead singers if they were in bluegrass at all," recalls Buffalo Gals founder Susie Monick. "Bluegrass has an aggressive feel, a male-dominated feel. All the people who started it were guys. Women didn't really do that. It was like you'd be a folksinger before you'd go and be a banjo player. . . . But I fell in with the wrong crowd."

The New York City native (b. 1952) became captivated by the banjo. Susie's college friend Debby Gabriel was learning guitar, so they practiced together: "We'd get in the elevator at the dormitory and see how many times we could do 'Foggy Mountain Breakdown' before the elevator went from the first floor to the top. A crowd started gathering. And that's how it all started. We had another girlfriend in college who played dulcimer [Carol Siegel]. We didn't purposefully make it a female band, but people started saying, 'Hey, won't you come and play in our club?' And we thought, 'Wow, you can even make money at having fun!' We started in 1970 as a trio."

Carol switched to mandolin; Debby left to concentrate on her painting; guitarist/singer Martha Trachtenberg and bassist Nancy Josephson signed on. By the time The Buffalo Gals made their first bluegrass festival appearance in 1974, they were joined by fiddler Sue Raines. The quintet released its LP the following year.

"It's a new thing," said Nancy in *Muleskinner News*. "There aren't too many women in bluegrass, let alone all-female bands, and of course we got all kinds of reactions. . . . After the initial shock wore off, they'd listen to the music." Added Martha, "Traditionally, women were supposed to keep to the softer music, and bluegrass is very hard, driving, even aggressive music. . . . Our music was all right, but we were getting jobs easily simply because we were a novelty. Happily enough, we were invited back to clubs on the strength of our music, not the gimmick."

Susie Monick, 1979.

Susie recalls some resentment from male pickers because of her band's rapid rise. "Guys would say, 'Well, you got on this big festival just because you were the only all-girl band.' And then we had to prove ourselves. I think that's what spurred us on to be more musicians. Also, one of our 'flaws' was we really didn't dress up girly-like. We almost underdressed. We wore blue jeans. We didn't want to make a statement like we were girls in miniskirts. Our music was the ultimate important thing. . . . And it wasn't a political message. We just figured the statement was that we were women doing it, driving on the road and being like a bunch of guys; we were living it. So it was neat. We were a bunch of girlfriends who liked to party and we enjoyed playing. We had a *lot* of fun, being the all-girl band at the festival. In the seventies there was a lot more partying than there is in the nineties."

"We're asked about it so often," said Nancy in 1976, "how we feel about the feminist movement and how it relates to us as musicians in a basically male field. I just want to make it clear that we are musicians. That is our job and our pleasure. Individually, we're into feminism at very different levels. We are entertainers and don't want to be a political band." Martha agreed with her: "The overall band feeling is that we make our statement for women simply by being competent musicians."

"Later, we began to attract a political audience," Susie recalls. "Something that was a big reward for us was that we would have women say, 'I didn't know I could do that. You're a role model.' And mostly I felt like the men were for us, too. [Bluegrass star] Sonny Osborne dressed up in a dress once so he could sit in with us. So did Tony Trischka." The Buffalo Gals summed up their party-girl spirit in their tune "Bluegrass and the Boys."

Susie, Nancy, Martha, mandolinist Lainie Lyle, and fiddler Kristin Wilkinson moved to Nashville in 1976. Nancy married guitar star David Bromberg. Kris became a successful Music Row session musician. Susie kept the band going for a while with various other women, but when she was the only original member left in 1979, she called it quits. By 1987 the banjo picker had picked up button accordion and mandolin and joined songwriter Richard Dobson's State of the Heart country-folk combo. In 1992 the group was chosen to represent Nashville at the world's fair at Seville, Spain.

The Buffalo Gals were rapidly joined by other all-girl bluegrass bands. Bluegrass Liberation was one of the earliest, but The Wildwood Pickers and Sidesaddle got the best reviews. "There is something good to say about everyone," stated *Bluegrass Unlimited* of The Wildwood Pickers' *First Harvest* collection of 1980, and the magazine was still raving when it reviewed the band again four years later. The core of this Chicago group was Mama Cory Koskela (bass) and her daughters Robin (lead vocals), Kim (banjo), and Sue (mandolin). Guitarist Muriel Anderson and fiddler Barb Good rounded out the lineup.

California's Sidesaddle also turned in splendid LPs. This all-female act was formed in 1979 and recorded its LP debut in 1986 with *Saratoga Gap,* which made the national bluegrass Top 10. The follow-up, 1988's *The Girl from the Red Rose Saloon,* featured reworkings of the Kitty Wells classic "She's No Angel" and Buffy-Sainte Marie's "Piney Wood Hills" among its many pleasures. Sidesaddle's core is Sonia Shell (banjo), Lee Anne Welch Caswell (fiddle), and Kim Elking (mandolin). Their instrumental flash was much in evidence on the third album, 1991's *Daylight Train.* In various band configurations these three have been abetted by bassists Karen Quick and Sheila Hogan McCormick and guitarists Jackie Miller and Diana Deininger.

"There are a lot of all-male bands, so why should this be so weird?" says Diana. Adds Sonia, "Sometimes guys will come in and say, 'Gee an all-girl band—and they're all good-lookin', too!' It just makes you want to spit. The other side of that is that we get so much work {because} we're so unique."

Kentucky's New Coon Creek Girls took its name from country's first all-girl string band, The Coon Creek Girls, which starred on the "Renfro Valley Barn Dance" in the thirties and forties. Its namesake was formed at Renfro in

1979. Original Coon Creek Girl founder Lily May Ledford heard the young-sters in 1980 and gave them her blessing to carry the name forward. Bassist Vicki Simmons was The New Coon Creek Girls' founder. Fiddler/guitarist Wanda Barnett joined in 1982, followed by mandolinist/singer Pam Perry and banjoist Annie Kaser. The band graduated from the barn dance in 1983 and became one of bluegrass music's showiest acts.

The female bluegrass revolution of the 1970s took place at almost exactly the same time as the old-time music revival. The string band touring circuit is closely aligned with bluegrass, and several performers are active in both musical settings. Women took an enthusiastic role in the movement to reintroduce and repopularize the sounds of parlor singers, string bands, hoedowns, family harmony, and mountain gospel. And like their bluegrass sisters, they found the "all-girl" band concept appealing. Several such groups were formed by the old-time preserva-tionists, including The Mountain Women's Cooperative Band, Bosom Buddies, The New Harmony Sisterhood Band, and The Reel World String Band.

A surprising number of female old-time revivalists came from the West Coast, not Appalachia. California's "all-girl" Any Old Time string band had a repertoire that incorporated female country chestnuts like "Dear Companion," "Hello Stranger," and "Cowboy Girl," as well as blues tunes. Sue Draheim, Genny Haley, and Kate Brislin were the core of this group. On its 1978 LP they were joined by Susie Rothfield and Valerie Mindel, while on 1981's *Ladies Choice* bassist Barbara Montoro rounded out the all-female lineup. The Delta Sisters, also Californians, were Frannie Leopold and Jeanie McLerie. Their 1981 LP included The Carter Family's "Texas Blues," a pair of Delmore Brothers revivals, and old-timey Cajun selections.

California singer Jane Voss combined feminism with her love of old-time music. Her 1976 collection, *An Album of Songs,* included homages to The Carter Family such as "My Clinch Mountain Home," "Bear Creek Blues," and "The Lover's Return," as well as Molly O'Day's "Too Late." But its most ear-catching number was her forceful, Sara Carter–meets–Gloria Steinem composition "Standing Behind a Man."

Even the name of the California string band The Good Ol' Persons reflected the impact of the women's movement. The group was formed in 1975 as an all-female San Francisco band, but soon evolved into a mixed group. "We thought it would be funny to put together an all-girl bluegrass band . . . and just knock their socks off," recalled founder Kathy Kallick. "We decided to play it really hard and really traditional, so we wouldn't sound like 'girls.' But," she added with a mock sigh, "the band

ALISON BROWN (BANJO)—Alison Krauss & Union Station, also led Michelle Shocked's country band

GLENDA FAYE (KNIPFER) (GUITAR)—The Right Combination, also recorded solo

OLD-TIME MUSIC FEMALE "SIDEMEN"

THE DRY BRANCH FIRE SQUAD (Mary Jo Leet)

HIGHWOODS STRING BAND (Ginny Cleland)

FUZZY MOUNTAIN (Sharon Poss)

HOLLOW ROCK (Bobbi Thompson)

BOOGER HOLE REVIVAL (Pat Epstein, Jan Kazor)

SANDY'S FANCY (Sandy Bradley)

YANKEE INGENUITY (Ruthie Dornfield, Mary Lea)

THE OLD KENTUCKY STRING BAND (Mary Williamson)

HESPERUS (Tina Chancey)

STILLHOUSE REELERS (Brooke Allen)

THE NASHVILLE JUG BAND (Jill Klein)

was infiltrated early on by men." The Good Ol' Persons' disc debut in 1977 featured rusticated versions of songs by everyone from Lefty Frizzell and Don Gibson to Carter Stanley and Merle Watson. Guitarist/singer Kathy Kallick and fiddler Paul Shelasky were the group mainstays. Dorothy Baxter, Barbara Mendelsohn, and future bluegrass star Laurie Lewis rounded out the sound in the 1970s. "It was definitely an oddity," Laurie recalls. "Men loved us because we were a group of girls; women loved us because we were a group of women." By 1980 the lineup was Kallick, Shelasky, dobro player Sally Van Meter, bassist/singer Bethany Raine, and mandolinist John Reischman. They recorded together in 1983 and 1986, increasingly spotlighting Kathy's original tunes

Banjo-picking champion Cathy Fink was another who combined old-time country music with feminism. She was the first old-time musician who researched and presented entire concerts of the music of country's female pioneers. "There are many different definitions of 'women's music,'" says Cathy. "There's a women's music scene that's focused toward women listeners, lesbian listeners, and feminist listeners. . . . The way I fit into all of this is hoping to bring to both the folk and the country scene a sort of reflection on some great [women's] stuff of the past." Cathy's multimedia shows "Women in Traditional Country Music" and "Songs of Working Women" introduced many to the classic sounds of Cousin Emmy, The DeZurick Sisters, The Coon Creek Girls, The Carter Family, and Patsy Montana.

Born in 1953 and raised in suburban Baltimore, Cathy was a folksinger until she attended McGill University in Montreal, where she fell in love with bluegrass and old-time sounds. She formed an old-timey duo with Duck Donald, toured Canada from 1974 through 1979, and recorded three LPs that demonstrated their fondness for hillbilly golden oldies. "We went about the task of learning every old-time duet that had ever come out," Cathy recalls. "We had a repertoire of five or six hundred old-time duets."

Cathy moved as a solo to Washington, D.C., after the duo broke up. In 1981 she became the first woman to win the West Virginia Old-Time Banjo Contest. "Years ago, I really got a lot of, 'Boy, she's really good *for a girl*.' But I've turned around people's attitudes about that, I think." Between 1980 and 1983 Cathy became active as a Smithsonian instrument demonstrator and old-time revivalist at clubs and festivals and began recording solo LPs. *Doggone My Time* (1982) featured "Coal Mining Woman" and "The Single Partner Waltz" alongside its fondly burnished country oldies. *The Leading Role* (1985) was a concept LP about country women that included "Queen of the Kitchen," "Payday at the Mill," and her feminist-bluegrass theme song "Little Darlin's Not My Name."

"It was very clear to me that in the bluegrass idiom there was very little material that women could sing with a sense of integrity," Cathy points out wryly. In 1984 and 1985 Cathy rounded up Ola Belle Reed, Alice Gerrard, and Patsy Montana to celebrate generations of women in country music at the Smithsonian. "A lot of country is geared to the male point of view," she said. "But this is not being promoted as a feminist event, although it is a feminist concept to highlight women's contributions. . . . We're showing that it's not such a fluke to have women who are good instrumentalists."

Cathy Fink's children's music is perhaps the major contribution of her career. She is the most important female source of kiddie records in country history. Her top-selling *Grandma Slid Down the Mountain* (1984), *I'm Gonna Tell* (1980), and *When the Rain Comes Down* (1987) are considered to be modern classics in this field. The albums contain songs about brushing teeth, breaking sex role stereotypes, counting, doing tongue twisters, and even learning to yodel. "Children's records have more longevity in the commercial marketplace," Cathy points out. "You know, there are new five-year-olds every day."

Cathy Fink, 1987.

Marcy Marxer's LPs *Jump Children* and *Kids All Over the World* of 1986 and 1988 were also widely praised. Bonded by their love of old-time country sounds and after years of working on each other's projects, she and Cathy joined forces in 1986. Marcy was born in Detroit in 1956 and developed her interest in old-time music as a college student in California. After eight years with the all-girl group Bosom Buddies, the guitarist/mandolinist moved to D.C. in 1982 to collaborate with Cathy in the band Rhythm Ranch, as well as in their duo.

Their LP *Cathy Fink & Marcy Marxer* appeared in 1989. In addition to fine versions of Ola Belle Reed's "I've Endured" and newcomer Mary-Chapin Carpenter's "I'm Not Alone Anymore," the record attracted some national attention with Cathy's song "Names," the first country song to address the topic of AIDS. It was written for the Names Quilt, a memorial to those who had died of the disease. Their follow-up CD as a duo was the children's collection *Help Yourself!* (1990). Its fun-filled songs are designed to inspire self-confidence in young children, to help them meet the challenges of growing up. Cathy coproduced the record, a role she has also assumed on albums by The Rude Girls, Critton Hollow String Band, Magpie, Si Kahn, the Children of Selma chorus, and the legendary Patsy Montana. In the early 1990s she and Marcy also started making instructional videos—*Kids Guitar, How to Sing Harmony, Making and Playing Homemade Instruments,* and *Learn to Yodel.* The last was reportedly used by Bette Midler so she could yodel in her film with Lily Tomlin, *Big Business.* Cathy also produced a five-part radio series called "Women in Country Music" for public radio.

In 1988 Cathy decided to do an "all-star" bluegrass women's album with Marcy, Good Ol' Persons alumni Laurie Lewis and Sally Van Meter, and Fiddle Fever's Molly Mason. The result, *Blue Rose,* won rave notices, and the band was chosen to showcase on The Nashville Network's national cable TV program "New Country." "Geraldine and Ruthie Mae," which was about two homeless bag ladies, was a standout track, as was the group's treatment of the female traditional "Careless Love." *Blue Rose* stands as a landmark recording in female-country annals.

"There's a long tradition for what we're doing," pointed out fiddler Laurie Lewis. "We aren't pioneers, but we are carrying on something important." Added organizer Cathy Fink, "It's about time for a record like this, because the last traditional music album by a women's group that is well known was Hazel and Alice, and they broke up at least twelve years ago."

There's no question that Hazel Dickens and Alice Gerrard were an overwhelming influence on many of the young women who were pouring into old-time and bluegrass music during this era. Their partnership, which yielded four LPs between 1967 and 1975, left a legacy of spine-tingling backwoods harmony; sturdy old-time revivals; and resonant, prowoman original songs. After Alice decided to go her own way, Hazel recorded a string of well-received solo LPs for Rounder Records and toured overseas.

In the late 1970s Alice joined the all-girl band movement by forming The Harmony Sisters with former Delta Sisters member Jeanie McLerie and classically trained cellist/violinist Irene Herrman. They issued a pair of LPs that were liberally dosed with Cajun tunes, notably the woman's complaint "Mon Neg' Est Pas Rive" and "La Femme Qui Jouait Aux Cartes," which is about a Cajun gal who prefers a life of drinking, card playing, and smoking cigarettes to her boyfriend. They spiced these with revivals of songs from Cousin Emmy and The Carter Family, as well as with Alice's working-girl portraits "Sky over Michigan" and "Payday at the Mill."

Alice also recorded in the 1980s with her husband, Mike Seeger, again emphasizing the compelling tunes gleaned from country music's pre–World War II "Golden Age." Since 1987 Alice has been based in

North Carolina as the publisher of the quarterly *Old Time Herald* and as a performer in an all-girl combo called The Herald Angels with Gail Gillespie and Hilary Dirlam.

Alice Gerrard is probably as well known for her old-time fiddling, guitar, and banjo-playing skills as she is as a singer/songwriter. The old-time revival included many other women instrumentalists. New York's Backwoods Band brought fiddler Susie Rothfield to the fore; Tennessee's Hit and Miss Folk Dance Band had banjo-pickin'-gal Patty Hall and singer/guitarist Judy Eron; Colorado's City Limits launched Lynn Morris, later the leader of her much-applauded bluegrass band. The unearthly beauty of West Virginia's Trapezoid belongs in part to Lorraine Duisit (mandola, mandolin, bowed psaltery, harp, guitar, vocals) and Freyda Epstein (violin, viola, vocals).

Women poured into this area of music. Many who might have become folkies a decade before found a home in the old-time revival. By 1985 there were more than twenty old-time bands spotlighting women. Fiddler Ramona Jones reemerged because of the movement and brought daughter Alisa to fame as a hammered-dulcimer virtuoso. Both women marketed solo albums. Phyllis Boyens performed coal-mining songs with her father, Nimrod Workman, then stepped out as a Rounder Records soloist and an actress, playing Loretta Lynn's mother in *Coal Miner's Daughter.*

The old-time boom vibrated through all of country's substyles. The male-dominated Cajun/zydeco field got its first female star around this time as Queen Ida (Guillory) rose to fame. The Austin-based Texana Dames are notable for bringing a female slant to Spanish-language Tex-Mex material. Country's western swing tradition got a female boost when the Maryland-based band Cowboy Jazz introduced the talents of fiddler Denise Carlson, pianist/singer Deanna Bogart, and guitarist/singer Kate Bennett. "The two words we hate the most are 'chick singers,'" said Kate. The most positive response I get is from other women, who are so excited to see women playing music onstage." Formed in 1979, Cowboy Jazz became a Rounder Records act in the 1980s, reviving everything from Ella Mae Morse's "Cow-Cow Boogie" and Cindy Walker's "Sugar Moon" to The Davis Sisters' "Rock-a-Bye Boogie," as well as introducing Kate Bennett's original tunes such as "A Cowgirl's Dream." Another repercussion of the old-time boom was renewed interest in buck and clog dancing, partly as a result of such fleet-footed females as Jacky Christian, Beverly Cotton, and "The Grand Ole Opry"'s Margaret Smathers.

Excepting North Carolina's Red Clay Ramblers, the greatest of all the old-time revival bands was probably Ohio's Hotmud Family, which

The Hotmud Family, 1981.

boasted the silver-voiced Suzanne Edmundson as its star attraction. "She is one of the best singers in bluegrass, not best 'girl' singers," declared one reviewer. Bluegrass, yes, but honky-tonk, Appalachian balladry, blues, mountain gospel, folk, and modern country were all easily within her grasp, as well. She was also a gifted multi-instrumentalist.

The Hotmuds were formed in 1970 when Suzanne, husband Dave Edmundson, and banjo picker Rick Good got together to play old-timey tunes. "We were sitting around singing Carter Family songs and thinking about how we're a 'family,' how we all fit together, and trying on different family names," Suzanne recalled. "We looked at our astrological signs and saw earth, fire, and water. We thought, 'What would you get if you mixed all three of those things?' And out came hot mud." The group found instant success in the early seventies around its home area of Dayton/Yellow Springs, Ohio. Many of its early jobs were in elementary schools, talking to kids about American musical history. They also starred in their own local radio show before becoming touring stars on the bluegrass/old-time festival circuit in the mid-1970s. Suzanne shifted from instrument to instrument as she moved more to the fore as the Hotmuds' focus. She plays fiddle, mandolin, autoharp, piano, and banjo, but was most often onstage with guitar as the group began to push her muscular, emotionally gripping alto into the spotlight.

Between 1974 and 1978 the Hotmud Family recorded a string of LPs for Cincinnati's Vetco label that virtually defined the old-time revival. A switch to Chicago's larger Flying Fish label brought greater sonic polish, an increasing emphasis on bluegrass, and the most ecstatic reviews of the band's career. *Live, As We Know It* (1979) and *Meat and Potatoes & Stuff Like That* (1981) garnered national attention with their effortless leaps between styles and dazzling musical finesse. But by 1982 The Hotmud Family was feeling worn and weary, frustrated that after a dozen years of performing it was no better off financially than the day it hit the road. Suzanne and Dave divorced, and the band dissolved around 1983.

Although these movements were never a part of the Nashville music business, both the female bluegrass revolution and the women of the old-time revival left a lasting legacy in commercial country music. One result of the all-girl band activity in bluegrass and old-time music was the reemergence of that tradition in mainstream country music, as well.

From the ranks of The New Coon Creek Girls came Pam Perry and Pam Gadd, the cornerstones of country's Grammy-nominated group Wild Rose. Wild Rose scored sizable hits with "Breaking New Ground" and "Go Down Swinging," and attracted much attention with its flashy "Everything He Touches" video, featuring the band's five women dressed in white and performing in a bright spotlight while beefcake workmen walk around the set.

"This idea that people have that women can't play aggravates me," says Kentucky-born banjoist/singer Pam Gadd (b. 1960). "They're so amazed that a woman can play. A guy came up to us after a show and said, 'You-all are really good. I have to admit, you're a lot better than I thought you would be.' Instantly, deep down, it hurt my feelings. And I thought, 'Well, what the heck is *that* supposed to mean?! You came here with the idea that we wouldn't be any good?' I just went, 'Oh, *really?*' And finally one of the other girls in the band said, 'Thank you.' I thought, 'Yes, just say thank you.' But I really thought, 'How insulting.'"

Comments Ohio-bred guitarist/singer Pam Perry (b. 1960). "There was a time when I tried out for a very well known bluegrass star, and he said, 'You're great. If you were a guy, I'd hire you, but you're a woman.'" Perry thinks a woman player has to be *better* than the average male to get noticed.

The two Pams are up front on stage, but Wild Rose is the brainchild of a multi-instrumental Jill-of-all-strings from Alabama named Wanda Vick. "I've always had the dream of having an all-girl band where we would be artists, not just the band backing the artists," says Wanda (b. 1961). She and Wild Rose's drummer, Pennsylvania native Nancy Given Prout (b. 1960), were members of Porter Wagoner's all-girl "Grand Ole Opry" backing band, The Right Combination. Bassist Kathy Mac, originally from Kentucky (b. 1959), was in an earlier all-female band, too, a Music City nightclub act called Tina Carroll & The Nashville Satins. Wanda recruited the other four for Wild Rose in 1987. At first they were called Miss Behavin'.

"We've had to prove ourselves," says Wanda, "because there just haven't been that many female musicians." Recalls Pam Gadd, "When I started playing banjo [in Kentucky] in 1974, I ran into very few female players. . . . There was Barbara Mandrell, and she was excellent in the entertainment kind of thing she did with the instruments, but as far as girls that picked

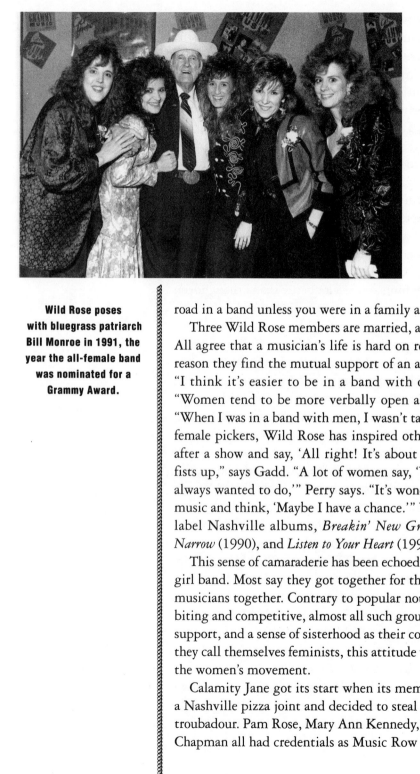

Wild Rose poses with bluegrass patriarch Bill Monroe in 1991, the year the all-female band was nominated for a Grammy Award.

for a living . . . it was unheard of." Pam Perry says she had the same trouble finding role models. "I used to work with The Carter Family. A long time ago Helen told me, 'If Mama Maybelle hadn't played, we never would have learned.' Women back then just didn't do that. You could learn to play the piano, but never learned a string instrument. And you would never travel on the road in a band unless you were in a family act."

Three Wild Rose members are married, and one, Perry, has children. All agree that a musician's life is hard on relationships, and that's one reason they find the mutual support of an all-female group important. "I think it's easier to be in a band with other women," says Perry. "Women tend to be more verbally open about things." Adds Gadd, "When I was in a band with men, I wasn't taken as seriously." Like most female pickers, Wild Rose has inspired other women. "They come up after a show and say, 'All right! It's about time!' and they raise their fists up," says Gadd. "A lot of women say, 'You-all are doing what I've always wanted to do,'" Perry says. "It's wonderful that they look at our music and think, 'Maybe I have a chance.'" Wild Rose has three major-label Nashville albums, *Breakin' New Ground* (1989), *Straight and Narrow* (1990), and *Listen to Your Heart* (1991).

This sense of camaraderie has been echoed by virtually every other all-girl band. Most say they got together for the sheer fun of being female musicians together. Contrary to popular notions that women are back-biting and competitive, almost all such groups cite cooperation, mutual support, and a sense of sisterhood as their cornerstones. Whether or not they call themselves feminists, this attitude was strongly emphasized in the women's movement.

Calamity Jane got its start when its members were drinking beer in a Nashville pizza joint and decided to steal the stage from the resident troubadour. Pam Rose, Mary Ann Kennedy, Mary Fielder, and Marshall Chapman all had credentials as Music Row songwriters, solo artists, or backup singers when they staged their takeover that night in 1981. Marshall wanted to remain independent, so when the act signed with CBS, former Miss Tennessee Linda Moore took her slot. *People* magazine dubbed the act "a hayseed version of The Go-Go's." "We like being women," Linda retorted, "but we're not going to sell sex." Instead, they wanted to live up to their namesake. "Calamity Jane was one of the first women to wear jeans," said Mary. "She drank beer when most women didn't and would sit there with Wild Bill Hickok, whom she was having an affair with. She was willing to be her own woman." The band issued its LP in 1982 and starred in one of country's first concept videos by using western-hero footage in its bluegrassy treatment of The Beatles' "I've Just Seen a Face." Pam and Mary Ann remained a team after the group dissolved, singing backup for Emmylou Harris in the 1980s and making a pop album for Sting's Pangaea label in 1990.

In addition to Wild Rose and Calamity Jane, several all-female bands have become active in country music of the eighties and nineties. These include such popular regional attractions as Baby Blue, Jeannie Wright & Her Western Wonders, and the wittily named Cheap Cologne. In 1992 the durable Roni Stoneman introduced her all-girl band The Daisy Mays.

Ranch Romance, based in Seattle, became a big attraction in the Pacific Northwest as the eighties drew to a close. "It started as a lark," recalls founder Jo Miller, "the all-star cowgirl revue." Jo, fiddler Barbara Lamb, bassist Nancy Katz, and mandolinist Lisa Theo were the core of Ranch Romance in 1987. The band was featured on The Nashville Network in 1988 and issued *Western Dream* on its own label in 1989. Canadian performer k.d. lang invited Ranch Romance to be her opening act later that year, and the band graduated to Sugar Hill Records with 1991's *Blue Blazes*.

The Dixie Chicks, based in Dallas, enjoyed a similarly rapid rise. Organized in 1989, the foursome was named Best Band at the 1990 Telluride Bluegrass Festival and by 1991 was ready with its debut CD, *Thank Heavens for Dale Evans.* The Dixie Chicks are Martie Erwin (fiddle), her sister Emily (banjo), Robin Lynn Macy (guitar, lead vocals), and Laura Lynch (bass). "It's a blast being an all-woman band," says Robin. "I mean, we get dressed together, we squeal together, we talk about 'you-know' together, everything. I just hope that ultimately people will appreciate the music."

Like Wild Rose, The Dixie Chicks and Ranch Romance have moved swiftly beyond bluegrass and old-timey sounds to enter the country mainstream. This is also true of Evangeline. Based in New Orleans, members Kathleen Steiffel, Sharon Leger, Beth McKee, Rhonda Lohmeyer, and Nancy Buchan were discovered playing in a Bourbon

Street bar by country-pop superstar Jimmy Buffett. He signed them to his Margaritaville Records company, issued their debut CD, and took them on the road as his opening act in 1992. Kathleen, Sharon, and Rhonda say they originally formed the group in 1988 after being inspired by Linda Ronstadt, Emmylou Harris, and Dolly Parton's *Trio* LP.

The explosion of females in the bluegrass and old-time fields created an extraordinary number of male-female duet teams who are still active in roots-music circles. Indiana's singing, fiddling, and banjo-playing Brad Leftwich & Linda Higginbotham are the most charmingly rustic of all these duos. Iowa's Nathan Bell & Susan Shore have pride of place for sheer wit, thanks to such hillbilly romps as "He's Been Drunk Ever Since His Wife Went Punk" and "Interstellar Cattle Call." Jeff & Sheri Easter are gospel stars. Georgian Sheri, born in 1963, is a second-generation country-gospel performer—her mother is Polly Lewis Williamson of The Lewis Family. Robin & Linda Williams achieved fame as regulars from 1975 to 1988 on the public-radio series "A Prairie Home Companion." Linda's dramatic, vibrato-laden alto attracted particular attention on the 1984 to 1988 LPs *Nine 'Til Midnight, Close As We Can Get,* and *All Broken Hearts Are the Same,* and the team's songs have been recorded by stars such as Emmylou Harris and Holly Near.

Most such duos of the seventies and eighties were folk revivalists who adopted country music as their style of choice, rather than the music of their childhoods. But at least one popular duo that grew from old-time music roots was steeped in the tradition from birth, The Kendalls. Royce and Floyce Kuykendall were a brother-duet act of the 1940s and 1950s called The Austin Brothers who came by the old-time style firsthand on a farm in Arkansas. When the duo broke up, Floyce became a salesman, and Royce and his wife, Melba, settled in St. Louis to become a barber and a beautician. Their daughter Jeannie was born in 1954.

By the time Jeannie was fifteen she was harmonizing with her father. They recorded a local single in 1969, then went to Nashville to record a country version of John Denver's folk tune "Leaving on a Jet Plane." It became a moderate hit in 1970, as did 1972 versions of the pop songs "Two Divided by Love" and "Everything I Own." Although this was the height of the pop-country, fancy-showroom era, Royce urged a return to a rootsier country sound. Jeannie's springtime-blossoms soprano and his bluegrassy, backwoods harmony moan were ideal on a 1977 remake of the Kitty Wells classic "Making Believe." They were even earthier on a honky-tonking toe-tapper called "Heaven's Just a Sin Away." The old-fashioned cheatin' song became a massive success, earning The Kendalls a Grammy and a CMA award.

In its wake, from 1975 to 1985 they unleashed an inspired string of wailing barroom masterpieces—"It Don't Feel Like Sinnin' to Me," "Pittsburgh Stealers," "You'd Make an Angel Want to Cheat," "Teach Me to Cheat," and "Cheater's Prayer." The Kendalls hit the charts thirty-seven times in all. They revived Dolly Parton's "Put It Off Until Tomorrow," Merle Haggard and Bonnie Owens's "Somewhere Between," and The Louvin Brothers' "My Baby's Gone," and enlisted Emmylou Harris as a third harmony voice on "Precious Love." They scored a dozen Top 10 hits. And in an increasingly sophisticated and complex business, they did it all on their own.

"We've never had a manager; we've done it all ourselves," says Royce. Jeannie says she's always trusted her father's judgment completely. "I don't want anything to do with the business end," she says. "It's still a man's world in the music industry." Music Row sharpies have encouraged the willowy, flaxen-haired Jeannie to go solo, but she "wasn't knocked over by that idea. We really believed in our sound together and thought that was our uniqueness." Their bluegrass-barroom fusion is one of country's catchiest.

The Kendalls, 1979.

Sharon and Cheryl White stuck with their dad, too. Along with Papa Buck, they make up one of the most successful groups to emerge from bluegrass into the country music mainstream. The Whites' female-dominated, family-harmony sound began captivating listeners when the girls were barely in their teens. Today the trio stars on "The Grand Ole Opry."

Buck was born in Oklahoma and raised in Texas in a musical stew of western swing, honky-tonk, gospel, bluegrass, Mexican, and blues, all of which he plays with assurance. He developed into one of country music's greatest honky-tonk pianists and bluegrass mandolinists while serving his apprenticeship in Lone Star State dives. Buck burned out on the honky-tonk life-style and became a pipe fitter in Arkansas, but music beckoned again when his daughters began picking and singing. Buck, his wife, Pat Goza White, and preteens Sharon (b. 1953) and Cheryl (b. 1955) formed The Down Home Folks as a family act in 1966. Sharon became a guitar picker; Cheryl took up bass. They were on the bluegrass festival circuit by 1968, and soon the girls were pressuring their father to jump back into music full-time. Sharon recalls 1971 as "the year that Cheryl and I said to Dad, 'Whenever you're ready, let's put the house up

for sale and go for it.' . . . We moved to Nashville in September 1971."

The Whites made their recording debut as Buck White & The Down Home Folks on County Records in 1972. But *Poor Folks Pleasure,* a 1978 collection on Sugar Hill, was the first to really capture the trio's lovely sunshine-and-wildflowers vocal blend. These early discs showcased the women reworking Jenny Lou Carson's "Jealous Heart," Wilma Lee and Stoney Cooper's "Come Walk with Me," Karla Bonoff's "Home," and other gems. Emmylou Harris discovered their special sound and invited The Whites to tour with her in 1979. Sharon fell in love with Emmy's bandleader, Ricky Skaggs, and married him in 1981. The Whites first made the charts with their revival of the golden oldie "Send Me the Pillow You Dream On" in 1981, and when Skaggs began producing his wife's group the following year, the big hits followed. "You Put the Blue in Me," "Hangin' Around," "Pins and Needles," and the Sharon White–Ricky Skaggs duet "Love Can't Ever Get Better Than This" all became radio favorites from 1982 to 1986. The Whites also had success with female-country tunes such as Jody Miller's "When the New Wears Off of Our Love," Connie Smith's "If It Ain't Love (Let's Leave It Alone)," and Gail Davies's "Hometown Gossip." The act was inducted into the Opry cast in 1984. The Whites switched successfully to gospel with *Doing It by the Book* and its award-winning single/video "It's Not What You Know" in 1988.

To date, only Sharon and Cheryl White have emerged from the female bluegrass revolution to become big mainstream country stars. But among country's less-flashy cousins in the bluegrass world, the revolution has had a profound effect. It is ironic that a style that so militantly opposed female participation is now being revitalized by its female performers. Many believe that women such as Alison Krauss, Claire Lynch, Laurie Lewis, and Rhonda Vincent are the brightest new stars in the bluegrass firmament and are the very future of bluegrass music.

When writers first called Alison Krauss the hottest young female talent in country music, they weren't kidding. Born in 1971 and raised in Illinois, Alison began entering fiddle contests at age eight, joined her first band at eleven, and won her first state fiddle championship at twelve. Rounder Records signed her as an artist when she was fourteen. She starred at the Newport Folk Festival at fifteen, and by sixteen she was fiddle champion in five states and a freshman majoring in voice at the University of Illinois. She placed first in national contests in 1984 and 1986. People were hailing her as "the next big thing" in bluegrass before she even had a driver's license.

"It's very, very strange to hear stuff like that," says the prodigy with the greased-lightning fiddle ability and the shimmering Appalachian vocal delivery. "I kind of feel undeserving. I know all these people—I'm friends with people that can kick my butt as singers and musicians, who haven't been lucky enough to have somebody make a video or whatever." She was, indeed, one of the first to make a bluegrass video, "I've Got That Old Feeling." Alison was the winner of The International Bluegrass Music Association's 1991 Entertainer of the Year award. She also won a Grammy Award that year. She was all of nineteen. By age twenty Alison Krauss had been written up in *Time, Newsweek, Musician, USA Today,* and *Rolling Stone,* an achievement no other bluegrass star of any age in any era can claim.

"Alison is the person who has done most in recent years to raise the profile of bluegrass music in the outside world," says Rounder executive Ken Irwin. Yet "the bluegrass community was slow to appreciate women vocalists. . . . In fact, we still get occasional cards from someone who says, 'Women can't sing bluegrass.'" He recalls that Alison was ready for stardom even as a child. "She was extremely professional. She must have been about thirteen at the time [the label began negotiating], but it was Alison, rather than her parents, that I dealt with each step of the way."

Between 1987 and 1990 she issued her first three albums, *Too Late to Cry, Two Highways,* and *I've Got That Old Feeling.* Folk star Michelle Shocked recruited Alison and her band, Union Station, for her *Arkansas Traveler* CD of 1992, and throughout that year Alison fended off the advances of the major country record labels. "I'm not striving for a hit," she said. "I just want to play bluegrass."

"I don't want people to listen because there's a kid there," she told one interviewer. "I want to be hired because of the sound we make, not because I'm younger than anybody else." To another she defended her style of choice by asserting, "Bluegrass is a killer. It's acoustic rock 'n' roll."

The second female bluegrass superstar-in-the-making might be Claire Lynch. Both solo and as a member of Alabama's Front Porch String Band, Claire has been turning heads for more than a decade. She joined

Alison Krauss, 1991.

The Front Porch String Band in the mid-1970s and married its mandolinist, Larry Lynch. The act issued three LPs and Claire's solo album on small regional labels between 1977 and 1981 before graduating to the bluegrass big time with *Lines and Traces* and *The Front Porch String Band* in 1990 and 1991 on Rebel Records.

Claire's expressive, bell-clear bluegrass voice has begun to attract attention in Music City. She has been commuting to Nashville from Alabama to sing backup on records by stars such as Patty Loveless, Skip Ewing, and Emmylou Harris. Patty recorded Claire's song "Some Morning Soon," and Kathy Mattea has issued Claire's "Hills of Alabam."

Rhonda Vincent is taking the big step toward country stardom by signing with Nashville's Giant Records, having served a long, long apprenticeship in bluegrass. Rhonda's parents, Johnny and Carolyn Vincent, began playing in the 1960s in a Kirksville, Missouri, band they formed with other family members. Rhonda was born in 1962. There was never any question about the girl's destiny. "I don't ever remember having a choice about playing music," Rhonda recalled. "When I got home from school, my grandpa and my dad were there waiting on me. So after school we played, and every night we had people over [to listen]. A lot of times I didn't enjoy it. . . . [But] I'm very thankful for that [experience] now. The audience response is worth it all."

Thanks to her father's rigorous instruction, Rhonda Vincent plays fiddle, mandolin, guitar, dobro, bass, banjo, and drums. She also possesses one of the most powerful voices in bluegrass. When she was five, the family got a local TV program, "The Sally Mountain Show." By 1971, when she was only nine, Rhonda Vincent was already a recording veteran, both as a member of "The Sally Mountain Show" and as the solo singer of Jimmie Rodgers's "Muleskinner Blues" on a single. The other relations dropped out, so Johnny and Carolyn added Rhonda's baby brothers to the band almost as soon as they could walk. "We take our babies off the bottle and put them on bluegrass," said Mama Carolyn. By 1985 Rhonda had recorded eight albums with her family.

Fiddler/singer/songwriter Laurie Lewis is the veteran of today's female bluegrass bandleaders. Born in 1950, Laurie came of age in Berkeley,

California, during the folk revival. She says she "just flipped" when she heard The Dillards in 1965 and became a bluegrass convert. She joined her first bluegrass band as a bass player for the Phantoms of the Opry in 1973, then became the fiddler in The Good Ol' Persons String Band from 1975 to 1977.

"I never thought of it as invading a field or girding my loins for battle," Laurie says. "It was part of the outgrowth of the women's movement for me. I grew up in the Bay Area, and that's always been a center of progressive thinking, [so] it didn't occur to me that there hadn't been bluegrass women in the past. By the time I ran up against any prejudice, I was already a professional." Laurie worked as a sideman for Barbara Dane, The Arkansas Sheiks, Robin Flower, Holly Near, and others and ran a Bay Area violin-repair shop. Her first LP with The Grant Street String Band appeared in 1983. She also portrayed the comedy character Bessie Mae Mucho in The Hot Rize band's goofball spin-off group Red Knuckles & The Trail Blazers.

Laurie issued her first solo LP in 1986. *Restless Rambling Heart* was marketed by Chicago's Flying Fish Records, for whom she also recorded 1989's *Love Chooses You* and 1990's *Singin' My Troubles Away.* The raves poured in for her driving fiddle virtuosity and luminous, yearning vocal presence. More than a dozen national publications perked up their ears to Laurie's extraordinary abilities. Country star Kathy Mattea recorded Laurie's song "Love Chooses You." Patsy Montana recorded "The Cowgirl's Song," and The Cowgirl Hall of Fame selected it as their official theme.

By the middle of 1990 songs by Laurie Lewis & Grant Street, Alison Krauss & Union Station, and Virginia's Lynn Morris Band occupied a third of the Top 25 positions on the national bluegrass chart, proof that the female revolution had succeeded. Laurie was also a participant in two other landmark events of the movement. The first was the all-star, all-girl *Blue Rose* project of 1988. The second was 1991's *Together,* a duo CD with Kathy Kallick, Laurie's old buddy from the Good Ol' Persons. Their reunion ripples with rich feminine harmony and first-rate picking.

Laurie Lewis has endured three decades as a woman in bluegrass music with her grace and wit unblemished. "I'm not planning on an overnight success," she once observed dryly. "I just want to play. . . . Music is a difficult living. I'm probably lucky in a way that I'm in a line of music . . . [with a] loyal, long-term audience." And as for women's position as bluegrass music's most important modern voices: "We respect tradition, but we are no longer singing about 'My Blue Ridge Cabin Home.' We're singing about relationships."

Laurie Lewis, 1992.

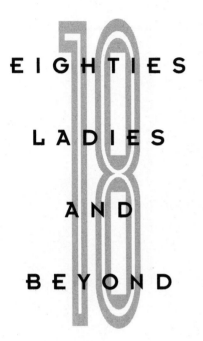

EIGHTIES LADIES AND BEYOND

Images for Our Times

Mary-Chapin Carpenter, 1992.

What is the image of the contemporary country music woman? Is it the homespun calico of the old-time music sweetheart or the fringe and buckskins of the singing cowgirl? Is it the sass of the rockabilly rebel, the cry of the honky-tonk victim, or the sophistication of the Nashville Sound chanteuse? The troubadour literacy of the folkie? The flash and zest of the bluegrassy all-girl band? The sequins of the show queen? The mountain wail of the gospel singer? The stylish hipness of the California country-rocker? The answer is "all of the above." Because for the present, anything goes. With the possible exception of the 1930s there has never been a greater period of experimentation in female country music than the 1980s and 1990s.

Most of the historical images are still in place; new ones are constantly being created, and image has never been more important. During the past ten years, country music has been profoundly influenced by the visual media. The era began in the early eighties with an explosion of country music films. These were not like the quickie singing-cowboy westerns of the forties or Nashville B-movies of the sixties, but were "A" films that played in suburban multiplexes, reaping millions in

profits and sometimes even Oscars—films like *Coal Miner's Daughter* (1980), *Tender Mercies* (1983), and *Sweet Dreams* (1985).

Similarly, country music on weekly TV graduated from formulaic, small-budget syndicated shows to classy network status. Series such as "Austin City Limits" (PBS), "Barbara Mandrell & The Mandrell Sisters" (NBC), "The Dukes of Hazzard" (CBS), and "Dolly!" (ABC) brought country personalities into millions of homes in the eighties.

Even more significant, both for the world of television and for the world of country music, was the development of the cable TV industry. The all-music cable channel MTV was born in 1981; within five years it would revolutionize popular music by creating a new breed of entertainer, the video star. Record companies noted that video exposure sold albums and, eventually, that the promotional clips themselves could be sold.

Nashville saw the handwriting on the wall. By the end of 1981 RCA and CBS were turning out both lip-synched "performance" clips and "concept" video pieces that illustrated songs' plots or moods. Charly McClain ("Sleeping with the Radio On"), Sylvia ("The Matador"), and Lacy J. Dalton ("Hard Times") were among the first with performance clips. The female pioneers in country concept videos were Calamity Jane ("I've Just Seen a Face"), Sylvia ("Snapshot"), and Juice Newton ("Love's Been a Little Bit Hard on Me"). Emmylou Harris broke ground in 1981 with country's first extended-length concept video, a minimovie that combined the innocent "Mr. Sandman" with the bitter "I Don't Have to Crawl."

By 1983 the beautiful Crystal Gayle was leading the way for women with five videos produced; and by 1985 she had ten. She was soon joined by such established hit makers as Dolly Parton ("Potential New Boyfriend"), The Kendalls ("Movin' Train"), Anne Murray ("A Little Good News"), and Janie Fricke ("The First Word in Memory Is Me").

It wasn't long before record companies deduced that the most effective use of the video clip was introducing new talent. In earlier eras it took years to build an image. With videos, a face was immediately connected to a song, making "instant stars" out of musicians. This dramatically accelerated the marketing of country music. The video age also demanded new faces; and this revolutionized a musical style known for its perennial personalities.

The new era officially began in March 1983, when cable television got two all-country channels in the same week. Country Music Television (CMT) came to life, initially via satellite dishes, offering twenty-four-hour-a-day exposure to the handful of country videos then available. The Nashville Network (TNN), a "country life-styles" channel, offered country variety programming, as well as videos. Both channels more than tripled their viewerships by the end of the decade. By 1986 all the major country labels were committed to videos.

What is the impact of this on country music women? If anything, video saturation has revealed their overall intelligence. Today's performers are bright, aware, take-charge ladies with enormous reserves of wit and wisdom. Women like K. T. Oslin, Pam Tillis, and Kathy Mattea are loved as much for their personalities as for their voices, thanks to videos and cable talk show apearances. They project a commonsense kind of smartness as down-to-earth sisters of song.

The Folkies

With this savvy new image in mind, it comes as no surprise that the largest group of country female stars of the eighties and nineties came from folk revival backgrounds, the daughters of Joan Baez and Linda Ronstadt. They've combined country's acoustic instruments, the strong personalities of the folk revivalists, and their own modern sensibilities to create powerfully appealing images. Mary-Chapin Carpenter, Kathy Mattea, Suzy Bogguss, and Wynonna Judd are at the center of this group of new country women. All have become celebrities by reaching to country fans with their heads, as well as their hearts.

Kathy Mattea was the pioneer with this new kind of image. She arrived in Nashville in late 1978 with clearheaded optimism, a strong sense of self, a healthy sense of humor, and a lustrous alto voice. Although she's from a working-class background, grew up in rural West Virginia, and even had an uncle who was a square dancer on the WWVA "Wheeling Jamboree," Kathy was candid about her musical influences—troubadours like Joni Mitchell and Buffy Sainte-Marie.

Kathy is the daughter of a chemical plant worker and his wife. She was raised in Cross Lanes, West Virginia, a tiny dot on the map that is "named for the stoplight; and I'm not kiddin'," Kathy says with a chuckle. Born in 1959, she comes from a large Italian-American clan; her mother delighted in seating her at the living room piano for impromptu recitals as a girl. Inspired by folkies, Kathy picked up the guitar in junior high and started singing in church at folk masses. Following the path of many other folk revival women, she joined a bluegrass group when she went to West Virginia University in 1976. When the act's principal songwriter graduated and moved to Nashville to try his luck, Kathy quit college to accompany him. After less than a year on Music Row, he abandoned music for medical school, but his

In addition, network television in the 1980s offered such made-for-TV successes as *The Gambler, Stand By Your Man, Living Proof, Murder in Music City, Amateur Night at the Dixie Bar & Grill, The Dollmaker, Murder in Coweta County, Country Gold, Burning Rage, The Baron,* and *Smokey Mountain Christmas.*

Kathy Mattea, 1988.

nineteen-year-old partner was made of tougher stuff. Kathy stayed.

Her natural friendliness and outgoing manner won her a job as a tour guide at the Country Music Hall of Fame. "I must've given that tour a million times," she recalls. "But, you know, the more I gave it and the more I listened to classic country music in the museum, the more I liked it." Kathy also took waitress and secretarial jobs during those early years in Music City, but she spent every moment of her off-work time accumulating recording studio experience. She sang jingles and song demo tapes for composers, and Mercury Records signed her in 1983.

Kathy groped for a musical identity and was bombarded with advice on how to dress, how to wear her hair, how to move, and how to act by Music Row's emerging army of image consultants. Her first album, *Kathy Mattea,* was a mix of styles that included sassy female numbers like "Street Talk," lush ballads such as "Someone Is Falling in Love," and even an evocatively poetic gospel song, "God Ain't No Stained Glass Window." All became moderate radio favorites, and Kathy entered the new country video field with a 1984 clip for "You've Got a Soft Place to Fall" that included discreet footage of her in a bubble bath. Her equally eclectic second LP, 1985's *From My Heart,* didn't significantly advance her reputation. Many critics were still comparing her to Anne Murray.

"The first two albums were, uh, floundering, if you wanna be, like, real specific," Kathy says. "You learn to sing lots of different styles of music, and then one day someone says to you, 'What's your artistic vision?' And you go, 'What?' It takes a while to find yourself." She followed her heart back to the acoustic sounds of her troubadour heroes, back to the simplicity of her Mountain State girlhood, and adopted a casual, folksy image. With *Walk the Way the Wind Blows* in 1986, Kathy Mattea became a star. The album's breakthrough hit was "Love at the Five and Dime," Nanci Griffith's tale of a working-class couple who find romance at Woolworth's. The album also included Kathy's own evocation of her coming of age, "Leaving West Virginia." The contemplative "Life As We Knew It" and "Goin' Gone" solidified her as a chart topper from 1986 to 1988. She won the hearts of truckers and retirees everywhere with "Eighteen Wheels and a Dozen Roses."

Kathy was named the Country Music Association's Female Vocalist of the Year in 1989 and 1990. She collected two gold record awards and scored fifteen Top 10 hits between 1986 and 1991. She knew she'd beaten the odds: "Take any week out of *Billboard* and count the number of women in the Top 10, or the Top 20 or even the Top 45. It's very difficult. There are a lot of radio stations that say, 'I'll play four women's records at a time. I can't add another woman to my playlist until I drop one.' I don't know how much of that is based on research or phone calls or what the public tells them. But I tell you, I know women can sell records. . . . The Judds are doing it right now. So is Emmylou Harris." Despite her ascent into the elite, Kathy kept her feet on the ground. She remains the most unassuming of Nashville celebrities. You might think of the words "winsome" or "good-humored" when you describe her, but not "starlike." You're still more likely to find her in a songwriter club than in a four-star restaurant. She lives in a modest old home, not a mansion, and she'd rather have a good guitar than a Mercedes. Kathy is country music's "star next door."

"What I find is that when people stop me and want to talk to me, it's not so much about this 'pedestal' thing as it is something just on a real human level. Someone wants to . . . say, 'I've got to tell you, this song meant so much to me because this is what I was going through when I heard it.' . . . One of the things about it is, the songs that I've had real success with haven't been 'ditties.' They've been songs that have made people feel emotions."

As she matured, Kathy gained the confidence to tackle lyrics, subjects, and styles that most Nashville acts avoided as too challenging or chancy. "You've gotta sing like you don't need the money," she sang in "Come from the Heart." In 1990 she sang "Where've You Been," which explored the lifelong devotion of a salesman and his wife, ending with their final meeting in a nursing home. With its offbeat subject and string-quartet arrangement the record was pretty left-field for country music, but it won her a Grammy and stacks of honors for its cowriter, Jon Vezner. Kathy and Jon were married on Valentine's Day 1988. The success of "Where've You Been" led to a whole album's worth of adventuresome material. *Time Passes By* (1991) included everything from the kooky biker-baby saga "Harley" to a stark portrait of a bowery bum called "Quarter Moon." Kathy's live shows are a collage, as well, incorporating Odetta's field-hand holler "Timber" and Colleen

Peterson's jazzy, tongue-tripping "You're Not the Only One."

She faced a career crisis in 1992 when a burst blood vessel in her vocal cords forced Kathy into surgery and silence. But Kathy has the grit to pull through such difficulties. "'Strong-willed' is *definitely* a word that has been used to describe me," she once told an interviewer. "I'm not fierce about feminism, but I am firm about being a strong person. So many people think feminism means giving up things that make men and women different and interesting to each other. I don't think that's so. . . . I had my parents always telling me that I could do anything. So I didn't get socialized to think that men could do things that women couldn't do."

Kathy Mattea led a parade of folk revival women onto the country charts. They were more urban and more educated than many of their predecessors, reflecting the changes in the working class itself, but their road to success was no easier. Texas tunesmith Nanci Griffith struggled for years making her own small-label albums, touring the folk circuit as a woman alone, and standing firm against the commercial pressures of the music business.

Born in 1954, Nanci was raised in an artsy, educated environment. Her father was a textbook and magazine publisher; her mother worked in real estate. Nanci took her first steps toward the life of a wandering minstrel when she picked up guitar at age six. She was captivated by the folksinging of sixties revivalists Carolyn Hester and Odetta, as well as by the lyrics and image of Loretta Lynn. "Loretta was the first person that inspired me that I didn't have to play other people's songs, that I could write my own dadgum songs and play my own rhythm guitar," Nanci recalled. "Her songs were little incredibly vivid stories that hit their subjects right on the nail's head.

"I started playing in honky-tonks when I was fourteen. I dearly love playing in bars, rowdy places. . . . I've always had to be aggressive. I didn't have a booking agent. . . . I toured constantly and did all my own business. . . . On the road, I think I'm a fairly intimidating person. Promoters don't cuss around me or do that sort of thing." Nanci's quiet Texas drawl, doelike eyes, and willowy brunet looks mask a strong-willed woman with a clear sense of self. "There's a lot of the schoolmistress in me," she once observed. Nanci's degree from the University of Texas is in education, and she initially taught kindergarten by day while playing the beer halls at night. Eventually she realized "there wasn't a whole lot of difference between dealing with a room full of kindergartners and a barroom full of drunks." At age twenty-one she married Texas folksinger Eric Taylor, but she divorced him and became a full-time musician in

1980. With two homemade LPs to her credit (from 1978 and 1982), she attracted national attention among folk fans with her penetrating, bell-like soprano, easygoing showmanship, and remarkable lyrics. Festival and club appearances paved the way for her 1984 Rounder Records LP *Once in a Blue Moon,* her first Nashville record. *The Last of the True Believers* (1985) introduced Kathy Mattea's later Number 1 hits "Love at the Five and Dime" and "Goin' Gone." To Nanci's surprise, the big-time MCA label offered her a country contract when she moved to Music City. The label marketed her sound as "folkabilly." Seven singles made the country charts. Her striking video of "I Knew Love" hit Number 3 on Country Music Television (CMT) in 1988.

By the middle of that year Nanci had three albums in the country music Top 10 in England, including the chart-topping *Little Love Affairs.* In the United States, MCA issued her version of Julie Gold's peace anthem "From a Distance," which Nanci included on both *Lone Star State of Mind* and *One Fair Summer Evening.* Unfortunately, country radio stations treated the yearning plea for international brotherhood as though it were a Christmas song, severely limiting its U.S. airplay. But Nanci's disc became a Number 1 hit in Ireland in 1989, beginning the song's remarkable journey around the world. She recorded German, Spanish, French, and Italian renditions of "From a Distance," and it hit the charts everywhere from Israel to England. In 1990 pop star Bette Midler made it a Number 1 U.S. hit and won it a Grammy Award.

Nanci remains her own businesswoman. She publishes Julie's international song phenomenon, as well as her own compositions. Evangeline, Bruce Springsteen, Willie Nelson, and Emmylou Harris have recorded her "Gulf Coast Highway." Suzy Bogguss turned her "Outbound Plane" into a hit.

Nanci Griffith poses on record album jackets with books by Eudora Welty, Thomas Wolfe, and Carson McCullers, and her own songs are populated by characters who seem to spring from short-story pages. "Salt-of-the-earth" folks, they have tender hearts, tough souls, and hard-working hands. "Portraying people who have resilience is important," she says. "'It's a Hard Life Wherever You Go,' you know? And unless you are someone who has strength within yourself . . . you don't survive in this world." Nanci Griffith's vivid cast of characters stakes a claim for her as one of the greatest songwriters in country music history.

Nanci had country music intentions but eventually found herself embraced by the pop music world. The opposite happened to Mary-Chapin Carpenter, who had pop intentions but was embraced by country music. This Washington, D.C., folk troubadour (b. 1958) candidly admitted she knew little about the country field and expressed amazement when she became a Nashville star. Yet her songwriting clarity, conversational delivery, and down-to-earth manner earned her two gold records, the Top New Female award from the Academy of Country Music, a string of major country hits, and a Grammy between 1989 and 1992.

"I have to be brutally honest and say that mainstream country music is not what I grew up with," says Chapin. "I can't look someone straight in the eye and claim it as my heritage. It is one of the things I like, but I like pop music, too. I do have my heart in acoustic music. What I feel most comfortable describing myself as is an acoustic musician with pop and country influences. . . . But I don't feel uncomfortable being called 'country.'"

She is the daughter of a *Life* magazine staffer and spent her childhood in Princeton, New Jersey; Tokyo, Japan; and Washington, D.C. Chapin was an introspective child who spent hours listening to Judy Collins records, teaching herself to play along on guitar. She also liked her mother's LPs by The Weavers. "I was a jock in high school, but otherwise I was a failure. I just sat in my room and played my guitar." She earned a degree in American Civilization from Brown University.

After graduation Chapin worked as a coffeehouse folksinger. She developed an alcohol problem, pulled herself back, then took a job as a grants consultant for an arts organization in D.C. When Chapin resumed her nighttime career, she began introducing audiences to her original songs of lost love, careworn women, lonely travelers, and wistful dreamers. Along the way, she became a local star, and figured she should have a record to sell at her shows. "It was really just going to be a homegrown project to put in my back pocket and sell at gigs. . . . I wasn't looking for" recording fame. Impressed by her sound, CBS offered her a Music Row contract. Thunderstruck, she signed with the company and issued her *Hometown Girl* in 1987. She quit her job in 1989 for the life of a touring musician.

The first LP found favor with college radio stations and music critics. The second, 1989's *State of the Heart,* brought her widespread acceptance with country fans. The combination of her hearty alto voice, taut acoustic-guitar sound, and warmly personal songwriting did the trick. "How Do," Chapin's sly come-on to a new boy in town, hit the country Top 20. Next, the bitter breakup song "Never Had It So Good" crashed into the Top 10, marking her "arrival" as a country star. "My parents . . . were reassured; I'm not sure I am," she said at the time. "I'm keeping my typing skills up and remembering all my computer programming." "Quittin' Time" and "Something of a Dreamer" also emerged from the *State of the Heart* collection as hits, and the nostalgic "This Shirt" became a popular video.

The steady, reserved singer/writer didn't find the transition to stardom smooth. "I'm not witty. It doesn't come easy to talk. It's sometimes hard to go along with the obligations that go along with getting your music heard." The fact that several of the songs on *State of the Heart* dealt with getting dumped by her boyfriend didn't help. "I want to talk about the songs, but I don't want everybody to know that I got 'slam-dunked' or went through 'unscheduled open-heart surgery.' A lot of the tunes came from being involved with someone and it ending badly."

She created a national sensation on the 1990 Country Music Association Awards when she sang the wry "Opening Act." Then "You Win Again" bounded up the charts as the lead-off single to her third album. National TV programs clamored to book her. *Rolling Stone, Elle, The Wall Street Journal,* and *Cosmopolitan* featured her. Raved Ralph Novak in *People,* "One of the virtues of these modern liberated times is that women can—in country music anyway—be sensitive, smart, aggressive and wholesome, all at the same time. . . . You're never sure if you want to buy her a glass of milk or a double bourbon, but a little uncertainty in life never hurt." *Shooting Straight in the Dark* spanned moods from the r&b romp "Right Now" to the contemplative "The Moon and St. Christopher." The album's Grammy-winning Cajun romp "Down at the Twist and Shout" and modern-woman number "Going Out Tonight" stampeded up the country charts in 1991 and 1992 as her career accelerated.

In the summer of 1992 Mary-Chapin Carpenter previewed her fourth album, *Come On Come On,* with the rollicking, good-natured, and downright sexy "I Feel Lucky." The whoop-it-up woman's number became an instant radio favorite and brought down the house at the country Fan Fair celebration. "There's always a dark side, but I was determined to show that I don't take myself that seriously. . . . When I start writing, I just sit down and look inward."

The wittiest entertainer of all these folk-country ladies is Cheryl Wheeler, who won a Capitol contract in 1990 after issuing three small-label LPs. Cheryl addressed her heavyset, plain-Jane looks by putting retouchers' marks all over her face on her major-label album jacket and calling it *Circles and Arrows.* She made a video of "Estate Sale" and won critical kudos, but failed to captivate the country audience. The New Englander found favor as a writer, however. Dan Seals scored a hit with her "Addicted," and Suzy Bogguss did the same with Cheryl's song "Aces."

Golden-voiced Texas folkie Katy Moffatt has also flirted with country stardom. She hit the charts in 1976 with "I Can Almost See Houston from Here," did some sterling work on the soundtrack of the 1981 movie *Hard Country,* and toured as a backup singer for Tanya Tucker and Lynn Anderson in 1982. In 1983 and 1984 she issued a series of country singles; in 1985 she garnered a Top New Female award nomination, and in 1989 and 1990 she found a niche as a Rounder Records folkie with the albums *Walkin' on the Moon* and *Child Bride.*

Louisiana-bred Lucinda Williams is the daughter of a college professor/poet. She began recording in 1979. She reemerged in 1988 with *Lucinda Williams,* and music mavens fell over one another praising her sweet-sad, throaty-twangy vocals and tough-tender tunes. Country star Patty Loveless did a single and video of Lucinda's "The Night's Too Long," Mary-Chapin Carpenter recorded "Passionate Kisses," and Linda Thompson sang "Abandoned," but the songwriter herself has yet to step into the country limelight. "You just get used to being broke all the time," says Lucinda. "It's a drag, and you get sick of it. [But] I've committed this much of my life, I can't quit now. Once you've already been married and divorced and been through a couple of things and decided you're not gonna settle down and have kids, you just keep on workin' on it. . . . I've played blues bars, country bars, college coffeehouses. I never wanted to be an elitist and be too intellectual. So truck drivers can understand what I'm saying."

Political pop-folk troubadour Michelle Shocked experimented with country with her 1992 CD *Arkansas Traveler.* It included collaborations with Norman & Nancy Blake, Alison Krauss, and The Red Clay Ramblers. The album was self-produced, as is often the case with the work of the folk-gone-country women. Nanci, Mary-Chapin, and Lucinda have also produced their own albums.

Suzy Bogguss has done it her way, too. In addition to coproducing her own albums, she climbed the country music ladder by booking her own shows, selling her own cassettes, and even hanging up her own promotional posters. Her pluck and "can-do" attitude made her one of Nashville's fastest-rising female stars of the early 1990s. She's a self-described "second-generation revivalist" who learned of country's charms by listening to the records of ex-folkies Linda Ronstadt and Emmylou Harris. Suzy's crystalline voice is adaptable to everything from swing tunes to torch songs, but she always earns ovations with her cowgirl yodeling.

Susan Kay Bogguss was born in 1956 in Aleda, Illinois, the kind of Main Street, U.S.A., town where neighbors leave their doors unlocked and children walk safely home from the movies at night. She describes her midwestern childhood with a chuckle as "Colgate toothpaste and

Sunbeam bread." She was a Girl Scout, a high school cheerleader, and a homecoming queen. But she had a solitary side, as well. Suzy is eight years younger than her closest brother. Her machinist father and secretary mother both worked, so she grew up as a "latchkey" kid, taking care of herself until they came home from their jobs thirty-five miles away. Suzy took up guitar and began to sing as a teenager. She majored in art at Illinois State University (and still designs and makes her own jewelry), but she was increasingly drawn to music.

After graduation Suzy headed west on a summer camping trip with some schoolteacher friends. "I took a little amplifier along, and whenever I felt like playing, I'd go in and say, 'Look, why don't you let me perform here tonight for fifty dollars? I'll even go out on the town square today and play for a while and put up signs and stuff like that.' We went all around through Colorado, Wyoming, Montana, Oregon, and California." The friends went home when summer ended. Suzy stayed on the road alone for the next five years, traveling in a camper and protected only by her "guard dog," Duchess, and her "attack cat," Chaucer. There were low points, such as the winter of 1981, which she spent in a Wyoming cabin chopping her own wood, going hungry, and feeling lonely. But that was

Suzy Bogguss, 1989.

also the winter she taught herself to yodel and learned western songs such as "Night Rider's Lament" from a band of ranch hands.

About a year later Suzy began to knock on Nashville's door. "I came down to visit for two days. I had made an album in Peoria, so in the daytime I got a map of the stars' homes and went around and left my album off at everybody's house. Like that was gonna get me a record deal, you know?" she adds with a laugh. "I left one at Loretta's and at Tammy Wynette's and at The Whites' and at Johnny Cash's. Barbara Mandrell's husband even let me in the house. I know it sounds funny, but you just don't know what to do [to crack the music business]." Back on the road she began a program of self-education. "Wherever I was, I'd turn that TNN channel on, and I would watch all these shows, getting a grasp on what a producer was, what a publisher was. It was sorta like watching 'Sesame Street' or something." In late 1984 she felt confident enough to try again. The day after arriving, Suzy landed a job singing in a restaurant near Music Row, sleeping out back in her camper with her pets. Word began to spread about the gleaming voice of this newcomer, and songwriters sought her out to sing their "demo" tapes. One of them, Doug Crider, was totally smitten and began courting her. They married in 1986. In the meantime Suzy landed the headlining slot at Dolly Parton's then-new Dollywood theme park. Capitol Records talent scouts caught her wowing audiences there and picked up a copy of another homemade cassette Suzy was peddling from the stage. The company offered her a contract.

She bowed on the country charts in 1987 with a languid re-creation of the 1941 cabaret chestnut "I Don't Want to Set the World on Fire." In 1988 she revived Patsy Montana's "I Want to Be a Cowboy's Sweetheart," giving country radio its first dose of yodeling in decades. The performances earned her the Academy of Country Music's Top New Female Vocalist award for 1988. Suzy was almost too tired to appreciate the moment: She'd stayed up the whole night before sewing beads on her dress. Her 1989 debut album, *Somewhere Between,* contained the lilting "Cross My Broken Heart," which became her first big hit. She stumbled commercially with her second collection in 1990, but rebounded strongly the following year with the hit-packed *Aces.* Suzy Bogguss versions of Ian Tyson's "Someday Soon," Nanci Griffith's "Outbound Plane," and Cheryl Wheeler's "Aces" all became big radio favorites, as did a melodic duet with Lee Greenwood called "Hopelessly Yours." Suzy's star-making album included her own composition "Yellow River Road," a thrilling exaltation called "Music on the Wind," and the affecting "Letting Go," which tells of a mother's and a daughter's melancholy as the latter packs to leave home for college.

"At Dollywood I got to meet a lot of hard-core country fans and kind of learned what makes them tick," she told the *Chicago Tribune.* "I think I learned what they want, what really makes them happy. Which is real simple, and not something that demographic statistics or anything else can figure out. They just want people who sing to them genuinely. . . . If you can do that, I think they're gonna give you all the love you need to keep you going."

By far the most successful of all the women who came to country after being inspired by the folk revivalists is Wynonna Judd. Both in a spectacularly successful duo with her mother, Naomi, and as a solo star, Wynonna built on the vivid songs and musical warmth of the folk revival. Her inspirations are poetic Joni Mitchell and blues-rocker Bonnie Raitt; Wynonna fused their sensibilities with a country approach to become the most electrifying Nashville singer of her generation.

For many years after Wynonna achieved stardom, her tale was over-shadowed by the remarkable odyssey of Naomi. Mama was born Diana Ellen Judd in 1946. She had mountaineer kin, but was raised in middle-class circumstances in middle-size Ashland, Kentucky, as the daughter of a filling-station owner and his wife. "I was extremely shy," Naomi/Diana recalls. "They always called me 'the china doll' because I was very fragile and had the porcelain skin. And I made straight A's. I wanted to be liked, so I got along with everybody from the cheerleaders to the delinquents." When she was in high school, her older brother, Brian, was diagnosed with cancer, which apparently tore the family apart. Papa Glen Judd turned to alcohol, and after Brian's death he and Polly Judd divorced. Naomi got pregnant and married high school sweetheart Mike Ciminella. She had daughter Christina Claire Ciminella, later Wynonna, the week before high school graduation in 1964.

After Mike finished college, the Ciminellas moved to Los Angeles. A second daughter, Ashley, was born there in 1968. Four years later the young couple divorced, leaving the Kentucky beauty alone in the California megalopolis with two young children and few resources. During the next several years Naomi scrambled from job to job, tenaciously surviving and dreaming ever more creative dreams. "It was those seven years in Hollywood that made us realize what we had," Naomi said later. "When we went out there, I thought everybody had an Aunt Zora who had never taken a bath in her life, that everybody knew what a copperhead looked like and how to chop its head off." She may be given to exaggeration, but there is little doubt that Naomi's Kentucky accent and down-to-earth values stood out in the psychedelic hippie culture then prevalent on the West Coast.

She learned astrology, adopted vegetarianism, and managed a health food store. Naomi also took jobs as a receptionist for the pop-soul act The Fifth Dimension, as a shoe model, and as a millionaire's secretary. Through it all, she came to appreciate her Appalachian heritage. To protect her kids from L.A. decadence, Naomi moved to an idyllic mountain home in tiny Morrill, Kentucky. She went to nursing school in nearby Berea from 1975 to 1977.

Wynonna began to play guitar. "I realized there just wasn't anything around and no TV to watch," the junior Judd recalled. "That's when I got into music. I realized it was going to take something that I did to entertain myself. . . . [In L.A.] I was the all-American kid. Hung out with friends . . . ate Ding-Dongs . . . watched 'The Brady Bunch.' . . . Did what all teens do." Wynonna was a moody child, prone to dark clouds of resentment and rebellion. She was not a particularly good student nor an especially popular one, but when she found music, she found meaning. "Music saved my life," she said years later. "I'm just an emotional hurricane. If it wasn't for music, I would have been one screwed-up kid. It gave me focus, it gave me something to do, to put all my energy into." Naomi began harmonizing with her daughter, teaching her old hymns and folk tunes, encouraging her musical development, and exposing her to country culture. While little Ashley played with her dolls, Naomi and Wynonna learned to chop wood, make lye soap, weave on a loom, bake bread, and live without telephone or newspaper. "I wanted them to see a vanishing way of life," Naomi explained.

Berea College is a hotbed of traditional Appalachian arts and music. Naomi started buying folk music, notably the LPs of Hazel and Alice, bluegrass records, the neotraditionalist works of Emmylou Harris, and the performances of the old-time country team The Delmore Brothers. A female duo was born.

Diana petitioned to have her legal name restored to Judd and to change her first name to Naomi to symbolize the rebirth she planned. Daughter Christina decided to become Wynonna. In 1977 they'd moved again, this time to Marin County, north of San Francisco. Naomi finished her nursing degree, appeared in *More American Graffiti* as a Vietnam protester, and got a job as the film's production secretary. During her northern California sojourn, Wynonna broadened her musical diet to include the sounds of Raitt, Ronstadt, The Eagles, and Little Feat. Naomi met some musicians who gave the thirteen-year-old girl her first recording studio experiences.

In 1979 the gypsy Judds moved to Middle Tennessee. Naomi took a nursing job at a hospital south of Nashville and rented a Victorian farmhouse. Within months, Naomi and Wynonna were singing on Ralph Emery's 5:30 A.M. local TV show as a duo he dubbed "The Soap Sisters." "Every now and then one of the kids at school would come up to me and say they'd seen me on TV," Wynonna remembers. "But even after that, it was still, 'Oh, yeah, you're gonna be a star. You and a million others.'" Her classmates hadn't reckoned on Naomi's determination. Convinced that her daughter was more than a little gifted, Mama Judd badgered the music industry during the next two years with steely will, ferocious persistence, and astonishing tenacity. Armed with nothing more than a tape made on a thirty-dollar recorder in her kitchen, her beauty, and her powerful southern-belle charm, Naomi did the nearly impossible. Without a backer, a contact, or an influence peddler, she made Music Row listen. She was propositioned, sexually harassed, insulted, and dismissed, but she refused to give up. She knocked on doors, hustled tapes to strangers, and gently but firmly asserted her daughter's right to a fair hearing. It was 1981, and Nashville was beginning to awake from its pop dream of Vegas glitz and get back in touch with its roots. Emmylou Harris, Ricky Skaggs, The Kendalls, Jeanne Pruett, Vern Gosdin, and The Whites were proving that there was still a market for simpler sounds. Even if there wasn't, Naomi would

Mama Naomi, left, and daughter Wynonna, The Judds, as they do their final concert together in 1991. Wynonna has gone on to solo stardom.

have pursued her romanticized folk vision just the same. When she wasn't at work, she was often in the Country Music Hall of Fame's library, researching old tunes like "The Sweetest Gift," "Cowboy's Sweetheart," and "Tom Dooley."

After nursing the daughter of a record producer, she coaxed him to the farmhouse to listen as she and Wynonna harmonized in the kitchen by the light of an oil lamp. The producer was charmed. The RCA and Curb executives were similarly bedazzled when The Judds next auditioned live in their offices. The two labels teamed up to market the act. Naomi's smoky harmony and Wynonna's fiery lead singing leaped from radio speakers in late 1983, and country listeners were captivated, too. During the next eight years they would make The Judds country's top-selling and most-awarded women.

The sound was a traditional-yet-modern concoction of acoustic guitars, spunky rhythms, cleverly crafted lyrics, and a swooping, bluesy lead voice that could trumpet, coo, shout, sigh, moan, growl, and sass. Wynonna Judd was only nineteen when the hits began, but she was a fully developed stylist of breathtaking range, spectacular emotive ability, and striking originality. The songs often spoke of strong, self-assertive women who insisted on being taken on their own terms. The personalities in "Girls' Night Out" (1985), "Turn It Loose" (1988), "Why Not Me" (1984), "One Man Woman" (1989), "Give a Little Love" (1988), and "One Hundred and Two" (1991) were plainspoken, fun-loving dames with no-nonsense approaches to life and love. Even when they wailed of being wronged in love, The Judds somehow seemed sassy and resilient: "Have Mercy" (1985), "Cry Myself to Sleep" (1986), and "Born to Be Blue" (1990) all have a burning ember of toughness. The mother-daughter duo was also quite effective on chin-up, inspirational material such as "I Know Where I'm Going" (1987) and "Love Can Build a Bridge" (1990). Naomi's idealized rural values shone in such sweetly sentimental lyrics as "Guardian Angels" (1990), "Young Love" (1989), and "Grandpa"(1986).

The videos were stunning, too. The Judds brought a high sense of style to female country music. Their fashionable outfits were sophisticated, individualistic, and hip, yet never excessively glamorous. The duo's visual presentations were also innovative. Their TV special "Across the Heartland" was artfully designed, incorporating baby Judd Ashley's home-movie footage. The Judds issued music's first 3-D home video collection.

In the early days especially, Naomi carried the interviews, dealt with the executives, and did most of the onstage talking. Wynonna was the singer, but Naomi was the show. Mama Judd was youthful, ravishing, flirtatious, and outgoing. Wynonna was chunky, irritable, and sometimes sullen. In early 1986 Mama turned forty, and Daughter was twenty-one. By then they were spatting openly in interviews "like two cats with their tails tied together thrown over a clothesline," as they put it. Interviews became like therapy sessions, with both participants candidly discussing their differences and difficulties. Wynonna resented being told to act like a demure country music lady. Naomi's penchant for melodramatic embellishment and hokum homilies irritated her. But as her career ascended to stratospheric levels, Wy began referring to Naomi as "the world's coolest mom."

"My counselor said I was kind of an emotional battlefield," Wynonna reflected. "There's a lot of sadness and darkness in my life, but yet I see the light. If it wasn't for Mom . . . surrounding me with . . . unconditional love, I would have gone off the deep end and probably turned into the biggest alcoholic or druggie in the world."

Both women were deeply touched by the impact their lives and their music seemed to have on others. Said Naomi, "We want to say to the people, 'You have forever changed us, and I hope you see yourselves in us. Because you made us.' . . . I have been through so much in my life. I've had people die in my arms, I've been divorced, fired, slam-dunked, and shot at. . . . I have crawled over broken glass to get here. . . . The fans validated me." And how. The Judds sold ten million albums and won more than fifty show-business awards, including four Grammys and eight CMA statuettes. In 1989 Naomi married gospel singer Larry Strickland. The following year Wynonna announced her engagement to singer/songwriter Tony King. After a stint as a fashion model, little sister Ashley landed a role on the network TV series "Sisters." Personally and professionally The Judds were on top of the world.

But in 1990 Naomi Judd learned she had a form of chronic hepatitis, a debilitating liver disease that can be fatal. In October of that year the duo held a tearful press conference in the same RCA office where they'd auditioned seven years before. "I have to resign; I have to retire from the music business I love so much," Naomi sobbed. Wynonna cried; the music executives choked up; the reporters blubbered; photographers got misty-eyed. The Judds staged a farewell tour throughout 1991 so that the fans could say good-bye. "We're going to share this with them because we come from them," Naomi said. "I have been a nurse and a secretary and a model and a housewife. . . . I have worked for minimum wage. . . . We came through the ranks. . . . Sometimes I look down and see someone out there who is my age who is maybe a schoolteacher or something, someone who has a dream." Naomi's dream ended in December 1991 at a concert that became a popular home video and cable TV special; proceeds went to the American Liver Foundation.

"The guilt of going on without her overwhelmed me," Wynonna said. "I always felt Mom deserved this more than I did. She worked for it." But when the hour of decision came, Wynonna was ready. "I'm just now learning how to have an identity. I'm twenty-seven years old and just now learning how to walk." She broke her engagement, took up motorcycle riding, and launched her solo career with the million-selling *Wynonna* in 1992. Its steaming mixture of blues, rock, and gospel won her crossover success on the pop album chart, as well as country hits such as "She Is His Only Need" and "I Saw the Light."

The All-Girl Sound

The Judds' harmony blend was one of several that reinvigorated country's "all-girl" tradition. Indeed, one of the hallmarks of the eighties was the proliferation of harmonizing female groups.

Doris King, Diane Williams, Tammy Stephens, and Cindy Nixon formed Belle in 1982 and began doing ad jingles, entertaining at Opryland, singing backup on others' records, and working the nightclub circuit. "A lot of places don't care if you can sing . . . or whatever, as long as you're four women," Tammy recalled. "They just say, 'Give us a pretty picture we can look at.'" The quartet learned to deal with drunk men yelling, "Take it off!" and sleazy promoters who wanted to "touch the merchandise" they were hiring. "We just kept our mind on our record deal," says Doris. "We were workin' toward what we knew was gonna come." With a name change to The Girls Next Door, the quartet made the country charts from 1986 to 1990 by applying their creamy Lennon Sisters–type blend to singles such as "Love Will Get You Through Times with No Money," "Slow Boat to China," and "How 'Bout Us."

Georgia's redheaded Burch Sisters hit the radio airwaves with the feisty "kiss-off" number "Everytime You Go Outside I Hope It Rains (1988)." Ethel & The Shameless Hussies were even sassier, adopting saucy stage characters to sing their risqué 1988 ditties "Last Night I Really Laid Down the Law," "Smokin' in Bed," and "Give Me a Younger Man."

The McCarter Sisters came to Music City from eastern Tennessee. Their mountain harmonies were heard on three major hits of 1988 and 1989, "Timeless and True Love," "The Gift," and "Up and Gone."

The all-girl Chantilly, Comanchi, Evangeline, and Wild Rose bands also specialize in female harmony.

By far the most successful multifemale harmony sound belongs to The Forester Sisters, who achieved fifteen Top 10 radio hits between 1985 and 1992. Kathy, June, Kim, and Christy Forester stand out from the pack because of Kim's ultraresonant, low alto harmony and Kathy's distinctively drawling, behind-the-beat lead vocals. They have also consistently selected intriguingly "different" female lyrics. As *Elle* magazine put it, "The images they've chosen to project, musically and visually, are perfectly post-feminist: ladylike but not passive, strong but not confrontational."

The group's breakthrough was the rhythmic "(That's What You Do) When You're in Love" (1985), in which a woman welcomed her wandering man back home with the suggestion that maybe she'd been slyly slipping around, too. The up-tempo "Leave It Alone" (1989) and the ballad "Old Enough to Know" (1990) were both "I'm-wise-to-you" songs. On the other hand, "Lyin' in His Arms Again" (1987) was a cheating song from the female side of the fence. Also in their hit

repertoire are celebrations of romance ("I Fell in Love Again Last Night") and sexy toe-tappers ("Mama's Never Seen Those Eyes"). Perhaps the quartet's finest moment on disc is "Letter Home" (1988). This brilliant piece of writing by Foresters producer Wendy Waldman conveys the regret and hope of a "high school star" who ran off to marry at eighteen, had kids, and was deserted ("Children and rent—there was no time for tears, just time to carry on"). She sits alone in front of her TV at night and writes her mom for the first time in years: "Work in a place with some other girls, and we're all doin' all right," she tells her. "We raise our kids, and our jeans still fit, and sometimes we go out at night." There is no finer song anywhere about single motherhood.

The Foresters' 1992 album title tune was "I Got a Date," a number about a suddenly single woman who finds herself "back on the market." Feistiest of all the sisters' country-feminist outings is their 1991 hit "Men." The bluesy, tongue-in-cheek song says, "They'll buy you dinner, open the door / Other than that, what are they good for?" and "You can't beat 'em up 'cause they're bigger than you / You can't live with 'em and you just can't shoot 'em. Men." "I don't think any honest woman in the world can say they can't relate with that song," says Christy.

The Foresters are clear-eyed, apple-cheeked country women with sunny dispositions who hail from Lookout Mountain, Georgia, just outside Chattanooga, Tennessee. "We're working-class," says Christy. "Daddy's a farmer, and he's been working a lot for the Chattanooga water company for, like, fifteen years. Mother works in a mill." Kim continues, "In fact, one of our goals was to make enough money to get her out of there." Mama encouraged them to sing gospel songs, and from childhood Kathy, June, Kim, and Christy were "stars" in their tiny mountain hamlet of New Salem. Long a fixture at church socials, they formed a band in 1978 and began playing in clubs.

"The first time I ever sang in a bar, I almost cried," Kim recalls. "I was used to having all the attention focused on us. In church everyone was quiet and listened. This was, get 'em a drink, go to the bathroom, smoke a cigarette, talkin'. It was a real culture shock." At the time, June was teaching grade school, Kathy was teaching music, Kim was in college and majoring in anthropology, and Christy was studying sociology. They saved their pennies to make a tape, which caught the ear of Warner Bros. in 1984. Their first single became a major hit, and the Foresters were catapulted overnight from Sunday school to stardom. They were named Top Vocal Group of 1986 by the Academy of Country Music. Then came five years on the road. "Everybody thinks it's so glamorous," Kathy says. "If I had to put it in a pie, I'd say that it would be like five percent glamour and ninety-five percent back-breaking hard road work. But, you know, I have ninety percent fond memories of it." Adds Kathy, "We get along fairly well. When one's having a bad day, the others leave her alone. We take turns doing the interviews by drawing straws." A supportive aunt handles child-care duties on the crowded tour bus.

A gospel album called *All I Need* and a Christmas collection titled *A Christmas Card* have kept the Foresters in touch with their religious music roots. But do not be misled: "Because we grew up singing in church, I think people always think there was no spunk or gumption in us," says Kathy. "We have had so many people that have been shocked when they come to see the show. . . . We're just not afraid to do anything or whatever it takes."

The Country-Rockers and California Girls

The "all-girl" country group is nothing new in country music, but one development of the 1980s is an innovation. That is the unprecedented proliferation of female-fronted bands. North Carolina's Dixiana (lead singer, Cindy Murphy), Wisconsin's Molly & The Heymakers (lead singer Molly Scheer), Arkansas's Grayghost (lead singer Lacey Schaffer), and Minnesota's Live 'n' Kickin' (lead singer Julie Strandemo) are examples of this trend. All arrived as a result of breakthroughs by Baillie & The Boys and Highway 101.

Baillie & The Boys came to country music by way of Pepsi-Cola, Gladys Knight, Ford, The Ramones, Burger King, and the Talking Heads, all of whom hired them as studio singers in New York City. Lead singer Kathie Baillie was raised in Connecticut, and her partners, Michael Bonagura and Alan LeBoeuf, were from New Jersey, but throughout their early career on the East Coast, listeners told them they sounded "country." Kathie married Michael in 1977, and they moved south three years later.

He delivered pizza, worked for a moving company, and waited tables in a restaurant. She taught aerobics classes and worked as a receptionist. Alan soon joined them, and gradually the three began getting work singing backups on records by Anne Murray, Vince Gill, Randy Travis, and others. In 1986 they were signed by RCA. Kathie's ardent, yearning soprano propelled "Oh Heart" into the country Top 10 in 1987, and it was followed by the similarly successful "Wilder Days" and "Long Shot" in 1988. Alan quit, but the act was so defined by Kathie's voice that it sounded just the same.

The bitter 1989 lyric of "She Deserves You" was inspired by her sister's divorce. Although she is particularly effective on heartache material, such as "I Can't Turn the Tide" (1989) and "Fool Such As I" (1990), Kathie's marriage to Michael is apparently a happy one. "Michael and I have a great relationship, as best friends, as husband and wife, and now as mother and father," she says. "I'm not really sure how we get along so well on the road, but we do. Not that we don't argue left and right; we do. But maybe that's what keeps our relationship strong." In 1991 she sang the intensely passionate "Treat Me Like a Stranger," the plea of a woman seeking to inject romance into the secure predictability of her marriage.

The strongest female songwriting, singing, and stage personality fronting a contemporary country band was unquestionably Paulette Carlson, who rode to fame as the voice of the country-rocking Highway 101 from 1987 to 1990. Often dubbed "the Stevie Nicks of country music" because of a husky, smoky vocal quality she shares with the Fleetwood Mac singer, Paulette is a blend of tender and tough. She's all airy femininity and shy-sweetheart charm, but her songs are often as assertive as the works of Loretta Lynn and Dolly Parton.

Born in 1954, Paulette was raised in the farmlands of Minnesota and

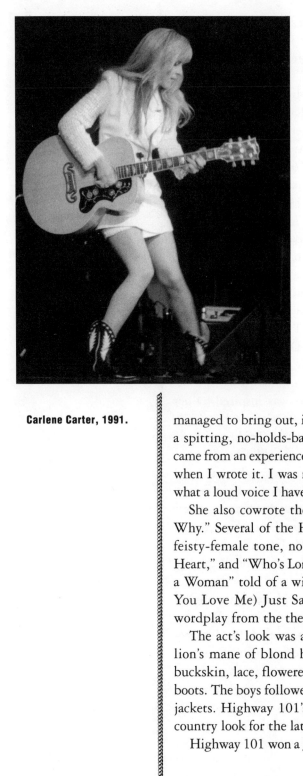

Carlene Carter, 1991.

came of age playing in country bar bands there. She moved to Nashville in 1978 and found work as a staff songwriter for The Oak Ridge Boys' publishing company and as a backup singer for Gail Davies. Paulette hungered for her own recording contract, but her 1983 and 1984 RCA solo singles, "You Gotta Get to My Heart," "I'd Say Yes," and "Can You Fool," all failed.

Dejected and disappointed, she returned north in 1985. "I was not happy. . . . I moved up to a farm in Minnesota to be with my mom. . . . We watched the winter roll in and kinda hibernated." Meanwhile manager Chuck Morris was building a band around her distinctive voice, enlisting California country-rockers Curtis Stone, Cactus Moser, and Jack Daniels. Warner Bros. Records issued Highway 101's single of Paulette's sassy composition "The Bed You Made for Me," and it rocketed into the country Top 10 in early 1987. "That song sort of set the pattern of what we were going to be. . . . It was a strong song. It's an attitude, and that is what we managed to bring out, is the attitude." "The Bed You Made for Me" was a spitting, no-holds-barred performance about infidelity that she says came from an experience with an ex-boyfriend. "I was feeling pretty huffy when I wrote it. I was ready to start swinging." She added, "People say what a loud voice I have. There's no problem . . . singing a sassy song."

She also cowrote the 1988 "leaving-lady" ballad "All the Reasons Why." Several of the Highway 101 tunes she didn't write also had a feisty-female tone, notably 1989's "Setting Me Up," "Honky-Tonk Heart," and "Who's Lonely Now." The 1987 hit "Whiskey If You Were a Woman" told of a wife's battle with her husband's alcoholism. "(Do You Love Me) Just Say Yes" (1988) was a coy, clever tease using wordplay from the then-current Just Say No campaign against drugs.

The act's look was as up to date as its sound. Paulette topped her lion's mane of blond hair with gaucho hats and cavorted in fringed buckskin, lace, flowered vests, denim jeans, prairie skirts, and cowgirl boots. The boys followed suit in snappy western shirts and embroidered jackets. Highway 101's casual-yet-flashy garb virtually defined a new country look for the late 1980s.

Highway 101 won a gold record and was named country's Group of the

Year in 1988, 1989, and 1990. The members began migrating to Nashville, beginning with Paulette's relocation in 1987. In late 1989 she married Alaskan construction engineer Randy Smith, and they had a daughter in 1991. Paulette went solo, and her debut CD, *Love Goes On,* was her sassiest collection of songs yet, featuring such strong female statements as "I'll Start with You," "The Chain Just Broke," and "Not with My Heart You Don't." She coproduced the album and cowrote seven of its ten tunes, making *Love Goes On* her most personal statement to date.

Highway 101 motored onward, recruiting ravishing redhead Nikki Nelson to replace Paulette. Nikki was just twenty-two when she became an instant country-rock princess, but she handled herself with aplomb. She'd been performing since age fourteen in her father's Nevada band, Goldrush, and had been waitressing and tending bar in Nashville since eighteen. She fronted Highway 101 on its spunky 1991 and 1992 hits "Big Bang Boom" and "Baby I'm Missing You," and showed she could handle ballads with "The Blame" and a remake of Tammy Wynette's "Till I Get It Right."

The sass and spunk of Paulette Carlson and Nikki Nelson were echoed by virtually every other frontwoman of this period. Significantly, all of these female-fronted groups performed in country-rock modes. The style became massively popular on the country airwaves in the eighties as California reasserted its country heritage of rowdy energy. Despite the best efforts of Linda Ronstadt and Emmylou Harris, few country-rockers had broken through in the seventies. Now the style came into its own.

The two women who profited most from the trend both grew from Tennessee roots to flower in the California sunshine. They are stepsisters Carlene Carter and Rosanne Cash.

Carlene's return to her Nashville birthplace in 1987 was the return of the prodigal daughter. "I was as wild as a guinea," admits the free-spirited singer/songwriter. She is an heiress of country music's greatest dynasty, but spent ten years and five LPs as the pioneer of a musical hybrid that combined rock's new wave attitude, rockabilly energy, country heart, and power-pop rhythm. Pulsing underneath her rock sass was the most distinguished bloodline in country music. Carlene is the granddaughter of Country Music Hall of Fame member Mother Maybelle Carter. She is the daughter of 1950s honky-tonk hero Carl Smith and Maybelle's daughter June, and her stepfather is Johnny Cash. As a youngster Carlene went along with Aunt Helen, Aunt Anita, Mama June, and Grandma Maybelle when they performed as Mother Maybelle & The Carter Sisters. "I just remember Grandma always having a fantastic sense of humor. She never seemed to get real upset about nothin'. She taught me how to do some of my favorite things—how to fish, how to bowl, how to play poker, and how to play the guitar." Mama June "brought me up to think that I could be anything I want to be, to be real comfortable about being myself."

She was born Rebecca Carlene Smith in 1955. June and Carl Smith divorced when Carlene was two. June married Nashville contractor Rip Nix three years later and wed Johnny Cash when Carlene was twelve. Carlene and her half-sister Rosey Nix joined Cash's daughters Rosanne, Kathy, Tara, and Cindy in the musical Cash-Carter household. Carlene's big number as a kid in the family road show was The Coasters' rock-'n'-roll classic "Charlie Brown." She withdrew from the clan as a teenager, and embarking on a series of ricochet romances, musical experiments, and headline-grabbing escapades, Carlene became one of the most colorful characters in the country-rock pantheon. Carlene quit school and married Joe Simpkins in 1971 at fifteen. "You get married then either because you're stupid or you're pregnant," she once said. "Unfortunately, I was both." Carlene bore daughter Tiffany, got a high school equivalency degree and a divorce, attended Belmont College, and started hanging out with the barhopping Music Row songwriting crowd. She married songwriter Jack Routh at age nineteen and had a son named Jackson. After that marriage went sour, she went on the road singing backup for Cash with half-sister Rosey and stepsister Rosanne. Their big number together was "Silver Threads and Golden Needles." Backstage they bickered jealously.

By the time she was twenty-two, Carlene had divorced a second time, quit college, headed for Los Angeles, and landed a rock recording contract. "When it came time for me to make records, I realized that there weren't any more male Carters. I'm proud of my dad's name, but I really felt more attached to the Carter name, being a female Carter, because it's always been, like, Carter Family women. . . . For so long I didn't realize how much Grandmother had changed things in her own little way. She was the first woman out there picking her guitar and going out on the road with these big ol' boys, and I just think she opened the way for lots of other women to do the same thing."

Carlene blazed a trail, too. Her debut LP, *Carlene Carter* (1978), was recorded in London with the rock band The Rumour. When she returned home from touring with the band, she was a committed rocker, and Nashville's conservative country folks thought she was the most wanton daughter of Dixie they'd ever seen. "They thought I was absolutely nuts. They still do." Carlene recorded *Two Sides to Every*

Woman (1979) with the aid of Doobie Brothers rockers. When she showcased its tunes at the Bottom Line in New York, Carlene boasted to the crowd that her "swingers" number "Swap-Meat Rag" would "put the cunt back into country." She married British rocker Nick Lowe in 1979 and moved to London to plunge into the rock life-style with gusto.

Meanwhile Carlene gained increasing respect as a songwriter. Her compositions were recorded by Emmylou Harris, The Go-Go's, The Doobie Brothers, and others. As a recording artist, Carlene came into her own with 1980's forward-looking *Musical Shapes.* The critically applauded collection was on the frontier of a new fusion between country and alternative rock and was hailed as one of the most adventurous albums of the year. Carlene offered a cluster of her engaging, infectious country-punk compositions, as well as an evocation of her heritage called "Appalachian Eyes." The LP also included a stomping run-through of her mother's famous composition "Ring of Fire," a rocked-up rendition of The Carter Family standard "Foggy Mountain Top," and a duet with rocker Dave Edmunds on the blue-collar love celebration "Baby Ride Easy." *Musical Shapes* was the forerunner of the young-country sound that Nashville would embrace enthusiastically a decade later, but at the time it was a commercial failure. "Basically, I felt like I got my teeth kicked in by country radio and by pop radio, because it was too rock for country and too country for rock. . . . I really loved that record a lot. I kind of got wounded, and I just said, 'Okay, I can't do what I want to do in country, so I'll try to do what I want to do in rock' . . . [but] you can't take the country out of the girl."

As her pop career waned, Carlene's third marriage ended, and she was increasingly debilitated by drugs and alcohol. In 1986 Helen, June, and Anita Carter came to England to sing. Carlene joined them for one performance and wound up staying with the group for two years. "It was at a time when I was really down, musically and emotionally. My marriage had broken up. . . . I had no job. . . . I didn't know what to do. . . . I was frustrated and confused." Being with the Carters gave her an emotional rock to stand on and the support she badly needed. It also put her back in touch with country music. "Being on the road with Helen and Anita and June was the greatest experience of my life. . . . When I worked with them, I got really sort of extra-proud of my roots." The quartet recorded an album called *Wildwood Flower* in 1988.

In 1989 Carlene teamed up with the country-rocking Southern Pacific on a bouncy hit called "Time's Up." It reintroduced her to country fans and paved the way for 1990's hit album *I Fell in Love.* Carlene's light-hearted charm and easygoing sense of humor were showcased in a sprightly, distinctive video of the rockabilly title tune. Both it and its follow-up, "Come On Back," made the Top 10. The poignant "The Sweetest Thing" became her first ballad hit, in 1991. The collection also included a reworking of the 1936 Carter Family classic "My Dixie Darlin'," a version of her dad's 1956 hit "You Are the One," and Carlene's own "Easy from Now On." Her witty personality, telegenic looks, country-hip manner, and acceptability to rock fans led to a 1991 job as the host of a country video show on the VH-1 cable channel.

"Men used to be the focus of my life. I was caught up in that southern-woman idea that once you had your man, then your life was figured out. Then one day it dawned on me that my life is what I make it, not what someone else makes it." The thrice-divorced Carlene calls her pickers The Better-Than-a-Husband Band, "because they don't give me no shit."

The substance that fueled Carlene's wild years went by many names in Music City. She called it "bat food." Studio pickers called it "go fast." Others called it "blow," "toot," "coke," or "crank." It was the stimulant cocaine, and at one point it seemed like half the music industry was snorting the Peruvian powder. Drugs had been part of the country scene ever since it emerged from its innocent infancy after World War II. Everything from morphine to marijuana was available during the honky-tonk era of the forties and fifties. While alcohol was generally the drug of choice, Nashville stars were particularly drawn to prescription amphetamines. These kept them awake during the long overnight drives from town to town in those pre-interstate days. They made all-night recording and songwriting sessions lively with ideas. They chased away the blues when you just didn't feel like smiling for yet another audience on the endless round of one-night stands. The country crowd's pill-popping heyday was the 1960s. The cocaine craze of the late 1970s coincided with the "outlaw" movement and lasted until the "new sobriety" trend of the late 1980s replaced it with "twelve-step" programs.

"Cocaine itself is an insidious drug," observed Rosanne Cash after her recovery. "It's like a snake. It's really awful. My God, the time you waste with drugs. Getting 'em, doing 'em, recovering from 'em." Rosanne, Carlene Carter, Karen Brooks, Tanya Tucker, Marshall Chapman, Lacy J. Dalton, Linda Hargrove, and dozens of other female stars confronted substance abuse.

Drug-induced feelings of energy and creativity were a big part of cocaine's lure. But for Rosanne there was an element of rebellion involved, as well. Born in Memphis in 1955, she is the daughter of the legendary Johnny Cash; he became a star when she was two and was a superstar by the time she was ten. Her mother is Vivian Liberto, an Italian Catholic with strict religious values and a protective nature. The Cashes moved to southern California in 1959, by which time Johnny had a substantial pill-popping habit and a wild reputation. Rosanne and her younger sisters, Tara, Kathy, and Cindy, were raised as Valley Girls while their father was off raising hell. After numerous domestic disputes, Johnny and Vivian divorced when Rosanne was eleven. She became a lonely, angry, moody adolescent, smoking pot by age fourteen and taking psychedelic drugs soon after. As *Village Voice* writer Jan Hoffman once put it, Rosanne was "a champion bad-Catholic-girl troublemaker." Her new stepfather, ironically, worked in law enforcement.

Rosanne Cash, 1986.

"There was no permissiveness whatsoever, so naturally I rebelled," Rosanne said. "Take my word for it, I was mean. I hated my teenage years. Just one massive conflict. I wallpapered my room with demerits. I remember the principal saying, 'It seems that Miss Cash doesn't have much respect for our institution. Why is that?' And I said, 'Well, you don't have much respect for Miss Cash, is why.'"

When Rosanne graduated from high school in 1973, she joined her father's road show as a laundress, then a backup singer. Carlene was emerging as the Carter-Cash clan's next likely superstar in those days. "Carlene and I were very competitive at one time," says Rosanne. "It was damaging to our friendship, and it was unnecessary. It was unfortunate. It was just what happens between young girls, though, who are just starting out." With money from Johnny, Rosanne went to live in London. When he pulled the plug on her partying there, she enrolled at Vanderbilt University in Nashville, then at the Lee Strasberg Theatre Institute in Hollywood. A German record label approached her about making an album. Carlene was dating hot-shot songwriter/producer Rodney Crowell, and Rosanne recruited him to help her begin the project. During her subsequent sojourn in Germany, Rosanne and Rodney became steady pen pals. Rosanne returned to the United States the night of the party for Carlene's debut album. And there she found Rodney waiting for her arrival. Within weeks they were living together, recording together, and doing drugs together. They married in 1979 and moved to Nashville in 1981.

With Rodney as her producer, Rosanne issued her first U.S. LP in 1979. She scored a moderate hit with Karen Brooks's female leaving song "Couldn't Do Nothin' Right," had duet success with Bobby Bare on "No Memories Hangin' Round," and recorded spirited country-rock versions of the feminist calypso oldie "Man Smart, Woman Smarter" and of her father's "Big River." But to the record company's dismay, Rosanne had daughter Caitlin instead of touring to promote her collection *Right or Wrong*.

In 1981 she issued *Seven Year Ache*. The LP's "My Baby Thinks He's a Train" and "Blue Moon with Heartache" became Number 1 hits. So did its sardonic title tune, evidently an indictment of her philandering husband. The album earned a gold record and was hailed as a cornerstone work of the "young-country" movement. Rosanne adopted rock-'n'-roll clothes and dyed her brown hair inky black, eggplant purple, and bright orange in succession. She became "queen of country's hip parade," as one observer quipped. Rodney surrounded his wife's liquid vocals with swirling, contemporary keyboard and electric guitar sounds, making her an influential force in an emerging American music style that fused alternative rock with acoustic country. Writers began referring to her as the leading light of the "new Nashville," a collection of cutting-edge music makers who were breaking down the barriers between country, rock, pop, and folk. Women, in particular, were drawn to Rosanne's confessional writing style and openhearted honesty.

Essentially private by nature, Rosanne found herself thrust into a media whirl of interviews and besieged by curious fans. "That's always been a problem for me. I don't like being recognized, for instance. When I'm in a grocery store or at the post office or something, it makes me feel like I've got something on the back of my dress. It's not a pleasant feeling." Rosanne had always assumed that Rodney would become the major star, and she stated repeatedly that her family and her writing were more important to her than the trappings of country stardom. She resisted the notion that country acts are expected to be close and intimate with their fans. In fact, she wasn't even certain she wanted to be part of the country community. The Beatles and Joni Mitchell were at least as influential to her as her father, and she made no bones about saying so.

Somewhere in the Stars arrived in stores in 1982. As with her previous efforts, there was one openly feminist tune, Susanna Clark's cowritten "Oh

Yes I Can," plus a clutch of radio hits—"Ain't No Money," "I Wonder," and "It Hasn't Happened Yet." With its novel use of special effects, the dreamy "I Wonder" became one of country's first truly creative video clips, and thereafter Rosanne remained a video innovator. She starred in the good-natured fashion parade "I Don't Know Why You Don't Want Me," the back-porch folkie "Tennessee Flat Top Box," the sexy duet with Rodney "It's Such a Small World," and the gorgeous, painterly "What We Really Want," among other memorable videos. Again in 1982 there was no tour: Rosanne had second daughter Chelsea instead.

Despite overwhelming success as a writer for others, Rodney's recording career foundered as his wife's soared. Both were doing a lot of cocaine by this time. She became ever more troubled and ambivalent about stardom and ever more inward-looking, anxious, and self-involved as a writer. Gaunt, mentally scattered, and suffering from low blood pressure, Rosanne was forced into drug treatment in 1984. "I count drug rehab as where my life started," she admitted to interviewer Lucy Kaylin.

"I went through a lot of bullshit and wrote an album about it," she added when the deeply personal *Rhythm & Romance* LP appeared in 1985. Her sunshine-and-shadow personality spoke from its every groove; its lyrics of recovery, adultery, inner pain, female strength, and emotional weakness put her psyche on view. "Just because I make records and write songs, I don't want to throw my private life open for inspection," she argued. "Yet I use songwriting in a real self-indulgent way, as therapy. And once I sing it, I have to live with it. . . . What's particularly hard is that after that part of my life is over with, I look at the song and say, 'I don't feel like that anymore, thank God.' But then I've got to go into an interview and talk about it. . . . I went through it: I got off drugs. I love my life now. I love reality. I'm so glad I did it. And that's really the end of the story."

The *Rhythm & Romance* song "Halfway House" directly addressed her problem. "My Old Man" was a moving tribute to her father, who also went through drug treatment during this period. Her tough-female song on the LP was "Hold On," which won BMI's award as the most-played country song of 1985. When she'd lost at the 1983 Grammy Awards to Juice Newton, Rosanne had turned to her husband and said something like, "I've got my new dress, I've got my new shoes tonight: I don't know why they don't want me." That line became the basis for "I Don't Know Why You Don't Want Me," the *Rhythm & Romance* song that won the 1985 female-country Grammy.

Rosanne returned to the studio and quickly ripped through the creation of 1987's *King's Record Shop,* a stripped-down acoustic disc that is her most overt homage to country music. Four of its singles became Number 1 hits, including a sprightly remake of her father's 1962 hit "Tennessee Flat Top Box." This time, the tough-woman performance was the Rodney Crowell composition "I Don't Have to Crawl." She also included a female hot-rodder number called "Green, Yellow and Red" and a song against domestic violence titled "Rosie Strike Back." Rosanne also took public stands against nuclear power, child abuse, and artistic censorship, and in favor of world peace, music education, and the environment. "It's very simple," she explained. "The truth is, my environmental work is an extension of mothering. It's knowing that I'm going to have grand-children on this planet who may not have clean air and clean water." She bore third daughter Carrie in late 1988. The "It's Such a Small World" duet with Rodney became a Number 1 record, and her *Hits 1979–1989* collection reached the Top 10. Rodney at last broke through to stardom in 1988. Rosanne began to paint and had her first exhibition. Her Acme Pictures video company with Joanne Gardner was enormously suc-cessful, and her songwriting income was soaring.

But by 1990 Rosanne was chafing at the conservative constraints of Nashville and feeling trapped by her country stardom. She hated fans' tour buses' going by her house, disliked the whole idea of Fan Fair, resented playing marketing games with her music, and was feeling restless. Her *Interiors* album (1990) signaled her spiritual malaise. It was her first collection made up entirely of her own compositions. Pop music critics hailed the brooding, richly textured song cycle as her masterwork. Country radio programmers rejected the collection outright. "I don't think that dark questions are necessarily depressing," she protested, "and I don't think that bringing up pain is necessarily depressing. I think it can be really healing. See, women are more in tune with that. To have a good cry is healing to us. And I think there is healing in this record. It's intimate. I think it's hopeful."

In late 1991 Rodney filed for divorce and Rosanne moved to New York City, maintaining a Nashville apartment. The school-aged daughters stayed in Music City, and she and baby Carrie frequently flew back to see them. "I just need some time by myself to sort it all out," she said. The divorce was finalized in the spring of 1992. She and Rodney are still good friends.

That acts such as Rosanne Cash, Carlene Carter, The Judds, and Highway 101 were deeply influenced by West Coast music trends is not insignificant. During the 1980s California reemerged as a country music force. The scene yielded Jan Browne, J. J. White, and Karen Tobin as new female voices, all of whom demonstrated a deep commitment to hard-edged, pure country sounds. Tish Hinojosa and Rosie Flores brought Hispanic heritage to their styles, bringing forward the female Mexican music tradition of Depression-era star Louise Massey. The influential *A Town South of Bakersfield* LPs of 1985 and 1988 showcased L.A. country women Candye Kane, Lucinda Williams, Katy Moffatt, Anne Harvey, Ree Van Vleck, Kathy Robertson, Camille Henry, and Patty Quinn, as well as Flores, Browne, and Tobin.

In 1992 Rosie Flores and Candye Kane were the country representatives on *Cause,* an album sponsored by the Los Angeles–based Rock for Choice movement. Proceeds were earmarked for The Feminist Majority's efforts to retain women's reproductive freedom in an increasingly anti-abortion political climate.

California's renewed country climate was also reflected in films. Such movie stars as Sissy Spacek, Meryl Streep, and Sean Young expressed themselves in country song, and personalities as diverse as Jessica Lange, Debra Winger, Sally Field, Jane Fonda, and Dyan Cannon portrayed country characters on the screen. In addition, TV actresses Rebecca Holden, Kim Grayson, and Susan Anton released records for the country market.

Country singer Lane Brody had success with both film and television themes. Born Eleni Connie Voorlas, she is a singer/songwriter of Greek descent who was raised in Wisconsin. Lane broke into show biz as a Chicago jingle singer before moving to Hollywood. In 1982 she provided the singing voice for Linda Hamilton in the made-for-TV movie *Country Gold* and sang the Emmy-nominated "Just a Little More Love" on the soundtrack of the TV movie *The Gift of Life.* Next, Lane wrote the title tune for the 1983 film *Tough Enough.* But Lane tired of being the singer who everybody heard but nobody knew. "I got so frustrated out there," she says. "My blues roots, my country roots, were never in my L.A. records." She and longtime companion Thom Bresh moved to Music City in 1983. Lane concentrated on Nashville recording, but ironically continued to get her big breaks back in Los Angeles.

A stylist of startling power and versatility, she is capable of arching soprano leaps and of forceful, resonant ballad belting. When producers of the Oscar-winning country movie *Tender Mercies* (1984) needed a female singer for the soundtrack album's "Over You," they called Lane. The song was nominated for an Academy Award and became her biggest solo hit to date. The producers of the TV series "The Yellow Rose" needed a theme singer and called her, too. So Lane wrote new verses to the folk song "The Yellow Rose of Texas" and sang lead in a duet of it with Johnny Lee. It became a Number 1 smash in 1984. The pair's follow-up, "I Could Get Used to This," was even more exciting, featuring Lane raising goose bumps at the finale in ecstatic, clarion soprano shouts. But both acts were dropped by their record companies just as the record was issued. After that debacle she starred and sang on the TV series "Heart of the City" in 1986, toured the world for the Department of Defense in 1990 and 1991, worked up a concert act with Bresh, sang jingles, and marketed records on her own.

As the California country scene regained its vitality, the style began producing odd offshoots. Several bands fused rough-edged rock with raw country emotionalism. They were dubbed "punkabilly" or "cow punk" by journalists. Among those featuring female voices were Lone Justice, The Knitters, and Pearl Harbor & The Explosions. Rubber Rodeo hailed from the Rhode Island School of Design, and the Last Roundup were "Ma and Pa Kettle on Manhattan's Lower-East-Side," as one writer put it. Rachel Sweet forged her punkabilly style in Ohio. Tennessee was home to Susan Marshall and Kristi Rose. The goal of all these women was to bring country's passion to rock audiences. Although none achieved mainstream success, several had a cultural impact. Lone Justice singer Maria McKee introduced "Don't Toss Us Away," which became a Nashville hit for Patty Loveless. The kitschy, fun-filled costuming of Rubber Rodeo's Trish Milliken later turned up in retro-chic outfits sported by Carlene Carter, Pam Tillis, and other stars of the 1990s. Pearl Harbor (Pearl Gates) revived Wanda Jackson's rockabilly classic "Fujiyama Mama," and Rachel Sweet sang rockabilly in the campy teen film *Cry Baby*.

The Rockabillys

Long into the 1980s female musicians were still trying to find a way to integrate the excitement, sexuality, and aggression of rock into their styles. For most, this meant adopting the sex-object images of Madonna, The Go-Go's, or Blondie's Debbie Harry. Just as it had been in the 1950s, rockabilly became an option for women seeking an alternative. This was just as true for women inside the country fold as it was for the "cow punk" rockers.

Becky Hobbs (b. 1950) of Bartlesville, Oklahoma, got her first professional experience as a teenager performing in miniskirts and go-go boots in the all-female rock band Surprise Package. She moved to L.A. in 1973, writing and recording three pop LPs before relocating to Nashville in 1982 to sing material more in keeping with her Okie roots. In Music City she developed a sizzling style that fused hard-hitting honky-tonk songs with an electrifying rockabilly stage presentation showcasing her as a Jerry Lee Lewis–style piano pounder. The blond whirlwind began billing her style as "Rockabecky" and issued an album in Europe by that title. *All Keyed Up,* her album of 1988, featured frisky wailing on the title tune and yielded the hit "Jones on the Jukebox." Becky's "Mama Was a Working Man" and "She Broke Her Promise" were strong, profemale compositions.

"Some of these songs are pretty ballsy little rascals," says the prolific composer. "I think I've touched upon a couple of subjects that as far as I know haven't been written about before." Becky's biggest hit as a singer was a 1983 duet with honky-tonker Moe Bandy, "Let's Get Over Them Together." She has had even more success as a writer. Conway Twitty sings a show-stopping version of her "I Want to Know You Before We Make Love." Shelly West, Lacy J. Dalton, George Jones, and others have also sung Hobbs's works. She is affectionately called "The Beckaroo" on Music Row, and she is quite popular as a performer in Europe and Africa. "A Woman Needs," "Hottest 'Ex' in Texas," "Do You Feel the Same Way Too," and her revivals of classic rockabilly have earned Becky the Swiss sobriquet "Das Energie Bundel."

The California-bred Sweethearts of the Rodeo participated in the female rockabilly revival, as well. Sisters Janis Oliver Gill (b. 1953) and Kristine Oliver Arnold (b. 1955) were middle-class girls of suburban Los Angeles who began singing together when they were nine and eleven. When the sisters were in high school, The Byrds issued the landmark country-rock LP *Sweetheart of the Rodeo,* inspiring the duo's name. Janis began playing guitar, and Kristine began developing her throaty lead-vocal style. Together they planned stardom. In 1980 Janis married future star Vince Gill, and Kristine married guitarist Leonard Arnold. But neither one set aside career for family.

"When we took time out to have children, we tried to have them close to each other so the kids could be with each other while we're working," Kristine says. Adds Janis, "It kind of irks our husbands a little bit because we consult each other before we consult with them. But you have to understand: We fantasized about this for some fifteen years." Both families moved to Nashville in 1983. Sweethearts of the Rodeo won a talent contest and a CBS contract. They bowed on the charts with a remake of The Everly Brothers' "Hey Doll Baby" in 1986 and followed it with a string of Top 10 tunes that were mostly female frolics with zesty rhythms—"Midnight Girl/Sunset Town," "Satisfy You," "Chains of Gold," and "Blue to the Bone."

"We believe in a very modern female, which we are," Kristine told interviewer Sandy Lovejoy. "We're mothers; we're wives; we're working. We do it all, just like the majority of women in the United States do. Therefore, we live a very strong female life-style, and our music reflects this."

Several of their songs were prominently showcased in the 1987 Kim Basinger movie *Nadine,* and the video of "Since I Found You" featured footage from the film. The sisters were video naturals with their hip California looks and the stylish outfits they design and sew themselves. "The way we look is a big part of it," says Kristine. But Janis adds, "I hope that people won't dismiss us as being two pretty faces. I really want to be taken seriously as a musician, as a guitar player, as a song-writer, as a singer." They adopted a particularly sophisticated, high-fashion image in the 1990 video of "You Look at Love That Way." The Sweethearts returned to a friskier style in 1991 with the singles "Hard-Headed Man" and "Devil and Your Deep Blue Eyes."

This rockabilly-as-fashion idea was also part of the appeal of young Kelly Willis of Austin, Texas. As a sixteen-year-old "army brat" in Annandale, Virginia, she auditioned for her boyfriend's rock band singing a Wanda Jackson oldie. A year later Kelly moved to Austin and began wowing the college kids with her aggressive delivery. Singer/songwriter Nanci Griffith alerted MCA Records in Nashville, and the label issued Kelly's debut album when she was twenty-one in 1990. Kelly belted bodaciously in her video of "River of Love," and though *Rolling Stone, The Village Voice,* and the *New York Times* all raved, the tune didn't click with country radio. A sex-kitten-in-a-motel video for "The Heart That Love Forgot" didn't help her second album, despite the album's excellent versions of Joe Ely's "Settle for Love" and Janis Martin's female-rock-abilly classic "Bang Bang." Kelly's most-heard performance to date is probably "Little Honey," which had a prime spot on the soundtrack of the landmark female outlaw/buddy movie *Thelma and Louise* in 1991.

No one embodied the female rockabilly spirit better than Tanya Tucker, who staged a spectacular comeback on the country charts beginning in 1986. Although indisputably a big celebrity, she had few big hits between 1980 and 1983 and was completely absent from the charts in 1984 and 1985. Tanya reemerged in the country Top 10 with the autobiographical-sounding "One Love at a Time," "Just Another Love," and "I'll Come Back as Another Woman." She'd introduce the last in concert by saying, "I'd like to dedicate this to my next ex-boyfriend," which drew a rousing round of laughter from audiences well acquainted with her scarlet reputation.

"If I had done half the things people say I do, I'd be dead," Tanya says with a throaty chuckle. "I'm just a fun-loving girl, a Texas girl." The supermarket tabloids gobbled up her every indiscretion, tracked her cocaine and booze escapades, and reported her rambunctious romantic romps. "It hurt a little at the time," she admits. "But, really, they sustained me and kept my name out there when there weren't any hit records. You know the old saying, 'As long as they spell your name right.'"

Always a hard worker, the former teen star spent her late twenties and early thirties rebuilding her career by racking up an astonishing eighteen Top 10 hits and working up one of country's finest stage shows. Many of her numbers between 1988 and 1992 were kiss-off songs like "If It Don't Come Easy" and "Down to My Last Teardrop." Another favorite song style of hers is the sexy come-on, as in "Call on Me," "My Arms Stay Open All Night," and her smoldering duet with T. Graham Brown "Don't Go Out." In fact, the finest female rockabilly singles of recent years are in these two modes, Tanya's bopping kiss-off "Walking Shoes" and zesty suggestion "If Your Heart Ain't Busy Tonight."

What is a Tanya Tucker song? "I've asked myself that," she answered interviewer Teresa George. "It's just a feel, I guess. When I listen to the song, I have to like what it says. I'm not much on 'poor little me' songs like, 'Oh, baby, you broke my heart.'" Still, her husky, unmistakable alto has been wrapped around some tender tunes—the lovelorn "It's Only Over for You" and "Love Me Like You Used To," the insightful romantic anthem "Strong Enough to Bend," and the farm-crisis statement "Bidding America Goodbye." And despite her tough reputation, Tanya has a vulnerable side. "It's a lonely business, bein' ballsy," she admits. "I don't think I really am that way."

During her late-1980s comeback Tanya pulled back from her on-the-edge life-style, and in 1988 she checked in to the Betty Ford Center for rehabilitation. "It wasn't my decision. I had nothing to do with it. It was a decision that was made for me. A bunch of my friends ganged up on me and said it was time to cut out my wild-livin' ways. They were concerned. I don't know if it was rightfully so or not, 'cause it's my life. But they love me and care about me, and it took a lot of courage on their part to confront me. I still like to go out and have fun, but it's not to the magnitude that it was. And you know what? You can really have a lot of fun straight, too. . . . Going through rehab, you sit there and hear about other people and their life stories, how unloved they were . . . and that's what led them into drugs and drinking and all that. . . . I just liked to have a good time . . . I had more [love] than I needed probably."

Today's new-country converts think of Tanya as one of their stars. Some are only dimly aware of her first career as the sultry, pubescent singer of such "adult" songs as "Would You Lay with Me" and "Delta Dawn" in 1973 and 1974. "I don't know, I feel like I'm part of the old

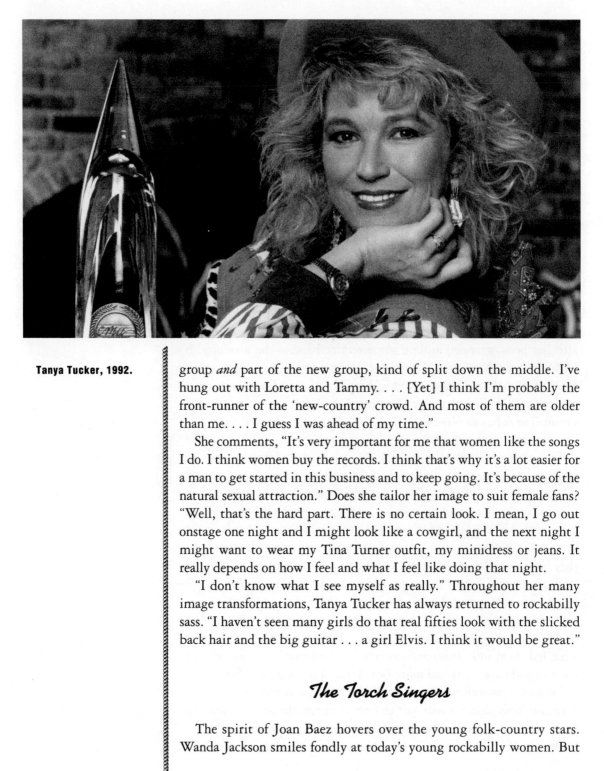

group *and* part of the new group, kind of split down the middle. I've hung out with Loretta and Tammy. . . . [Yet] I think I'm probably the front-runner of the 'new-country' crowd. And most of them are older than me. . . . I guess I was ahead of my time."

She comments, "It's very important for me that women like the songs I do. I think women buy the records. I think that's why it's a lot easier for a man to get started in this business and to keep going. It's because of the natural sexual attraction." Does she tailor her image to suit female fans? "Well, that's the hard part. There is no certain look. I mean, I go out onstage one night and I might look like a cowgirl, and the next night I might want to wear my Tina Turner outfit, my minidress or jeans. It really depends on how I feel and what I feel like doing that night.

"I don't know what I see myself as really." Throughout her many image transformations, Tanya Tucker has always returned to rockabilly sass. "I haven't seen many girls do that real fifties look with the slicked back hair and the big guitar . . . a girl Elvis. I think it would be great."

The Torch Singers

The spirit of Joan Baez hovers over the young folk-country stars. Wanda Jackson smiles fondly at today's young rockabilly women. But no female star of the past tugs stronger at today's stylists than Patsy Cline. Her emotional delivery, nonconformist personality, and pop appeal still fascinate more than thirty years after her death. Her torch tradition has many bearers today.

One of them, Marsha Thornton, made her debt explicit with a 1990 single titled "A Bottle of Wine and Patsy Cline." Another, Reba McEntire, included a Patsy song on each of her first three LPs and repopularized "Sweet Dreams" as a single. Nashville nightclub chanteuse Sharon Haynes re-creates Patsy's looks, singing, costumes, and gestures in a popular theatrical tribute. Rosie Flores sang "Lovin' in Vain," and Mary Miller sang "I Fall to Pieces." Prior to her headline-making affair with country star/sausage king Jimmy Dean, Music City's Donna Meade revived Patsy's "Leavin' on Your Mind" (1988).

And then there was k.d. lang, who believed she was Patsy's reincarnation and named her band "the reclines." When Kathy Dawn Lang first came to Nashville as a tourist, she sought out Patsy's photo on the wall at Tootsie's Orchid Lounge and signed it. The arty Canadian didn't seem to know much about Tammy or Loretta or Dolly. In fact, she was virtually ignorant of every star in country music but one. Patsy.

Actually, k.d. lang couldn't be her idol's reincarnation, no matter how fervently she wished it. Patsy Cline died two years after k.d. was born in 1961. Even though k.d. was raised in the small Alberta farming town of Consort, she didn't grow up a country music fan. Her mother taught school, and her father, who deserted the family when she was twelve, was a pharmacist. The first concert k.d. ever attended was by Anne Murray, but she didn't become seriously interested in country sounds until she was in college. While attending Alberta's Red Deer College in 1982, the classically trained k.d. landed a role in a theater production based on Patsy Cline. To help her prepare, a friend bought her a Patsy album. She flipped, later claiming that she experienced a spiritual communion with the late Nashville Sound queen.

She formed "the reclines," adopted the lowercase spelling of her name, recorded the Canadian LP *A Truly Western Experience,* and became an overnight sensation north of the border in 1984. The disc included Patsy's "Stop Look and Listen," the first of several homages to come. But more to the point were k.d. lang's own tunes, such as "Hanky Panky." They suggested the raucous stage show with which she bowled over audiences in her march from the prairie to stardom. She was a bona fide country kook, cavorting in square-dance dresses, western shirts, and cutoff cowboy boots. With one foot in the honky-tonk and one foot in performance-art bohemia, k.d. shouted while doing a whirling-dervish polka and wailed while doubled over, fetus-style. With her close-cropped hair and sparse makeup, she looked a whole lot more like Buddy Holly than Barbara Mandrell.

After her tourist visit to Nashville in 1986, k.d. got an American recording contract. She returned to Music City to showcase her U.S. LP *Angel with a Lariat* in 1987, and to her surprise she won over the conservative country moguls. Minnie Pearl and Harlan Howard both proclaimed themselves fans, and the rest of the usually reserved Music Row attendees rewarded her with two standing ovations. Her songs are often ironic, sideways-looking, and half-humorous—it isn't every country ditty that has lines about dancing while dodging cow-pies ("Watch Your Step Polka") or being lassoed by a celestial being ("Angel with a Lariat"). In performance she "hit the deck" in the middle of the girlfriend-slugging "Johnny Get Angry," barked loudly during "Damned Old Dog," do-si-do'd with band members during "Turn Me Round," and camped it up with cigarette props on Patsy's torch oldie "Three Cigarettes in an Ashtray." Her vocal pyrotechnics did the rest. Her clear, powerful voice is capable of both full-throttle ferocity and trembling, heart-in-throat tenderness. It is equal parts hillbilly twang, comedic goofing, punk-rock intensity, and torrid blues emoting.

Her eccentric, left-field stage approach shattered all sorts of preconceptions about what a country female should do. "I'm not trying to be different," k.d. said. "I'm just trying to do what I do. This is part of my personality. It's my natural way of doing country music. This is a new form of country music. People are afraid of change." Some were. Her record sold well and her concerts were packed, but few country radio stations played her debut single, a remake of Lynn Anderson's "Rose Garden." Her 1988 duet with Roy Orbison on "Crying" won a Grammy Award, but it never cracked the Top 40. She was named Entertainer of the Year by the Canadian Country Music Association and became a Johnny Carson favorite on "The Tonight Show," yet mainstream U.S. radio men branded her as too wacky, oddball, and, well, *different*. Her 1988 LP *Shadowland* teamed k.d. with the legendary Nashville Sound producer Owen Bradley. Superstars Kitty Wells, Brenda Lee, and Loretta Lynn joined her on it for a "Honky-Tonk Angels' Medley." The album won a gold record, but country radio stations gave its country-classic re-creations "I'm Down to My Last Cigarette" and "Lock, Stock and Teardrops" the cold shoulder. Was she too quirky for heartland America?

Hardly. When k.d. lang appeared at the Fan Fair festival in 1989 she created a sensation among the diehard country traditionalists there. The same scene was repeated whenever she faced country crowds. After a few notes, everybody seemed to forget they were watching a gender bender in a decidedly male brush cut. "I think my persona definitely has caused attention. . . . And I think it's good, because I think a lot of women have felt trapped for a long time, felt the need to conform to the sequined gowns and stuff. I'm aware of how alternative my looks are in comparison with other women. I get flak for it. . . . But what is paradoxical about it to me is that country's always been the vehicle for honesty. I've been like this all my life. I dressed like this when I was five. . . . All of us are constantly in comparison to the perfect model. . . . Look at yourself in the mirror and say, well, 'I'm okay.'"

Her big-as-all-outdoors voice and song-writing talent found their fullest expression in her gold record LP of 1989 *Absolute Torch and Twang.* Her original tunes for the collection were the best country compositions of her career. As always she reinterpreted country chestnuts, notably "Three Days" and "Big Big Love," and as always country radio stations shied away from her sounds while consumers gobbled up the album. *Absolute Torch and Twang* won the 1990 Grammy for Best Female Country Performance of the year. She followed it in mid-1990 with a long-form video called

Canada's k.d. lang, the first openly lesbian country singer, wows the Fan Fair festival attendees in 1988.

Harvest of Seven Years, which also sold well. Her single with the jazz a cappella group Take 6 of "Ridin' the Rails" had just been issued from the *Dick Tracy* soundtrack in the summer of 1990 when a media controversy erupted over k.d.'s "Meat Stinks" TV ad promoting vegetarianism and kindness to animals. "If you knew how meat was made, you'd probably lose your lunch," she said. Even though the ad never aired, cattlemen howled in protest. Stations in beef-producing states announced that they were banning her records, a bogus gesture, since they'd never played them in the first place.

Intriguingly, that flap was much bigger than the mild stir that followed k.d. lang's revelation that she was a lesbian. She was so androgynous-looking that most fans had probably already assumed it. Music Row moguls merely shrugged and said, "So what?" "I think there's a few of my fans who are lesbians, maybe more than a few," said Loretta Lynn in *Coal Miner's Daughter*. "But they're my fans . . . and it don't bother me." Dolly Parton has also embraced her homosexual following. Country music insiders have long whispered among themselves when one of their own is known to be homosexual—indeed, at least eight other important female figures in country history are said to be gay—but no one in country music had spoken publicly about their sexual preference until k.d. gave an interview to *The Advocate* in the summer of 1992. At the time she was on movie screens portraying a half-Eskimo in *Salmonberries*. Her character had a lesbian nude scene, which naturally prompted questioning. She subsequently told the *Boston Globe* that she "came out" because she wanted "to have the issue over with. It's always been an undercurrent, the question of androgyny. I'm a little tired of it and I want people to focus on my music rather than to someday have to be defensive about it in *The National Enquirer* or something." She told *The Advocate* that she didn't want lesbianism to define her. "I feel like it's a part of my life, my sexuality, but . . . it certainly isn't my cause," she said. "There's a lot of straight women at my shows. I am a feminist. I don't care if the women I reach are lesbians or not. . . . I'm offering something that they don't have a lot of: a strong example, something that's geared more to women's feelings."

Ingenue, a collection of pop ballads that she called "postnuclear cabaret," was released in 1992. "I think I have actually drained my country resources for a while," she said. "I don't know if it's forever."

Canada's other major torch singer of the 1990s was Michelle Wright, who broke through with the hits "Take It Like a Man" and "One Time Around" in 1992. The smoky-voiced Toronto star, born in 1961, was raised to sing by her mother, Monica, who was also a performer. Michelle paid her dues en route to Nashville with nine years of road work in pop and country bands and a sustained bout with alcoholism, addressing the latter in the song "As Far as Lonely Goes." Michelle's notable "He Would Be 16" is the meditation of a woman recalling the son she gave up for adoption. In 1993, Michelle read Patsy Cline's letters for the soundtrack of the video documentary "Remembering Patsy."

There is more than a little r&b in Michelle Wright's singing style, which is true of many of the country torch singers of the eighties and nineties. Blind Georgia pianist/singer Terri Gibbs (b. 1954) emerged with her country-soul fusion in 1980 with the sultry "Somebody's Knockin'." Terri had a drawling, bluesy tone that was particularly effective on 1982's "Mis'ry River," "Ashes to Ashes," and "Some Days It Rains All Night Long." She turned to gospel music in 1987, then married and began a family. Gus Hardin was a longtime favorite in Tulsa nightclubs before her discovery by RCA in 1983. Born Carolyn Ann Blankenship in 1945, she had a tough, raspy quality that sounded gripping on "After the Last Goodbye" (1983), "If I Didn't Love You" (1983), and "My Mind Is on You" (1985). But Gus was as rough as her voice. After she reportedly boozed it up and told off one too many influential radio men, the label dropped her. Dana McVicker's blue-eyed soul belting bore the unmistakable stamp of Nashville Sound great Brenda Lee. After becoming quite popular as a song demo singer on Music Row, Dana won a Capitol contract in 1987. But despite compelling efforts like "Call Me a Fool" and "Rock-a-Bye Heart," she didn't strike radio pay dirt and returned to her anonymous studio work.

If heartache is the hallmark of a great country torch diva, diminutive Shelby Lynne has had more than enough for greatness. Her dramatic, demon-possessed alto is the window into a dark soul, and her feisty, ferocious stage attitude is the armor around a battered heart. Shelby Lynn Moorer was raised by country-singing parents in small-town southern Alabama. Her ex-Marine father had a violent streak. When he drank, he beat her mother, as well as Shelby and her little sister. Mama took the girls and left, but Papa kept harassing them. Shelby and her mother sang duets and dreamed of emulating The Judds, but in 1986, when Shelby was seventeen, her father showed up at their home in Mobile. Her mother went outside to talk to him on the driveway. He shot and killed her, then turned the gun on himself.

Shelby was still in therapy when she scorched the country scene with her flamethrower voice a year later. A producer/songwriter wrangled an appearance on cable TV's "Nashville Now," and the next day she had four record-label offers. Shelby is just five foot one and weighs a hundred pounds, but she's a mountain of bitterness, defiance, melancholy, and unadulterated intensity when she sings. Critics groped for adjectives to describe her 1989 LP debut. Shelby was just twenty and going through a divorce when she began doing shows and interviews.

Her rage, suffering, confusion, and hurt leaped from the grooves of such searing performances as "The Hurtin' Side" and "I Love You So Much It Hurts." On tour, opening for Randy Travis, Shelby would start her shows in total darkness singing "I'm So Lonesome I Could Cry." She went for less-is-more charisma, standing with leather-clad legs planted apart to turn "Heartbreak Hotel" and "I Can't Stop Loving You" into infernos of emotion. Although she moves only a little, Shelby somehow conveys an assertive physicality. "I go by the gut," she says, "by instinct, totally."

Reba McEntire became her booster. George Jones selected her as his

duet partner on "If I Could Bottle This Up." Ricky Van Shelton featured her on his TV special. But widespread industry support could not melt her flinty heart. "I do not trust anybody," Shelby says. "It's almost like I'm angry. Sometimes I'll do a TV show or somethin' and then go back and look at it and think, 'God, who's *that?*' I scare myself." She flatly declined the advice of show-biz stylists, coaches, and consultants. She wouldn't wear dresses. She chopped off her hair. She refused to take media-training lessons. She wouldn't kowtow to executives. She spoke her mind. She didn't do slick stage patter at her concerts. She wouldn't smile for the camera. "I don't play games," she says. "I do nothin' but sing. . . . I'm gonna go out there and do my thing . . . and you can like it or you can not like it. I really could care less, because I'm happy at this one time. . . . I just let the feelin's take over."

In the late eighties, Shelby Lynne was the youngest woman signed to a major recording contract in Nashville. At the other end of the spectrum was K.T. Oslin. None of the modern country torch singers reached out to women as directly or as compellingly as this former Broadway chorine. Unlike their counterparts in pop music, dozens of country women have remained stars into middle age. But K.T. is the only one who *began* her hit-making career at age forty-five. She became the inspiration for every middle-aged woman who felt vibrant yet overlooked; who believed she had wisdom, sex appeal, and something to offer; who yearned for recognition of her experience.

K.T. Oslin did it with sass, smarts, and savvy. She charmed audiences with her heart-of-gold manner, self-mocking wisecracks, brassy attitude, keen wit, and joie de vivre. She wrote songs with a sharp eye for emotional truth and a willingness to bend conventions. She had class, but could roar with earthy laughter. Friends dubbed her "diva." She called herself "dirt diva."

Beneath all truly funny people is a recognition of sadness. Kay Toinette Oslin laughs to ease her loneliness. She was born in Crosett, Arkansas, in 1942, and her father died when she was five. She became a shy, withdrawn child as her lab-technician mother raised Kay and her brother in Mobile and Houston. Mama sang swing tunes on local radio.

Kay's tastes ran to Patsy Cline and Kay Starr as a youngster, then to folk music as a college student. She overcame her "loner" personality when she discovered the stage. With radio producer Chuck Jones and songwriter Guy Clark, Kay formed a Houston folk trio in 1962. Her big number at the time was the ageless Appalachian love lyric "Barbara Allen." Then she formed a folk duo with Frank Davis and tested the waters in Hollywood, but their L.A. LP was never issued. Kay put her drama degree to use by joining the *Hello, Dolly!* road company. When the tour ended in 1966, she found herself in Manhattan.

"I got off the bus with my A-line skirt, my matching luggage, my cat, and my perfect hairdo, and winos start spillin' booze on my shoes," she recalls with a laugh. "I thought, 'Girl, what have you *done?!*' Can you imagine how ridiculous I must have looked, standing there in the middle of Greenwich Village in my . . . matching shoes and handbag?" For the next twenty years she soaked up New York sophistication, blending its style and moxie with her down-home, breezy Texas charm. She had small roles in *Promises, Promises,* a revival of *West Side Story,* and other musicals. She sang jingles. She lived spartanly and auditioned a lot. "That pulling-back period is when I started to write. I had to entertain myself some way. I didn't have any money to do anything else, and you can only watch so much television. So I turned to the piano." Inspired by Tanya Tucker's "Delta Dawn," Kay began noodling at the keyboard, teaching herself chord patterns and putting words together. She took a tape to the performance rights organization SESAC. SESAC's Nashville executive Dianne Petty thought it sounded country. Old buddy Guy Clark hired Kay to sing on his 1978 LP, and Petty began circulating Kay's songs around Music Row.

But Petty recalls with some bitterness how difficult it was to get record companies to sign K.T. Oslin to sing her own songs. "It was always, 'Oh, this is great. How old is she?' I understood why they said it, but I still hated it," Petty says. Elektra Records put out "Clean Your Own Tables" and "Younger Men" as "Kay T. Oslin" singles in 1981 and 1982, then dropped her. Kay returned to New York defeated. While she warbled for Sanka, Coca-Cola, and other products, Petty kept pitching in Nashville. In short order K.T.'s tunes were recorded by Gail Davies ("Round the Clock Lovin'"), Sissy Spacek ("Lonely but Only for You"), Dottie West ("Where Is a Woman to Go?"), and The Judds ("Old Pictures"). Meanwhile Kay was getting depressed and gaining weight. She began landing roles in TV ads, playing frumpy housewives. "One day I woke up and said, 'Do I wanna spend my life bein' the Fix-o-Dent lady on a roller coaster, and havin' my head stuck in a john saying I-can-

LIFE AFTER 40

Female performers who
made the national country
charts past age forty:

MAYBELLE CARTER
64
KITTY WELLS
60
BONNIE GUITAR
56
PATTI PAGE
55
MINNIE PEARL
54
LORETTA LYNN
53
DOTTIE WEST
53
SUE THOMPSON
50
JEANNE PRUETT
50
TAMMY WYNETTE*
49
K.T. OSLIN*
49
JAN HOWARD
48
MELBA MONTGOMERY
48
JUNE CARTER
47
CRISTY LANE
47
BILLIE JO SPEARS
47
MARGO SMITH
46
ANNE MURRAY
46
DOLLY PARTON*
46
JEAN SHEPARD
45
SKEETER DAVIS
45
CONNIE FRANCIS
45
NAOMI JUDD
45

see-my-dishes-in-here, and worryin' about ring-around-the-collar and the smell in the house air, and talkin' about cleansers?' I thought, 'Oh, my God: I'm going to die, and the only thing I'll be remembered for is a hemorrhoid commercial. Girl, you have *got* to give this singin' thing one more try.'"

She dropped forty pounds, borrowed seven thousand dollars from a stockbroker aunt, and staged a showcase on Music Row in a last-ditch effort for a record deal. RCA's Joe Galante invited her to lunch. "You wanted to see the old dame in person, didn't you?" she wisecracked. "You know," he said later, "I don't care how old she is. I think she's kinda sexy."

The label introduced her with a yearning remake of the Gus Hardin single "Wall of Tears" that was a modest radio hit in early 1987. But when K.T. Oslin was let loose with her own song "80's Ladies" as her second RCA effort, women throughout America responded. "We've been educated, we got liberated," Kay sang as she summed up the experiences of "girls of the fifties" who lived through rock 'n' roll, children, divorces, and consciousness-raising. "We burned our bras and we burned our dinners." Sung with throbbing conviction and backed with a pounding rhythm track, "80's Ladies" became the anthem of a generation. It sold a million copies and won a Grammy. Its video was honored by the Academy of Country Music as best of the year, and its singer was named Top New Female Vocalist. In 1988 K.T. Oslin became the first female songwriter in history to win Song of the Year from the Country Music Association. She also triumphed as its Female Vocalist of the Year.

"Do Ya," the song of a long-married woman wondering if she still has sex appeal, hit Number 1 in late 1987, followed by the sensuous "I'll Always Come Back." "Hold Me" repeated the theme of the middle-aged couple struggling to keep romance alive. It, too, hit Number 1, and it propelled the album *This Woman* to million-selling status. Both the song and Kay's performance of it were honored with Grammys. "I'm overworked and I'm overweight," Kay sang in another of the *This Woman* singles. "I can't remember when I last had a date." This exploration of loneliness, "Didn't Expect It to Go Down This Way," became her first performance video, allowing millions to see her saucy, graceful stage style. As she vamped across America in concert, Kay dressed in stylish suits and high heels, adopting gloves and fans as trademarks. Her mastery of performance technique is matched by few.

She kicked off her third collection, *Love in a Small Town,* with the wry "Come Next Monday." Its video is one of the most hilarious in the annals of popular music, featuring Kay camping it up as the Bride of

Frankenstein. "Come Next Monday" hit Number 1 in 1990 and brought her her third consecutive million-selling album. She populated the album with lonely people who are too choosy for love ("Mary and Willi"), frisky rednecks ("Cornell Crawford"), and a woman who drinks and remembers ("Still on My Mind"). She turned the rock-'n'-roll oldie "Love Is Strange" into a slow, slinky sashay and tossed off the 1946 chestnut "You Call Everybody Darling" with vaudeville panache.

In 1990 Kay guest-starred on the TV western "Paradise" as a demented backwoods mother who sings "Down in the Valley" as she seeks revenge. She turned her "New Way Home" into a duet with Carol Burnett on the latter's variety series the following year. Her tour of military installations in Latin America for the USO in late 1991 became a Nashville Network cable special in 1992. RCA also marketed *Great Video Hits,* a collection of her popular, personality-packed clips.

"I try to write about things that I understand, so of course I write from a woman's standpoint," said K.T. Oslin to interviewer Janet Williams. "Somebody asked me, 'Why do you always write songs about women?' I said, 'What do you mean? I *am* a woman.' I don't know how a man's mind works. If I did, I'd be a millionaire—I'd sell a tip sheet." She said in *USA Today,* "I like the women in my songs to be strong and straight-ahead." To writer Holly Gleason she added, "While there've always been women singers in country music, they've always been singing songs written by men that reflect the way men *think* women feel. Now you find that people are finally saying, 'Hey, the women songwriters have something to say.' The songs are truly from a woman's point of view."

Music Row Songwriters

K.T. was part of an eighties invasion of female songwriting talent into Nashville. Today virtually every major song publisher in Music City has female staff writers. Some of them double as entertainers; others are strictly tunesmiths who ply their trade in relative anonymity.

At Nashville's Bluebird Cafe, female songwriters have banded together in humorous response to the "Writers in the Round" shows inaugurated by Thom Schuyler, Paul Overstreet, Don Schlitz, and Fred Knobloch. "Women in the Round" shows featured such gifted and quick-witted tunesmiths as Karen Staley, Tricia Walker, Ashley Cleveland, and Pam Tillis in a circle trading quips and songs by turns. Other clubs host all-female songwriter evenings, too. Hit composer

DELIA BELL
45
CONNIE SMITH
44
LACY J. DALTON*
44
EMMYLOU HARRIS*
44
SAMMI SMITH
43
LIZ ANDERSON
43
BARBARA MANDRELL
43
JANIE FRICKE
42
LYNN ANDERSON
42
HELEN CORNELIUS
42
JOY FORD
42
SUSAN RAYE
42
LINDA RONSTADT*
42
CRYSTAL GAYLE*
41
BRENDA LEE*
41
GUS HARDIN
41
WILMA LEE COOPER
40
LEONA WILLIAMS
40

*Still recording for major country music record companies as of 1992.

Wendy Waldman has parlayed her craftsmanship into a position as one of Nashville's few female record producers. Alice Randall translated her songwriting abilities into screenwriting; she is also unusual as a black woman in the country composing field. The most prolific hit composers among Nashville's "80's Ladies" were Susan Longacre, Mary Sharon Rice, Matraca Berg, Nancy Montgomery, Beth Nielsen Chapman, Beckie Foster, Victoria Shaw, and the singing-writing duo Pam Rose and Mary Ann Kennedy.

Of all the nonperforming female composers, none has been more successful than Rhonda Kye Fleming, whose song catalog reads like a contemporary country "greatest-hits" package. Born in 1951, Kye is a native of Fort Smith, Arkansas, who began writing songs at fourteen and performing as a folksinger by her late teens. She moved to Nashville in 1977 and hit pay dirt instantly when song publisher Tom Collins teamed her with former Minnesota farm boy Dennis Morgan. Between 1977 and 1984 they were a hit factory, and Kye blossomed from a fey Joni Mitchell–style folkie into a beaming, self-confident professional. Three of Barbara Mandrell's torchiest ballads were Fleming/Morgan collaborations, "Years," "Love Is Fair," and "The Best of Strangers." Charley Pride's seemingly autobiographical "Roll on Mississippi" was by the team; and Steve Wariner established his youthful, jaunty image with their "Kansas City Lights." Ronnie Milsap sang himself back to his Appalachian roots with their "Smoky Mountain Rain." The sensuous Jim Ed Brown/Helen Cornelius duet "Morning Comes Too Early" was also penned by them. Sylvia's gentle renditions of their "Tumbleweed" led to her style's being dubbed "prairie music."

Fleming and Morgan were named Songwriters of the Year three times in the early 1980s by the Nashville Songwriters Association International. Their "Nobody," recorded by Sylvia, was BMI's most-performed country song of 1983. "Sleeping Single in a Double Bed," sung by Mandrell, was *Billboard*'s Country Song of the Year in 1978, and the same star's "I Was Country When Country Wasn't Cool" was nominated for both Grammy and CMA awards in 1981.

Both writers became wealthy, but creatively restless. Since their parting in 1984, Kye has collaborated with a variety of others, turning out such hits as Michael Johnson's "Give Me Wings" (1987), Willie Nelson's "There You Are" (1989), and Crystal Gayle's "Nobody Wants to Be Alone" (1985). Such stars as The Nitty Gritty Dirt Band, The Judds, Kathy Mattea, Lee Greenwood, Amy Grant, Olivia Newton-John, Charlie Daniels, John Schneider, and Janie Fricke have recorded Kye's recent tunes. In the late 1980s she began a successful collaboration with songwriting legend Janis Ian.

Two major singers emerged from Music Row's song factories of the eighties, Deborah Allen and Holly Dunn. Both women had careers as Nashville songwriters before achieving mass popularity as performers.

Deborah is a former Memphis beauty queen. Born Deborah Lynn Thurmond in 1953, she migrated to Music City at age nineteen. Deborah Allen first starred on disc in 1979 as an ethereal harmony singer with the late Jim Reeves when RCA redid the music behind Reeves's vocals on "Don't Let Me Cross Over," "Oh How I Miss You Tonight," and "Take Me in Your Arms and Hold Me," all of which became Top 10 "duet" hits. By this time Deborah was writing steadily. She met young tunesmith Rafe Van Hoy on Music Row in 1978, and they began collaborating. John Conlee, Lee Greenwood, Janie Fricke, and Tanya Tucker scored big hits with their songs. They married in 1982.

"When people say to me, 'How does it feel to be a female songwriter?' I say, 'Well, I guess not that much different than it does to be a male songwriter,'" Deborah remarks. "There have been people who have tried to organize female writers' nights, and for some people I guess that's good. But for me, that's sort of like having a black Miss America contest. It's obviously setting yourself apart. . . . I think it's a little demeaning for the female population. . . . That's the way I feel about it, and I guess that's why I have such a good reputation with the guys around town, because I don't try to say, 'Look, I'm a girl, and I think I deserve a little extra attention.'"

Deborah is effusive, vivacious, and flirty. And unlike most of her country contemporaries, she was willing to adopt an openly sexual image to appeal to men rather than women. She posed in unclothed Eve-like innocence, holding an apple, on the jacket of her 1980 LP *Trouble in Paradise.* The collection was totally written by Deborah, but it brought her no hits. A subsequent string of country-pop singles for Capitol Records also failed to ignite her solo career. She switched to RCA in 1983 and blasted to the top with "Baby I Lied." The single had a big, booming, wall-of-sound quality, with Deborah wailing soulfully from deep in a sonic cavern. Its thundering, crashing, ear-jolting power attracted considerable pop airplay. "I always say 'Baby I Lied' was a pop record that crossed over into the country chart," she said later. Husband Rafe produced her two Top 10 country follow-ups.

The couple continued to collaborate in crafting her 1984 LP *Let Me Be the First.* From the damply sexual, Deborah-in-bed cover photo to the synthesizer-drenched arrangements, the album served notice that she was ready to step beyond the country marketplace. Deborah marked time in the country field with a rockabilly video for "Rockin' Little Christmas" while asking to be transferred to RCA's pop roster. She resurfaced in 1987, outfitted like Madonna and singing to sassy funk rhythms on *Telepathy*. The LP's title tune was produced and written for her by Prince. But by 1992 she was back with a new country contract.

Holly Dunn served a somewhat longer apprenticeship in the songwriting trenches. She labored on Music Row as a studio singer, demo maker, and publishing staff writer for six years before getting a recording contract, then for two more years before she was allowed to pursue her natural country-folk style. Holly is a preacher's daughter from San Antonio (b. 1957) who attended Abilene Christian College as an advertising/public relations major. Two weeks after her college graduation in 1979 she moved to Nashville, where her older brother, Chris Waters, was already a songwriting professional. "My first real job in the music business was at CBS Songs/April Blackwood. I was just a receptionist—receptionist and sexual harassment victim," she adds with a rueful laugh. Although Dunn is genial and humorous, she also has a cool, gracious poise that borders on primness. "I think I put off an aura of being very nice, but 'Don't mess with me.' I can't really say I've never been discriminated against; there have been a few times when I felt like I wasn't being taken seriously." Holly sang song demos for other writers, gradually assembling a compilation tape of her clear, expressive soprano. Louise Mandrell, Cristy Lane, Marie Osmond, Sylvia, Terri Gibbs, and The Whites recorded her early songs.

MTM Records signed her and issued the mostly glossy, country-pop *Holly Dunn* as her debut album in 1985. "I felt like there was some miscommunication between me and the higher-ups about who I am musically," she recalls. "They saw me mistakenly as a pop person. I really fought hard to get 'Daddy's Hands' to be put out" as a single. Written as a Father's Day gift to her dad, the tune was the only folk thing on the album. After three other songs from the collection failed, the label agreed with her wishes to issue it as a single and video in 1986. It became a smash, vindicating Holly and eventually leading to her coproducing her own albums. Both "Daddy's Hands" and "A Face in the Crowd," her 1987 duet with Michael Martin Murphey, were nominated for Grammys. Holly won the Top New Female Vocalist award from the Academy of Country Music in 1986, the Horizon Award from the Country Music Association in 1987, and the Country Songwriter of the Year award from BMI in 1988.

The last award was in recognition of the long string of hits she'd composed. These include "Love Someone Like Me," "Only When I

Love," and the achingly gorgeous ballads "Strangers Again" and "Someday," all taken from her *Cornerstone* and *Across the Rio Grande* LPs of 1987 and 1988. Emmylou Harris and Dolly Parton were among her harmony singers. Comments Holly, "I looked to Dolly and to people like Emmylou and Gail Davies for being kind of female pioneers" who controlled their own records. "That'd be real flattering if they [other music women] thought of me that way." Holly survived the sinking of the MTM music ship in 1989. She signed with Warner Bros., was honored with "Grand Ole Opry" cast membership, and sailed ahead with more Number 1 hits. But she ran aground on the rocks of controversy when she issued the teasing "Maybe I Mean Yes" in 1991. In it she suggested that love should be "a little hard to get" and that when she says no to an ardent male, perhaps she really doesn't mean it. The song sparked criticism from fans and women's groups who thought its lyrics encouraged date

Holly Dunn, 1990.

rape. Holly didn't see it that way, but rather than capitalize on the brouhaha, she asked that broadcasters withdraw the single. She said her decision "was reached due to the continued misunderstanding of the intent . . . and also my belief that music should be a positive experience." She added that "the subject of rape is an important issue that needs to be discussed, and if my song has served as a vehicle toward that discussion, then perhaps that is the silver lining to this controversy." It was all rather ironic, for Holly Dunn has always been one of Nashville's strongest supporters of women's issues. "I try not to do songs that put women in a bad light," she told *Tennessean* reporter Thomas Goldsmith. "I'm very respectful of women and what we've had to overcome."

"It's a different business for women than it is for men," says Holly Dunn. "A man can 'come out of the box' and sell a million. . . . On the other hand, the changing of the guard with the men is much quicker than it is with the women. . . . We're in the trenches slugging it out year after year. The guys tend to be more flashes."

This became abundantly true at the end of the 1980s when a procession of "country hunks" topped the charts. One good-looking cowboy after another became an overnight million-seller, vastly increasing country's share of the music marketplace and creating a major American entertainment craze. By 1989 the country record market was humming to the tune of five hundred million dollars a year, and during the next two years it would soar to one and a half billion dollars. Clint Black, Garth Brooks, Alan Jackson, Travis Tritt, Billy Ray Cyrus, and dozens of other handsome honky-tonk pin-ups rose to superstardom.

But in Music Row's frenzy to sign and promote these hunks, the women of country music lost almost all the hard-won ground they'd gained during the previous three decades. Between 1981 and 1989 female acts had finally moved beyond having only 10 to 20 percent of a given year's hit records, to occupying 25 to 35 percent of the charts. But in 1990 men muscled them aside and women's share of the charts dived to 12 percent, its lowest level since the early sixties. Perennial favorites such as Crystal Gayle, Emmylou Harris, Barbara Mandrell, Tammy Wynette, and Anne Murray were suddenly struggling for survival. Even Dolly Parton's place in the Top 10 was no longer assured.

The Show Queens

Only one female country performer could compete head-to-head with the men in country record and concert ticket sales during this "hot hunk" period—Reba McEntire. The redheaded diva rose slowly to prominence in the 1980s, fine-tuning her image as she overwhelmed audiences with her bigger-than-life vocal power, highly ornamented phrasing, tear-stained lyrics, and ever more elaborate stage shows. Reba began her Nashville career as a wide-eyed cowgirl innocent; adopted a Patsy Cline heartache style; helped lead country's "new traditionalist" crusade; reemerged as a glamorous show queen; emoted mightily in videos; and became a business empress with her own booking, management, publishing, and transportation companies.

It was quite a journey, one that demanded unshakable self-confidence and ambition. The trip began in the backseat of a 1960s sedan as her parents drove from rodeo to rodeo out west. To keep her children occupied during the long hauls, Jackie McEntire taught them to sing harmonies. Reba, born in 1955, was raised to hoist feed sacks and ride herd just like her dad and older brother, Pake. Home was a 7,100-acre cattle ranch ten miles south of Kiowa, Oklahoma, population 754. Father Clark McEntire was a three-time world's-champion calf roper; Grandpa John was a national rodeo celebrity; Pake eventually went on the circuit, and so did sisters Alice, Reba, and Susie. Tomboy Reba was hardheaded and competitive like her father, but Mama Jackie's artistic influence prevailed. Deeply impressed by the style of Patsy Cline, Jackie was a good enough singer herself to have been a professional. Reba has often said that she is living out her mother's dream. By the time she was in high school, the kids had formed The Singing McEntires and won every talent contest around. In 1971 they made a locally distributed tribute record to their famous granddad called "The Ballad of John McEntire," and in 1974 Reba was invited to sing the national anthem at the National Rodeo Finals in Oklahoma City. Country star Red Steagall heard her, and afterward at a party the nineteen-year-old impressed him with her rendition of Dolly Parton's "Joshua."

Steagall invited Reba and her mother to Music City and financed a demonstration recording session. Mercury Records was looking for a new female act and signed Reba in late 1975. She recorded "I Don't Want to Be a One Night Stand" in early 1976, then went home to Oklahoma. Burly national bulldogging (steer wrestling) champion Charlie Battles was courting her. The rodeo star was ten years her senior and divorced with two sons. Reba married him that June, and they spent their honeymoon competing in rodeos and visiting country stations to promote her single. It went nowhere, and Reba finished college to get a teaching certificate. Her Nashville recording sessions continued, resulting in two more dud singles in 1977 and an album that introduced what became her early-career trademark, a revival of a Patsy Cline number ("Why Can't He Be You"). In 1979 the melodically curvy "Runaway Heart" provided Reba with her first real vocal showcase, and her Patsy Cline remake "Sweet Dreams" became her first Top 20 hit. Along with the assertive Maria Muldaur/Peggy Lee favorite "I'm a Woman," they became the centerpieces of her second LP. Reba finally hit the Top 10 with "(You Lift Me) Up to Heaven" in 1980 and "Today All Over Again" in 1981. Her third LP had "A Poor Man's Roses" as her Patsy tribute.

She was slowly making progress, but these were frustrating days.

Reba McEntire, 1991.

"There's lots of times when I would get aggravated and disgusted, still out of money and still overdrawn. Once after everything screwed up at a show I got back in the van and said, 'Oh, that just makes me so mad, I can hardly stand it.' And my cousin said, 'Why don't you quit?' I said, 'That's the stupidest thing I've ever heard in my life. I'll *never* quit.' And it just dawned on me then, 'Well, Reba, quit gripin', quit bitchin', and go *do* it. You know you want to.'"

Reba McEntire came to maturity on the LPs *Feel the Fire* (1980), *Heart to Heart* (1981), and *Unlimited* (1982). She has a remarkable voice that is like a bird in flight, swooping, gliding, and fluttering through melodies, decorating them with tiny "cries," octave leaps, and bent sustains. It can ache with desire, murmur tenderness, or spit anger. Reba sings with a heart-in-throat intensity that brings conviction to even the most mundane love lyrics. But her golden voice, fresh-faced looks, and howdy-neighbor personality were just about all she had going for her at first. "I didn't know absolutely *anything* when I came to Nashville," she says. "I didn't know what the music business was like. All I'd ever been associated with was ranchin' and rodeoin'." Gazing at the succession of LP jackets from then is like looking at a photo gallery of cookie-cutter country starlets. Make her hair redder. Give her a permanent. Lay on the eye makeup. Put her in a silk chemise. Dress her in sequined evening gowns. Give her the soft-focus, romantic look. Pile her tresses on top of her head. Tease 'em up. Let 'em fall. The first thing she did with her Number 1 hit-making status was take charge.

"Let's put it this way: I've sorta taken my career into control myself," she said. "I don't want to be a puppet anymore." She signed with MCA Records and issued the intense affirmation of blue-collar devotion "Just a Little Love" and the vaulting declaration of freedom "He Broke Your Memory Last Night" in 1984. Then came the LP *My Kind of Country,* which put her in the forefront of Nashville's back-to-basics rejuvenation. The album contained the oldies of Connie Smith, Ray Price, Carl Smith, and Faron Young, as well as her Number 1 hits "How Blue" and "Somebody Should Leave." It won her the Female Vocalist of the Year honor at the CMA awards of 1984. Reba sobbed as the audience stood in ovation. She said, "When me and my mama first came to town, she told me, 'Reba, I couldn't do this, so I'm livin' my dreams through you.'" Raising the statuette, she added, "This is for me and my mama."

Reba wore the CMA Female Vocalist crown three more years in succession, more than anyone in history. She was invited to join "The Grand Ole Opry" cast and won a Grammy. The accolades spurred her into a rigorous campaign to upgrade her stage show, become an actress, and expand her horizons. In 1986 Reba was named country's Entertainer of the Year and began collecting a string of gold and platinum record awards for her increasing sales achievements. She conquered New York with a triumphant appearance at Carnegie Hall and entered the music video era by enacting a hurt and suspicious housewife in "Whoever's in New England" (1986). Since then, she has portrayed a suburban widow in "What Am I Gonna Do About You," a glamorous chanteuse singing Jo Stafford's "Sunday Kind of Love," and an inspiring waitress/wife/mother who goes back to school to get her degree in "Is There Life Out There." She showcased her cowgirl skills in the video for "You Lie." She emoted effectively as Bobbi Gentry's prostitute-gone-uptown in "Fancy," and in re-creating Vicki Lawrence's murderess in "The Night the Lights Went Out in Georgia." The videos led to roles in the feature *Tremors,* the TV movie *The Gambler IV,* and the soap opera "One Life to Live."

"I want to take charge," she said. "I'm always greedy. I want to do more. I've never been content with my life. . . . I'm very competitive, very ambitious. Who don't like to win? You show me a person who don't like to win." More than any of her contemporaries, Reba McEntire seems consumed by her music, her career, her showmanship, her image, her audience, her profession. In 1987 she divorced Charlie Battles. She moved to Nashville from her Oklahoma ranch; fired her manager; took over total control of her career; started coproducing her albums; and opened her own office, incorporating a song publishing firm, booking agency, management company, fan-club organization, and private-jet leasing business. "The way I look at it now, it's 'Let's kick this into high gear.' Now we can do this and that. It's great momentum. . . . It's just something to do constantly in the music business. It's a 24-hour, 365-day-a-year job." Reba had blossomed from a green Okie hick into a savvy, hard-nosed businesswoman. "The lesson I learned . . . is not a good one," she confessed. "It was not to trust anybody. Take care of yourself. . . . The hard times . . . made me stronger, more independent." The "new" Reba found a new man. Her former-steel-guitarist-turned-road-manager, Narvel Blackstock, got a divorce shortly after she did. They married in 1989 and had baby son Shelby in 1990. Together, Reba and Narvel built her empire.

In her fifteen years of climbing the country music ladder, Reba went from "the pickup trucks and campers, and U-Haul trailers to vans . . . goin' six and seven hundred miles all piled in there with me bein' the only woman and six or seven guys traveling from Oregon to Texas overnight to do shows. Then, finally, to a tour bus" in the eighties and on to private planes in the nineties. In March 1991 Reba and her entourage chartered private jets to bring them back to Nashville from a show in San Diego. The first plane hit a mountainside on takeoff, killing seven of Reba's band members, her road manager, and its pilot and copilot. Reba, Narvel, and the two other band members were booked on other flights. Among the dead were bandleader Kirk Cappello; songwriter Chris Austin; and singer Dana McVicker's husband, Michael Thomas. Two days after the crash Reba did an interview for *People* that resulted in her first cover story in the widely read magazine. She organized a memorial service, auditioned a new band, and got a standing ovation for singing "I'm Checking Out" on the Oscar telecast nine days later. She resumed touring two weeks after the tragedy. "I'm not going to quit, because there are too many opportunities that I have open to me," she said. "Staying busy is the best thing for all of us."

Today Reba is the queen of the show queens. Former manager Bill Carter hired some stage and image consultants for her in the mid-1980s; and she dug into their advice like a trail-weary cowpuncher at a banquet. By the 1990s her touring production featured multiple costume changes, fancy choreography, elaborate sets, flashy lighting effects, video screens, and scripted patter. She surprised country fans by singing and dancing the Aretha Franklin/Otis Redding soul oldie "Respect" and adopting pop sounds. She said that high-style gowns made her feel sassy and powerful onstage. She began doing more adventurous material, addressing such issues as troubled children ("I Heard Her Crying"), battered women ("The Stairs"), nursing homes ("All Dressed Up"), divorce, widowhood, prostitution, cheating, and sex. "I'm trying to sing songs for women, to say for them what they can't say for themselves," she told the *Chicago Tribune*'s Jack Hurst. "But I'm trying to do it for the '80s and '90s. Before, a lot of women identified with 'Don't Come Home a-Drinkin' With Lovin' on Your Mind.' Now, it's, 'Don't even think about coming home, 'cause I ain't gonna be here. I ain't gonna put up with that kind of carrying on.' Women today are more independent. They're not slapped around as much. They don't take it as much as they used to.

"I want to be those women's friend. You know, they've got problems. Like if I was a woman whose husband was cheatin' on me, or who worked nine to five, sick to death of my job, sick to death of the kids, sick to death of my husband, sick to death of what I'm havin' to go through— that's the kind of songs I'd pick. There's a lot of women out there who just want to have that three minutes of rebellion." Like Loretta Lynn, Janie Fricke, and Emmylou Harris before her, Reba goes out of her way to find songs by female songwriters, in hopes of giving them a break in the male-dominated music world. "I really do think it's just as tough for women now as it was when I started," she told reporter Michael McCall. "Women still have to struggle, still have to prove themselves four times as much as a man does." She says her secret is her rodeo-cowgirl background: "The thing that helped me so much in the music business is that I'd competed with men. It got me ready. It helped me to know how they think. Just 'cause you're a girl, they're not gonna cut you any slack, so I never asked for it from the beginning."

Reba's survival in the increasingly competitive country market was matched by few other show queens. Dottie's daughter Shelly West (b. 1958) gave it a shot with some Top 10 duets with David Frizzell from 1981 to 1983, followed by some "party-girl" solo numbers such as "Jose Cuervo" and "Somebody Buy This Cowgirl a Beer." Former Memphis session singer Judy Rodman (b. 1951) enjoyed a flurry of radio activity from 1985 to 1988 with songs including the feisty "Girls Ride Horses Too" and "Goin' to Work." Native Nashvillian Robin Lee (Irwin) (b. 1963) specialized in country interpretations of pop songs such as "Angel in Your Arms" and "Black Velvet" from 1984 to 1990.

But it became increasingly tough to crack the new, hunk-dominated charts. All country music women felt the pinch as the industry swung back to its macho, honky-tonk roots in the early 1990s. With the exceptions of superstars such as Reba McEntire, Wynonna Judd, and Tanya Tucker and the breakthroughs of a few hardy folkies, female acts were shoved aside.

Daughters of Dolly

As always country music was reflecting a larger American trend. It was hard times for women everywhere, for this same period marked the "feminization" of poverty. Women's advances of the 1970s were halted by the economic realities of the 1980s and 1990s, when the rich got richer and the poor got poorer. With the top 5 percent of the population controlling 60 percent of its wealth, the nation slid slowly into an economic recession. Poverty, hunger, and homelessness became major social issues for the first time since the Great Depression. The Reagan and Bush administrations cut income maintenance programs, food stamps, and health care expenditures. Those most affected were poor women, their children, and the elderly. The statistics are alarming: Fully half the families with female heads of households in the United States are below the poverty level. And while the popular image of the poor is of a black mother and her kids in an urban ghetto, the reality is that of the 32.5 million poor, nearly 70 percent of them are white. Two out of every three adults in poverty in America are women; one-quarter of all women working full-time earn less than $10,000 a year, well below the poverty level.

As poverty increased in the eighties wealth was concentrated into fewer and fewer hands. The rich were glamorized by the enormously popular 1980s TV shows "Dynasty," "Dallas," "Knots Landing," and "Falcon Crest." Millionaires such as Donald Trump, Ted Turner, and Malcolm Forbes became media stars. Mega-million-dollar mergers consolidated hundreds of businesses into international cartels—Nashville was a microcosm of this as small independent companies were squeezed out and six major conglomerates took control of the country recording industry.

George Bush graduated to the presidency in 1988. Vice president Dan Quayle promoted "family values" and suggested that America's problems were because of declining morality. Increasingly, he blamed women for social ills. Although only one million families receive Aid to Families with Dependent Children (AFDC) money for more than five years in a row, Quayle singled out welfare mothers as damaging our moral fiber, apparently leading a nation of 250 million away from its values of "family, hard work, integrity and personal responsibility," as he put it. In 1990, one in four babies was born to an unmarried mother, compared to one in 20 in 1960. Abortion became a major Quayle issue. Yet after TV's "Murphy Brown" character made the decision in 1992 to have a baby without marriage rather than an abortion, Quayle railed.

"Who is Dan Quayle to go after single mothers?" shot back Tanya Tucker. Country's most famous unwed mom fumed in the *New York Daily News,* "What in the world does he know of what it's like to go through pregnancy and have a child with no father for the baby? Who is he to call single mothers tramps? I wanted to grow up, fall in love, get married, have two kids, drive a station wagon, and live in a house with a white picket fence. Every woman in America wants that. It doesn't always happen, though. . . . I make a lot of money . . . [but] what about the poor single mothers of this country—and there are so many of them—that Dan Quayle is yelling about? They can't afford anything. Their men left them alone to bring up children in a hard world. What about them? Why harass them? The real trouble with these situations isn't the women having children out of wedlock; it's men with no backbone—like Dan Quayle—who don't understand their plight."

In reality, "family values" had become isolation from society, alienation from public service, and rugged individualism. In the absence of political leaders and philanthropic businessmen, music stars became the champions of causes embodying the old-fashioned values of community, charity, social justice, and humanity. They raised their voices for the environment, crusaded against homelessness and hunger, promoted AIDS research, raised money for the beleaguered farmers, supported Amnesty International, and battled nuclear power. These efforts made headlines for pop and rock stars, but they were nothing new for country music. Its stars have been doing benefits for prisoners, disaster victims, and the impoverished as long as there has been country music. Compassion and generosity toward the needy have always been a large part of the country tradition.

So Minnie Pearl became an enthusiastic participant in the Comic Relief benefits for the homeless. Among those singing at Farm Aid shows have been Tanya Tucker, K.T. Oslin, Emmylou Harris, The Forester Sisters, Suzy Bogguss, Lacy J. Dalton, Rosanne Cash, Kathy Mattea, and Nanci Griffith. The Nashville women's shelter has been aided in song by Gail Davies, Lynn Anderson, Pam Tillis, Kathy Mattea, Karen Brooks, and others. Dozens of Music Row women have performed at the annual prochoice Nashville benefits to aid Tennesseans Keeping Abortion Legal and Safe. Emmylou stars at concerts to fund food banks. Barbara Mandrell crusaded on behalf of organ donation and seat belt safety. Rosanne Cash spearheaded a national environmental awareness campaign and joined Mary-Chapin Carpenter, Maura O'Connell, Kate and Anna McGarrigle, Emmylou Harris, and others on *'Til Their Eyes Shine Again,* a 1992 CD to aid the Voiceless Victims program for children of war-torn countries. Country stars especially embraced the issue of literacy. In the wake of new statistics revealing that twenty-seven million Americans are functionally illiterate, Paul Overstreet penned "Billy Can't Read" for a national campaign, and Trisha Yearwood and Pam Tillis were among those who launched it at a 1992 benefit show.

The high school dropout rate in Sevier County, Tennessee, is 35 percent, and Appalachia as a whole is poorly educated. Dolly Parton, who was the first member of her family to get a diploma, set up a scholarship fund to encourage kids to stay in school. Dolly also funds a county health-care program. She viewed the 1986 opening of her Dollywood theme park in her native mountains as a way of providing more jobs for the economically depressed region.

"I think if a person just remembers who they are and where they came from, and tries to develop those good qualities and tries to remember that we all feel the same things, they can be a good success," she says. "They say a mind is a terrible thing to waste. Well, I say a dream is a terrible thing to waste. And I've always been a big dreamer. I was born a dreamer."

As her fame spread, Dolly grinned from the covers of *Redbook, McCall's, Interview, Vanity Fair, People,* and *Playboy. Ms.* magazine declared

Dolly Parton, 1991.

her its Woman of the Year in 1987. And then there were *The National Enquirer, Star, Globe, National Examiner,* and every other supermarket tabloid. "I am the boob queen and the tabloid queen," Dolly cracked on TV's "A Current Affair," "so if there's something going on about boobs, of course I'm going to be plastered on the cover. . . . There's a real scare about breast implants and me. . . . But it's not true about me having problems with anything to do with my breasts, other than they seem to be killing a lot of other people. But they're not bothering me at all." Almost all of the big-city media were fascinated by her looks. "The first time my Mama saw me all done up with blond bleached hair all piled up, and my lips, cheeks, and nails as red as I could get them, she screamed to the Lord, 'Why are you testing me this way?' And she told me the Devil must have made me do it. 'Heck no,' I told Mama. 'Let's give credit where it's due: I did this all myself!'"

Dolly shrewdly capitalized on the public's fascination. She spent the eighties climbing from country stardom to multimedia superstardom. Her working-girl character Doralee in the smash hit 1980 movie *9 to 5* was the first in a series of strong, positive female parts she played during her subsequent silver-screen career. Dolly never claimed to be a great thespian; she always maintained she was playing variations on her personality, taking roles that brought the self-assertive women in her country songs to life. There was Miss Mona, the heart-of-gold madam of *The Best Little Whorehouse in Texas* (1982), and Jake Ferris, the feisty country singer of *Rhinestone* (1984). Dolly's role as Truvy, the beautician, in *Steel Magnolias* (1989) was the wisecracking center of a circle of strong female characters played by Olympia Dukakis, Shirley MacLaine, Sally Field, Daryl Hannah, and Julia Roberts. In *Straight Talk* (1992), her Doctor Shirlee was an Arkansas loser who became a Chicago winner by dishing out homespun humor and wisdom as a radio psychologist. In the TV movie *Wild*

Texas Wind (1991), she was a battered woman who finds strength.

A Smoky Mountain Christmas got the highest ratings of any ABC TV movie in two years when it aired in 1986. The network then gambled forty-four million dollars in 1987 that Dolly could revive the dead network variety series concept. It was the first attempt at this kind of weekly show since another country queen, Barbara Mandrell, had bowed out five years earlier. "Dolly" put its star in comedy bits and production numbers, but only really came alive when she interacted with audience members during the show's question-and-answer sessions. It was not renewed. Indomitable Dolly pushed forward with a new restaurant business in Hawaii and investments in hogs, hardware stores, and macadamia nuts. Her Sandollar film company produced the Oscar-winning 1989 *Common Threads,* a documentary about the AIDS quilt.

Her most successful enterprise was Dollywood. Opened in 1986, the four-hundred-acre attraction hosted more than a million visitors its first year and has continued to be a major tourist draw since. In addition to rides and musical shows, Dollywood features Appalachian crafts and a Dolly Parton museum. "Other people look at me like a star," she reflects, "but I didn't ever. It never dawned on me until I went through that museum they built for me at Dollywood. I saved all this junk over the years. . . . Seein' it all put together, I got very emotional. I think that was the first time in my life that it hit me that I was a star. It kind of jarred things inside me." The feelings, she adds, were not altogether pleasant; she felt an existential tinge of futility. Although she seldom shows it, Dolly has a melancholy side. Fans were surprised when she admitted going through a profound depression in the mid-1980s. Gynecologic problems and a heartbreak she wouldn't specify gave her a bad case of the bedridden blues. After she caught herself eyeing the gun she keeps at her bedside, "I said to myself, either you get up off your fat ass and get past this point in your life, or kill yourself already. In the end," she added in a *Life* magazine interview, "I just had to shut my trap." By steadfastly limiting her food intake to tiny portions at a sitting, Dolly shed forty pounds between 1983 and 1987. Her svelte reemergence coincided with the filming of *Steel Magnolias* and the reinvigoration of her recording career. She still regards that transformation as her greatest accomplishment. "Conquering my weight problem has been one of the biggest achievements of my life. The battle I had was within myself. Anybody with a weight problem will know exactly what I mean."

Her music during this period became erratic. Dolly experimented with pop sounds. The insightful "Single Women" (1982) came from TV's "Saturday Night Live." The touching "Hard Candy Christmas" (1982) was from Carol Hall's *Best Little Whorehouse* musical score. Her million-selling "Islands in the Stream" (1983) duet with Kenny Rogers was penned by The Bee Gees. *The Great Pretender* (1984) was an LP of pop oldies.

Yet sprinkled through her albums was evidence that her songwriting gift was undimmed. "Hollywood Potters" moralized about the show-business world that abused and bruised starry-eyed hopefuls. "Appalachian Memories" was the saga of displaced mountain folks lost in northern cities. She also waxed nostalgic on her Number 1 hit "Tennessee Homesick Blues" in *Rhinestone*. The *Trio* album with Linda Ronstadt and Emmylou Harris was a triumphant return to her mountain roots, spawning four Top 10 hits and a slew of awards from 1987 to 1988. *Trio, 9 to 5,* and *Steel Magnolias* were all-female projects, as was a 1993 recording with Tammy Wynette and Loretta Lynn, her fellow break-through country women of the sixties. "I don't know, I seem to have my best luck working with other women," she says.

As she entered her mid-forties, Dolly seemed to gain vigor. "It's like I wake up young because my thoughts are young. . . . Don't be scared of your age, 'cause it's not gonna do you a damn bit of good. You might as well have a good attitude, 'cause we *are* gonna get older. . . . Of course I would like to stay young forever, and I want to look as good as I can for as long as I can, as long as there's money and plastic surgery and doctors and collagen or whatever it takes to make me feel better about myself. . . . I have been proud of my age."

She reconquered the charts by enlisting Kentuckian Ricky Skaggs as her producer on *White Limozeen* (1989). Its "Why'd You Come in Here Lookin' Like That?" inspired a delightfully comedic video. The album's "What Is It My Love" comes from the point of view of a cruelly victimized woman. "I'll probably get killed for saying this, but I wrote the song because so many of my brothers, my dad, and a lot of my people are men with macho, redneck attitudes. . . . This song was inspired by my family and how some of 'em treat their women. . . . I've had a couple of those men in my own life, too. And this is like so many people I know." In 1991 Dolly issued the strongly feminist single and video "Eagle When She Flies."

Her Number 1 hit from the *Eagle When She Flies* album was a duet with Ricky Van Shelton called "Rockin' Years." But the collection had another duet partner—Lorrie Morgan, with whom Dolly sang on the female-competition tune "Best Woman Wins." Although Dolly was off to Hollywood by the time Lorrie joined the Opry in 1984, the superstar has long been the youngster's guardian angel from afar. When Lorrie was trying to break into the business, Dolly urged manager Sandy Gallin to help. She watched Lorrie on The Nashville Network and predicted

stardom when most of Music Row was still
ignoring the singer. So when the two women
shared a flight to L.A. in 1990, Dolly cracked open
a bottle of champagne and vowed to write them a
duet. "I thought, 'Well, this is just the champagne
talking,'" Lorrie recalls. "'We ain't ever gonna do
this.' I thought, 'This is like Let's-Do-Lunch.'" But
Dolly meant it. "Best Woman Wins" appeared on
both women's subsequent CDs as one of the only
female-star duets in country history. Like Dolly,
Lorrie has a will-to-win attitude, a likable
directness, and a spunky, independent streak. But
there's a seldom-seen tender side to her self-
sufficiency.

"There are some days when I feel like I could
just conquer the world, but—and I know the
women's libbers are going to hate me for this—
there are other times when the woman in me
comes out, when I feel weak and alone, and I feel
like I need somebody to lean on." Lorrie is a self-
described "survivor" who lost her father at sixteen,
was making a living in music before her high
school graduation, became a divorced single mom, climbed to stardom
for fifteen years, and was widowed by country star Keith Whitley just as
her career was about to blossom.

Lorrie Morgan reaches
for an admirer's message
during the 1990 Fan Fair
celebration in Nashville.

Lorrie was born in Nashville in 1959, the fifth and final child of "Grand
Ole Opry" star George Morgan and his wife, Anna. She grew up watching
her dad sing "Candy Kisses" and "Room Full of Roses" on the hallowed
stage and made her own Opry debut at age thirteen singing the Marie
Osmond/Anita Bryant favorite "Paper Roses." Chronically truant at her
Catholic school and never much of a student, Lorrie realized early that
singing was her destiny. "I was working nightclubs when I was fifteen
years old. So while other people were doing homework, I was out. I went
through a wild period. I guess I grew up real quick. . . . When I was seventeen years old, I bought my very first car, with my own money that I
made working nightclubs. I had a *good* time. Every now and then I still get
that little itch to be wild. . . . Hippies intrigued me a lot. I think that's
why I liked Harley riders. Something about them guys with long hair
and helmets; it really turns me on. It's a fantasy thing of mine. . . . I look
at them and envy them because I would love to get on a bike and just say
good-bye." After her father died following heart surgery in 1976, Lorrie

became even more committed to singing. She married George Jones's steel player, Ron Gaddis, when she was twenty, but the union ended in divorce a year later, leaving her with a baby daughter to raise.

"I think in a way that it was a blessing that I got pregnant with Morgan, because I was definitely headed down the wrong road of life," she told reporter Sandy Smith. "I did a little too much drinking and a little too much partying. And when I had Morgan, it changed. My kids have put everything into perspective. . . . I thought I needed a crutch. My nerves have always been real bad . . . and I'd think, 'I can't go through this.' There were times when I tried a drink before I'd go onstage. And I can't drink. Alcoholism runs in my family. My dad wasn't an alcoholic, but I had some uncles who died of alcohol."

She sang at Opryland. She sang at The Nashville Palace. She sang on TV. She recorded singles for Columbia, Four-Star, Hickory, and MCA, all of which stiffed. "They treated me like I was a nobody." A season on the road opening shows and singing duets with the hard-living Jones was particularly rugged. "And so I got out. When I left George Jones, I literally almost had a nervous breakdown because of the pressures of a bad marriage and the Jones show. I got out of the music business for about two years. Went back to my mom's house. Gave up trying. I think that was my first realization of what drugs and alcohol can do to a person."

Nashville Network star Ralph Emery helped her get back on her feet with regular spots on the then-new TNN cable channel. During Fan Fair in 1984, Lorrie was invited to become an Opry regular, which at least brought regular paychecks if not stardom. The Opry's queens had always been her biggest influences, and they embraced the youngster they'd watched growing up backstage. "As far as the women at the Opry, Jeannie Seely is a wonderful friend of mine. When nobody's around and it's like woman-to-woman, she's real, real supportive. She was very supportive of me at the Opry, as were Jean Shepard and Jeanne Pruett." Seely, Shepard, and Lorrie costarred in a three-ages-of-woman country musical called *Takin' It Home* in 1986. Otherwise, Lorrie's career became a grind of one-night stands. "My mom stayed home with us kids, and I'm not doing that for mine. . . . I missed a lot of Morgan's baby years, which made me feel real guilty. But then again, I had to work. . . . There was no choice." Working-mother guilt still sometimes overwhelms Lorrie: "I want to tell you from the heart, it is the pits."

Her life brightened when she met singer Keith Whitley backstage at the Opry. They dated and married; Lorrie had their son, Jesse, during Fan Fair week in 1987. She got an RCA recording contract. Everything was going great. But Whitley had a dangerous alcohol problem. The honky-tonk star was a binge drinker who downed huge quantities when he was off by himself. Lorrie thought her love could change him. She threw away his booze and tied his leg to hers in bed so he couldn't sneak away. But in 1989 she went on tour to Alaska to promote her new RCA ballad "Dear Me." Alone in their house, Keith Whitley drank himself to death. She buried him as fans wept for the storybook country sweethearts. Lorrie's sad "Dear Me" seemed suddenly painfully autobiographical. It shot toward the Top 10 while factories were pressing copies of *Leave the Light On,* her debut album. The widow was caught in the situation of trying to launch her career, provide for her family, and deal with her grief all at once. Lorrie shouldered her load without complaint, first turning to her Opry sisters for solace, then to the loyal country fans. "There were many days when I thought I was going to give up," she confided in the pages of *Country America.* "But with two kids, I knew I couldn't do that. . . . I did it for them. I had to pull myself up . . . and say, 'You will go on. You will continue. . . . You are not going to be this way. You're stronger than this.'" The woman-to-woman "Out of Your Shoes," the shape-up-or-ship-out "Five Minutes," and the sweetly romantic "He Talks to Me" all followed "Dear Me" into the Top 10; *Leave the Light On* won a gold record.

Lorrie set up the Keith Whitley Memorial Fund at the Vanderbilt Institute for the Treatment of Addictions in 1989, and since then she and her band have played charity softball games against country radio stations to raise funds for antidrug and alcohol abuse programs.

In 1991 she followed *Leave the Light On* with the even more powerful *Something in Red.* It included the up-tempo hits "We Both Walk" and "Except for Monday," the memorable female lyric "Something in Red," and a devastating remake of George Jones's country oldie of abject desolation "A Picture of Me Without You." "You know, when we first started accepting material for this album, every song that was pitched was morbid. I mean, it was all kinds of dying songs. I said, 'I'm not doing that. I'm not basing my career on a tragedy. I *live* the tragedy, every day, without it being in my music.'" *Something in Red* became her second gold record. In 1990 Lorrie's "'Til a Tear Becomes a Rose" duet with her late husband won a CMA Award.

While touring in 1991, Lorrie fell in love with Clint Black's bus driver, Brad Thompson. He proposed during Fan Fair, and they married that October. A month later the new bride was hospitalized for ovarian surgery and underwent a hysterectomy at age thirty-two. Lorrie was back on the road within weeks, making her way in the world and refusing to see herself as anything but a dedicated working woman. "Most of my life I have provided financially for myself," she says. "I'm just out bustin' my butt, trying to make it work."

PATTY LOVELESS
11
SKEETER DAVIS
11
SYLVIA
11
DAVE & SUGAR
11
17. **LINDA RONSTADT**
10
JEAN SHEPARD
10
HIGHWAY 101
10
18. **BRENDA LEE**
9
PATSY CLINE
9
HOLLY DUNN
9
JUICE NEWTON
9
MARGARET WHITING
9 (all with Jimmy Wakely)
19. **LORRIE MORGAN**
8
MARGO SMITH
8
20. **LACY J. DALTON**
7
K.T. OSLIN
7
SWEETHEARTS OF THE RODEO
7
HELEN CORNELIUS
7 (all with Jim Ed Brown)
CRISTY LANE
7
OLIVIA NEWTON-JOHN
7
SUSAN RAYE
7
SHELLY WEST
7

Lorrie and Dolly maintain country's blue-collar, good-ol'-girl character. They're part of a growing group of women who wear their hillbilly credentials with dignity. Bluegrass-rooted singers Alison Krauss, Irene Kelley, and Rhonda Vincent share this proud-to-be-country attitude, as do such stylists as "Hee Haw"'s Vickie Bird, Alaskan Vickie Sanders, Ohio's yodeling Ethel Delaney, and native Tennessean Dianne Davis.

The most unusual story of all belongs to Jett Williams. She began touring with Hank Williams's legendary band The Drifting Cowboys in 1989, an event that climaxed her decade-long quest for identity. Adopted children often fantasize that their parents are famous entertainment stars. Jett says she dreamed that as a child. In 1985 she learned she was Hank's illegitimate daughter, and seven years later the courts ruled that she was entitled to a share of the millions generated annually by his estate.

Jett was born five days after the superstar's death in 1953. Her mother was a Nashville secretary named Bobbie Jett. Before his death Hank signed a document acknowledging that the pregnant Bobbie's baby was his, stating that he wanted custody after the birth, and agreeing to provide for the child. Instead, Hank's mother, Lillian Stone, adopted the newborn. But she died a year later. Jett was put up for adoption in Alabama, and her papers were sealed in the Montgomery County courthouse. Her existence had been whispered about in Nashville for years, but the Williams heirs conspired to keep the knowledge from her. "I was like the only one who didn't know about me," Jett says. "I was the best-kept secret in country music."

Jett recounted her tale in the 1990 book *Ain't Nothin' as Sweet as My Baby,* then sold her compelling saga to the movies. In concert Jett sings "Your Cheatin' Heart," "Hey Good Lookin'," "Kaw-Liga," and the other songs of her famous father. Given her remarkable life, Jett Williams might be the woman who's proudest of all to be country.

Patty Loveless rode this sentiment to fame, as well. Like Lorrie and Jett, she traces her social and musical roots directly back to the classic stylists of Nashville's "golden era." She learned at the feet of the greats. "I have never made a habit of goin' around saying, 'I'm Loretta Lynn's cousin.' I don't want people to think I'm playin' off that," says the Kentucky native. Nevertheless, "It all started for me with people like Porter Wagoner and Dolly Parton and The Wilburn Brothers helping me and encouraging me." She started life as Patty Ramey (b. 1957), the daughter of a coal miner. When she was twelve, Patty formed a country duo with her brother Roger. She was headlining in Louisville by age fourteen and making trips to Nashville a year later. After cousin Loretta left the Wilburns' fold, the brothers signed Patty to their publishing company and hired her to perform in their road show. She married Wilburn drummer Terry Lovelace, dropped out of country music, and moved to North Carolina to sing rock for seven years. Her stage name, Loveless, is a variation on her married name.

After her divorce Patty decided to give Nashville another try. "You just can't take that traditional sound out of my voice. It's there. Even when I was singing rock 'n' roll." Brother Roger became her manager. He talked his way into MCA Records in 1985, and a year later the company issued her debut LP. The album failed, but its ballad "I Did" attracted a good deal of attention from critics and radio programmers. "There wasn't really any female singers out there doin' this form of traditional kind of music—it really was a hard-core country song. . . . That's when the public accepted me as an artist."

The pump was primed for a breakthrough. Her second album, *If My Heart Had Windows,* established Patty as a Top 10 act, and her follow-up LP, *Honky-Tonk Angel* (1989), became a gold record thanks to "The Blue Side of Town," "Chains," and "Timber I'm Falling in Love." All had a rock edge, and Patty admits that country-rocker Linda Ronstadt was as big an influence as Dolly and Loretta. "I feel like there's a lot of spunk to her," she said. "She's a fighter. You know, a lot of women in country music need some up-tempo tunes."

Patty took her own rockin' advice on *Up Against My Heart* (1991) and *On Down the Line* (1990), collections that included such firecracker performances as "Jealous Bone," "On Down the Line," "The Night's Too Long," and "I'm That Kind of Girl." She began dressing more provocatively, changed her hair from dark blond to reddish brown, and opened shows for the rowdy Hank Williams, Jr. Following vocal surgery, Patty Loveless returned to hard-core country singing with 1993's sassy romp "Blame It on Your Heart."

"I have a traditional sound, but I think I have an edge to it—a gutsy kind of sound," Patty believes. Her favorite offstage activity? "A lot of women will probably think I'm crazy, but I enjoy just cleanin' up around the house and gettin' my hands into things. It's work for some, but I don't look at it as work. I look at it as somethin' that's helpin' me to ease my mind."

Sounds and Styles for the Nineties

Like Lorrie Morgan, Carlene Carter, and Rosanne Cash, Nashville-bred Pam Tillis was born into country music. But Pam spent the years of her musical development running as far away from her natural style as she

could. She applied her fiery heartache soprano to rock, jazz, disco, pop, new wave, and r&b. She sang everything from jingles to soul songs, refusing for the first dozen years of her professional life to claim her country birthright. Pam is the daughter of Mel Tillis, the country king named Entertainer of the Year in 1976. Born in 1957, she made her first public performance singing "Tom Dooley" at "The Grand Ole Opry" when she was eight.

She was self-conscious and insecure as a youngster. Of the five Tillis children, firstborn Pam became the introspective loner. Mel was always on the road, so Doris Tillis raised the kids on her own. When Mel was home, he and Doris battled constantly. "I would sit in my room and make up mournful songs," Pam recalls. Just as important, she began exercising the big, shimmering, soul-piercing voice that later paid her bills. Pam was determined to steer an independent course from her dad. As Nashville went into its show-queen era in the seventies, she became a rebellious rocker. A car wreck in high school sent her face-first through a windshield and into plastic surgery. She recovered, but she didn't slow down.

"My majors in college were music and partying," Pam says. "The first week on campus, I signed up for a rock 'n' roll group and my classes, in that order." After singing in a pop duo with future rocker Ashley Cleveland, Pam dropped out of the University of Tennessee and moved to San Francisco. She launched a free-form jazz/rock combo and sang with The Ramsey Lewis Trio. She married Rick Mason, got pregnant, and split up with him three weeks after son Ben was born in 1978. "Single mother, thy name is Guilt," quips Pam. "But I had to make a living." To make ends meet, she went on the road with Mel as his backup singer. "Pat and Debby [Boone] we're definitely not," she says, summing up the clash of wills that ensued. Barbara Fairchild had a minor country hit with Pam's song "The Other Side of the Morning," but the songwriter kept on a zigzag course from style to style. Pam found work fronting a motel-lounge "Top 40" band. "I've sung Donna Summer's greatest hits a million times each." In the 1980s her vocal reputation spread on Music Row, and Pam became the gal to call for an injection of soul into an ad jingle or a song demo tape. She issued a disco-ish single in 1981 and a new wave rock LP in 1983. There was also a brief stint as a Billie Holiday–style torch chanteuse and even a fling in a Nashville production of *Jesus Christ, Superstar.* With the exception of the musical, all of these projects failed. "Maybe the universe was trying to tell me something, and I finally started saying, 'Hey, God, I can take a hint,'" says Pam, who inherited her father's wacky wit, as well as his music talent.

In 1986 she developed a good-natured, Opry-style revue called Twang Night that married hillbilly oldies with a hip, youthful sensibility. These shows prefigured the breakthroughs of such cool-to-be-country acts as Marty Stuart and Dwight Yoakam. Among Pam's show stoppers were the Kitty Wells classic "Amigo's Guitar" and the Loretta Lynn favorite "You Ain't Woman Enough to Take My Man." "Nobody's doin' the honky-tonk stuff that I grew up ignoring," she said at the time. Her Twang Night collaborator Janis Carnes explained, "Twang is what you feel the emotion from in country music. As 'soul' is to rhythm and blues, 'twang' is to country. And they're losing that around here." Pam did Twang Night shows for fun, but they wound up changing her life. "I was 'channeling' Loretta Lynn, and somehow that physically connected me with all this [country] stuff again. The more I got into it, the harder it got to switch [musical] hats convincingly. Now all the other 'Pam Tillises' are on sabbatical. They're on the beach in Bora-Bora."

She signed with Warner Bros., but a succession of fine country singles for the label in 1986 and 1987 all died. Among them was "Those Memories," later a smash for Dolly, Linda, and Emmylou, and "One of Those Things," which became a Top 10 hit when Pam rerecorded it in 1991. She also sang on the soundtrack LP for the western *Rustlers' Rhapsody.* Later, her Warners tune "Drawn to the Fire" popped up in a scene in *Thelma and Louise,* whose screenplay was written by Pam's friend Callie Khouri, a former Nashville waitress. Despite disc disappointment, Pam's songwriting reputation bloomed. She penned the Highway 101 hit "Someone Else's Troubles Now" and Judy Rodman's "Goin' to Work," plus songs for Juice Newton, The Forester Sisters, Wild Rose, and Janie Fricke.

The activity resulted in an Arista Records contract in 1990. Pam rocketed to the top of the charts in 1991 and 1992 with the feisty, ironic "Don't Tell Me What to Do"; the throbbing, torrid "Maybe It Was

Memphis"; and three other singles from her CD *Put Yourself in My Shoes.* On it Pam unleashed her explosive range, fierce tonal attack, and simmering passion. The album was declared a gold record. *Homeward Looking Angel* followed in 1992, with its sexy lead-off single and video "Shake the Sugartree." She made peace with Papa Mel, and married songwriter/guitarist Bob DiPiero.

"I just don't think women are as ready to go for their old stereotypes," says Pam. "They are not following the old patterns. What are the stereotypes in rock 'n' roll? Sex vixen? Country women aren't into doing that. It seems like if there's any kind of stereotypical image [in the nineties], it would be that I'm the completely nonthreatening, safe girl next door. Even Lorrie Morgan could be your manicurist that you hang out with after work and go have drinks with. . . . K.T. Oslin reminds me of Madge the Beautician. . . . But the country market is so 'schitzed-out' right now. I play a lot of shows where it's an older crowd, and you don't want to alienate those people. Then you've got your new people who are hungry and rumbling and maybe would love somebody with a little more kick-butt image. The thing that I think is easiest is to just dispense with an image and be yourself." Pam's searing soulfulness as a singer and offbeat personality forged a charming new star style for the 1990s.

There are others. Virginia's Cee Cee Chapman and Canada's Lori Yates bring raspy vocal conviction and hip, casual fashion sense to the contemporary country female image. Mary-Chapin Carpenter's intelligent folkiness, Wynonna Judd's bluesy toughness, and Tanya Tucker's rebel sexiness have all met with million-selling disc success in the nineties. Martina McBride and Ronna Reeves are sleek, petite, brunet beauties with eager-to-please verve in their hearts and startling, Ronstadt-like power in their throats. Martina, born in 1966, grew up singing in a family band on the Kansas plains. She sold T-shirts at Garth Brooks concerts before releasing her debut CD in 1992. Ronna, born in 1967, is a tiny Texas lass who graduated from regional child star to national recording artist in 1991.

The seventies music of Linda Ronstadt and Emmylou Harris is probably the most powerful influence on the young women coming to country music today. Emerging stars Joy White, Faith Hill, Lisa Stewart, and Lari White all cite them as their inspiration. Million-selling Trisha Yearwood surprised Emmylou when they taped TNN's "American Music Shop" together. Emmy marveled at how well the young woman knew her harmonies. "I've been singing with you all my life," Trisha replied. She also knows just about every note of every Ronstadt album ever made. She describes Linda as her "megahero, mainly because of the power and the emotion she sings with. And even though she didn't write the things she recorded, she made them sound like she had written every word." Trisha is blessed with that same gift. She has a big, swaggering, self-confident wallop of a voice that tosses off challenging rockers as if they were so many skipping stones. She transforms ballads into epic emotional essays. Trisha turns phrases with striking effect, yet seems to be hardly trying, as though there is a well of vocal strength she hasn't even touched yet.

In 1992 billboards sprouted all over downtown Nashville proclaiming Trisha Yearwood "Platinum Blonde." When Trisha's "She's in Love with the Boy" went to Number 1 in 1991, it was the first time a woman's debut single had topped the charts in country music since Connie Smith's "Once a Day" in 1964. And when the *Trisha Yearwood* CD sold a million, it was country's first female platinum debut since Donna Fargo's twenty years before.

"I know that I've been real lucky, and it's kind of scary," says the overnight star. She doesn't seem frightened. Trisha Yearwood is self-assured, disarmingly candid, good-humored, a little sassy, and enormously likable. She's the girl next door with some "attitude." She's calm, poised, sensible, and composed, yet somehow earthy, approachable, and small-town. Trisha is a statuesque five-foot-eight-inch beauty whose fans include preteen girls who clamor for autographs at her shows. "I wish you could see the letters I get; they are so precious. I'm like the den mother of country music."

Trisha has often said in interviews that she thinks she's "too normal" to be a music star. "I wasn't the most popular girl in school, and I wasn't the 'dog.' I was kind of normal and in the middle and involved in everything. I made good grades, but I wasn't the brainy one that nobody liked. And I wasn't the homecoming queen, either." Born in 1964, she is the daughter of a small-town Georgia banker and a schoolteacher. After high school and two years of junior college, Trisha moved to Nashville in 1985 to study in Belmont College's music-business program. Her student internship was in the publicity department at MTM Records, and after graduation she continued at the company as a receptionist. Meanwhile her electrifying voice was attracting attention in the Music Row songwriting community. Taping songwriters' demos for two years prepared her for the big time. An unknown named Garth Brooks was also a studio singer at the time. When both got recording contracts, he asked her to sing on his albums, and she asked him to sing on hers. In 1991 she became superstar Garth's opening act on tour.

"Some people think he found me in a ditch somewhere and gave me a

LAMAR

PLATINUM BLONDE — *Trisha Yearwood*

MCA

Billboards throughout
Music City proclaimed
the overnight stardom of
Trisha Yearwood in 1992.

life. He really did help me as far as getting me in front of a bunch of people. But up to that point, I had really done everything myself. I was my own boss." Trisha's song of country romance "She's in Love with the Boy" became a sing-along sensation in 1991. Garth harmonized on her frankly sexual ballad "Like We Never Had a Broken Heart." She trumpeted about a modern gal's dream boy in "That's What I Like About You," pleaded for her individuality on "The Woman Before Me," and snarled determination in "Wrong Side of Memphis." All became massive radio hits. "I don't like wimpy lyrics," she says. "I like to find things women don't normally say or are afraid to say." The video script for "That's What I Like About You" called for her to kiss the guy in his hammock. Instead, Trisha playfully dumped him out of it. "When we do that song live, the women just go crazy."

"Trisha Yearwood is an authentic phenomenon, a woman singer who has helped rewrite the book on women singers," said *Country Music* magazine. "Move over, boys, here comes a star," said *The Tennessean.* In the midst of country's hot-hunks marketing fever, Trisha's remarkable sales success made headlines everywhere. "I heard all the time when I was starting out that women don't sell records," Trisha told writer Michael Bane. She said to Thomas Goldsmith, "I've heard for six years, 'Don't expect to sell as many records as George Strait, because women just don't do that.'" To interviewer Noel Davis she complained, "There is a mentality in Nashville that women don't sell as well as men"; and, "if you don't think it is going to happen, it is surely not going to happen."

In fact, country music's conventional wisdom was just an unsubstantiated myth. This attitude has vexed Music Row women for decades, and in 1992 one executive decided to investigate it. Arista Records publicist Merissa Ide had a gut feeling that even though they were in the vast minority, country's women were selling proportionally as well as the men were. So she tallied all the gold and platinum sellers then active. At the time, only 36 women were recording artists on major labels, but 15 of them had won these sales awards (42 percent). Men and male groups, on the other hand, represented 117 album-making acts, of whom 44 had sold in the millions (38 percent). That women were doing as well as men as country record sellers didn't surprise Merissa. She reasoned that if she enjoyed women's recordings, other women must, too. In pop music, women were among the biggest sellers. Could country fans be so different from their pop counterparts?

"The women of country music are going to be coming forward, and five years from now you'll see a parity there," predicts Liberty Records President Jimm Bowen. Speaking at *Music Row* magazine's "Industry Summit '92" seminar, Bowen said, "Women are going to get a chance to . . . take charge of their music. . . . Women haven't sold in the past because men told them what to sing. But when a woman like Reba [McEntire] gets control, it changes. . . . When that happens, they . . . reach the female consumer."

Dolly Parton's take-charge approach includes understanding what other women want. "People don't come to the shows to see you be you," Dolly says. "They come to see you be *them* and what they want to be. I've always believed that."

Bibliography

1. The Spirit of the Mountains

EMMA BELL MILES

Kay Baker Gaston, *Emma Bell Miles* (Signal Mountain, Tenn.: Walden's Ridge Historical Association, 1985).

Emma Bell Miles, *The Spirit of the Mountains* (Knoxville: University of Tennessee Press, 1975, reprint of 1905 edition).

Emma Bell Miles, *Our Southern Birds* (Chattanooga: National Book Co., 1919).

CHIPETA

P. David Smith, *Ouray Chief of the Utes* (Ouray, Colo.: Wayfinder Press, 1986).

ALMEDA RIDDLE

Roger D. Abrahams, ed., *A Singer and Her Songs* (Baton Rouge: Louisiana State University Press, 1970).

JEAN RITCHIE

Jean Ritchie, *Singing Family of the Cumberlands* (New York: Oxford University Press, 1955).

Jean Ritchie, *Children's Songs and Games from the Southern Mountains* LP liner notes (New York: Folkways Records, 1957).

Jean Ritchie, *British Traditional Ballads in the Southern Mountains Vol. 2* LP liner notes (New York: Folkways Records, 1961).

Jean Ritchie, *Precious Memories* LP liner notes (New York: Folkways Records, 1962).

Anonymous, *The Ritchie Family of Kentucky* LP liner notes (New York: Folkways Records, 1958).

DOROTHY SCARBOROUGH

Dorothy Scarborough, *A Song Catcher in Southern Mountains* (New York: Columbia University Press, 1937).

BELLE STARR

Richard K. Fox, *Belle Starr the Bandit Queen* (Austin, Tex.: The Steck Co., 1960).

Phillip W. Steele, *Starr Tracks: Belle and Pearl Starr* (Gretna, La.: Pelican Publishing, 1989).

MAUDE MINNISH SUTTON

Maude Minnish Sutton, "The Old English Ballads in North Carolina," *The Charlotte Observer,* Sept. 23, 1928.

Maude Minnish Sutton, papers and diaries at University of North Carolina (see Archives cited).

JEAN THOMAS

Jean Thomas, *American Folk Song Festival* LP liner notes (New York: Folkways Records, 1960).

Jean Thomas, *Ballad Makin' in the Mountains of Kentucky* (New York: Henry Holt Co., 1939).

Jean Thomas and Joseph A. Leeder, *The Singin' Gatherin'* (New York: Silver Burdett Co., 1939).

WOMEN FOLKLORISTS

D. K. WILGUS, *Anglo-American Folksong Scholarship Since 1898* (New Brunswick, N.J.: Rutgers University Press, 1959).

FOLK SONGS

Louise Rand Bascom, "Ballads and Songs of Western North Carolina," *Journal of American Folklore,* vol. 22, no. 84, April–June 1909.

Olive Woolley Burt, *American Murder Ballads and Their Stories* (New York: Oxford University Press, 1958).

Arthur Kyle Davis, ed., *Traditional Ballads of Virginia* (Cambridge, Mass.: Harvard University Press, 1929).

Duncan Emrich, *Folklore on the American Land* (Boston: Little, Brown Co., 1972).

Philip S. Foner, *American Labor Songs of the 19th Century* (Urbana, Ill.: University of Illinois Press, 1975).

Samuel L. Forcucci, *A Folk Song History of America* (Englewood Cliffs, N.J.: Prentice-Hall, 1984).

Tom Glazer, *A New Treasury of Folk Songs* (New York: Bantam Books, 1961).

Alan Lomax, *The Folk Songs of North America* (Garden City, N.Y.: Doubleday, 1975).

John A. Lomax and Alan Lomax, *Folk Song U.S.A.* (New York: Signet/New American Library, 1947).

Flora L. McDonell, *Folk Dances of Tennessee* (Delaware, Ohio: Cooperative Recreation Services, n.d.).

Reginald Nettel, *Seven Centuries of Popular Song* (London: Phoenix House, Ltd., 1956).

John Jacob Niles, *One Ballad Book of John Jacob Niles* (New York: Bramhall House, 1960).

Louise Pound, *American Ballads and Songs* (New York: Charles Scribner's Sons, 1972).

Leo Rainey, *Songs of the Ozark Folk* (Branson, Mo.: The Ozarks Mountaineer, 1972).

Carl Sandburg, *The American Songbag* (New York: Harcourt Brace & Co., 1927).

Cecil Sharp and Maud Karpeles, *Eighty Appalachian Folk Songs* (Winchester, Mass.: Faber & Faber, 1968).

Frank Shay, *My Pious Friends and Drunken Companions* (New York: Dover Publications, 1961).

COWBOY SONGS

Guy Logsdon, *The Whorehouse Bells Were Ringing and Other Songs Cowboys Sing* (Urbana, Ill.: University of Illinois Press, 1989).

J. A. Lomax and Alan Lomax, *Cowboy Songs and Other Frontier Ballads* (New York: Macmillan Publishing, 1910).

N. Howard Thorp, *Songs of the Cowboys* (Cambridge, Mass.: Riverside Press, 1908).

Jim Bob Tinsley, *He Was Singin' This Song* (Orlando, Fla.: University Presses of Florida, 1981).

John I. White, *Git Along Little Dogies* (Urbana, Ill.: University of Illinois Press, 1975).

ARCHIVES

Appalachian State University, Boone, N.C.—Appalachian Collection; The Greer Collection.

Country Music Foundation, Nashville.

The Library of Congress, Washington, D.C.—Archive of Folk Song.

University of Arizona, Tucson—Western Folksong Collection.

University of Arkansas, Fayetteville—Folklore Collection; Otto Ernest Rayburn Collection.

University of New Mexico Library, Albuquerque—J. D. Robb Collection.

University of North Carolina, Chapel Hill—Howard Odum papers; John Charles Campbell and Olive Dame Campbell papers; Edward Vernon Howell papers; Maude Minnish Sutton folders; Annabell Morris Buchanon papers; The North Carolina Archive of Folk Lore and Music.

University of Southern California, Los Angeles—The John Edwards Memorial Foundation.

University of Virginia, Fredericksburg—University of Virginia Collection of Folk Music.

Utah State University, Logan—Austin and Alta Fife collection of western folk songs.

OTHER SOURCES

Eric H. Davidson and Paul Newman, *Bluegrass from the Blueridge* LP liner notes (New York: Folkways Records, 1967).

Kenneth Goldstein, *The Unfortunate Rake* LP liner notes (New York: Folkways Records, n.d.).

Cecily Hancock, "Unexpected Antiquity," *Autoharp,* vol. 3, no. 5, May 24, 1963.

Roger Lax and Frederick Smith, *The Great Song Thesaurus* (New York: Oxford University Press, 1984).

Alan Lomax, *Ballads and Breakdowns from the Southern Mountains* LP liner notes (Bergenfield, N.J.: Prestige Records, n.d.).

Alan Lomax, *Blue Ridge Mountain Music* LP liner notes (New York: Atlantic Records, n.d.).

Russell Sanjek, *American Popular Music and Its Business* (New York: Oxford University Press, 1988).

Jerry Silverman, *The Liberated Woman's Songbook* (New York: Collier Books, 1971).

Joe Wilson, "Rachel and the Eighth of January," *Bluegrass Unlimited,* May 1988.

Anonymous, *Ballads and Songs of the Blue Ridge Mountains* LP liner notes (New York: Asch Records, n.d.).

2. Southern Sentiments

THE CHERRY SISTERS

Martin Gottfried, *In Person* (New York: Harry N. Abrams, 1985).

Lynn Sherr and Jurate Kazickas, *The American Woman's Gazetteer* (New York: Bantam Books, 1976).

Anthony Slide, *Selected Vaudeville Criticism* (Metuchen, N.J.: The Scarecrow Press, 1988).

LOTTA CRABTREE

Lotta Crabtree files, New York Public Library Theater Collection.

David Dempsy, *The Triumphs and Trials of Lotta Crabtree* (New York: William Morrow & Co., 1968).

Linda Martin and Kerry Segrave, *Women in Comedy* (Secaucus, N.J.: Citadel Press, 1986).

Lois Rather, *Lotta's Fountain* (Oakland, Calif.: The Rather Press, 1979).

Constance Rourke, *Troupers of the Gold Coast or The Rise of Lotta Crabtree* (New York: Harcourt, Brace & Co., 1928).

Silvia Anne Sheafer, *Women of the West* (Reading, Mass.: Addison-Wesley Publishing Co., 1980).

Mary Unterbrink, *Funny Women* (Jefferson, N.C.: McFarland & Co., 1987).

Anonymous, Lotta pamphlet (n.p., 1890).

FANNY CROSBY

Fanny Crosby, *Fanny Crosby's Life Story* (New York: Every Where Publishing Co., 1903).

Fanny J. Crosby, *Memories of Eighty Years* (Boston: James H. Earle & Co., 1906).

John Loveland, *Blessed Assurance: The Life and Hymns of Fanny Crosby* (Nashville: Boardman Press, 1978).

MOMMY GRAY

Phillip Fortune, "Otto Gray & His Oklahoma Cowboys," typescript (n.p., n.d.).

Otto Gray, advertisement, *Billboard*, Sept. 7, 1929.

Otto Gray, ad flyer/press kit, n.d.

Otto Gray and His Oklahoma Cowboys, *Old Time Songs* (St. Louis: Jensen Printing Co., n.d.).

Otto Gray and His Oklahoma Cowboys, *Songs* (n.p., n.d.).

Leslie A. McGill, "Music in Oklahoma by the Billy McGinty Cowboy Band," *The Chronicles of Oklahoma*, vol. 38, no. 1, Spring 1960.

Glenn Shirley, "Daddy of Cowboy Bands," *Oklahoma Today*, vol. 9, no. 4, Fall 1959.

Elsie Shoemaker, "Otto Gray Severs Part of His Connections with Stillwater," *Stillwater Oklahoma News-Press*, Oct. 30, 1966.

Anonymous, "Otto Gray Cowboys Set for RKO Tour," *Billboard*, Sept. 7, 1929.

Anonymous, "Otto Gray, Cowboys Click Well in East," *Billboard*, Nov. 8, 1930.

JANE GREEN

Brad Kay, *Jane Green—Wild Romantic Blues* LP liner notes (Venice, Calif.: Superbatone Records, 1989).

ADELYNE HOOD

Mary Bufwack and Robert K. Oermann, "Adelyne Hood: The Amalgamation of Vaudeville and Folk Traditions in Early Country Music," *JEMF Quarterly*, vol. 18, nos. 67–68, Fall/Winter 1982.

Robert Coltman, "Carson Robison: First of the Rural Professionals," *Old Time Music*, no. 29, Summer 1978.

Fred Goldrup, letter to the authors, Feb. 27, 1980.

Walter Darrell Haden, "Vernon Dalhart: Commercial Country Music's First International Star," *JEMF Quarterly*, vol. 11, pt. 2–3, Summer/Autumn 1975.

Robert R. Olson, letter to the authors, March 6, 1980.

Catherine Robison, letter to the authors, Apr. 12, 1980.

Catherine Robison, letter to the authors, Mar. 27, 1981.

Jim Walsh, "Vernon Dalhart," *Hobbies*, May–Dec. 1960.

Anonymous, "Ex Radio Singer Dies," *The Pittsburgh Post-Gazette*, Apr. 12, 1958.

Anonymous, *The Pittsburgh Press*, Mar. 5, 1944.

Anonymous, "Newsfront," *The Bulletin Index*, Mar. 19, 1942.

Anonymous, "Aunt Caroline of Radio Dies in Oakland," *The Pittsburgh Press*, Apr. 11, 1958.

THE HUTCHINSON FAMILY

Carol Brink, *Harps in the Wind: The Story of the Singing Hutchinsons* (New York: Da Capo Press, 1980).

Dale Cockrell, ed., *Excelsior: Journals of the Hutchinson Family Singers, 1842–1846* (Stuyvesant, N.Y.: Pendragon Press, 1989).

Philip D. Jordan, *Singin' Yankees* (Minneapolis: University of Minnesota Press, 1946).

ADA JONES

Milford Fargo, letter to the authors, Apr. 20, 1981.

Jim Walsh, "Favorite Pioneer Recording Artists: Ada Jones," *Hobbies*, June–July 1954.

Ulysses (Jim) Walsh, "Favorite Pioneer Recording Artists: Ada Jones," *Hobbies*, June 1946–Jan. 1947.

ROSE MELVILLE

Rose Melville, "Sis Hopkins' Sayings," *Billboard*, Feb. 1, 1908.

Anonymous, "Sis Hopkins Experiences," *Kalem Klip Sheet*, Jan. 28, 1916.

Anonymous, "Rose Melville—The Feminine Denman Thompson," clipping (n.p., 1908).

Anonymous, "Rose Melville and Sis Hopkins," clipping (n.p., 1908).

FIDDLIN' POWERS AND FAMILY

Charles K. Wolfe, "Fiddlin' Powers and His Family," *Old Time Music*, Fall 1985.

RAE SAMUELS

Anthony Slide, *Selected Vaudeville Criticism* (Metuchen, N.J.: The Scarecrow Press, 1988).

SOPHIE TUCKER

Sophie Tucker, *Some of These Days* (n.p., 1945).

THE WEAVER BROTHERS AND ELVIRY

James Saxon Childers, "Professional Rubes Tell Adventures: Old Fashioned Show Still Liked by the Public," *Old Time Country*, vol. 5, no. 4, Winter 1988.

Camille Gavin, "Retired Star of Vaudeville, Film Recalls 'Good Old Days,'" *Old Time Country*, vol. 5, no. 4, Winter 1988 (reprint of 1975 article in *The Bakersfield Californian*).

Joseph Lenz, "Familiar Faces," *Old Time Country*, vol. 5, no. 4, Winter 1988.

Bill Sachs, "Country Personals Had Start in Vaude and Tabloid Fields," *Country Music Who's Who* (Denver: Heather Enterprises, 1960).

Loretta Weaver Torbett, "Weaver Brothers and Elviry," *Old Time Country*, vol. 5, no. 4, Winter 1988.

VAUDEVILLE/EARLY SHOW BUSINESS

Gerald Bordman, *American Musical Theatre* (New York: Oxford University Press, 1978).

John E. DiMeglio, *Vaudeville U.S.A.* (Bowling Green, Ohio: Bowling Green University Press, 1973).

Marjorie Farnsworth, *The Ziegfeld Follies* (New York: Bonanza Books, 1956).

Douglas Gilbert, *American Vaudeville* (New York: Dover Publications, 1968).

Abel Green and Joe Laurie, Jr., *Show Biz from Vaude to Video* (New York: Henry Holt & Co., 1951).

Mary C. Henderson, *Broadway Ballyhoo* (New York: Harry N. Abrams, 1989).

Philip C. Lewis, *Trouping, How the Show Came to Town* (New York: Harper & Row, 1973).

Charles and Louise Samuels, *Once Upon a Stage* (New York: Dodd, Mead & Co., 1974).

Russell Sanjek, *American Popular Music and Its Business* (New York: Oxford University Press, 1988).

Anthony Slide, *The Vaudevillians* (Westport, Conn.: Arlington House, 1981).

William Lawrence Slout, *Theatre in a Tent* (Bowling Green, Ohio: Bowling Green University Popular Press, 1972).

Bernard Sobel, *A Pictorial History of Vaudeville* (New York: The Citadel Press, 1961).

Charles W. Stein, ed., *American Vaudeville as Seen by Its Contemporaries* (New York: Da Capo Press, 1984).

Robert C. Toll, *Blacking Up* (New York: Oxford University Press, 1974).

EARLY RECORDING

Norm Cohen, *Minstrels & Tunesmiths* LP liner notes (Los Angeles: JEMF Records, 1981).

Roland Gelatt, *The Fabulous Phonograph, 1877–1977* (New York: Macmillan Publishing, 1977).

Oliver Read and Walter L. Welch, *From Tin Foil to Stereo* (Indianapolis: Howard W. Sams & Co., 1959).

Russell Sanjek, *American Popular Music and Its Business* (New York: Oxford University Press, 1988).

Richard K. Spottswood, "Country Music & the Phonograph," *Bluegrass Unlimited*, Feb. 1987.

WOMEN SONGWRITERS/NINETEENTH-CENTURY SONGS

C. A. Browne, *The Story of Our National Ballads* (New York: Thomas Y. Crowell Co., 1931).

Richard Crawfod, *The Civil War Songbook* (New York: Dover, 1977).

Paul Glass and Louis C. Singer, *Singing Soldiers* (New York: Da Capo Press, 1975).

Dorothy Horstman, *Sing Your Heart Out Country Boy* (Nashville: Country Music Foundation, 1986).

Helen Kendrick Johnson, *Our Familiar Songs and Those Who Made Them* (New York: Arno Press, 1974, reprint of 1909 edition).

Maymie R. Krythe, *Sampler of American Songs* (New York: Harper & Row, 1969).

Roger Lax and Frederick Smith, *The Great Song Thesaurus* (New York: Oxford University Press, 1984).

Robert Lissauer, *Lissauer's Encyclopedia of Popular Music in America* (New York: Paragon House, 1991).

Theodore Raph, *The Songs We Sang* (New York: Castle Books, 1964).

Norton Stillman, *Trust Me with Your Heart Again* (New York: Simon & Schuster, 1971).

3. Single Girl, Married Girl

THE BLUE RIDGE MOUNTAIN SINGERS

Charles Wolfe and Patty Hall, *Banjo Pickin' Girl* LP liner notes (Somerville, Mass.: Rounder Records, 1979).

SAMANTHA BUMGARNER

Charles Wolfe, "Samantha Bumgarner: The Original Banjo Pickin' Girl," *The Devil's Box,* vol. 12, no. 1, Mar. 1, 1978.

Charles Wolfe and Patty Hall, *Banjo Pickin' Girl* LP liner notes (Somerville, Mass.: Rounder Records, 1979).

Anonymous, "Aunt Samantha Bumgarner, Fiddlin' Ballad Woman Dies," Associated Press wire obituary, Dec. 26, 1960.

Anonymous, Columbia Records ad, *Talking Machine World,* June 15, 1924.

THE CARTER FAMILY

John Atkins, Bob Coltman, Alec Davidson, and Kip Lornell, *The Carter Family* London: Old Time Music Books, 1973).

Janette Carter, interview with the authors, May 1978.

Janette Carter, interview in "Southern Songbirds," PBS radio series, 1990.

Joe Carter, interview with the authors, May 1978.

June Carter, "I Remember the Carter Family," *Country Song Roundup,* Oct.–Dec. 1965.

June Carter, interview with Robert K. Oermann, May 1987.

June Carter, interview with Robert K. Oermann, June 1989.

Maybelle Carter, "Maybelle Carter: Woman Behind the Clan," *Music City News,* Aug. 1966.

Maybelle Carter, interview on LP *Mother Maybelle Carter* (Nashville: Columbia Records, 1973).

Sara Carter, interview with Henry Young on LP *An Interview with Sara Carter* (Temple, Tex.: Museum Records, 1971).

Archie Green, William H. Koon, and Norm Cohen, *The Carter Family on Border Radio* LP liner notes (Los Angeles: JEMF Records, 1972).

Charles Hirschberg, "The Ballad of A.P. Carter," *Life,* Dec. 1991.

Gladys Carter Millard, interview with the authors, May 1978.

Gladys Carter Millard, "I Remember Daddy," *The Sunny Side Sentinel,* c. 1961.

Michael Orgill, *Anchored in Love: The Carter Family Story* (Old Tappan, N.J.: Fleming H. Revell Co., 1975).

Nolan Porterfield, "Hey, Hey, Tell 'Em 'Bout Us: Jimmie Rodgers Visits the Carter Family," in *Country: The Music and the Musicians* (New York: Abbeville Press, 1988).

Tony Russell, *The Carter Family* LP liner notes (Alexandria, Va.: Time-Life Records, 1982).

William R. Smith, "The Original Carter Family," *Country Music People,* Dec. 1961.

Charles Wolfe, "No Depression in Heaven: Carter Family Gospel," *Rejoice!,* vol. 1, no. 1, Winter 1987.

THE JENKINS FAMILY

Wayne W. Daniel, *Pickin' on Peachtree: The History of Country Music in Atlanta, Georgia* (Urbana, Ill.: University of Illinois Press, 1990).

Archie Green, "Commercial Music Graphics 8," *JEMF Quarterly,* vol. 5, pt. 1, no. 13, Spring 1969.

Gene Wiggins, *Fiddlin' Georgia Crazy* (Urbana, Ill.: University of Illinois Press, 1987).

BILLIE MAXWELL

Charles Wolfe, "Billie Maxwell: The First Singing Cowgirl," *Old Time Country,* vol. 6, no. 2, Summer 1989.

MOONSHINE KATE

Bob Coltman, "Look Out, Here He Comes," *Old Time Music,* no. 9, Summer 1973.

Wayne W. Daniel, *Pickin' on Peachtree* (Urbana, Ill.: University of Illinois Press, 1990).

Wayne W. Daniel, "Women's Lib and the George Old-Time Fiddlers' Conventions," *The Devil's Box,* vol. 16, no. 1, Mar. 1, 1982.

Charles Salter, "Hillbilly Memories," *The Atlanta Journal,* Sept. 13, 1976.

Jimmy Townsend, "Fiddlin' John Carson and Moonshine Kate," clipping (n.p., n.d.).

Gene Wiggins, *Fiddlin' Georgia Crazy* (Urbana, Ill.: University of Illinois Press, 1987).

Mark Wilson, *The Old Hen Cackled & The Rooster's Gonna Crow: Fiddlin' John Carson* LP liner notes (Somerville, Mass.: Rounder Records, 1973).

THE PERRY COUNTY MUSIC MAKERS

Steve Davis, "In Memoriam," *The Devil's Box,* vol. 11, no. 3, Sept. 1, 1977.

Nonnie Presson, *Going Back to Tennessee: The Perry County Music Makers* LP liner notes (Clarksville, Tenn.: Davis Unlimited Records, 1976).

Charles Wolfe, "The Perry County Music Makers," *The Devil's Box,* no. 26, Sept. 1, 1974.

Charles Wolfe, "We Play to Suit Ourselves," *Old Time Music,* no. 14, Autumn 1974.

Charles Wolfe, *Sunset Memories: The Perry County Music Makers* LP liner notes (Clarksville, Tenn.: Davis Unlimited Records, 1974).

THE PICKARD FAMILY

Joe Bleeden, "The Pickard Family," *Western and Country Music,* Jan. 1952.

Garnett Ladlaw Eskew, "The Pickards," *Radio Digest,* vol. 25, no. 6, Oct. 1930.

Ed Kahn, "Tapescript: Interview with Charlie, Bubb, and Lucille Pickard," *JEMF Newsletter,* vol. 4, pt. 4, no. 12, Dec. 1968.

Obed Pickard, *Pickard Family Album* (Chicago: Ava-Adams-Vee & Abbott, 1929).

Tex Ritter, *The Pickard Family Sing Song Hits of Yesterday* LP liner notes (Los Angeles, Verve Records, n.d.).

Anonymous, "Folksong's Favorite Family," *Country Song Roundup,* vol. 1, no. 11, Apr. 1951.

ROBA STANLEY

Roba Stanley, interview with Robert K. Oermann, April 1987.

Charles Wolfe, "Roba Stanley: The First Country Sweetheart," *Old Time Music,* no. 26, Autumn 1977.

Charles Wolfe and Patty Hall, *Banjo Pickin' Girl* LP liner notes (Somerville, Mass.: Rounder Records, 1979).

THE STONEMAN FAMILY

Norman Cohen, Eugene W. Earle, and Graham Wickham, *The Early Recording Career of Ernest V. Stoneman* (Los Angeles: John Edwards Memorial Foundation, 1978).

Tony Russell, *Ernest V. Stoneman and The Blue Ridge Corn Shuckers* LP liner notes (Somerville, Mass.: Rounder Records, n.d.).

4. "The National Barn Dance"

COUSIN EMMY

John Cohen, *The New Lost City Ramblers with Cousin Emmy* LP liner notes (New York: Folkways Records, 1968).

Cousin Emmy, *Cousin Emmy's Song Book* (n.p.: c. 1945).

Wayne W. Daniel, "Cousin Emmy," *Bluegrass Unlimited,* Oct. 1985.

Grandpa Jones, interview with Robert K. Oermann, Nov. 1990.

John Lair, *Chimney Corner Songs* (Chicago: John Lair, 1936).

Alan Lomax, *Kentucky Mountain Ballads Sung by Cousin Emmy* LP liner notes (New York: Decca Records, 1947).

Time-Life Records editors, *The Women* LP liner notes (Alexandria, Va.: Time-Life Records, 1981).

Ivan M. Tribe, *Mountaineer Jamboree: Country Music in West Virginia* (Lexington: University Press of Kentucky, 1984).

Charles K. Wolfe, *Kentucky Country* (Lexington: University Press of Kentucky, 1982).

Anonymous, "Versatile Emmy," *Stand By!,* July 18, 1936.

Anonymous, "Cousin Emmy," *Time,* Dec. 6, 1943.

THE DeZURICK SISTERS

Robert K. Oermann, "DeZurick Sisters Biography" typescript at The Country Music Foundation Library & Media Center, June 1979.

Time-Life Records editors, *The Women* LP liner notes (Alexandria, Va.: Time-Life Records, 1981).

Anonymous, "The DeZurick Sisters," *National Jamboree,* Aug. 1949.

Anonymous, "Yodeling Sisters," *Stand By!,* Sept. 11, 1937.

THE GIRLS OF THE GOLDEN WEST

Peter Feldman, *The Girls of the Golden West* LP liner notes (Santa Barbara, Calif.: Sonyatone Records, 1978).

Millie Good, interview in "Southern Songbirds," PBS radio series, 1990.

Tony Russell and Charles Wolfe, "Two Cowgirls on the Lone Prairie," *Old Time Music,* no. 43, Winter 1986/87.

Mary Jean Shurtz, "Girls of the Golden West," *Mountain Broadcast & Prairie Recorder*, Nov. 1946.

Ivan M. Tribe, *Millie and Dolly Good: Songs of the West* LP liner notes (Brighton, Mich.: Old Homestead Records, 1981).

Anonymous, "Golden West Girl," *Stand By!*, Jan. 9, 1937.

Anonymous, "Merrymaker," *Stand By!*, Jan. 16, 1937.

LILY MAY LEDFORD

Charles Faurot, *The Coon Creek Girls* LP liner notes (New York: County Records, 1968).

Allesa Clay High, "The Coon Creek Girl from Red River Gorge: An Interview with Lily May Pennington," *Adena*, vol. 2, no. 1, Spring 1977.

Kenneth Hull, *Lily May—A Legend in Our Time* (Paris, Ky.: K. Hull, 1970).

Kenneth Hull, *Lily May & The Coon Creek Girls with Pioneer Women in Country Music* (Mayfield, Ky.: Kenneth Hull, 1985).

Lily May Ledford, *Coon Creek Girl* (Berea, Ky.: Berea College Appalachian Center, 1980).

Lily May Ledford, *Banjo Pickin' Girl* LP liner notes (Chicago: Greenhays Records, 1983).

Robert K. Oermann, "Country Music Pioneer Dead at 68," *The Tennessean*, July 18, 1985.

Virginia Seeds, "Lily May's in Town!," *Stand By!*, Sept. 26, 1936.

Charles K. Wolfe, *Kentucky Country* (Lexington: University Press of Kentucky, 1982).

Anonymous, "Fiddlin' Gal," *Stand By!*, Apr. 3, 1937.

Anonymous, "Last of the Coon Creek Girls Dies," *Renfro Valley Bugle*, vol. 41, no. 12, Aug. 1987.

Anonymous, "Lily May Ledford: 1917–1985," *Bluegrass Unlimited*, Sept. 1985.

Anonymous, "Lily May Pennington Wins Arts Award," *Renfro Valley Bugle*, vol. 39, no. 11, July 1985. ,

LOUISIANA LOU

Zeke Clements, interview with Robert K. Oermann, July 1987.

John McCormick, "The Veterans' Sweetheart," *Rural Radio*, vol. 2, no. 4, May 1939.

Robert K. Oermann, "Louisiana Lou," *Old Time Music*, no. 34, Summer–Autumn 1980.

Vic Willis, interview with Robert K. Oermann, Nov. 1982.

Charles Wolfe and Patty Hall, *Banjo Pickin' Girl* LP liner notes (Somerville, Mass.: Rounder Records, 1979).

LULU BELLE

Craig Baguley, "Lula Belle: Tender Memories Recalled," *Country Music People*, vol. 22, nos. 4–5, April–May 1991.

Wayne W. Daniel, "Lulu Belle and Scotty: Have I Told You Lately That I Love You?," *Bluegrass Unlimited*, March 1986.

Jake Lambert, "Where Are They Now?," *Big Country News*, Nov. 1969.

William E. Lightfoot, "The Belle of the Barn Dance: Reminiscing with Lulu Belle Wiseman Stamey," *Journal of Country Music*, vol. 12, no. 1, 1987.

Lulu Belle, "Lulu Belle's Autobiography," *Stand By!*, Apr. 12, 1949.

Lulu Belle, "The Royal Family," *Stand By!*, Oct. 31, 1936.

John W. Morris, *Lulu Belle and Scotty Early and Great Vol. 1* LP liner notes (Brighton, Mich.: Old Homestead Records, 1985).

Bob Powel, "Lulu Belle and Scotty by Themselves," *Country Music People*, Dec. 1972.

William Welch, "Lula Belle Tells Grim Rape Story," Associated Press wire story, May 5, 1977.

North Carolina Manual, 1975 (Raleigh: Secretary of State Pub., 1975).

Anonymous, *Lulu Belle & Scotty: The Sweethearts of Country Music* LP liner notes (Nashville: Starday Records, c. 1965).

Anonymous, "Girl on the Cover," *Stand By!*, July 27, 1935.

Anonymous, "Hitched! Wedding Bells for Lulu Belle," *Stand By!*, Feb. 2, 1935.

Anonymous, "Lulu Belle and Scotty . . . Tops in Troupers," *National Jamboree*, Aug. 1949.

FIBBER MCGEE AND MOLLY

Charles Stumpf and Tom Price, *Heavenly Days!: The Story of Fibber McGee and Molly* (Waynesville, N.C.: The World of Yesterday, 1987).

LOUISE MASSEY

Louise Massey, interview with Elvis E. Fleming—Chaves County Historical Society, Mar. 1976.

Louise Massey, "History of Louise Massey (Mabie): Louise Massey and the West-erners," undated typescript, Country Music Foundation Library & Media Center.

Peer International, *Louise Massey and the Westerners Song Folio* (New York: Peer International Corp., 1941).

PATSY MONTANA

Mary Bufwack and Robert K. Oermann, *The Very Early Patsy Montana & the Prairie Ramblers* LP liner notes (Sulzheim, Germany: Cattle Records, 1981).

Chris Comber, "The Prairie Ramblers," *Country Music Review*, Dec. 1973.

Chris Comber, "Patsy Montana: The Cowboys' Sweetheart," *Old Time Music*, no. 4, Spring 1972.

Patsy Montana, letter to Robert K. Oermann, Mar. 27, 1980.

Patsy Montana, interview with Robert K. Oermann, May 1984.

Patsy Montana, interview with the authors, June 1984.

Patsy Montana, interview in "Southern Songbirds," PBS radio series, 1990.

Patsy Montana, letter to Robert K. Oermann, Sept. 13, 1985.

Robert K. Oermann, *Patsy Montana & the Prairie Ramblers: Columbia Historic Edition* LP liner notes (Nashville: CBS Records, 1984).

Robert K. Oermann and Mary A. Bufwack, "Patsy Montana and the Development of the Cowgirl Image," *Journal of Country Music*, vol. 8, no. 3, 1981.

Bob Powel, "Patsy Montana," *Country Music People*, Sept. 1978.

Art Satherley, letter to Jo Walker, Sept. 9, 1967.

Walt Trott, "Patsy Montana: The Lady & the Legend," *Country Scene*, Nov. 1987.

Anonymous, "Girl on the Cover," *Stand By!*, Nov. 30, 1935.

LINDA PARKER

John Lair, "Notes from the Music Library," *Stand By!*, Nov. 11, 1936.

John Lair, "Notes from the Music Library," *Stand By!*, Aug. 21, 1937.

Anonymous, "Linda Parker, Singer, Dead," *South Bend Tribune*, Aug. 12, 1935.

Anonymous, "Sunbonnet Girl," *Stand By!*, Aug. 24, 1935.

Letters to the editor, "Listeners' Mike," *Stand By!*, Aug. 24, 1935.

THE THREE LITTLE MAIDS

Jenny Lou Carson, *Jenny Lou Carson Song Book* (Chicago: M.M. Cole Publishing, 1944).

Jimmy Snow, *I Cannot Go Back* (Plainfield, N.J.: Logos International, 1977).

Tennessean reporters, "Sally's Husband Sues Foley for $100,000," *The Tennessean*, Apr. 17, 1952.

Tennessean reporters, "Foley Settles Suit Charging Alienation," "Sally Sweet Sues for Alimony," "Sally Sweet Divorce to be Heard Monday," *The Tennessean*, May 20, May 24, and June 24, 1952.

GRACE WILSON

Don Finlayson, "She Has a Million Friends," *Rural Radio*, June 1939.

Anonymous, "Meet Grace Wilson," *Radio Varieties*, Feb. 1940.

Anonymous, "Girl on the Cover," *Stand By!*, Apr. 13, 1935.

WLS AND "THE NATIONAL BARN DANCE"

Zeke Clements, interview with Robert K. Oermann, July 1987.

James F. Evans, *Prairie Farmer and WLS* (Urbana, Ill.: University of Illinois Press, 1969).

Jack Hurst, "Barn Dance Days: Chicago's National Barn Dance," *Bluegrass Unlimited*, Mar. 1986.

William E. Lightfoot, "The Belle of the Barn Dance: Reminiscing with Lulu Belle Wiseman Stamey," *Journal of Country Music*, vol. 12, no. 1, 1987.

Patsy Montana, "Portraits from the Most Popular Country Show on the Air, 1924–1939," *Journal of Country Music*, vol. 10, no. 3, 1985.

Patsy Montana, interview with Robert K. Oermann, Aug. 1985.

Stand By! magazine, Feb. 16–June 25, 1938.

WLS Family Album annuals, 1931–1957.

1930s SHOW BUSINESS AND RADIO LORE

Eric Barnouw, *A Tower in Babel: A History of Broadcasting in the United States* (New York: Oxford University Press, 1966).

Thomas A. DeLong, *The Mighty Music Box* (Los Angeles: Amber Crest Books, 1980).

Philip K. Eberly, *Music in the Air: America's Changing Tastes in Popular Music, 1920–1980* (New York: Hastings House, 1982).

Roger D. Kinkle, *The Complete Encyclopedia of Popular Music and Jazz, 1900–1950* (Westport, Conn.: Arlington House, 1974).

Tom Lewis, *Empire of the Air: The Men Who Made Radio* (New York: Harper-Collins/Edward Burlingame Books, 1991).

Dick Perry, *Not Just a Sound: The Story of WLW* (Englewood Cliffs, N.J.: Prentice-Hall, 1971).

William McKinley Randle, *History of Radio Broadcasting and Its Social and Economic Effect on the Entertainment Industry, 1920–1930* (Cleveland: Ph.D. thesis, Western Reserve University, 1966).

Russell Sanjek, *American Popular Music and Its Business* (New York: Oxford University Press, 1988).

Ivan M. Tribe, *Mountaineer Jamboree* (Lexington: University Press of Kentucky, 1984).

THE DEPRESSION

Ann Banks, *First Person America* (New York: Vintage Books, 1981).

Thomas R. Frazier, ed., *The Private Side of American History* (New York: Harcourt Brace Jovanovich, 1975).

Meridel Le Sueur, *Women on the Breadlines* (Cambridge, Mass.: West End Press, 1977).

Arthur M. Schlesinger and Dixon Ryan Fox, eds., *The History of American Life* (New York: The Macmillan Company, 1948).

David A. Shannon, ed., *The Great Depression* (Englewood Cliffs, N.J.: Prentice-Hall, 1960).

Studs Terkel, *Hard Times* (New York: Pantheon Books, 1986).

Tom E. Terrill and Gerrold Hirsch, eds., *Such As Us: Southern Voices of the Thirties* (Chapel Hill: University of North Carolina Press, 1978).

Susan Ware, *Holding Their Own: American Women in the 1930s* (Boston: Twayne Publishers, 1982).

5. Hungry Disgusted Blues

LITA AND RAY AUVILLE

R. Serge Denisoff, *Great Day Coming* (Baltimore: Penguin Books, 1973).

JUDY CANOVA

Kyle Crichton, "Hillbilly Judy," *Colliers,* May 16, 1942.

Robert Kendall, "Judy Canova: Will She Yodel in 'No No Nanette'?," *Hollywood Studio,* Jan. 1972.

James Robert Parish, *The Slapstick Queens* (New York: Castle Books, 1973).

James Robert Parish and Michael R. Pitts, *Hollywood Songsters* (New York: Garland Publishing, 1991).

Robbins Music Corp. *Famous Radio Hill-Billies Ann, Judy and Zeke Collection of Original Songs of the Hills and Popular Old Time Mountain Tunes* (New York: Robbins Music Corp., 1934).

J.S., "Annie, Judy and Zeke" New Acts review, *Billboard,* May 30, 1931.

Thomas Burnett Swann, *The Heroine or the Horse* (Cranbury, N.J.: A.S. Barnes & Co., 1977).

THE CARTER FAMILY

June Carter, "I Remember the Carter Family," *Country Song Roundup,* Oct. 1965, Dec. 1965.

Gene Fowler and Bill Crawford, *Border Radio* (Austin: Texas Monthly Press, 1987).

Archie Green, William H. Koon, and Norm Cohen, *The Carter Family on Border Radio* LP liner notes (Los Angeles: JEMF Records, n.d.).

Ed Romaniuk, *The Original Carter Family from 1936 Radio Transcripts* LP liner notes (Brighton, Mich.: Old Homestead Records, n.d.).

Tony Russell, *The Carter Family Country & Western Classics* LP liner notes (Alexandria, Va.: Time-Life Records, 1982).

Ivan M. Tribe, *The Carter Family in Texas Vol. 2* LP liner notes (Brighton, Mich.: Old Homestead Records, 1978).

AGNES "SIS" CUNNINGHAM

Kristin Baggelaar and Donald Milton, *Folk Music: More Than a Song* (New York: Thomas Y. Crowell, 1976).

Jim Capaldi, "The Struggle Continues," *Folkscene,* vol. 4, no. 12, Feb. 1977.

A. Cunningham and G. Friesen, *Sundown* LP liner notes (New York: Folkways Records, 1976).

NANCY DIXON

Archie Green, *Babies in the Mill* LP liner notes (Chicago: Testament Records, 1964).

SARAH OGUN GUNNING

Kristin Baggelaar and Donald Milton, *Folk Music: More Than a Song* (New York: Thomas Y. Crowell, 1976).

Guy Carawan, *Come All You Coal Miners* LP liner notes (Somerville, Mass.: Rounder Records, 1973).

Jim Garland, *The Silver Dagger* LP liner notes (Somerville, Mass.: Rounder Records, 1976).

Archie Green, *Girl of Constant Sorrow* LP liner notes (Huntington, Vt.: Folk-Legacy Records, 1965).

AUNT MOLLY JACKSON

Kristin Baggelaar and Donald Milton, *Folk Music: More Than a Song* (New York: Thomas Y. Crowell, 1976).

John Greenway, *The Songs and Stories of Aunt Molly Jackson* LP liner notes (New York: Folkways Records, 1961).

The Rounders, *Aunt Molly Jackson Library of Congress Recordings* LP liner notes (Somerville, Mass.: Rounder Records, 1971).

Charles K. Wolfe, *Kentucky Country* (Lexington: University Press of Kentucky, 1982).

ZORA LAYMAN

Time-Life Records editors, *The Women* LP liner notes (Alexandria, Va.: Time-Life Records, 1981).

Gerald F. Vaughn, "Ray Whitley's Tribute to Frank Luther," *JEMF Quarterly,* pt. 1, 1976.

Gerald F. Vaughn, letter to Danny Hatcher and Robert K. Oermann, Nov. 1981.

THE PICKARD FAMILY

Joe Bleeden, "The Pickard Family," *Western & Country Music,* Jan. 1952.

Gene Fowler and Bill Crawford, *Border Radio* (Austin: Texas Monthly Press, 1987).

Ed Kahn, "Tapescript: Interview with Charlie, Bubb and Lucille Pickard," *JEMF Newsletter,* vol. 4, pt. 4, no. 2, Dec. 1968.

Tex Ritter, *Pickard Family: Song Hits of Yesterday* LP liner notes (Los Angeles: Verve Records, 1957).

Anonymous, "Folksong's Favorite Family," *Country Song Roundup,* vol. 1, no. 11, Apr. 1951.

FLORENCE REECE

William Serrin, "Woman Who Wrote Labor Song, Now Frail, Is Still a Fighter," *The New York Times,* Mar. 18, 1984.

Anonymous, Florence Reece obituary, *Sing Out!,* vol. 32, no. 2, 1986.

BORDER RADIO

Gene Fowler and Bill Crawford, *Border Radio* (Austin: Texas Monthly Press, 1987).

Archie Green, William H. Koon, and Norm Cohen, *The Carter Family on Border Radio* LP liner notes (Los Angeles: JEMF Records, n.d.).

Tom Lewis, *Empire of the Air: The Men Who Made Radio* (New York: Harper-Collins/Edward Burlingame Books, 1991).

FOLK MUSIC AND THE LABOR MOVEMENT

Richard O. Boyer and Herbert M. Morais, *Labor's Untold Story* (New York: United Electrical, Radio and Machine Workers of America, 1955).

Suzanne Crowell, *Appalachian People's History Book* (Louisville: Mountain Education Associates/Southern Conference Educational Fund, 1971).

R. Serge Denisoff, *Great Day Coming* (Baltimore: Penguin Books, 1973).

Roberta Ash Garner, *Social Movements in America* (Chicago: Rand McNally, 1977).

Archie Green, *Only a Miner* (Urbana: University of Illinois Press, 1972).

Waldemar Hille, ed., *The People's Song Book* (New York: Oak Publications, 1961).

Frances Fox Piven and Richard A. Cloward, *Poor People's Movements* (New York: Random House, 1977).

Pete Seeger and Bob Reiser, *Carry It On!* (New York: Simon & Schuster, 1985).

Howard Zinn, *A People's History of the United States* (New York: Harper & Row, 1980).

6. Hollywood Hayride

ROSALIE ALLEN

Rosalie Allen, "The Life Story of Rosalie Allen, Radio's New Singing Star, as Told to Ellsworth Newcomb," undated scrapbook clipping, Country Music Foundation Library & Media Center.

Rosalie Allen, "Disc'Cussion," *Hoedown,* vol. 1, no. 4, Dec. 1953.

Anonymous, *Starring Elton Britt and Rosalie Allen* LP liner notes (Los Angeles: Grand Award Records, 1966, originally released 1955).

Anonymous, "Rosalie Allen Sings," *National Jamboree,* vol. 1, no. 1, June 1949.

Anonymous, "Miss Rosalie Allen: Champion Girl Yodeler of America," *National Hillbilly News,* Nov.–Dec. 1947.

Anonymous, "Rosalie Allen: Queen of the Yodelers," undated press kit, Country Music Foundation Library & Media Center.

Anonymous, "Queen of Hillbilly Deejays," *Record Roundup,* vol. 2, no. 7, July 1948.

Anonymous, "Gal Hilljockey Favorite in N.Y.," *Record Roundup,* vol. 1, no. 9, Aug. 1947.

THE AMBURGEY SISTERS

Martha Carson, interview with Robert K. Oermann, May 1990.

Wayne W. Daniel, *Pickin' on Peachtree* (Urbana: University of Illinois Press, 1990).

Martha Fogarty, ". . . To Sing Again After 15 Years," *The Knoxville Journal,* July 27, 1976.

Robert K. Oermann, "'Young' Martha Carson: 'From Neon to Nashville,'" *The Tennessean,* May 26, 1990.

Various writers, "I Am Woman: A Tribute to Women in Music," *BMI The Many Worlds of Music,* no. 4, 1977.

Anonymous, "Mr. & Mrs.: Salty & Mattie," *Cowboy Songs,* vol. 1, no. 23, Nov. 1952.

EDITH BERBERT

Dorothy Horstman, *Sing Your Heart Out, Country Boy* (New York: E.P. Dutton, 1975).

JUDY CANOVA

Kyle Crichton, "Hillbilly Judy," *Colliers,* May 16, 1942.

Glenn Esterly, "She's a Big Girl Now: Diana Canova," *TV Guide,* vol. 28, no. 50, Dec. 13, 1980.

Richard Maurice Hurst, *Republic Studios: Between Poverty Row and the Majors* (Metuchen, N.J.: Scarecrow Press, 1979).

James Robert Parish, *The Slapstick Queens* (New York: Castle Books, 1973).

James Robert Parish and Michael R. Pitts, *Hollywood Songsters* (New York: Garland Publishing, 1991).

Thomas Burnett Swann, *The Heroine or the Horse* (Cranbury, N.J.: A.S. Barnes & Co., 1977).

Anonymous, "Pigtail Pagliacci: Country Gal Yearns for Siren Roles," *Record Roundup,* vol. 1, no. 6, May 1947.

JENNY LOU CARSON

Jenny Lou Carson, *The Jenny Lou Carson Song Book* (Chicago: M.M. Cole Publishing, 1944).

Jenny Lou Carson, *Songs by Jenny Lou Carson Album No. 2* (Beverly Hills: Hill and Range Songs, 1949).

MOTHER MAYBELLE AND THE CARTER SISTERS

June Carter, "I Remember The Carter Family," *Country Song Roundup,* Dec. 1965.

June Carter Cash, *From the Heart* (New York: Prentice-Hall Press, 1987).

June Carter Cash, *Among My Klediments* (Grand Rapids, Mich.: Zondervan Publishing, 1979).

Michael Orgill, *Anchored in Love: The Carter Family Story* (Old Tappan, N.J.: Fleming H. Revell Co., 1975).

Tony Russell, *The Carter Family* LP liner notes (Alexandria, Va.: Time-Life Records, 1982).

CAROLINA COTTON

Gordon Anderson, "Bakersfield Teacher a Star in Singing Cowboy Films," *Bakersfield Californian,* n.d.

Bobbie Bennett and Hinton Bradbury, "Carolina Cotton Is Top Box Office Attraction!" publicity kit, 1953.

Mario A. DeMarco, "Cowboy Song Stars," *Cowboy Songs,* vol. 1, no. 22, Sept. 1952.

Bea Terry, "Folk Music and Its Folks," undated clipping, Country Music Foundation Library & Media Center.

Ivan M. Tribe, "Carolina Cotton: Hollywood's Yodeling Sweetheart," *Old Time Country,* vol. 7, no. 3, Summer 1991.

Anonymous, "Curvacious Carolina Cotton," *Cowboy Songs,* no. 11, Nov. 1950.

Anonymous, "One Career That Was Worth Yodeling About," *Bakersfield Californian,* July 1, 1980.

DIXIE DARLING

Gladys Rupert, "The Dixie Darling Show," *The Mountain Broadcast and Prairie Recorder,* Mar. 1946.

GAIL DAVIS

Tim Brooks and Earle Marsh, *The Complete Directory to Prime Time Network TV Shows* (New York: Ballantine, 1988).

Steve Oney, "The Last Roundup," *California,* Nov. 1982.

THE DINNING SISTERS

Jean Dinning, interview with Robert K. Oermann, July 1987.

Bob Greene, "Dreamgirls," *Esquire,* May 1987.

Frank Lenger, *The Dinning Sisters Vol. 2* LP liner notes (Paris, France: Capitol Records, 1985).

Frank Lenger, *The Dinning Sisters: Songs We Sang at The National Barn Dance* LP liner notes (Sulzheim, Germany: Cattle Records, 1986).

Frank Lenger, *The Dinning Sisters and Friends* LP liner notes (Sulzheim, Germany: Cattle Records, 1988).

Frank Lenger, *The Dinning Sisters: Swingin' at the Barn Dance* LP liner notes (Sulzheim, Germany: Cattle Records, 1989).

Don Lewis, "Listen Up!," *The Milwaukee Journal,* Jan. 26, 1986.

Robert K. Oermann, "Revival Surprises Retired Dinning Sisters," *The Tennessean,* July 12, 1987.

James Robert Parish and Michael R. Pitts, *Hollywood Songsters* (New York: Garland Publishing, 1991).

Michael Pitts, "Nostalgia Soundtrack," *Classic Images,* no. 171, n.d.

Mike Wyma, "Dinnings' Music Revived by Sound of 1 Fan Clapping," *Los Angeles Times,* June 4, 1987.

ESMERELDY

WHBQ Radio, "Esmereldy: WHBQ Announcement Record," undated Memphis radio station typescript, Country Music Foundation Library & Media Center.

Anonymous, "Esmereldy: The Streamlined Hillbilly," *National Jamboree,* Aug. 1949.

Anonymous, "Behind the Scenes with Esmereldy," *Cowboy Songs,* no. 20, May 1952.

DALE EVANS

Frank Henderson, "New Star of Western Pictures," *The Mountain Broadcast and Prairie Recorder,* Mar. 1945.

James Robert Parish and Michael R. Pitts, *Hollywood Songsters* (New York: Garland Publishing, 1991).

Dale Evans Rogers, *Dale: My Personal Picture Album* (Old Tappan, N.J.: Fleming H. Revell Co., 1971).

Roy Rogers and Dale Evans with Carlton Stowers, *Happy Trails* (Waco, Tex.: Word Books, 1979).

David Rothel, *The Roy Rogers Book* (Madison, N.C.: Empire Publishing, 1987).

Thomas Burnett Swann, *The Heroine or the Horse* (Cranbury, N.J.: A.S. Barnes & Co., 1977).

Anonymous, "Intimate Facts About the Queen: Meet the Real Dale," *National Jamboree,* Nov.–Dec. 1949.

Anonymous, "Queen of the Westerners: Dale Evans," *Cowboy Songs,* no. 12, Jan. 1951.

Anonymous, "Dale Evans Deserts Lead Western Roles," *Record Roundup,* vol. 1, no. 4, Mar. 1947.

Anonymous, "Wedding Bells Ring for Dale and Roy," *Record Roundup,* vol. 2, no. 2, Feb. 1948.

ELLA MAE EVANS

Randall Riese, *Nashville Babylon* (New York: Congdon & Weed, 1988).

Nick Tosches, *Country* (New York: Stein & Day, 1977).

MARY FORD

Donald Clarke, ed., *The Penguin Encyclopedia of Popular Music* (New York: Viking, 1989).

Rich Kienzle, *Great Guitarists* (New York: Facts on File, 1985).

George T. Simon & Friends, *The Best of the Music Makers* (Garden City, N.Y.: Doubleday, 1979).

Joe Smith, *Off the Record* (New York: Warner Books, 1988).

J. R. Young, *The World Is Still Waiting for the Sunrise* LP liner notes (Hollywood: Capitol Records, 1974).

Anonymous, "Guest Stars: Les Paul–Mary Ford," *Cowboy Songs,* vol. 1, no. 27, July 1953.

SALLY FOSTER

Dick C. Land, "Sally Foster: The Girl with the Smile in Her Voice," *The Mountain Broadcast and Prairie Recorder,* June 1945.

Anonymous, "Girl on the Cover," *Stand By!,* Jan. 25, 1936.

THE HICKORY SISTERS

Anonymous, "The Hickory Sisters," *The Mountain Broadcast and Prairie Recorder,* June 1946.

POLLY JENKINS

Polly Jenkins and Her Plow Boys, *Heart Throbs of the Hills* (New York: Bob Miller, 1937).

Dick C. Land, "Polly Jenkins and Her Pals," *The Mountain Broadcast and Prairie Recorder,* Jan. 1947.

MA AND PA KETTLE

Leslie Halliwell, *The Filmgoers' Companion* (New York: Equinox/Avon, 1971).

Ephraim Katz, *The Film Encyclopedia* (New York: Perigee, 1979).

Leonard Maltin, ed., *Leonard Maltin's TV Movies and Video Guide* (New York: Signet/New American Library, 1986).

David Quinlan, *The Illustrated Encyclopedia of Character Actors* (New York: Harmony/Crown, 1985).

PATSY LEE

Benny Karr, "Our Own Patsy Lee," *Cowboy Music World*, Nov.–Dec. 1944.

THE LOG CABIN GIRLS

Frankie More, *Frankie More's Log Cabin Girls* (Wheeling, W.Va.: Frankie More/WWVA, 1938).

Asher Sizemore, *Log Cabin Songs as Sung by Frankie More's Log Cabin Boys* (Louisville: Kentucky Home Publishing Co., 1936).

Ivan M. Tribe, *Mountaineer Jamboree* (Lexington: University Press of Kentucky, 1984).

LULU BELLE

Craig Baguley, "Lulu Belle: Tender Memories Recalled," *Country Music People*, vol. 22, nos. 4–5, April–May 1991.

Wayne W. Daniel, "Lulu Belle and Scotty: Have I Told You Lately That I Love You?," *Bluegrass Unlimited*, Mar. 1986.

Jake Lambert, "Where Are They Now?," *Big Country News*, Nov. 1969.

LAURA LEE OWENS MCBRIDE

John Pugh, "Laura Lee—The Queen of Swing," *Music City News*, Mar. 1973.

Cecil Remington, *Queen of Western Swing Laura Lee* LP liner notes (Nacogdoches, Tex.: Delta Records, 1984).

Charles R. Townsend, *San Antonio Rose: The Life and Music of Bob Wills* (Urbana: University of Illinois Press, 1976).

THE MCKINNEY SISTERS

Dean and Evelyn, *Favorite Songs of the Progressive Farmerettes* (Raleigh, N.C.: Progressive Farmer, 1944).

ELSIE MCWILLIAMS

Gordon Cotton, "Father of Country Music Born in Sister-in-Law's Songs," Associated Press story in *Kansas City Star*, Nov. 30, 1975.

Elsie McWilliams, interview with the authors, April 1978.

Elsie McWilliams, letter to Jim Evans, in *America's Blue Yodeler: Jimmie Rodgers Fan Club Journal*, vol. 1, no. 4, Fall 1953.

Nolan Porterfield, *Jimmie Rodgers* (Urbana: University of Illinois Press, 1979).

Anonymous, "Mrs. Elsie McWilliams," *Hillbilly Folk Record Journal*, April–May–June 1954.

ROSE MADDOX

Wayne W. Daniel, "The Saga of the Maddox Brothers and Rose: A Country Music Success Story," *Bluegrass Unlimited*, Dec. 1990.

Garth Gibson, "Rose Maddox," *Country & Western Spotlight*, no. 1, Summer 1974.

Rose Maddox, interview with Robert K. Oermann, July 1989.

Robert K. Oermann, "Country Pioneer Rose Maddox Yearns for Nashville Laurels," *The Tennessean*, Aug. 6, 1989.

Keith Olesen, *Maddox Brothers and Rose 1946–1951, Vols. 1–2* LP liner notes (El Cerrito, Calif.: Arhoolie Records, 1976).

Charlie Seemann, *Maddox Brothers and Rose Columbia Historic Edition* LP liner notes (Nashville: Columbia Records, 1985).

Chris Strachwitz, *The Maddox Brothers & Rose on the Air, Vol. 2* LP liner notes (El Cerrito, Calif.: Arhoolie Records, 1985).

Johnny Whiteside, "The Manifest Destiny of The Maddox Brothers and Rose," *Journal of Country Music*, vol. 11, no. 2, 1986.

Anonymous, "Family Folks: Maddox Bros. & Rose," *Country Song Roundup*, vol. 1, no. 21, Dec. 1952.

Anonymous, "From Southern Rags to Western Riches," *Country Song Roundup*, vol. 1, no. 9, Dec. 1950.

Anonymous, "Rose Maddox: The Flower of Country Music," *Cowboy Songs*, vol. 12, no. 66, May 1961.

Anonymous, *The One Rose* LP liner notes (Los Angeles: Capitol Records, 1958).

PATTI PAGE

Donald Clarke, ed., *The Penguin Encyclopedia of Popular Music* (New York: Viking, 1989).

Stephen Holden, "Pop Pioneer Patti Page Retains Perennial Appeal," New York Times News Service story in *The Tennessean*, Aug. 7, 1988.

Jack Rael, "Overdub Pioneer Patti Page," letter to *Grammy* magazine, vol. 8, no. 1, Jan. 1990.

George T. Simon & Friends, *The Best of the Music Makers* (Garden City, N.Y.: Doubleday, 1979).

Joe Smith, *Off the Record* (New York: Warner Books, 1988).

Joel Whitburn, *Top Country Singles, 1944–1988* (Menomonee Falls, Wisc.: Record Research, 1989).

Anonymous, *Go On Home* LP liner notes (Nashville: Mercury Records, 1962).

THE POE SISTERS

Nelle Poe Yandell and Howard Vokes, *The Poe Sisters: Early Stars of the Grand Ole Opry* LP liner notes (Sulzheim, Germany: Cattle Records, 1989).

THE RHODES FAMILY

Wayne W. Daniel, "Well Traveled Rhodes: Meet Dusty and Dot," *Bluegrass Unlimited*, Jan. 1990.

DOROTHY SHAY

Philip K. Scheuer, "This Hillbilly's Svelte! No One-Hoss Shay, She," *Los Angeles Times*, Jan. 21, 1951.

Anonymous, "Dorothy Shay, 'Park Avenue Hillbilly,' Dies," Associated Press obituary in *The Tennessean*, Oct. 23, 1978.

DINAH SHORE

Emily Belser, "Dinah Shore Says Year's Free Singing Was Experience Worth Million Dollars," INS wire story in *The Tennessean*, May 29, 1959.

Donald Clarke, ed., *The Penguin Encyclopedia of Popular Music* (New York: Viking, 1989).

Gene Handsaker, "Dinah Shore . . . Almost Legend," Associated Press story in *The Tennessean*, May 25, 1961.

Charles Higham, "Nothin' Could Be Finah for Dinah Shore," *The New York Times*, Aug. 27, 1972.

Nellie Kenyon, "Nashville Home Dinah's Target," *The Tennessean*, Jan. 4, 1957.

Cynthia Lowry, "Dinah Keeps Mind Open, Stays Young," Associated Press story in *The Tennessean*, Apr. 13, 1969.

Robert K. Oermann, "'Dinah Comes Home Again Tonight' on TNN," *The Tennessean*, Apr. 17, 1990.

Robert K. Oermann, "Dinah: Is Anyone Finah?," *The Tennessean*, May 20, 1990.

Vernon Scott, "Dinah and Chevy Announce Parting," Associated Press story in *The Tennessean*, Feb. 17, 1961.

Vernon Scott, "Politics Aside, It's Still Dinah and Burt," Associated Press story in *The Tennessean*, Oct. 15, 1972.

Dinah Shore, interview with Robert K. Oermann, Apr. 1990.

George T. Simon & Friends, *The Best of the Music Makers* (Garden City, N.Y.: Doubleday, 1979).

Bob Thomas, "Working Wives Happier, Busy Dinah Shore Says," Associated Press story in *The Tennessean*, Nov. 18, 1951.

Anonymous, "Nashville Girl Makes It as Singer . . . Fanny Rose Shore Finds Career in New York," *The Tennessean*, Jan. 1, 1940.

Anonymous, "Dinah Shore and Actor Now in Army Wed," *The Tennessean*, Dec. 7, 1943.

Anonymous, "Dinah Shore Chosen Top Woman Singer," *The Tennessean*, Feb. 25, 1944.

Anonymous, "Dinah Charges Mental Cruelty," "Divorce Fails to Dampen Dinah's Spirit," "Dinah Shore's Marriage Ends," "Dinah Shore Weds Again," "Dinah Shore Sues 2nd Husband for Divorce," "Dinah Shore Sheds Second Husband," "Adultery Charged to Dinah," "Dinah Cleared of Adultery" Associated Press stories in *The Tennessean*, 1962–1965.

JO STAFFORD

Donald Clarke, ed., *The Penguin Encyclopedia of Popular Music* (New York: Viking, 1989).

Tom Colborn, *Introducing Jo Stafford* LP liner notes (London: EMI/Capitol Records, 1987).

George T. Simon & Friends, *The Best of the Music Makers* (Garden City, N.Y.: Doubleday, 1979).

Anonymous, "Guest Star: Jo Stafford," *Cowboy Songs*, no. 26, May 1953.

Anonymous, "Jo Stafford," *Record Roundup*, vol. 3, no. 1, Jan. 15, 1949.

KAY STARR

Gino Falzarano, "The Fabulous Favorite Miss Kay Starr," *DISCoveries*, vol. 4, no. 9, Sept. 1991.

Gary Giddins, "A Star Is Reborn," *Village Voice*, Nov. 12, 1985.

Robert K. Oermann, "Versatile Starr Brightens Show," *The Tennessean*, Mar. 23, 1986.

Steve Sanders, "Concert Review: Kay Starr," *Hollywood Reporter*, Aug. 3, 1988.

George T. Simon & Friends, *The Best of the Music Makers* (Garden City, N.Y.: Doubleday, 1979).

Anonymous, *Kay Starr Again!* LP liner notes (Hollywood: Capitol Records, 1974).

UNCLE PETE AND LOUISE

J.V.H., "The Story of Uncle Pete and Louise," in *Uncle Pete and Louise Songbook* (New York: n.p., c. 1934).

CINDY WALKER

Hinton Bradbury, "Cindy Walker: Tater Pie Gal," undated magazine clipping, authors' collection.

Royce Korsak, "With a Song in Her Heart," *Dallas Times Herald*, Oct. 3, 1973.

Walt Trott, "Cindy Walker Loves Lone Star Lifestyle," *Country Scene*, n.d., c. 1987.

Cindy Walker, *Cindy Walker's Folio of Songs No. 1* (Portland, Oreg.: American Music, 1942).

Cindy Walker, *Song Souvenirs Bob Wills & The Texas Playboys* (Winona, Minn.: Hal Leonard Publishing, 1976).

Cindy Walker, interview with Robert K. Oermann, June 1991.

Anonymous, "Speaking of Songwriters: Cindy Walker," *Hoedown*, vol. 1, no. 6, Feb. 1954.

Anonymous, "Life Is a Song for Cindy," *Country Song Roundup*, vol. 1, no. 4, Feb. 1950.

Anonymous, "Mother of Songwriter Walker to Be Buried in Texas Today," *The Tennessean*, June 6, 1991.

WEAVER BROTHERS AND ELVIRY

James Saxon Childers, "Professional Rubes Tell Adventures: Old Fashioned Show Still Liked by the Public," *Old Time Country*, vol. 5, no. 4, Winter 1988.

Camille Gavin, "Retired Star of Vaudeville, Film Recalls 'Good Old Days,'" *Old Time Country*, vol. 5, no. 4, Winter 1988 (reprint of 1975 article in *The Bakersfield Californian*).

Richard Maurice Hurst, *Republic Studios: Between Poverty Row and the Majors* (Metuchen, N.J.: Scarecrow Press, 1979).

Joseph Lenz, "Familiar Faces," *Old Time Country*, vol. 5, no. 4, Winter 1988.

Loretta Weaver Torbett, "Weaver Brothers and Elviry," *Old Time Country*, vol. 5, no. 4, Winter 1988.

Anonymous, Elviry Weaver obituary, *Hollywood Reporter*, Dec. 12, 1977.

MARGARET WHITING

Robert K. Oermann, "Will Durable Stylist Whiting Steal the Show," *The Tennessean*, Aug. 17, 1986.

Stephen Ross, "Margaret Whiting," *Yesterday*, no. 9, c. 1991.

Margaret Whiting and Will Holt, *It Might as Well Be Spring* (New York: William Morrow & Co., 1987).

COUNTRY MUSIC AND THE MOVIES

Daily Variety, various issues, 1940–1955.

Billy Doyle, "Lost Players," *Classic Images*, no. 175, n.d.

Gene Fernett, *Poverty Row* (Satellite Beach, Fla.: Coral Reef Publishers, 1973).

Hollywood Reporter, various issues, 1940–1955.

Richard Maurice Hurst, *Republic Studios: Between Poverty Row and the Majors* (Metuchen, N.J.: Scarecrow Press, 1979).

Don Miller, *B Movies* (New York: Ballantine Books, 1987).

Ted Okuda, *Grand National, Producers Releasing Corporation and Screen Guild/Lippert* (Jefferson, N.C.: McFarland & Co., 1989).

David Rothel, *The Singing Cowboys* (La Jolla, Calif.: A.S. Barnes, 1978).

Robert Sklar, *Movie-Made America: A Cultural History of American Movies* (New York: Vintage/Random House, 1975).

Thomas Burnett Swann, *The Heroine or the Horse* (Cranbury, N.J.: A.S. Barnes & Co., 1977).

Maurice Terenzio, Scott MacGillivray, and Ted Okuda, *The Soundies Distributing Corporation of America: A History and Filmography* (Jefferson, N.C.: McFarland & Co., 1991).

Alan Warner, *Who Sang What on the Screen* (North Ryde, NSW, Australia: Angus & Robertson Publishing, 1984).

CALIFORNIA AND THE DUST BOWL

Bruce Henstell, *Sunshine and Wealth: Los Angeles in the Twenties and Thirties* (San Francisco: Chronicle Books, 1984).

Walter J. Stein, *California and the Dust Bowl Migration* (Westport, Conn.: Greenwood Press, 1973).

WORLD WAR II/THE 1940s

Rosalyn Baxandall, Linda Gordon, and Susan Reverby, eds., *America's Working Women* (New York: Vintage/Random House, 1976).

Patrick Carr, ed., *The Illustrated History of Country Music* (Garden City, N.Y.: Doubleday, 1979).

John Costello, *Love, Sex and War: Changing Values, 1939–45* (London: William Collins Sons & Co., 1985).

Linnell Gentry, *A History and Encyclopedia of Country, Western and Gospel Music* (Nashville: Clairmont Corp., 1969).

Susan M. Hartmann, *The Home Front and Beyond: American Women in the 1940s* (Boston: Twayne Publishers, 1982).

Bill C. Malone, *Country Music U.S.A.* (Austin: University of Texas Press, 1968).

Steven Mintz and Susan Kellogg, *Domestic Revolutions: A Social History of American Family Life* (New York: Free Press/Macmillan, 1988).

Ronnie Pugh, "Country Across the Country," in *Country: The Music and the Musicians* (New York: Abbeville Press, 1988).

Robert Shelton, *The Country Music Story* (Secaucus, N.J.: Castle Books, 1966).

Carol Ward and Judith Papachristou, *Myth America: Picturing American Women, 1865–1945* (New York: Pantheon/Random House, 1975).

Joel Whitburn, *Pop Memories, 1890–1954* (Menomonee Falls, Wisc.: Record Research, 1986).

7. Honky-tonk Girl

CHARLINE ARTHUR

Bob Allen, *Welcome to the Club* LP liner notes (Bremen, Germany: Bear Family Records, 1986).

Charline Arthur, interview with Bob Pinson and Robert K. Oermann, June 1979.

Alice M. Michaels, letter to Robert K. Oermann, Sept. 1988.

Richard Weize, letter/press release, Jan. 1988.

Anonymous, "Dallas Bombshell: Charline Arthur," *Cowboy Songs*, no. 43, Oct. 1956.

Anonymous, "Women in the News," *Cowboy Songs*, Dec. 1953.

BETTY CODY

Reimar Binge, *Betty Cody's Souvenir Album* LP liner notes (Sulzheim, Germany: Cattle Records, 1985).

Anonymous, "Betty Cody," RCA Victor Records publicity bio, 1953.

WILMA LEE AND STONEY COOPER

Robert Cogswell, "We Made Our Name in the Days of Radio," *JEMF Quarterly*, vol. 11, pt. 2, no. 38, Summer 1975.

Wilma Lee Cooper, interview with Robert K. Oermann, Sept. 1980.

Chris Gladden, "Nothing but Country in Its Purest Form," *Roanoke Times & World News*, Aug. 20, 1979.

Douglas B. Green, "Wilma Lee and Stoney Cooper," *Bluegrass Unlimited*, March 1974.

Robert K. Oermann, "Mountain Courage Helped Wilma Lee Deal with Death," *The Tennessean*, Oct. 29, 1979.

Robert K. Oermann, *Wilma Lee Cooper* LP liner notes (Somerville, Mass.: Rounder Records, 1981).

Ray Thigpen, "Wilma Lee Cooper," *Bluegrass Unlimited*, Nov. 1988.

DAISY MAE AND OLD BROTHER CHARLIE

Anonymous, "Daisy Mae and Old Brother Charlie Starring in WDAE's Barn Dance," *National Jamboree*, vol. 1, no. 4, Nov.–Dec. 1949.

Anonymous, "Mr. and Mrs. Music!," *Cowboy Songs*, no. 21, July 1952.

Anonymous, "Daisy Mae and Old Brother Charlie," *Country Song Roundup*, vol. 1, no. 17, Apr. 1952.

GOLDIE HILL

Goldie Hill, interview with Mary A. Bufwack and Robert K. Oermann, Oct. 1989.

Pat Twitty, *Goldie Hill* LP liner notes (Nashville: Decca Records, 1958).

Anonymous, "Goldie Hill: Beauty and Brains," *Country & Western Jamboree*, Oct. 1956.

ANN JONES

Carl Hayden, "Country Western Singer Ann Jones Recalls Early Days on the Road," *Idaho Statesman*, June 22, 1975.

Huey Jones, "Ann Jones" publicity flyer (Marana, Ariz.: Huey Jones, n.d.).

Thurston Moore, ed., *Scrapbook of Hillbilly and Western Stars* (Cincinnati: Artists Publications, 1952).

H. B. Teeter, "Glamor and Sex Ain't No Use to Wimmin Who Want to Hire Out in Country Music," *The Tennessean*, Nov. 19, 1954.

Anonymous, "A Laugh in Her Voice: Ann Jones," *Cowboy Songs*, vol. 1, no. 16, Sept. 1951.

Anonymous, "Dee Jay Special," biographical notes on King Records nos. 961 and 972 (Cincinnati: King Records, 1951).

ROSE MADDOX

Wayne W. Daniel, "The Saga of the Maddox Brothers and Rose: A Country Music Success Story," *Bluegrass Unlimited*, Dec. 1990.

Rose Maddox, interview with Robert K. Oermann, July 1989.

Robert K. Oermann, "Country Pioneer Rose Maddox Yearns for Nashville Laurels," *The Tennessean*, Aug. 6, 1989.

Keith Olesen, *Maddox Brothers and Rose 1946–1951, Vols. 1–2* LP liner notes (El Cerrito, Calif.: Arhoolie Records, 1976).

Charlie Seemann, *Maddox Brothers and Rose Columbia Historic Edition* LP liner notes (Nashville: Columbia Records, 1985).

Chris Strachwitz, *The Maddox Brothers & Rose on the Air, Vol. 2* LP liner notes (El Cerrito, Calif.: Arhoolie Records, 1985).

JOE AND ROSE LEE MAPHIS

Dorothy Horstman, *Sing Your Heart Out, Country Boy* (Nashville: Country Music Foundation, 1986).

Rose Lee Maphis, interview with Robert K. Oermann, Oct. 1988.

Don Pierce, *Mr. and Mrs. Country Music* LP liner notes (Nashville: Starday Records, n.d.).

Paul F. Wells, *Dim Lights, Thick Smoke* LP liner notes (Los Angeles: CMH Records, 1978).

Anonymous, "Singing Newlyweds," *Cowboy Songs*, Dec. 1953.

Anonymous, "Meet Joe & Rose Lee Maphis," undated magazine clipping.

ABBIE NEAL AND THE RANCH GIRLS

Abbie Neal and Gene Johnson, "Biographical Sketch of Abbie Neal," promotional booklet (Pittsburgh: n.p., n.d.).

Ivan M. Tribe, *Mountaineer Jamboree: Country Music in West Virginia* (Lexington: University Press of Kentucky, 1984).

Anonymous, "A Leave of Absence for Abbie Neal," *National Jamboree* clipping (c. 1957).

MOLLY O'DAY

John Atkins, "Molly O'Day: One of Country's Greatest Female Voices," *Country Music People*, Mar. 1977.

Dave Peyton, "Country World Singing Praises of Molly, Lynn," *Huntington Herald-Dispatch*, July 20, 1975.

Dave Peyton, "Molly O'Day: A Living Legend," *Pickin'*, Sept. 1979.

Don Rhodes, "Mac Wiseman," *Bluegrass Unlimited*, vol. 10, no. 1, July 1975.

Ivan M. Tribe, *Molly O'Day Radio Favorites* LP liner notes (Brighton, Mich.: Old Homestead Records, n.d.).

Ivan M. Tribe, *A Sacred Collection: Molly O'Day* LP liner notes (Brighton, Mich.: Old Homestead Records, 1979).

Ivan Tribe and John Morris, *The Soul of Molly O'Day, Vols. 1 & 2* LP liner notes (Brighton, Mich.: Old Homestead Records, 1984).

Ivan M. Tribe and John W. Morris, "Molly O'Day and Lynn Davis: A Strong Influence on Bluegrass Music," *Bluegrass Unlimited*, vol. 9, no. 3, Sept. 1974.

Ivan Tribe and John Morris, "Molly O'Day: On the Threshold of Greatness," *The Journal*, vol. 1, no. 6, Dec. 1991.

Anonymous, "Country Music Legend Molly O'Day Dies," Associated Press obituary in *The Tennessean*, Dec. 7, 1987.

JEAN SHEPARD

Jean Hollabaugh, "Jean Shepard—Special Effort to Comeback," *The Tennessean*, Nov. 3, 1964.

Jack Hurst, "Now Jean Can Be Other Woman," *The Chicago Tribune*, Apr. 11, 1975.

Robert K. Oermann, "Country's Jean Shepard Makes Vietnam Veterans Her Cause," *The Tennessean*, May 21, 1988.

Jean Shepard, interview with Robert K. Oermann, May 1988.

Ginger Willis, "A Shepard Catches a Hawk," *Country Song Roundup*, May 1961.

SUNSHINE SUE

Jan Edwards, "Memories of Sunshine Sue and the Old Dominion Barn Dance," *Bluegrass Unlimited*, June 1991.

Norman Rowe, "A Firm, Final Bow for Sunshine Sue is Due Next Sunday," *Richmond Times-Dispatch*, Mar. 16, 1975.

Norman Rowe, "Sunshine, Sue Return; Crowd Packs Mosque," *Richmond Times-Dispatch*, Mar. 24, 1975.

WRVA, "Sunshine Sue," press releases (Richmond: n.d.).

WRVA, *Old Dominion Barn Dance Picture Album* (Richmond: W.R. Thompson & Co., n.d.).

Anonymous, "We're From Ioway!," *Stand By!*, Nov. 17, 1936.

Anonymous, "Sunshine Sue the Personality Queen," *Rustic Rhythm*, Apr. 1957.

Anonymous, "Sunshine Sue Workman Dies of Heart Attack," Associated Press obituary in *The Tennessean*, June 15, 1979.

TEXAS RUBY

Ruth M. Charon and Curly Fox, "Miss Texas Ruby," publicity bio, n.p., 1963.

Zeke Clements, interview with Robert K. Oermann, July 1987.

Curly Fox and Texas Ruby, *21 of Our Best Songs* (Nashville: WSM, n.d.).

Sydney Nathan, *Favorite Songs of Texas Ruby* LP liner notes (Cincinnati: King Records, 1963).

Ivan M. Tribe, "Curly Fox: Old Time and Novelty Fiddler Extraordinary," *The Devil's Box*, no. 27, Dec. 1, 1974.

Anonymous, "Curly Fox and Texas Ruby on King," *Record Roundup*, vol. 2, May 1948.

Anonymous, *Traveling Blues/Original Recordings of Texas Ruby and Curly Fox/Memorial Tribute to Texas Ruby* LP liner notes (Nashville: Harmony/Columbia Records, 1963).

Anonymous, "Folk Singer Texas Ruby Dies in Trailer Fire," UPI wire story, Mar. 30, 1963.

Anonymous, "Death Hits Opry 6th Time," UPI wire story, Mar. 30, 1963.

KITTY WELLS

Olan Bassham, "Kitty Wells: Queen of Country Music," *Big Country News*, vol. 1, no. 4, Nov. 1969.

Mary Bufwack, "The Feminist Sensibility in Post-War Country Music," *Southern Quarterly*, vol. 22, no. 3, Spring 1984.

Joan Dew, *Singers & Sweethearts* (Dolphin/Doubleday, 1977).

A. C. Dunkleburger, *Queen of Country Music: The Life Story of Kitty Wells* (Nashville: Ambrose Printing, 1977).

Thomas Goldsmith, "Queen of Country Music Winner at Grammy Awards," *The Tennessean*, Feb. 17, 1991.

Douglas B. Green, "Kitty Wells," *BMI: The Many Worlds of Music*, no. 4, 1976.

Charles Newman, "The Kitty Wells Story," *Country News and Views*, vol. 2, no. 4, April 1964.

Robert K. Oermann, "Golden Memories Day for Kitty, Johnny," *The Tennessean*, Oct. 30, 1987.

Robert K. Oermann, "Back in the Country, 1952: Kitty Wells Becomes the Queen of Country Music," *Country Song Roundup*, vol. 35, no. 303, Oct. 1984.

Robert K. Oermann, "Honky-Tonk Angels: Kitty Wells and Patsy Cline," in *Country: The Music and the Musicians* (New York: Abbeville Press, 1988).

Robert K. Oermann and Mary A. Bufwack, *Kitty Wells: The Golden Years* LP liner notes (Somerville, Mass.: Rounder Records, 1982).

Bob Pinson, Richard Weize, and Charles Wolfe, *The Golden Years: Kitty Wells* LP booklet (Achtern Dahl, Germany: Bear Family Records, 1987).

Walt Trott, "Kitty Wells/Sweet Dreams," typescript, Oct. 1, 1985.

Walt Trott, "Kitty Wells," Entertainment Unlimited press release, Oct. 1991.

Kitty Wells and Sue Sturdivant, *Kitty's Country Cookbook* (Nashville: Wright's Enterprises, n.d.).

Kitty Wells and Johnny Wright, interview with Robert K. Oermann, Oct. 1987.

AUDREY WILLIAMS

Dale Vinicur, *Audrey Williams: Ramblin' Gal* (Vollersode, Germany: Bear Family Records, 1988).

Lycretia Williams and Dale Vinicur, *Still in Love with You* (Nashville: Rutledge Hill Press, 1989).

WOMEN AND HONKY-TONK MUSIC

Patrick Carr, ed., *The Illustrated History of Country Music* (Garden City, N.Y.: Doubleday, 1979).

Dorothy Horstman, *Sing Your Heart Out, Country Boy* (Nashville: Country Music Foundation, 1986).

Otto Kitsinger, *The Early Country Charts* (Nashville: Otto Kitsinger, 1987).

Bill C. Malone, *Country Music U.S.A.* (Austin: University of Texas Press, 1968).

Robert K. Oermann, *The Greatest Country Music Recordings of All Time: Honky-Tonk, Vol. 1* LP liner notes (Franklin Center, Pa.: Franklin Mint Record Society, 1983).

Joel Whitburn, *Top Country Singles, 1944–1988* (Menomonee Falls, Wisc.: Record Research, 1989).

Anonymous, "Kitty & Goldie Start Country-Girl Search," *Billboard*, June 20, 1953.

Anonymous, "Show Biz Sexes War in Offing? Fems Show Discrimination False," *Billboard*, Nov. 5, 1949.

POSTWAR AMERICA

William Chafe, *The American Woman* (New York: Oxford University Press, 1972).

Ely Chinoy, *Automobile Workers and the American Dream* (Boston: Beacon Press, 1955).

John Costello, *Love, Sex and the War* (London: Collins, 1985).

Helene Deutsch, *The Psychology of Women* (New York: n.p., 1944).

Barbara Ehrenrich, *The Hearts of Men* (Garden City, N.Y.: Doubleday, 1983).

Marynia Farnham and Ferdinand Lundberg, *Modern Woman: The Lost Sex* (New York: n.p., 1947).

Betty Friedan, *The Feminine Mystique* (New York: Dell Publishing, 1983).

Louis Gordon and Alan Gordon, *American Chronicle* (New York: Crown, 1990).

Dorothy Horstman, *Sing Your Heart Out, Country Boy* (Nashville: Country Music Foundation, 1986).

Oliver Jensen, *The Revolt of American Women* (New York: Harcourt, Brace, Jovanovich, 1971).

C. Wright Mills, *White Collar* (New York: Oxford University Press, 1951).

Steven Mintz and Susan Kellogg, *Domestic Revolutions* (New York: Free Press, 1988).

Glenda Riley, *Inventing the American Woman* (Arlington Heights, Ill.: Harlan Davidson Publishing, 1986).

Agnes Rogers, *Women Are Here to Stay* (New York: Harper & Bros., 1949).

8. All-Day Sing

TAMMY FAYE BAKKER

Joe E. Barnhart, *Jim & Tammy: Charismatic Intrigue Inside PTL* (Buffalo: Prometheus Books, 1988).

Robert Barr, "Contributors Will Be Televangelists' Jury," Associated Press wire story in *The Tennessean*, Mar. 29, 1987.

Art Harris, "Tammy's Love for Singer," *Washington Post* wire story in *The Nashville Banner*, Apr. 2, 1987.

Larry Martz and Ginny Carroll, *Ministry of Greed* (New York: Weidenfeld & Nicolson/Newsweek Books, 1988).

John Omicinski, "Is Televangelists' War Drying Up the Coffers?," Gannett News Service story in *The Tennessean*, Apr. 5, 1987.

Carol Richards, "The Ladies of Televangelism," Gannett News Service story in *The Tennessean*, Mar. 29, 1987.

William E. Schmidt, "For Bakkers, Excess Wiped Out Climb," New York Times News Service story in *The Tennessean*, May 24, 1987.

Karen S. Schneider, Nina Burleigh, et al., "Tammy's Troubled Waters," *People*, Apr. 6, 1992.

Tom Shales, "Bakkers Lived and Died by the Tube," *Washington Post* wire story in *The Tennessean*, Apr. 29, 1990.

Tammie Smith, "Album's 'Best Tune' Sets Record Straight," *The Tennessean*, Sept. 12, 1987.

MARTHA CARSON

Martha Carson, interview with Robert K. Oermann, May 1990.

Robert K. Oermann, "'Young' Martha Carson: 'From Neon to Nashville,'" *The Tennessean*, May 26, 1990.

THE CHUCK WAGON GANG

Roy Carter, interview with Robert K. Oermann, July 1983.

Elbert Haling, "Rolling Along with the Chuck Wagon Gang," *Rural Radio*, vol. 1, no. 6, July 1938.

Robert K. Oermann, "Chuck Wagon Gang Rolls onto Charts," *The Tennessean*, July 19, 1983.

Sandy Smith, "Chuck Wagon Gang Serves Gospel Oldies," *The Tennessean*, Feb. 19, 1989.

Bob Terrell, *The Chuck Wagon Gang: A Legend Lives On* (Nashville: Roy Carter and Bob Terrell, 1990).

Harold Timmons, *Chuck Wagon Gang: Columbia Historic Edition* LP liner notes (Nashville: Columbia Records, 1985).

THE HAPPY GOODMAN FAMILY

Joe Edwards, "Happy Goodman Family Reunites," Associated Press story, Sept. 9, 1990.

Anonymous, "Happy Goodman Family," *The Singing News*, July 1989.

THE HUMBARD FAMILY

Walter Carter, "Humbard: World Evangelism," *The Tennessean*, June 8, 1979.

Lisa Hemby, "Success at '25': 'Avoid Religion,'" *The Tennessean*, May 15, 1977.

Joe McKnight, "Humbard, with 540 Stations, Shows TV Evangelists," Associated Press story in *The Tennessean*, Dec. 8, 1977.

Clifford Terry, "It's a Far Cry from the Church in the Wildwood," *TV Guide*, Oct. 2, 1971.

Anonymous, "Rex Humbard Ministry Background," press kit (Akron, Ohio: Rex Humbard Foundation, 1979).

Anonymous, "Rex Humbard Biographical Information," publicity bio (Akron, Ohio: Rex Humbard Foundation, 1978).

Anonymous, "Introducing Rex Humbard," publicity bio (Akron, Ohio: Rex Humbard Foundation, 1978).

THE JOHNSON FAMILY SINGERS

Anonymous, *Old Time Religion by the Johnson Family Singers* LP liner notes (Nashville: RCA Records, 1955).

Anonymous, *The Touch by Betty Johnson* LP liner notes (Chicago: Bally Records, c. 1957).

Anonymous, *Faith of Our Fathers: The Johnson Family Singers Featuring Betty Johnson* LP liner notes (Nashville: Columbia Records, n.d.).

KATHRYN KUHLMAN

Ann Butler, "She Believes in Miracles," *The Pittsburgh Press*, Feb. 3, 1974.

Bohdan Hodiak, "Kuhlman's Radio Voice Falls Silent," *Pittsburgh Post-Gazette*, Apr. 24, 1982.

Helen K. Hosier, *Kathryn Kuhlman: The Life She Led, the Legacy She Left* (Old Tappan, N.J.: Fleming H. Revell, 1976).

William A. Nolen, "In Search of a Miracle," *McCall's*, Sept. 1974.

Evan Pattak, "The Last Miracle Show," *Pittsburgh*, Apr. 1976.

Allen Spraggett, *Kathryn Kuhlman: The Woman Who Believes in Miracles* (Cleveland: World Publishing Co., 1970).

Anonymous, "Religion: 'I Believe,'" *The Bulletin Index*, Nov. 6, 1948.

Anonymous, "Miracle Woman," *Time*, Sept. 14, 1970.

Anonymous, "Kathryn Kuhlman," *Current Biography*, July 1974.

THE LeFEVRES

Jesse Burt and Duane Allen, *The History of Gospel Music* (Nashville: K&S Press, 1971).

Gospel Music Association, *Gospel Music '79* (Nashville: Gospel Music Association, 1979).

Pierce LeFevre, "A Word Portrait: Eva Mae," *Music City News*, Aug. 1966.

THE LEWIS FAMILY

Jesse Burt and Duane Allen, *The History of Gospel Music* (Nashville: K&S Press, 1971).

Don Cusic, "Lewis Family Maintains an Enduring Career," *Music City News*, Jan. 1987.

Don Rhodes, "30 Years of Music," *Augusta Chronicle*, Apr. 28, 1984.

LITTLE ELLER LONG

Anonymous, "WNAX Missouri Valley Barn Dance," *National Jamboree*, Aug. 1949.

Anonymous, "The Long and Short of It," *Radio Varieties*, Feb. 1940.

THE NEWCOMER TWINS

Ruth Lee Miller, "The Newcomer Twins," *The Mountain Broadcast and Prairie Recorder*, no. 4, June 1945.

Ivan M. Tribe, *Mountaineer Jamboree: Country Music in West Virginia* (Lexington: University Press of Kentucky, 1984).

THE SINGING RAMBOS

Bob Battle, "Rambos' Daughter Reba on Different Gospel-Singing Path," *The Nashville Banner*, Jan. 1, 1980.

Jesse Burt and Duane Allen, *The History of Gospel Music* (Nashville: K&S Press, 1971).

Laura Eipper, "Reba Sings New Christian Music," *The Tennessean*, Feb. 27, 1979.

Jack Hurst, "Gospel Group Rose on Slick Tires, Miracles," *The Tennessean*, Apr. 11, 1971.

Various writers, "I Am Woman: A Tribute to Women in Music," *BMI: The Many Worlds of Music*, no. 4, 1977.

THE SPEER FAMILY

Faye Brock and Ben Speer, interview with Robert K. Oermann, Mar. 1991.

Bob Darden, "Sixty-Seven Years of Speers," *Rejoice!*, Winter 1989.

Robert K. Oermann, "Speers: 70-Year Legacy to Future," *The Tennessean*, Apr. 6, 1991.

Deana Surles, "The Speers," *The Singing News*, Apr. 1990.

DOC AND CHICKIE WILLIAMS

Doc Williams, letter to *The Tennessean*, May 1987.

Anonymous, *Chickie Williams Sings the Old Songs* LP liner notes (Wheeling, W.Va.: Wheeling Records, 1959).

THE "RENFRO VALLEY BARN DANCE"

Donald E. Allen, ed., *Renfro Valley Keepsake* (Renfro Valley Enterprises, 1940).

[John Lair], *Renfro Valley Keepsake* (Renfro Valley Enterprises, 1947).

SOUTHERN GOSPEL MUSIC

Jesse Burt and Duane Allen, *The History of Gospel Music* (Nashville: K&S Press, 1971).

Don Cusic, *The Sound of Light* (Bowling Green, Ohio: Bowling Green State University Popular Press, 1990).

Gene Gideon, "Olde Time Camp Meetin' Days," in *Olde Time Camp Meetin' Songs* (Camdenton, Mo.: Albert E. Brumley & Sons, 1971).

Gene Gideon, "All-Day Singin' and Dinner on the Ground," in *All-Day Singin' and Dinner on the Ground Traditional Songs and Recipes* (Camdenton, Mo.: Albert E. Brumley & Sons, 1972).

Gospel Music Association, *Gospel Music '79* (Nashville: Gospel Music Association, 1979).

H. B. Teeter, "Glamor and Sex Ain't No Use to Wimmin Who Want to Hire Out in Country Music," *The Tennessean*, Nov. 19, 1954.

Charles Wolfe, "'Gospel Boogie': White Southern Gospel Music in Transition, 1945–55," in *Popular Music 1: Folk or Popular?* (Cambridge: Cambridge University Press, 1981).

THE PENTECOSTAL MOVEMENT

Robert Mapes Anderson, *Vision of the Disinherited* (New York: Oxford University Press, 1974).

Walter J. Hollenweger, *The Pentecostals* (Minneapolis: Augsburg Publishing House, 1972).

Weston LaBarre, *They Shall Take Up Serpents* (Minneapolis: University of Minnesota Press, 1962).

Liston Pope, *Millhands and Preachers* (New Haven: Yale University Press, 1942).

9. Rockabilly Women

BONNIE LOU

F. B. Gillis, "Bonnie Lou Loves Home and Hayride," *Country and Western Jamboree*, June 1956.

Randy McNutt, *We Wanna Boogie: An Illustrated History of the American Rockabilly Movement* (Hamilton, Ohio: HHP Books, 1988).

Mary Jean Shurtz, "Meet Bonnie Lou," *The Mountain Broadcast and Prairie Recorder*, Nov. 1946.

Mary Wood, "Bonnie a Lou-Lou Investment," *Cincinnati Enquirer*, Feb. 18, 1967.

Anonymous, "Bonnie Lou at Home," *Cincinnati Enquirer*, July 10, 1955.

Anonymous, "Bonnie Rings the Bell," *Country Song Roundup*, vol. 1, no. 26, Oct. 1953.

Anonymous, "Women in the News," *Cowboy Songs*, vol. 1, no. 28, Sept. 1953.

JO-ANN CAMPBELL

Big Bopper Bill, "The Blonde Bombshell," *Paul's Record Magazine*, Apr. 1976.

Jo-Ann Campbell, interview with Mary A. Bufwack, Oct. 1986.

Bill Griggs, "Jo Ann Campbell: The Blonde Bombshell," *Rockin' 50's*, no. 15, Dec. 1988.

Adam Komorowski, *Jo-Ann Campbell, Miss Reet Petite* LP liner notes (London: Charly Records, 1986).

Robert K. Oermann and Mary A. Bufwack, "Rockabilly Women," *Journal of Country Music*, vol. 8, no. 1, May 1979.

Bruce Pollock, *When Rock Was Young* (New York: Holt, Rinehart and Winston, 1981).

JEAN CHAPEL

Ben A. Green, "West Says 'All Nashville Bursting with Pride'; Knowles Home Happy," *The Nashville Banner*, Aug. 30, 1956.

Randy McNutt, *We Wanna Boogie: An Illustrated History of the American Rockabilly Movement* (Hamilton, Ohio: HHP Books, 1988).

Anonymous, "Jean Chapel 'Rocks' Huge Brooklyn Theater Audience at Singing Debut," Associated Press story in *The Nashville Banner*, Aug. 30, 1956.

Anonymous, "Jean Chapel Scores with First Sun Record Release, to Sign with New York Gale Agency," *Country Music Reporter*, vol. 1, no. 1, Aug. 18, 1956.

Various writers, "I Am Woman: A Tribute to Women in Music," *BMI: The Many Worlds of Music*, no. 4, 1977.

THE COLLINS KIDS

Stuart Colman, "The Collins Kids," *Now Dig This*, no. 104, Nov. 1991.

Wayne Russell, "The Collins Kids: Town Hall Party," *New Kommotion*, vol. 2, no. 10, Summer 1978.

Wayne Russell, "The Collins Kids," *Now Dig This*, no. 22, Jan. 1985.

Joel Selvin, *Ricky Nelson: Idol for a Generation* (Chicago: Contemporary Books, 1990).

Anonymous, "Growing Up with the Collins Kids," *Trail*, c. 1957.

Anonymous, "So Whatever Happened to Larry Collins' Record of 'Delta Dawn,'" *Nevada State Journal*, Mar. 15, 1974.

JESSI COLTER/MIRRIAM JOHNSON

Jim Grant, "Duane Eddy Discography," *New Kommotion*, Summer 1978.

Robert K. Oermann and Mary A. Bufwack, "Rockabilly Women," *Journal of Country Music*, vol. 8, no. 1, May 1979.

JACKIE DESHANNON

Martin Cerf, "Jackie DeShannon," *Phonograph Record Magazine*, January 1978.

Donald Clarke, ed., *The Penguin Encyclopedia of Popular Music* (New York: Viking Penguin, 1989).

Brian Gari, "What the World Needs Now Is Jackie DeShannon," *Goldmine*, Sept. 6, 1991.

Spencer Leigh, "Jackie DeShannon," *Who Put the Bomp*, Spring 1976.

Parke Puterbaugh, *The Best of Jackie DeShannon* CD liner notes (Los Angeles: Rhino Records, 1992).

Wayne Russell, *Footsoldiers and Kings* (Brandon, Manitoba, Canada: Wayne Russell/Leech Printing, n.d.).

Arnold Shaw, "Jackie DeShannon," *BMI: The Many Worlds of Music*, Mar. 1970.

Irwin Stambler, *Encyclopedia of Pop, Rock & Soul* (New York: St. Martin's Press, 1977).

Anonymous, "The Jackie Dee Story," *Folk and Country Songs*, vol. 4, no. 14, Feb. 1959.

WANDA JACKSON

Mary Bufwack, *Rock 'n' Roll Away Your Blues* LP liner notes (Somerville, Mass.: Rounder Records, 1986).

Gilbert Dumas, *Les Pionniers du Rock: Wanda Jackson* LP liner notes (Paris: Capitol Records, n.d.).

Lee Fuller, "Rock-a-Chicka," *Not Fade Away*, no. 13, 1978.

Bob Garbutt, *Rockabilly Queens* (Toronto: Dovetail Press, 1979).

Wanda Jackson, interview with Mary A. Bufwack, Apr. 1986.

Wanda Jackson, interview with Robert K. Oermann, Nov. 1986.

Wanda Jackson and Wendell Goodman, *Called Together* (Del City, Okla.: Spirit Press, 1990).

Rip Lay, "The Wanda Jackson Story," *Big Town Review*, Apr.–May 1972.

Miriam Linna, "Wanda Jackson," *Kicks*, no. 4, 1985.

Robert K. Oermann, "Rockabilly Queen Reclaiming Throne," *The Tennessean*, Jan. 10, 1987.

Ben Townsent, "The Magic Wanda," *Hoedown*, vol. 1, no. 1, May 1966.

BRENDA LEE

David Dalton and Lenny Kaye, *Rock 100* (New York: Grosset & Dunlap, 1977).

Lee Fuller, "Rock-a-Chicka," *Not Fade Away*, no. 13, 1978.

Bob Garbutt, "Brenda Lee—The Early Years," *New Kommotion*, vol. 2, no. 8, Winter 1978.

Bob Garbutt, *Rockabilly Queens* (Toronto: Dovetail Press, 1979).

Ben A. Green, "Success: One Step at a Time," *Country and Western Jamboree*, July 1957.

Virginia Keathley, "Teacher's Understanding Aided Brenda's Career," *The Tennessean*, Oct. 12, 1980.

Brenda Lee, interview with Robert K. Oermann, Oct. 1983.

Brenda Lee, interview with Robert K. Oermann, Apr. 1991.

Robert K. Oermann, "Little Miss Dynamite Sparks the Rock of Ages," *The Tennessean*, May 26, 1991.

Robert K. Oermann and Mary A. Bufwack, "Rockabilly Women," *Journal of Country Music*, vol. 8, no. 1, May 1979.

John Smith III, "Spotlight on Brenda Lee," *Rockin' 50s*, no. 5, Apr. 1987.

David Zimmerman, "Little Brenda Lee Back in a Big Way," *USA Today*, Aug. 29, 1991.

Anonymous, *Brenda Lee* souvenir booklet (n.p., 1977).

Anonymous, "Fashions on Parade," *Rustic Rhythm*, May 1957.

ALIS LESLEY

Bill Millar, *Hollywood Rock & Roll: Era Records* LP liner notes (London: Chiswick Records, n.d.).

LINDA GAIL LEWIS

Jimmy Guterman, *Rockin' My Life Away* (Nashville: Rutledge Hill, 1991).

Linda Gail Lewis, interview with Robert K. Oermann and Pete Loesch, June 1989.

Myra Lewis with Murray Silver, *Great Balls of Fire* (New York: Quill, 1982).

Colin Phillips, "Blood on the Keys," *Now Dig This,* no. 102, Sept. 1991.

ROSE MADDOX

Randy McNutt, *We Wanna Boogie: An Illustrated History of the American Rockabilly Movement* (Hamilton, Ohio: HHP Books, 1988).

Rose Maddox, interview with Robert K. Oermann, July 1989.

JANIS MARTIN

Freida Barter, "Janis Martin: Acclaim Is Wonderful," *Country & Western Jamboree,* Sept. 1956.

Ed Bayes, "Janis Martin," *Goldmine,* Jan.–Feb. 1977.

Ed Bayes, *Rockin' Rollin' Janis* LP liner notes (The Netherlands: Country Classics Library, 1976).

Bob Garbutt, *Rockabilly Queens* (Toronto: Dovetail Press, 1979).

Adam Komorowski, "My Girl Janis," *New Kommotion,* Winter 1977.

Robert K. Oermann and Mary A. Bufwack, "Rockabilly Women," *Journal of Country Music,* vol. 8, no. 1, May 1979.

THE MILLER SISTERS

Colin Escott and Martin Hawkins, *Catalyst: The Sun Records Story* (London: Aquarius, 1975).

Colin Escott, Martin Hawkins, and Hank Davis, *The Sun Country Years* LP liner notes (Bremen, West Germany: Bear Family Records, 1986).

SPARKLE MOORE

Miriam Linna, "Wow! Sparkle!" *Kicks,* no. 6, 1988.

'NITA, RITA, AND RUBY

Robert K. Oermann, *Rock Love* LP liner notes (Bremen, West Germany: Bear Family Records, 1985).

Ruby Wright, interview with Robert K. Oermann, June 1985.

BARBARA PITTMAN

Barry Buckley-Williams, "I Need a Man," *Big Beat of the Fifties,* no. 68, Sept. 1991.

Trevor Cajiao, "Swinging Baby Doll," *Now Dig This,* no. 28, July 1985.

Randy McNutt, *We Wanna Boogie: An Illustrated History of the American Rockabilly Movement* (Hamilton, Ohio: HHP Books, 1988).

M. M. Mike, "Barbara Pittman," *Mean Mountain Music,* vol. 4, no. 1, n.d.

REVEREND JIMMY SNOW

Jimmy Snow, *I Cannot Go Back* (Plainfield, N.J.: Logos, 1977).

Jimmy Snow, sermon excerpt in *Rock and Roll: The Early Days,* video (Burbank, Calif.: RCA/Columbia Pictures Home Video, 1985).

LUCILLE STARR

Doug Kibble, "Bob & Lucille (Canadian Sweethearts)," *New Kommotion,* vol. 2, no. 6, Summer 1977.

Robert K. Oermann, "Parlez-Vous Francais in Nashville?," *The Tennessean,* May 7, 1987.

Lucille Starr, interview with Robert K. Oermann, Apr. 1987.

MAGGIE SUE WIMBERLY/SUE RICHARDS

Colin Escott, Martin Hawkins, and Hank Davis, *The Sun Country Years* LP liner notes (Bremen, West Germany: Bear Family Records, 1986).

Jim Roden, "Singer Revives Country Career," *Dallas Times Herald,* June 20, 1975.

ANITA WOOD

Wayne Russell, "His Latest Flame," *Now Dig This,* no. 32, Nov. 1985.

Anonymous, "Elvis: $7,700 Paid for Love Letter Singer Wrote," Associated Press story in *The Nashville Banner,* Aug. 30, 1991.

ROCKABILLY WOMEN

Mary A. Bufwack and Robert K. Oermann, *Wild Wild Young Women* LP liner notes (Somerville, Mass.: Rounder Records, n.d.).

Collector Records, *Rock & Roll Girls* LP liner notes (Rotterdam, The Netherlands: White Label Records, n.d.).

Colin Escott and Martin Hawkins, *Catalyst: The Sun Records Story* (London: Aquarius, 1975).

Colin Escott with Martin Hawkins, *Good Rockin' Tonight* (New York: St. Martin's Press, 1991).

Colin Escott, Martin Hawkins, and Hank Davis, *The Sun Country Years* LP liner notes (Bremen, West Germany: Bear Family Records, 1986).

Lee Fuller, "Rock-a-Chicka," *Not Fade Away,* no. 13, 1978.

Bob Garbutt, *Rockabilly Queens* (Toronto: Dovetail Press, 1979).

Don R. Kirsch, *Rock n' Roll Obscurities* (Tacoma, Wash.: Don Kirsch, 1981).

Randy McNutt, *We Wanna Boogie: An Illustrated History of the American Rockabilly Movement* (Hamilton, Ohio: HHP Books, 1988).

Robert K. Oermann and Mary A. Bufwack, "Rockabilly Women," *Journal of Country Music,* vol. 8, no. 1, May 1979.

THE 1950s/EARLY ROCK 'N' ROLL CULTURE

Alan Betrock, *The I Was a Teenage Juvenile Delinquent Rock 'n' Roll Horror Beach Party Movie Book* (New York: St. Martin's Press, 1986).

Tim Brooks and Earl Marsh, *The Complete Directory to Prime Time Network TV Shows 1946–Present* (New York: Ballantine Books, 1988).

David Ehrenstein and Bill Reed, *Rock on Film* (New York: Delilah, 1982).

Herb Hendler, *Year by Year in the Rock Era* (New York: Praeger, 1987).

Mark Thomas McGee, *The Rock and Roll Movie Encyclopedia of the 1950s* (Jefferson, N.C.: McFarland & Co., 1990).

Norm N. Nite, *Rock On Almanac* (New York: Harper & Row, 1989).

Bruce Pollock, *When Rock Was Young* (New York: Holt, Rinehart and Winston, 1981).

Linda J. Sandahl, *Rock Films* (New York: Facts on File, 1987).

Jan Stacy and Ryder Syvertsen, *Rockin' Reels* (Chicago: Contemporary Books, 1984).

Nick Tosches, *Unsung Heroes of Rock 'n' Roll* (New York: Charles Scribner's Sons, 1984).

Ed Ward, Geoffrey Stokes, and Ken Tucker, *Rock of Ages* (New York: Rolling Stone Press, 1986).

10. The Nashville Sound

ALCYONE BATE BEASLEY

John Pugh, "Background Singers Come to Front," *Music City News,* Mar. 1973.

Anonymous, "Alcyone Beasley, 1st Woman Opry Singer, Dies," *Nashville Banner,* Oct. 18, 1982.

WILMA BURGESS

Irwin Stambler and Grelun Landon, *Encyclopedia of Folk, Country and Western Music* (New York: St. Martin's Press, 1969).

Anonymous, "Wilma Burgess" bio, *Country Music Who's Who* Programming Service (Denver: Heather Publications, n.d.).

PATSY CLINE

Owen Bradley, interview with Robert K. Oermann, Sept. 1991.

Owen Bradley, interview with Robert K. Oermann, Jan. 1992.

Meredith S. Buel, "Hillbilly with Oomph," *The Washington Star,* Mar. 18, 1956.

Mary Bufwack, "The Feminist Sensibility in Post-War Country Music," *The Southern Quarterly,* vol. 22, no. 3, Spring 1984.

June Carter Cash, *From the Heart* (New York: Prentice-Hall, 1987).

Charlie Dick, interview with Robert K. Oermann, Oct. 1985.

Charlie Dick, interview with Robert K. Oermann, Nov. 1986.

Hallway Productions, *The Real Patsy Cline,* video documentary (Nashville: Hallway Productions, 1986).

Don Hecht, "I Remember Patsy Cline," *Country Music,* Oct. 1973.

Jan Howard, interview with Robert K. Oermann, July 1987.

Jan Howard, *Sunshine and Shadow* (New York: Richardson & Steirman, 1987).

Joli Jensen, *Patsy Cline's Recording Career: The Search for a Sound* (Urbana-Champaign: University of Illinois Institute of Communications Research thesis, 1981).

Joli Jensen, "Patsy Cline's Recording Career: The Search for a Sound," *Journal of Country Music,* vol. 9, no. 2, 1982.

Paul Kingsbury, *The Patsy Cline Collection* CD liner notes (Nashville: MCA/Country Music Foundation, 1991).

Brenda Lee, interview with Robert K. Oermann, Apr. 1991.

Loretta Lynn, *I Remember Patsy* LP liner notes (Nashville: MCA Records, 1977).

Loretta Lynn, "I Remember Patsy Cline," *Your Friend Loretta Lynn Yearbook* (Wild Horse, Colo.: Loretta Lynn International Fan Club, 1967).

Loretta Lynn with George Vecsey, *Coal Miner's Daughter* (Chicago: Contemporary Books, 1976).

Barbara Mandrell with George Vecsey, *Get to the Heart* (New York: Bantam, 1990).

Bob Millard, "Patsy Cline: Owen Bradley Remembers," *Goldmine,* Dec. 4, 1987.

Ellis Nassour, *Patsy Cline: An Intimate Biography* (New York: Tower Books, 1981).

Ellis Nassour, "Patsy Cline: In the Beginning," *Journal of Country Music,* vol. 8, no. 3, 1981.

Ellis Nassour, "Nashville Remembers Patsy Cline," *Music City News,* June 1980.

Robert K. Oermann, "Honky-Tonk Angels: Kitty Wells and Patsy Cline," in *Country: The Music and the Musicians* (New York: Abbeville, 1988).

Robert K. Oermann, "Documentary Tells Patsy Cline's 'Real' Story," *The Tennessean,* Nov. 19, 1986.

Jay Orr, *Patsy Cline Live at the Opry* LP liner notes (Nashville: MCA Records, 1988).

Ronnie Pugh, *Patsy Cline Live: Volume Two* (Nashville: MCA Records, 1989).

George Vecsey with Leonore Fleischer, *Sweet Dreams* (New York: St. Martin's Press, 1985).

Dottie West, interview with Robert K. Oermann, Apr. 1983.

SKEETER DAVIS

Jerry Bailey, "Who Is the Real Skeeter Davis?," *The Tennessean,* July 2, 1974.

Laura Eipper, "Skeeter Enjoys 'Rebel' Tag," *The Tennessean,* Nov. 2, 1979.

Thomas Goldsmith, "Skeeter Davis Weds Rocker Spampinato," *The Tennessean,* Jan. 30, 1987.

Thomas Goldsmith, "Ralph's New Kiss and Tell Irks Skeeter," *The Tennessean,* Sept. 7, 1991.

Bill Hance, "Skeeter Told to Forego Opry Appearance Tonight," *Nashville Banner,* Dec. 15, 1973.

Gene Roe, "Tribute to B.J.," *Country Song Roundup,* vol. 1, no. 28, Jan. 1954.

Jean Shepard, interview with Robert K. Oermann, Mar. 1988.

Melvin Shestack, *The Country Music Encyclopedia* (New York: Thomas Y. Crowell, 1974).

Anonymous, "The Singing Sweethearts: Life Story of the Great Davis Sisters," *Hoedown,* vol. 1, no. 2, Oct. 1953.

BONNIE GUITAR

Bonnie Guitar, interview with Mary A. Bufwack, July 1979.

JAN HOWARD

Jan Howard, interview with Robert K. Oermann, July 1987.

Jan Howard, *Sunshine and Shadow* (New York: Richardson & Steirman, 1987).

Ellis Nassour, *Patsy Cline: An Intimate Biography* (New York: Tower Books, 1981).

Robert K. Oermann, "Opry Star's Ups and Downs Make a Life of 'Sunshine and Shadow,'" *The Tennessean,* July 9, 1987.

Karen Trotter, "Jan Howard: Shedding Light on a Lifetime of Dark Shadows," *Nashville Scene,* July 20, 1988.

Anonymous, "Jan Howard," *West Plains Gazette,* no. 7, Summer 1980.

ANITA KERR

Patrick Carr, ed., *The Illustrated History of Country Music* (Garden City, N.Y.: Doubleday, 1979).

Dave Dexter, Jr., "Anita Kerr—Music: That's What My Life's All About," *Billboard,* Apr. 28, 1979.

BRENDA LEE

Brenda Lee, interview with Robert K. Oermann, Oct. 1983.

Brenda Lee, interview with Robert K. Oermann, Aug. 1985.

Brenda Lee, interview with Robert K. Oermann, Nov. 1987.

Brenda Lee, interview with Robert K. Oermann, June 1988.

Brenda Lee, interview with Robert K. Oermann, Apr. 1991.

John Smith III, "Spotlight on Brenda Lee," *Rockin' 50s,* no. 5, Apr. 1987.

JUDY LYNN

Irwin Stambler and Grelun Landon, *Encyclopedia of Folk, Country and Western Music* (New York: St. Martin's Press, 1969).

Anonymous, *The Judy Lynn Show Plays Again* LP liner notes (Nashville: Musicor Records, 1965).

JOHNNY AND JONIE MOSBY

Tony Byworth, "Johnny and Jonie Mosby," *Country Music People,* Nov. 1971.

Karen Schneider and Nancy Matsumoto, "Birth at 52," *People,* May 18, 1992.

Anonymous, *Make a Left and Then a Right* LP liner notes (Hollywood: Capitol Records, 1967).

Anonymous, *Mr. & Mrs. Country Music* LP liner notes (New York: Harmony Records, n.d.).

Anonymous, "Jonie Mosby Becomes Mom Again at Age 52," Associated Press story in *The Nashville Banner,* Apr. 1, 1992.

MINNIE PEARL

Paul Bryant, "The Belle of Grinder's Switch," *The Mountain Broadcast and Prairie Recorder,* Oct. 1946.

Pat Harris, "Minnie Pearl Talks to Minnie Pearl," *Chicago Sun-Times,* Nov. 16, 1980.

Jack Hurst, "Minnie Pearl Edits Out 'Seamy Details,'" *Cincinnati Enquirer,* Jan. 21, 1980.

Judy Mizell, "Minnie Pearl: Grand Ole Opry's Crown Jewel," *Inside Opryland USA,* vol. 8, no. 10, Nov. 1990.

Robert K. Oermann, "Back in the Country, 1940: Minnie Pearl Joins the Grand Ole Opry," *Country Song Roundup,* Oct. 1983.

Minnie Pearl, interview with Robert K. Oermann, May 1984.

Minnie Pearl, interview with Robert K. Oermann, Jan. 1986.

Minnie Pearl, interview with Robert K. Oermann, Apr. 1989.

Minnie Pearl, *Minnie Pearl's Diary* (n.p., 1953).

Minnie Pearl, *Christmas at Grinders Switch* (Nashville: Abingdon Press, 1963).

Minnie Pearl with Joan Dew, *Minnie Pearl* (New York: Simon and Schuster, 1980).

Don Pierce, *America's Beloved Minnie Pearl* LP liner notes (Nashville: Starday Records, 1966).

Leah Rozen, "Minnie Pearl," *People,* Oct. 26, 1987.

Anonymous, "College Graduate Scores on Opry as Girl Hillbilly," *Record Roundup,* vol. 1, no. 8, July 1947.

Anonymous, "Hats On for Minnie Pearl," *National Jamboree,* June 1949.

Anonymous, "Minnie Pearl BB's Country Man of Year," *Billboard,* Oct. 29, 1966.

Anonymous, "Minnie Pearl" bio, *Country Music Who's Who* Programming Service (Denver: Heather Publications, n.d.).

SARIE AND SALLIE

Wayne W. Daniel, "Happy Hal Burns and the Garrett's Snuff Vanities," *Bluegrass Unlimited,* Nov. 1989.

Jack Hurst, *Nashville's Grand Ole Opry* (New York: Harry N. Abrams, 1975).

Red O'Donnell, column in *The Nashville Banner,* July 10, 1980.

Anonymous, "The New Party Line," *Rural Radio,* vol. 1, no. 1, Feb. 1938.

Anonymous, "Sarie and Sallie See the City," *Stand By!,* July 10, 1937.

SUE THOMPSON

Rich Kienzle, "The Checkered Career of Hank Penny," *Journal of Country Music,* vol. 8, no. 2, 1980.

Bea Terry, "Sue Thompson" publicity bio (Hollywood: Bea Terry Publicity and Promotion, c. 1953).

Anonymous, "Close Up of Sue Thompson," *Cowboy Songs,* no. 70, Winter 1962–1963.

Anonymous, "Sweet Sue," *Cowboy Songs,* no. 20, May 1952.

Anonymous, "Crowd Pleaser," *Country Song Roundup,* vol. 1, no. 14, Oct. 1951.

Anonymous, "Sue Thompson Biography" publicity bio, n.p., 1974.

Anonymous, "Sue Thompson—Not 'Itty Bitty' Anymore," publicity bio (Nashville: Hickory Records, c. 1970).

Anonymous, "Sue Thompson" publicity bio (Independence, Kans.: Jim Halsey Agency, n.d.).

RACHEL VEACH

Jack Harris, "Roy Finds the Right Girl," *Rural Radio,* vol. 2, no. 5, June 1939.

Elizabeth Schlappi, *Roy Acuff: The Smoky Mountain Boy* (Gretna, La.: Pelican Publishing, 1978).

DOTTIE WEST

Jim Albrecht, "The Wild West," *CountryStyle,* May 1981.

Michael Bane, "Dottie West: Country's Singing Swinger!," *Oui,* Jan. 1983.

Scott Cain, "Dottie West: Happy Again," *The Atlanta Journal,* Apr. 17, 1981.

Rochelle Carter and Robert K. Oermann, "Trustee Seeks Out Dottie West Stash," *The Tennessean,* Mar. 28, 1991.

Carol Davis, "West Had Planned Album of Duets," *Nashville Banner,* Sept. 6, 1991.

Thomas Goldsmith, "Stars She Befriended Mourn Dottie," *The Tennessean,* Sept. 5, 1991.

Thomas Goldsmith, "Fans, Friends Celebrate West's Life," *Nashville Banner,* Sept. 8, 1991.

Dennis Hunt, "Dottie Going Solo—On Record," *Los Angeles Times,* June 10, 1981.

David Kepple, "At 47, Beautiful Dottie Is Finding Her Best Success," *Birmingham, Ala., News,* Oct. 5, 1981.

Frances Meeker, "Bill, Dottie West Beat Hard Times," *Nashville Banner,* Jan. 26, 1967.

Brice Minnigh, "Auction Brings Tears, Cash," *The Tennessean,* June 14, 1991.

Ellis Nassour, *Patsy Cline: An Intimate Biography* (New York: Tower Books, 1981).

Robert K. Oermann, "Dottie, Shelly and Tess—West Gals Team Up," *The Tennessean,* May 7, 1983.

Robert K. Oermann, "The Frizzell-West Dynasty," *Country Rhythms,* Sept. 1983.

Robert K. Oermann, "Singer Dottie West Marries Steady Boyfriend," *The Tennessean,* July 2, 1983.

Robert K. Oermann, "Glamorous Dottie Remains a Role Model," *The Tennessean*, Nov. 10, 1984.

Robert K. Oermann, "Dottie: Looking Up, Though She's Down," *The Tennessean*, Aug. 4, 1990.

Robert K. Oermann, "Manager: Dottie Endures Tough Times," *The Tennessean*, July 25, 1991.

Jay Orr, "Stars Mourn West," *Nashville Banner*, Sept. 4, 1991.

Marty Racine, "At Her Peak," *Houston Chronicle*, Aug. 30, 1981.

Joe Rich, "Dottie West Can't Pay Creditors," *The Tennessean*, Aug. 21, 1990.

Dottie West, interview with Robert K. Oermann, Apr. 1983.

Dottie West, interview with Robert K. Oermann, Aug. 1990.

Dru Wilson, "West Was Raised on Cornbread and on Fiddles," *Gazette Telegraph*, Aug. 28, 1981.

Anonymous, *Headed West* (Nashville: Dottie West Fan Club, 1966).

Anonymous, "Dottie West" bio, *Country Music Who's Who* Programming Service (Denver: Heather Publications, n.d.).

DEL WOOD

Pat Harris, "Del Wood: Country as a Shoe, Gracious as a Slipper," *The Tennessean*, Oct. 5, 1989.

Ellis Nassour, *Patsy Cline: An Intimate Biography* (New York: Tower Books, 1981).

Robert K. Oermann, "Opry's 'Queen of the Ivories' Dies," *The Tennessean*, Oct. 4, 1989.

Robert K. Oermann, "Del Wood Celebrates Opry Career," *The Tennessean*, Nov. 18, 1988.

Robert K. Oermann, "Queen of Ivories Off to Bermuda," *The Tennessean*, Jan. 21, 1983.

Del Wood, interview with Robert K. Oermann, Nov. 1988.

Del Wood, interview with Robert K. Oermann, Jan. 1983.

Del Wood, interview with Robert K. Oermann, Aug. 1983.

Anonymous, "Down Yonder Girl: Del Wood," *Country Song Roundup*, vol. 1, no. 16, Feb. 1952.

Anonymous, "The Fanning Bee," *Country Song Roundup*, vol. 1, no. 34, Sept. 1954.

Anonymous, "Miss Del Wood: Mistress of the Keyboard," *Rustic Rhythm*, May 1957.

Anonymous, "Del Wood Has Her Own Special Style," *The Tennessean*, Dec. 25, 1981.

THE GRAND OLE OPRY

Chet Hagan, *Grand Ole Opry* (New York: Henry Holt, 1989).

Jack Hurst, *Nashville's Grand Ole Opry* (New York: Harry N. Abrams, 1975).

William R. McDaniel and Harold Seligman, *Grand Ole Opry* (New York: Greenberg, 1952).

Jerry Strobel, ed., *Grand Ole Opry WSM Picture-History Book* (Nashville: WSM, 1976).

Jerry Strobel, ed., *Grand Ole Opry WSM Picture-History Book* (Nashville: Opryland USA, 1984).

Myron Tassin and Jerry Henderson, *Fifty Years at the Grand Ole Opry* (Gretna, La.: Pelican Publishing, 1975).

Charles K. Wolfe, *The Grand Ole Opry: The Early Years, 1925–35* (London: Old Time Music, 1975).

WSM, *Grand Ole Opry History Picture Book* (Nashville: WSM, 1957).

WSM, *Official WSM Grand Ole Opry History-Picture Book* (Nashville, WSM, 1961).

THE NASHVILLE SOUND

Patrick Carr, ed., *The Illustrated History of Country Music* (Garden City, N.Y.: Doubleday, 1979).

Bill Ivey, "The Bottom Line: Business Practices That Shaped Country Music," in *Country: The Music and the Musicians* (New York: Abbeville, 1988).

Robert K. Oermann, "Listening to Country Music," in *The Country Music Book* (New York: Charles Scribner's Sons, 1985).

Robert K. Oermann with Douglas B. Green, *The Listener's Guide to Country Music* (New York: Facts on File, 1983).

11. The Folk Revival

JOAN BAEZ

Joan Baez, *And a Voice to Sing With* (New York: New American Library, 1987).

Joan Baez, *Come from the Shadows* LP liner notes (Beverly Hills: A&M Records, 1972).

Joan Baez, *Daybreak* (New York: Avon Books, 1966).

Kristin Baggelaar and Donald Milton, *Folk Music: More Than a Song* (New York: Thomas Y. Crowell, 1976).

Ray Bonds, ed., *The Harmony Illustrated Encyclopedia of Rock* (New York: Harmony Books, 1982).

Jim Crockett, "Joan Baez," in *Artists of American Folk Music* (New York: GPI/Quill/William Morrow, 1986).

Bob Dylan, *Joan Baez in Concert: Part 2* LP liner notes (New York: Vanguard Records, 1963).

Charles J. Fuss, "Joan Baez: An American Artist," *Goldmine*, vol. 15, no. 17, Aug. 25, 1989.

Thomas Goldsmith, "Baez Sends Soviets a Message of Hope," *The Tennessean*, Aug. 21, 1991.

Barry Lazell, ed., *Rock Movers & Shakers* (New York: Billboard Publications, 1989).

Pamela Little, "Baez Takes Own Road to Success," Gannett News Service story, May 10, 1991.

Rob Moritz, "Joan Baez Sends Songs of Spirit," *The Nashville Banner*, Aug. 21, 1991.

Robert Santelli, *Aquarius Rising: The Rock Festival Years* (New York: Dell Publishing, 1980).

THE BROWNS

Bill Williams, *20 of the Best the Browns* LP liner notes (Germany: RCA Records, 1985).

Charles Wolfe, *Looking Back to See* LP liner notes (Bremen, West Germany: Bear Family Records, 1986).

ANITA CARTER

Otto Kitsinger, *Ring of Fire* CD liner notes (Vollersode, West Germany: Bear Family Records, 1989).

JANETTE CARTER

Appalshop Film & Video, *Sunny Side of Life*, video documentary (Whitesburg, Ky.: Appalshop Films, 1985).

Janette Carter, interview with Mary A. Bufwack and Robert K. Oermann, May 1978.

Janette Carter, interview in "Southern Songbirds," PBS radio series, 1990.

Anne Gilbert, *Joe and Janette Carter* LP liner notes (Floyd, Va.: County Records, 1966).

Tony Russell, *The Carter Family* LP liner notes (Alexandria, Va.: Time-Life Records, 1982).

MAYBELLE CARTER

Kristin Baggelaar and Donald Milton, *Folk Music: More Than a Song* (New York: Thomas Y. Crowell, 1976).

Maybelle Carter, "The Show Goes on for Mother Maybelle," *Music City News*, Sept. 1966.

Douglas B. Green, "Maybelle Carter: Linking Mountain Folk with Modern Country," *Pickin'*, vol. 6, no. 2, Mar. 1979.

Tony Russell, *The Carter Family* LP liner notes (Alexandria, Va.: Time-Life Records, 1982).

Charles Wolfe, *Sara & Maybelle Carter* CD liner notes (Vollersode, West Germany: Bear Family Records, 1991).

Anonymous, "Johnny Cash Will Officiate at Carter Rites," *Nashville Banner*, Oct. 24, 1978.

JUDY COLLINS

Vivian Claire, *Judy Collins* (New York: Flash Books, 1977).

Judy Collins, "Going Home Again," *Ms.*, Apr. 1973.

Judy Collins, *Trust Your Heart* (Boston: Houghton Mifflin Co., 1987).

Barry Lazell, ed., *Rock Movers & Shakers* (New York: Billboard Publications, 1989).

Lillian Roxon, *Lillian Roxon's Rock Encyclopedia* (New York: Grosset & Dunlap, 1971).

BARBARA DANE

Kristin Baggelaar and Donald Milton, *Folk Music: More Than a Song* (New York: Thomas Y. Crowell, 1976).

Barbara Dane, *Anthology of American Folk Songs* LP liner notes (Los Angeles: Tradition Records, 1959).

Barbara Dane and Irwin Silber, *I Hate the Capitalist System* LP liner notes (Brooklyn, N.Y.: Paredon Records, 1973).

Irwin Silber, *Barbara Dane Sings the Blues* LP liner notes (New York: Folkways Records, 1964).

HAZEL DICKENS

Alice Gerrard, *Hazel & Alice* LP liner notes (Somerville, Mass.: Rounder Records, 1977).

Alice Gerrard, Len Stanley, and Richard Harrington, "Hazel Dickens, the Working-Class Conscience of Harlan County U.S.A.," *Unicorn Times,* Aug. 1977.

Richard Harrington, "Hazel Dickens' Songs for Hard-Hit People," *The Washington Post,* Mar. 29, 1981.

Jan Hoffman, "Union Blues," *Village Voice,* Sept. 1, 1987.

Ralph Rinzler, *Hard Hitting Songs for Hard Hit People* LP liner notes (Somerville, Mass.: Rounder Records, 1980).

Neil V. Rosenberg, *Won't You Come and Sing for Me?* LP liner notes (New York: Folkways Records, 1973).

Richard K. Spottswood, *Strange Creek Singers* LP liner notes (Berkeley, Calif.: Arhoolie Records, 1972).

Bill Vernon, *Who's That Knocking?* LP liner notes (New York: Verve Forecast Records, c. 1967).

ZILPHIA HORTON

R. Serge Denisoff, *Great Day Coming: Folk Music and the American Left* (Baltimore: Penguin Press, 1971).

Todd Gitlin, *The Sixties: Years of Hope, Days of Rage* (New York: Bantam, 1987).

Pete Seeger and Bob Reiser, *Carry It On* (New York: Simon & Schuster, 1985).

Juan Williams, *Eyes on the Prize* (New York: Viking Penguin, 1987).

JANIS IAN

Susan Ahrens, "Janis Ian: Plug Her into Something," *The Music Gig,* Oct. 1976.

Art Harris, "Janis Ian Becomes Society's Grownup," *Rolling Stone,* July 17, 1975.

Janis Ian, interview with Robert K. Oermann, May 1989.

Janis Ian, interview with Robert K. Oermann, Nov. 1989.

Daisann McLane, "Janis Ian: Society's Child Gains Acceptance," *Circus,* Dec. 30, 1975.

Brian Mansfield, "Janis Ian Adjusts to Nashville," *The Nashville Scene,* June 29, 1989.

Robert K. Oermann, "Through Good Times and Bad, Janis Ian Abides in Her Music," *The Tennessean,* June 18, 1989.

Robert K. Oermann, "Poor Health Postpones Ian's Comeback," *The Tennessean,* Nov. 12, 1989.

Bob Sarlin, "Janis Ian at 24," *Crawdaddy,* Feb. 1976.

Geoffrey Stokes, "Janis Ian," *Zoo World,* June 20, 1974.

IAN AND SYLVIA

Kristin Baggelaar and Donald Milton, *Folk Music: More Than a Song* (New York: Thomas Y. Crowell, 1976).

David Browne, "Where Are They Now?/Ian and Sylvia," *Rolling Stone,* Sept. 10, 1987.

Bob Palmer, *The Best of Ian & Sylvia* LP liner notes (New York: Columbia Records, 1973).

Irwin Stambler and Grelun Landon, *The Encyclopedia of Folk, Country & Western Music* (New York: St. Martin's Press, 1983).

Sylvia Tyson, interview with Robert K. Oermann, Feb. 1983.

RAMONA JONES

Nancy Cardwell, "Ramona Jones and the Grandpa Jones Dinner Theater," *Bluegrass Unlimited,* June 1988.

Grandpa Jones, interview with Robert K. Oermann, Nov. 1990.

Louis M. "Grandpa" Jones with Charles K. Wolfe, *Everybody's Grandpa* (Knoxville: University of Tennessee Press, 1984).

Charles Wolfe, "Grandpa and Ramona Jones: Two Lives, One Music," *The Devil's Box,* vol. 13, no. 4, Dec. 1, 1979.

Charles Wolfe, *Ramona Jones: Lady's Fancy* LP liner notes (Floyd, Va.: County Records, 1984).

KATHY KAHN

Kathy Kahn, "The One-Woman Traveling Road Show," *Country Music,* July 1974.

Kathy Kahn, *Hillbilly Women* (New York: Avon Books, 1972).

KATIE LEE

American Society of Composers, Authors and Publishers, *ASCAP Biographical Dictionary* (New York: R.R. Bowker, 1980).

Katie Lee, *Love's Little Sisters* LP liner notes (Jerome, Ariz.: Katydid Records, 1975).

MELANIE

Erik Himmelsbach, "Melanie: Bubble Earth Mother," *Goldmine,* vol. 13, no. 14, July 3, 1987.

Jon E. Johnson, "Melanie: Prematurely Blonde," *DISCoveries,* vol. 3, no. 1, Jan. 1990.

JONI MITCHELL

Donald Clarke, ed., *The Penguin Encyclopedia of Popular Music* (New York: Viking/Penguin, 1989).

Anthony Fawcett, *California Rock California Sound* (Los Angeles: Reed Books, 1978).

Barry Lazell, ed., *Rock Movers & Shakers* (New York: Billboard Publications, 1989).

Steve Pond, "Wild Things Run Fast: Joni Mitchell," *Rolling Stone,* Nov. 25, 1982.

Irwin Stambler and Grelun Landon, *The Encyclopedia of Folk, Country & Western Music* (New York: St. Martin's Press, 1983).

MARIA MULDAUR

Susan Benson, "The Sunny Sessions: Maria Muldaur Croons for Kids," *Entertainment Weekly,* Aug. 31, 1990.

Maria Muldaur, interview with Robert K. Oermann, May 1986.

Maria Muldaur, interview with Robert K. Oermann, Apr. 1990.

Robert K. Oermann, "Maria Muldaur to Debut Tonight in Nashville," *The Tennessean,* May 29, 1986.

Robert K. Oermann, "It's Back to Work for Maria Muldaur," *The Tennessean,* Apr. 12, 1990.

TRACY NELSON

Tim Kaihatsu, "Tracy Nelson Sings the Blues," *Musicians' Industry,* Feb./Mar. 1981.

Tracy Nelson, interview with Robert K. Oermann, Sept. 1983.

Tracy Nelson, interview with Robert K. Oermann, May 1987.

Robert K. Oermann, "Soulful Tracy Nelson Takes Fresh Look at Music City," *The Tennessean,* Sept. 16, 1983.

Robert K. Oermann, "Critics' Darling Tracy Nelson No Longer Singing the Blues," *The Tennessean,* June 7, 1987.

Derk Richardson, "Tracy Nelson's Special Memories of Bay Area," *Berkeley Gazette,* Oct. 27, 1982.

ODETTA

Odetta, interview with Robert K. Oermann, Dec. 1986.

Robert K. Oermann, "Folk Singer Odetta Turns to Country," *The Tennessean,* Dec. 18, 1986.

Robert Yelin, "Odetta," in *Artists of American Folk Music* (New York: GPI/Quill/William Morrow, 1986).

RAY AND INA PATTERSON

David Freeman, *Old-Time Songs: Volume 2* LP liner notes (Floyd, Va.: County Records, c. 1968).

Bill Vernon, *Old-Time Ballads & Hymns* LP liner notes (New York: County Records, 1966).

OLA BELLE REED

Isaac Rehert, "A 'Hillbilly' Doctorate," *Baltimore Sun,* June 13, 1978.

Toby Thompson, "A True Appalachian Contralto," *The Washington Post,* Apr. 21, 1976.

David Whisnant, *Ola Belle Reed & Family* LP liner notes (Somerville, Mass.: Rounder Records, n.d.).

MALVINA REYNOLDS

Jim Capaldi, "All the World's Children Are Hers," *Folkscene,* vol. 5, no. 8, Dec. 1977.

Jim Crockett, "Malvina Reynolds," in *Artists of American Folk Music* (New York: GPI/Quill/William Morrow, 1986).

Gene Lees, "The Passion of Malvina Reynolds," *Hi Fi,* May 1968.

Malvina Reynolds, "A Ribbon Bow," *Sing Out,* Summer 1963.

Robert Shelton, *Malvina Reynolds Sings the Truth* (New York: Columbia Records, 1966).

Rosalie Sorrels, *Mama Lion* LP liner notes (Berkeley, Calif.: Cassandra Records, 1980).

JEAN RITCHIE

Kristin Baggelaar and Donald Milton, *Folk Music: More Than a Song* (New York: Thomas Y. Crowell, 1976).

Donald Clarke, ed., *The Penguin Encyclopedia of Popular Music* (New York: Viking/Penguin, 1989).

Alanna Nash, "Jean Ritchie: Queen of the Dulcimer," *Frets,* Feb. 1980.

J. W. Williamson, "Jean Ritchie on *Next of Kin,*" *Now and Then,* vol. 8, no. 3, Fall 1991.

BUFFY SAINTE-MARIE

American Society of Composers, Authors and Publishers, *ASCAP Biographical Dictionary* (New York: R.R. Bowker, 1980).

Kristin Baggelaar and Donald Milton, *Folk Music: More Than a Song* (New York: Thomas Y. Crowell, 1976).

Jerry Bailey, "Buffy's Music Off the Warpath," *The Tennessean,* Apr. 14, 1984.

Mary Campbell, "Buffy Sainte-Marie Combines Indian and Mainstream Music," Associated Press story in *The Tennessean,* Aug. 16, 1987.

Lynn Harvey, "Sainte-Marie Making Home in Nashville," *The Tennessean,* Jan. 13, 1975.

Red O'Donnell, "Buffy Despaired, Now a Rising Star," *Nashville Banner,* Apr. 21, 1969.

Kathy Sawyer, "Buffy Braves a Blizzard to Keep a Date with Chet," *The Tennessean,* Jan. 10, 1968.

Maynard Solomon, *It's My Way!* LP liner notes (New York: Vanguard Records, 1964).

Irwin Stambler and Grelun Landon, *The Encyclopedia of Folk, Country & Western Music* (New York: St. Martin's Press, 1983).

PEGGY SEEGER

Charles Seeger, *Folk Songs of Courting & Complaint* LP liner notes (New York: Folkways Records, 1955).

Peggy Seeger, *American Folksongs for Christmas* LP liner notes (Cambridge, Mass.: Rounder Records, 1989).

Peggy Seeger, *Penelope Isn't Waiting Anymore* LP liner notes (Somerville, Mass.: Rounder Records, c. 1976).

THE STONEMANS

Wayne W. Daniel, "The Serious Side of Roni Stoneman," *Bluegrass Unlimited,* June 1990.

Darryl Hicks, "Donna Stoneman—Free from the Burden," in *God Comes to Nashville* (Harrison, Ark.: New Leaf Press, 1979).

Robert K. Oermann, "Daughter Battles to Keep Stoneman Music Alive," *The Tennessean,* July 31, 1987.

Will Smith, "The Stoneman Family, an Interview with Patsy Stoneman," *Autoharpoholic,* vol. 12, no. 2, Spring 1991.

Patsy Stoneman, interview with Robert K. Oermann, July 1987.

Ivan M. Tribe, "Patsy Stoneman, Portrait of a Survivor," *Bluegrass Unlimited,* Mar. 1989.

Anonymous, *The Stonemans* (Nashville: Patsy Stoneman, c. 1985).

HEDY WEST

Kristin Baggelaar and Donald Milton, *Folk Music: More Than a Song* (New York: Thomas Y. Crowell, 1976).

Hedy West, *Hedy West* LP liner notes (New York: Vanguard Records, 1961).

Hedy West, *Old Times and Hard Times* LP liner notes (Sharon, Conn.: Folk-Legacy Records, 1968).

Hedy West, *Love, Hell and Biscuits* LP liner notes (Bremen, West Germany: Bear Family Records, 1976).

THE FOLK REVIVAL

Pat Arnow, "A Sound from the Past," *Now and Then,* vol. 2, no. 3, Fall 1985.

Kristin Baggelaar and Donald Milton, *Folk Music: More Than a Song* (New York: Thomas Y. Crowell, 1976).

R. Serge Denisoff, *Great Day Coming: Folk Music and the American Left* (Baltimore: Penguin Books, 1973).

Craig Harris, *The New Folk Music* (Crown Point, Ind.: White Cliffs Media, 1991).

Charles Hirschberg, "The Ballad of A.P. Carter," *Life,* Dec. 1991.

Phil Hood, ed., *Artists of American Folk Music* (New York: GPI/Quill/William Morrow, 1986).

Jerome L. Rodnitzky, *Minstrels of the Dawn* (Chicago: Nelson-Hall, 1976).

Neil V. Rosenberg, *Bluegrass: A History* (Urbana: University of Illinois Press, 1985).

Larry Sandberg and Dick Weissman, *The Folk Music Sourcebook* (New York: Alfred A. Knopf, 1976).

Pete Seeger and Bob Reiser, *Carry It On!* (New York: Simon and Schuster, 1985).

Irwin Stambler and Grelun Landon, *The Encyclopedia of Folk, Country & Western Music* (New York: St. Martin's Press, 1983).

Jacques Vassal, *Electric Children: Roots and Branches of Modern Folkrock* (New York: Taplinger Publishing, 1976).

Eric Von Schmidt and Jim Rooney, *Baby Let Me Follow You Down* (Garden City, N.Y.: Anchor/Doubleday, 1979).

WOMEN'S SONGS

Evelyn Alloy, *Working Women's Music* (Somerville, Mass.: New England Free Press, 1976).

Mary Bufwack, "Songs of Women's Work," unpublished typescript, 1981.

Mary A. Bufwack and Robert K. Oermann, *Songs of Self-Assertion: Women in Country Music* (Somerville, Mass.: New England Free Press, 1980).

Joyce Cheney, Marcia Deihl, and Deborah Silverstein, eds., *All Our Lives: A Women's Songbook* (Baltimore: Diana Press, 1976).

Kathy Henderson, Frankie Armstrong, and Sandra Kerr, *My Song Is My Own* (London: Pluto Press, 1979).

Polly Parsons, *Songs for the Liberated Woman* (London: Kahn & Averill, 1973).

Jerry Silverman, *The Liberated Woman's Songbook* (New York: Collier Books, 1971).

Hilda E. Wenner and Elizabeth Freilicher, *Here's to the Women* (Syracuse, N.Y.: Syracuse University Press, 1987).

Various authors, "Women and Music," *Heresies,* no. 10, 1980.

THE 1960s

William H. Chafe, *Women and Equality* (New York: Oxford University Press, 1977).

R. Serge Denisoff, *Great Day Coming: Folk Music and the American Left* (Baltimore: Penguin Books, 1973).

Sara Evans, *Personal Politics* (New York: Vintage, 1980).

Todd Gitlin, *The Sixties: Years of Hope, Days of Rage* (New York: Bantam, 1987).

Michael W. Miles, *The Radical Probe* (New York: Atheneum, 1973).

12. You're Lookin' at Country

KAY ADAMS

Cliffie Stone, *Alcohol and Tears* LP liner notes (Los Angeles: Tower Records, 1967).

Joel Whitburn, *Top Country Singles, 1944–1988* (Menomonee Falls, Wisc.: Record Research, 1989).

LORETTA LYNN

Owen Bradley, interview with Robert K. Oermann, Jan. 1992.

Rick Cornett, "Loretta Lynn Sings Her Mind and Beats the Odds: Female Viewpoint No Longer a Stranger to Country Music Charts," *Record Collector's Monthly,* no. 23, Sept. 1984.

Joan Dew, *Singers & Sweethearts* (New York: Country Music Magazine/Dolphin/Doubleday/KBO, 1977).

Joe Edwards, "The One Thing Loretta Lynn Hasn't Learned," Associated Press story, Oct. 31, 1991.

Douglas B. Green, "Loretta Lynn: An Historical Retrospective," *Country Song Roundup,* June 1980.

Hallway Productions, *Loretta Lynn: Honky-Tonk Girl,* video documentary (Nashville: Hallway Productions, 1990).

Hallway Productions, *The Real Patsy Cline,* video documentary (Nashville: Hallway Productions, 1986).

Loretta Lynn, interview with Robert K. Oermann, Nov. 1982.

Loretta Lynn, interview with Robert K. Oermann, July 1986.

Loretta Lynn with George Vecsey, *Coal Miner's Daughter* (New York: Warner Books, 1976).

Robert K. Oermann, "Loretta's First Visit to a Beauty Shop," *Inside Country Music,* June 1983.

Robert K. Oermann, "Loretta Lynn Takes Country Music to the Big Apple for TV Special," *The Tennessean,* Nov. 7, 1983.

Robert K. Oermann, "Awards Queen Loretta Lynn Mines More Golden Memories," *The Tennessean,* July 13, 1986.

Laurence J. Zwisohn, *Loretta Lynn's World of Music* (Los Angeles: John Edwards Memorial Foundation/Palm Tree Library, 1980).

Anonymous, "Owen Bradley: 'She Was Like a Female Hank Williams,'" *Country Song Roundup,* June 1980.

NORMA JEAN

Norma Jean, interview with Robert K. Oermann, Oct. 1984.

Norma Jean, *I Guess That Comes from Being Poor* LP liner notes (Nashville: RCA Records, 1972).

Robert K. Oermann, "Norma Jean Out of Retirement," *The Tennessean,* Nov. 1, 1984.

Anonymous, "Norma Jean" bio, *Country Music Who's Who* Programming Service (Denver: Heather Publications, n.d.).

JEANNE PRUETT

Jack Hurst, "Jeanne Pruett Weathers Crossover Phenomenon," *St. Paul Pioneer Press,* Mar. 16, 1980.

Robert K. Oermann, "Independent Lady, Independent Label," *Nashville Gazette,* vol. 1, no. 2, May 1980.

Robert K. Oermann, "Female Cast Takes Over Opry Stage," *The Tennessean,* Feb. 14, 1986.

Robert K. Oermann, "Sweet Taste of Success for Jeanne Pruett," *The Tennessean,* May 6, 1988.

Jeanne Pruett, *Feedin' Friends Cookbook* (Franklin, Tenn.: Jeanne Pruett/Harris Press, 1986).

Jeanne Pruett, *Feedin' Friends Cookbook II* (Franklin, Tenn.: Jeanne Pruett/Harris Press, 1988).

Jeanne Pruett, *Pen Friends* fan club newsletter, vol. 1, no. 1, May 1986.

Jeanne Pruett, interview with Robert K. Oermann, Apr. 1980.

Jeanne Pruett, interview with Robert K. Oermann, Feb. 1986.

Jeanne Pruett, interview with Robert K. Oermann, May 1988.

JEANNIE C. RILEY

David Hazard, "CBN Corner," *Nevada State Journal and Reno Evening Gazette*, June 2, 1978.

Laura Eipper Hill, "Jeannie's Mountaintop Reached with Religion," *The Tennessean*, May 12, 1981.

Robert K. Oermann, "Jeannie C.'s 'Honest Book' in Paperback," *The Tennessean*, Mar. 23, 1983.

Jeannie C. Riley, interview with Robert K. Oermann, Mar. 1983.

Jeannie C. Riley with Jamie Buckingham, *From Harper Valley to the Mountaintop* (Lincoln, Va.: Chosen Books, 1981).

BOBBIE ROY

Joel Whitburn, *Top Country Singles, 1944–1988* (Menomonee Falls, Wisc.: Record Research, 1989).

Anonymous, *I'm Your Woman* LP liner notes (Nashville: Capitol Records, 1972).

BILLIE JO SPEARS

Kathy Batts, "Billie Jo—She's as Country as They Come," *Springfield Leader & Press*, Mar. 11, 1978.

Jack Hurst, "Billie Jo Spears: A Rising Country Star Who Has the World on a String—Of Hits," *Chicago Tribune*, Nov. 10, 1976.

Murray Kash, *Murray Kash's Book of Country* (London: Star Books, 1981).

Irwin Stambler and Grelun Landon, *The Encyclopedia of Folk, Country & Western Music* (New York: St. Martin's Press, 1983).

Tony Tyworth, "Billie Jo Spears," *Country Music People*, Oct. 1975.

Anonymous, "Presenting Billie Jo Spears," publicity bio (Nashville: United Talent, n.d.).

LEONA WILLIAMS

Kelly Delaney, "Songstress Has Lived Many of the Songs She Writes," *American Songwriter*, Oct. 1984.

Merle Haggard with Peggy Russell, *Sing Me Back Home* (New York: Times Books, 1981).

Marina Nickerson, "Leona Williams," *The El Paso Times*, Feb. 7, 1981.

Robert K. Oermann, "Leona Williams: More Than Mrs. Haggard," *Country Song Roundup*, Mar. 1983.

Robert K. Oermann, "Busy Leona Williams Starts 1985 Off Right," *The Tennessean*, Jan. 12, 1985.

Leona Williams, interview with Robert K. Oermann, Oct. 1982.

Leona Williams, interview with Robert K. Oermann, Jan. 1985.

William J. Zmudka, "Leona Williams: A Heart as Big as the Country," *Country Music News*, Oct. 1984.

RUBY WRIGHT

Robert K. Oermann, *Rock Love* LP liner notes (Bremen, West Germany: Bear Family Records, 1985).

Ruby Wright, interview with Robert K. Oermann, June 1985.

WORKING-CLASS 1960s AMERICA

Mary Bufwack, "Songs of Women's Work," unpublished typescript, 1981.

William H. Chafe, *Women and Equality* (New York: Oxford University Press, 1977).

Mary Frank Fox and Sharlene Hesse-Biber, *Women at Work* (Mayfield Publishing Company, 1984).

Steven Mintz and Susan Kellogg, *Domestic Revolutions* (New York: Free Press, 1988).

Karin Stallar, Barbara Ehrenreich, and Holly Sklar, *Poverty in the American Dream* (Boston: South End Press, 1983).

Howard Zinn, *A People's History of the United States* (New York: Harper & Row, 1980).

13. The Heroines of Heartbreak

SHIRLEY BOONE

Pat Boone, *Together: 25 Years with the Boone Family* (Nashville: Thomas Nelson Publishers, 1979).

Shirley Boone, *One Woman's Liberation* (Carol Stream, Ill.: Creation House, 1972).

ANITA BRYANT

Anita Bryant, interview with Robert K. Oermann, May 1990.

Anita Bryant, *Mine Eyes Have Seen the Glory* (Old Tappan, N.J.: Fleming H. Revell Co., 1970).

Anita Bryant, *The Anita Bryant Story* (Old Tappan, N.J.: Fleming H. Revell Co., 1977).

Robert K. Oermann, "Survivor Bryant Comes Full Circle," *The Tennessean*, May 16, 1990.

HELEN CORNELIUS

Bob Battle, "Singer Says Work Built Character," *The Nashville Banner*, July 28, 1981.

Bob Battle, "Helen Cornelius—A Woman of Character," *The Nashville Banner*, Jan. 5, 1982.

Andrew "Ace" Collins, "Far Beneath the Bitter Snows," *Plus: The Magazine of Positive Thinking*, Apr. 1989.

Suzanne Crane and Rochelle Friedman, "Jim Ed & Helen: Sticking Together," *Country Music*, Sept. 1980.

Laura Eipper, "Jim Ed and Helen Sing Swan Song," *The Tennessean*, Sept. 26, 1980.

Laura Eipper, "Singer Helen Cornelius' Show Will Go On," *The Tennessean*, Oct. 4, 1980.

Thomas Goldsmith, "Brown and Cornelius Revive Team," *The Tennessean*, Apr. 29, 1988.

Bill Hance, "Songstress on Road, Looking Back to Family," *The Nashville Banner*, June 24, 1972.

David Henry, "Jim Ed Brown Divorce Case Takes 1st Step," *The Nashville Banner*, Oct. 3, 1980.

Jim Jerome, "For a Song . . . ," *People*, Aug. 29, 1977.

Bill Littleton, "Jim Ed and Helen: Low Key and High Energy," *Country Song Roundup*, May 1979.

Bill Littleton, "Helen Cornelius: Ready to Fly," *Performance*, Dec. 1980.

Bob Millard, "She's Had More Heartaches Than a Soap Opera Heroine," *The Nashville Banner*, Sept. 30, 1983.

Red O'Donnell, "Helen Cornelius Ready for 'Single,'" *The Nashville Banner*, Sept. 29, 1980.

BARBARA FAIRCHILD

Barbara Fairchild, interview with Robert K. Oermann, Feb. 1986.

Robert K. Oermann, "1970s Country Queen Makes 1980s Comeback," *The Tennessean*, Mar. 13, 1986.

Anonymous, "Barbara Fairchild: Exclusive Interview," *Nashville Reporter*, Oct. 1982.

Anonymous, "Barbara Fairchild," publicity bio, 1986.

CRISTY LANE

James Albrecht, "Bucking the Odds," *CountryStyle*, June 1979.

Ellen Brooks, "Cristy Lane: Fulfilling Dreams, Forgetting Images," *CountryStyle*, June 1981.

Thomas Goldsmith, "Singer Doesn't Belt Them Out, but She's Heard Far and Wide," *The Tennessean*, June 20, 1987.

Ruth Ann Leach, "Mail-Order Record Queen's Courage," *The Nashville Banner*, Jan. 15, 1986.

John Lomax III, "Cristy Lane the Hardest Way," *Country Song Roundup*, June 1981.

Sandy Neese, "TV Ads Brought Stardom to Cristy Lane," *The Tennessean*, Sept. 15, 1983.

Lee Stoller with Pete Chaney, *Cristy Lane: One Day at a Time* (Madison, Tenn.: LS Records, 1983).

LORETTA LYNN

Hallway Productions, *Loretta Lynn: Honky-Tonk Girl*, video documentary (Nashville: Hallway Productions, 1990).

Loretta Lynn, interview with Robert K. Oermann, July 1986.

Carol Offen, comp., "The Big Speakout," *Country Music*, July 1974.

MELBA MONTGOMERY

Tony Byworth, "Melba Montgomery," *Country Music People*, Dec. 1974.

Geoff Lane, "Melba Montgomery Hits the Country Spot," *Country Music*, Sept. 1974.

Bill Melody, "Melba Montgomery Was Born to Sing," *Levittown-Bristol Pa. Courier-Times*, Oct. 6, 1988.

Anonymous, "Melba Montgomery: Sugar & Spice & Everything Nice," *Country Song Roundup*, May 1968.

Anonymous, "Melba Montgomery Works with the Pros," *Country Song Roundup*, Feb. 1966.

DOLLY PARTON AND PORTER WAGONER

Leonore Fleischer, *Dolly: Here I Come Again* (Toronto: PaperJacks, 1987).

Dave Hickey, "Dolly Triumphant!" *Country Music*, July 1974.

Alanna Nash, *Dolly* (Los Angeles: Reed Books/Country Music, 1978).

Lola Scobey, *Dolly Parton: Daughter of the South* (New York: Zebra/Kensington, 1977).

SANDY POSEY

Tony Byworth, "Whatever Happened to Sandy Posey?" *Country Music People*, June 1975.

Carolyn [Posey], *Why Don't We Go Somewhere and Love* LP liner notes (Nashville: Columbia Records, 1972).

Martha Sharp, interview with Robert K. Oermann, Feb. 1992.

Irwin Stambler and Grelun Landon, *The Encyclopedia of Folk, Country & Western Music* (New York: St. Martin's Press, 1983).

SUSAN RAYE

[Tony Byworth] unbylined, "Susan Raye Interviewed," *Country Music People*, May 1974.

Thomas Goldsmith, "Life's Bustling for Singer Susan Raye," *The Tennessean*, Dec. 25, 1985.

Anonymous, "Susan Raye," *Country Song Roundup Annual*, 1974.

JEANNIE C. RILEY

Carol Offen, comp., "The Big Speakout," *Country Music*, July 1974.

JEANNIE SEELY

Tony Byworth, "Jack Greene, Jeannie Seely," *Country Music People*, June 1973.

[Walter Carter] unbylined, "Opry's Jeannie Seely a Fighter," *The Tennessean*, Feb. 20, 1981.

Dixie Deen, "The Success Story of Jeannie Seely," *Music City News*, Oct. 1966.

Laura Eipper, "Jeannie's Aiming to Please," *The Tennessean*, Sept. 3, 1977.

Bill Hance, "The Cochrans' Farmhouse: Homey as an Old Barn," *The Nashville Banner*, Feb. 16, 1973.

Jack Hurst, "Opry's Jeannie Seely No Fairy-Tale Doll," *The Tennessean*, May 11, 1969.

Robert K. Oermann, "Willie & Jeannie Are 'On the Road Again,'" *The Tennessean*, Sept. 24, 1982.

Robert K. Oermann, "Seely Earns Her Place on 'Cowboy' Album," *The Tennessean*, Oct. 28, 1983.

Robert K. Oermann, "Miss Country Soul Opens Nightclub," *The Tennessean*, June 7, 1985.

Robert K. Oermann, "Outspoken Jeannie Seely Collects Her 'Wits,'" *The Tennessean*, Oct. 20, 1988.

Robert K. Oermann, "Jeannie Says Goodbye to Rose Room," *The Tennessean*, Aug. 18, 1989.

Jeannie Seely, interview with Robert K. Oermann, June 1985.

Jeannie Seely, interview with Robert K. Oermann, Oct. 1988.

Jeannie Seely, interview with Robert K. Oermann, Aug. 1989.

Jeannie Seely, *Pieces of a Puzzled Mind* (Nashville: Publications Jeannie Seely Songs, 1987).

JEAN SHEPARD

Jack Hurst, "Now Jean Can Be Other Woman," *The Chicago Tribune*, Apr. 11, 1975.

Carol Offen, comp., "The Big Speakout," *Country Music*, July 1974.

CONNIE SMITH

Steve Casey, "Country Singer Places Family over Show Biz," *San Diego Evening Tribune*, Mar. 3, 1978.

Edward W. Cotton, "A Hoosier Charmer, Country Style," *Indianapolis Star*, Jan. 16, 1966.

Kathleen Gallagher, "Connie Smith: I've Had a Chance to Live My Life Over," *Country Music*, Dec. 1973.

Darryl Hicks, "Connie Smith Haynes—Successful Overnight but Not Happy," in *God Comes to Nashville* (Harrison, Ark.: New Leaf Press, 1979).

Mary Ellen Moore, "Connie Smith: A Traditionalist Comes Back to the Fold," *Country Music*, Mar.–Apr 1985.

Robert K. Oermann, "Electrifying Connie Smith Back at Last," *The Tennessean*, Apr. 27, 1984.

Robert K. Oermann, "Connie Smith's in Quest of Her Crown," *The Tennessean*, Oct. 11, 1986.

Carol Offen, comp., "The Big Speakout," *Country Music*, July 1974.

Darrell Rowlett, "Connie Smith: A Young Lady Complete with a Music and a Message," *Country Song Roundup*, Oct. 1973.

Darrell Rowlett, "Connie Smith Prefers Evangelism, Housekeeping to Selling Records," *The Greenville Sun*, May 2, 1973.

Connie Smith, interview with Robert K. Oermann, Sept. 1986.

Genevieve J. Waddell, "Meet Connie Smith: Grand Ole Opry Christian," *People*, Nov. 1972.

TAMMY WYNETTE

Joan Dew, "Tammy Wynette: Heroine of Heartbreak," *Cosmopolitan*, Apr. 1978.

Joan Dew, *Singers & Sweethearts* (New York: Doubleday, 1977).

Stuart Goldman, "Penthouse Interview: Tammy Wynette," *Penthouse*, Sept. 1980.

Peter Guralnick, "Tammy: The Only Time I'm Really Me," *Country Music*, Mar. 1979.

Suzie Guymon, "I'd Do It All Over Again!" *Las Vegas Sun*, Jan. 11, 1980.

Stan Leventhal, "The Tammy Wynette Interview," *Country Rhythms*, Feb. 1983.

Alanna Nash, "Tammy Wynette: Country Music's Heroine of Heartbreak," *The Country Gentleman*, Spring 1981.

Robert K. Oermann, "The Heartbreak's Over: Tammy's Finally Happy," *The Tennessean*, Aug. 13, 1983.

Robert K. Oermann, "First Lady Tammy Wynette Makes Charity First Priority," *The Tennessean*, Aug. 25, 1985.

Robert K. Oermann, "Tammy Wynette Steps Up onto 'Higher Ground' for Fresh Start," *The Tennessean*, Nov. 8, 1987.

Robert K. Oermann, "Tammy Bound for Mu Mu Land," *The Tennessean*, Mar. 8, 1992.

Carol Offen, comp., "The Big Speakout," *Country Music*, July 1974.

George Richey, interview with Robert K. Oermann, Feb. 1992.

Tammy Wynette, interview with Robert K. Oermann, July 1983.

Tammy Wynette, interview with Robert K. Oermann, Aug. 1985.

Tammy Wynette, interview with Robert K. Oermann, Oct. 1987.

Tammy Wynette, interview with Robert K. Oermann, Feb. 1992.

Tammy Wynette with Joan Dew, *Stand by Your Man* (New York: Simon & Schuster, 1979).

COUNTRY DUETS

Mary A. Bufwack, *The Greatest Country Music Recordings of All Time: The Great Duets* LP liner notes (Franklin Center, Pa.: Franklin Mint Record Society, 1983).

THE WOMEN'S MOVEMENT

Susan Faludi, *Backlash: The Undeclared War Against American Women* (New York: Crown, 1991).

Suzanne Levine and Harriet Lyons, eds., *The Decade of Women: A Ms. History of the 70s* (New York: Paragon, 1980).

CONSERVATISM AND THE SOUTH

Paul DiMaggio, Richard A. Peterson, and Jack Esco, Jr., "Country Music: Ballad of the Silent Majority," in *The Sounds of Social Change* (Chicago: Rand McNally and Co., 1972).

Todd Gitlin, *The Sixties: Years of Hope, Days of Rage* (New York: Bantam, 1987).

Allen Hunter, "In the Wings: New Right Ideology and Organization," *Radical America*, vol. 15, nos. 1–2, Spring 1981.

Kirk Loggins, "Father Ordered to Stop Talking White Supremacy to Sons," *The Tennessean*, Feb. 2, 1992.

Bobby Lord, *Hit the Glory Road!* (Nashville: Broadman Press, 1969).

Jens Lund, "Fundamentalism, Racism and Political Reaction in Country Music," in *The Sounds of Social Change* (Chicago: Rand McNally and Co., 1972).

Charles P. Roland, *The Improbable Era: The South Since World War II* (Lexington: University Press of Kentucky, 1975).

Kirkpatrick Sale, *Power Shift: The Rise of the Southern Rim* (New York: Random House, 1975).

Nick Tosches, *Country the Biggest Music in America* (New York: Stein & Day, 1977).

F. Clifton White and William J. Gill, *Why Reagan Won: A Narrative History of the Conservative Movement* (Chicago: Regnery, 1981)..

14. Just Because I'm a Woman

LIZ ANDERSON

Jay Hoffer, *Like a Merry-Go-Round* LP liner notes (Nashville: RCA Records, 1968).

Mira Smith and Margaret Lewis, "The Country Music Writer: Liz Anderson," *Country Song Roundup*, Aug. 1975.

Walt Trott, "Mama Never Promised Me a Rose Garden," *Country Scene*, Mar. 1987.

BOUDLEAUX AND FELICE BRYANT

Boudleaux Bryant, interview with Robert K. Oermann, Mar. 1986.

Wayne W. Daniel, "Rocky Top," *Bluegrass Unlimited*, Apr. 1982.

Kelly Delaney, "Boudleaux & Felice Bryant: All They Had to Do Was Dream," *Songwriter*, Dec. 1978.

Mike Hyland, "Bryants Starting a New Career," *Billboard*, Feb. 9, 1980.

Paul Kingsbury, *Standards from House of Bryant* CD liner notes (Nashville: House of Bryant, 1990).

Bob Oermann, "Boudleaux Bryant: Georgia Music Hall of Famer," *BMI: The Many Worlds of Music*, n.d.

Robert K. Oermann, "Writers of 'Rocky Top' Hall of Fame Inductees," *The Tennessean*, Mar. 4, 1986.

Lee Rector, "Writers Felice & Boudleaux Review 30 Years," *Music City News*, Feb. 1980.

Tom Roland, "Boudleaux & Felice Bryant: A Winning Combination," *BMI Music World*, Fall 1991.

H. H. Teeter, "Boudleaux & Felice," *The Tennessean*, Jan. 8, 1956.

Ed Ward, "Country Music's Roots Wrapped Around Couple," *Austin American*, Oct. 23, 1981.

Anonymous, "25 Years of Harmony," *Billboard*, Jan. 26, 1974.

DONNA FARGO

Donna Fargo, interview with Robert K. Oermann, Oct. 1982.

Donna Fargo, interview with Robert K. Oermann, June 1985.

Jack Hurst, "Some of Donna's Views Aren't Off the Record," *Chicago Tribune*, Aug. 4, 1976.

Jack Hurst, "Donna Fargo's Back, and Still the Happiest Girl," *Chicago Tribune*, Dec. 6, 1978.

Robert K. Oermann, "Donna Fargo May Be Down, but You Can't Count Her Out," *The Tennessean*, Nov. 6, 1982.

Robert K. Oermann, "Donna Fargo's Not 'The Happiest Girl,'" *The Tennessean*, June 26, 1985.

Keith Tuber, "Donna Fargo," *Los Angeles Herald Examiner*, Apr. 21, 1980.

Gloria Tulley, "Fargo Billed for Two-Day Annual Music Festival," *San Jose News*, June 10, 1977.

Robert Windeler, "Donna Fargo: The Schoolmarm Who Went Country," *People*, Aug. 19, 1974.

Anonymous, Warner Bros. Records publicity bio, July 1980.

Anonymous, RCA Records publicity bio, June 1982.

Anonymous, Mercury Records publicity bio, Aug. 1986.

BOBBIE GENTRY

Penny F. Anderson, "Bobbie Gentry's Summer," *Rochester N.Y. Democrat and Chronicle*, June 16, 1974.

Texas Jim Cooper, "Bobbie Gentry: Pop with a Country Sound," *Country Song Roundup*, June 1968.

Howard Elson and John Brunton, *Whatever Happened To?* (New York: Proteus, 1981).

Don Lee Keith, *Fancy* LP liner notes (Los Angeles: Capitol Records, 1969).

Jon Pareles and Patricia Romanowski, eds., *Rolling Stone Encyclopedia of Rock & Roll* (New York: Rolling Stone/Summit, 1983).

Kathy Sawyer, "Bobbie's a One-Man Woman," *The Tennessean*, Oct. 29, 1967.

Irwin Stambler, *Encyclopedia of Pop, Rock & Soul* (New York: St. Martin's Press, 1977).

Irwin Stambler and Grelun Landon, *The Encyclopedia of Folk, Country & Western Music* (New York: St. Martin's Press, 1969).

Irwin Stambler and Grelun Landon, *The Encyclopedia of Folk, Country & Western Music* (New York: St. Martin's Press, 1983).

Anonymous, "A Gutsy Voice, a Grim Song Made Her an Instant Hit," *Life*, Nov. 10, 1967.

Anonymous, "What Does Billy Joe Really Mean?," *The Tennessean*, Aug. 27, 1967.

LINDA HARGROVE

Bob Battle, "She Honors Country Roots," *Wheeling Intelligencer*, May 5, 1979.

Edith Carter, "Women Making It," *Stereo*, Spring 1975.

Barbara Charone, "Linda Hargrove, Pedal Pusher," *Rolling Stone*, Jan. 2, 1975.

Thomas Goldsmith, " 'Blue Jean Country Queen' Leaves Hard Living Behind," *The Tennessean*, Apr. 25, 1990.

Patty Hall, "Linda Hargrove: The Blue Jean Country Queen," *Folkscene*, vol. 5, no. 6, Aug. 1977.

Will Hardesty, "She'd Put the French Horn in Country Music," *Rocky Mountain News*, Mar. 7, 1976.

Linda Hargrove, interview with Robert K. Oermann, July 1989.

Linda Hargrove, interview with Robert K. Oermann, July 1992.

Jack Hurst, "A Lyric Wrote Linda Hargrove's Ticket," *Chicago Tribune*, Mar. 10, 1976.

Jack Hurst, "Hargrove's Writing Takes Turn for Success," *Chicago Tribune*, July 6, 1977.

Alan Wilson, "Linda Hargrove Made It in Nashville . . . ," *Denver Post*, May 13, 1973.

LORENE MANN

Grant Turner, *A Mann Named Lorene* LP liner notes (Nashville: RCA Records, 1969).

Anonymous, "Lorene Mann" bio, *Country Music Who's Who* Programming Service (Denver: Heather Publications, n.d.).

DOLLY PARTON

Robert K. Oermann, "Dolly Parton's Work in Progress," *The Aquarian*, Mar. 31, 1982.

Robert K. Oermann, "The Dolly Parton Interview," *Country Rhythms*, June 1982.

Robert K. Oermann, "The Dolly Parton Interview: Pt. 2," *Country Rhythms*, Sept. 1982.

Robert K. Oermann, "Dolly Parton Is Alive & Well," *The Tennessean*, Nov. 11, 1982.

Robert K. Oermann, "Dolly's Back in Town!," *USA Today*, Nov. 12, 1982.

Robert K. Oermann, "Dolly and Band Bid Farewell on HBO Special from London," *The Tennessean*, June 19, 1983.

Robert K. Oermann, "Dolly," *Inside Country Music*, Feb. 1983.

Robert K. Oermann, "Rhinestone," *Country Rhythms*, Mar. 1984.

Robert K. Oermann, "Kenny, Dolly Celebrate Early Yuletide," *The Tennessean*, Dec. 2, 1984.

Robert K. Oermann, "Tennessee Mountain Memories Bring Dolly Parton Back Home Again," *The Tennessean*, June 22, 1986.

Robert K. Oermann, "Dolly Parton: Here She Comes Again," *Country Sounds*, May 1987.

Robert K. Oermann, "Dreamer Dolly Comes Home," *The Tennessean*, Feb. 14, 1988.

Robert K. Oermann, "The Unsinkable Dolly Stays Afloat," *The Tennessean*, Mar. 19, 1988.

Robert K. Oermann, "Dolly: Sweet, Savvy and Sassy," *The Tennessean*, Apr. 23, 1989.

Robert K. Oermann, "Dolly Rides Back into Country in 'Limozeen,'" *The Tennessean*, July 8, 1989.

Robert K. Oermann, "A Christmas Dolly," *The Tennessean*, Dec. 16, 1990.

Dolly Parton, press conference, Jan. 1980.

Dolly Parton, interview with Robert K. Oermann, Apr. 1982.

Dolly Parton, press conference, Nov. 1982.

Dolly Parton, interview with Robert K. Oermann, Oct. 1983.

Dolly Parton, interview with Robert K. Oermann, June 1984.

Dolly Parton, press conference, June 1984.

Dolly Parton, press conference, Dec. 1984.

Dolly Parton, press conference, June 1986.

Dolly Parton, interview with Robert K. Oermann, Mar. 1987.

Dolly Parton, press conference, Feb. 1988.

Dolly Parton, interview with Robert K. Oermann, Apr. 1989.

Dolly Parton, interview with Robert K. Oermann, Dec. 1990.

DOLLY PARTON (SECONDARY)

Joan Dew, *Singers & Sweethearts* (New York: Doubleday, 1977).

Leonore Fleischer, *Dolly: Here I Come Again* (Toronto: PaperJacks, 1987).

Frank Gannon, "Here She Comes Again," *Philip Morris Magazine*, Summer 1987.

Lawrence Grobel, "Playboy Interview—Dolly Parton," *Playboy*, vol. 25, no. 10, Oct. 1978.

Cindi Hoelzle, "Dolly Parton," *The Gavin Report*, July 7, 1989.

Leo Janos, "Dolly Parton: No Frets, No Regrets!" *Cosmopolitan*, Sept. 1980.

Marguerite Michaels, "I'm Not Going, I'm Just Growing," *Parade*, Nov. 2, 1980.

Maura Moynihan and Andy Warhol, "Dolly Parton," *Interview*, July 1985.

Alanna Nash, *Dolly* (Los Angeles: Reed Books/Country Music, 1978).

Carol Offen, comp., "The Big Speakout," *Country Music*, July 1974.

Lola Scobey, *Dolly Parton: Daughter of the South* (New York: Zebra/Kensington, 1977).

Kevin Sessums, "Good Golly, Miss Dolly!" *Vanity Fair*, June 1991.

William Stadiem, "Daisy Mae in Hollywood," *Interview*, July 1990.

Jean Vallely, "On the Rock Road with Dolly Parton," *Time*, Apr. 18, 1977.

Willadeene, *In the Shadow of a Song* (New York: Bantam, 1985).

Anonymous, "Biography of Dolly Parton," Solters/Roskin/Friedman, Inc., 1987.

FRANCES PRESTON

Darienne L. Dennis, "In the Music Biz, a Star Behind the Scenes," *Fortune,* Jan. 5, 1987.

Susan Nadler, "St. Frances of Nashville," *Savvy,* Jan. 1989.

Robert K. Oermann, "Frances Preston Marks 25th Year in Blaze of Glory," *The Tennessean,* Oct. 12, 1983.

Robert K. Oermann, "BMI Names Preston to No. 2 Position," *The Tennessean,* Mar. 27, 1985.

Robert K. Oermann, "Nashville's Frances Preston President of BMI," *The Tennessean,* Apr. 30, 1986.

Robert K. Oermann, "Frances Preston Among Most Powerful Women," *The Tennessean,* Nov. 4, 1990.

Barbara Pepe, "Licensed to Bill," *Hits,* June 8, 1987.

Frances Preston, interview with Robert K. Oermann, Oct. 1983.

Frances Preston, interview with Robert K. Oermann, Mar. 1985.

Frances Preston, interview with Robert K. Oermann, Apr. 1986.

Frances Preston, interview with Robert K. Oermann, Nov. 1990.

Jim Sparks, "Frances Preston," *Advantage,* Oct. 1982.

Anonymous, "Paying the Pipers," *Broadcasting,* Mar. 29, 1987.

JO WALKER-MEADOR

Thomas Goldsmith and Robert K. Oermann, "Banquet Honors CMA's Retiring Walker-Meador," *The Tennessean,* Nov. 14, 1991.

Robert K. Oermann, "CMA Chief's Success Behind the Scenes," *The Tennessean,* Nov. 10, 1991.

Jo Walker-Meador, interview with Robert K. Oermann, Nov. 1991.

MARIJOHN WILKIN

Tom T. Hall, *The Soul of a Singer* LP liner notes (Nashville: Dot Records, 1967).

Bill Hance, "Marijohn Wilkin," *BMI: The Many Worlds of Music,* Fall 1975.

Darryl E. Hicks, *Lord, Let Me Leave a Song* (Nashville: Message Press, 1978).

COUNTRY MUSIC AND TELEVISION

Stephen Cox, *The Beverly Hillbillies* (Chicago: Contemporary Books, 1988).

Robert K. Oermann, "Country Conquers the Tube," *Country Rhythms,* Mar. 1982.

Robert K. Oermann, "Cool Medium Warms Up to Nashville," *Billboard,* Oct. 17, 1981.

Robert K. Oermann, "Music & Video," *Video Systems,* Aug. 1982.

Robert K. Oermann, "Back in the Country, 1948: Country Music Goes on National TV," *Country Song Roundup,* June 1984.

Anonymous, "Television's Role in Country Music, 1948–1987: Beginnings," *CMA Close-Up,* Jan. 1988.

Anonymous, "Television's Role in Country Music, 1948–1987: Programming Trends of the 1950s," *CMA Close-Up,* Feb. 1988.

Anonymous, "Television's Role in Country Music, 1948–1987: Commercial Developments of the 1960s," *CMA Close-Up,* June 1988.

Anonymous, "Television's Role in Country Music, 1948–1987: Programming Trends of the 1970s," *CMA Close-Up,* Oct. 1988.

WOMEN IN THE WORK FORCE

Mary Frank Fox and Sharlene Hesse-Biber, *Women at Work* (n.p.: Mayfield Publishing Co., 1984).

Nancy Gibbs, "The War Against Feminism," *Time,* Mar. 9, 1992.

Sara E. Rix, ed., *The American Woman 1990–91* (New York: W.W. Norton & Co., 1990).

Anonymous, "More Working Women Projected," Associated Press story in *The Tennessean,* Aug. 17, 1978.

WOMEN IN THE MUSIC BUSINESS

Robert K. Oermann, "Warner Bros. Names Two Female V.P.s," *The Tennessean,* Apr. 4, 1984.

Robert K. Oermann, "Music Row Women Get Teed Off," *The Tennessean,* May 31, 1989.

David Ross, ed., "In Charge: Music Row's Decision Makers," *Music Row,* May 8, 1990.

David Ross, ed., "In Charge: Music Row's Decision Makers," *Music Row,* Apr. 23, 1991.

Jackie White, "Women of Calibre," *Country Music,* July 1974.

Bill Williams, "The Ladies of Nashville," *Billboard,* Oct. 17, 1970.

Bill Williams, "Nashville Battle Scene of Sexes; Gal Writers Click," *Billboard,* May 10, 1969.

Charles Wolfe, *Lefty Frizzell: Life's Like Poetry* CD liner notes (Vollersode, Germany: Bear Family Records, 1992).

15. Hollywood, Tennessee

LYNN ANDERSON

Lynn Anderson, interview with Robert K. Oermann, July 1987.

Tony Byworth, "Tony Byworth Tells the Story of Lynn Anderson," *Country Music People,* Mar. 1973.

Duren Cheek, "Ex-Husband Says Singer Was Abusive," *The Tennessean,* July 13, 1991.

Dixie Hall, "A Conversation with Lynn Anderson," *Country Music,* Nov. 1972.

Kirk Loggins, "Judge Won't Quit Singer's Custody Case," *The Tennessean,* Sept. 13, 1990.

Kirk Loggins, "Singer, Ex-Mate Testify to Cocaine Use," *The Tennessean,* Nov. 17, 1990.

Robert K. Oermann, "Country Queen Faces Career Crossroads," *The Tennessean,* Aug. 6, 1987.

Robert K. Oermann, "Country Queens Confront Legal Battles," *The Tennessean,* Oct. 21, 1988.

Robert K. Oermann, "Judge Refuses Return of Kids to Anderson," *The Tennessean,* Sept. 15, 1990.

Carol Offen, comp., "The Big Speakout," *Country Music,* July 1974.

Jan Read, "Anderson's Ex Tries to Cancel Summer Visits," *The Tennessean,* June 14, 1991.

Peggy Russell, "Lynn Anderson," *Country Song Roundup,* Mar. 1973.

Walt Trott, "Mama Never Promised Me a Rose Garden," *Country Scene,* Mar. 1987.

Anonymous, "Lawyer Wants Lynn Anderson's Ex-Husband to Pay for Her Time," *The Tennessean,* Feb. 21, 1991.

SHEILA ANDREWS

Jack Hurst, "Sheila Andrews Has a Voice You Can't Forget," *Chicago Tribune,* Jan. 16, 1980.

JACK BLANCHARD AND MISTY MORGAN

Doug Davis, "Mr. & Mrs. B. Seeking a Hit," *Dallas Morning News,* July 1, 1972.

Jim Roden, "A New Musical Team," *Dallas Times Herald,* Aug. 9, 1974.

Anonymous, "'Tennessee Bird Walk'—10 Minute Decision," *The Tennessean,* Apr. 12, 1970.

Anonymous, "Jack and Misty," *Music City News,* May 1970.

DEBBY BOONE

Debby Boone, *So Far* (Nashville: Thomas Nelson Publishers, 1981).

Pat Boone, *Together: 25 Years with the Boone Family* (Nashville: Thomas Nelson Publishers, 1979).

Cherry Boone O'Neill, *Starving for Attention* (New York: Continuum Publishing, 1982).

Joseph Farah, "Debby Boone," *Contemporary Christian Magazine,* Dec. 1983.

Rich Wiseman, "God Is Debby Boone's Copilot," *Rolling Stone,* Jan. 12, 1978.

TONI BROWN AND TERRY GARTHWAITE

Steve Chapple and Reebee Garofalo, *Rock 'n' Roll Is Here to Pay* (Chicago: Nelson-Hall, 1977).

JUNE CARTER

Joan Dew, *Singers & Sweethearts* (Dolphin/Doubleday, 1977).

SAMI JO COLE

Steve Chapple and Reebee Garofalo, *Rock 'n' Roll Is Here to Pay* (Chicago: Nelson-Hall, 1977).

DAVE AND SUGAR

Mark Dawidziak, "Dave Minus Sugar Sweet Too," *Kingsport Times-News,* Aug. 13, 1982.

Kim Moore, "Group's Songs Have to Gel," *Hutchinson, Kansas News,* Sept. 15, 1980.

George M. Newton, "Marshville Music Festival . . . ," *Monroe, N.C., Enquirer-Journal,* Aug. 2, 1990.

Sue Powell, interview with Robert K. Oermann, Apr. 1981.

Jerry Sharpe, "Dave and Sugar Sweet Sound," *Pittsburgh Press,* July 12, 1981.

Anonymous, "Dave Rowland & Sugar" publicity bio, Top Billing International, 1982.

Anonymous, "Dave & Sugar" publicity bio, Dot Records, 1980.

JANIE FRICKE

Janie Fricke, interview with Robert K. Oermann, May 1985.

Nick Krewen, "Janie Makes Even Jingles Sound Good," *The Hamilton Spectator*, Feb. 16, 1985.

Jack Lloyd, "It's Her Choice: She Can Be a Star if She Wants To," *Philadelphia Inquirer*, Nov. 17, 1978.

Robert K. Oermann, "Four Kings and Country Queen Wow Murfreesboro," *The Tennessean*, Oct. 25, 1982.

Robert K. Oermann, "'Lucky' Janie Fricke Showcases for Charity . . . ," *The Tennessean*, June 2, 1985.

Anonymous, "Janie Fricke" publicity bio, Kathy Gangwisch & Associates, 1985.

CRYSTAL GAYLE

Chet Flippo, "The Problem with Crystal," *Playboy*, Nov. 1981.

Crystal Gayle, interview with Robert K. Oermann, Nov. 1987.

Robert K. Oermann, "Classical Honor for Crystal," *The Tennessean*, Nov. 15, 1987.

Robert K. Oermann, "Magic, Music of Crystal Gayle to Sparkle During the Holidays," *The Tennessean*, Nov. 29, 1987.

Anonymous, "Crystal Gayle" publicity bio, Columbia Records, 1981.

Anonymous, "Crystal Gayle" publicity bio, Elektra Records, 1982.

BRENDA LEE

Brenda Lee, interview with Robert K. Oermann, Apr. 1991.

Brenda Lee, interview with Robert K. Oermann, June 1980.

Robert K. Oermann, "Brenda Lee: Still Pickin' Hits, as Usual," *Nashville Gazette*, July 1980.

Robert K. Oermann, "Brenda Lee Is Nashville's Song Magnet," *Music City News*, Dec. 1981.

LORETTA LYNN

Carol Offen, comp., "The Big Speakout," *Country Music*, July 1974.

CHARLY McCLAIN

Lucinda Cornelius, "This Year's Baby Becomes Next Year's Star," *Memphis Press-Scimitar*, Dec. 29, 1978.

Charly McClain, interview with Robert K. Oermann, Apr. 1983.

Robert K. Oermann, "Charly: A New Career & a New LP," *The Tennessean*, Apr. 23, 1983.

Neil Pond, "Sexy Charly McClain Wins the Female Fans, Too," *Music City News*, Mar. 1982.

Jane Sanderson, "When Charly Sleeps with the Radio On . . . ," *People*, Dec. 14, 1981.

Anonymous, "Charly McClain" publicity bio, Epic Records, 1983.

Anonymous, "Female Singer Becomes a Star Alone," n.p., 1982 (unbylined clipping in *Music City News* files).

Anonymous, "Time to Can Sex Talk, Claims McClain," *The Nashville Banner*, Feb. 4, 1982.

REBA McENTIRE

Don Cusic, *Reba: Country Music's Queen* (New York: St. Martin's Press, 1991).

Reba McEntire, interview with Robert K. Oermann, Dec. 1986.

Bob Millard, "Reba's Star Is on the Rise," *Nashville Banner*, Sept. 1, 1983.

Sandy Neese, "Oklahoma Cowgirl Starts New Year in a Big Way," *The Tennessean*, Jan. 8, 1983.

Robert K. Oermann, "Reba McEntire: Return of the Singing Cowgirl," *Country Digest*, 1980.

BARBARA MANDRELL

Barbara Mandrell, "Nashville Sounds" *WCMS* radio newsletter, Oct. 1970.

Barbara Mandrell with George Vecsey, *Get to the Heart* (New York: Bantam Books, 1990).

Barbara Mandrell, interview with Robert K. Oermann, Feb. 1984.

Barbara Mandrell, press conference, Jan. 1985.

Barbara Mandrell, interview with Robert K. Oermann, Dec. 1986.

Barbara Mandrell, interview with Robert K. Oermann, May 1988.

Barbara Mandrell, interview with Robert K. Oermann, Sept. 1990.

Louise Mandrell and Ace Collins, *The Mandrell Family Album* (Nashville: Thomas Nelson Publishers, 1983).

Sandy Neese and Robert K. Oermann, "The Lady Is a Champ," *The Tennessean*, Aug. 5, 1983.

Robert K. Oermann, "The Barbara Mandrell Interview," *Country Rhythms*, May 1984.

Robert K. Oermann, "Choked Up Barbara Back: 'I Thank God I'm Alive,'" *The Tennessean*, Jan. 4, 1985.

Robert K. Oermann, "Barbara with Dolly: A Fantastic Comeback," *The Tennessean*, Mar. 3, 1986.

Robert K. Oermann, "Barbara Mandrell Gearing Up for Fan Fair Activities," *The Tennessean*, June 5, 1986.

Robert K. Oermann, "Mandrell Breakfast Fetes Fans," *The Tennessean*, June 13, 1986.

Robert K. Oermann, "Barbara Mandrell Saluted by Her Fan Club Members," *The Tennessean*, June 14, 1985.

Robert K. Oermann, "Barbara Mandrell and Family Invite Viewers to Holiday Fest," *The Tennessean*, Dec. 21, 1986.

Robert K. Oermann, "Barbara Mandrell's Palatial Fontanel," *The Tennessean*, Feb. 9, 1989.

Robert K. Oermann, "Barbara Mandrell Takes Stars Out to the Old Ballgame," *The Tennessean*, May 29, 1988.

Robert K. Oermann, "Barbara Tries Country in New LP, Log Home," *The Tennessean*, Nov. 19, 1988.

Robert K. Oermann, "Mandrell's Candor Lands Her Best Seller," *The Tennessean*, Oct. 7, 1990.

Robert K. Oermann, "Mandrell's Life Story 'Gets to the Heart,'" *The Tennessean*, Oct. 16, 1990.

BARBARA MANDRELL (SECONDARY)

Jon Bream, "Mandrell: Hectic Schedule Keeps Her Up and Running," *Minneapolis Star*, Apr. 26, 1981.

Charles Paul Conn, *The Barbara Mandrell Story* (New York: Berkley Books, 1988).

Joe Edwards, "Barbara Mandrell Eyes Comeback," Associated Press story, Nov. 15, 1985.

Douglas B. Green, "Barbara Mandrell: Picker/Singer," *Pickin'*, vol. 5, no. 8, Sept. 1978.

Robert Macy, "New Priorities, Old Pizazz for Barbara Mandrell," Associated Press story, Feb. 4, 1988.

Holly Miller, "Barbara Mandrell: Fire and Faith," *Saturday Evening Post*, Apr. 1982.

Carol Offen, comp., "The Big Speakout," *Country Music*, July 1974.

Ellen Torgerson Shaw, "She's Just Plain Folks," *TV Guide*, Apr. 18, 1981.

Anonymous, "Country Artists Rap Top-40 Lists," *Variety*, Nov. 10, 1976.

Anonymous, "Barbara Mandrell" publicity bio, Columbia Records, 1969.

Anonymous, "Barbara Mandrell" publicity bio, Peter Simone Public Relations, 1973.

Anonymous, "Barbara Mandrell Fact Sheet," MCA Records, 1982.

Anonymous, "Barbara Mandrell" publicity bio, MCA Records, 1984.

ANNE MURRAY

Mary Campbell, "Anne Murray Going Semi-Hip," *The Tennessean*, Jan. 20, 1974.

Thomas Goldsmith, "Murray Might Be a Superstar, but Back Home She's 'Just Anne,'" *The Tennessean*, Nov. 5, 1989.

Anne Murray, interview with Robert K. Oermann, Aug. 1986.

Anne Murray, interview with Robert K. Oermann, Sept. 1988.

Anne Murray, interview with Robert K. Oermann, Aug. 1990.

Robert K. Oermann, "Cool Canadian Anne Murray Warms Hearts," *The Tennessean*, Feb. 19, 1985.

Robert K. Oermann, "Hit Queen Anne Murray Prevails Despite Fads of Pop Music Scene," *The Tennessean*, Aug. 17, 1986.

Robert K. Oermann, "Anne Murray Plans a Benefit," *The Tennessean*, Sept. 22, 1988.

Robert K. Oermann, "Canada's Sweetheart Anne Murray Debunks 'National Treasure' Title," *The Tennessean*, Nov. 13, 1988.

Robert K. Oermann, "Anne Murray Shares 20 Years of Memories," *The Tennessean*, Nov. 17, 1988.

Robert K. Oermann, "Anne Murray Returns to Country," *The Tennessean*, Oct. 20, 1990.

Robert K. Oermann, "Audience Rapport Keeps Murray in the Spotlight," *The Tennessean*, Apr. 14, 1991.

OLIVIA NEWTON-JOHN

Jerry Bailey, "Olivia Emigrates to Country Music," *The Tennessean*, Aug. 25, 1974.

Peter J. Boyer, "Country Olivia Opened Doors," Associated Press story in *The Tennessean*, Apr. 3, 1977.

Laura Eipper, "Olivia N-J Tries Out as Radio Interviewer," *The Tennessean*, Oct. 14, 1977.

Bill Hance, "Olivia a Little Nervous over Place," *The Nashville Banner*, Mar. 24, 1975.

Bill Hance, "Country Controversy Inspires 'Olivia' Song," *The Nashville Banner*, Jan. 29, 1975.

Lynn Harvey, "Olivia, Al Go Country," *The Tennessean*, Mar. 25, 1975.

Mike Howie, "Olivia: Physical and Fit," *Champaign News Gazette*, Sept. 10, 1982.

Red O'Donnell, "Olivia Newton-John a Refreshing Breeze," *The Nashville Banner*, Aug. 20, 1974.

LaWayne Satterfield, "Cease-Fire in Nashville," *Country Rambler*, Sept. 23, 1976.

Timothy White, "Olivia's Story," *Crawdaddy*, July 1978.

Robert Windeler, "Nashville Resented Her . . . ," *People*, July 31, 1978.

Eve Zibart, "Olivia: Ready for the Country," *The Tennessean*, July 15, 1976.

MARIE OSMOND

Doris Klein Bacon, "Dig Out the Diapers, Donny . . . ," *People*, Jan. 17, 1983.

Robert K. Oermann, "For Marie Osmond, a Busy Three Years," *The Tennessean*, Feb. 23, 1985.

Robert K. Oermann, "Things Are Going Well for Marie," *The Tennessean*, Nov. 1, 1986.

Robert K. Oermann, "On Her Own and On Her Way," *USA Weekend*, Aug. 8–10, 1986.

Marie Osmond, interview with Robert K. Oermann, Feb. 1985.

Marie Osmond, interview with Robert K. Oermann, Oct. 1986.

Neil Pond, "Marie Grows Up," *Music City News*, Aug. 1987.

Neil Pond, "The Princess of Oz," *Country America*, Dec. 1990/Jan. 1991.

Shawn Williams, "Marie Osmond: Rebounding Into Country Stardom . . . ," *Music City News*, Sept. 1986.

Shawn Williams, "Marie Osmond Works Hard for Her Money," *Music City News*, Sept. 1988.

MARY KAY PLACE

Chet Flippo, "The Real Mary Kay Place Stands Up," *Rolling Stone*, Jan. 26, 1978.

Anonymous, "Loretta Haggers," *Country Music*, Aug. 1976.

Anonymous, "Mary Kay Place/Loretta Haggers," *Music Gig*, Dec. 1976.

Anonymous, "Swap the Old Lady for a New Woman," *New Woman*, vol. 8, no. 1, Jan./Feb. 1978.

JEANNIE SEELY

Tony Byworth, "Jack Greene, Jeannie Seely," *Country Music People*, June 1973.

JEAN SHEPARD

Jack Hurst, "Now Jean Can Be Other Woman," *The Chicago Tribune*, Apr. 11, 1975.

Carol Offen, comp., "The Big Speakout," *Country Music*, July 1974.

Jean Shepard, interview with Robert K. Oermann, May 1988.

MARGO SMITH

Bob Battle, "Goodnight Gracie, Hello Star," *The Nashville Banner*, Feb. 17, 1981.

Charles Dibrell, "Singer's Fire Damage Could Total $500,000," *The Nashville Banner*, Feb. 7, 1985.

Laura Eipper, "Margo's Road from Teaching to Top-10," *The Tennessean*, Aug. 25, 1979.

Marsh Nichols, "Fired Manager Sues Country Artist," *The Nashville Banner*, Nov. 5, 1981.

Robert K. Oermann, "Margo Smith: I Want to Be a Superstar," *Country Song Roundup*, Dec. 1980.

Robert K. Oermann, "Margo Smith Brings Back the Yodel," *The Tennessean*, May 6, 1984.

Cletus Sickler, "Blaze Consumes Singer's Home," *The Tennessean*, Feb. 7, 1985.

Margo Smith, interview with Robert K. Oermann, Nov. 1980.

Margo Smith, interview with Robert K. Oermann, May 1984.

SISSY SPACEK

Robert K. Oermann, "Sissy's Back to Country," *The Tennessean*, Aug. 21, 1983.

Robert K. Oermann, "Sissy Spacek Goes Country for Real," *Country Rhythms*, Jan. 1984.

Sissy Spacek, interview with Robert K. Oermann, Aug. 1983.

BILLIE JO SPEARS

Bob Battle, "'There Is Nothing Like People,' Says Billie Jo Spears," *The Nashville Banner*, Jan. 29, 1980.

Tony Byworth, "Billie Jo Spears," *Country Music People*, Oct. 1975.

Bob Millard, "Billie Jo Spears Getting Ready to Climb U.S. Charts Again," *The Nashville Banner*, Dec. 23, 1983.

Ellis Nassour, "They Said Billie Jo Spears Would Never Sing Again," *Country Music*, Aug. 1977.

Mike Pigott, "Billie Jo Spears Scolded for Lying to Her Fans," *The Nashville Banner*, Feb. 28, 1979.

Joe Taylor, interview with Robert K. Oermann, Apr. 1992.

Anonymous, "Billie Jo Spears: A Country Star!!!," *Country Song Roundup*, Oct. 1976.

SYLVIA

Dolly Carlisle, "A Producer's Frumpy Secretary Becomes His Hot New Star," *People*, June 15, 1981.

Robert K. Oermann, "Country Bio: Sylvia," *Country Digest*, Nov. 1980.

Anonymous, "Sylvia" publicity bio, RCA Records, 1983.

DIANA TRASK

Chris Huizenga, "Diana Trask: Miss Country Soul Makes It Happen," *After Dark*, Aug. 1976.

Millie Jackson, interview with Robert K. Oermann, Sept. 1983.

Bob Powel, "Diana Trask Interviewed," *Country Music People*, Oct. 1974.

Anonymous, "Diana Trask" press kit, Buddy Lee Attractions, 1976.

DOTTIE WEST

Carol Offen, comp., "The Big Speakout," *Country Music*, July 1974.

Tammy Wynette, interview with Robert K. Oermann, Feb. 1992.

COUNTRY WOMEN OF THE 1970s

Noel Coppage, "Country Music's Traipsin' Women," *Stereo Review*, Dec. 1974.

Joan Dew, "Country Music's New Women," *Redbook*, vol. 144, no. 3, Jan. 1975.

Joan Dew, *Singers & Sweethearts* (New York: Dolphin/Doubleday, 1977).

Robert Hilburn, "Nashville Says Hello Dolly, Linda and . . . ," *Los Angeles Times*, Sept. 3, 1978.

Michael Kosser, *Those Bold & Beautiful Country Girls* (New York: Delilah/Mayflower,1979).

Tony Schwartz, "Country Girls," *Newsweek*, Apr. 17, 1978.

Bill Williams, "Female Country Acts Succeed," *Billboard*, Apr. 12, 1975.

Anonymous, "Ever Changing Country Music," *St. Louis Post-Dispatch*, Oct. 29, 1978.

Anonymous, "Women Have Hard Way to Go in Country," *Billboard*, Jan. 12, 1974.

Anonymous, "Female Artists Spur Gains Made by Country Market," *Billboard*, Feb. 6, 1971.

Various writers, "I Am Woman," *BMI: The Many Worlds of Music*, no. 4, 1977.

Various writers, "Songs of American Women," *Sing Out!*, vol. 25, no. 2, 1976.

THE ASSOCIATION OF COUNTRY ENTERTAINERS (ACE)

B. Drummond Ayers Jr., "Country Singers Kick Up a Fuss," *Champaign-Urbana Courier*, Jan. 2, 1975.

Jerry Bailey, "Artists Organize New Group, Want Country to Stay Country," *The Tennessean*, Nov. 13, 1974.

Jerry Bailey, "Group Misunderstands CMA: Member," *The Tennessean*, Nov. 14, 1974.

Jerry Bailey, "Country Music Group Defended," *The Tennessean*, Nov. 15, 1974.

Jerry Bailey, "New Group Gets CMA Voices," *The Tennessean*, Nov. 16, 1974.

Bill Hance, "New Country Group Picks 4 CMA Nominees," *The Nashville Banner*, Nov. 13, 1974.

Bill Hance, "Country Cliques, Politics Pique Stars," *The Nashville Banner*, Nov. 14, 1974.

Bill Hance, "ACE Trio to Oversee CMA Nominees," *The Nashville Banner*, Dec. 10, 1974.

Bill Hance, "ACE Lodges Complaint Against Stations," *The Nashville Banner*, Nov. 5, 1976.

Lynn Harvey, "Protesters Court CMA Boss," *The Tennessean*, Jan. 1, 1975.

Jean Shepard, interview with Robert K. Oermann, May 1988.

OPRYLAND U.S.A.

Hal Gieseking, *Opryland U.S.A.* (New York: McGraw-Hill, 1989).

Robert K. Oermann, "A Summer of Stars," *The Tennessean*, Mar. 3, 1991.

Robert K. Oermann, "Opryland's Star Alumni Return to Help Launch 13th Season," *The Tennessean*, Mar. 21, 1984.

Caleb Pirtle III, *The Grandest Day* (Nashville: Opryland U.S.A., 1979).

MUSIC INDUSTRY GROWTH

Philip K. Eberly, *Music in the Air* (New York: Hastings House, 1982).

Anonymous, *Inside the Recording Industry: A Statistical Overview* (New York: Recording Industry Association of America, 1985).

Anonymous, *Inside the Recording Industry: A Statistical Overview* (Washington, D.C.: Recording Industry Association of America, 1987).

Anonymous, *Inside the Recording Industry: A Statistical Overview* (Washington, D.C.: Recording Industry Association of America, 1988).

WOMEN'S GAINS OF THE 1970s

Judith Freeman Clark, *Almanac of American Women in the 20th Century* (New York: Prentice-Hall, 1987).

16. Back to Country

KAREN BROOKS

Karen Brooks, interview with Robert K. Oermann, June 1982.

Karen Brooks, interview with Robert K. Oermann, July 1992.

Robert K. Oermann, "Karen Brooks: Musician and Cowgirl," *The Tennessean,* May 21, 1983.

KIM CARNES

Kim Carnes, interview with Robert K. Oermann, Sept. 1987.

Robert K. Oermann, "Music Row Will Welcome Kim Carnes . . . ," *The Tennessean,* Oct. 1, 1987.

MARSHALL CHAPMAN

Walter Carter, "R&W Might Be the Answer to Singer's Identity Dilemma," *The Tennessean,* June 21, 1981.

Marshall Chapman, interview with Robert K. Oermann, Jan. 1987.

Marshall Chapman, interview with Robert K. Oermann, July 1989.

Laura Eipper, "Marshall's Much More Than One of the Boys," *The Tennessean,* Aug. 28, 1977.

Robert K. Oermann, "Marshall Chapman Celebrates Most Rockin' Year Ever," *The Tennessean,* Jan. 21, 1987.

JESSI COLTER

Andrew Cleary, "Jessi Colter Started with Tent Revivals," *Rocky Mountain News,* Feb. 11, 1978.

Joan Dew, "Jessi Colter's 'Ridin' Shotgun' . . . ," *The Tennessean,* Mar. 14, 1982.

Missy Harris, "'Outlaw' Jessi Colter Roams to Gospel Path," *Decatur Daily,* Apr. 28, 1985.

Jack Hurst, "Even If She Isn't Lisa, She Can Well Smile," *Philadelphia Inquirer,* June 1, 1975.

David Koppel, "Jessi Colter and Her Big, Gray Bus," *Chicago Sun-Times,* Aug. 6, 1978.

Richard Trubo, "Old Musical Exercise Yields Almost Instant Success," *Kansas City Star,* July 13, 1975.

Ellis Widner, "Jessi Raps About Music and Ole Waylon," *Country Rambler,* Dec. 10, 1976.

Anonymous, "Jessi Colter," *Song Hits,* Feb. 1977.

RITA COOLIDGE

Rita Coolidge, interview with Robert K. Oermann, Apr. 1983.

Robert K. Oermann, "Rita Coolidge Returns Home for a New LP and Old Friends," *The Tennessean,* May 1, 1983.

LACY J. DALTON

Elizabeth Benedict, "Something to Believe In," *Phillip Morris Magazine,* Fall 1986.

Jim Bessman, "I'm a Radical Environmentalist," *BMI: The Many Worlds of Music,* Summer 1989.

Lacy J. Dalton, interview with Robert K. Oermann, Sept. 1985.

Lacy J. Dalton, interview with Robert K. Oermann, Mar. 1989.

Lacy J. Dalton, interview with Robert K. Oermann, Aug. 1991.

Geoffrey Himes, "Blue-Collar Country," *The Washington Post,* Aug. 25, 1986.

Marjie McGraw, "Surviving in Music City," *Tune-In,* May 1989.

Alanna Nash, *Behind Closed Doors: Talking with the Legends of Country Music* (New York: Alfred A. Knopf, 1988).

Robert K. Oermann, "Lady Renegade Dalton Wins New Prizes," *The Tennessean,* Oct. 26, 1985.

Robert K. Oermann, "Lacy J. Dalton Battles Back as Gutsy Country 'Survivor,'" *The Tennessean,* May 21, 1988.

Anonymous, Lacy J. Dalton publicity bio, Columbia Records, May 1983.

GAIL DAVIES

Gail Davies, interview with Robert K. Oermann, July 1982.

Gail Davies, interview with Robert K. Oermann, Apr. 1984.

Gail Davies, interview with Robert K. Oermann, Aug. 1984.

Gail Davies, interview with Robert K. Oermann, Sept. 1986.

Gail Davies, interview with Robert K. Oermann, July 1987.

Robert K. Oermann, "A Nashville Afternoon with Gail Davies," *Country Rhythms,* Aug. 1982.

Robert K. Oermann, "Country's Gail Davies Sings, Speaks from the Heart," *The Tennessean,* Mar. 11, 1984.

Robert K. Oermann, "Gail Davies Gets Real with Wild Choir," *The Tennessean,* Sept. 27, 1986.

Robert K. Oermann, "Gail Davies' Musical Heart Lies Between a Rock, a Country Place," *The Tennessean,* July 19, 1987.

Anonymous, Gail Davies publicity bio, Capitol Records, Mar. 1990.

DOTTSY

Bill Oakey, "There Is Something You Should Know About Dottsy," *Country Song Roundup,* July 1979.

Bill Oakey, "Whatever Happened to Dottsy?" *Country Song Roundup,* Mar. 1981.

Red O'Donnell, "Dottsy Mixes Career . . . ," *The Nashville Banner,* July 24, 1981.

Doug Pullen, "Country Singer Rebuilds Career," *El Paso Herald-Post,* Feb. 5, 1982.

EMMYLOU HARRIS

Bob Allen, "Emmylou: The Ballad of Sally Rose," *Country Music,* no. 112, March/April 1985.

Michael Barackman, "Emmylou Harris," *Folkscene,* vol. 4, no. 2, Apr. 1976.

Ben Fong-Torres, *Hickory Wind: The Life and Times of Gram Parsons* (New York: Pocket Books, 1991).

Thomas Goldsmith, "Emmylou Makes Magic on Fabled Ryman Stage," *The Tennessean,* Jan. 12, 1992.

Emmylou Harris, interview with Robert K. Oermann, Nov. 1984.

Emmylou Harris, interview with Robert K. Oermann, Mar. 1987.

Emmylou Harris, interview with Robert K. Oermann, May 1987.

Emmylou Harris, interview with Robert K. Oermann, Sept. 1990.

Jennifer Harris, "The Ballad of Emmylou Harris," *Nashville,* June 1986.

Jack Hurst, "Emmylou Harris Offers a Rich Mix of Thought, Song," *St. Paul Pioneer Press,* Mar. 23, 1980.

Alanna Nash, *Behind Closed Doors: Talking with the Legends of Country Music* (New York: Alfred A. Knopf, 1988).

Robert K. Oermann, "Emmylou Harris Moving to Music City," *The Tennessean,* July 21, 1983.

Robert K. Oermann, "Emmylou Harris Readies for a Challenging 1985," *The Tennessean,* Dec. 8, 1984.

Robert K. Oermann, "Emmylou Harris: Life, Liberty and the Pursuit of Happiness," *Country Song Roundup,* May 1985.

Robert K. Oermann, "Emmylou, Kennerley Tie the Knot," *The Tennessean,* Nov. 16, 1985.

Robert K. Oermann, "Dolly, Linda and Emmylou: All for One and One for All," *The Tennessean,* Mar. 12, 1987.

Robert K. Oermann, "Emmylou's Beacon of Integrity Shines on Golden Gospel Songs," *The Tennessean,* July 5, 1987.

Robert K. Oermann, "Musical Mission Accomplished . . . ," *The Tennessean,* Sept. 23, 1990.

NICOLETTE LARSON

Kelly Delaney, "Nicolette Larson Pursues Her Country Roots," *Country News,* June 1985.

Nicolette Larson, interview with Robert K. Oermann, Mar. 1985.

Nicolette Larson, interview with Robert K. Oermann, Apr. 1986.

Nicolette Larson, interview with Robert K. Oermann, Apr. 1987.

Nicolette Larson, interview with Robert K. Oermann, Sept. 1988.

Robert K. Oermann, "Pop's Nicolette Larson Takes a Turn to Country," *The Tennessean,* Mar. 23, 1985.

Robert K. Oermann, "Nicolette's in 'Country for the Long Haul,'" *The Tennessean,* July 5, 1986.

Robert K. Oermann, "Larson Enjoys First Sitcom Acting Job," *The Tennessean,* Apr. 19, 1987.

Robert K. Oermann, "Singer Nicolette Larson Tours as Queen of the Road," *The Tennessean,* Oct. 2, 1988.

RATTLESNAKE ANNIE McGOWAN

Walter Carter, "Be It Rhinestones or Jeans, Annie McGowan's All Country," *The Tennessean,* Feb. 21, 1980.

Annie McGowan, interview with Robert K. Oermann, Nov. 1984.

Annie McGowan, interview with Robert K. Oermann, Aug. 1985.

Annie McGowan, interview with Robert K. Oermann, Mar. 1986.

Robert K. Oermann, "Rattlesnake Annie Takes Musical Message to Europe," *The Tennessean,* Nov. 19, 1984.

Robert K. Oermann, "Veteran & Newcomer Comprise Country's Newest Duet Team," *The Tennessean*, Sept. 3, 1985.

Robert K. Oermann, "'Pure Country' Rattlesnake Annie Carves Own Niche in Music World," *The Tennessean*, Mar. 20, 1986.

Anonymous, "Rattlesnake Annie," Columbia Records publicity bio, 1987.

JUICE NEWTON

Thomas Goldsmith, "Juice Squeezes Out Time for Work and Home," *The Tennessean*, July 2, 1989.

Juice Newton, interview with Robert K. Oermann, Oct. 1982.

Juice Newton, interview with Robert K. Oermann, Apr. 1986.

Juice Newton, interview with Robert K. Oermann, Aug. 1987.

Juice Newton, interview with Toby Goldstein, 1981.

Robert K. Oermann, "Country Music Opens Arms to Pop Singer Juice Newton," *The Tennessean*, Oct. 24, 1982.

Robert K. Oermann, "Juice Newton: Country or Not?" *Country Song Roundup*, July 1984.

Robert K. Oermann, "Juice Newton Balances Health, Home, Hits," *The Tennessean*, Oct. 24, 1987.

Robert K. Oermann, "Juice Newton's Sound Goes Country," *The Tennessean*, Mar. 1, 1986.

COLLEEN PETERSON

Robert K. Oermann, "Canadian Singer Ready to Make Her Mark," *The Tennessean*, June 11, 1983.

Robert K. Oermann, "Colleen Peterson Makes '84 Farewell . . . ," *The Tennessean*, Dec. 14, 1984.

Colleen Peterson, interview with Robert K. Oermann, May 1983.

Colleen Peterson, interview with Robert K. Oermann, Dec. 1984.

LINDA RONSTADT

Mark Bego, *Linda Ronstadt: It's So Easy!* (Austin, Texas: Eakin Press, 1990).

Vivian Claire, *Linda Ronstadt* (New York: Jove/Quick Fox, 1978).

Rod Davis, "I'm Not Good at Doing What I'm Told," *American Way*, Apr. 1, 1988.

Stephen Holden, "For Linda Ronstadt, the Past Continues to Inspire," *The New York Times*, Sept. 14, 1986.

Stephen Holden, "A 'Grown Up' Linda Ronstadt," New York Times News Service story, Jan. 1, 1988.

Elizabeth Kaye, "Linda Ronstadt: Why Is She the Queen of Lonely," *Redbook*, Feb. 1979.

Luisa Potenza Muniz, "Grammy Winner Linda Ronstadt Hails from Rich Tradition of Food and Song," New York Times News Service story in *The Tennessean*, Sept. 27, 1989.

Robert K. Oermann, "Linda Ronstadt Turning Back to Country?" *The Tennessean*, Aug. 24, 1985.

Robert K. Oermann, "Dolly, Linda and Emmylou: All for One and One for All," *The Tennessean*, Mar. 12, 1987.

Robert K. Oermann, "Whither Ronstadt?" *The Tennessean*, Mar. 26, 1987.

Anne M. Peterson, "Linda Ronstadt Expands on Musical Style Once Again," Associated Press story, Sept. 18, 1990.

Cliff Radel, "What Will Ronstadt Do Next?" Gannett News Service story, Aug. 31, 1990.

Bob Reiss, "Linda Ronstadt: When Will I Be Loved?" *The Washington Post Magazine*, Oct. 9, 1977.

Lisa Robinson, "I'm Still Sane, and Sensible Too," *Cal Today*, Aug. 16, 1981.

Linda Ronstadt, interview with Robert K. Oermann, Mar. 1987.

Stu Schreiberg, "To the Beat of a Different Drum," *USA Weekend*, Nov. 28, 1986.

SAMMI SMITH

Phil Burrows, "Sammi Smith Back on Country Circuit," *Muskogee Phoenix & Times Democrat*, Aug. 31, 1980.

Laura Eipper, "Sammi: There's More to It Than Music," *The Tennessean*, July 21, 1978.

Lew Holle, "Sammi Smith," *American Sound*, Nov. 1972.

Sherry Maves, "Sammi Is Not Just Another Singer," *Freeport, Ill., Journal-Standard*, June 29, 1985.

Robert K. Oermann, "Unsinkable Sammi," *Country Song Roundup*, Mar. 1982.

Sammi Smith, interview with Robert K. Oermann, July 1982.

Jerry Thompson, "She Wanted to Hang It Up," *The Tennessean*, June 13, 1974.

Anonymous, "Sammi Smith: The Girl Who's Turning on the World," *Country Song Roundup Annual*, 1971.

TANYA TUCKER

Victoria Balfour, "I'm Still a Party Girl," *Us*, June 2, 1986.

Jay Christian, "Tanya Tucker's Baby Joy," *The Star*, Oct. 22, 1991.

Robert K. Oermann, "Tanya: This Girl Is a Woman Now," *The Tennessean*, Mar. 26, 1983.

Robert K. Oermann, "Torrid Tanya," *The Tennessean*, Apr. 19, 1986.

Robert K. Oermann, "Tanya Celebrates Milestones in Life, Career," *The Tennessean*, Oct. 1, 1988.

Robert K. Oermann, "Tanya Tucker: Sexy Tabloid Queen or Cowgirl-Next-Door?," *The Tennessean*, Feb. 23, 1992.

Neil Pond, "Tanya Tucker Comes Back as Another Woman," *Music City News*, Nov. 1986.

Tanya Tucker, interview with Robert K. Oermann, Mar. 1983.

Tanya Tucker, interview with Robert K. Oermann, Mar. 1986.

Tanya Tucker, interview with Robert K. Oermann, Sept. 1988.

Tanya Tucker, interview with Robert K. Oermann, Jan. 1992.

JENNIFER WARNES

Walter Carter, "Warnes: The Hit Must Fit," *The Tennessean*, July 1, 1979.

Robert K. Oermann, "New 'Jenny Sings Lenny' Album Wins Singer's Long Uphill Fight," *The Tennessean*, Jan. 15, 1987.

Jennifer Warnes, interview with Robert K. Oermann, Jan. 1987.

COUNTRY MUSIC'S IDENTITY CRISIS

Everett J. Corbin, *Storm over Nashville: A Case Against Modern Country Music* (Nashville: Ashlar Press, 1980).

Robert K. Oermann, "Old vs. New Country: The Battle Is On," *Country Rhythms*, Sept. 1981.

Jean Shepard, interview with Robert K. Oermann, May 1988.

Justin Tubb, interview with Robert K. Oermann, Apr. 1989.

17. Little Darlin's Not My Name

MARTHA ADCOCK

Jack Hurst, "Bluegrass or Newgrass, the Adcocks' Roots Are Deep," *Chicago Tribune*, Mar. 1, 1981.

Mike Joyce, "The Eclectic Guitar Player," *The Washington Post*, Jan. 30, 1987.

Rich Kienzle, *The Acoustic Collection* LP liner notes (Los Angeles: CMH Records, 1988).

ANY OLD TIME

Any Old Time, *Any Old Time Stringband* LP liner notes (El Cerrito, Calif.: Arhoolie Records, 1978).

Jim S. Griffith, "Any Old Time *Stringband*" record review, *Bluegrass Unlimited*, Dec. 1978.

Les McIntyre, "Any Old Time *Ladies Choice*" record review, *Bluegrass Unlimited*, June 1981.

DELIA BELL

Barry Brower, "Bill Grant & Delia Bell . . . ," *Bluegrass Breakdown*, Winter 1988.

Jack Hurst, "Thank You Emmylou: The Tale of a Big Break," *Chicago Tribune*, Jan. 16, 1983.

Kathy Kaplan, *Bluer Than Midnight* LP liner notes (Floyd, Va.: County Records, 1978).

Arlie Metheny, "Bill & Juarez Grant's Salt Creek Park," *Bluegrass Unlimited*, Sept. 1988.

Walter V. Saunders, "Delia Bell *Bluer Than Midnight*" record review, *Bluegrass Unlimited*, Sept. 1979.

Anonymous, "Delia Bell" Warner Bros. Records publicity bio, 1982.

GLORIA BELLE

Bob Artis, *Bluegrass* (New York: Hawthorn Books, 1975).

Walter V. Saunders, "Gloria Belle *A Good Hearted Woman*" record review, *Bluegrass Unlimited*, Feb. 1979.

GINGER BOATWRIGHT

Ginger Boatwright, interview with Robert K. Oermann, Oct. 1991.

Bob Campbell, "Bushwackers: Female Quartet Sings Bluegrass," *Country Gazette*, no. 8, Mar. 1981.

George B. McCency, "Red, White & Blue (Grass) *Pickin' Up*" record review, *Bluegrass Unlimited*, Jan. 1975.

Frank Overstreet, "Red White & Blue (Grass)," *Bluegrass Unlimited*, July 1973.

THE BUFFALO GALS

Mike Greenstein, "Expanding the Horizons," *Bluegrass Unlimited*, Dec. 1976.

Susie Monick, interview with Robert K. Oermann, Apr. 1992.

Tony Trischka, "Buffalo Gals: Female Grass," *Muleskinner News*, n.d.

Tony Trischka, *Buffalo Gals First Borne* LP liner notes (Ferndale, N.Y.: Renovah Records, 1975).

BENNY AND VALLIE CAIN

Walter V. Saunders, "Betty and Vallie Cain," *Bluegrass Unlimited,* May 1972.

CALAMITY JANE

Walter Carter, "'Calamity Jane' Characteristic of Female Quartet's Nature," *The Tennessean,* Sept. 13, 1981.

Jack Hurst, "Calamity Jane: Energy Spills Over into Every Song," *Chicago Tribune,* Feb. 7, 1982.

Anonymous, "Spunky Calamity Jane," *People,* Dec. 28, 1981.

JUDY CARRIER

Judy Carrier, "Hangin' On," *Bluegrass Unlimited,* Apr. 1987.

Dick Kimmell, "Judy Carrier *From the Berkshires to the Smokies*" record review, *Bluegrass Unlimited,* July 1982.

COWBOY JAZZ

David Beaudouin, "Cowboy Jazz," *Unicorn Times,* Mar. 1980.

Kay Rios, "Kate Bennett Back Again," *Ft. Collins Triangle Review* (Colo.), vol. 7, no. 61, Dec. 5, 1979.

Linnell Smith, "Cowboy Jazz Has Swingin' Range of Sounds," *Baltimore Evening Sun,* Feb. 21, 1980.

THE DIXIE CHICKS

Bob Millard, "Hatching Success," *The Dallas Times Herald,* Dec. 14, 1990.

JEFF AND SHERI EASTER

Wayne W. Daniel, "Jeff & Sheri Easter," *Bluegrass Unlimited,* May 1988.

Jeff and Sheri Easter, interview with Robert K. Oermann, Sept. 1990.

Laura Lee, "A Winning Combination," *The Singing News,* Dec. 1987.

Robert K. Oermann, "Easters' Sound Restores Traditional Country Gospel," *The Tennessean,* Sept. 23, 1990.

Wayde Powell, "Home Folks," *Precious Memories,* May–June 1988.

Sandy Smith, "Picture Perfect Love," *The Singing News,* July 1989.

Kimmy Wix, "Jeff & Sheri Easter: To Know Them Is to Love Them," *Cash Box,* Aug. 26, 1989.

ELMO AND PATSY

Ken Beck, "'Grandma' Rings Out Yuletide," *The Tennessean,* Dec. 24, 1989.

Anonymous, "Elmo & Patsy Epic Records publicity bio, 1984.

EVANGELINE

Evangeline, interview with Robert K. Oermann, May 1992.

CATHY FINK

Lisa Bellamy, "Folksinger Sings 'The Songs of Working Women,'" *The Raleigh Times,* Oct. 1984.

Cathy Fink, interview with Robert K. Oermann, Aug. 1987.

Nat Hentoff, "An Eclectic Original," *The Progressive,* Oct. 1984.

Phil Hood, "Blue Rose," *Frets,* Mar. 1989.

Mike Joyce, "Marxer: Glad to Play in a Minor's Key," *The Washington Post,* Dec. 12, 1985.

Larry Kelp, "Cathy Fink & Marcy Marxer," *Sing Out!,* vol. 33, no. 4, Summer 1988.

Larry Kelp, "Blue Rose Flowers with Hot Picking and Harmonies," *The Tribune Calendar,* Nov. 6, 1988.

Norman Kerner, "Fink & Marxer: The Biggest Hearts in the Business," *Maryland Magazine,* Apr. 1990.

Bill Littleton, "Cathy Fink Breaks Barriers with Country/Folk Stylings," *Performance,* 1987 Country Talent Directory (Fort Worth: 1987).

Robert K. Oermann, "Cathy Fink Brings Women's Slant to Bluegrass World," *The Tennessean,* Aug. 6, 1987.

Katherine S. Seigenthaler, "Cathy Fink, Painting Women's Lives," *The Washington Post,* Oct. 26, 1984.

M. Scott Skinner, "Banjo-Picker Restores Life to Old Songs," *The Arizona Daily Star,* Feb. 21, 1985.

BETTY FISHER

Don Rhodes, "Born to Be Free—Betty Fisher," *Bluegrass Unlimited,* Nov. 1976.

Walter V. Saunders, "Betty Fisher & the Dixie Bluegrass Band *Carolina Mountain Home*" record review, *Bluegrass Unlimited,* Jan. 1976.

Anonymous, "Betty Fisher & the Dixie Bluegrass Band," *The Bluegrass Star,* Feb. 1973.

ALICE GERRARD

David Menconi, "On Stage, Page, She Fights to Keep Old-Time Music Young," *Bluegrass Unlimited,* Mar. 1992.

THE GOOD OL' PERSONS

J. D. Kleinke, "Omnigrass, Anyone?," *Bluegrass Unlimited,* Mar. 1991.

Laurie Lewis, interview with Robert K. Oermann, Aug. 1992.

Alan J. Steiner, "The Good Ol' Persons *I Can't Stand to Ramble*" record review, *Bluegrass Unlimited,* Apr. 1984.

THE HOTMUD FAMILY

D. P. Breckenridge, "Meat, Potatoes Music Fills Joyous Hotmud LP," *Kansas City Star,* Jan. 5, 1982.

Bob Cantwell, "It's Current to Us," *Bluegrass Unlimited,* Apr. 1977.

Dale Dempsey, "They Fiddle Around with Old-Timey Country," *Dayton Journal Herald,* July 10, 1982.

Sherri Gardner, "Hot Mudders Dig Wide Furrow in Musical Bluegrass Country," *Knoxville News-Sentinel,* July 4, 1977.

Frank J. Godbey, "The Hotmud Family *Till We Meet Here Again*" record review, *Bluegrass Unlimited,* July 1974.

Bruce Kaplan, interview with Robert K. Oermann, May 1992.

Dick Kimmel, "The Hotmud Family *Years in the Making*" record review, *Bluegrass Unlimited,* Jan. 1979.

Robert K. Oermann, "The Hotmud Family *Live as We Know It*" record review, *The Nashville Gazette,* Sept. 4, 1980.

John Thomas, "Mix Earth, Water, Fire: You Get Music," *Dayton Daily News,* Mar. 20, 1973.

Ron Thomason, "Fertile Ground with Deep Roots," *Bluegrass Unlimited,* Dec. 1983.

James Windell, "Hotmud Family's Music Clean Country Fun," *Oakland Press,* Oct. 30, 1981.

THE KENDALLS

Thomas Goldsmith, "Family Ties, Traditions Shape Kendalls' Career," *The Tennessean,* Aug. 26, 1989.

Mark Humphrey, "Kendalls Prove Two Parts Equal Harmony," *Los Angeles Daily News,* Mar. 29, 1985.

The Kendalls, interview with Robert K. Oermann, Dec. 1982.

The Kendalls, interview with Robert K. Oermann, May 1984.

Bob Millard, "No Cheatin' on New Kendalls LP?" *The Nashville Banner,* Sept. 16, 1983.

Robert K. Oermann, "Kendalls Have Big Plans for New Year," *The Tennessean,* Jan. 1, 1983.

Robert K. Oermann, "Dad and Daughter Kendall Back on the Charts," *The Tennessean,* May 19, 1984.

ALISON KRAUSS

Mike Boehm, "A Festival Fit for Fiddles," *Providence Journal-Bulletin,* Sept. 1987.

Bill Christophersen, "Catgut's Got Her Tongue," *Newsweek,* Oct. 1, 1990.

Thomas Goldsmith, "Alison Krauss Plays Second Fiddle to No One in Bluegrass," *The Tennessean,* Sept. 15, 1990.

Thomas Goldsmith, "Talented Krauss Adds 'Busy' to Growing List of Adjectives," *The Tennessean,* Dec. 20, 1991.

Jack Hurst, "Bluegrass Blueblood," *Chicago Tribune,* Jan. 19, 1992.

Alison Krauss, interview with Robert K. Oermann, May 1988.

Jim Macnie, "Alison Krauss," *Musician,* Feb. 1991.

Edward Morris, "Alison Krauss Is Kicking Bluegrass into the Big-Time," *Billboard,* Nov. 10, 1990.

Tim O'Brien, *Two Highways* LP liner notes (Cambridge, Mass.: Rounder Records, 1989).

Robert K. Oermann, "Alison Krauss Fiddles, Sings Her Way to the Top," *The Tennessean,* May 13, 1988.

Robert K. Oermann, "Bluegrass Association Awards Nashville's Krauss, Others," *The Tennessean,* Sept. 28, 1991.

Jay Orr, "Rising Bluegrass Star Krauss Has Her Feet on the Ground," *The Nashville Banner,* Sept. 21, 1990.

Claudia Perry, "Fiddling Around with Alison Krauss," *The Houston Post,* Oct. 20, 1991.

Jeff Qualls, "Alison Krauss Proves Why Bluegrass May Grow," *Cue Magazine,* May 2, 1991.

Sophronia Scott and Wendy Cole, "Fiddlin' Gal," *Time,* Mar. 4, 1991.

Jack Tottle, "Alison Krauss and Union Station," *Bluegrass Unlimited,* June 1991.

Tony Trischka, *Too Late to Cry* LP liner notes (Cambridge, Mass.: Rounder Records, 1987).

Anonymous, "Alison Krauss Is No Cornball . . . ," *People,* Aug. 11, 1986.

KATIE LAUR

Marty Godbey, "The Katie Laur Band," *Bluegrass Unlimited*, Jan. 1978.

LAURIE LEWIS

Calvin Ahlgren, "Laurie Lewis Finds Bluegrass Green Enough," *San Francisco Chronicle*, July 1, 1990.

Jim Gitlin, "Laurie Lewis and Grant Street: I'm Gonna Be the Wind," *Bluegrass Unlimited*, Apr. 1990.

Jim Hatlo, "Laurie Lewis *Restless Rambling Heart* " record review, *Frets*, June 1987.

Susan Herbert, "Laurie Lewis—With Fiddle and Song," *San Francisco Independent*, July 17, 1990.

Roland Kausen, "Laurie Lewis *Restless Rambling Heart*" record review, *Bluegrass Unlimited*, Sept. 1987.

Laurie Lewis, interview with Robert K. Oermann, Aug. 1992.

Robert K. Oermann, "Laurie Lewis *Love Chooses You*" record review, *The Tennessean*, Nov. 12, 1989.

Derk Richardson, "Love Chooses Laurie Lewis," *Berkeley Express*, June 16, 1989.

Eric A. Savage, "Laurie Lewis & Kathy Kallick *Together*" record review, *Bluegrass Unlimited*, Mar. 1992.

LILLIMAE

Frank J. Godbey, "Lillimae and the Dixie Gospelaires *There's a Big Wheel*," record review, *Bluegrass Unlimited*, Apr. 1976.

Walter V. Saunders, "Lillimae and the Dixie Gospelaires *Sing 'Working on a Road' Bluegrass Style*," record review, *Bluegrass Unlimited*, Feb. 1973.

Ivan and Deanna Tribe, "Lillimae: In the Men's World of Bluegrass," *Bluegrass Unlimited*, Aug. 1976.

CLAIRE LYNCH

Thomas Goldsmith, "Bluegrass' Claire Lynch Finding a Country Niche," *The Tennessean*, Oct. 26, 1991.

ROSE MADDOX

Ken Nelson, *Rose Maddox Sings Bluegrass* LP liner notes (Hollywood: Capitol Records, 1962).

THE MARSHALL FAMILY

Glenn Roberts, Jr., "The Marshall Family," *Bluegrass Unlimited*, June 1977.

John Roemer, "The Marshall Family *Requests*" record review, *Bluegrass Unlimited*, Feb. 1977.

John D. Rossbach, "The Marshall Family *Best Of Vol. 2*" record review, *Bluegrass Unlimited*, Apr. 1989.

LYNN MORRIS

Pete Wernick, *The Lynn Morris Band* LP liner notes (Cambridge, Mass.: Rounder Records, 1989).

THE NEW COON CREEK GIRLS

Roland Kausen, "New Coon Creek Girls *Pictures*" record review, *Bluegrass Unlimited*, Apr. 1989.

Alan J. Steiner, "New Coon Creek Girls *How Many Biscuits Can You Eat*" record review, *Bluegrass Unlimited*, Apr. 1984.

Alan J. Steiner, "New Coon Creek Girls *So I'll Ride*" record review, *Bluegrass Unlimited*, Nov. 1991.

RANCH ROMANCE

Patrick MacDonald, "Ranching Out," *The Seattle Times*, Feb. 2, 1988.

Jo Miller, interview with Robert K. Oermann, Sept. 1990.

Robert K. Oermann, "Ranch Romance Rewrites the Rules," *The Tennessean*, Sept. 4, 1990.

SIDESADDLE

Sam Mitchell, "Sidesaddle: Not Just Five More Pretty Faces," *Bluegrass Unlimited*, Nov. 1986.

Richard D. Smith, "Sidesaddle *Saratoga Gap*" record review, *Bluegrass Unlimited*, Jan. 1986.

Anonymous, *The Girl from the Red Rose Saloon* LP liner notes (Whitesburg, Ky.: Turquoise Records, 1988).

THE SULLIVAN FAMILY

Arlie Metheny, "The Sullivan Family Celebrates 40th Anniversary," *Bluegrass Unlimited*, Mar. 1990.

Walter V. Saunders, "The Sullivan Family *Working on a Building*" record review, *Bluegrass Unlimited*, Sept. 1972.

Ruth Stephens, "Picayune, Mississippi, Revisited," *Bluegrass Unlimited*, Mar. 1990.

Marty Stuart, *A Joyful Noise* CD liner notes (Nashville: Country Music Foundation Records, 1991).

Anonymous, "Jerry and Tammy Sullivan" Country Music Foundation publicity bio, 1991.

RHONDA VINCENT

Arlie Metheny, "Sally Mountain Show," *Bluegrass Unlimited*, July 1988.

Susan L. Rife, "Vincent Has Always Fiddled with Music," *Wichita Eagle*, Feb. 23, 1990.

John Roemer, "Rhonda Vincent New Dreams and Sunshine" record review, *Bluegrass Unlimited*, Mar. 1989.

Bob Rolfe, "Family Act Brings Musical Tradition to Southern Tier," *Corning Leader* (N.Y.), Aug. 22, 1988.

Alan J. Steiner, "Rhonda Vincent & The Sally Mountain Show *Bound for Gloryland*" record review, *Bluegrass Unlimited*, Feb. 1992.

Anonymous, "The Sally Mountain Show Honored," *Lancaster Excelsior* (Mo.), Jan. 27, 1988.

THE WHITES

Doug Green, *Buck White & The Down Home Folks* LP liner notes (Floyd, Va.: County Records, 1972).

Jack Hurst, "The Whites Aren't Prim . . . ," *Chicago Tribune*, June 9, 1985.

Robert K. Oermann, "From Clubs to Concert Halls, the Whites Climb to the Top," *The Tennessean*, June 26, 1983.

Robert K. Oermann, "Ricky and Sharon Chart Marital Bliss," *The Tennessean*, Aug. 1, 1987.

Sharon White, interview with Robert K. Oermann, July 1987.

The Whites, interview with Robert K. Oermann, June 1983.

Shawn Williams, "The Whites," *Gospel Voice*, Sept. 1988.

WILD ROSE

Linda Cearley, "A Band That's 'Breakin' New Ground,'" *Modesto Bee*, Nov. 17, 1989.

Lydia Dixon Harden, "Wild Rose Comes into Bloom," *Music City News*, Sept. 1990.

Robert K. Oermann, "For Women, a Free Wild Rose," *The Tennessean*, Nov. 17, 1990.

Sean Piccoli, "Wild Rose Blossoms onto Charts," *The Washington Times*, Aug. 16, 1990.

Neil Pond, "Wild Rose Blossoms," *Country America*, Feb. 1992.

Wild Rose, interview with Robert K. Oermann, Nov. 1990.

THE WILDWOOD PICKERS

A. T. Boland, "The Wildwood Pickers *Family Reunion*" record review, *Bluegrass Unlimited*, Feb. 1984.

Arlie Metheny, "The Wildwood Pickers," *Bluegrass Unlimited*, Nov. 1987.

Jim Scribbins, "The Wildwood Pickers *First Harvest*" record review, *Bluegrass Unlimited*, June 1980.

ROBIN AND LINDA WILLIAMS

Teresa Annas, "A Prairie Home in Middlebrook," *The Virginian-Pilot and the Ledger-Star*, Dec. 12, 1987.

Leslie Berman, "Down Home with a 'Prairie Home' Pair," *Newsday*, June 3, 1988.

Mike Hughes, "Home, Home from the 'Prairie' and on Stage," *Lansing State Journal*, Aug. 21, 1988.

Robert K. Oermann, "Robin, Linda Williams Share 'Prairie' Spirit," *The Tennessean*, Feb. 14, 1988.

Robin and Linda Williams, interview with Robert K. Oermann, Feb. 1988.

THE WILLIAMS SISTERS

Walter V. Saunders, "The Williams Sisters *The New Female Voices of Bluegrass*" record review, *Bluegrass Unlimited*, July 1973.

WOMEN IN BLUEGRASS

Thomas A. Adler, "Women in Bluegrass Music," unpublished paper presented at American Folklore Society meetings, Oct. 1986.

Bob Artis, *Bluegrass* (New York: Hawthorn Books, 1975).

John L. Boothroyd, comp., *Bluegrass LP Issues, 1957–1990* (Briar Hill, Victoria, Australia: John L. Boothroyd Publisher, 1990).

Ronni Lundy, "Spotlight On: Three Leaders in the Bluegrass Women's Movement," *Louisville Courier-Journal*, Mar. 19, 1989.

Neil V. Rosenberg, *Bluegrass: A History* (Urbana: University of Illinois Press, 1985).

18. EIGHTIES LADIES AND BEYOND

BAILLIE AND THE BOYS

Baillie & The Boys, interview with Robert K. Oermann, Jan. 1988.

Robert K. Oermann, "Trio Scores as Country Music Fans' Newest . . . ," *The Tennessean*, Feb. 6, 1988.

Anonymous, "Baillie & The Boys" publicity bio (Nashville: RCA Records, 1990).

Suzy Bogguss

Suzy Bogguss, interview with Robert K. Oermann, Apr. 1989.

Suzy Bogguss, interview with Robert K. Oermann, July 1990.

Suzy Bogguss, interview with Robert K. Oermann, Mar. 1992.

Kelley Gattis, "Horizon," *CMA Close Up,* Apr. 1990.

Thomas Goldsmith, "Suzy Bogguss Gives It Her All," *The Tennessean,* Mar. 14, 1992.

Jack Hurst, "Secret of Success," *Chicago Tribune,* July 19, 1987.

Robert K. Oermann, "'Top New Female Vocalist' Earns a Celebrity Fan Club," *The Tennessean,* Aug. 5, 1989.

Kimmy Wix, "Playing with a Winning Hand," *Music City News,* Apr. 1992.

Lane Brody

Lane Brody, interview with Robert K. Oermann, Apr. 1984.

Lane Brody, interview with Robert K. Oermann, Oct. 1986.

Robert K. Oermann, "This Year's Oscars Have Two Ties to Nashville," *The Tennessean,* Apr. 7, 1984.

Robert K. Oermann, "Nashville's Lane Brody Shines as Country Girl in Hollywood," *The Tennessean,* Oct. 19, 1986.

Mary-Chapin Carpenter

Mary-Chapin Carpenter, interview with Robert K. Oermann, Mar. 1988.

Mary-Chapin Carpenter, interview with Robert K. Oermann, Sept. 1989.

Mary-Chapin Carpenter, interview with Robert K. Oermann, Nov. 1990.

Kelley Gattis, "Horizon," *CMA Close Up,* Feb. 1990.

Alanna Nash, "Mary-Chapin Carpenter," *Stereo Review,* Jan. 1990.

Blythe Newlon, "The Music of Mary-Chapin Carpenter," *SongTalk,* Spring 1991.

Ralph Novak, "Mary-Chapin Carpenter *Shooting Straight in the Dark"* record review, *People,* Nov. 19, 1990.

Robert K. Oermann, "Folk Poet Finds New Country Audience," *The Tennessean,* Mar. 26, 1988.

Robert K. Oermann, "Mary-Chapin Carpenter Takes Country Road," *The Tennessean,* Nov. 18, 1989.

Robert K. Oermann, "Carpenter Redefines 'Opening Act,'" *The Tennessean,* Nov. 4, 1990.

Eliza Wing, "Country's Unlikely Star," *Rolling Stone,* Mar. 21, 1991.

Carlene Carter

Patrick Carr, "Carlene Carter's Back in Town," *Country Music,* Nov./Dec. 1991.

Carlene Carter, interview with Robert K. Oermann, Oct. 1987.

Carlene Carter, interview with Robert K. Oermann, Aug. 1990.

Jeffrey Cason, "Carlene Carter," *After Dark,* Nov. 1980.

Kelly Delaney, "Carlene Carter Has Heritage in Her Music," *Music City News,* Dec. 1980.

Cyndi Hoelzle, "Carlene Carter: Easy from Now On," *The Gavin Report,* Mar. 29, 1991.

Divina Infusino, "Seven-Year Itch," *Pulse!,* Sept. 1990.

Robert K. Oermann, "Carter Kin Reclaims Her Country Heritage," *The Tennessean,* Nov. 8, 1987.

Robert K. Oermann, "Country Carlene Reaches Back to Roots," *The Tennessean,* Sept. 22, 1990.

Jay Orr, "Carter's Country Is All Her Own," *The Nashville Banner,* Aug. 23, 1990.

Frank Rose, "The Carlene Carter Interview," *Oui,* May 1981.

Fred Schruers, "Urban Cowgirl," *New York News,* Dec. 28, 1980.

Rosanne Cash

Rosanne Cash, interview with Robert K. Oermann, Nov. 1990.

Rosanne Cash, interview with Robert K. Oermann, Jan. 1990.

Rosanne Cash, interview with Robert K. Oermann, Apr. 1989.

Rosanne Cash, interview with Robert K. Oermann, Nov. 1987.

Rosanne Cash, interview with Robert K. Oermann, Sept. 1987.

Rosanne Cash, interview with Robert K. Oermann, July 1985.

Rosanne Cash, interview with Robert K. Oermann, Mar. 1982.

Rosanne Cash, "Labeling of Records: Shades of McCarthy," letter to the editor, *The Tennessean,* Dec. 6, 1985.

Holly Gleason, "Rosanne Strikes Back," *Tune-In,* July 1987.

Holly Gleason, "Beyond Country," *Pulse!,* Aug. 1987.

Lydia Dixon Harden, "Rosanne Cash: Breaking New Ground," *Music City News,* 1986.

Jan Hoffman, "Some Girls Do," *The Village Voice,* vol. 33, no. 27, July 5, 1988.

Lucy Kaylin, "She Walks the Line," *GQ,* Sept. 1991.

Phyllis Martin, "Rosanne Cash," *Country Song Roundup,* Sept. 1980.

Robert K. Oermann, "Rosanne Cash: Profile," *BMI Music World,* Winter 1988.

Robert K. Oermann, "Citizen Cash," *The Tennessean,* Dec. 16, 1990.

Robert K. Oermann, "Joanne Gardner, Rosanne Cash Team Up with Acme Pictures," *The Tennessean,* Apr. 20, 1989.

Robert K. Oermann, "Cash, Crowell Making Music on Sunny Side," *The Tennessean,* July 30, 1988.

Robert K. Oermann, "Rosanne Cash Hits the Road with a New Sound," *The Tennessean,* Oct. 10, 1987.

Robert K. Oermann, "Private Rosanne Goes Public," *The Tennessean,* Aug. 4, 1985.

Robert K. Oermann, "Rosanne Cash: Free-Spirited Woman in a Man's World," *Country Song Roundup,* Apr. 1982.

Robert K. Oermann, "Rosanne Cash: *Somewhere in the Stars*" record review, *The Record,* Oct. 1982.

Robert K. Oermann, "Rosanne Cash Fills December Airwaves," *The Tennessean,* Dec. 15, 1985.

Joe Rich, "Cash Leads Fight Against New Labeling Bill," *The Tennessean,* July 20, 1990.

Holly Dunn

Holly Dunn, interview with Robert K. Oermann, May 1987.

Holly Dunn, interview with Robert K. Oermann, July 1989.

Thomas Goldsmith, "Dunn Achieves 'Milestones,'" *The Tennessean,* July 13, 1991.

Robert K. Oermann, "Holly Dunn Blossoms as 'Blue Rose' Star," *The Tennessean,* Sept. 9, 1989.

Robert K. Oermann, "'Daddy's Hands' Pointed Her in the Right Direction," *The Tennessean,* June 20, 1987.

Robert K. Oermann, "'SIX Holds Out, Plays Dunn's Song," *The Tennessean,* Aug. 1, 1991.

Cathy Straight and Robert K. Oermann, "Not a Dunn Deal . . . ," *The Tennessean,* July 27, 1991.

Ethel and The Shameless Hussies

Ethel & The Shameless Hussies, interview with Robert K. Oermann, Oct. 1987.

Ethel & The Shameless Hussies, interview with Robert K. Oermann, Nov. 1988.

Robert K. Oermann, "Ethel and Her Hussies Team Up for a Shameless Halloween Bash," *The Tennessean,* Oct. 25, 1987.

Robert K. Oermann, "Shameless Hussies: Talent and Trash," *The Tennessean,* Dec. 26, 1988.

The Forester Sisters

Denny Angelle, "Perfume, Ribbons & Pearls," *Tune-In,* Aug. 1986.

Lydia Dixon Harden, "The Forester Sisters Aren't Afraid to Try Anything," *Music City News,* Aug. 1991.

Laura Fissinger, "Family Ties," *Elle,* Mar. 1988.

The Forester Sisters, interview with Robert K. Oermann, June 1986.

The Forester Sisters, interview with Robert K. Oermann, Apr. 1985.

Jack Hurst, "Four Sisters from Lookout Mountain . . . ," *Chicago Tribune,* Sept. 22, 1985.

Robert K. Oermann, "Forester Sisters Move into Country's Top 10 in Cinderella Fashion," *The Tennessean,* May 6, 1985.

Robert K. Oermann, "Forester Sisters Working Hard for the Money," *The Tennessean,* July 12, 1986.

Linda Romine, "Forester Sisters Were Born to Sing Four-Part Harmony," Cox News Service story, Dec. 18, 1989.

Anonymous, "Forester Sisters" publicity bio (Nashville: Warner Bros. Records, 1990).

Anonymous, "Forester Sisters" publicity bio (Nashville: Warner Bros. Records, 1991).

Anonymous, "Forester Sisters" publicity bio (Nashville: Warner Bros. Records, 1992).

The Girls Next Door

The Girls Next Door, interview with Robert K. Oermann, Mar. 1986.

Jack Hurst, "Doris King Comes Out of Background . . . ," *Chicago Tribune,* Mar. 16, 1986.

Robert K. Oermann, "The Girls Next Door Reaching for Success," *The Tennessean,* May 22, 1986.

Nanci Griffith

Stephanie Beardsley, "High Notes," *New Texas,* Jan./Feb. 1983.

Bob Claypool, "No Big Rainbow," *The Houston Post,* June 12, 1982.

Bob Claypool, "Griffith's Music Career Doing Fine . . . ," *The Houston Post,* Nov. 18, 1983.

Thomas Goldsmith, "Nanci Griffith Finds Love in Faraway Places," *The Tennessean,* June 25, 1988.

Nanci Griffith, interview with Robert K. Oermann, Apr. 1985.

Nanci Grittith, interview with Robert K. Oermann, May 1986.

Nanci Griffith, interview with Robert K. Oermann, Apr. 1989.

David Hepworth, "Steel Magnolia," *Q,* n.d. [1991].

Stephen Holden, "The Pop Life," *The New York Times,* Feb. 10, 1988.

Peter Nelson, "The Queen of Folkabilly," *Rolling Stone,* May 7, 1987.

Robert K. Oermann, "Folk Singer Nanci Griffith Proud to Carry on the Tradition," *The Tennessean,* Apr. 25, 1985.

Robert K. Oermann, "Texas Folk Queen Embraced by Music City," *The Tennessean,* May 28, 1986.

Robert K. Oermann, "Sagas of Everyday People Propel Nanci Griffith to International Fame," *The Tennessean,* May 7, 1989.

Robert K. Oermann, "Midler Song Hits Hearts of the World," *The Tennessean,* Dec. 16, 1990.

HIGHWAY 101

John Butterfield, "Paulette Carlson's Turn," *USA Weekend,* Oct. 6, 1989.

Paulette Carlson, interview with Robert K. Oermann, Mar. 1987.

Thomas Goldsmith, "Attitude, Music Successfully Mix for Highway 101," *The Tennessean,* Jan. 27, 1990.

Thomas Goldsmith, "Highway 101's Cinderella," *The Tennessean,* July 6, 1991.

Highway 101, interview with Robert K. Oermann, Feb. 1989.

Highway 101, interview with Robert K. Oermann, Apr. 1992.

Robert K. Oermann, "Highway 101 Speeds to Success," *The Tennessean,* Apr. 5, 1987.

Robert K. Oermann, "Highway 101: Far More Than a One-Way Street," *The Tennessean,* Mar. 18, 1989.

Robert K. Oermann, "It's Full Speed Ahead," *The Tennessean,* May 9, 1992.

BECKY HOBBS

Becky Hobbs, interview with Robert K. Oermann, July 1988.

Robert K. Oermann, "Fans, Critics 'All Keyed Up' for Rockabilly's Becky Hobbs," *The Tennessean,* July 16, 1988.

THE JUDDS

Bob Allen, "The Judds: Wynonna and Naomi" publicity bio (Nashville: RCA Records, 1983).

Bob Allen, "The Judds: A Year of Long and Painful Goodbyes," *Country Music,* Nov./Dec. 1991.

Laura Fissinger, "Family Ties," *Rolling Stone,* July 2, 1987.

Thomas Goldsmith and Robert K. Oermann, "Ending on a High Note," *The Tennessean,* Dec. 5, 1991.

Jan Hoffman, "A Tie That Binds," *Village Voice,* Apr. 1, 1986.

Naomi Judd, "Fighting to Cast Off Death's Shadow," *People,* Nov. 26, 1990.

Wynonna Judd, "Mom Taught Me to Dream," *USA Weekend,* May 10, 1991.

Wynonna Judd, interview with Robert K. Oermann, Apr. 1992.

The Judds, interview with Robert K. Oermann, Dec. 1983.

The Judds, interview with Robert K. Oermann, Aug. 1984.

The Judds, interview with Robert K. Oermann, Jan. 1987.

The Judds, interview with Robert K. Oermann, Aug. 1988.

The Judds, interview with Robert K. Oermann, Apr. 1989.

The Judds, interview with Robert K. Oermann, Nov. 1991.

The Judds, press conference, Oct. 1990.

Alan Light, "Wynonna Leaves Home," *Rolling Stone,* June 25, 1992.

Bob Millard, *The Judds* (New York: Dolphin/Doubleday, 1988).

Ed Morris, "Mama Judd's Last Show?" *Billboard,* Sept. 28, 1991.

Robert K. Oermann, "Mother-Daughter Team Hits Charts with Top-20 Tune," *The Tennessean,* Feb. 25, 1984.

Robert K. Oermann, "Mother-Daughter Judds Find Quick Road to Success," *The Tennessean,* Sept. 8, 1984.

Robert K. Oermann, "Country Stars the Judds Take Their Rocketship Ride in Stride," *The Tennessean,* Mar. 1, 1987.

Robert K. Oermann, "Golden Harmony of the Judds Strikes Dual Chords in Real Life," *The Tennessean,* Dec. 11, 1988.

Robert K. Oermann, "Judds Give More Than Music," *The Tennessean,* Apr. 23, 1989.

Robert K. Oermann, "Naomi's Wedding," *The Tennessean,* May 8, 1989.

Robert K. Oermann, "Wynonna Judd to Wed Songwriter Tony King," *The Tennessean,* July 31, 1990.

Robert K. Oermann, "Illness Leads to Breakup of the Judds," *The Tennessean,* Oct. 18, 1990.

Robert K. Oermann, "The Judds: A Fond Farewell," *The Tennessean,* Dec. 1, 1991.

Robert K. Oermann, "Wynonna Looks Ahead," *The Tennessean,* Dec. 4, 1991.

Robert K. Oermann, "Wynonna's Hits Just Keep Comin'," *The Tennessean,* Apr. 15, 1992.

Robert K. Oermann, "Better, Bolder Wynonna," *The Tennessean,* May 24, 1992.

Robert K. Oermann and Thomas Goldsmith, "In Their Last Show, Judds Pour Their Hearts Out," *The Tennessean,* Dec. 5, 1991.

Jay Orr, "Totally Wynonna," *The Nashville Banner,* May 30, 1992.

John Reggero, "Here Come the Judds," *Us,* Feb. 25, 1985.

K.D. LANG

David Bauder, "k.d. lang Takes a Sharp Turn from Country," Associated Press wire story, May 1, 1992.

Jon Bream, "Lang Gives Nashville a Colorful New Face," *Minneapolis Star Tribune,* May 1987.

Michael Corcoran, "That Dang Lang," *American Way,* Oct. 1, 1989.

Robert Cross, "Uniquely InClined," *Chicago Tribune,* July 5, 1989.

k.d. lang, interview with Robert K. Oermann, May 1987.

k.d. lang, interview with Robert K. Oermann, June 1989.

Brendan Lemon, "Virgin Territory: k.d. lang," *The Advocate,* June 16, 1992.

Robert K. Oermann, "Kooky K.D. Gives Country a Kick," *The Tennessean,* May 14, 1987.

Robert K. Oermann, "K.D. Lang Committed Country Music," *The Tennessean,* July 1, 1989.

Robert K. Oermann, "Music Row on k.d. lang: 'So What?'" *The Tennessean,* June 6, 1992.

Michael Spector, "Patsy Cline Meets Judy Garland," *The New York Times,* July 23, 1992.

Jim Sullivan, "Making the Break from Country Music," *The Boston Globe* wire story, June 10, 1992.

PATTY LOVELESS

Sandy Adzgery, "Loveless No More," *Tune In,* Sept. 1991.

Lydia Dixon Harden, "Patty Loveless: Ready, Willing and Able," *Music City News,* Dec. 1989.

Thomas Goldsmith, "Fans' Favorite Patty Loveless Likes Her Country with an Edge," *The Tennessean,* July 29, 1990.

Sandy Lovejoy, "Patty Loveless Takes the Long View," *KNIX Country Spirit,* July 1991.

Patty Loveless, interview with Robert K. Oermann, June 1987.

Patty Loveless, interview with Robert K. Oermann, Sept. 1988.

Robert K. Oermann, "Patty Loveless Eyes Country Queendom," *The Tennessean,* Sept. 1, 1987.

Robert K. Oermann, "Patty Loveless: Today, She's the Latest Honky-Tonk Angel," *The Tennessean,* Nov. 12, 1988.

LORETTA LYNN

Loretta Lynn with George Vecsey, *Coal Miner's Daughter* (New York: Warner Books, 1976).

SHELBY LYNNE

Jack Hurst, "A Young Singer's Sorrows," *Chicago Tribune,* Dec. 3, 1989.

Sandy Lovejoy, "Up and Comer," *KNIX Country Spirit,* July 1991.

Shelby Lynne, interview with Robert K. Oermann, Dec. 1989.

Shelby Lynne, interview with Robert K. Oermann, Dec. 1991.

Brian Mansfield, "Good Things in a Small Package," *Nashville Scene,* Oct. 19, 1989.

Robert K. Oermann, "Misfortune's Child, Everybody's Darling," *The Tennessean,* Jan. 6, 1990.

David Zimmerman, "Her Sorrowful Style Comes from the Soul," *USA Today,* Feb. 28, 1990.

MARTINA MCBRIDE

Martina McBride, interview with Robert K. Oermann, July 1992.

THE MCCARTER SISTERS

Neil Pond, "Meet the McCarters," *Music City News,* Sept. 1988.

REBA MCENTIRE

Reba McEntire, interview with Robert K. Oermann, Oct. 1984.

Reba McEntire, interview with Robert K. Oermann, Feb. 1986.

Reba McEntire, interview with Robert K. Oermann, Nov. 1986.

Reba McEntire, interview with Robert K. Oermann, Dec. 1986.

Reba McEntire, interview with Robert K. Oermann, July 1988.

Reba McEntire, interview with Robert K. Oermann, Apr. 1989.

Robert K. Oermann, "Reba McEntire: The Return of the Singing Cowgirl," *Country Digest,* vol. 1, no. 1, 1980.

Robert K. Oermann, "Reba Follows Her Own Advice: 'Be Yourself,'" *The Tennessean,* Nov. 3, 1984.

Robert K. Oermann, "Why Did Reba Cry at Opry Induction?" *The Tennessean,* Feb. 7, 1986.

Robert K. Oermann, "'Whoever's in New England' with Reba," *The Tennessean,* Feb. 13, 1986.

Robert K. Oermann, "Hard Working Reba 'Having a Blast' at the Top," *The Tennessean,* Mar. 16, 1986.

Robert K. Oermann, "Entertainer of Year McEntire Rarin' to Face the Challenge," *The Tennessean,* Jan. 11, 1987.

Robert K. Oermann, "Reba's All 'Fired Up' About This," *The Tennessean,* Apr. 11, 1987.

Robert K. Oermann, "Young Country Proves a Crowd Pleaser," *The Tennessean,* June 27, 1987.

Robert K. Oermann, "Reba McEntire Will Soon Call Nashville Home," *The Tennessean,* Sept. 26, 1987.

Robert K. Oermann, "Queen Reba Reaches to Pop Fans from Atop Her Country Throne," *The Tennessean,* July 10, 1988.

Robert K. Oermann, "Reba McEntire Weds Manager," *The Tennessean,* June 6, 1989.

Robert K. Oermann, "Can Reba Swap Country Glitter for New Silver Screen Sparkle?" *The Tennessean,* July 23, 1989.

Robert K. Oermann, "Reba McEntire is Expecting," *The Tennessean,* Aug. 8, 1989.

Robert K. Oermann, "Reba Plans Memorial Service," *The Tennessean,* Mar. 18, 1991.

Robert K. Oermann, "Tears, Songs for McEntire Group," *The Tennessean,* Mar. 21, 1991.

Robert K. Oermann and Rochelle Carter, "City Grieves for Eight Killed," *The Tennessean,* Mar. 17, 1991.

REBA MCENTIRE (SECONDARY)

James Ring Adams, "Reba McEntire: Country Singer of the Year," *McCall's,* Jan. 1987.

Don Cusic, *Reba: Country Music's Queen* (New York: St. Martin's Press, 1991).

Steve Dougherty and Jane Sanderson, "Sweet Dreams No More," *People,* Apr. 1, 1991.

Mary H. J. Farrell and Jane Sanderson, "Reba's Rough Ride Back," *People,* Nov. 4, 1991.

Chet Flippo, "Get Your Life Straight," *USA Weekend,* Sept. 27, 1991.

Jack Hurst, "Cowgirl Reba McEntire Sticks to Her Guns," *Chicago Tribune,* Oct. 28, 1984.

Jack Hurst, "McEntire Uses Songs to Speak for Women," *Palm Beach Sun Sentinel,* Oct. 17, 1986.

Kathryn Jenson, "Reba," *Oklahoma Today,* May–June 1984.

Carol Leggett, *Reba McEntire the Queen of Country* (New York: Fireside/Simon & Schuster, 1992).

Edward Morris, "Reba Keeps High Profile," *Billboard,* Aug. 30, 1986.

Sandy Neese, "Oklahoma Cowgirl Starts New Year in a Big Way," *The Tennessean,* Jan. 8, 1983.

Sandy Neese, "Reba Runs a Mean Barrel," *The Tennessean,* Nov. 12, 1983.

Gerry Wood, "After Bucking the Rodeo Circuit, Singer Reba McEntire Finds Country Music a Cinch," *People,* Apr. 23, 1984.

KATHY MATTEA

Lydia Dixon Harden, "Kathy Mattea," *Music City News,* Feb. 1991.

Laura Fissinger, "Kathy Mattea Steadily Builds Her Career," *The Nashville Banner,* Dec. 3, 1987.

Kathy Mattea, interview with Robert K. Oermann, Apr. 1983.

Kathy Mattea, interview with Robert K. Oermann, Feb. 1985.

Kathy Mattea, interview with Robert K. Oermann, Jan. 1988.

Kathy Mattea, interview with Robert K. Oermann, Mar. 1991.

Kathy Mattea, interview with Robert K. Oermann, Nov. 1991.

Robert K. Oermann, "Kathy Mattea Sings Her Way from Country Starlet to Star," *The Tennessean,* Mar. 10, 1985.

Robert K. Oermann, "Kathy Mattea Hits No. 1," *The Tennessean,* Jan. 16, 1988.

Robert K. Oermann, "Kathy Mattea: Country Music Star-Next-Door," *The Tennessean,* Mar. 24, 1991.

Robert K. Oermann, "Mattea's Throat Now Seems OK," *The Tennessean,* Nov. 16, 1991.

Neil Pond, "Kathy Mattea: Life as She Knows It," *Music City News,* Apr. 1989.

KATY MOFFATT

Katy Moffatt, interview with Robert K. Oermann, Nov. 1988.

LORRIE MORGAN

Wiley Alexander, "Morgan Endures Heartbreak on Her Way to Stardom," *San Antonio Express-News,* Dec. 28, 1990.

Suzanne Gibson, "Horizon," *CMA Close Up,* Apr. 1989.

Jack Hurst, "At 24, Vocalist Lorrie Morgan Marks Decade in Show Business," *Chicago Tribune,* June 7, 1984.

Jim Lewis, "Lorrie Morgan Talks About Late Husband," United Press International wire story, May 26, 1989.

Zac Meadows, "Lorrie Morgan," *Country Music Parade,* Mar.–Apr. 1990.

Lorrie Morgan, interview with Sandy Smith, Apr. 1989.

Lorrie Morgan, interview with Robert K. Oermann, Apr. 1991.

Robert K. Oermann, "Lorrie Picks Up the Tempo," *The Tennessean,* June 1, 1991.

Robert K. Oermann, "Morgan Gets Engaged," *The Tennessean,* June 13, 1991.

Robert K. Oermann, "Lorrie Weds Old-Fashioned Way," *The Tennessean,* Oct. 28, 1991.

Neil Pond, "Starting Over," *Country America,* May 1991.

Janet Williams, "Lorrie Morgan: Up Close," *CMA Close Up,* Apr. 1992.

K.T. OSLIN

Mary Ellin Barritt, "K.T. Oslin, Offbeat Country Star," *USA Weekend,* Aug. 28, 1988.

Holly Gleason, "Just Plain Folks," *Standing Ovation* [?], [photocopy] [c. 1988].

Robert K. Oermann, "'Most Promising Songwriter' Changes Mind About Music City," *The Tennessean,* June 20, 1983.

Robert K. Oermann, "Mainstream Appeal Transforms K.T. Oslin into Country Diva," *The Tennessean,* Oct. 2, 1988.

Robert K. Oermann, "Dial in K.T. for Hours of New Country," *The Tennessean,* May 27, 1989.

Robert K. Oermann, "Operatic Oslin Emotes at Songwriter Benefit," *The Tennessean,* Nov. 30, 1989.

Robert K. Oermann, "K.T. Looks for 'Paradise,'" *The Tennessean,* Feb. 20, 1990.

Robert K. Oermann, "K.T. Oslin Salutes Her Military Fans," *The Tennessean,* Dec. 14, 1991.

K.T. Oslin, interview with Robert K. Oermann, Oct. 1986.

K.T. Oslin, interview with Robert K. Oermann, Aug. 1988.

K.T. Oslin, interview with Robert K. Oermann, Feb. 1990.

Neil Pond, "K.T. Oslin," *Music City News,* Apr. 1988.

Janet Williams, "Close-Up: K.T. Oslin," *CMA Close Up,* Aug. 1991.

Shawn Williams, "K.T. Oslin: This '80s Lady Takes a Slow Road to Stardom," *Music City News,* Aug. 1987.

David Zimmerman, "K.T. Oslin: '80s Lady," *USA Today,* Aug. 18, 1988.

Anonymous, "K.T. Oslin Returns to Music City," *The Tennessean,* Jan. 12, 1986.

Anonymous, "Kay T. Oslin," Warner Bros. Records bio, 1982.

Anonymous, "K.T. Oslin," RCA Records bio, 1986.

Anonymous, "K.T. Oslin," RCA Records bio, 1990.

Anonymous, "K.T. Oslin Goes to No. 1 Singing Her Own Songs," *The Tennessean,* Jan. 10, 1988.

Anonymous, "K.T. Oslin Clicks in Country," *The Tennessean,* Aug. 20, 1989.

DOLLY PARTON

Robert K. Oermann, "Tennessee Mountain Memories Bring Dolly Parton Back Home Again," *The Tennessean,* June 22, 1986.

Robert K. Oermann, "Dreamer Dolly Comes Home," *The Tennessean,* Feb. 14, 1988.

Robert K. Oermann, "The Unsinkable Dolly Stays Afloat," *The Tennessean,* Mar. 19, 1988.

Robert K. Oermann, "Dolly: Sweet, Savvy and Sassy," *The Tennessean,* Apr. 23, 1989.

Robert K. Oermann, "Dolly Rides Back into Country in 'Limozeen,'" *The Tennessean*, July 8, 1989.

Robert K. Oermann, "A Christmas Dolly," *The Tennessean*, Dec. 16, 1990.

Robert K. Oermann, "It's 'Straight Talk' from Dolly," *The Tennessean*, Mar. 28, 1992.

Dolly Parton, interview with Robert K. Oermann, Apr. 1982.

Dolly Parton, press conference, Nov. 1982.

Dolly Parton, interview with Robert K. Oermann, Oct. 1983.

Dolly Parton, interview with Robert K. Oermann, June 1984.

Dolly Parton, press conference, June 1984.

Dolly Parton, press conference, Dec. 1984.

Dolly Parton, press conference, June 1986.

Dolly Parton, interview with Robert K. Oermann, Mar. 1987.

Dolly Parton, press conference, Feb. 1988.

Dolly Parton, interview with Robert K. Oermann, Apr. 1989.

Dolly Parton, interview with Robert K. Oermann, Dec. 1990.

Dolly Parton, interview with Robert K. Oermann, Mar. 1992.

DOLLY PARTON (SECONDARY)

Cindy Adams, "Dolly's Dazzling Comeback," *Ladies' Home Journal*, Mar. 1984.

Joe Brown, "Rhinestone Cowgirl," *The Washington Post*, Mar. 8, 1984.

Susan Cheever, "I Will Show the People Who I Am—Good and Bad," *TV Guide*, Oct. 17, 1987.

Lydia Dixon Harden, "Dolly Parton: Back to the Country," *Music City News*, Mar. 1991.

Tom Green, "Plucky Parton Running the Show at ABC," *USA Today*, Sept. 25, 1987.

Donna E. Haupt, "Dolly," *Life*, Mar. 1987.

Nanci Hellmich, "Parton's Park: A Dream Come True," *USA Weekend*, May 2, 1986.

Mike Hughes, "Looking for Fame in All the Right Places," *The Tennessean*, Sept. 23, 1991.

Mike Hughes, "Farrah Focuses Again on Abuse," *The Tennessean*, Sept. 25, 1991.

Jane Lieberman, "Parton & Gallin's Sandollar Lines Up Pix with Majors," *Variety*, Mar. 15, 1989.

Deanna Starkey and Andrea Dzik, "Dolly's Magic Touch," *Country Music*, July/Aug. 1987.

Gloria Steinem, "Dolly Parton," *Ms.*, Jan. 1987.

Peter Travers, "Dolly Parton Gives 'Whorehouse' a Texas Send-Off," *People*, Aug. 2, 1982.

Sheila Wissner, "From Humiliation Comes Inspiration," *The Tennessean*, Mar. 28, 1990.

Jeanne Wolf, "Dolly Parton," "A Current Affair" TV interview, May 20, 1992.

RONNA REEVES

Ronna Reeves, interview with Robert K. Oermann, Aug. 1991.

SWEETHEARTS OF THE RODEO

Jack Hurst, "Nashville Scene Spurs Revival of the Sweethearts," *Chicago Tribune*, Mar. 20, 1986.

Sandy Lovejoy, "Sweethearts Ready to Pounce," *KNIX Country Spirit*, July 1991.

Marjie McGraw, "Changing Times: Two Nashville Sweeties Capture Country Music's Heart," *Tune-In*, Feb. 1990.

Robert K. Oermann, "Sweethearts of the Rodeo Take Show on the Road," *The Tennessean*, Mar. 19, 1986.

Robert K. Oermann, "Every Day Is Valentine's Day for Sweethearts of the Rodeo," *The Tennessean*, Feb. 13, 1988.

Sweethearts of the Rodeo, interview with Robert K. Oermann, Mar. 1986.

Sweethearts of the Rodeo, interview with Robert K. Oermann, Jan. 1988.

Shawn Williams, "Sweethearts of the Rodeo See a Dream Come True," *Music City News*, Mar. 1990.

PAM TILLIS

Thomas Goldsmith, "Pam Tillis Singing Out as Rep's Mary Magdalene," *The Tennessean*, May 12, 1988.

Robert K. Oermann, "Child of Nashville Country Opts for Rockin' & Rollin'," *The Tennessean*, Dec. 5, 1982.

Robert K. Oermann, "Pam Tillis Rocks on as Nashville's Kingpin," *The Tennessean*, July 10, 1983.

Robert K. Oermann, "Pam Tillis: 'Versatile' Is Her Middle Name," *The Tennessean*, Jan. 7, 1986.

Robert K. Oermann, "'The Twang's the Thang' Say Tillis and Her Pals," *The Tennessean*, Apr. 26, 1987.

Robert K. Oermann, "Pam Tillis," *The Tennessean*, May 11, 1991.

Jay Orr, "Meet Another Hard Working Tillis," *The Nashville Banner*, June 8, 1992.

Pam Tillis, interview with Robert K. Oermann, June 1981.

Pam Tillis, interview with Robert K. Oermann, May 1983.

Pam Tillis, interview with Robert K. Oermann, Jan. 1986.

Pam Tillis, interview with Robert K. Oermann, Apr. 1987.

Pam Tillis, interview with Robert K. Oermann, Mar. 1991.

Jeff Woods, "Pam Tillis Grows Up," *Music City News*, May 1991.

Anonymous, "Pam Tillis," Elektra Records bio, 1981.

Anonymous, "Pam Tillis," Warner Bros. Records bio, 1983.

Anonymous, "Pam Tillis," Arista Records bio, 1990.

TANYA TUCKER

Teresa George, "Up Close with Tanya Tucker," *CMA Close Up*, Feb. 1990.

Robert K. Oermann, "Torrid Tanya," *The Tennessean*, Apr. 19, 1986.

Robert K. Oermann, "Tanya Celebrates Milestones in Life, Career," *The Tennessean*, Oct. 1, 1988.

Robert K. Oermann, "Tanya Tucker," *The Tennessean*, Feb. 23, 1992.

Neil Pond, "Tanya Tucker Comes Back as Another Woman," *Music City News*, Nov. 1988.

Tanya Tucker, interview with Robert K. Oermann, Mar. 1986.

Tanya Tucker, interview with Robert K. Oermann, Sept. 1988.

Tanya Tucker, interview with Robert K. Oermann, Jan. 1992.

CHERYL WHEELER

Steve Hochman, "Wheeler's Songs Have It Both Ways," *Los Angeles Times*, Apr. 22, 1987.

Jim Kelton, "Singer Becomes Underground Success," *Everett* (Wash.) *Herald*, Dec. 13, 1986.

JETT WILLIAMS

Jeffrey A. Frank, "Her Cheated Heart," *The Washington Post Magazine*, Dec. 3, 1989.

Thomas Goldsmith and Robert K. Oermann, "Claim to Williams Royalties 'Surprises' Music Industry," *The Tennessean*, July 11, 1985.

Martha Hume, "Jett Williams Takes the Stage," *Southern Magazine*, Dec. 1988.

Robert K. Oermann, "Lost Daughter of Hank Williams Stakes Claim," *The Tennessean*, Nov. 19, 1987.

Robert K. Oermann, "Court Rules Hank Sr.'s Illegitimate Daughter Can Pursue Royalty Claims," *The Tennessean*, June 19, 1990.

Robert K. Oermann, "'Sweet' Days for Jett Williams," *The Tennessean*, Nov. 3, 1990.

Jett Williams, interview with Robert K. Oermann, Nov. 1987.

Jett Williams, interview with Robert K. Oermann, Oct. 1990.

David Zimmerman, "She Seeks Legitimacy Lost at Birth," *USA Today*, Mar. 26, 1990.

LUCINDA WILLIAMS

Arion Berger, "The Singer and the Song," *L.A. Weekly*, Nov. 1, 1988.

Robert K. Oermann, "Lucinda Williams Finally Gets Noticed," *The Tennessean*, Apr. 19, 1989.

Lucinda Williams, interview with Robert K. Oermann, Apr. 1989.

TRISHA YEARWOOD

Michael Bane, "20 Questions with Trisha Yearwood: Banker's Genes," *Country Music*, July/Aug. 1992.

Noel Davis, "Yearwood Is at Home in Fairy Tale," *The Orange County Register*, Feb. 7, 1992.

Earl Dittman, "Not Just a Passing Thing," *Tune In*, Sept. 1991.

Joe Edwards, "Life Seems Perfect for Trisha Yearwood," Associated Press wire story, Mar. 6, 1992.

Thomas Goldsmith, "Yearwood Takes Off," *The Tennessean*, Aug. 31, 1991.

Thomas Goldsmith, "Trisha Yearwood Turns the Tables," *Music City News*, Dec. 1991.

Robert K. Oermann, "Yearwood Gets Sexy, Sassy in Concert," *The Tennessean*, Apr. 16, 1992.

Robert K. Oermann, "Trisha Yearwood: Move Over Boys, Here Comes a Star," *The Tennessean*, June 20, 1992.

Neil Pond, "Trisha Yearwood: Country's Hottest Girl Next Door," *Country America*, Aug. 1992.

Trisha Yearwood, interview with Robert K. Oermann, Apr. 1992.

VIDEOS IN COUNTRY MUSIC

Joanne Gardner, interview with Robert K. Oermann, Mar. 1990.

Kip Kirby, "View '82 Rise in Country Films," *Billboard,* Dec. 12, 1981.

Kip Kirby, "Cable Getting Still More Country," *Billboard,* Apr. 9, 1983.

Mary Matthews, interview with Robert K. Oermann, Mar. 1990.

Kitty Moon, interview with Robert K. Oermann, Mar. 1990.

Bob Oermann, "Shaping Video for Music," *Video Systems,* Aug. 1982.

Robert K. Oermann, "You're Lookin' at Country" columns, *Country Rhythms,* Jan.–June 1984.

Robert K. Oermann, "Video Business Booming for All," *The Tennessean,* Jan. 26, 1986.

Robert K. Oermann, "Jon Small Makes Music Videos Work," *The Tennessean,* Feb. 20, 1986.

Robert K. Oermann, "Music Videos Shine in the Spotlight," *The Tennessean,* Nov. 15, 1989.

Robert K. Oermann, "Video Next Hot Area for Country," *The Tennessean,* Nov. 20, 1991.

Robert K. Oermann, "From Music to Screen in Tennessee," *The Hollywood Reporter,* Mar. 1990.

Robert K. Oermann, "Cable's Pop VH-1 Goes 'Country,'" *The Tennessean,* Jan. 31, 1990.

Lloyd Werner, "Television: Helping Country Music Sing a Sweeter Tune," speech at National Academy of Television Arts and Sciences Luncheon in New York, Apr. 8, 1992 (reprinted by The Nashville Network).

Scott Yarbrough, dir., *Music Row Video* series, UPI Media, 1983–1984.

THE COUNTRY MUSIC INDUSTRY

Broadcast Music Inc., *BMI Songs* (New York: BMI, 1988).

Lisa Gubernick and Peter Newcomb, "The Wal-Mart School of Music," *Forbes,* Mar. 2, 1992.

Robert K. Oermann, "Music Keeps the Economy Fit as a Fiddle," *The Tennessean,* Oct. 7, 1990.

Robert K. Oermann, "Numbers Say a Mouthful in Nashville," *The Journal of Country Music,* Fall 1990.

Robert K. Oermann, "Twelve Good Reasons Why Country's Hot," *The Tennessean,* Feb. 22, 1992.

Robert K. Oermann, "How Garth Conquered America: Marketing the New Nashville," *Journal of Country Music,* vol. 14, no. 3, 1992.

Robert K. Oermann and Thomas Goldsmith, "Business Is Booming for Nashville Music," *The Tennessean,* Jan. 24, 1988.

Priscilla Painton, "Country Rocks the Boomers," *Time,* Mar. 30, 1992.

THE FEMINIZATION OF POVERTY

Mary A. Bufwack, "Welfare-Mother Bashing," *The Nashvillian,* July 2, 1992.

Barbara Ehrenreich, "Who's on Main Street?," *Mother Jones,* July/Aug. 1992.

Barbara Ehrenreich, *Fear of Falling: The Inner Life of the Middle Class* (New York: Harper Collins, 1989).

Susan Faludi, *Backlash: The Undeclared War Against American Women* (New York: Crown Publishers, 1991).

Lois Gordon and Alan Gordon, *American Chronicle* (New York: Crown Publishers, 1990).

Sylvia Ann Hewlett, *A Lesser Life* (New York: W. Morrow, 1986).

Katherine S. Newman, *Falling from Grace: The Experience of Downward Mobility in the American Middle Class* (New York: Vintage/Random House, 1988).

Photo Credits

Academy of Motion Picture Arts & Sciences: 160

Authors' Collection: 3, 14, 15, 16, 17, 19, 25, 29, 31, 32, 35, 36, 39, 40, 41, 46, 49, 59, 62, 63, 67, 81, 82, 83, 84, 87, 94, 97, 100, 103, 104, 116, 122, 125, 127, 131, 136, 137, 139, 144, 147, 148, 150, 153, 156, 159, 165, 171, 177, 181, 189, 192, 195, 197, 199, 200, 203, 206, 207, 208, 209, 211, 218, 224, 231, 234, 235, 241, 248, 250, 261, 262, 266, 268, 271, 274, 276, 279, 282, 285, 287, 289, 293, 295, 296, 298, 305, 314, 316, 317, 320, 321, 322, 324, 327, 332, 346, 349, 354, 358, 361, 364, 372, 375, 378, 379, 382, 387, 389, 392, 394, 409, 410, 412, 413, 414, 418, 421, 430, 437, 438, 445, 450, 455, 458, 460, 463, 467, 475, 476, 479, 522

Bear Family Records: 173, 215, 229

Broadcast Music Inc.: 386

Mary Bufwack: 428, 449, 550

Jo-Ann Campbell: 220

Jean Miles Catino and Kay Baker Gaston: 22

Country Music Association: 385

Country Music Foundation: 34, 51, 61, 75, 107, 183, 244

P. Casey Daley: 212

Flying Fish Records: 470

Beth Gwinn: 398, 424, 472, 478, 481, 499, 516, 531, 538

Historical Center of Southeast New Mexico: 91

Gerald Holly: 381

Mars Hill College/Lunsford Collection: 72

Alan L. Mayor: 325, 407, 415, 432, 441, 484, 491, 495, 502, 507, 519, 529, 541, 546

Music City News: 186, 222, 297, 341, 345, 350, 416

Robert K. Oermann: 453

George Pikow: 6, 299

Rounder Records: 8, 109, 113, 117, 301

The Tennessean: 446

Gene Wiggins: 65

Charles Wolfe: 71, 120

Index